THE ESSENTIAL WORLD HISTORY

VOLUME I: TO 1800

William J. Duiker
The Pennsylvania State University

Jackson J. Spielvogel
The Pennsylvania State University

 CENGAGE

Australia • Brazil • Mexico • Singapore • United Kingdom • United States

The Essential World History,
Volume I: to 1800
Ninth Edition
William J. Duiker and
Jackson J. Spielvogel

Product Manager: Joseph D. Potvin

Senior Content Manager: Philip Lanza

Learning Designer: Kate MacLean

Product Assistant: Haley Gaudreau

Marketing Manager: Valerie Hartman

Senior IP Analyst: Alexandra Ricciardi

IP Project Manager: Betsy Hathaway

Production Service/Compositor:
MPS Limited

Art Director: Sarah Cole

Text Design: Deborah Dutton/
Dutton & Sherman Design

Cover Design: Sarah Cole

Cover Image: A hot air balloon flies over
the Pyramid of the Sun at the Teotihuacan
archaeological site in San Juan Teotihuacan,
Mexico during a festival held on the spring
equinox.

Credit: RONALDO SCHEMIDT/Getty Images.

For product information and technology assistance, contact us at
Cengage Customer & Sales Support, 1-800-354-9706
or **support.cengage.com.**

For permission to use material from this text
or product, submit all requests online
at **www.cengage.com/permissions.**

Library of Congress Control Number: 2018955890
Student Edition:
ISBN: 978-0-357-02686-1
Loose-leaf Edition:
ISBN: 978-0-357-02695-3

Cengage
20 Channel Center Street
Boston, MA 02210
USA

Cengage is a leading provider of customized learning solutions with
employees residing in nearly 40 different countries and sales in more
than 125 countries around the world. Find your local representative at
www.cengage.com.

Cengage products are represented in Canada by Nelson Education, Ltd.

To learn more about Cengage platforms and services, register or access
your online learning solution, or purchase materials for your course,
visit **www.cengage.com.**

Printed in the United States of America
Print Number: 01   Print Year: 2018

ABOUT THE AUTHORS

WILLIAM J. DUIKER is liberal arts professor emeritus of East Asian studies at The Pennsylvania State University. A former U.S. diplomat with service in Taiwan, South Vietnam, and Washington, D.C., he received his doctorate in Far Eastern history from Georgetown University in 1968, where his dissertation dealt with Chinese educator and reformer Cai Yuanpei. At Penn State, he has written widely on the history of Vietnam and modern China, including the widely acclaimed *The Communist Road to Power in Vietnam* (revised edition, Westview Press, 1996), which was selected for a Choice Outstanding Academic Book Award in 1982–1983 and 1996–1997. Other recent books are *China and Vietnam: The Roots of Conflict* (Berkeley, 1987); *U.S. Containment Policy and the Conflict in Indochina* (Stanford, 1995); *Sacred War: Nationalism and Revolution in a Divided Vietnam* (McGraw-Hill, 1995); and *Ho Chi Minh: A Life* (Hyperion, 2000), which was nominated for a Pulitzer Prize in 2001. While his research specialization is in the field of nationalism and Asian revolutions, his intellectual interests are considerably more diverse. He has traveled widely and has taught courses on the history of communism and non-Western civilizations at Penn State, where he was awarded a Faculty Scholar Medal for Outstanding Achievement in the spring of 1996. In 2002 the College of Liberal Arts honored him with an Emeritus Distinction Award.

TO YVONNE,
FOR ADDING SPARKLE TO THIS BOOK, AND TO MY LIFE
W.J.D.

JACKSON J. SPIELVOGEL is associate professor emeritus of history at The Pennsylvania State University. He received his Ph.D. from The Ohio State University, where he specialized in Reformation history under Harold J. Grimm. His articles and reviews have appeared in such journals as *Moreana*, *Journal of General Education*, *Catholic Historical Review*, *Archiv für Reformationsgeschichte*, and *American Historical Review*. He has also contributed chapters or articles to *The Social History of the Reformation*, *The Holy Roman Empire: A Dictionary Handbook*, *Simon Wiesenthal Center Annual of Holocaust Studies*, and *Utopian Studies*. His work has been supported by fellowships from the Fulbright Foundation and the Foundation for Reformation Research. At Penn State, he helped inaugurate the Western civilization courses as well as a popular course on Nazi Germany. His book *Hitler and Nazi Germany* was published in 1987 (seventh edition, 2014). He is the author of *Western Civilization*, first published in 1991 (tenth edition, 2018). Professor Spielvogel has won five major university-wide teaching awards. During the year 1988–1989, he held the Penn State Teaching Fellowship, the university's most prestigious teaching award. In 1996, he won the Dean Arthur Ray Warnock Award for Outstanding Faculty Member and in 2000 received the Schreyer Honors College Excellence in Teaching Award.

TO DIANE,
WHOSE LOVE AND SUPPORT MADE IT ALL POSSIBLE
J.J.S.

BRIEF CONTENTS

PART I

THE FIRST CIVILIZATIONS AND THE RISE OF EMPIRES (PREHISTORY TO 500 C.E.)   2

PART II

NEW PATTERNS OF CIVILIZATION (500–1500 C.E.)   136

PART III

THE EMERGENCE OF NEW WORLD PATTERNS (1500–1800)   340

CONTENTS

17 THE EAST ASIAN WORLD 417

18 THE WEST ON THE EVE OF A NEW WORLD ORDER 442

MAPS

DOCUMENTS

FEATURES

PREFACE

FOR SEVERAL MILLION YEARS after primates first appeared on the surface of the earth, human beings lived in small communities, seeking to survive by hunting, fishing, and foraging in a frequently hostile environment. Then suddenly, in the space of a few thousand years, there was an abrupt change of direction as human beings in a few widely scattered areas of the globe began to master the art of cultivating food crops. As food production increased, the population in those areas rose correspondingly, and people began to gather in larger communities. They formed governments to provide protection and other needed services to the local population. Cities appeared and became the focal point of cultural and religious development. Historians refer to this process as the beginnings of civilization.

For generations, historians in Europe and the United States pointed to the rise of such civilizations as marking the origins of the modern world. Courses on Western civilization conventionally began with a chapter or two on the emergence of advanced societies in Egypt and Mesopotamia and then proceeded to ancient Greece and the Roman Empire. From Greece and Rome, the road led directly to the rise of modern civilization in the West.

There is nothing inherently wrong with this approach. Important aspects of our world today can indeed be traced back to these early civilizations, and all human beings the world over owe a considerable debt to their achievements. But all too often this interpretation has been used to imply that the course of civilization has been linear in nature, leading directly from the emergence of agricultural societies in ancient Mesopotamia to the rise of advanced industrial societies in Europe and North America. Until recently, most courses on world history taught in the United States routinely focused almost exclusively on the rise of the West, with only a passing glance at other parts of the world, such as Africa, India, and East Asia. The contributions made by those societies to the culture and technology of our own time were often passed over in silence.

Two major reasons have been advanced to justify this approach. Some have argued that it is more important that young minds understand the roots of their own heritage than that of peoples elsewhere in the world. In many cases, however, the motivation for this Eurocentric approach has been the belief that since the time of Socrates and Aristotle Western civilization has been the sole driving force in the evolution of human society.

Such an interpretation, however, represents a serious distortion of the process. During most of the course of human history, the most advanced civilizations have been not in the West, but in East Asia or the Middle East. A relatively brief period of European dominance culminated with the era of imperialism in the late nineteenth century, when the political, military, and economic power of the advanced nations of the West spread over the globe. During recent generations, however, that dominance has gradually eroded, partly as a result of changes taking place within Western societies and partly because new centers of development are emerging elsewhere on the globe—notably in Asia, with the growing economic strength of China and India and many of their neighbors.

World history, then, has been a complex process in which many branches of the human community have taken an active part, and the dominance of any one area of the world has been a temporary rather than a permanent phenomenon. It will be our purpose in this book to present a balanced picture of this story, with all respect for the richness and diversity of the tapestry of the human experience. Due attention must be paid to the rise of the West, of course, since that has been the most dominant aspect of world history in recent centuries. But the contributions made by other peoples must be given adequate consideration as well, not only in the period prior to 1500 when the major centers of civilization were located in Asia, but also in our own day, when a multipolar pattern of development is clearly beginning to emerge.

Anyone who wishes to teach or write about world history must decide whether to present the topic as an integrated whole or as a collection of different cultures. The world that we live in today, of course, is in many respects an interdependent one in terms of economics as well as culture and communications, a reality that is often expressed by the phrase "global village." The convergence of peoples across the surface of the earth into an integrated world system began in early times and intensified after the rise of capitalism in the early modern era. In growing recognition of this trend, historians trained in global history, as well as instructors in the growing number of world history courses, have now begun to speak and write of a "global approach" that turns attention away from the study of individual civilizations and focuses instead on the "big picture" or, as the world historian Fernand Braudel termed it, interpreting world history as a river with no banks.

On the whole, this development is to be welcomed as a means of bringing the common elements of the evolution of human society to our attention. But this approach also involves two problems. For the vast majority of their time on earth, human beings have lived in partial or virtually total isolation from each other. Differences in climate, location, and geographic features have created human societies vastly different from each other in culture and historical experience. Only in relatively recent times (the commonly accepted date has long been the beginning of the age of European exploration at the end of the fifteenth century, but some would now push it back to the era of the Mongol Empire or even further) have cultural interchanges begun to create a common "world system," in which events taking place in one part of the world are rapidly transmitted throughout the globe, often with momentous consequences. In recent generations, of course, the process of global interdependence has been proceeding even more rapidly. Nevertheless, even now the process is by no means complete, as ethnic and regional differences continue to exist and to shape the course of world history. The tenacity of these differences and sensitivities is reflected not only in the rise of internecine conflicts in such divergent areas as Africa, India, and eastern Europe, but also in the emergence in recent years of such regional organizations as the African Union, the Association for the Southeast Asian Nations, and the European Union.

The second problem is a practical one. College students today are all too often not well informed about the distinctive character of civilizations such as China and India and, without sufficient exposure to the historical evolution of such societies, will assume all too readily that the peoples in these countries have had historical experiences similar to ours and will respond to various stimuli in a similar fashion to those living in western Europe or the United States. If it is a mistake to ignore those forces that link us together, it is equally a mistake to underestimate those factors that continue to divide us and to differentiate us into a world of diverse peoples.

Our response to this challenge has been to adopt a global approach to world history while at the same time attempting to do justice to the distinctive character and development of individual civilizations and regions of the world. The presentation of individual cultures is especially important in Parts I and II, which cover a time when it is generally agreed that the process of global integration was not yet far advanced. Later chapters begin to adopt a more comparative and thematic approach, in deference to the greater number of connections that have been established among the world's peoples since the fifteenth and sixteenth centuries. Part V consists of a series of chapters that center on individual regions of the world while at the same time focusing on common problems related to the Cold War and the rise of global problems such as terrorism, climate change, and environmental pollution.

We have sought balance in another way as well. Many textbooks tend to simplify the content of history courses by emphasizing an intellectual or political perspective or, most recently, a social perspective, often at the expense of sufficient details in a chronological framework. This approach is confusing to students whose high school social studies programs have often neglected a systematic study of world history. We have attempted to write a well-balanced work in which political, economic, social, religious, intellectual, cultural, and military history have been integrated into a chronologically ordered synthesis.

FEATURES OF THE TEXT

To enliven the past and let readers see for themselves the materials that historians use to create their pictures of the past, we have included **primary sources** (boxed documents) in each chapter that are keyed to the discussion in the text. The documents, appearing in two features called **Historical Voices** and **Opposing Viewpoints**, include examples of the religious, artistic, intellectual, social, economic, and political aspects of life in different societies and reveal in a vivid fashion what civilization meant to the individual men and women who shaped it by their actions. Questions at the end of each source aid students in analyzing the documents.

Each chapter has a **lengthy introduction** to help maintain the continuity of the narrative and to provide a synthesis of important themes. Anecdotes in the chapter introductions dramatically convey the major theme or themes of each chapter. A **timeline** at the end of each chapter enables students to see the major developments of an era at a glance and within cross-cultural categories, while the more **detailed chronologies** reinforce the events discussed in the text.

Updated maps and extensive illustrations serve to deepen the reader's understanding of the text. **Detailed map captions** are designed to enrich students' awareness of the importance of geography to history, and numerous spot maps enable students to see at a glance the region or subject being discussed in the text. Map captions also include a question to guide students' reading of the map. To facilitate understanding of cultural movements, illustrations of artistic works discussed in the text are placed near the discussions. A **Chapter Outline and Focus Questions**, as well as **Critical Thinking** questions at the beginning of each chapter give students a useful overview and guide them to the main subjects of each chapter. The focus questions are then repeated at the beginning of each major section in the chapter to reinforce the main themes. A focus question entitled **Connections to Today** is intended to help students appreciate the relevance of history by asking them to draw connections between the past and present. A **glossary of important terms** (boldfaced in the text when they are introduced and defined) is provided at the back of the book to maximize reader comprehension. A **guide to pronunciation** is provided in parentheses in the text following the first mention of a complex name or term.

Comparative Essays, keyed to the seven major themes of world history (see p. xxix), enable us to more concretely draw comparisons and contrasts across geographic, cultural, and chronological lines. Some new essays have been added to the ninth edition. **Comparative Illustrations,** also keyed to the seven major themes of world history, continue to be a feature in each chapter. Both the comparative essays and the comparative illustrations conclude with focus questions to help students develop their analytical skills. We hope that the comparative essays and the comparative illustrations will assist instructors who wish to encourage their students to adopt a comparative approach to their understanding of the human experience. The **Film & History** feature, included in many chapters, now appears in a new, brief format.

The **Opposing Viewpoints** feature presents a comparison of two or three primary sources to facilitate student analysis of historical documents. This feature has been expanded and now appears in almost every chapter. Focus questions are included to guide students in evaluating the documents.

To help students examine how and why historians differ in their interpretation of specific topics, new historiographical subsections were introduced in the eighth edition. Each of these sections is now preceded by the heading **Historians Debate** to make students more aware of the interpretive nature of history.

End-of-chapter elements, first added in the seventh edition, provide study aids for class discussion, individual review, and/or further research. The **Chapter Summary** is illustrated with thumbnail images of chapter illustrations. **Reflection Questions** and the **Chapter Timeline** aid students in reviewing the chapter.

New to This Edition

After reexamining the entire book and analyzing the comments and reviews of many colleagues who have found the book to be a useful instrument for introducing their students to world history, we have also made a number of other changes for the ninth edition.

We have continued to strengthen the global framework of the book, but not at the expense of reducing the attention assigned to individual regions of the world. New material has been added to most chapters to help students

be aware of similar developments globally, including new comparative sections. New illustrations appear in every chapter. A number of the Part I through Part V opening essays have been substantially revised, and questions relating to the issues discussed in these essays have been added in the chapters that follow. The enthusiastic response to the primary sources (boxed documents) led us to evaluate the content of each document carefully and add new documents throughout the text, including new comparative documents in the Opposing Viewpoints features.

To keep up with the ever-growing body of historical scholarship, new or revised material has been added throughout the book on the following topics:

Chapter 1 Possible discovery of new hominids in Indonesia; Neanderthals and modern humans; cave painting; new Historians Debate section "Why did Early Civilizations Develop?"; the Hebrew Bible, including the Documentary Hypothesis; new illustration and material on the Ten Commandments.

Chapter 2 A new opening vignette focusses on the Indus Valley Civilization; section on Indian religion and the Comparative Essay have been revised; new document "The Duties of a King."

Chapter 3 The comparative essay on metals has been revised; new document "The Mandate of Heaven."

Chapter 4 Minoan Crete; Mycenaean Greece; the so-called "Dark Age" in Greece; the *polis*; Greek cultural identity; Greek settlements abroad; the Persian Wars; role of Persian threat for a growing sense of Greek cultural identity; growing sense of Greek cultural identity due to athletic games; new document feature "The Character of Alexander"; Hellenistic political institutions.

Chapter 5 Aeneas and Romulus and Remus and the legendary founding of Rome; citizenship policy and the Roman army; Roman imperialism; comparison of Augustus and Julius Caesar; revolts against Roman rule during the *Pax Romana*; new Historians Debate section "What was Romanization?"; contacts with Han China; Roman women; revolts against Roman rule in Judaea.

Chapter 6 The section on stateless societies has been revised and repositioned in the chapter; comparative essay on the environment revised; added material on Inka civilization; new document "The Legend of the Feathery Serpent."

Chapter 7 Revised opening vignette on Muhammad; new Historians Debate question on reasons for Islamic expansion; new document "Ibn Khaldun: Islam's Greatest Historian."

Chapter 8 New document "Beware the Troglodytes."

Chapter 9 The section on Indian religion has been substantially revised; new Historians Debate section "The

Indian Economy: Promise Unfulfilled?"; much new material has been added on early statehood in Southeast Asia and the role of the region in the maritime trade network; new document "Education of a Brahmin."

Chapter 10 New material on Empress Wu; revised section on traditional society in China; new document "Confucianism and its Enemies"; section on Admiral Zheng He revised and expanded.

Chapter 11 Revised section on Japanese borrowing from China; added information on Korean technology; two new documents: "Seduction of the Akashi Lady" and "The First Vietnam War."

Chapter 12 Monks as missionaries, particularly St. Patrick; Charlemagne as emperor; new Historians Debate section "What was Feudalism?"; peasant women; role of agriculture in the development of trade in the High Middle Ages; Bernard of Clairvaux; the Fourth Crusade; new material in Historians Debate section "What were the Effects of the Crusades?"

Chapter 13 The Fourth Crusade; new Historians Debate section "Why did the Eastern Roman Empire (Byzantine Empire) Last a Thousand Years Longer Than the Western Roman Empire?"; the English use of the longbow; the Great Schism; new C-head section "The Artist and Social Status"; new document feature "The Genius of Michelangelo."

Chapter 14 Revised introduction; new document "For God, Gold, and Glory in the Age of Exploration." New information on maritime trade in Asia and the motives for European exploration.

Chapter 15 Luther; the Jesuits; women and witchcraft; the Thirty Years' War; new document feature "The Destruction of Magdeburg in the Thirty Year's War."

Chapter 16 New document "A Portrait of Suleyman the Magnificent;" added discussion on Ottoman technology; revised and expanded section on Safavid Persia; revised comparative essay on war; new Historians Debate section "The Ottoman Empire: A Civilization in Decline?"

Chapter 17 New Historians Debate section "The Qing Economy: Ready for Takeoff?" New Opposing Viewpoints document "The Debate over Christianity."

Chapter 18 Women and the Scientific Revolution; Rococo art; global trade; the consumer revolution; new Historians Debate section "Was There an Agricultural Revolution?"; Jamestown; the Seven Years' War; new document feature "Frederick the Great and His Father"; the Three Estates; the French clergy; the Reign of Terror.

Chapter 19 New document feature "The Steam Engine and Cotton"; early railroad transportation; the Industrial Revolution on the Continent; British policies in India.

Chapter 20 Latin America; the United States; new document feature "A Radical Critique of the Land Problem in Mexico"; new Film & History feature, *Suffragette;* Courbet; Impressionism; Mary Cassatt; Japanese influence in the arts.

Chapter 21 Revised opening vignette on Cecil Rhodes; new Film & History vignette *A Passage to India*; revised discussion on colonial policies in Africa; new Historians Debate section "Imperialism: Drawing up the Balance Sheet."

Chapter 22 Two new Historians Debate sections "Was the October Revolution a Success or a Failure?" and "The Meiji Restoration: A Revolution from Above?" New documents "An Insignificant and Detestable Race" and "The Rules of Good Citizenship in Meiji Japan."

Chapter 23 New document "The Reality of War: The Views of British Poets"; life in the trenches; the end of World War I; the Great Depression.

Chapter 24 New opening vignette on Lenin and the East; revised section on the early Nanjing Republic; new Historians Debate section "Taisho Democracy: An Aberration?"; revised section on communism in Asia.

Chapter 25 New material on socialism and the rise of fascism in Italy and Germany; the Enabling Act; economic differences between fascism and communism; the Nazi economy; the Soviet economy; naval battles, including Battle of North Atlantic and Battle of Leyte Gulf; new B-head section "The Impact of Technology"; Japan and war crimes.

Chapter 26 New opening vignette on the rise of the Iron Curtain; new information on the Soviet takeover of Eastern Europe; new Film & History vignette *Bridge of Spies;* new information on the collapse of Soviet power in Eastern Europe; new closing section on "The Revenge of History."

Chapter 27 New document feature "One Day in the Life of Ivan Denisovich"; sections on Eastern Europe moved to Chapter 26; revised section on the collapse of the USSR; substantial updating and revision of material on contemporary China.

Chapter 28 French politics and immigration; France and terrorism; Germany, Great Britain and Brexit, Poland, Czech Republic, and Russia; the European Union; Canada; Argentina and Mexico; the Women's Movement; terrorism; immigration; new document feature "The West and Islam"; the environment; technology; new C-head section on "Art in the Contemporary World."

Chapter 29 New opening vignette on terrorism in West Africa; substantial revisions and updating of contemporary situation in Africa; new document on the OAU; fully revised an updated material on politics, economics, religion, and the recent crisis in the Middle East; new material on the Syrian civil war; revised Comparative Essay "Religion and Society."

Chapter 30 Revised opening vignette; revised section on communalism in India; new document "The Golden Throat of President Sukarno"; current conditions in South Asia, Southeast Asia, Japan, and the Little Tigers substantially revised. New Historians Debate section "The East Asian Miracle: Fact or Myth?"

Epilogue New material on the global economy.

Instructor Resources

✦ MINDTAP MindTap for *The Essential World History* 9e is a flexible, online learning platform that provides students with a relevant and engaging learning experience that builds their critical thinking skills and fosters their argumentation and analysis skills. Through a carefully designed chapter-based learning path, MindTap supports students as they develop historical understanding, improve their reading and writing skills, and practice critical thinking by making connections between ideas.

Students read sections of the ebook and take Check Your Understanding quizzes that test their reading comprehension. They put higher-level critical thinking skills into practice to complete chapter tests. They also use these skills to analyze textual and visual primary sources in each chapter through an autograded image primary source activity and a manually graded short essay in which students write comparatively about multiple primary sources.

Beyond the chapter-level content, students can increase their comfort in analyzing primary sources through thematically-organized primary source autograded activities that span the text. They also practice synthesizing their knowledge and articulating what they have learned through responding to essay prompts that span broader themes in the book.

MindTap also allows instructors to customize their content, providing tools that seamlessly integrate YouTube clips, outside websites, and personal content directly into the learning path. Instructors can assign additional primary source content through the Instructor Resource Center and Questia, primary- and secondary-source databases located on the MindTap app dock that house thousands of peer-reviewed journals, newspapers, magazines, and books.

The additional content available in MindTap mirrors and complements the authors' narrative, but also includes primary-source content and assessments not found in the printed text. To learn more, ask your Cengage sales representative to demo it for you—or go to **www.cengage .com/mindtap**.

Instructor's Companion Website   The Instructor's Companion Website, accessed through the Instructor Resource Center (login.cengage.com), houses all of the supplemental materials you can use for your course. This includes a Test Bank, Instructor's Manual, and PowerPoint Lecture Presentations. The Test Bank contains essay, multiple-choice, true-or-false, and historical identification questions for each chapter. The Instructor's Resource Manual includes instructional objectives and focus questions, chapter summaries, suggested lecture topics, map exercises, discussion questions for the primary sources, topics for student research, relevant websites, suggestions for additional videos, and online resources for information on historical sites. Finally, the PowerPoint Lectures are ADA-compliant slides that collate the key takeaways from the chapter in concise visual formats perfect for in-class presentations or for student review.

Cengage.com/student   Save your students time and money. Direct them to www.cengage.com/student for a choice in formats and savings and a better chance to succeed in your class. Cengage.com/student, Cengage's online store, is a single destination for more than 10,000 new textbooks, ebooks, study tools, and audio supplements. Students have the freedom to purchase à la carte exactly what they need when they need it. Students can save up to 70% off on the ebook electronic textbook.

✦ CENGAGE
UNLIMITED   We now offer CENGAGE UNLIMITED, the first-of-its-kind digital subscription designed specifically to lower costs. Students get everything Cengage has to offer—in one place. For $119.99 per term (or $179.99 per year), students have access to:

- Award-winning products proven to boost outcomes and increase engagement
- Over 20,000 digital products, covering 70 disciplines and 675 courses
- A free print rental with any activated digital learning product (like MindTap)
- Dozens of study guides matched to the most common college courses
- Twelve-month free access for up to six ebooks

Currently available in selected markets. For more information, please contact your local Learning Consultant or visit **cengage.com/unlimited**

Learn more at Cengage.com about books that build skills in doing history, including:

- *Doing History: Research and Writing in the Digital Age*, 2e (ISBN: 9781133587880) Prepared by Michael J. Galgano, J. Chris Arndt, and Raymond M. Hyser of James Madison University.

- *Writing for College History,* 1e (ISBN: 9780618306039) Prepared by Robert M. Frakes of Clarion University.

- *The Modern Researcher,* 6e (ISBN: 9780495318705) Prepared by Jacques Barzun and Henry F. Graff of Columbia University.

Reader Program Cengage publishes a number of readers. Some contain exclusively primary sources, others are devoted to essays and secondary sources, and still others provide a combination of primary and secondary sources. All of these readers are designed to guide students through the process of historical inquiry. Visit **www .cengage.com/history** for a complete list of readers.

Custom Options Nobody knows your students like you, so why not give them a text that is tailor-fit to their needs? Cengage offers custom solutions for your course—whether it's making a small modification to *The Essential World History* 9e, to match your syllabus or combining multiple sources to create something truly unique. Contact your Cengage representative to explore custom solutions for your course.

ACKNOWLEDGMENTS

Both authors gratefully acknowledge that without the generosity of many others, this project could not have been completed.

William Duiker would like to thank Kumkum Chatterjee and On-cho Ng for their helpful comments about issues related to the history of India and premodern China. His long-time colleague Cyril Griffith, now deceased, was a cherished friend and a constant source of information about modern Africa. Art Goldschmidt has been of invaluable assistance in reading several chapters of the manuscript, as well as in unraveling many of the mysteries of Middle Eastern civilization. He would like to thank Charles Ingrao for providing information on Spanish policies in Latin America, and Tony Hopkins and Dan Baugh for their insights on British imperial policy. Finally, he remains profoundly grateful to his wife, Yvonne V. Duiker, Ph.D. She has not only given her usual measure of love and support when this appeared to be an insuperable task, but she has also contributed her own time and expertise to enrich the sections on art and literature, thereby adding life and sparkle to this edition, as well as the earlier editions of the book. To her, and to his daughters Laura and Claire, he will be forever thankful for bringing joy to his life.

Jackson Spielvogel would like to thank Art Goldschmidt, David Redles, and Christine Colin for their time and ideas. Daniel Haxall of Kutztown University provided valuable assistance with materials on postwar art, popular culture, Postmodern art and thought, and the digital age. He is especially grateful to Kathryn Spielvogel for her work as research associate. Above all, he thanks his family for their support. The gifts of love, laughter, and patience from his daughters, Jennifer and Kathryn; his sons, Eric and Christian; his daughters-in-law, Liz and Laurie; and his sons-in-law, Daniel and Eddie, were especially valuable. He also wishes to acknowledge his grandchildren, Devyn, Bryn, Drew, Elena, Sean, Emma, and Jackson, who bring great joy to his life on a daily basis. Diane, his wife and best friend, provided him with editorial assistance, wise counsel, and the loving support that made a project of this magnitude possible.

Thanks to Cengage's comprehensive review process, many historians were asked to evaluate our manuscript. We are grateful to the following for the innumerable suggestions that have greatly improved our work:

Henry Abramson
Florida Atlantic University

Eric H. Ash
Wayne State University

William Bakken
Rochester Community College

Suzanne Balch-Lindsay
Eastern New Mexico University

Michael E. Birdwell
Tennessee Technological University

Eric Bobo
Hinds Community College

Michael Bonislawski
Cambridge College

Connie Brand
Meridien Community College

Eileen Brown
Norwalk Community College

Paul Buckingham
Morrisville State College

Ted Butler
Darton State College

Kelly Cantrell
East Mississippi Community College

Thomas Cardoza
University of California, San Diego

Alistair Chapman
Westmont College

Nupur Chaudhuri
Texas Southern University

Richard Crane
Greensboro College

Wade Dudley
East Carolina University

E. J. Fabyan
Vincennes University

Kenneth Faunce
Washington State University

Jamie Garcia
Hawaii Pacific University

Steven Gosch
University of Wisconsin—Eau Claire

Donald Harreld
Brigham Young University

Janine C. Hartman
University of Connecticut

Greg Havrilcsak
University of Michigan—Flint

Thomas Hegerty
University of Tampa

Sanders Huguenin
University of Science and Arts of Oklahoma

Ahmed Ibrahim
Southwest Missouri State University

C. Barden Keeler
Gulf Coast High School

Marilynn Fox Kokoszka
Orchard Ridge Campus, Oakland Community College

James Krippner-Martinez
Haverford College

Oscar Lansen
University of North Carolina—Charlotte

David Leinweber
Oxford College, Emory University

Susie Ling
Pasadena City College

Moira Maguire
University of Arkansas at Little Rock

Jason McCollom
University of Arkansas

Andrew McGreevy
Ohio University

Daniel Miller
Calvin College

Michael Murdock
Brigham Young University

Lopita Nath
University of the Incarnate Word

Mark Norris
Grace College

Elsa A. Nystrom
Kennesaw State University

S. Mike Pavelec
Hawaii Pacific University

Matthew Phillips
Kent State University

Randall L. Pouwels
University of Central Arkansas

Margaret Power
Illinois Institute of Technology

Pamela Sayre
Henry Ford Community College

Jenny Schwartzberg
Delgado Community College

Philip Curtis Skaggs
Grand Valley State University

Laura Smoller
University of Arkansas at Little Rock

Beatrice Spade
University of Southern Colorado

Jeremy Stahl
Middle Tennessee State University

Clif Stratton
Washington State University

Kate Transchel
California State University, Chico

Justin Vance
Hawaii Pacific University

Lorna VanMeter
Ball State University

Michelle White
University of Tennessee at Chattanooga

Edna Yahil
Washington State University—Swiss Center

The following individuals contributed reviews for the ninth edition:

Connie Brand
Meridian Community College

Brett Brinegar
Copiah-Lincoln Community College

Stephen P. Budney
University of Pikeville

Kelly Cantrell
East Mississippi Community College

Shawn Dry
Oakland Community College

Steven Patterson
Mississippi College

Melissa Ryckman
Martin Methodist College

Jason Toy
Cecil College

The authors are truly grateful to the people who have helped us to produce this book. The editors at Cengage have been both helpful and congenial at all times. We especially wish to thank Kate MacLean who thoughtfully, wisely, efficiently, and pleasantly guided the overall development of this edition. We also thank Philip Lanza for his valuable managerial skills. Kayci Wyatt of MPS Limited was as cooperative and cheerful as she was competent in matters of production management. And finally, we wish to thank Clark Baxter, whose initial faith in our ability to do this project was inspiring.

THEMES FOR UNDERSTANDING WORLD HISTORY

AS THEY PURSUE THEIR CRAFT, historians often organize their material according to themes that enable them to ask and try to answer basic questions about the past. Such is our intention here. In preparing the ninth edition of this book, we have selected several major themes that we believe are especially important in understanding the course of world history. Thinking about these themes will help students to perceive the similarities and differences among cultures since the beginning of the human experience.

In the chapters that follow, we will refer to these themes frequently as we advance from the prehistoric era to the present. Where appropriate, we shall make comparisons across cultural boundaries or across different time periods. To facilitate this process, we have included a comparative essay in each chapter that focuses on a particular theme within the specific time period covered by that chapter. For example, the comparative essay in Chapter 6 deals with the human impact on the natural environment during the premodern era, while the essay in Chapter 30 discusses the same issue in the contemporary world. Each comparative essay is identified with a particular theme, although many essays touch on multiple themes.

We have sought to illustrate these themes using comparative illustrations in each chapter. These illustrations are comparative in nature and seek to encourage the reader to think about thematic issues in cross-cultural terms, while not losing sight of the unique characteristics of individual societies. Our seven themes, each divided into two subtopics, are listed below.

Politics & Government
1. Politics and Government The study of politics seeks to answer certain basic questions that historians have about the structure of a society: How were people governed? What was the relationship between the ruler and the ruled? What people or groups of people (the political elites) held political power? What actions did people take to guarantee their security or change their form of government?

Art & Ideas
2. *Art and Ideas* We cannot understand a society without looking at its culture, or the common ideas, beliefs, and patterns of behavior that are passed on from one generation to the next. Culture includes both high culture and popular culture. High culture consists of the writings of a society's thinkers and the works of its artists. A society's popular culture encompasses the ideas and experiences of ordinary people. Today, the media have embraced the term *popular culture* to describe the current trends and fashionable styles.

Religion & Philosophy
3. *Religion and Philosophy* Throughout history, people have sought to find a deeper meaning to human life. How have the world's great religions, such as Hinduism, Buddhism, Judaism, Christianity, and Islam, influenced people's lives? How have they spread to create new patterns of culture in other parts of the world?

Family & Society
4. *Family and Society* The most basic social unit in human society has always been the family. From a study of family and social patterns, we learn about the different social classes that make up a society and their relationships with one another. We also learn about the role of gender in individual societies. What different roles did men and women play in their societies? How and why were those roles different?

Science & Technology
5. *Science and Technology* For thousands of years, people around the world have made scientific discoveries and technological innovations that have changed our world. From the creation of stone tools that made farming easier to advanced computers that guide our airplanes, science and technology have altered how humans have related to their world.

Earth & Environment
6. *Earth and the Environment* Throughout history, peoples and societies have been affected by the physical world in which they live. Climatic changes alone have been an important factor in human history. Through their economic activities, peoples and societies, in turn, have also made an impact on their world. Human activities have affected the physical environment and even endangered the very existence of entire societies and species.

7. *Interaction and Exchange* Many world historians believe that the exchange of ideas and innovations is the driving force behind the evolution of human societies. Knowledge of agriculture, writing and printing, metalworking, and navigational techniques, for example, spread gradually from one part of the world to other regions and eventually changed the face of the entire globe. The process of cultural and technological exchange took place in various ways, including trade, conquest, and the migration of peoples.

A NOTE TO STUDENTS ABOUT LANGUAGES AND THE DATING OF TIME

One of the most difficult challenges in studying world history is coming to grips with the multitude of names, words, and phrases in unfamiliar languages. Unfortunately, this problem has no easy solution. We have tried to alleviate the difficulty, where possible, by providing an English-language translation of foreign words or phrases, a glossary, and a pronunciation guide in parentheses in the text. The issue is especially complicated in the case of Chinese because two separate systems are commonly used to transliterate the spoken Chinese language into the Roman alphabet. The Wade-Giles system, invented in the nineteenth century, was the most frequently used until recent years, when the pinyin system was adopted by the People's Republic of China as its own official form of transliteration. We have opted to use the latter, as it appears to be gaining acceptance in the United States.

In our examination of world history, we also need to be aware of the dating of time. In recording the past, historians try to determine the exact time when events occurred. World War II in Europe, for example, began on September 1, 1939, when Adolf Hitler sent German troops into Poland, and ended on May 7, 1945, when Germany surrendered. By using dates, historians can place events in order and try to determine the development of patterns over periods of time.

If someone asked you when you were born, you would reply with a number, such as 2000. In the United States, we would all accept that number without question, because it is part of the dating system followed in the Western world (Europe and the Western Hemisphere). In this system, events are dated by counting backward or forward from the birth of Christ (assumed to be the year 1). An event that took place 400 years before the birth of Christ would commonly be dated 400 B.C. (before Christ). Dates after the birth of Christ are labeled as A.D. These letters stand for the Latin words *anno domini,* which mean "in the year of the Lord" (or the year of the birth of Christ). Thus, an event that took place 250 years after the birth of Christ is written A.D. 250, or in the year of the Lord 250. It can also

be written as 250, just as you would not give your birth year as A.D. 2000, but simply as 2000.

Some historians now prefer to use the abbreviations B.C.E. ("before the common era") and C.E. ("common era") instead of B.C. and A.D. This is especially true of world historians who prefer to use symbols that are not so Western or Christian oriented. The dates, of course, remain the same. Thus, 1950 B.C.E. and 1950 B.C. are the same year, as are A.D. 40 and 40 C.E. In keeping with the current usage by many world historians, this book will use the terms B.C.E. and C.E.

Historians also make use of other terms to refer to time. A decade is 10 years; a century is 100 years; and a millennium is 1,000 years. The phrase "fourth century B.C.E." refers to the fourth period of 100 years counting backward from 1, the assumed date of the birth of Christ. Since the first century B.C.E. would be the years 100 B.C.E. to 1 B.C.E., the fourth century B.C.E. would be the years 400 B.C.E. to 301 B.C.E. We could say, then, that an event in 350 B.C.E. took place in the fourth century B.C.E.

The phrase "fourth century C.E." refers to the fourth period of 100 years after the birth of Christ. Since the first period of 100 years would be the years 1 to 100, the fourth period or fourth century would be the years 301 to 400. We could say, then, for example, that an event in 350 took place in the fourth century. Likewise, the first millennium B.C.E. refers to the years 1000 B.C.E. to 1 B.C.E.; the second millennium C.E. refers to the years 1001 to 2000.

The dating of events can also vary from people to people. Most people in the Western world use the Western calendar, also known as the Gregorian calendar after Pope Gregory XIII, who refined it in 1582. The Hebrew calendar, on the other hand, uses a different system in which the year 1 is the equivalent of the Western year 3760 B.C.E., considered by Jews to be the date of the creation of the world. Thus, the Western year 2018 is the year 5778 on the Jewish calendar. The Islamic calendar begins year 1 on the day Muhammad fled from Mecca, which is the year 622 C.E. on the Western calendar.

THE FIRST CIVILIZATIONS AND THE RISE OF EMPIRES (PREHISTORY TO 500 C.E.)

FOR HUNDREDS OF THOUSANDS OF YEARS, human beings lived in small groups or villages, surviving by hunting, fishing, and foraging in an often hostile environment. Then, in the space of a few thousand years, an abrupt change occurred as people in a few areas of the world began to master the art of cultivating food crops. As food production increased, the population in these areas grew, and people began to live in larger communities. Cities appeared and became centers of cultural and religious development. Historians refer to these changes as the *beginnings* of civilization.

How and why did the first civilizations arise? What role did cross-cultural contacts play in their development? What was the nature of the relationship between these permanent settlements and nonagricultural peoples living elsewhere in the world? Finally, what brought about the demise of these early civilizations, and what legacy did they leave for their successors in the region? The first civilizations that emerged in Mesopotamia, Egypt, India, and China in the fourth and third millennia B.C.E. all shared several basic characteristics. Perhaps most important was that each developed in a river valley that provided the agricultural resources needed to maintain a large population.

The emergence of these sedentary societies had major effects on the social organizations, religious beliefs, and ways of life of the peoples living in them. As populations increased and cities sprang up, centralized authority became a necessity. And in the cities, new forms of livelihood arose to satisfy the growing demand for social services and consumer goods. Some people became artisans or merchants; others became warriors, scholars, or priests. In some cases, the early cities reflected the hierarchical character of the society as a whole, with a central royal palace surrounded by an imposing wall to separate the rulers from the remainder of the urban population.

Although the emergence of the first civilizations led to the formation of cities governed by elites, the vast majority of the population consisted of peasants or slaves working on the lands of the wealthy. In general, the changes affected rural peoples less than their urban counterparts. Farmers continued to live in simple mud-and-thatch huts, and many continued to face legal restrictions on their freedom of action and movement. Slavery was common in virtually every ancient society.

Within these civilizations, the nature of social organization and relationships also began to change. As the concept of private property spread, people were less likely to live in large kinship groups, and the nuclear family became increasingly prevalent. Gender roles came to be differentiated, with men working in the fields or at various specialized occupations and women remaining in the home. Wives were less likely to be viewed as partners than as possessions under the control of their husbands.

These new civilizations were also the sites of significant religious and cultural developments. All of them gave birth to new religions that sought to explain and even influence the forces of nature. Winning the approval of the gods was deemed crucial to a community's

I.1

success, and a professional class of priests emerged to handle relations with the divine world.

Writing was an important development in the evolution of these new civilizations. Eventually, all of them used writing as a means of communication and as an avenue of creative expression.

From the beginnings of the first civilizations around 3000 B.C.E., the trend was toward the creation of larger territorial states with more sophisticated systems of control. This process reached a high point in the first millennium B.C.E. Between 1000 and 500 B.C.E., the Assyrians and Persians amassed empires that encompassed large areas of the Middle East. The conquests of Alexander the Great in the fourth century B.C.E. created an even larger, if short-lived, empire that soon divided into four kingdoms. Later, the western portion of these kingdoms, along with the Mediterranean world and much of Western Europe, fell subject to the mighty empire of the Romans. At the same time, much of India became part of the Mauryan Empire. Finally, in the last few centuries B.C.E., the Qin and Han Dynasties of China created a unified Chinese empire.

At first, these new civilizations had relatively little contact with peoples in the surrounding regions. But evidence is growing that a regional trade had started to take hold in the Middle East, and probably in southern and eastern Asia as well, at an early date. As the population increased, the volume of trade rose with it, and the new civilizations moved outward to acquire new lands and access needed resources. As they expanded, they began to encounter peoples along the periphery of their empires.

Little evidence has survived to show us the nature of these first encounters, but the results probably varied widely according to time and place. In some cases, the growing civilizations found it relatively easy to absorb the isolated communities of agricultural or food-gathering peoples they encountered. Such was the case in southern China and southern India. But in other instances, notably among the nomadic or seminomadic peoples in the Central and northeastern parts of Asia, the problem was more complicated and often resulted in bitter and extended conflict.

Over a long period of time, contacts between these nomadic or seminomadic peoples and settled civilizations gradually developed. At least initially, the relationships were mutually beneficial because each needed goods produced by the other. As early as 3000 B.C.E., nomadic peoples in Central Asia also served as an important link for goods and ideas transported over distances between sedentary civilizations. Overland trade throughout southwestern Asia was already well established by the third millennium B.C.E.

Eventually, the relationship between the settled peoples and the nomadic peoples became increasingly tense. Where conflict occurred, the governments of the sedentary civilizations used a variety of techniques to resolve their problems, including negotiations, conquest, and alliances with other pastoral peoples to isolate their primary tormentors.

In the end, these early civilizations collapsed not only as a result of nomadic invasions but also because of their own weaknesses, which made them increasingly vulnerable to attacks along the frontier. Some of their problems were political, and others were related to climatic change or environmental problems.

The fall of the ancient empires did not mark the end of civilization, of course, but rather served as a transition to a new stage of increasing complexity in the evolution of human society.

Chapter Outline and Focus Questions

Source: Essam Al-Sudani/AFP/Getty Images

1.1 Excavation of Warka Showing the Ruins of Uruk

Critical Thinking

Q *In what ways were the civilizations of Mesopotamia and North Africa alike? In what ways were they different? What accounts for the similarities and differences?*

Connections to Today

Q *What lessons can you learn from the decline and fall of early civilizations in Mesopotamia, Egypt, Assyria, and Persia, and how do those lessons apply to today's civilizations?*

IN 1849, A DARING YOUNG ENGLISHMAN made a hazardous journey into the deserts and swamps of southern Iraq. Braving high winds and temperatures that reached 120 degrees Fahrenheit, William Loftus led a small expedition southward along the banks of the Euphrates River in search of the roots of civilization. As he said, "From our childhood we have been led to regard this place as the cradle of the human race."

Guided by native Arabs into the southernmost reaches of Iraq, Loftus and his small band of explorers were soon overwhelmed by what they saw. He wrote, "I know of nothing more exciting or impressive than the first sight of one of these great piles, looming in solitary grandeur from the surrounding plains and marshes." One of these piles, known to the natives as the mound of Warka, contained the ruins of Uruk, one of the first cities in the world and part of the world's first civilizations.

Southern Iraq, known to the ancient Greeks as *Mesopotamia*, was one of the areas in the world where civilization began. In the fertile valleys of large rivers—the Tigris and Euphrates in Mesopotamia, the Nile in Egypt, the Indus in India, and the Yellow in China— intensive agriculture became capable of supporting large groups of people. In these regions, civilization was born. The first civilizations emerged in western Asia (now known as the Middle East) and Egypt, where people developed organized societies and created the ideas and institutions that we associate with civilization.

Before considering the early civilizations of western Asia and Egypt, however, we must briefly examine our prehistory and observe how human beings made the shift from hunting and gathering to agricultural communities and ultimately to cities and civilizations.

1-1 THE FIRST HUMANS

 Focus Question: How did the Paleolithic and Neolithic Ages differ, and how did the Neolithic Revolution affect the lives of men and women?

The earliest humanlike creatures—known as **hominids**— lived in Africa some 3 million to 4 million years ago. Called *Australopithecines* (aw-stray-loh-PITH-uh-synz), or "southern ape men," by their discoverers, they flourished in eastern and southern Africa and were the first hominids to make simple stone tools. Australopithecines may also have been bipedal—that is, they may have walked upright on two legs—a trait that would have enabled them to move over long distances and make use of their arms and legs for different purposes.

In 1959, Louis and Mary Leakey discovered a new form of hominid in Africa that they labeled *Homo habilis* ("skilled human"). The Leakeys believed that *Homo habilis*, which had a brain almost 50 percent larger than that of

the Australopithecines, was the earliest toolmaking hominid. Their larger brains and ability to walk upright allowed these hominids to become more sophisticated in searching for meat, seeds, and nuts for nourishment.

New hominids continue to be found, although considerable controversy often surrounds those discoveries. The contention that a 2003 discovery in Indonesia of a distinct hominid species known as the "hobbit" because of its small body is a distinct hominid species has been challenged by other scientists.

A new phase in early human development occurred around 1.5 million years ago with the emergence of *Homo erectus* ("upright human"). As a more advanced human form, *Homo erectus* made use of larger and more varied tools and was the first hominid to leave Africa and move into Europe and Asia.

1-1a The Emergence of *Homo sapiens*

Around 250,000 years ago, a crucial stage in human development began with the emergence of *Homo sapiens* (HOH-moh SAY-pee-unz) ("wise human being"). The first anatomically modern humans—*Homo sapiens sapiens* ("wise, wise human being")— appeared in Africa between 200,000 and 150,000 years ago. Recent evidence indicates that they began to spread outside Africa around 70,000 years ago. Map 1.1 on p. 6 shows probable dates for different movements, although many of these are still controversial.

These modern humans, who were our direct ancestors, soon encountered other hominids such as the Neanderthals, whose remains were first found in the Neander Valley in Germany. Neanderthal remains have since been found in both Europe and western Asia and have been dated to between 200,000 and 30,000 B.C.E. New genetic evidence indicates that European humans interbred with Neanderthals—and East Asian humans even more so. Neanderthals relied on a variety of stone tools and were the first early people to bury their dead. By 30,000 B.C.E., *Homo sapiens sapiens* had replaced the Neanderthals, who had largely become extinct.

The Spread of Humans: Out of Africa or Multiregional? The movements of the first modern humans were rarely sudden or rapid. Groups of people advanced beyond their old hunting grounds at a rate of only two to three miles per generation. This was enough, however, to populate the world in some tens of thousands of years. Some scholars who advocate a multiregional theory have suggested that advanced human creatures may have emerged independently in different parts of world rather than in Africa alone. But the latest genetic, archaeological, and climatic evidence strongly supports the out-of-Africa theory as the

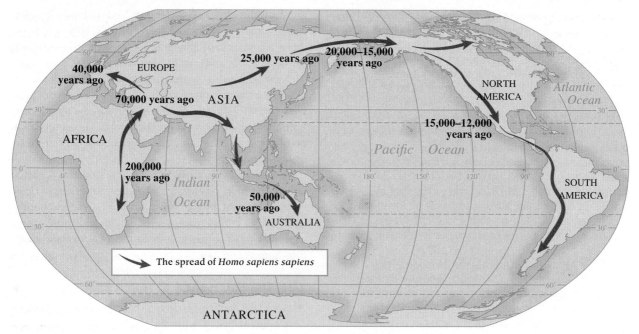

Map 1.1 The Spread of *Homo sapiens sapiens*. *Homo sapiens sapiens* spread from Africa beginning some 70,000 years ago. Living and traveling in small groups, these anatomically modern humans were hunter-gatherers.

 Given that some diffusion of humans occurred during ice ages, how would such climate change affect humans and their movements, especially from Asia to Australia and Asia to North America?

most likely explanation of human origin. In any case, by 10,000 B.C.E., members of *Homo sapiens sapiens* could be found throughout the world. By that time, only the human species was left. All humans today—whether Europeans, Australian Aborigines, or Africans—belong to the same subspecies of human being.

1-1b The Hunter-Gatherers of the Paleolithic Age

One of the basic distinguishing features of the human species is the ability to make tools. The earliest tools were made of stone, and so this early period of human history (ca. 2,500,000–10,000 B.C.E.) has been designated the **Paleolithic Age** (*paleolithic* is Greek for "old stone").

For hundreds of thousands of years, humans relied on gathering and hunting for their daily food. Paleolithic peoples had a close relationship with the world around them, and over time they came to know which plants to eat and which animals to hunt. They gathered wild nuts, berries, fruits, and a variety of wild grains and green plants. Around the world, they captured and consumed various animals, including buffalo, reindeer, and fish.

Gathering wild plants and hunting animals no doubt led to certain patterns of living. Paleolithic people probably lived in small bands of twenty or thirty. They were

nomadic, moving from place to place to follow animal migrations and vegetation cycles. Over the years, their tools became more refined and more useful. The invention of the spear and later the bow and arrow made hunting considerably easier. Harpoons and fishhooks made of bone increased the catch of fish.

Both men and women were responsible for finding food—the chief work of Paleolithic people. Because women bore and raised the children, they generally stayed close to the camps, but they played an important role in acquiring food by gathering berries, nuts, and grains. Men hunted for wild animals, an activity that often took them far from camp. Because both men and women played important roles in providing for the band's survival, many scientists believe that a rough equality existed between men and women.

Some groups of Paleolithic people found shelter in caves, but over time they also created new types of shelter. Perhaps the most common was a simple structure of wood poles or sticks covered with animal hides. The systematic use of fire, which archaeologists believe began around 500,000 years ago, made it possible for the caves and human-made structures to have light and heat. Fire also enabled early humans to cook their food, which made it taste better, last longer, and, in the case of some plants such as wild grain, easier to chew and digest.

The making of tools and the use of fire—two important technological innovations of Paleolithic peoples—remind us how adaptation is crucial to human survival. But Paleolithic peoples did more than just survive. The cave paintings of large animals found in southwestern France and northern Spain bear witness to the cultural activity of Paleolithic peoples. A cave discovered in southern France in 1994 contains more than 300 paintings of lions, oxen, owls, bears, and other animals. Most of these are animals that Paleolithic people did not hunt, which suggests that the paintings were made for religious or even decorative purposes. To make their paintings, Paleolithic artists used stone lamps that burned animal fat to illuminate the cave walls and mixed powdered mineral ores with animal fat to create red, yellow, and black pigments. Some artists even made brushes out of animal hairs to apply their paints.

1-1c The Neolithic Revolution, ca. 10,000–4000 B.C.E.

The end of the last ice age around 10,000 B.C.E. was followed by what is called the **Neolithic Revolution**, a significant change in living patterns that occurred in the New Stone Age. The name *New Stone Age* is misleading, however. Although Neolithic peoples made a new type of polished stone axes, this was not the most significant change they introduced.

A Revolution in Agriculture   The biggest change was the shift from gathering plants and hunting animals for sustenance (food gathering) to producing food by systematic agriculture (food production). Planting grains and vegetables provided a regular supply of food, whereas the domestication of animals such as sheep, goats, cattle, and pigs added a steady source of meat, milk, and fibers such as wool for clothing. Growing crops and taming food-producing animals created new relationships between humans and nature, something historians have described as an agricultural revolution (see the Comparative Essay "From Hunter-Gatherers and Herders to Farmers," p. 8). Revolutionary change is dramatic and requires great effort, but the ability to acquire food on a regular basis gave humans greater control over their environment and enabled them to give up their nomadic ways of life and live in settled communities. The increase in food supplies also led to a noticeable expansion of the population.

Systematic agriculture developed independently in different areas of the world between 8000 and 5000 B.C.E. Inhabitants of the Middle East began cultivating wheat and barley and domesticating pigs, cattle, goats, and sheep by 8000 B.C.E. From the Middle East, farming spread into southeastern Europe and by 4000 B.C.E. was well established in Central Europe and the coastal regions of the Mediterranean. The cultivation of wheat and barley also spread from western Asia into the Nile River Valley of Egypt by 6000 B.C.E. and soon spread up the Nile to other areas of Africa. In the woodlands and tropical forests of Central Africa, a separate farming system emerged, based on the cultivation of tubers or root crops such as yams. The cultivation of wheat and barley also moved eastward into the highlands of northwestern and Central India between 7000 and 5000 B.C.E. By 5000 B.C.E., rice was being cultivated in Southeast Asia, and from there it spread into southern China. In northern China, the cultivation of millet and the domestication of pigs and dogs seemed well established by 6000 B.C.E. In the Western Hemisphere, Mesoamericans (inhabitants of present-day Mexico and Central America) domesticated beans, squash, and maize (corn) as well as dogs and fowl between 7000 and 5000 B.C.E.

Consequences of the Neolithic Revolution   Growing crops on a regular basis gave rise to more permanent settlements that historians refer to as *Neolithic* farming villages or towns. Although they appeared in Europe, India, Egypt, China, and Mesoamerica, the oldest and most extensive Neolithic villages were in the Middle East. Çatal Hüyük (chaht-ul hoo-YOOK) in modern Turkey had walls that enclosed thirty-two acres, and its population probably reached 6,000 inhabitants during its high point from 6700 to 5700 B.C.E. People lived in simple mud-brick houses that were built so close to one another that there were few streets. To get to their homes, people had to walk along the rooftops and enter their homes through holes in their roofs.

Religious shrines housing figures of gods and goddesses have been found at Çatal Hüyük, as have many female statuettes. Molded with noticeably large breasts and buttocks, these "earth mothers" perhaps symbolically represented the fertility of both "our mother" Earth and human mothers. The shrines and the statues point to the important role of religious practices in the lives of these Neolithic peoples.

The Neolithic agricultural revolution had far-reaching consequences. Once people settled in villages or towns, they built houses for protection and other structures to store goods. As organized communities stored food and accumulated material goods, they began to engage in trade. People also began to specialize in certain crafts, and a division of labor developed. Pottery was made from clay and baked in a fire to make it hard. The pots were used for cooking and to store grains. Stone tools became more refined as flint blades were used to make sickles and hoes for use in the fields. Vegetable fibers from such plants as flax and cotton were used to make thread that

From Hunter-Gatherers and Herders to Farmers

Earth & Environment Some 10,000 years ago, human beings began to cultivate crops and domesticate animals. The first farmers undoubtedly used simple techniques and still relied primarily on other forms of food production such as hunting, foraging, and pastoralism (herding). The real breakthrough came when farmers began to cultivate crops along the floodplains of river systems. The advantage was that crops grown in such areas were not as dependent on rainfall and therefore produced more reliable harvests. In addition, sediments carried by river waters deposited nutrients in soils, enabling farmers to cultivate single plots of ground for many years without moving to new locations. Thus, the first truly sedentary (nonmigratory) societies were born.

The spread of river valley agriculture in various parts of Asia and Africa was the decisive factor in the rise of the first civilizations. The increase in food production in these regions made possible a significant growth in population, while efforts to control the flow of water to maximize the irrigation of cultivated areas and to protect the local inhabitants from hostile forces outside the community led to the first cooperative activities on a large scale. The need to oversee the entire process brought about the emergence of an elite that was eventually transformed into a government.

We shall investigate this process in the next several chapters as we explore the rise of civilizations in the Mediterranean, the Middle East, South Asia, China, and the Americas. We shall also raise many important questions: Why did some human communities not take the leap to farming even though they had the capacity to support agriculture? Why did other groups that mastered the cultivation of crops not take the next step and create large and advanced societies? Finally, what happened to the existing communities of hunter-gatherers who were overrun or driven out as the agricultural revolution spread throughout the world?

Over the years, many possible explanations—some biological and others cultural or environmental in nature—have been advanced to answer such questions. According to Jared Diamond in *Guns, Germs, and Steel: The Fates of Human Societies,* the ultimate causes of such differences lie not within the character or cultural values of the resident population but in the nature of the local climate and topography. These influence the degree to which local crops and animals can be put to human use and then transmitted to adjoining regions. In Mesopotamia, for example, the widespread availability of edible crops such as wheat and barley helped promote the transition to agriculture in the region. At the same time, the absence of land barriers between Mesopotamia and neighbors to the east and west facilitated the rapid spread of agricultural techniques and crops to climatically similar regions in the Indus River Valley and Egypt.

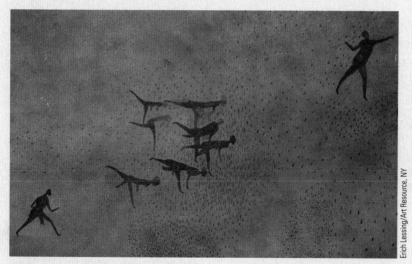

Erich Lessing/Art Resource, NY

1.2 Women's Work. This rock painting from a cave in modern-day Algeria, dating from around the fourth millennium B.C.E., shows women harvesting grain.

 What role did agriculture play in the emergence of civilization?

was woven into cloth. Many of the food plants consumed today began to be cultivated in the Neolithic Age.

The change to systematic agriculture in the Neolithic Age also had consequences for the relationship between men and women. Men assumed the primary responsibility for working in the fields and herding animals, jobs that kept them away from the home. Women remained behind, grinding grain into flour, caring for the children, weaving clothes, and performing other household tasks that required considerable labor. In time, as work outside the home was increasingly perceived as more important than work done at home, men came to play the more dominant role in society, which gave rise to the practice of **patriarchy** (PAY-tree-ark-ee), or a society dominated by men, a basic pattern that has persisted to our own times.

Other patterns set in the Neolithic Age also proved to be enduring elements of human history. Fixed dwellings, domesticated animals, regular farming, a division of labor, men holding power—all of these are part of the human story. For all of our scientific and technological progress, human survival still depends on growing and storing food, an accomplishment of people in the Neolithic Age. The Neolithic Revolution was truly a turning point in human history.

Between 4000 and 3000 B.C.E., significant technical developments began to transform Neolithic towns. The invention of writing enabled records to be kept, and the use of metals marked a new level of human control over the environment and its resources. Already before 4000 B.C.E., artisans had discovered that metal-bearing rocks could be heated to liquefy metals that could then be cast in molds to produce tools and weapons that were more useful than stone instruments. Although copper was the first metal to be used for producing tools, after 4000 B.C.E. metalworkers in western Asia discovered that combining copper and tin formed bronze, a much harder and more durable metal than copper alone. Its widespread use has led historians to speak of the Bronze Age from around 3000 to 1200 B.C.E.; thereafter, bronze was increasingly replaced by iron.

At first, Neolithic settlements were hardly more than villages, but as their inhabitants mastered the art of farming, more complex human societies gradually emerged. As wealth increased, these societies began to develop armies and wall off their cities for protection. By the beginning of the Bronze Age, the concentration of larger numbers of people in river valleys was leading to a whole new pattern for human life.

Erich Lessing/Art Resource, NY

1.3 Statue from Ain Ghazal. This life-sized statue made of plaster and bitumen was discovered in 1984 in Ain Ghazal, an archaeological site near Amman, Jordan. Dating from 6500 B.C.E., it is among the oldest known statues of the human figure. Although it appears lifelike, the features are too generic to represent a particular individual. The purpose and meaning of this sculpture may never be known.

1-2 THE EMERGENCE OF CIVILIZATION

Focus Question: What are the characteristics of civilization, and where did the first civilizations emerge?

As human societies grew and developed greater complexity, civilization came into being. A **civilization** is a complex culture in which large numbers of people share a variety of common elements. Historians have identified many basic characteristics of civilization, including the following:

1. *An urban focus.* Cities became the centers for political, economic, social, cultural, and religious development.
2. *New political and military structures.* An organized government bureaucracy arose to meet the administrative demands of the growing population, and armies were organized to acquire land and power and for defense.
3. *A new social structure based on economic power.* Although kings and an upper class of priests, political leaders, and warriors dominated, large groups of free common people (farmers, artisans, craftspeople) also existed. At the bottom of the social hierarchy was a class of slaves.
4. *The development of more complexity in a material sense.* Surpluses of agricultural crops freed some people to work in occupations other than farming. Demand among ruling elites for luxury items encouraged the creation of new products. And as urban populations exported finished goods in exchange for raw materials from neighboring populations, organized trade grew substantially.
5. *A distinct religious structure.* The gods were deemed crucial to the community's success, and a professional priestly class, serving as stewards of the gods' property, regulated relations with the gods.
6. *The development of writing.* Kings, priests, merchants, and artisans began to use writing to keep records.

7. *New forms of significant artistic and intellectual activity.* For example, monumental architectural structures, usually religious, occupied a prominent place in urban environments.

The first civilizations that developed in Mesopotamia and Egypt will be examined in detail in this chapter. *But civilizations also developed independently in other parts of the world.* Between 3000 and 1500 B.C.E., the valleys of the Indus River in India supported a flourishing civilization that extended hundreds of miles from the Himalayan Mountains to the coast of the Arabian Sea (see Chapter 2). Another river valley civilization emerged along the Yellow River in northern China around 4,000 years ago (see Chapter 3). Under the Shang Dynasty, whose kings ruled from around 1570 B.C.E. to 1045 B.C.E., this civilization contained impressive cities with huge city walls and royal palaces.

Scholars have long believed that civilization emerged only in these four areas: the fertile river valleys of the Tigris and Euphrates Rivers, the Nile River, the Indus River, and the Yellow River. *Recently, however, archaeologists have discovered other early civilizations.* One of these flourished in Central Asia (in what are now the republics of Turkmenistan and Uzbekistan) around 4,000 years ago. People in this civilization built mud-brick buildings, raised sheep and goats, had bronze tools, used a system of irrigation to grow wheat and barley, and developed a writing system. Another early civilization was discovered in the Supe River Valley of Peru in South America. At the center of this civilization was the city of Caral, which flourished around 2600 B.C.E. (see Chapter 6). It contained buildings for officials, apartment buildings, and grand residences, all built of stone.

HISTORIANS DEBATE 1-2a Why did Early Civilizations Develop?

Because civilizations developed independently in different parts of the world, can general causes be identified that would explain why all of these civilizations emerged? Several possible explanations of how civilization began have been suggested. One theory maintains that challenges forced human beings to make efforts that resulted in the rise of civilization. Some scholars have adhered to a material explanation and have argued that material forces such as the accumulation of food surpluses made possible the specialization of labor and development of large communities with bureaucratic organization. But some areas such as the Fertile Crescent, where civilization emerged in Southwest Asia, were not naturally conducive to agriculture. Abundant food could be produced only through a massive human effort to manage vast amounts of water, an undertaking that required organization and

bureaucratic control and led to civilized cities. Other historians have argued that nonmaterial forces, primarily religious, provided the sense of unity and purpose that made such organized activities possible. Finally, some scholars doubt that we will ever discover the actual causes of early civilization.

1-3 CIVILIZATION IN MESOPOTAMIA

 Focus Question: How are the chief characteristics of civilization evident in ancient Mesopotamia?

The Greeks called the valley between the Tigris and Euphrates Rivers *Mesopotamia* (mess-uh-puh-TAY-mee-uh), the "land between the rivers." The region receives little rain, but the soil of the plain of southern Mesopotamia was enlarged and enriched over the years by layers of silt deposited by the two rivers. In late spring, the Tigris and Euphrates overflow their banks and deposit their fertile silt, but because this flooding depends on the melting of snows in the upland mountains where the rivers begin, it is irregular and sometimes catastrophic. In such circumstances, farming could be accomplished only with human intervention in the form of irrigation and drainage ditches to control the flow of the rivers and produce the crops. Large-scale irrigation made possible the expansion of agriculture in this region, and the abundant food provided the material base for the emergence of civilization in Mesopotamia.

1-3a The City-States of Ancient Mesopotamia

The creators of the first Mesopotamian civilization were the Sumerians (soo-MER-ee-unz or soo-MEER-ee-unz), a people whose origins remain unclear. By 3000 B.C.E., they had established several independent cities, including Eridu, Ur, Uruk, Umma, and Lagash (see Map 1.2). As these cities expanded, they came to exercise political and economic control over the surrounding countryside, forming city-states, the basic units of Sumerian civilization.

Sumerian Cities Sumerian cities were surrounded by walls. Uruk, for example, was encircled by a wall six miles long with defense towers located every thirty to thirty-five feet along its length. City dwellings built of sun-dried bricks included both the small flats of peasants and the larger dwellings of civic and priestly officials. Although Mesopotamia had little stone or wood for building purposes, it did have plenty of mud. Mud bricks, easily shaped by hand, were left to bake in the hot sun until they were

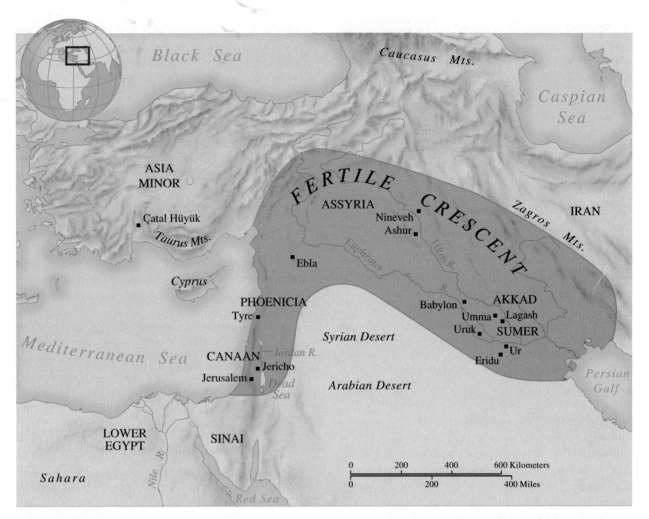

Map 1.2 The Ancient Near East. The Fertile Crescent encompassed land with access to water at the Persian Gulf, the Mediterranean Sea, and the Tigris and Euphrates Rivers. Employing flood management and irrigation systems, the peoples of the region established civilizations based on agriculture. These civilizations developed writing, law codes, and economic specialization.

 What geographic aspects of the Mesopotamian city-states made conflict between them likely?

hard enough to use for building. People in Mesopotamia were remarkably creative with mud bricks, inventing the arch and the dome and constructing some of the largest brick buildings in the world.

The most prominent building in a Sumerian city was the temple, which was dedicated to the chief god or goddess of the city and often built atop a massive stepped tower called a **ziggurat** (ZIG-uh-rat). The Sumerians believed that gods and goddesses owned the cities, and much wealth was used to build temples as well as elaborate houses for the priests and priestesses who served the deities. Because they supervised the temples and their property, these priests and priestesses had great power. Ruling power in

Sumerian city-states, however, was primarily in the hands of kings.

Sumerians viewed kingship as divine in origin. Kings, they believed, derived their power from the gods and were their agents. As one person said in a petition to his king, "You in your judgment, you are the son of Anu [god of the sky]; your commands, like the work of a god, cannot be reversed. Your words, like rain pouring down from heaven, are without number."[1] Regardless of their origins, kings had power—they led armies and organized workers for the irrigation projects on which Mesopotamian farming depended. The army, the government bureaucracy, and the priests and priestesses all aided the kings in their rule.

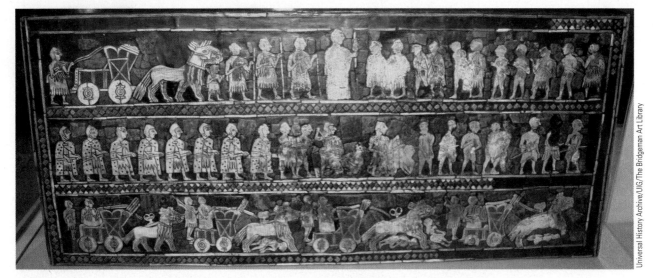

1.4 The "Royal Standard" of Ur. This detail is from the "Royal Standard" of Ur, a box dating from around 2700 B.C.E. that was discovered in a stone tomb from the royal cemetery of the Sumerian city-state of Ur. The scenes on one side of the box depict the activities of the king and his military forces. Shown in the bottom panel are four Sumerian battle chariots. Each chariot held two men, one holding the reins and the other armed with a spear for combat. A special compartment in the chariot held several spears. The charging chariots are seen defeating the enemy. In the middle band, the Sumerian soldiers round up the captured enemies. In the top band, the captives are presented to the king, who has alighted from his chariot and is shown standing above all the others in the center of the panel.

1-3b Economy and Society

The economy of the Sumerian city-states was primarily agricultural, but commerce and industry became important as well. The people of Mesopotamia produced woolen textiles, pottery, and metalwork. The Sumerians imported copper, tin, and timber in exchange for dried fish, wool, barley, wheat, and metal goods. Traders traveled by land to the eastern Mediterranean to the west and by sea to India in the east. The introduction of the wheel, which had been invented around 3000 B.C.E. by nomadic people living in the region north of the Black Sea, led to carts with wheels that made transporting goods easier.

Sumerian city-states probably contained four major social groups: elites, dependent commoners, free commoners, and slaves. Elites included royal and priestly officials and their families. Dependent commoners included the elites' clients, who worked for the palace and temple estates. Free commoners worked as farmers, merchants, fishers, scribes, and craftspeople. Probably 90 percent or more of the population were farmers. Slaves belonged to palace officials, who used them in building projects; to temple officials, who used mostly female slaves to weave cloth and grind grain; and to rich landowners, who used them for farming and domestic work.

1-3c Empires in Ancient Mesopotamia

As the number of Sumerian city-states grew and the states expanded, new conflicts arose as city-state fought city-state for control of land and water. Located in the flatland of Mesopotamia, the Sumerian city-states were also open to invasion. To the north of the Sumerian city-states were the Akkadians (uh-KAY-dee-unz). We call them a Semitic people because of the type of language they spoke (see Table 1.1). Around 2340 B.C.E., Sargon, leader of the Akkadians, overran the Sumerian city-states and established an empire that included most of Mesopotamia as well as lands westward to the Mediterranean. Attacks from neighboring hill peoples eventually caused the Akkadian empire to fall, and its end by 2100 B.C.E. brought a return to independent city-states and renewed conflicts between them. It was not until 1792 B.C.E. that a new empire came to control much of Mesopotamia under Hammurabi (ham-uh-RAH-bee), who ruled over the Amorites or Old Babylonians, a large group of Semitic-speaking seminomads.

TABLE 1.1	Some Semitic Languages	
Akkadian	Assyrian	Hebrew
Arabic	Babylonian	Phoenician
Aramaic	Canaanitic	Syriac

Note: Languages in italics are no longer spoken.

Hammurabi's Empire Hammurabi (1792–1750 B.C.E.) employed a well-disciplined army of foot soldiers who carried axes, spears, and copper or bronze daggers. He learned to divide his opponents and subdue them one by one. Using such methods, he gained control of Sumer and Akkad, creating a new Mesopotamian kingdom with its capital at Babylon.

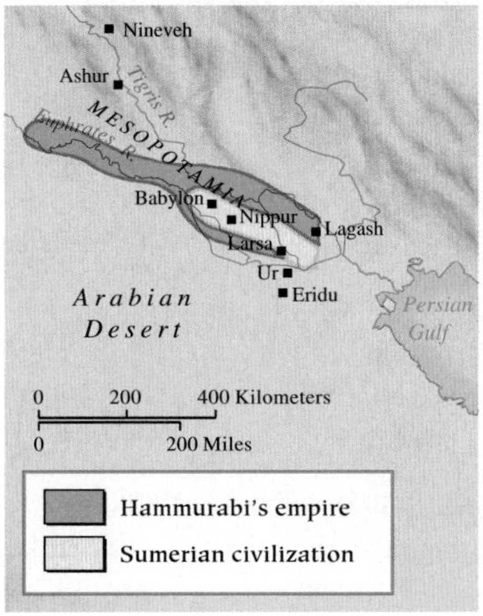

Hammurabi, the man of war, was also a man of peace who took a strong interest in state affairs. He built temples, defensive walls, and irrigation canals; encouraged trade; and brought about an economic revival. Indeed, Hammurabi saw himself as a shepherd to his people: "I am indeed the shepherd who brings peace, whose scepter is just. My benevolent shade was spread over my city. I held the people of the lands of Sumer and Akkad safely on my lap."[2] After his death, however, a series of weak kings were unable to keep Hammurabi's empire united, and it finally fell to new invaders.

Map 1.3 Hammurabi's Empire

The Code of Hammurabi: Society in Mesopotamia Hammurabi is best remembered for his law code, a collection of 282 laws. Although many scholars today view Hammurabi's collection less as a code of laws and more as an attempt by Hammurabi to portray himself as the source of justice to his people, the code still gives us a glimpse of the values of the Mesopotamian society of his time (see Historical Voices, "The Code of Hammurabi," p. 14).

The Code of Hammurabi reveals a society with a system of strict justice. Penalties for criminal offenses were severe and varied according to the social class of the victim. A crime against a member of the upper class (a noble) by a member of the lower class (a commoner) was punished more severely than the same offense against a member of the lower class. Moreover, the principle of "an eye for an eye, a tooth for a tooth" was fundamental to this system of justice. This meant that punishments should fit the crime: "If a free man has destroyed the eye of a member of the aristocracy, they shall destroy his eye" (Code of Hammurabi, No. 196). Hammurabi's code also had an impact on legal ideas in Southwest Asia for hundreds of years, as the following verse from the Hebrew Bible demonstrates: "If anyone injures his neighbor, whatever he has done must be done to him: fracture for fracture, eye for eye, tooth for tooth. As he has injured the other, so he is to be injured" (Leviticus 24:19–20).

The largest category of laws in the Code of Hammurabi focused on marriage and the family. Parents arranged marriages for their children. After the marriage, the parties involved signed a marriage contract; without it, no one was considered legally married. The husband provided a bridal payment to the bride's parents, and the woman's parents were responsible for a dowry to the new husband.

As in many patriarchal societies, women possessed fewer privileges and rights in the married relationship than men. A woman's place was in the home, and failure to fulfill her expected duties was grounds for divorce. If she was not able to bear children or tried to leave home to engage in business, her husband could divorce her. Furthermore, a wife who was a "gadabout, . . . neglecting her house [and] humiliating her husband, shall be prosecuted" (Code of Hammurabi, No. 143).

Sexual relations were strictly regulated as well. Husbands but not wives were permitted sexual activity outside marriage. A wife and her lover caught committing adultery were pitched into the river, although if the husband pardoned his wife, the king could pardon the guilty man. Incest was strictly forbidden. If a father had incestuous relations with his daughter, he would be banished. Incest between a son and his mother resulted in both being burned.

Fathers ruled their children as well as their wives. Obedience was duly expected: "If a son has struck his father, he shall cut off his hand" (Code of Hammurabi, No. 195). If a son committed a serious enough offense, his father could disinherit him.

1-3d The Culture of Mesopotamia

A spiritual worldview was of fundamental importance to Mesopotamian culture. To the peoples of Mesopotamia, the gods were living realities who affected all aspects of life. It was crucial, therefore, that correct hierarchies be observed. Leaders could prepare armies for war, but success really depended on a favorable relationship with the gods. This helps explain the importance of the priestly class and the reason why even kings took great care to dedicate offerings and monuments to the gods.

The Importance of Religion The physical environment obviously affected the Mesopotamian view of the universe. Ferocious floods, heavy downpours, scorching winds, and oppressive humidity were all part of the Mesopotamian

The Code of Hammurabi

 Family & Society

ALTHOUGH IT IS NOT THE EARLIEST MESOPOTAMIAN LAW CODE, Hammurabi's is the most complete. The code emphasizes the principle of retribution ("an eye for an eye") and punishments that vary according to social status. Punishments could be severe. The following examples illustrate these concerns.

The Code of Hammurabi

25. If a fire break out in a man's house and a man, who goes to extinguish it cast his eye on the furniture of the owner of the house, and take the furniture of the owner of the house, that man shall be thrown into that fire.

129. If the wife of a man be taken in lying with another man, they shall bind them and throw them into the water. If the husband of the woman would save his wife, or if the king would save his male servant (he may).

131. If a man accuse his wife, and she has not been taken in lying with another man, she shall take an oath in the name of god and she shall return to her house.

196. If a man destroy the eye of another man, they shall destroy his eye.

198. If one destroy the eye of a freeman or broke the bone of a freeman, he shall pay one mina of silver.

199. If one destroy the eye of a man's slave or break the bone of a man's slave, he shall pay one-half his price.

209. If a man strike a man's daughter and bring about a miscarriage, he shall pay ten shekels of silver for her miscarriage.

210. If that woman die, they shall put his daughter to death.

211. If through a stroke, he brings about a miscarriage to the daughter of a freeman, he shall pay five shekels of silver.

212. If that woman die, he shall pay one-half mina of silver.

213. If he strike the female slave of a man and bring about a miscarriage, he shall pay two shekels of silver.

214. If that female slave die, he shall pay one-third mina of silver.

 What do these points of law from the Code of Hammurabi reveal to you about Mesopotamian society?

Source: Hammurabi, *The Code of Hammurabi, King of Babylon*, ed. R. F. Harper, 2nd ed. (Chicago: The University of Chicago Press, 1904).

climate. These conditions and the resulting famines easily convinced Mesopotamians that this world was controlled by supernatural forces, which often were not kind or reliable. In the presence of nature, people in Mesopotamia could easily feel helpless, as this poem relates:

The rampant flood which no man can oppose,
Which shakes the heavens and causes earth to tremble,
In an appalling blanket folds mother and child,
Beats down the canebrake's full luxuriant greenery,
And drowns the harvest in its time of ripeness.[3]

The Mesopotamians discerned cosmic rhythms in the universe and accepted its order but perceived that it was not completely safe because of the presence of willful, powerful cosmic powers that they identified with gods and goddesses.

With its numerous gods and goddesses animating all aspects of the universe, Mesopotamian religion was a form of **polytheism**. The four most important deities were An, god of the sky and hence the most important force in the universe; Enlil (EN-lil), god of wind; Enki (EN-kee), god of the earth, rivers, wells, and canals, as well as inventions and crafts; and Ninhursaga (nin-HUR-sah-guh), a goddess associated with soil, mountains, and vegetation, who came to be worshiped as a mother goddess, the "mother of all children." Ninhursaga manifested her power by giving birth to kings and conferring the royal insignia on them.

The Cultivation of Writing and Sciences The realization of writing's great potential was another aspect of Mesopotamian culture. Around 3000 B.C.E., the Sumerians invented a **cuneiform** (kyoo-NEE-uh-form) ("wedge-shaped") system of writing. Using a reed stylus, they made wedge-shaped impressions on clay tablets, which were then baked or dried in the sun. Once dried, these tablets were virtually indestructible, and the several hundred thousand that have been found so far have been a valuable source of information for modern scholars. Sumerian writing evolved from pictures of concrete objects to simplified and stylized signs, leading eventually

Early Writing

Art & Ideas

CUNEIFORM SCRIPT FROM AN EARLY SUMERIAN DYNASTY covers the upper part of the cone of Uruinimgina, as shown in Image 1.5a. The first Egyptian writing was also pictographic, as shown in the hieroglyphs in the detail from the mural in the tomb of Ramesses I in Image 1.5b. In Central America, the Maya civilization had a well-developed writing system, also based on hieroglyphs, as seen in 1.5c in the text carved on a stone platform in front of the Palace of the Large Masks in Kabah, Mexico.

Q *What common feature is evident in these early writing systems? How might you explain that?*

©Sandro Vannini/CORBIS

1.5b

RMN/Art Resource, NY

1.5a

Erich Lessing/Art Resource, NY

1.5c

to a phonetic system that made possible the written expression of abstract ideas.

Writing enabled a society to keep records and maintain knowledge of previous practices and events (see Comparative Illustration, "Early Writing"). Writing also allowed people to communicate ideas in new ways, which is especially evident in the most famous piece of Mesopotamian literature, the *Epic of Gilgamesh,* an epic poem that records the exploits of a legendary king, Gilgamesh (GILL-guh-mesh), who embarks on a search for the secret of immortality. But his efforts fail and Gilgamesh remains mortal. The desire for immortality,

one of humankind's great searches, ends in complete frustration. "Everlasting life," as this Mesopotamian epic makes clear, is only for the gods.

People in Mesopotamia also made outstanding achievements in mathematics and astronomy. In math, the Sumerians devised a number system based on 60, using combinations of 6 and 10 for practical solutions. Geometry was used to measure fields and erect buildings. In astronomy, the Sumerians made use of units of 60 and charted the heavenly constellations. Their calendar was based on twelve lunar months and was brought into harmony with the solar year by adding an extra month from time to time.

1-4 EGYPTIAN CIVILIZATION: "THE GIFT OF THE NILE"

 Focus Questions: What are the basic features of the three major periods of Egyptian history? What elements of continuity are evident in the three periods? What are their major differences?

"The Egyptian Nile," wrote one Arab traveler, "surpasses all the rivers of the world in sweetness of taste, in length of course and usefulness. No other river in the world can show such a continuous series of towns and villages along its banks." The Nile River was crucial to the development of Egyptian civilization (see Historical Voices, "The Significance of the Nile River and the Pharaoh," p. 17). Egypt, like Mesopotamia, was a river valley civilization.

1-4a The Importance of Geography

The Nile is a unique river, beginning in the heart of Africa and coursing northward for thousands of miles. The longest river in the world, the Nile was responsible for creating an area several miles wide on both banks of the river that was fertile and capable of producing abundant harvests. The "miracle" of the Nile was its annual flooding. The river rose in the summer from rains in Central Africa, crested in Egypt in September and October, and left a deposit of silt that enriched the soil. The Egyptians called this fertile land the "Black Land" because it was dark in color from the silt and the crops that grew on it so densely. Beyond these narrow strips of fertile fields lay the deserts (the "Red Land"). Around 100 miles before it empties into the Mediterranean, the river splits into two major branches, forming the Delta, a triangular-shaped territory called Lower Egypt to distinguish it from Upper Egypt, the land upstream

to the south (see Map 1.4). Egypt's important cities developed at the apex of the Delta.

Unlike with Mesopotamia's rivers, the flooding of the Nile was gradual and usually predictable, and the river itself was seen as life enhancing, not life threatening. Although a system of organized irrigation was still necessary, the small villages along the Nile could create such systems without the massive state intervention that was required in Mesopotamia. Egyptian civilization consequently tended to remain more rural, with many small population centers congregated along a narrow band on both sides of the Nile.

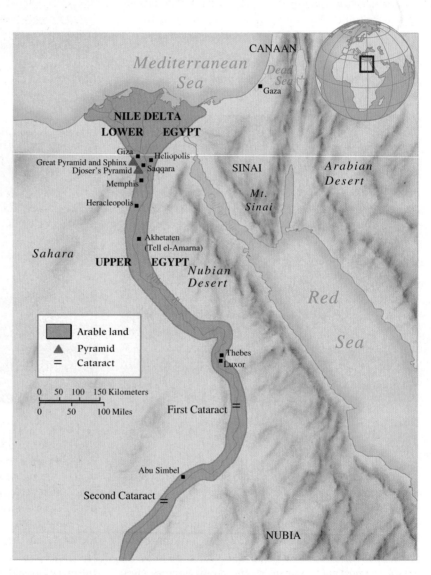

Map 1.4 Ancient Egypt. Egyptian civilization centered on the life-giving water and flood silts of the Nile River, with most of the population living in Lower Egypt, where the river splits to form the Nile Delta. Most of the pyramids, built during the Old Kingdom, are clustered south and west of Cairo.

 How did the lands to the east and west of the river help protect Egypt from invasion?

The Significance of the Nile River and the Pharaoh

Religion & Philosophy

TWO OF THE MOST IMPORTANT SOURCES OF LIFE for the ancient Egyptians were the Nile River and the pharaoh. Egyptians perceived that the Nile made possible the abundant food that was a major source of their well-being. This *Hymn to the Nile*, probably from the nineteenth and twentieth dynasties in the New Kingdom, expresses the gratitude Egyptians felt for the Nile.

Hymn to the Nile

Hail to you, O Nile, that issues from the earth and comes to keep Egypt alive! . . .

He that waters the meadows which Re created, in order to keep every kid alive.

He that makes to drink the desert and the place distant from water: that is his dew coming down from heaven. . . .

The lord of fishes, he who makes the marsh-birds to go upstream. . . .

He who makes barley and brings emmer [wheat] into being, that he may make the temples festive.

If he is sluggish, then nostrils are stopped up, and everybody is poor. . . .

When he rises, then the land is in jubilation, then every belly is in joy, every backbone takes on laughter, and every tooth is exposed.

The bringer of good, rich in provisions, creator of all good, lord of majesty, sweet of fragrance. . . .

He who makes every beloved tree to grow, without lack of them.

The Egyptian king, or pharaoh, was viewed as a god and the absolute ruler of Egypt. His significance and the gratitude of the Egyptian people for his existence are evident in this hymn from the reign of Sesotris III (ca. 1880–1840 B.C.E.).

Hymn to the Pharaoh

He has come to us, he has taken the land of the well, the double crown [crown of Upper and Lower Egypt] is placed on his head.

He has come, he has united the two lands, he has joined the kingdom of the upper land with the lower.

He has come, he has ruled Egypt, he has placed the desert in his power.

He has come, he has protected the two lands, he has given peace in the two regions.

He has come, he has made Egypt to live, he has destroyed its afflictions.

He has come, he has made the aged to live, he has opened the breath of the people. He has come, he has trampled on the nations, he has smitten the [enemies], who knew not his terror.

He has come, he has protected his frontier, he has rescued the robbed.

 How do these two hymns underscore the importance of the Nile River and the institution of the pharaoh to Egyptian civilization?

Sources: Pritchard, James B., ed., *Ancient Near Eastern Texts Relating to the Old Testament*, 3rd Edition with Supplement. Copyright © 1950, 1955, 1969, renewed 1978 by Princeton University Press. W. M. Flinders-Petrie, *A History of Egypt*, Fifth Edition (Methuen & Co.: London, 1903), Vol. 1, p. 183.

The surpluses of food that Egyptian farmers grew in the fertile Nile Valley made Egypt prosperous. But the Nile also served as a unifying factor in Egyptian history. In ancient times, the Nile was the fastest way to travel through the land, making both transportation and communication easier. Winds from the north pushed sailboats south, and the current of the Nile carried them north.

Unlike Mesopotamia, which was subject to constant invasion, Egypt had natural barriers that gave it some protection from invasion. These barriers included deserts to the west and east; cataracts (rapids) on the southern part of the Nile, which made defense relatively easy; and the Mediterranean Sea to the north. These barriers, however, were only effective when they were combined with Egyptian fortifications at strategic locations. Nor did barriers prevent the development of trade.

The regularity of the Nile floods and the relative isolation of the Egyptians created a sense of security and a feeling of changelessness. To the ancient Egyptians, when the Nile flooded each year, "the fields laugh and people's faces light up." Unlike people in Mesopotamia, Egyptians faced life with a spirit of confidence in the stability of things. Ancient Egyptian civilization was characterized by a remarkable degree of continuity for thousands of years.

1-4b The Importance of Religion

The Egyptians had no word for religion because it was an inseparable element of the world order, the universal cosmic scheme to which their society belonged. The pharaoh was the divine being whose function was to maintain Egypt's stability within that cosmic order. He did this by supervising the sacred ceremonies that his deputies, the priests, performed in the temples to appease the gods and goddesses who controlled the universe. Daily rituals involved focusing on an image of the deity and providing it with food and sustenance.

The Egyptians were polytheistic and had large numbers of gods associated with heavenly bodies and natural forces, hardly surprising in view of the importance to Egypt's well-being of the sun, the river, and the fertile land along its banks. The sun was the source of life and hence worthy of worship. The sun god took on different forms and names, depending on his specific role. He was worshiped as Atum in human form and as Re (RAY), who had a human body but the head of a falcon. The Egyptian ruler took the title of Son of Re, since he was seen as an earthly form of Re.

1-4c The Course of Egyptian History: The Old, Middle, and New Kingdoms

Modern historians have divided Egyptian history into three major periods known as the Old Kingdom, the Middle Kingdom, and the New Kingdom. These periods of long-term stability were characterized by strong monarchical authority, competent bureaucracy, freedom from invasion, extensive construction of temples and pyramids, and considerable intellectual and cultural activity. But between the periods of stability were eras of instability known as the Intermediate Periods.

The Old Kingdom   The history of Egypt begins around 3100 B.C.E. when King Menes united the villages of both Upper and Lower Egypt into a single kingdom and created the first Egyptian royal dynasty. Henceforth, the ruler would be called "king of Upper and Lower Egypt," and one of the royal crowns would be the Double Crown, combining the White Crown of Upper Egypt and the Red Crown of Lower Egypt. Just as the Nile served to unite Upper and Lower Egypt physically, the king served to unite the two areas politically.

The Old Kingdom encompassed the fourth through eighth dynasties of Egyptian kings, lasting from around 2575 to 2125 B.C.E. It was an age of prosperity and splendor that was visible in the construction of the greatest and largest pyramids in Egypt's history. Kingship was a divine institution in ancient Egypt and formed part of a universal scheme: "What is the king of Upper and Lower Egypt? He is a god by whose dealings one lives, the father and mother of all men, alone by himself, without an equal."[4] In obeying their king, subjects helped maintain the cosmic order.

Among the various titles of Egyptian kings, that of **pharaoh** (originally meaning "great house" or "palace," referring to the royal palace) eventually came to be the most common.

Although theoretically absolute in their power, in practice Egyptian kings did not rule alone. By the fourth dynasty, a bureaucracy with regular procedures had developed. In time, Egypt was divided into provinces or *nomes*, as they were later called by the Greeks—twenty-two in Upper Egypt and twenty in Lower Egypt. A governor, called a *nomarch* by the Greeks, was head of each nome and was responsible to the king.

The Pyramids   One of the great achievements of Egyptian civilization, the building of pyramids, occurred in the time of the Old Kingdom. Pyramids were built as part of a larger complex of buildings dedicated to the dead—in effect, a city of the dead. The area included a large pyramid for the king's burial, as well as smaller structures for his family and the pharaoh's noble officials.

The tombs were well prepared for their residents, their rooms furnished and stocked with numerous supplies, including chairs, boats, chests, weapons, games, dishes, and a variety of foods. The Egyptians believed that human beings had two bodies—a physical one and a spiritual one, which they called the *ka*. If the physical body was properly preserved (by mummification) and the tomb was furnished with all the objects of regular life, the ka could return, surrounded by earthly comforts, and continue its life despite the death of the physical body.

The largest and most magnificent of all the pyramids was built under King Khufu (KOO-foo). Constructed at Giza around 2540 B.C.E., this famous Great Pyramid covers 13 acres, measures 756 feet at each side of its base, and stands 481 feet high (see Comparative Illustration, "The Pyramid," p. 141 in Chapter 6). Its four sides are almost precisely oriented to the four points of the compass. The interior included a grand gallery to the burial chamber, which was built of granite and contained a lidless sarcophagus for the pharaoh's body. The Great Pyramid still stands as a visible symbol of the power of Egyptian kings of the Old Kingdom and the spiritual conviction that underlay Egyptian society. No later pyramid ever matched its size or splendor. The pyramid was not only the king's tomb but also an important symbol of royal power. It could be seen from miles away, reminding people of the glory, might, and wealth of the ruler who was regarded as a living god on earth.

The Middle Kingdom   Despite the theory of divine order, the Old Kingdom eventually collapsed, ushering in a period of disorder that lasted some 125 years. Finally, a new royal dynasty managed to pacify all Egypt and inaugurated the Middle Kingdom, a new period of stability lasting from about 2010 to 1630 B.C.E. Egyptians later portrayed the Middle Kingdom as a golden age, a clear indication of its stability.

The Middle Kingdom was characterized by a new concern of the pharaohs for the people. In the Old Kingdom, the pharaoh had been viewed as an inaccessible god-king. Now he was portrayed as the shepherd of his people and responsible for building public works and providing for the public welfare. Pharaohs of the Middle Kingdom undertook many helpful projects such as draining the swampland in the Nile Delta to provide thousands of acres of new farmland.

Disorder and a New Order: The New Kingdom

The Middle Kingdom came to an end around 1630 B.C.E. with the invasion of Egypt by a people from western Asia known to the Egyptians as the Hyksos (HIK-sohs). The Hyksos used horse-drawn war chariots and overwhelmed the Egyptian soldiers, who fought from donkey carts. For almost 100 years, the Hyksos ruled much of Egypt, but the conquered took much from their conquerors. From the Hyksos, the Egyptians learned to use bronze in making new farming tools and weapons. They also mastered the military skills of the Hyksos, especially the use of horse-drawn war chariots.

Eventually, a new line of pharaohs—the eighteenth dynasty—made use of the new weapons to throw off Hyksos domination, reunite Egypt, establish the New Kingdom (ca. 1539–1069 B.C.E.), and launch the Egyptians along a new militaristic path. During the period of the New Kingdom, Egypt created an empire and became the most powerful state in the Middle East.

The power of the New Kingdom pharaohs was aided by massive wealth, which they showed by building new temples. Queen Hatshepsut (hat-SHEP-soot) (ca. 1503–1480 B.C.E.), one of the first women to become pharaoh in her own right, built a great temple at Deir el Bahri (dayr ahl BAH-ree) near Thebes. Hatshepsut was succeeded by her nephew, Thutmosis (thoot-MOH-suss) III (ca. 1480–1450 B.C.E.), who led seventeen military campaigns into Syria and Canaan and even reached the Euphrates River. Egyptian forces occupied Canaan and Syria and also moved westward into Libya.

The eighteenth dynasty was not without its troubles, however. One source of conflict was the pharaoh Amenhotep (ah-mun-HOH-tep) IV (ca. 1364–1347 B.C.E.), who introduced the worship of Aten, god of the sun disk, as the supreme god and later in his reign as the only god. In the pharaoh's eyes, he and Aten had become co-rulers of Egypt, and he pursued his worship with great enthusiasm, changing his own name to Akhenaten (ah-kuh-NAH-tun) ("servant of Aten") and closing the temples of other gods. Nevertheless, his attempt at religious change failed. Egyptians were unwilling to abandon their traditional ways and beliefs, especially because they saw the destruction of the old gods as subversive of the very cosmic order on which Egypt's survival depended. At the same time, Akhenaten's preoccupation with his religious revolution caused him to ignore foreign affairs and led to the loss of both Syria and Canaan. Akhenaten's changes were soon undone after his death by the boy-pharaoh Tutankhamun (too-tang-KAH-mun), who restored the old gods. The eighteenth dynasty soon came to an end.

The nineteenth dynasty managed to restore Egyptian power one more time. Under Ramesses (RAM-uh-seez) II (ca. 1279–1213 B.C.E.), the Egyptians regained control of Canaan, but new invasions in the thirteenth century by the "Sea Peoples," as the Egyptians called them, destroyed Egyptian power in Canaan and drove the Egyptians back within their old frontiers. The days of Egyptian empire were ended, and the New Kingdom itself expired with the end of the twentieth dynasty in 1069 B.C.E. For the next thousand years, despite periodic revivals of strength, Egypt was dominated by Libyans, Nubians, Persians, and finally Macedonians after the

Bildarchiv Steffens/The Bridgeman Art Library

1.6 Statues of Ramesses II at Abu Simbel. After being driven out of Canaan and Syria by the Hittites, the Egyptian empire grew to power one final time under Ramesses II. He succeeded in reconquering Canaan but was unable to restore the boundaries of the previous empire. The massive Temple of Ramesses II, located at Abu Simbel, was carved out of a cliff of Nubian sandstone. The giant statues represent Ramesses II.

conquest of Alexander the Great (see Chapter 4). In the first century B.C.E., Egypt became a province in Rome's mighty empire.

1-4d Society and Daily Life in Ancient Egypt

For thousands of years, Egyptian society managed to maintain a simple structure, organized along hierarchical lines with the god-king at the top. An upper class of nobles and priests aided the king and participated in the elaborate rituals of life that surrounded the pharaoh. This ruling class ran the government and managed its own landed estates, which provided much of its wealth.

Below the upper classes were merchants and artisans. Merchants engaged in an active trade up and down the Nile as well as in town and village markets. Some merchants also engaged in international trade; the king sent them to Crete and Syria, where they obtained wood and other products. Expeditions traveled into Nubia for ivory and down the Red Sea to Punt for incense and spices. Eventually, trade links were established between ports on the Red Sea and lands as far away as the Indonesian archipelago. Egyptian artisans made an incredible variety of well-built and beautiful goods: stone dishes; painted boxes made of clay; wooden furniture; gold, silver, and copper tools and containers; paper and rope made of papyrus; and linen clothes.

By far, the largest number of people in Egypt simply worked the land. Although in theory the king owned all the land, he granted portions of it to his subjects. Large sections were in the possession of nobles and the temple complexes. Most of the lower classes were serfs or common people, bound to the land, who cultivated the estates. They paid taxes in the form of crops to the king, nobles, and priests; lived in small villages or towns; and provided military service and forced labor for building projects.

Ancient Egyptians had a highly positive attitude toward daily life on Earth. They married young (girls at twelve, boys at fourteen) and established a home and family. The husband was master in the house, but wives were respected and in charge of the household and education of the children. From a book of wise sayings (which the Egyptians called "instructions") came this advice: "If you are a man of standing, you should found your household and love your wife at home as is fitting. Fill her belly; clothe her back. . . . Make her heart glad as long as you live."[5] Women's property and inheritance remained in their hands, even in marriage. Although most careers and public offices were closed to women, some did operate businesses. Peasant women worked long hours in the fields and at numerous domestic tasks. Upper-class women could function as priestesses, and four queens even became pharaohs in their own right.

1-4e The Culture of Egypt: Art and Writing

Commissioned by kings or nobles for use in temples or tombs, Egyptian art was largely functional. Wall paintings and statues of gods and kings in temples served a spiritual purpose. They were an integral part of the performance of ritual, which was thought necessary to preserve the cosmic order and hence the well-being of Egypt. Likewise, the mural scenes and sculptured figures found in the tombs had a specific function: to assist the journey of the deceased into the afterworld.

Writing emerged in Egypt during the first two dynasties. The Greeks later labeled Egyptian writing **hieroglyphics** (HY-uh-roh-glif-iks), meaning "priest carvings" or "sacred writings." Hieroglyphs were sacred characters that were used as picture signs to depict objects as well as impart a sacred value. Although hieroglyphs were later simplified for writing purposes into two scripts, they never developed into an alphabet. Egyptian hieroglyphs were initially carved in stone, but later the two simplified scripts were written on papyrus, paper made from the reeds that grew along the Nile.

1.7 The Making of Jewelry. In ancient Egypt, people used jewelry for self-adornment and to indicate social status. This photo of a wall fragment from a tomb in Thebes around 1400 B.C.E. shows jewelers and metal craftsmen at work. At the top, jewelers are seen drilling holes in hard stone beads with three or four bow drills. The beads were then polished and strung in collars, as seen in the lower panel.

1-4f The Spread of Egyptian Influence: Nubia

The civilization of Egypt affected other peoples in the lands of the eastern Mediterranean. Egyptian products have been found in Crete, and Cretan products were known in Egypt (see Chapter 4). The Egyptians also affected the south in sub-Saharan Africa in Nubia (the northern part of modern Sudan). In fact, some archaeologists have recently suggested that the African kingdom of Nubia may have arisen even before the kingdoms of Egypt.

Contacts between the Upper and Lower Nile had been established by the late third millennium B.C.E., when Egyptian merchants traveled to Nubia to obtain ivory, ebony, frankincense, and leopard skins. A few centuries later, Nubia had become an Egyptian tributary. At the end of the second millennium B.C.E., Nubia profited from the disintegration of the Egyptian New Kingdom to become the independent state of Kush. Egyptian influence continued, however, as Kushite culture borrowed extensively from Egypt, including religious beliefs, the practice of interring kings in pyramids, and hieroglyphs.

But in the first millennium B.C.E., Kush also directly affected Egypt. During the second half of the eighth century B.C.E., Kushite monarchs took control of Egypt and founded the twenty-fifth dynasty of Egyptian rulers. Not until 663 B.C.E. was the last Kushite ruler expelled from Egypt.

Although its economy was probably founded primarily on agriculture and animal husbandry, Kush developed into a major trading state in Africa that endured for hundreds of years. Its commercial activities were stimulated by the discovery of iron ore in a floodplain near the river at Meroë (MER-oh-ee or MER-uh-wee). Strategically located at the point where a land route across the desert to the south intersected the Nile River, Meroë eventually became the capital of the state. In addition to iron products, Kush and Meroë supplied goods from Central and eastern Africa—notably ivory, gold, ebony, and slaves—to the Roman Empire, Arabia, and India.

1-5 NEW CENTERS OF CIVILIZATION

 Focus Questions: What was the significance of the Indo-Europeans? How did Judaism differ from the religions of Mesopotamia and Egypt?

Mesopotamia and North Africa have dominated our story of civilization so far, but significant developments were also taking place on the fringes of these civilizations. By 4000 B.C.E., Neolithic peoples in southern France, Central Europe, and the coastal regions of the Mediterranean had domesticated animals and begun to farm largely on their own.

One outstanding feature of late Neolithic Europe was the erection of **megaliths** (*megalith* is Greek for "large stone"). The first megalithic structures were built around 4000 B.C.E., more than 1,000 years before the great pyramids were built in Egypt. Between 3200 and 1500 B.C.E., standing stones were erected throughout the British Isles and northwestern France, typically placed in circles or lined up in rows. Stonehenge in England was the most famous megalithic construction, but others have been found as far north as Scandinavia and as far south as the islands of Corsica, Sardinia, and Malta. Archaeologists have demonstrated that the stone circles were used as observatories not only to detect such simple astronomical phenomena as the midwinter and midsummer sunrises but also to make such sophisticated observations as the major and minor standstills of the moon.

1-5a Nomadic Peoples: Impact of the Indo-Europeans

On the fringes of civilization lived nomadic peoples who depended on hunting and gathering, herding, and sometimes a bit of farming for their survival. Most important were the *pastoral nomads* who on occasion overran civilized communities and forged their own empires. Pastoral nomads domesticated animals for both food and clothing and moved along regular migratory routes to provide steady sources of nourishment for their animals.

Among the most important nomadic peoples were the Indo-Europeans, groups that spoke languages derived from a single parent tongue. Indo-European languages include Greek, Latin, Persian, Sanskrit, and the Germanic languages (see Table 1.2). The original Indo-European-speaking peoples were probably based somewhere in the steppe region north of the Black Sea or in southwestern Asia in modern Iran or Afghanistan, but around 2000 B.C.E. they began to move into Europe, India, and western Asia. The domestication of horses and the importation of the wheel and wagon from Mesopotamia facilitated the Indo-European migrations to other lands.

One group of Indo-Europeans who moved into Asia Minor and Anatolia (modern Turkey) around 1750 B.C.E. coalesced with the native peoples to form the Hittite kingdom, with its capital at Hattusha (Bogazköy in modern Turkey). Between 1600 and 1200 B.C.E., the Hittites created their own empire in western Asia and even threatened the power of the Egyptians. The Hittites were the first of the Indo-European peoples to use iron; the widespread availability of iron ore enabled them to construct

TABLE 1.2	Some Indo-European Languages
Subfamily	**Languages**
Indo-Iranian	*Sanskrit,* Persian
Balto-Slavic	Russian, Serbo-Croatian, Czech, Polish, Lithuanian
Hellenic	Greek
Italic	*Latin,* Romance languages (French, Italian, Spanish, Portuguese, Romanian)
Celtic	Irish, Gaelic
Germanic	Swedish, Danish, Norwegian, German, Dutch, English

Note: Languages in italics are no longer spoken.

weapons that were stronger and cheaper to make than earlier weapons.

1-5b Territorial States in Western Asia: The Phoenicians

During its heyday, the Hittite Empire was one of the great powers in western Asia. But around 1200 B.C.E., it was destroyed by new waves of invading Indo-European peoples. The destruction of the Hittite kingdom and the weakening of Egypt around 1200 B.C.E. left no dominant powers in western Asia, allowing a patchwork of petty kingdoms and city-states to emerge, especially in the area of Syria and Canaan. The Phoenicians (fuh-NEE-shunz) were one of these peoples.

A Semitic-speaking people (see Table 1.1, p. 12), the Phoenicians lived in the area of Canaan along the Mediterranean coast on a narrow band of land 120 miles long. Their newfound political independence after the demise of Hittite and Egyptian power helped the Phoenicians expand the trade that was already the foundation of their prosperity. They improved their ships and became great international sea traders, charting new routes, not only in the Mediterranean but also in the Atlantic Ocean, where they sailed north to Britain and south along the west coast of Africa. The Phoenicians established several colonies in the western Mediterranean; Carthage, the most famous colony, was located on the north coast of Africa.

Culturally, the Phoenicians are best known as *transmitters*. Instead of using pictographs or signs to represent whole words and syllables as the Mesopotamians and Egyptians did, the Phoenicians simplified their writing by using twenty-two different signs to represent the sounds of their speech. These twenty-two characters or letters could be used to spell out every word in

the Phoenician language. Although the Phoenicians were not the only people to invent an alphabet, theirs would have special significance because it was eventually passed on to the Greeks. From the ancient Greek alphabet came the modern Greek, Roman, and Cyrillic alphabets in use today.

1-5c The "Children of Israel"

To the south of the Phoenicians lived another group of Semitic-speaking people known as the Israelites. Although they were a minor factor in the politics of the region, their **monotheism**—belief in one God—later influenced both Christianity and Islam and flourished as a world religion in its own right. The Israelites had a tradition concerning their origins and history that was eventually written down as part of the Hebrew Bible, known to Christians as the Old Testament.

Many scholars today doubt that the biblical account reflects the true history of the early Israelites. The Hebrew Bible is a collection of twenty-four books written over hundreds of years. Dating of the biblical books is problematic, although scholars have advanced a documentary hypothesis that maintains that a series of authors wrote different books of the Bible over hundreds of years until the books were finally consolidated around 250 B.C.E. They argue that the early books of the Bible were written centuries after the events described and preserve only the cultural memory of what the Israelites came to believe about themselves and that recent archaeological evidence often contradicts the details of the biblical account. There is, for example, no archaeological or other evidence for the exodus from Egypt. These scholars also argue that the Israelites were not nomadic invaders but indigenous peoples in the Canaanite hill country. What is generally agreed, however, is that between 1200 and 1000 B.C.E., the Israelites emerged as a distinct group of people, possibly organized into tribes or a league of tribes.

HISTORIANS DEBATE **Was There a United Kingdom of Israel?** According to the Hebrew Bible, the Israelites established a united kingdom of Israel beginning with Saul and David. By the time of Solomon (ca. 970–930 B.C.E.), the son of David, the Israelites had supposedly established control over all of Canaan and made Jerusalem the capital of a united kingdom. According to the biblical account, Solomon did even more to strengthen royal power by expanding the government and army and extending the Israelites' trading activities. Solomon is portrayed as a great builder responsible for the Temple in the city of Jerusalem. The Israelites viewed the Temple as the symbolic center of their religion and hence of the kingdom of Israel itself. Under Solomon, ancient Israel supposedly reached the height of its power

The accuracy of this biblical account of the united kingdom of Israel under Saul, David, and Solomon has recently been challenged by a new generation of archaeologists and historians. Although they mostly accept Saul, David, and Solomon as historical figures, they view them more as chief warlords than as kings. If a kingdom of Israel did exist during these years, it was not as powerful or as well organized as the Hebrew Bible says. Furthermore, they argue, no definitive archaeological evidence proves that Solomon built the Temple in Jerusalem.

The Kingdoms of Israel and Judah Whether or not there was a united kingdom of Israel, in the aftermath of Solomon's death tensions between northern and southern tribes in Israel led to the establishment of two separate kingdoms—the kingdom of Israel, composed of the ten northern tribes, with its capital eventually at Samaria, and the kingdom of Judah, consisting of two southern tribes, with its capital at Jerusalem (see Map 1.5). In 722 or 721 B.C.E., the Assyrians (uh-SEER-ee-unz) overran the kingdom of Israel and deported many Israelites to other parts of the Assyrian Empire. These dispersed Israelites ("the ten lost tribes") merged with neighboring peoples and gradually lost their identity.

The southern kingdom of Judah managed to retain its independence for a while as Assyrian power declined, but a new enemy soon appeared on the horizon. The Chaldeans (kal-DEE-unz) defeated Assyria, conquered the kingdom of Judah, and completely destroyed Jerusalem in 586 B.C.E. Many upper-class people from Judah were deported to Babylon; the memory of their exile is still evoked in the stirring words of Psalm 137:

> By the rivers of Babylon, we sat and wept when we remembered Zion. . . .
>
> How can we sing the songs of the Lord while in a foreign land?
>
> If I forget you, O Jerusalem, may my right hand forget its skill.
>
> May my tongue cling to the roof of my mouth if I do not remember you,
>
> If I do not consider Jerusalem my highest joy.[6]

But the Babylonian captivity of the people of Judah did not last. A new set of conquerors, the Persians, destroyed the Chaldean kingdom and allowed the people of Judah to return to Jerusalem and rebuild their city and Temple. The revived kingdom of Judah remained under Persian control until the conquests of Alexander the Great in the fourth century B.C.E. The people of Judah survived, eventually becoming known as the Jews and giving their name to Judaism, the religion of Yahweh (YAH-way), the Israelite god.

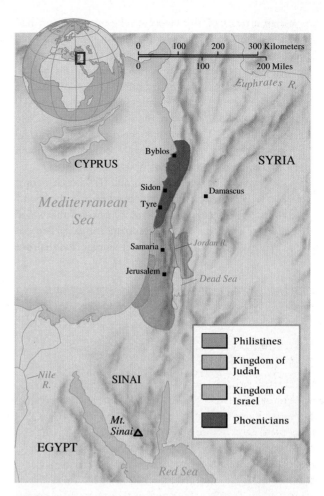

Map 1.5 The Israelites and their Neighbors in the first Millennium B.C.E. After Solomon's death, tensions between the tribes in Israel led to the creation of two kingdoms—a northern kingdom of Israel and a southern kingdom of Judah. With power divided, the Israelites could not resist invasions, and many were dispersed from Canaan. Some, such as the "ten lost tribes," never returned. Others were sent to Babylon but were later allowed to return under the rule of the Persians.

Q Why was Israel more vulnerable than Judah to the Assyrian Empire?

The Spiritual Dimensions of Israel According to the Hebrew conception, there is but one god called Yahweh, who created the world and everything in it. This omnipotent creator was not removed from the life he had created but was a just and good God who expected goodness from his people. If they did not obey his will, they would be punished. But he was primarily a god of mercy and love: "The Lord is gracious and compassionate, slow to anger and rich in love. The Lord is good to all; he has compassion on all he has made."[7] Each individual could have a personal relationship with this being.

Three aspects of the Hebrew religious tradition had special significance: the covenant, the law, and the prophets. The Israelites believed that during the exodus from Egypt, when biblical tradition holds that led his people out of bondage and into the promised land, God made a covenant or contract with the tribes of Israel, who believed that Yahweh had spoken to them through Moses (see Historical Voices, "The Covenant and the Law," p. 25). The Israelites promised to obey Yahweh; in return, Yahweh promised to take special care of his chosen people.

This covenant between Yahweh and his chosen people could be fulfilled, however, only by obedience to the law of God. Most important were the ethical concerns that stood at the center of the law. These commandments spelled out God's ideals of behavior: "You shall not murder. You shall not

1.8 Moses and the Ten Commandments. As we have seen, according to the Hebrew Bible, God gave to Moses a set of commandments for the Israelites to obey. Although these commandments are interpreted and numbered differently by religious groups, the early Christian church came to consider the Ten Commandments given to Moses by God as a summary of God's law and a standard for ethical behavior. This is evident in this sixth-century detail of Moses and the Ten Commandments in the Eastern Roman (later known as Byzantine) church of San Vitale in Italy. The Israelites shown in the photo are, of course, garbed in the clothing styles of the sixth century.

Alfredo Dagli Orti/Art Resource, NY

commit adultery. You shall not steal."[8] True freedom consisted of following God's moral standards voluntarily. If people chose to ignore the good, then suffering and evil would follow.

The Israelites believed that certain religious teachers called *prophets* were sent by God to serve as his voice to his people. The golden age of prophecy began in the mid-eighth century B.C.E. and continued during the time when the people of Israel and Judah were threatened by Assyrian and Chaldean conquerors. These "men of God" went through the land warning the Israelites that they had failed to keep God's commandments and would be punished for breaking the covenant.

Out of the words of the prophets came new concepts that enriched the Jewish tradition. The prophets embraced a concern for all humanity. All nations would someday come to the God of Israel: "All the earth shall worship you." This vision encompassed the establishment of peace for all the nations of the world. In the words of the prophet Isaiah: "He will judge between the nations and will settle disputes for many people. They will beat their swords into plowshares and their spears into pruning hooks. Nation will not take up sword against nation, nor will they train for war anymore."[9]

Although the prophets developed a sense of universalism, the demands of the Jewish religion (the need to obey God) eventually encouraged a separation between the Jews and their non-Jewish neighbors. Unlike most other peoples of the Middle East, the Jews could not simply be amalgamated into a community by accepting the gods of their conquerors and their neighbors. To remain faithful to the demands of their god, they might even have to refuse loyalty to political leaders.

1-6 THE RISE OF NEW EMPIRES

Q **Focus Question:** What methods and institutions did the Assyrians and Persians use to amass and maintain their respective empires?

Small and independent states could exist only as long as no larger state dominated western Asia. New empires soon arose, however, and conquered vast stretches of the ancient world.

1-6a The Assyrian Empire

The first of these empires emerged in Assyria, located on the upper Tigris River. The Assyrians were a Semitic-speaking people who exploited the use of iron weapons to establish an empire that by 700 B.C.E. included Mesopotamia, parts of the Iranian plateau, sections of

The Covenant and the Law: The Book of Exodus

Religion & Philosophy

ACCORDING TO THE BIBLICAL ACCOUNT, the Israelites supposedly made their covenant with Yahweh during their exodus from Egypt. They agreed to obey their god and follow his law. In return, Yahweh promised to take special care of his chosen people. This selection from the biblical book of Exodus describes the making of the covenant and God's commandments to the Israelites.

Exodus 19:1–8

In the third month after the Israelites left Egypt—on the very day—they came to the desert of Sinai. After they set out from Rephidim, they entered the desert of Sinai, and Israel camped there in the desert in front of the mountain. Then Moses went up to God, and the Lord called to him from the mountain, and said, "This is what you are to say to the house of Jacob and what you are to tell the people of Israel: 'You yourselves have seen what I did to Egypt, and how I carried you on eagles' wings and brought you to myself. Now if you obey me fully and keep my covenant, then out of all nations you will be my treasured possession. Although the whole earth is mine, you will be for me a kingdom of priests and a holy nation.' These are the words you are to speak to the Israelites." So Moses went back and summoned the elders of the people and set before them all the words the Lord had commanded him to speak. The people all responded together, "We will do everything the Lord has said." So Moses brought their answer back to the Lord.

Exodus 20:1–3, 7–17

And God spoke all these words, "I am the Lord your God, who brought you out of Egypt, out of the land of slavery. You shall have no other gods before me. . . . You shall not misuse the name of the Lord your God, for the Lord will not hold anyone guiltless who misuses his name. Remember the Sabbath day by keeping it holy. Six days you shall labor and do all your work, but the seventh day is a Sabbath to the Lord your God. On it you shall not do any work, neither you, nor your son or daughter, nor your manservant or maidservant, nor your animals, nor the alien within your gates. For in six days the Lord made the heavens and the earth, the sea, and all that is in them, but he rested on the seventh day. Therefore the Lord blessed the Sabbath day and made it holy. Honor your father and your mother, so that you may live long in the land the Lord your God is giving you. You shall not murder. You shall not commit adultery. You shall not steal. You shall not give false testimony against your neighbor. You shall not covet your neighbor's house. You shall not covet your neighbor's wife, or his manservant or maidservant, his ox or donkey, or anything that belongs to your neighbor."

 What was the nature of the covenant between Yahweh and the Israelites? What was its moral significance for the Israelites? How does it differ from Hammurabi's code, and how might you explain those differences?

Source: The Holy Bible, New International Version, (Colorado Springs, Colorado, Biblica, 1973).

Asia Minor, Syria, Canaan, and Egypt down to Thebes (see Map 1.6). But in less than a century, internal strife and resentment of Assyrian rule led subject peoples to rebel against it. The capital city of Nineveh fell to a coalition of Chaldeans and Medes in 612 B.C.E., and in 605 B.C.E., the rest of the empire was finally divided between the two powers.

At the Assyrian Empire's height, kings ruled with absolute power. To administer their empire more effectively, the Assyrians established a network of staging posts throughout the empire and used relays of horses (mules or donkeys in the mountains) to carry messages.

The Assyrians were outstanding conquerors. Over many years of practice, they developed effective military leaders and fighters. The Assyrian army was large, well

organized, and disciplined. It included a standing army of infantry as its core, accompanied by cavalry and horse-drawn war chariots that were used as mobile platforms for shooting arrows. Moreover, the Assyrians had the first large armies equipped with iron weapons.

Another factor in the effectiveness of the Assyrian military machine was its use of terror as an instrument of warfare (see Opposing Viewpoints, "The Governing of Empires: Two Approaches," p. 27). As a matter of regular policy, the Assyrians laid waste to the land in which they were fighting, smashing dams, looting and destroying towns, setting crops on fire, and cutting down trees, particularly fruit trees. They were especially known for committing atrocities against their captives.

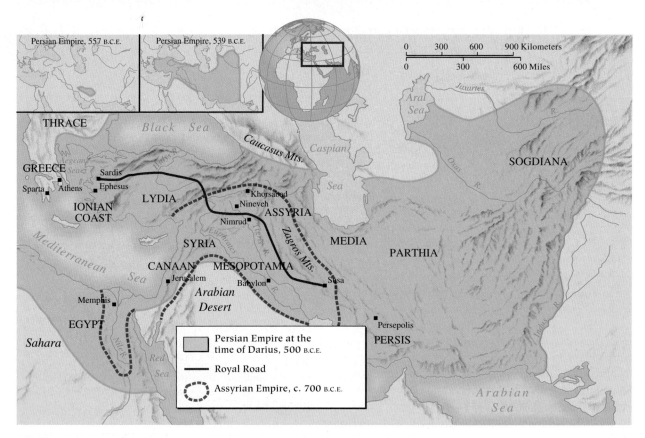

Map 1.6 The Assyrian and Persian Empires. Cyrus the Great united the Persians and led them in a successful conquest of much of the Near East, including most of the lands of the Assyrian Empire. By the time of Darius, the Persian Empire was the largest the world had yet seen.

 Based on your examination of this map of the Assyrian and Persian Empires, what do you think would be the challenges of governing a large empire?

1-6b The Persian Empire

After the collapse of the Assyrian Empire, the Chaldeans, under their king Nebuchadnezzar (neb-uh-kud-NEZZ-ur) II (605–562 B.C.E.), made Babylonia the leading state in western Asia. Nebuchadnezzar rebuilt Babylon as the center of his empire, giving it a reputation as one of the great cities of the ancient world. But the splendor of Chaldean Babylonia proved to be short-lived when Babylon fell to the Persians in 539 B.C.E.

The Persians were an Indo-European–speaking people who lived in southwestern Iran. Primarily nomadic, they were organized in tribes until the Achaemenid (ah-KEE-muh-nud) Dynasty managed to unify them. One of the dynasty's members, Cyrus (559–530 B.C.E.), created a powerful Persian state that stretched from Asia Minor in the west to western India in the east. In 539, Cyrus entered Mesopotamia and captured Babylon. His treatment of Babylonia showed remarkable restraint and wisdom. Babylonia was made into

a Persian province, but many government officials were kept in their positions. Cyrus also issued an edict permitting the Jews, who had been brought to Babylon in the sixth century B.C.E., to return to Jerusalem with their sacred temple objects and to rebuild their Temple as well.

To his contemporaries, Cyrus the Great deserved to be called the Great. He must have been an unusual ruler for his time, a man who demonstrated considerable wisdom and compassion in the conquest and organization of his empire. Unlike the Assyrian rulers of an earlier empire, he had a reputation for mercy. Medes, Jews, and Babylonians all accepted him as their legitimate ruler.

Cyrus's successors extended the territory of the Persian Empire. His son Cambyses (kam-BY-seez) (530–522 B.C.E.) undertook a successful invasion of Egypt. Darius (duh-RY-uss) (521–486 B.C.E.) added a new Persian province in western India that extended to the Indus River and then moved into Europe, conquering Thrace and creating the

The Governing of Empires: Two Approaches

Politics & Government

BOTH THE ASSYRIANS AND THE PERSIANS CREATED LARGE EMPIRES that encompassed large areas of the ancient Near East. Although both Assyrian and Persian rulers used military force and violence to attain their empires, their approaches to conquest and ruling sometimes differed. Assyrian rulers were known for their terror tactics and atrocities, as described in the first two selections. Although the kings of Persia also used terror when needed, they also had a reputation for less cruelty and more tolerance. Especially noteworthy was Cyrus, as is evident in this selection from a decree (known as the Cyrus Cylinder) that he issued in 538 B.C.E. The propaganda value of his words is also apparent, however.

King Sennacherib (704–681 B.C.E.) Describes His Siege of Jerusalem (701 B.C.E.)

As to Hezekiah, the Jew, he did not submit to my yoke, I laid siege to [forty-six] of his strong cities, walled forts and to the countless small villages in their vicinity, and conquered them by means of well-stamped earth-ramps, and battering-rams brought thus near to the walls combined with the attack by foot soldiers, using mines, breaches as well as sapper work. I drove out of them 200,150 people, young and old, male and female, horses, mules, donkeys, camels, big and small cattle beyond counting, and considered them booty. . . .

King Ashurbanipal (669–627 B.C.E.) Describes His Treatment of Conquered Babylon

I tore out the tongues of those whose slanderous mouths had uttered blasphemies against my god Ashur and had plotted against me, his god-fearing prince; . . . The others, I smashed alive with the very same statues of protective deities with which they had smashed my own grandfather Sennacherib—now finally as a belated burial sacrifice for his soul. I fed their corpses, cut into small pieces, to dogs, pigs, . . . vultures, the birds of the sky and also to the fish of the ocean. After I . . . thus made quiet again the hearts of the great gods, my lords, I removed the corpses of those whom the pestilence had felled, whose leftovers after the dogs and pigs had fed on them were obstructing the streets, filling the places of Babylon, and of those who had lost their lives through the terrible famine.

The Cyrus Cylinder

I am Cyrus, king of the world, great king, legitimate king, king of Babylon, king of Sumer and Akkad, king of the four corners of the earth. . . .

When I entered Babylon as a friend and when I established the seat of the government in the palace of the ruler under jubilation and rejoicing, Marduk, the great lord [the chief Babylonian god], caused the magnanimous inhabitants of Babylon to love me, and I was daily endeavoring to worship him. My numerous troops walked around in Babylon in peace. I did not allow anybody to terrorize any place of the country of Sumer and Akkad. I strove for peace in Babylon and in all his other sacred cities. As to the inhabitants of Babylon . . . I brought relief to their dilapidated housing, putting thus an end to their main complaints. . . .

 Both Ashurbanipal and Cyrus entered Babylon as conquerors. How did their treatment of the conquered city differ? How do you explain the differences? Which method do you think was more effective? Why?

Sources: Pritchard, James B., ed., *Ancient Near Eastern Texts Relating to the Old Testament,* Third Edition with Supplement. © 1950, 1955, 1969, renewed 1978 by Princeton University Press. Reprinted by permission of Princeton University Press.

largest empire the world had yet seen. His contact with the Greeks led him to undertake an invasion of the Greek mainland (see Chapter 4).

Civil Administration and the Military Darius strengthened the basic structure of the Persian government by creating a more rational division of the empire into twenty provinces called *satrapies.* Each **satrapy** (SAY-truh-pee) was ruled by a governor or satrap (SAY-trap), literally a "protector of the kingdom." Satraps collected tributes, were responsible for justice and security, raised military levies for the royal army, and normally commanded the military forces within their satrapies. In terms of real power, the satraps were miniature kings who created courts imitative of the Great King's.

An efficient system of communication was crucial to sustaining the Persian Empire. Well-maintained roads facilitated the rapid transit of military and government

1.9 Darius, the Great King. Darius ruled the Persian Empire from 521 to 486 B.C.E. He is shown on his throne in Persepolis, the new capital city he built. In his right hand, he holds the royal staff; his left grasps a lotus blossom with two buds, a symbol of royalty.

personnel. One in particular, the so-called Royal Road (see Map 1.6), stretched from Sardis, the center of Lydia in Asia Minor, to Susa, the chief capital of the Persian Empire. Like the Assyrians, the Persians established way stations equipped with fresh horses for the king's messengers.

In this vast administrative system, the Persian king occupied an exalted position. All subjects were the king's servants, and he, the Great King, was the source of all justice, possessing the power of life and death over everyone. At its height, much of the power of the Persian Empire depended on the military. By the time of Darius, the Persian monarchs had created a standing army of professional soldiers that was truly international in character, composed of contingents from the various peoples who made up the empire. At its core were a cavalry force of 10,000 and an elite infantry force of the same size known as the *Immortals* because they were never allowed to fall

below 10,000 in number. When one was killed, he was immediately replaced.

After Darius, Persian kings became more and more isolated at their courts, surrounded by luxuries paid for by the immense quantities of gold and silver that flowed into their treasuries, located in the capital cities. Both their hoarding of wealth and their later overtaxation of their subjects are seen as crucial factors in the ultimate weakening of the Persian Empire.

Persian Religion: Zoroastrianism Of all the Persians' cultural contributions, the most original was their religion, **Zoroastrianism**. According to Persian tradition, Zoroaster (ZOR-oh-ass-tur) was born in 660 B.C.E. After a period of wandering and solitude, he experienced revelations that caused him to be revered as a prophet of the "true religion." His teachings were eventually written down in the third century B.C.E. in the Zend Avesta, the sacred book of Zoroastrianism.

Zoroaster's spiritual message was basically monotheistic. To Zoroaster, the religion he preached was the only perfect one, and Ahuramazda (uh-HOOR-uh-MAHZ-duh) (the "Wise Lord") was the only god, the supreme deity, the "creator of all things." According to Zoroaster, Ahuramazda also possessed qualities that all humans should aspire to such as good thought, right action, and piety. Although Ahuramazda was supreme, he was not unopposed; this gave a dualistic element to Zoroastrianism. At the beginning of the world, the good spirit of Ahuramazda was opposed by the evil spirit later identified as Ahriman.

Humans also played a role in this cosmic struggle between good and evil. Ahuramazda, the creator, gave all humans free will and the power to choose between right and wrong. The good person chooses the right way of Ahuramazda. Zoroaster taught that there would be an end to the struggle between good and evil. Ahuramazda would eventually triumph, and the final separation of good and evil would occur at the last judgment at the end of the world. Individuals, too, would be judged. Each soul faced a final evaluation of its actions. The soul of a person who had performed good deeds would achieve paradise; but if the deeds had been evil, the person would be thrown into an abyss of torment. Some historians believe that Zoroastrianism, with its emphasis on good and evil, heaven and hell, and a last judgment, affected Christianity, a religion that eventually surpassed it in significance.

Humanlike creatures first emerged in Africa around 3 million to 4 million years ago. Over time, Paleolithic peoples learned to create sophisticated tools, to use fire, and to adapt to and even change their physical world. They were primarily nomads who hunted animals and gathered wild plants for survival. The agricultural revolution of the Neolithic Age, which began around 10,000 B.C.E., dramatically changed human patterns of living. The growing of food on a regular basis and the taming of animals enabled humans to stop their nomadic ways and settle in permanent settlements, which gave rise to more complex human societies.

These more complex human societies, which we call the first civilizations, emerged around 3000 B.C.E. in the river valleys of Mesopotamia, Egypt, India, and China.

An increase in food production in these regions led to a significant growth in human population and the rise of cities. The peoples of Southwest Asia and Egypt developed cities and struggled with the problems of organized states as they moved from individual communities to larger territorial units and eventually to empires. They invented writing to keep records and created literature. They constructed monumental buildings to please their gods, give witness to their power, and preserve their culture. They developed new political, military, social, and religious structures to deal with the basic problems of human existence and organization. These first civilizations left detailed records that allow us to view how they grappled with three of the fundamental problems that humans have pondered: the nature of human relationships, the nature of the universe, and the role of divine forces in that cosmos.

By the middle of the second millennium B.C.E., much of the creative impulse of the Mesopotamian and Egyptian civilizations was beginning to wane. Around 1200 B.C.E., many small states emerged, but all of them were eventually overshadowed by the rise of the great empires of the Assyrians and Persians. The Assyrian Empire was the first to unite almost all of the ancient Middle East. Even larger, however, was the empire of the Great Kings of Persia. The many years of peace that the Persian Empire brought

to the Middle East facilitated trade and the general well-being of its peoples. It is no wonder that many peoples expressed their gratitude for being subjects of the Great Kings of Persia. Among these peoples were the Hebrews, who created no empire but nevertheless left an important spiritual legacy. The embrace of monotheism created in Judaism one of the world's greatest religions, one that went on to influence the development of both Christianity and Islam.

REFLECTION QUESTIONS

Q What were the achievements of early humans during the Paleolithic and Neolithic Ages, and how did those achievements eventually make possible the emergence of civilization?

Q What roles did geography, environmental conditions, religion, politics, economics, and women and families play in the civilizations of Southwest Asia and Egypt?

Q Compare and contrast the administrative and military structure and attitudes toward subject peoples of the Assyrian and Persian Empires.

CHAPTER TIMELINE

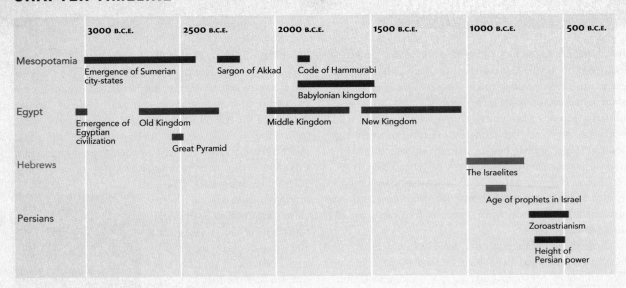

	3000 B.C.E.	2500 B.C.E.	2000 B.C.E.	1500 B.C.E.	1000 B.C.E.	500 B.C.E.

Mesopotamia
Emergence of Sumerian city-states
Sargon of Akkad
Code of Hammurabi
Babylonian kingdom

Egypt
Emergence of Egyptian civilization
Old Kingdom
Great Pyramid
Middle Kingdom
New Kingdom

Hebrews
The Israelites
Age of prophets in Israel

Persians
Zoroastrianism
Height of Persian power

CHAPTER NOTES

1. Quoted in A. Kuhrt, The *Ancient Near East, c. 3000–330 B.C.* (London, 1995), vol. 1, p. 68.

2. Quoted in M. Van de Mieroop, *A History of the Ancient Near East, ca. 3000–323 B.C.* (Oxford, 2004), p. 106.

3. Quoted in T. Jacobsen, "Mesopotamia," in H. Frankfort et al., *Before Philosophy* (Baltimore, 1949), p. 139.

4. Quoted in M. Covensky, *The Ancient Near Eastern Tradition* (New York, 1966), p. 51.

5. Ibid., p. 413.

6. Psalms 137:1, 4–6.

7. Psalms 145:8–9.

8. Exodus 20:13–15.

9. Isaiah 2:4.

MindTap® is a fully online, highly personalized learning experience built upon Cengage Learning content. MindTap combines student learning tools—readings, multimedia, activities, and assessments—into a singular Learning Path that guides students through the course and helps students develop the critical thinking, analysis, and communication skills that are essential to academic and professional success.

Chapter Outline and Focus Questions

2-1 The Emergence of Civilization in India: The Indus Valley Society

Q What were the chief features of the Indus Valley civilization, and in what ways was it similar to the civilizations that arose in Egypt and Mesopotamia?

2-2 The Aryans in India

Q What were some of the distinctive features of the class system introduced by the Aryan peoples, and what effects did it have on Indian civilization?

2-3 Escaping the Wheel of Life: The Religious World of Ancient India

Q What are the main tenets of Brahmanism and Buddhism? How did they differ, and how did each religion influence Indian civilization?

2-4 The Rule of the Fishes: India After the Mauryas

Q Why was India unable to maintain a unified empire in the first millennium B.C.E., and how was the Mauryan Empire temporarily able to overcome the tendencies toward disunity?

2-5 The Exuberant World of Indian Culture

Q In what ways did the culture of ancient India resemble and differ from the cultural experience of ancient Mesopotamia and Egypt?

Borromeo/Art Resource, NY

2.1 Mohenja-Daro: Ancient city on the Indus

Critical Thinking

Q What role did geography and the local environment play in affecting the nature of the first civilization that developed in the South Asian subcontinent? In what ways were these factors different from those that affected the civilizations discussed in Chapter 1?

Connections to Today

Q How would you compare the class system in ancient India as described in the Law of Manu with that of the United States at the present time? What do you think accounts for the differences?

IN THE EARLY 1920S, an archaeological team led by John Marshall, a British colonial official, uncovered the remains of an ancient city that had been buried under the silt of the Indus River for more than 3,000 years. Suddenly, the fabled civilizations in

Mesopotamia and the Nile River Valley (see Chapter 1) had a contemporary equivalent far to the east on the edge of the Indian subcontinent. As excavations continued, diggers at the site discovered the skeletal remains of several human beings caught in positions of sudden flight, provoking the assumption that the ancient city—now dubbed Mohenjo-Daro or "City of the Dead"—had come to an abrupt end as the result of an invasion by nomadic peoples who began arriving in the region around 1500 B.C.E. Over the next several hundred years, these immigrants, who called themselves the *Aryans*, set out to create the civilization that we know today as India.

Today, nearly a century after the Marshall team began its labors, much about the Indus Valley civilization—as this ancient culture is now commonly labeled by specialists—still remains a mystery, mainly because its writing system, inscribed on clay seals and tablets found at various sites in the region, remains undeciphered, and the connections between it and the later culture that developed in the Indian subcontinent under the Aryans remains in dispute among historians (see section 2-2a, "Who Were the Aryans?," p. 36). Nevertheless, many scholars today agree with John Marshall's conclusion at the time that many aspects of this long-dead civilization still persist among the peoples, culture, and values of the Indian people today.

2-1 THE EMERGENCE OF CIVILIZATION IN INDIA: THE INDUS VALLEY SOCIETY

 Focus Question: What were the chief features of the Indus Valley civilization, and in what ways was it similar to the civilizations that arose in Egypt and Mesopotamia?

The vast region of the Indian subcontinent is home to a great variety of peoples: people speaking one of the languages in the Dravidian family, who probably descended from the Indus River culture that flourished at the dawn of Indian civilization, more than 4,000 years ago; Aryans, descended from the pastoral peoples who flooded southward from Central Asia in the second millennium B.C.E.; and hill peoples, who may have lived in the region before the rise of organized societies and thus may have been the earliest inhabitants of all.

Although today this beautiful mosaic of peoples and cultures has been broken up into many separate independent states, the region still possesses a coherent history that is recognizably Indian despite its internal diversity.

2-1a A Land of Diversity

India was and still is a land of diversity that is evident in its languages and cultures as well as its physical characteristics. India possesses an incredible array of languages. It has a deserved reputation, along with the Middle East, as a cradle of religion. Two of the world's major religions, Hinduism and Buddhism, originated in India.

In its size and diversity, India seems more like a continent than a single country. That diversity begins with the geographic environment. Shaped like a spade hanging from the southern ridge of Asia, the Indian subcontinent is composed of several core regions. In the far north are the Himalayan and Karakoram mountain ranges, home to the highest mountain peaks in the world. Directly south of the Himalayas and the Karakoram range is the rich valley of the Ganges (GAN-jeez), India's "holy river" and one of the core regions of Indian culture. To the west is the Indus River Valley. Today, the latter is a relatively arid plateau that forms the backbone of the modern state of Pakistan, but in ancient times it enjoyed a more temperate climate and served as the cradle of Indian civilization.

South of India's two major river valleys lies the Deccan (DEK-uhn), a region of hills and an upland plateau that extends from the Ganges Valley to the southern tip of the Indian subcontinent. The interior of the plateau is relatively hilly and dry, but the eastern and western coasts are occupied by lush plains, which are historically among the most densely populated regions of India. Off the southeastern coast is the island known today as Sri Lanka. Although Sri Lanka is now a separate country quite distinct politically and culturally from India, the island's history is intimately linked with that of its larger neighbor.

2-1b The Indus Valley Civilization: A Fascinating Enigma

The first signs that an ancient civilization had emerged in the Indus River Valley appeared in the early nineteenth century, when archaeologists discovered the remains of an urban settlement at Harappa, a town located several hundred miles north of the site at Mohenjo-Daro. Today, more than 1,000 small agricultural settlements have been unearthed in the region, many of them dating back more than 9,000 years. Those small mud-brick villages eventually gave rise to the sophisticated human communities that historians call the Indus Valley civilization. Although today the area is relatively arid, during the third and fourth millennia B.C.E., it evidently received much more abundant rainfall, and the valleys of the Indus River and its tributaries supported a thriving civilization that may have covered a total area of more than 700,000 square miles from the Himalayas to the coast of the Indian Ocean. More than seventy sites have been unearthed since the area was first discovered in the 1850s, but the main sites are at the two major cities, Harappa in the Punjab (pun-JAHB) and Mohenjo-Daro nearly 400 miles to the south near the mouth of the Indus River (see Map 2.1).

Political and Social Structures In several respects, the Indus Valley civilization closely resembled the cultures of Mesopotamia and the Nile Valley. Like them, it probably began in tiny farming villages scattered throughout the river valley, some dating back to as early as 6500 or 7000 B.C.E. These villages thrived and grew until, by the middle of the third millennium B.C.E., they could support a privileged ruling elite living in walled cities of considerable magnitude and affluence. The center of power was the city of Harappa, which was surrounded by a brick wall more than forty feet thick at its base and more than 3.5 miles in circumference. The city was laid out on an essentially rectangular grid, with some streets as wide as thirty feet. Most buildings were constructed of kiln-dried mud bricks

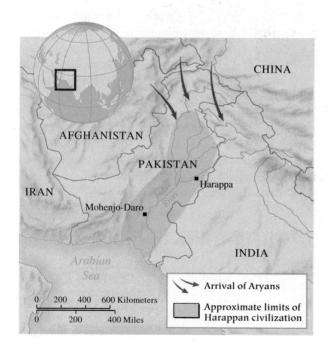

Map 2.1 Ancient Indus Valley civilization. This map shows the location of the first civilization that arose in the Indus River Valley, which today is located in Pakistan.

Q Based on this map, why do you think the Indus Valley civilization resembled the civilizations of Mesopotamia and Egypt?

and were square in shape, reflecting the grid pattern. At its height, the city may have had as many as 80,000 inhabitants, making it as large as some of the most populous Sumerian urban centers.

Both Harappa and Mohenjo-Daro were divided into large walled neighborhoods, with narrow lanes separating the rows of houses. Houses varied in size, with some as high as three stories, but all followed the same general plan based on a square courtyard surrounded by rooms. Bathrooms featured an advanced drainage system that carried wastewater out to drains under the streets and thence to sewage pits beyond the city walls.

Unfortunately, the Indus Valley writing system has not yet been deciphered, so historians know relatively little about the organization of the Indus society and not even the name it called itself (Sumerian sources referred to it as *Meluhha*). Recent archaeological evidence, however, suggests that unlike its contemporaries in Egypt and Sumer, the Indus Valley society was not a centralized monarchy claiming divine origins but a collection of more than 1,500 towns and cities loosely connected by ties of trade and alliance and ruled by a coalition of landlords and rich merchants. There were no royal precincts or imposing burial monuments and few surviving stone or terra-cotta images that might represent kings, priests, or military commanders. It is possible, however, that religion had advanced beyond the stage of spirit worship to belief in a single god or goddess of fertility. Carvings of animals on many of the clay seals suggest the possibility of animal sacrifice at ceremonies undertaken to maintain the fertility of the soil and guarantee the annual harvest (see Image 2.2).

As in Mesopotamia and Egypt, the Indus Valley economy was based primarily on agriculture, and evidence shows that grain crops such as wheat, barley, and rice, as well as peas, were cultured as early as 7,000 years ago. The presence of cotton seeds at various sites suggests that the Indus Valley peoples may have been the first to master the cultivation of this useful crop and possibly introduced it, along with rice, to other societies in the region. But they also developed an extensive trading network that extended to Sumer and other civilizations to the west. Textiles and foodstuffs were apparently imported from Sumer in exchange for metals such as copper, lumber, precious stones, and various types of luxury goods. Much of this trade was conducted by ship via the Persian Gulf, although some undoubtedly went by land.

Indus Valley Culture Archaeological remains indicate that the Indus Valley peoples possessed a culture as sophisticated in some ways as that of the Sumerians to the west. The aesthetic quality of some Indus Valley pottery and sculpture is superb, rivaling equivalent work produced elsewhere. Sculpture was probably the region's highest artistic achievement. Some artifacts possess a wonderful vitality of expression. Fired clay seals show a deft touch in carving animals such as elephants, tigers, rhinoceroses, and antelope, and figures made of copper or terracotta show a lively sensitivity and a sense of grace and movement.

Writing was another achievement of Indus Valley society and dates back at least to the beginning of the third millennium B.C.E. (see Comparative Essay, "Writing and Civilization," p. 35). Unfortunately, the only surviving examples of Indus Valley writing are the pictographic symbols inscribed on the clay seals and tablets. The script contained more than 400 characters, but most are too stylized to be identified by their shape, and scholars have made little progress in deciphering them. There are no apparent links with Mesopotamian scripts. Although, as in Mesopotamia, the primary purpose of writing may have been to record commercial transactions, some of the clay seals appear to have been intended to portray religious ceremonies. Until the script is deciphered, much about the Indus Valley civilization must remain, as one historian termed it, a fascinating enigma.

The Collapse of the Indus Valley Civilization One of the great mysteries of the Indus Valley civilization is how it came to an end. The once popular theory that the city of Mohenjo-Daro was invaded and destroyed by marauding Aryan warriors has now been widely dismissed because the Aryan peoples apparently did not begin to arrive in northwest India until about 1500 B.C.E., at least four centuries after the apparent abandonment of Mohenjo-Daro. More likely, Indus Valley civilization had already fallen on hard times, probably as a result of natural causes. Archaeologists have found clear signs of social decay, including evidence of trash in the streets, neglect of public services, and overcrowding in urban neighborhoods. Mohenjo-Daro itself may have been destroyed by an epidemic or by natural phenomena such as floods, an earthquake, or a shift in the course of the Indus River. Some climatologists speculate that the monsoon rains that regularly water the region had weakened at the outset of the second millennium B.C.E. If that was the case, any migrating peoples arrived in the area after the greatness of Indus Valley civilization had already passed.

2.2 A mother goddess. During its period of florescence, from 2600 to 1900 B.C.E., the craftsmen of the Indus Valley civilization created a variety of terra cotta objects, including whimsical toy animals, whistles, tops, and dice for children. Most enigmatic, however, are the numerous female figurines such as the one shown here with elaborate headdresses and numerous strands of necklaces. Their meaning and purpose, however, remain elusive. Were they representatives of an Earth goddess like many other female deities throughout the ancient world? Although the evidence is inconclusive, a fertility goddess was probably worshipped in the Indus Valley, as it was in other river valleys throughout the region.

© DeA Picture Library/Art Resource, NY

In recent years, a new theory has been proposed by some historians in India, who contend that the Aryan peoples did not migrate into the Indian subcontinent from Central Asia, but were in fact descendants of the indigenous population that had originally created the Indus Valley civilization. Most scholars, however, continue to support the migration hypothesis, although the evidence is not conclusive. They point out that the spoken language of the Aryan people, known as *Sanskrit*, is widely recognized as a branch of the Indo-European family of languages (see Chapter 1). Moreover, the earliest account produced by the Aryan people themselves, the Rig Veda (RIK VA-duh) (see next section), describes a culture based primarily on pastoralism, a pursuit not particularly suited to the Indus River valley. Significantly, the tradition of buffalo sacrifice, inscribed on innumerable seals throughout the Indus River Valley, is not mentioned in the Rig Veda. A definitive solution to the debate will have to await further evidence.

2-2 THE ARYANS IN INDIA

Q **Focus Question:** What were some of the distinctive features of the class system introduced by the Aryan peoples, and what effects did they have on Indian civilization?

Assuming the Aryans arrived from elsewhere to settle in India, they gradually adapted to the geographic realities of their new homeland and abandoned the pastoral life for agricultural pursuits. They were assisted by the introduction of iron, which probably came from the Middle East,

Writing and Civilization

Art & Ideas

When evidence of the complexity and sophistication of the Indus Valley civilization began to emerge in the early twentieth century, among the most tantalizing objects to appear were the clay seals and tablets that contained mysterious inscriptions in a written language that has not yet been deciphered. Without a greater understanding of the meaning of these enigmatic signs, our knowledge of Indus Valley civilization must remain rudimentary. This challenge is a testament to the importance of a written language and how it enables historians to uncover the secrets of ancient cultures.

According to prehistorians, human beings invented the first spoken language around 50,000 years ago. As human beings spread from Africa to other continents, that initial language gradually fragmented and evolved into innumerable separate tongues. By the time the agricultural revolution began around 10,000 B.C.E., there were perhaps nearly twenty distinct language families in existence around the world.

During the later stages of the agricultural revolution, the first writing systems also began to emerge in various places around the world (see Map 2.2). The first successful efforts were apparently achieved in Mesopotamia and Egypt, but knowledge of writing soon spread to peoples along the shores of the Mediterranean and in the Indus River Valley in South Asia. Wholly independent systems were also invented in China and Mesoamerica. Writing was used for a variety of purposes. It enabled a ruler to communicate with his subjects on matters of official concern, as when the Egyptian king Scorpion in about 3250 B.C.E. ordered that a decree announcing a major military victory over rivals in the region be inscribed on a limestone cliff in the Nile River Valley. In other cases, the purpose was to enable human beings to communicate with supernatural forces. In China and Egypt, for example, priests used writing to communicate with the gods. In Mesopotamia and in the Indus River Valley, merchants apparently used writing to mark official events or to record commercial and other legal transactions. Finally, writing was also used to present ideas in new ways, giving rise to such early Mesopotamian literature as *The Epic of Gilgamesh*.

How did these early written languages evolve into the complex systems in use today? In almost every case, the

Scala/Art Resource, NY

2.3 Indus Valley seals. Like their contemporaries in Mesopotamia, the Indus Valley peoples developed a writing system to record their spoken language. Unfortunately, it has not yet been deciphered. Most extant examples of early writing from the area are found on fired clay seals depicting human figures and animals. These seals have been found in houses and were probably used to identify the owners of goods for sale. Other seals may have been used as amulets or have had other religious significance. Several depict religious figures or ritualistic scenes of sacrifice.

first systems consisted of pictographs, pictorial images of various concrete objects such as trees, water, cattle, body parts, and the heavenly bodies. Eventually, the pictographs became more stylized to facilitate transcription—much as we often use a cursive script instead of block printing today. Finally, and most important for their future development, these pictorial images began to take on specific phonetic meanings so they could represent sounds in the written language. Most sophisticated written systems eventually evolved to a phonetic script based on an alphabet of symbols that represented all sounds in the spoken language, but others went only part way by adding phonetic signs to the individual character to suggest pronunciation while keeping part of the original pictograph to indicate meaning. Most of the latter systems, such as hieroglyphics in Egypt and cuneiform in Mesopotamia, eventually became extinct, but the ancient Chinese writing system survives today, although in greatly altered form.

 For what purposes were writing systems developed in the ancient world? What appears to have been the initial purpose of the Indus Valley peoples' script?

where it had been introduced by the Hittites (see Chapter 1) around 1500 B.C.E. The invention of the iron plow, along with the development of irrigation, enabled the Aryans and their indigenous subjects to clear the dense jungle growth along the Ganges River and transform the Ganges Valley into one of the richest agricultural regions in South Asia. The Aryans also developed their own writing system based on the Aramaic (ar-uh-MAY-ik) script of the Middle East and were thus able to transcribe the legends that previously had been passed down from generation to generation by memory (see Map 2.2). Most of what is known about the early Aryans is based on oral traditions passed on the aforementioned Rig Veda, an ancient work that was written down after the Aryans arrived in India (it is one of several Vedas, or collections of sacred instructions and rituals).

HISTORIANS DEBATE ## 2-2a Who Were the Aryans?

Historians know relatively little about the origins of the Aryan peoples. The traditional view is that they were Indo-European speakers who had once inhabited vast areas in the steppes north and east of the Black and Caspian Seas. The Indo-Europeans were primarily pastoral peoples who migrated from season to season in search of fodder for their herds. Historians have credited them with many technological achievements, including the invention of horse-drawn chariots and the stirrup, both of which were eventually introduced throughout much of the Eurasian supercontinent.

Although many other Indo-European-speaking peoples moved westward and eventually settled throughout Europe, the Aryans began to settle in an area around the Oxus River in Central Asia and then moved south across the Hindu Kush mountain range into the plains of northern India. Between 1500 and 1000 B.C.E., they gradually advanced eastward from the Indus Valley and across the fertile plain of the Ganges River, and some migrated southward into the Deccan Plateau. Eventually, they extended their political mastery over the entire subcontinent and its mainly Dravidian-speaking inhabitants, although the indigenous culture undoubtedly survived to remain a prominent element in the evolution of traditional Indian civilization.

Based on the Comparative Essay, "Writing and Civilization," p. 35, in what ways were these first writing systems similar, and how were they different?

2-2b From Chieftains to Kings

As in other Indo-European societies, each of the various Aryan groups was led by a chieftain called a **raja** (RAH-juh) ("prince"), who was assisted by a council of elders composed of other leading members of the community. Like the elders, the raja was normally a member of the warrior class called the **kshatriya** (kshuh-TREE-yuh). The chief derived his power from his ability to protect his people from rival groups, an ability that was crucial in the warring kingdoms and shifting alliances that were typical of early Aryan society. Though the rajas claimed to be

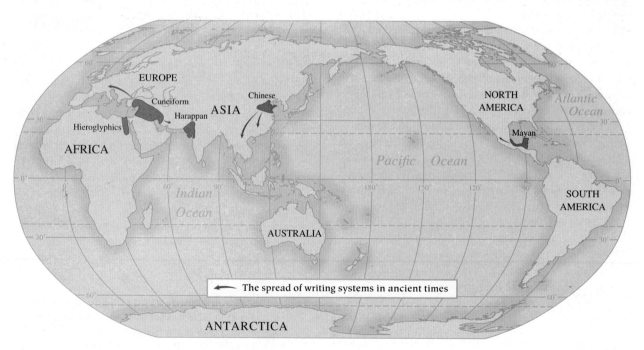

Map 2.2 Writing systems in the ancient world. A chief characteristic of the first civilizations was the development of a system of written communication.

representatives of the gods, they were not viewed as gods themselves.

As Indian society grew in size and complexity, the chieftains began to be transformed into kings, usually called **maharajas** (mah-huh-RAH-juhs) ("great princes"). Nevertheless, the tradition that the ruler did not possess absolute authority remained strong. Like all human beings, the ruler was required to follow the *dharma* (DAR-muh), a set of laws that established behavioral standards for all individuals and classes in Indian society.

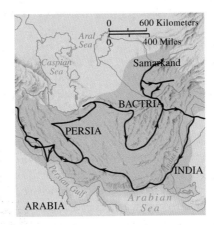

Map 2.3 Alexander the Great's movements in Asia

The Impact of The Greeks While competing groups squabbled for precedence in India, powerful new empires were rising to the west. First came the Persian Empire of Cyrus and Darius. Then came the Greeks. After two centuries of sporadic rivalry and warfare, the Greeks achieved a brief period of regional dominance in the late fourth century B.C.E. with the rise of Macedonia under Alexander the Great. Alexander had heard of the riches of India, and in 330 B.C.E., after conquering Persia, he launched an invasion of the east (see Chapter 4). In 326 B.C.E., his armies arrived in the plains of northwestern India. They departed almost as suddenly as they had come, leaving in their wake Greek administrators and a veneer of cultural influence that would affect the area for generations to come. (See Map 2.3.)

2-2c The Mauryan Empire

The Alexandrian conquest was only a brief interlude in the history of the Indian subcontinent, but it played a formative role; on the heels of Alexander's departure rose the first dynasty to control much of the region. The founder of the new state, who took the royal title Chandragupta Maurya (chun-druh-GOOP-tuh MOWR-yuh) (324–301 B.C.E.), drove out the Greek administrators who had remained after the departure of Alexander and solidified his control over the northern Indian plain. He established the capital of his new Mauryan Empire at Pataliputra (pah-tah-lee-POO-truh) (modern Patna) in the Ganges Valley (see Map 2.4).

Little is known of Chandragupta Maurya's empire. Most accounts of his reign rely on the scattered remnants of a lost work written by Megasthenes (muh-GAS-thuh-neez), a Greek ambassador to the Mauryan court, in about 302 B.C.E. Chandragupta Maurya was apparently advised by a brilliant court official named Kautilya (kow-TIL-yuh), whose name has been attached to a treatise on politics called the *Arthasastra* (ar-thuh-SAS-truh).

The work actually dates from a later time, but it may well reflect Kautilya's ideas.

Although the author of the *Arthasastra* follows Aryan tradition in stating that the happiness of the king lies in the happiness of his subjects, the treatise also asserts that when the sacred law of the dharma and practical politics collide, the latter must take precedence: "Whenever there is disagreement between history and sacred law or between evidence and sacred law, then the matter should be settled in accordance with sacred law."

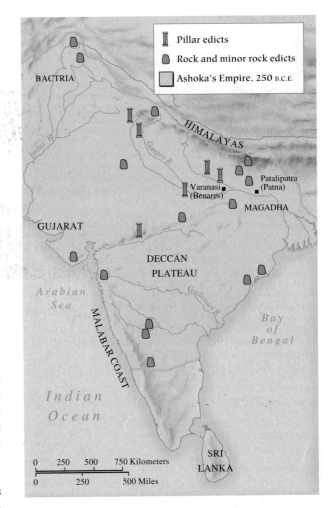

Map 2.4 The empire of Ashoka. Ashoka, the greatest Indian monarch, reigned over the Mauryan Empire in the third century B.C.E. This map shows the extent of his empire and the location of the pillar edicts that were erected along major trade routes.

Q *Why do you think the pillars and rocks were placed where they were?*

In the Beginning

Religion & Philosophy **AS THE INDIANS BEGAN TO SPECULATE** about the nature of the cosmic order, they came to believe in the existence of a single monistic force in the universe, a form of ultimate reality called *Brahman*. Today the early form of Hinduism is sometimes called Brahmanism. In the Upanishads (oo-PAHN-ih-shahds), the concept began to emerge as an important element of Indian religious belief. It was the duty of the individual self—called the *Atman*—to achieve an understanding of this ultimate reality so that after death the self would merge in spiritual form with *Brahman*. Sometimes *Brahman* was described in more concrete terms as a creator god—eventually known as Vishnu—but more often in terms of a shadowy ultimate reality. In the following passage from the Upanishads, the author speculates on the nature of ultimate reality.

The Upanishads

In the beginning . . ., this world was just being, one only, without a second. Some people, no doubt, say: "In the beginning . . ., this world was just nonbeing, one only,

without a second; from that nonbeing, being was produced." But how indeed . . . could it be so? How could being be produced from nonbeing? . . .

In the beginning this world was being alone, one only, without a second. Being thought to itself: "May I be many, may I procreate." It produced fire. That fire thought to itself: "May I be many, may I procreate." It produced water. Therefore, whenever a person grieves or perspires, then it is from fire [heat] alone that water is produced. That water thought to itself: "May I be many, may I procreate." It produced food; it is from water alone that food for eating is produced. . . . That divinity (Being) thought to itself: "Well, having entered into these three divinities [fire, water, and food] by means of this living self, let me develop names and forms."

 How would you compare this passage from the Upanishads with the accounts about the origins of life from Egyptian and Hebrew sources as cited in Chapter 1?

Source: From *The Upanishads*, tr. Juan Mascaro. Viking Press, 1965.

But whenever sacred law is in conflict with rational law, then reason shall be held authoritative."[1] The *Arthasastra* also emphasizes ends rather than means, achieved results rather than the methods employed. For this reason, it has often been compared to Machiavelli's famous political treatise, *The Prince*, written more than 1,000 years later during the Italian Renaissance (see Chapter 15).

As described in the *Arthasastra*, Chandragupta Maurya's government was highly centralized and even despotic: "It is power and power alone which, only when exercised by the king with impartiality, and in proportion to guilt, over his son or his enemy, maintains both this world and the next."[2] The king possessed a large army and a secret police responsible to his orders (according to the Greek ambassador Megasthenes, Chandragupta Maurya was chronically fearful of assassination, a not unrealistic concern for someone who had allegedly come to power by violence). Reportedly, all food was tasted in his presence, and he made a practice of never sleeping twice in the same bed in his sumptuous palace. To guard against corruption, a board of censors was empowered to investigate cases of possible malfeasance and incompetence within the bureaucracy.

2-2d Caste and Class: Social Structures in Ancient India

When the Aryans arrived in India, they already possessed a strong class system based on a ruling warrior class and other social groupings characteristic of a pastoral society. In the subcontinent, they encountered peoples living by farming or by other pursuits such as fishing, hunting, or food gathering. The ultimate result was a set of social institutions and class divisions that have continued to have relevance down to the present day.

The Class System At the crux of the social system that emerged from the clash of cultures was the concept of a hierarchical division of society that placed each individual within a ritual framework that defined the person's occupation and status within the broader community. In part, this division may have been an outgrowth of attitudes held by the Aryan peoples with regard to the indigenous population. The Aryans, who followed primarily pastoral pursuits, tended to look askance at their new neighbors, who lived by tilling the soil. Further, the Aryans, a mostly light-skinned people, were contemptuous of the indigenous peoples, who were darker. Light skin came to imply high status, whereas dark skin suggested the opposite.

The concept of color, however, was only the physical manifestation of a division that took place in Indian society on the basis of economic functions. Indian classes (called *varna*, literally "color" but commonly and mistakenly translated as "castes" in English) did not simply reflect an informal division of labor. Instead, at least in theory, they were a set of rigid social classifications that determined not only one's occupation but also one's status in society and one's hope for ultimate salvation (see "2-3 Escaping the Wheel of Life" later in this chapter). There were five major varna in Indian society in ancient times. At the top were two classes that were collectively viewed as the aristocracy and clearly represented the ruling elites in Aryan society before their arrival in India: the priests and the warriors.

Members of the priestly class were known as the *brahmins* and were usually considered to be at the top of the social scale. Descended from seers who had advised the ruler on religious matters in Aryan tribal society—*brahmin* meant "one possessed of **Brahman** (BRAH-mun)," a term for the supreme god in the Hindu religion—they were eventually transformed into an official class after their religious role declined in importance. Megasthenes described this class as follows:

> After their birth the children are in the care of one person after another, and as they advance in years their masters are men of superior accomplishments. The philosophers reside in a grove in front of the city within a moderate-sized enclosure. They live in a simple style and lie on pallets of straw and [deer] skins. They abstain from animal food and sexual pleasures, and occupy their time in listening to serious discourse and in imparting knowledge to willing ears.[3]

The second class was the kshatriya, the warriors. Although often listed below the brahmins in social status,

many kshatriyas were probably descended from the ruling warrior class in Aryan society before the conquest of India and thus may have originally ranked socially above the brahmins, although they were ranked lower in religious terms. Like the brahmins, the kshatriyas were originally identified with a single occupation—fighting—but as the character of Aryan society changed, they often switched to other forms of employment.

The third-ranked class in Indian society was the *vaisya* (VISH-yuh) (literally, "commoner"). The vaisyas were usually viewed in economic terms as the merchant class. Some historians have speculated that they were originally guardians of the tribal herds but many of them moved into commercial pursuits after settling in India. Megasthenes noted that members of this class "alone are permitted to hunt and keep cattle and to sell beasts of burden or to let them out on hire. In return for clearing the land of wild beasts and birds which infest sown fields, they receive an allowance of corn from the king. They lead a wandering life and dwell in tents."[4] Although this class ranked below the first two in social status, it shared with them the privilege of being considered *twice-born*, a term used to refer to males who had undergone a ceremony at puberty whereby they were initiated into adulthood and introduced into Indian society.

Below the three twice-born classes were the *sudras* (SOO-druhs *or* SHOO-druhs), who represented the great bulk of the Indian population. The sudras were not considered fully Aryan, and the term probably originally referred to the indigenous population. Most sudras were peasants or artisans or worked at other forms of manual labor. They had only limited rights in society.

At the lowest level of Indian society, and in fact not even considered a legitimate part of the class system itself, were the untouchables (also known as *outcastes*, or *pariahs*). The untouchables probably originated as a slave class consisting of prisoners of war, criminals, ethnic minorities, and other groups considered outside Indian society. Even after slavery was outlawed, the untouchables were given menial and degrading tasks that other Indians would not accept such as collecting trash, handling dead bodies, or serving as butchers or tanners. One historian estimates that they may have accounted for a little more than 5 percent of the total population of India in antiquity.

The life of the untouchables was extremely demeaning. They were not considered fully human, and their very presence was considered polluting to members of the other varna. No Indian of a higher class would touch or eat food handled or prepared by an untouchable. Untouchables lived in special ghettos and, according to one foreign observer, were required to tap two sticks together to announce their presence when they traveled outside their quarters so that others could avoid them.

CHRONOLOGY	Ancient India
Indus Valley civilization	ca. 2600–1900 B.C.E.
Arrival of the Aryans	ca. 1500 B.C.E.
Life of Gautama Buddha	ca. 560–480 B.C.E.
Invasion of India by Alexander the Great	326 B.C.E.
Mauryan Dynasty founded	324 B.C.E.
Reign of Chandragupta Maurya	324–301 B.C.E.
Reign of Ashoka	269–232 B.C.E.
Collapse of Mauryan Dynasty	183 B.C.E.
Rise of Kushan kingdom	ca. first century C.E.

Technically, the class divisions were absolute. Individuals supposedly were born, lived, and died in the same class. In practice, some upward or downward mobility probably took place, and there was undoubtedly some flexibility in economic functions. But throughout most of Indian history, class taboos remained strict. Members were generally not permitted to marry outside their class (although in practice, men were occasionally allowed to marry below their class but not above it).

The Jati   The people of ancient India did not belong to a particular class as individuals but as part of a larger kinship group commonly referred to as the *jati* (JAH-tee) (in Portuguese, *casta,* which evolved into the English term *caste*), a system of extended families that originated in ancient India and still exists in somewhat changed form today. Although the origins of the jati system are unknown (there are no indications of strict class distinctions in Indus Valley society), the jati eventually became identified with a specific kinship group living in a specific area and carrying out a specific function in society. Each jati was identified with a particular varna, and each had its own separate economic function, at least in theory.

The jatis were thus the basic social organization into which traditional Indian society was divided. Each jati was itself composed of hundreds or thousands of individual nuclear families and was governed by its own council of elders. Membership in this ruling council was usually hereditary and based on the wealth or social status of particular families within the community.

In theory, each jati was assigned a particular form of economic activity. Obviously, though, not all families in a given jati could take part in the same vocation; as time went on, members of a single jati commonly engaged in several different lines of work. Sometimes an entire jati would have to move its location to continue performing a particular form of activity. In other cases, a jati would adopt an entirely new occupation to remain in a certain area. Such changes in habitat or occupation introduced the possibility of movement up or down the social scale. In this way, an entire jati could sometimes engage in upward mobility, even though that normally was not possible for individuals, who were tied to their class identity for life.

The class system in ancient India may sound highly constricting, but there were persuasive social and economic reasons why it survived for so many centuries. In the first place, it provided an identity for individuals in a highly hierarchical society. Although an individual might rank lower on the social scale than members of other classes, it was always possible to find others ranked even lower. Perhaps equally important, the jati was a primitive form of welfare system. Each jati was obliged to provide for any of its members who were poor or destitute. The jati also provided an element of stability in a society that all too often was in a state of political instability.

2-2e Daily Life in Ancient India

Beyond these rigid social stratifications was the Indian family. Not only was life centered around the family, but also the family, not the individual, was the most basic unit in society.

The Family   The ideal social unit was an extended family with three generations living under the same roof. It was essentially patriarchal, except along the Malabar coast, near the southwestern tip of the subcontinent, where a matriarchal form of social organization prevailed down to modern times. In the rest of India, the oldest male traditionally possessed legal authority over the entire family

2.4 Female Earth spirit. This Earth spirit, carved on a gatepost of the Buddhist stupa at Sanchi (SAHN-chee) 2,200 years ago, illustrates how earlier Indian representations of the fertility goddess were incorporated into Buddhist art. Women were revered as powerful fertility symbols and considered dangerous when menstruating or immediately after giving birth. Voluptuous and idealized, this Earth spirit was believed to be able to cause a tree to blossom by wrapping her leg around the trunk or even merely touching a branch with her arm.

The Position of Women in Ancient India

Family & Society THE AMBIVALENT ATTITUDE TOWARD WOMEN IN ANCIENT INDIA is evident in this passage from the *Law of Manu*, which states that respect for women is the responsibility of men. At the same time, it also makes clear that a woman's place is in the home.

The *Law of Manu*

Women must be honored and adorned by their father, brothers, husbands, and brother-in-laws who desire great good fortune.

Where women, verily, are honored, there the gods rejoice, where, however they are not honored, there all sacred rites prove fruitless.

Where the female relations live in grief—that family soon perishes completely; where, however, they do not suffer from any grievance—that family always prospers. . . .

The father who does not give away his daughter in marriage at the proper time is censurable; censurable is the husband who does not approach his wife in due season; and after the husband is dead, the son, verily is censurable, who does not protect his mother.

Even against the slightest provocations should women be particularly guarded; for unguarded they would bring grief to both the families.

Regarding this as the highest dharma of all four classes, husbands though weak, must strive to protect their wives.

His own offspring, character, family, self, and dharma does one protect when he protects his wife scrupulously. . . .

The husband should engage his wife in the collections and expenditure of his wealth, in cleanliness, in dharma, in cooking food for the family, and in looking after the necessities of the household. . . .

Women destined to bear children, enjoying great good fortune, deserving of worship, the resplendent lights of homes on the one hand and divinities of good luck who reside in the houses on the other—between these there is no difference whatsoever.

 How do these attitudes toward women compare with those we have encountered in the Middle East and North Africa?

Source: Manu Smrti 3.55–57: Ed. J. Jolly. London: Trubner, 1887 (Trubner Oriental Series)

---

unit (see Historical Voices, "The Position of Women in Ancient India," above).

The family was linked together in a religious sense by a series of commemorative rites to ancestral members. These rituals originated in the Vedic era and consisted of family ceremonies to honor the departed and link the living with the dead. The male family head was responsible for leading the ceremonies. At his death, his eldest son had the duty of conducting the funeral rites.

The importance of the father and the son in family ritual underlined the importance of males in Indian society. Male superiority was expressed in a variety of ways. Women could not serve as priests (although in practice, some were accepted as seers), nor were they normally permitted to study the Vedas. In general, males had a monopoly on education because the primary goal of learning to read was to carry on family rituals. In high-class families, young men began Vedic studies with a **guru** (teacher). Some then went on to higher studies in major cities. The goal of such an education might be either professional or religious.

The Role of Women In general, only males could inherit property, except in a few cases when there were no sons. According to law, a woman was always considered a minor. Divorce was prohibited, although it sometimes took place. According to the *Arthasastra*, a wife who had been deserted by her husband could seek a divorce. Polygamy was fairly rare and apparently occurred mainly among the higher classes, but husbands were permitted to take a second wife if the first was barren. Producing children was an important aspect of marriage, both because children provided security for their parents in old age and physically proved male potency. Child marriage was common for young girls, whether because of the desire for children or because daughters represented an economic liability to their parents. But perhaps the most graphic symbol of women's subjection to men was the ritual of **sati** (suh-TEE) (often written *suttee*), which encouraged the wife to throw herself on her dead husband's funeral pyre and follow him into death. The Greek visitor Megasthenes reported "that he had heard from some persons of wives burning themselves along with their deceased husbands and doing so gladly; and that those women who refused to burn themselves were held in disgrace."[5] All in all, it was undoubtedly a difficult existence. According to the Law of Manu, an early treatise on social organization and behavior in ancient India, probably written in the first or second century B.C.E., a woman was subordinated to men throughout her life and, as a wife, should "worship her lord as a god."[6]

At the root of female subordination to the male was the practical fact that, as in most agricultural societies, men did most of the work in the fields. Females were viewed as having little utility outside the home and indeed were considered an economic burden because parents were obliged to provide a dowry to acquire a husband for a daughter. Female children also appeared to offer little advantage in maintaining the family unit because they joined the families of their husbands after their wedding ceremonies.

Despite all of these indications of female subjection to the male, there are numerous signs that women often played influential roles in Indian society, and the code of behavior set out in the Law of Manu stressed that they should be treated with respect (see the preceding "The Position of Women in Ancient India"). Indians appeared to be fascinated by female sexuality, and tradition held that women often used their sexual powers to achieve domination over men. The author of the Mahabharata, a vast epic of early Indian society, complained that "the fire has never too many logs, the ocean never too many rivers, death never too many living souls, and fair-eyed woman never too many men." Despite the legal and social constraints, women often played an important role within the family unit, and many were admired and honored for their talents. It is probably significant that paintings and sculpture from ancient and medieval India frequently show women in roles equal to those of men.

2-2f The Economy

The arrival of the Aryans did not drastically change the economic character of Indian society. Not only did most Aryans eventually take up farming, but also it is likely that agriculture expanded rapidly under Aryan rule with the invention of the iron plow and the spread of northern Indian culture into the Deccan Plateau. One consequence of this process was to shift the focus of Indian culture from the Indus Valley farther eastward to the Ganges River Valley, which even today is one of the most densely populated regions on Earth. The flatter areas in the Deccan Plateau and in the coastal plains were also turned into cropland.

Indian Farmers For most Indian farmers, life was harsh. Among the most fortunate were those who owned their own land, although they were required to pay taxes to the state.

Many others were sharecroppers or landless laborers. They were subject to the vicissitudes of the market and often paid exorbitant rents to their landlords. Concentration of land in large holdings was limited by the tradition of dividing property among all the sons, but large estates worked by hired laborers or rented out to sharecroppers were not uncommon, particularly in areas where local rajas derived much of their wealth from their property.

Another problem for Indian farmers was the unpredictability of the climate. India is in the monsoon zone. The monsoon is a seasonal wind pattern in southern Asia that blows from the southwest during the summer months and from the northeast during the winter. The southwest monsoon, originating in the Indian Ocean, is commonly marked by heavy rains. When the rains were late, thousands starved, particularly in the drier areas, which were especially dependent on rainfall. Strong governments attempted to deal with such problems by building state-operated granaries and maintaining the irrigation works; but strong governments were rare, and famine was probably all too common. The staple crops in the north were wheat, barley, and millet, with wet rice farming common in the fertile river valleys. In the south, grain and vegetables were supplemented by various tropical products, cotton, and spices such as pepper, ginger, cinnamon, and saffron.

Trade and Manufacturing By no means were all Indians farmers. As time passed, India became one of the most advanced trading and manufacturing civilizations in the ancient world. After the rise of the Mauryas, India's role in regional trade began to expand, and the subcontinent became a major transit point in a vast commercial network that extended from the rim of the Pacific to the Middle East and the Mediterranean Sea. This regional trade went both by sea and by camel caravan. Overland trade via what is now known as the Silk Road was underway by at least the first millennium B.C.E. Maritime commerce based on the seasonal monsoon winds across the Indian Ocean may have begun as early as the fifth century B.C.E. It extended eastward as far as Southeast Asia and China and southward as far as the straits between Africa and the island of Madagascar. Westward went spices, teakwood, perfumes, jewels, textiles, precious stones and ivory, and wild animals. In return, India received gold, tin, lead, and wine. The subcontinent had, indeed, become a major crossroads of trade in the ancient world.

India's expanding role as a manufacturing and commercial hub of the ancient world was undoubtedly a spur to the growth of the state. Under Chandragupta Maurya, the central government became actively involved in commercial and manufacturing activities. It owned mines and vast crown lands and undoubtedly earned massive profits from its role in regional commerce. Nevertheless, a significant private sector also flourished that was dominated by great caste guilds that monopolized key sectors of the economy. A money economy probably came into operation during the second century B.C.E. when copper and gold coins were introduced from the Middle East. This, in turn, led to the development of banking. But village trade continued to be conducted by means of barter or cowry shells (highly polished shells used as a medium of exchange throughout much of Africa and Asia) throughout the ancient period.

2-3 ESCAPING THE WHEEL OF LIFE: THE RELIGIOUS WORLD OF ANCIENT INDIA

 Focus Questions: What are the main tenets of Brahmanism and Buddhism? How did they differ, and how did each religion influence Indian civilization?

As with Indian politics and society, Indian religion is a blend of Aryan and Dravidian culture. The intermingling of those two civilizations gave rise to an extraordinarily complex set of religious beliefs and practices filled with diversity and contrast. Out of this cultural mix came two of the world's great religions, Buddhism and Hinduism, and several smaller ones, including Jainism and Sikhism. Early Aryan religious beliefs, however, are known to historians as **Brahmanism**.

2-3a Brahmanism

Although little is known about the form of religion practiced in the Indus Valley civilization, evidence about the earliest religious beliefs of the Aryan peoples is better documented and comes primarily from sacred texts such as the Vedas, a set of four collections of hymns and religious ceremonies originally transmitted by memory through the centuries by Aryan priests and systematized in written form by about 1000 B.C.E. Many of these religious ideas were probably common to all of the Indo-European peoples before their separation into different groups at least 4,000 years ago. Early Aryan beliefs were based on the common concept of a pantheon of gods and goddesses representing great forces of nature similar to the immortals of Greek mythology. The Aryan ancestor of the Greek father-god Zeus, for example, may have been the deity known in early Aryan tradition as Dyaus (DYOWS) (see Chapter 4).

The parent god Dyaus was a somewhat distant figure, however, and was eventually overshadowed by other, more functional gods possessing more familiar human traits. For awhile, the primary Aryan god was the great warrior god

Indra. Indra summoned the Aryan tribal peoples to war and was represented in nature by thunder. Later, Indra declined in importance and was replaced by Varuna (vuh-ROO-nuh), lord of justice. Other gods and goddesses represented various forces of nature or the needs of human beings such as fire, fertility, and wealth. During Vedic times, the concept of sacrifice was a key means of communicating with celestial forces. As in many other ancient cultures, the practice may have begun as human sacrifice, but animals were later used as substitutes. The priestly class, the brahmins, played a key role in these ceremonies. Another element of Indian religious belief in ancient times was the ideal of asceticism.

Although there is no reference to such practices in the Vedas, by the sixth century B.C.E. self-discipline, which involved subjecting oneself to painful stimuli or even self-mutilation, had begun to replace sacrifice as a means of communicating with the gods. Apparently, the original motive for asceticism was to achieve magical powers, but later, in the Upanishads (oo-PAHN-ih-shahds)—a set of commentaries on the Vedas compiled in the sixth century B.C.E.— it was seen as a means of spiritual meditation that would enable the practitioner to reach beyond material reality to a world of truth and bliss beyond earthly joy and sorrow (see Opposing Viewpoints: "The Search for Truth," p. 44). It is possible that another motive was to permit those with strong religious convictions to communicate directly with metaphysical reality without having to rely on the priestly class at court.

Asceticism, of course, has been practiced in other religions, including Christianity and Islam, but it seems particularly identified with **Hinduism**, the religion that emerged from early Indian religious tradition (see Image 2.5). Eventually, asceticism evolved into the modern practice of body training that we know as *yoga* ("union"), which is accepted today as a meaningful element of Hindu religious practice.

Reincarnation Another new concept—**reincarnation**— also probably began to appear around the time the Upanishads were written. This is the idea that the individual soul is reborn in a different form after death and progresses through several existences on the wheel of life until it reaches its final destination in a union with the Great World Soul, Brahman. Because life is harsh, this final release is the objective of all living souls. From this concept comes the term *Brahmanism*, referring to the early form of Aryan religious tradition.

A key element in this process is the idea of *karma*—that one's rebirth in a next life is determined by one's karma (actions) in this life. As it emerged from Brahmanism in the first century C.E., Hinduism placed all living species on a vast scale of existence, including the four classes and the untouchables in human society. The current status of an

The Search for Truth

Religion & Philosophy   **WHEN THE RIG VEDA WAS ORIGINALLY COMPOSED** in the second millennium B.C.E., brahmins at court believed that the best way to communicate with the gods was through sacrifice, a procedure that was carried out through the intermediation of the fire god Agni. The first selection is an incantation uttered by priests at the sacrificial ceremony.

By the middle of the first millennium B.C.E., however, the tradition of offering sacrifices had come under attack by opponents, who argued that the best way to seek truth and tranquility was by renouncing material existence and adopting the life of a wandering mendicant. In the second selection, from the *Mundaka Upanishad*, an advocate of this position forcefully presents his views. The similarity with the fervent believers of early Christianity, who renounced the corrupting forces of everyday life by seeking refuge in isolated monasteries in the desert, is striking.

The *Rig Veda*

I extol Agni, the household priest, the divine minister of the sacrifice, the chief priest, the bestower of blessings.

May that Agni, who is to be extolled by ancient and modern seers, conduct the gods here.

Through Agni may one gain day by day wealth and welfare which is glorious and replete with heroic sons.

O Agni, the sacrifice and ritual which you encompass on every side, that indeed goes to the gods.

May Agni, the chief priest, who possesses the insight of a sage, who is truthful, widely renowned, and divine, come here with the gods.

O Agni, O Angiras ["messenger"], whatever prosperity you bring to the pious is indeed in accordance with your true function.

O Agni, illuminator of darkness, day by day we approach you with holy thought bringing homage to you.

Presiding at ritual functions, the brightly shining custodian of the cosmic order [rta], thriving in your own realm.

O Agni, be easy of access to us as a father to his son. Join us for our well-being.

The *Mundaka Upanishad*

Unsteady, indeed, are those boats in the form of sacrifices, eighteen in number, in which is prescribed only the inferior work. The fools who delight in this sacrificial ritual as the highest spiritual good go again and again through the cycle of old age and death.

Abiding in the midst of ignorance, wise only according to their own estimate, thinking themselves to be learned, but really obtuse, these fools go round in a circle like blind men led by one who is himself blind.

Abiding manifoldly in ignorance they, all the same, like immature children think to themselves: "We have accomplished our aim." Since the performers of sacrificial ritual do not realize the truth because of passion, therefore, they, the wretched ones, sink down from heaven when the merit that qualified them for the higher world becomes exhausted.

Regarding sacrifice and merit as most important, the deluded ones do not know of any other higher spiritual good. Having enjoyed themselves only for a time on top of the heaven won by good deeds [sacrifice, etc.] they reenter this world or a still lower one.

Those who practice penance [*tapas*] and faith in the forest, the tranquil ones, the knowers of truth, living the life of wandering mendicancy—they depart, freed from passion, through the door of the sun, to where dwells verily . . . the imperishable Soul [*Atman*].

Having scrutinized the worlds won by sacrificial rites, a brahmin should arrive at nothing but disgust. The world that was not made is not won by what is done [i.e., by sacrifice]. For the sake of that knowledge he should go with sacrificial fuel in hand as a student, in all humility to a preceptor [guru] who is well versed in the [Vedic] scriptures and also firm in the realization of Brahman.

Unto him who has approached him in proper form, whose mind is tranquil, who has attained peace, does the knowing teacher teach, in its very truth, that knowledge about Brahman by means of which one knows . . . the only Reality.

 In which passages in these two documents do you find a reference to the idea of karma (see the discussion under "Reincarnation" in the text)? Which document makes use of the concept, and how? What role does asceticism play in these documents?

Source: From *Sources of Indian Tradition*, Vol. 1, 2e, by Ainslee Embree. Copyright © 1988 by Columbia University Press.

2.5 The searcher. In their search for truth and the ultimate reality, some early followers of Brahmanism embarked on a lifelong retreat from the material world. The holy scripture for such early ascetics was the Upanishads, a collection of writings dating from the middle of the first millennium B.C.E. that extolled a life of privation and self-denial. The practice continues today, as this photograph of an Indian mendicant wandering in the mountains of the Deccan Plateau attests.

William J. Duiker

The ultimate goal of achieving "good" karma, as we have seen, was to escape the cycle of existence. To the sophisticated, the nature of that release was a spiritual union of the individual soul with the Great World Soul, Brahman, described in the Upanishads as a form of dreamless sleep, free from earthly desires. Such a concept, however, was undoubtedly too ethereal for the average Indian, who needed a more concrete form of heavenly salvation, a place of beauty and bliss after a life of disease and privation.

What about the religious beliefs of the vast majority of the Indian people during this formative stage in South Asian society? In all likelihood, popular religion during the first millennium B.C.E. broadly resembled that of peoples elsewhere throughout the world at that time. Belief in the existence of spirits related to natural events such as thunder or rainfall or to natural objects such as mountains or trees was probably commonplace. By the end of the first millennium B.C.E., many primary deities had begun to appear, including the so-called trinity of gods: Brahman the Creator, Vishnu the Preserver, and Shiva (SHIV-uh) (originally the Vedic god Rudra) the Destroyer. Although Brahman (sometimes in his concrete form called *Brahma*) was considered to be the highest god, Vishnu and Shiva eventually began to take precedence in the devotional exercises of many Hindus, who could be roughly divided into Vishnuites and Shaivites (see Image 2.6).

Over the centuries, religious practices among Aryan elites changed radically from its origins in Aryan pastoral society. The early belief in deities representing forces of nature gradually gave way to a more formalized system as described above, with a priestly class at court performing sacrifices in order to obtain heavenly favors. But during the first millennium B.C.E., religious belief began to evolve into a more personal experience for some people, with an emphasis on ethics as a means of obtaining a union between *Atman* (AHT-mun), the individual soul, and Brahman, the ultimate reality.[7]

The average Indian, however, would probably have thought of heavenly salvation in more concrete terms, as a place where the hardships of earthly life would give way to pleasure and delight. In later centuries, the Brahmanical beliefs and practices of early Aryan society would gradually be replaced by a more popular faith that henceforth would become known as *Hinduism*. We will discuss that transformation in Chapter 9.

individual soul, then, is not simply a cosmic accident but the inevitable result of actions that that soul has committed in a past existence.

The concept of karma is governed by the *dharma*, a law regulating human behavior. The dharma imposes different requirements on different individuals depending on their status in society. Those high on the social scale such as brahmins and kshatriyas are held to a more strict form of behavior than are sudras. The brahmin, for example, is expected to abstain from eating meat because that would entail the killing of another living being, thus interrupting its karma.

At the same time, the concept of reincarnation provided certain compensations for those lower on the ladder of life. For example, it gave hope to the poor that if they behaved properly in this life, they might improve their condition in the next. It also provided a means for unassimilated groups such as ethnic minorities to find a place in Indian society while simultaneously maintaining their distinctive way of life.

2-3b Buddhism: The Middle Path

In the sixth century B.C.E., a new doctrine appeared in northern India that soon began to rival the popularity of Brahmanical beliefs throughout the subcontinent. This new doctrine was called **Buddhism**.

The Life of Siddhartha Gautama The historical founder of Buddhism, Siddhartha Gautama (si-DAR-tuh GAW-tuh-muh), was a native of a small principality in the foothills of the Himalaya Mountains in what is today southern Nepal. He was born in the mid-sixth century B.C.E., the son of a ruling kshatriya family (see Comparative Illustration, "The Buddha and Jesus," p. 47).

According to tradition, the young Siddhartha was raised in affluent surroundings and trained, like many other members of his class, in the martial arts. On reaching maturity, he married and began to raise a family. At age twenty-nine, however, he suddenly discovered the pain of illness, the sorrow of death, and the degradation caused by old age in the lives of ordinary people and exclaimed, "Would that sickness, age, and death might be forever bound!" From that time on, he decided to dedicate his life to determining the cause and seeking the cure for human suffering.

To find the answers to these questions, Siddhartha abandoned his home and family and traveled widely. At first, he tried to follow the model of the ascetics, but he eventually decided that self-mortification did not lead to a greater understanding of life and abandoned the practice. Then one day, after a lengthy period of meditation under a tree, he finally achieved enlightenment as to the meaning of life and spent the remainder of his life preaching it. As embodied in his teachings, his conclusions became the philosophy (or, as some would have it, the religion) of Buddhism. According to legend, the Devil (the Indian term is *Mara*) attempted desperately to tempt him with political power and the company of beautiful girls. But Siddhartha Gautama resisted:

> *Pleasure is brief as a flash of lightning*
> *Or like an autumn shower, only for a moment. . . .*
> *Why should I then covet the pleasures you speak of?*
> *I see your bodies are full of all impurity:*
> *Birth and death, sickness and age are yours.*
> *I seek the highest prize, hard to attain by men—*
> *The true and constant wisdom of the wise.*[8]

2.6 The three faces of Shiva. In the first centuries C.E., Hindus began to adopt the technique of rock art. One outstanding example is at the Elephanta Caves, near the modern city of Mumbai (Bombay). Dominating the cave is this 18-foot-high triple-headed statue of Shiva, representing the Hindu deity in all his various aspects. The central figure shows him in total serenity, enveloped in absolute knowledge. The angry profile on the left portrays him as the destroyer, struggling against time, death, and other negative forces. The right-hand profile shows his loving and feminine side in the guise of his beautiful wife, Parvati.

William J. Duiker

Buddhism and Brahmanism How much the modern doctrine of Buddhism resembles the original teachings of Siddhartha Gautama is open to debate because so much time has elapsed since his death and original texts relating his ideas are lacking. Nor is it certain that Siddhartha even intended to found a new religion or doctrine. In some respects, his ideas could be viewed as a reformist form of Brahmanism that was designed to transfer responsibility from the priests to the individual, much as sixteenth-century German monk Martin Luther saw his ideas as a reformation of Christianity. Siddhartha accepted much of the belief system of Brahmanism, if not all of its practices. For example, he accepted the concept of reincarnation and the role of karma as a means of influencing the movement of individual souls up and down the scale of life. He praised nonviolence and borrowed the idea of living a life of simplicity and chastity from the ascetics. Moreover, his vision of metaphysical reality—commonly known as **nirvana**—is closer to the Aryan concept of Brahman than it is to the Christian concept of heavenly salvation. Nirvana involves an extinction of selfhood and a final reunion with the Great World Soul, and it is sometimes likened to a dreamless sleep or to a kind of "blowing out" (as of a candle). Buddhists occasionally remark that someone who asks for a description does not understand the concept.

At the same time, however, the new doctrine differed from existing practices in several key ways. To begin with, Siddhartha denied the existence of an individual soul. To him, the concept of Atman—the individual soul—meant that the soul was subject to rebirth and thus did not achieve a complete liberation from the cares of this world. In fact, Siddhartha denied the ultimate reality of the material world in its entirety and taught that it was an illusion to be transcended. Siddhartha's idea of achieving nirvana was based on his conviction that the pain, poverty, and sorrow that afflict human beings are caused essentially by their attachment to the things of this world. Once worldly cares are abandoned, pain and sorrow can be overcome. With this knowledge

The Buddha and Jesus

Religion & Philosophy

AS BUDDHISM EVOLVED, transforming Siddhartha Gautama, known as the Buddha, from mortal to god, Buddhist art changed as well. Statuary and relief panels began to illustrate the story of his life. Image 2.7a shows a frieze from the second century C.E., in which the infant Siddhartha is seen emerging from the hip of his mother, Queen Maya. Although dressed in draperies that reflect Greek influences from Alexander the Great's brief incursion into northwestern India, her sensuous stance and the touching of the tree evoke the female Earth spirit of traditional Indian art. Image 2.7b shows a Byzantine painting depicting the infant Jesus with his mother, the Virgin Mary, dating from the sixth century C.E. Notice that a halo surrounds the head of both the Buddha and Jesus. The halo—a circle of light—is an ancient symbol of divinity. In Hindu, Greek, and Roman art, the heads of gods were depicted emitting sunlike divine radiances. Early kings adopted crowns made of gold and precious gems to symbolize their own divine authority.

Q *What similarities and differences do you see in these depictions of the mothers of key religious figures?*

William J. Duiker

2.7a

Erich Lessing/Art Resource, NY

2.7b

How to Achieve Enlightenment

Religion & Philosophy | **ONE OF THE MOST FAMOUS PASSAGES** in Buddhist literature is the sermon at Sarnath, which Siddhartha Gautama delivered to his followers in a deer park outside the holy city of Varanasi (Benares), in the Ganges River Valley. Here he set forth the key ideas that would define Buddhist beliefs for centuries to come. During an official visit to Sarnath nearly three centuries later, Emperor Ashoka ordered the construction of a stupa (reliquary) in honor of the Buddha's message.

The Sermon at Benares

Thus have I heard: at one time the Lord dwelt at Benares at Isipatana in the Deer Park. There the Lord addressed the five monks:

> "These two extremes, monks, are not to be practiced by one who has gone forth from the world. What are the two? That conjoined with the passions and luxury, low, vulgar, common, ignoble, and useless; and that conjoined with self-torture, painful, ignoble, and useless. Avoiding these two extremes the Tathagata has gained the enlightenment of the Middle Path, which produces insight and knowledge and tends to calm, to higher knowledge, enlightenment, Nirvana.
>
> "And what, monks, is the Middle Path, of which the Tathagata has gained enlightenment, which produces insight and knowledge, and tends to calm, to higher knowledge, enlightenment, Nirvana? This is the noble Eightfold Way: namely, right view, right intention, right speech, right action, right livelihood, right effort, right mindfulness, right concentration. This, monks, is the Middle Path, of which the Tathagata has gained enlightenment, which produces insight and knowledge, and tends to calm, to higher knowledge, enlightenment, Nirvana.

> "1. Now this, monks, is the noble truth of pain: birth is painful, old age is painful, sickness is painful, death is painful, sorrow, lamentation, dejection, and despair are painful. Contact with unpleasant things is painful, not getting what one wishes is painful. In short the five groups of graspings are painful.
>
> "2. Now this, monks, is the noble truth of the cause of pain: the craving, which tends to rebirth, combined with pleasure and lust, finding pleasure here and there; namely, the craving for passion, the craving for existence, the craving for nonexistence.
>
> "3. Now this, monks, is the noble truth of the cessation of pain, the cessation without a remainder of craving, the abandonment, forsaking, release, nonattachment.
>
> "4. Now this, monks, is the noble truth of the way that leads to the cessation of pain: this is the noble Eightfold Way; namely, right view, right intention, right speech, right action, right livelihood, right effort, right mindfulness, right concentration.
>
> "And when, monks, in these four noble truths my due knowledge and insight with its three sections and twelve divisions was well purified, then, monks, . . . I had attained the highest complete enlightenment. This I recognized. Knowledge arose in me, insight arose that the release of my mind is unshakable; this is my last existence; now there is no rebirth."

 How did Siddhartha Gautama reach the conclusion that following the "four noble truths" was the proper course for living a moral life? How do his ideas compare with the commandments that God gave to the Israelites (see Chapter 1)?

Source: From *The Teachings of the Compassionate Buddha,* E. A. Burtt, ed. Copyright 1955 by Mentor. Used by permission of the E. A. Burtt Estate.

comes **bodhi** (BOH-dee), or wisdom (source of the term *Buddhism* and the familiar name for Gautama the Wise: Gautama Buddha).

Achieving this understanding is a key step on the road to nirvana, which, as in Brahmanism, is a form of release from the wheel of life. According to tradition, Siddhartha transmitted this message in a sermon to his disciples in a deer park at Sarnath (see Historical Voices, "How to Achieve Enlightenment," above), not

far from the modern city of Benares (buh-NAHR-is *or* buh-NAHR-eez)—also known as Varanasi (vah-RAH-nah-see). Like so many messages, it is deceptively simple and is enclosed in four noble truths: (1) life is suffering, (2) suffering is caused by desire, (3) the way to end suffering is to end desire, and (4) the way to end desire is to avoid the extremes of a life of vulgar materialism and a life of self-torture and to follow the **Middle Path**. Also known as the Eightfold Way, the Middle Path calls for right knowledge, right purpose, right speech, right conduct, right occupation, right effort, right awareness, and right meditation.

Buddhism also differed in its relative egalitarianism. Although Siddhartha accepted the idea of reincarnation (and hence the idea that human beings differ as a result of karma accumulated in a previous existence), he rejected the division of humanity into rigidly defined classes based on previous reincarnations and taught that all human beings could aspire to nirvana as a result of their behavior in this life—a message that likely helped Buddhism win support among people at the lower end of the social scale.

In addition, Buddhism was much simpler than existing beliefs. Siddhartha rejected the panoply of gods that had become identified with Brahmanism and forbade his followers to worship his person or his image after his death. In fact, many Buddhists view Buddhism as a philosophy rather than a religion.

After Siddhartha Gautama's death in 480 B.C.E., dedicated disciples carried his message the length and breadth of India. Buddhist monasteries were established throughout the subcontinent, and temples and **stupas** (STOO-puhs) (stone towers housing relics of the Buddha) sprang up throughout the countryside.

Women were permitted to join the monastic order but only in an inferior position. As Siddhartha had explained, women are "soon angered," "full of passion," and "stupid": "that is the reason . . . why women have no place in public assemblies . . . and do not earn their living by any profession." Still, the position of women tended to be better in Buddhist societies than it was elsewhere in ancient India.

Jainism During the next centuries, Buddhism began to compete actively with the existing Aryan beliefs; it also competed with another new faith known as **Jainism** (JY-ni-zuhm), whose founder, Mahavira (mah-hah-VEE-ruh), was a contemporary of Siddhartha Gautama. Resembling Buddhism in its rejection of the reality of the material world, Jainism was more extreme in practice. However, Siddhartha Gautama called for the "middle way" between passion and luxury and pain and self-torture, Mahavira preached a doctrine of extreme simplicity to his followers, who kept no possessions and relied on begging for a living. Some even rejected clothing and wandered through the world naked.

Ashoka, A Buddhist Monarch Buddhism received an important boost when Ashoka (uh-SHOH-kuh), the grandson of Chandragupta Maurya, converted to Buddhism in the third century B.C.E. Ashoka (r. 269–232 B.C.E.) is widely considered the greatest ruler in the history of India. By his own admission, as noted in rock edicts placed around his kingdom, Ashoka began his reign conquering, pillaging, and killing, but he began to regret his bloodthirsty past and attempted to rule benevolently after his conversion to Buddhism.

Ashoka directed that banyan trees and shelters be placed along the road to provide shade and rest for weary travelers. He sent Buddhist missionaries throughout India and ordered the erection of stone pillars with official edicts and Buddhist inscriptions to instruct people in the proper way (see Map 2.3). According to tradition, his son converted the island of Sri Lanka to Buddhism, and the peoples there accepted a tributary relationship with the Mauryan Empire.

Detail from an Ashoka Pillar (photo), Indian school (third century b.c.e.)/Sarnath, Uttar Pradesh, India/The Bridgeman Art Library

2.8 The Lions of Sarnath. Their beauty and Buddhist symbolism make the Lions of Sarnath the most famous of the capitals topping Ashoka's pillars. Sarnath was the holy site where the Buddha first preached, and these roaring lions echo the proclamation of Buddhist teachings to the four corners of the world. The wheel not only represents the Buddha's laws but also proclaims Ashoka's imperial legitimacy as the enlightened Indian ruler.

2-4 THE RULE OF THE FISHES: INDIA AFTER THE MAURYAS

Focus Question: Why was India unable to maintain a unified empire in the first millennium B.C.E., and how was the Mauryan Empire temporarily able to overcome the tendencies toward disunity?

After Ashoka's death in 232 B.C.E., the Mauryan Empire began to fragment into separate states. In 183 B.C.E., the last Mauryan ruler was overthrown by one of his military commanders, and India reverted to disunity. Several new kingdoms, some of them perhaps influenced by the memory of the Alexandrian conquests, arose along the fringes of the subcontinent in Bactria, known today as Afghanistan. In the first century C.E., Indo-European–speaking peoples fleeing from the nomadic Xiongnu (SHYAHNG-noo) warriors in Central Asia seized power in the area and proclaimed the new Kushan (koo-SHAHN) Kingdom (see Chapter 9). For the next two centuries, the Kushanas extended their political sway over northern India as far as the central Ganges Valley, while other kingdoms scuffled for predominance elsewhere on the subcontinent. India would not see unity again for another 500 years.

Several reasons for India's failure to maintain a unified empire have been proposed. Some historians suggest that a decline in regional trade during the first millennium C.E. may have contributed to the growth of small land-based kingdoms that drew their primary income from agriculture. The tenacity of the Aryan tradition with its emphasis on tribal rivalries may also have contributed. Although the Mauryan rulers tried to impose a more centralized organization, clan loyalties once again came to the fore after the collapse of the Mauryan Dynasty. Furthermore, the behavior of the ruling class was characterized by what Indians call the "rule of the fishes," which glorified warfare as the natural activity of the king and the aristocracy. The *Arthasastra,* which set forth a model of a centralized Indian state, assumed that war was the "sport of kings." Still, this was not an uneventful period in the history of India; Indo-Aryan ideas continued to spread toward the south, and both Brahmanism and Buddhism evolved in new directions.

2-5 THE EXUBERANT WORLD OF INDIAN CULTURE

Focus Question: In what ways did the culture of ancient India resemble and differ from the cultural experience of ancient Mesopotamia and Egypt?

Few cultures in the world are as rich and varied as India's. Most societies excel in some forms of artistic and literary achievement and not in others, but India has produced great works in almost every field of cultural endeavor—art and sculpture, science, architecture, and literature.

2-5a Literature

The earliest known Indian literature consists of the four Vedas, which were passed down orally from generation to generation until they were finally written down after the Aryans arrived in India. The Rig Veda dates from the second millennium B.C.E. and consists of more than 1,000 hymns used at religious ceremonies. The other three Vedas were written considerably later and contain instructions for performing ritual sacrifices and other ceremonies.

The language of the Vedas was **Sanskrit** (SAN-skrit), a member of the Indo-European family of languages. After the Aryans entered India, Sanskrit gradually declined as a spoken language and was replaced in northern India by a simpler tongue known as **Prakrit** (PRAH-krit). Nevertheless, Sanskrit continued to be used as the language of the bureaucracy and literary expression for many centuries after that. Like Latin in medieval Europe, it also served as a common language of communication between various regions of India. In the south, a variety of Dravidian languages continued to be spoken.

After the development of a new writing system sometime in the first millennium B.C.E., India's holy literature was probably inscribed on palm leaves stitched together into a book somewhat similar to the first books produced on papyrus or parchment in the Mediterranean region. Also written for the first time were India's great historical epics, the Mahabharata and the Ramayana (rah-mah-YAH-nah). Both of these epics may have originally been recited at religious ceremonies, but they are essentially historical writings that recount the martial exploits of great Aryan rulers and warriors.

The Mahabharata consists of more than 90,000 stanzas and was probably written around 100 B.C.E., describing in great detail a war between cousins for control of the kingdom around 1000 B.C.E. Interwoven in the narrative are many fantastic legends of the Hindu gods. Above all, the Mahabharata is a tale of moral confrontations. The most famous section of the book is the Bhagavad Gita, a sermon by the legendary Indian figure Krishna on the eve of a major battle. In this sermon, Krishna sets forth one of the key ethical maxims of Indian society: in taking action, one must be indifferent to success or failure and consider only the moral rightness of the act itself.

The Ramayana, written at about the same time, is much shorter than the Mahabharata. It is an account of a semilegendary ruler named Rama (RAH-mah) who, as the result of a palace intrigue, is banished from the kingdom and forced to live as a hermit in the forest. Later, he fights the demon-king of Sri Lanka (Ceylon), who has kidnapped his beloved wife, Sita (SEE-tuh). Like the Mahabharata, the Ramayana is strongly imbued with religious and moral significance. Rama himself is portrayed as the ideal Aryan hero, a perfect ruler and an ideal son, while Sita projects the supreme duty of female chastity and wifely loyalty to her husband. The Ramayana is a story of the triumph of good over evil, duty over self-indulgence, and generosity over selfishness. It combines filial and erotic love, conflicts of human passion, character analysis, and poetic descriptions of nature.

2-5b Architecture and Sculpture

After literature, the greatest achievements of early Indian civilization were in architecture and sculpture. Some of the earliest examples of Indian architecture stem from the time of Emperor Ashoka, when Buddhism became the religion of the state. Until the time of the Mauryas, Aryan buildings had been constructed of wood. With the rise of the empire, stone began to be used as artisans arrived in India seeking employment after the destruction of the Persian Empire by Alexander. Many of these stone carvers accepted the patronage of Emperor Ashoka, who used them to spread Buddhist ideas throughout the subcontinent.

There were three main types of religious structures: the pillar, the stupa, and the rock chamber. During Ashoka's reign, many stone columns were erected alongside roads to commemorate the events in the Buddha's life and mark pilgrim routes to holy places. Weighing as many as fifty tons each and rising as high as thirty-two feet, these polished sandstone pillars were topped with a carved capital, usually depicting lions uttering the Buddha's message. Ten remain standing today.

A stupa was originally meant to house a relic of the Buddha such as a lock of his hair or a branch of the famous bodhi tree, and it was constructed in the form of a burial mound (the pyramids in Egypt also derived from burial mounds). Eventually, the stupa became a place for devotion and the most familiar form of Buddhist architecture. Stupas rose to considerable heights and were surmounted

Hidekazu Nishibata/SuperStock

2.9 Sanchi gate and stupa. Constructed during the reign of Emperor Ashoka in the third century B.C.E., the stupa at Sanchi was enlarged over time, eventually becoming the greatest Buddhist monument in the Indian subcontinent. Originally intended to house a relic of the Buddha, the stupa became a holy place for devotion and a familiar form of Buddhist architecture. Sanchi's four elaborately carved stone gates, each more than forty feet high, tell stories of the Buddha set in joyful scenes of everyday life. Christian churches would later portray events in the life of Jesus to instruct the faithful.

Experience an interactive version of this period in ⁙ MINDTAP with a spire, possibly representing the stages of existence en route to nirvana. According to legend, Ashoka ordered the construction of 84,000 stupas throughout India to promote the Buddha's message. A few survive today, including one at Sarnath and its more elaborate prototype at Sanchi, which were begun under Ashoka and completed two centuries later.

The final form of early Indian architecture is the rock chamber carved out of a cliff on the side of a mountain. Ashoka began the construction of these chambers to provide rooms to house monks or wandering ascetics and to serve as halls for religious ceremonies. The chambers were rectangular in form, with pillars, an altar, and a vault, making them reminiscent of Roman basilicas in the West (see Comparative Illustration, "Rock Architecture," in Chapter 9, p. 224).

All three forms of architecture were embellished with decorations permeated with a sense of nature and the vitality of life. Many reflect an amalgamation of popular and sacred themes, of Buddhist, Vedic, and pre-Aryan religious motifs such as male and female Earth spirits. In its sensuousness and exuberance, Indian art was meant to express otherworldly delights, not the pleasures of this world. Until the second century C.E., however, Siddhartha Gautama was represented only through symbols, such as the wheel of life, the bodhi tree, and the footprint, perhaps because artists deemed it improper to portray him in human form because he had escaped his corporeal confines into enlightenment. After the spread of Mahayana Buddhism in the second century, when the Buddha began to be portrayed as a god, his image began to appear in stone as an object for divine worship (see Chapter 9).

2-5c Science

Our knowledge of Indian science is limited by the paucity of written sources, but it is evident that ancient Indians had amassed an impressive amount of scientific knowledge in many areas. Especially notable was their work in mathematics, where they devised the numerical system that we know as "Arabic numerals" and use today. In astronomy, they charted the movements of the heavenly bodies and recognized the spherical nature of Earth at an early date. Their ideas of physics were similar to those of the Greeks; matter was divided into the five elements of earth, air, fire, water, and ether. Many of their technological achievements are impressive, notably the quality of their textiles and the massive stone pillars erected during the reign of Ashoka. The pillars weighed as many as fifty tons each and were transported many miles to their final destination.

2.10 Symbols of the Buddha. Early Buddhist sculptures depicted the Buddha only through visual symbols that represented his life on the path to enlightenment. In this relief from the stupa at Bharhut, carved in the second century B.C.E., we see four devotees paying homage to the Buddha, who is portrayed as a giant wheel dispensing his "wheel of the law." The riderless horse on the left represents Siddhartha Gautama's departure from his father's home as he set out on his search for the meaning of life.

William J. Duiker

While the peoples of North Africa and the Middle East were actively building the first civilizations, a similar process was getting under way in the Indus River Valley. Much has been learned about the nature of the Indus Valley civilization in recent years, but the lack of written records limits our understanding. How did the Indus Valley people deal with the fundamental human problems mentioned at the close of Chapter 1? The answers remain tantalizingly elusive.

As often happened elsewhere, however, the collapse of Harappan civilization did not lead to the total disappearance of its culture. The new society that eventually

emerged throughout the subcontinent after the coming of the Aryans was an amalgam of two highly distinctive cultures, each of which made a significant contribution to the politics, social institutions, and creative impulse of ancient Indian civilization.

With the rise of the Mauryan dynasty in the fourth century B.C.E., the distinctive features of a great civilization begin to be clearly visible. It was extensive in its scope, embracing the entire Indian subcontinent and eventually, in the form of Buddhism and Hinduism, spreading to China and Southeast Asia. But the underlying ethnic, linguistic, and cultural diversity of the Indian people posed a constant challenge to the unity of the state. After the collapse of the Mauryas, the subcontinent would not come under a single authority again for several hundred years.

In the meantime, another great experiment was taking place far to the northeast across the Himalaya Mountains. Like many other civilizations of antiquity, the first Chinese state was concentrated on a major river system. And also like them, its political and cultural achievements eventually spread far beyond their original habitat. In the next chapter, we turn to the civilization of ancient China.

REFLECTION QUESTIONS

Q What is the debate over the origins of the Aryan peoples, and why do many historians of India consider it to be such an important question?

Q Why was Buddhism able to make such inroads among the Indian people at a time when Brahmanical beliefs had long been dominant in the subcontinent?

Q What were some of the main characteristics of Indian politics and government during the first millennium B.C.E., and how can they be compared and contrasted with those of ancient Egypt and Mesopotamia?

CHAPTER TIMELINE

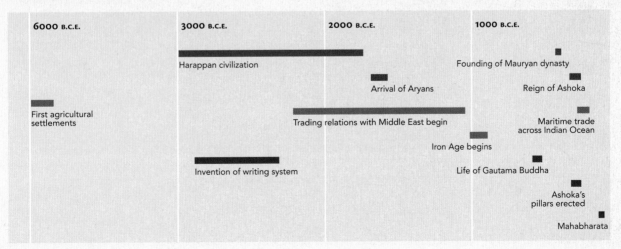

| 6000 B.C.E. | 3000 B.C.E. | 2000 B.C.E. | 1000 B.C.E. |

Harappan civilization

Arrival of Aryans

Founding of Mauryan dynasty

Reign of Ashoka

First agricultural settlements

Trading relations with Middle East begin

Maritime trade across Indian Ocean

Iron Age begins

Invention of writing system

Life of Gautama Buddha

Ashoka's pillars erected

Mahabharata

CHAPTER NOTES

1. Quoted in R. Lannoy, *The Speaking Tree: A Study of Indian Culture and Society* (London, 1971), p. 318.
2. The quotation is from ibid., p. 319. Note also that the Law of Manu says that "punishment alone governs all created beings. . . . The whole world is kept in order by punishment, for a guiltless man is hard to find."
3. Strabo's *Geography*, bk. 15, quoted in M. Edwardes, *A History of India: From the Earliest Times to the Present Day* (London, 1961), p. 55.
4. Ibid., p. 54.
5. Ibid., p. 57.
6. From the Law of Manu, quoted in A. L. Basham, *The Wonder That Was India* (London, 1961), pp. 180–181.
7. According to historian of religion Karen Armstrong, a gradual shift of emphasis from sacrificial rites to ethics was characteristic of many early belief systems during the first millennium B.C.E. For a discussion, see her *The Great Transformation: The Beginning of our Religious Traditions* (New York, 2006).
8. Quoted in A. K. Coomaraswamy, *Buddha and the Gospel of Buddhism* (New York, 1964), p. 34.

MINDTAP From Cengage

MindTap® is a fully online, highly personalized learning experience built upon Cengage Learning content. MindTap combines student learning tools—readings, multimedia, activities, and assessments—into a singular Learning Path that guides students through the course and helps students develop the critical thinking, analysis, and communication skills that are essential to academic and professional success.

CHINA IN ANTIQUITY

Chapter Outline and Focus Questions

Image Asset Management Ltd./Alamy

政始目始皇乙卯即王位庚辰併天下稱皇帝
年居王位二十五年即帝位十二年壽五十

3.1 The First Emperor of Qin

Critical Thinking

Q *The civilization of ancient China resembled those of its contemporaries in Mesopotamia and North Africa in several respects, but the contrasts were equally significant. What were some of these differences, and how might geography and the environment have helped to account for them?*

Connections to Today

Q *Which aspects of Confucian thought as depicted in the* Analects *appear to have particular relevance to today's world? What lessons can we learn today from the teachings of Master Kong?*

HIS AMBITION WAS LIMITLESS. After mounting the throne of his native state of Qin at the age of thirteen, he immediately set out to conquer all the neighboring states in the region and unite all of China under his rule. Achieving that objective in the year 221 B.C.E., he then sought to create a highly regimented society

according to his own plan. Potential rivals were executed, and their writings were destroyed. Peasants and workers were organized to serve the interests of the state, and thousands of laborers were mobilized to build a gigantic mausoleum, guarded by thousands of molded terra-cotta warriors, to provide for his afterlife. But the vaulting ambitions of the ruler known as Qin Shi Huang-di (chin shee hwang-DEE), or the First Emperor of Qin—as he styled himself—were ultimately destined to be thwarted. After he died at the age of forty-nine in 210 B.C.E., Qin Shi Huang-di's empire rapidly fell apart, and the Qin Dynasty was broadly reviled by later generations of historians as an unfortunate aberration in the long course of Chinese history. Nevertheless, the First Emperor's legacy lived on in the form of a strong and centralized empire that survived over two millennia and has traditionally been viewed as one of the greatest civilizations of human history.

3-1 THE DAWN OF CHINESE CIVILIZATION

 Focus Questions: How did geography influence the civilization that arose in China? To what degree do geographical realities explain the unique characteristics that differentiate China from other civilizations in the ancient world?

According to a familiar legend, Chinese society was founded by a series of rulers who brought the first rudiments of civilization to the region nearly 5,000 years ago. The first was Fu Xi (foo SHEE), the ox tamer who "knotted cords for hunting and fishing," domesticated animals, and introduced the beginnings of family life (for an explanation regarding the transliteration of the Chinese written language, see "A Note to Students About Language and the Dating of Time," p. xxxiv). The second was Shen Nong (shun NOONG), the divine farmer who "bent wood for plows and hewed wood for plowshares." Shen Nong taught the people the techniques of agriculture. Last came Huang Di (hwahng DEE), the Yellow Emperor, who "strung a piece of wood for the bow, and whittled little sticks of wood for the arrows." Legend credits Huang Di with creating the Chinese system of writing and with inventing the bow and arrow.[1] Modern historians, of course, do not accept the literal accuracy of such legends but view them instead as part of the process whereby early peoples attempted to make sense of the world and their

role in it. Nevertheless, such re-creations of a mythical past often contain an element of truth. Although there is no clear evidence that the "three sovereigns" actually existed, their achievements do symbolize some of the defining characteristics of Chinese civilization: the interaction between nomadic and agricultural peoples, the importance of the family as the basic unit of Chinese life, and the development of a unique system of writing.

3-1a The Land and People of China

Although human communities have existed in China for several hundred thousand years, the first *Homo sapiens* arrived in the area sometime after 40,000 B.C.E. as part of the great migration out of Africa. Around the eighth millennium B.C.E., the early peoples living on the hillsides and along the riverbanks of northern and central China began to master the cultivation of crops, especially dry crops such as millet and sorghum, which required little water and had a short growing season. Many of these early agricultural settlements were in the neighborhood of the Yellow River, where they gave birth to two Neolithic societies known to archaeologists as the **Yangshao** (yahng-SHOW ["ow" as in "how"]) and the **Longshan** (loong-SHAHN) cultures (sometimes identified in terms of their pottery as the painted and black pottery cultures, respectively). Similar communities began to appear in the Yangzi Valley in central China and along the coast to the south. The southern settlements were based on the cultivation of rice, which had been domesticated as early as the sixth millennium B.C.E. Thus, agriculture, and perhaps other elements of early civilization, may have developed spontaneously in several areas of China rather than radiating outward from one central region.

At first, these simple Neolithic communities were hardly more than villages, but as the inhabitants mastered the rudiments of agriculture, they gradually gave rise to more sophisticated and complex societies. In a pattern that we have seen elsewhere, civilization gradually spread from these nuclear settlements in the valleys of the Yellow and Yangzi Rivers to other lowland areas of eastern and central China. The two great river valleys, can thus be considered the core regions in the development of Chinese civilization (see Map 3.1).

Although these densely cultivated valleys eventually became among the great food-producing areas of the ancient world, China is more than a land of fertile fields. In fact, only 12 percent of the total land area is arable, compared with 23 percent of the United States. Much of the remainder consists of mountains and deserts that ring the country on its northern and western frontiers.

This often arid and forbidding landscape is a dominant feature of Chinese life and has played a significant role in

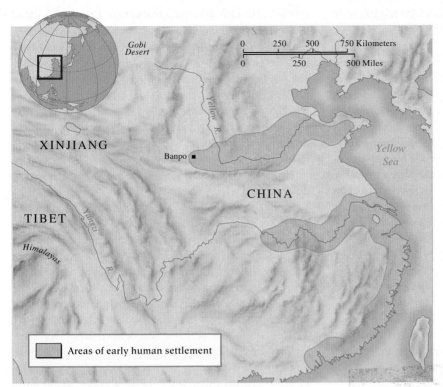

Map 3.1 **Neolithic China.** Like the ancient civilizations that arose in northern Africa and western Asia, early Chinese society emerged along the banks of two major river systems, the Yellow and the Yangzi. Because China was separated from other civilizations by snowcapped mountains and forbidding deserts, it was compelled to develop essentially on its own and without contacts from other societies going through a similar process.

Q *Based on the discussions in the preceding chapters, what are the advantages and disadvantages of close contact with other human societies?*

Chinese history. These geographic barriers served to isolate the Chinese people from advanced agrarian societies in other parts of Asia. The frontier regions in the Gobi (GOH-bee) Desert, Central Asia, and the Tibetan plateau were sparsely inhabited by peoples of Mongolian, Indo-European, or Turkic extraction. Most were primarily pastoral societies, and relations between the Chinese and the steppe peoples, like the contacts between other ancient river valley civilizations and their neighbors, were intermittent and frequently unstable. Although less numerous than the Chinese, many of these peoples possessed impressive skills in warfare and were sometimes aggressive in seeking wealth or territory in the settled regions south of the Gobi Desert. Over the next 2,000 years, the northern and northwestern frontier became one of the great fault lines of conflict in Asia as Chinese forces attempted to protect precious farmlands from marauding peoples operating beyond their borders. When China was unified and blessed with capable rulers, it could usually keep the nomadic intruders at bay and even bring them under a loose form of Chinese administration. But in times of internal weakness, China was vulnerable to outside attack, and nomadic peoples succeeded on several occasions in overthrowing Chinese rulers and setting up their own regimes.

From other directions, China normally had little to fear. To the east lay the China Sea, a lair for pirates and the source of powerful typhoons that occasionally ravaged the coast but otherwise rarely a source of concern. South of the Yangzi River was a hilly region inhabited by a mixture of peoples of varied language and ethnic stock who lived by farming, fishing, or food gathering. They were gradually absorbed in the inexorable expansion of Chinese civilization.

3-1b The Shang Dynasty

Historians of China have traditionally dated the beginning of Chinese civilization to the founding of the Xia (shee-AH) Dynasty some 4,000 years ago. Although the precise date for the rise of the Xia has been disputed, recent archaeological evidence from various sites in north-central China provides credence for its existence. Legend maintains that the founder was a ruler named Yu, who is also credited with introducing irrigation and draining the floodwaters that periodically threatened to inundate the northern China plain. The Xia Dynasty eventually was replaced by a second dynasty, the Shang (SHAHNG), around the sixteenth century B.C.E. The late Shang capital at Anyang (ahn-YAHNG), just north of the Yellow River in north-central China, has been excavated by archaeologists. Among the finds were thousands of so-called oracle bones, ox and chicken bones or turtle shells that were used by Shang rulers for divination (seeking to foretell future events by interpreting divine signs) and to communicate with the gods. The inscriptions on these oracle bones are the earliest known form of Chinese writing and provide much of our information about the beginnings of civilization in China. They portray a culture gradually emerging from the Neolithic to the early Bronze Age.

Political Organization China under the Shang Dynasty was a predominantly agricultural society ruled by an aristocratic class whose major concerns were war and maintaining control over key resources such as metal and salt.

One ancient chronicler complained that "the big affairs of state consist of sacrifice and soldiery."[2] Combat was carried on by means of two-horse chariots. The appearance of chariots in China in the mid-second millennium B.C.E. coincides roughly with similar developments elsewhere in Asia, leading some historians to suggest that the Shang ruling class may originally have invaded China from far to the west. But items found in Shang burial mounds are similar to Longshan pottery, implying that the Shang ruling elites were linear descendants of the indigenous Neolithic peoples in the area. If that was the case, the Shang probably acquired their knowledge of horse-drawn chariots through contact with peoples of neighboring regions, some of whom may have been Indo-European speakers.

The Shang king ruled with the assistance of a central bureaucracy in the capital city. His realm was divided into many territories governed by chieftains, but the king appointed these chieftains and could apparently depose them at will. He was also responsible for the defense of the realm and controlled large armies to achieve that purpose. The transcendent importance of the ruler was graphically displayed in the ritual sacrifices undertaken immediately after his death, when hundreds of his retainers were buried with him in the royal tomb.

3-1c Shang China

As the inscriptions on the oracle bones make clear, the Shang ruling elite believed in the existence of supernatural forces and thought they could communicate with those forces to obtain divine intervention on matters of this world. Evidence from the oracle bones suggests that the king was already being viewed as an intermediary between heaven and earth. In fact, an early Chinese character for king (王)consists of three horizontal lines connected by a single vertical line; the middle horizontal line represents the king's place between human society and the divine forces in nature. The early Chinese also had a clear sense of life in the hereafter (see Comparative Illustration, "The Afterlife and Prized Possessions," p. 59).

Social Structures In the Neolithic period, the farm village was apparently the basic social unit of China. Villages were organized by clans rather than by nuclear family units, and all residents probably took the common clan name of the entire village. In some cases, a village may have included more than one clan. At Banpo, an archaeological site near modern Xian (shee-AHN) that dates back at least 8,000 years, individual dwellings housed nuclear families, but a larger building in the village was apparently used as a clan meeting hall. The clan-based origins of Chinese society may help explain the continued importance of the joint family in traditional China, as well as the relatively small number of family names in Chinese society. Even today only some 400 family names are used in a society of more than 1 billion people, and the colloquial name for the common people in China today is "the old hundred names."

By Shang times, the classes were becoming increasingly differentiated. Poorer peasants probably did not own their farms but were obliged to work the lands of the chieftain and other elite families in the village. The aristocrats not only made war and served as officials (indeed, the first Chinese character for *official* originally meant "warrior") but also were the primary landowners. In addition to the aristocratic elite and the peasants, there were a small number of merchants and artisans, as well as slaves, probably consisting primarily of criminals or prisoners taken in battle.

The Shang are perhaps best known today for their mastery of bronze casting. Utensils, weapons, and ritual objects made of bronze have been found in royal tombs in urban centers throughout the area under Shang influence (see Comparative Essay, "The Use of Metals," p. 62). The Shang also created a sophisticated writing system that would eventually spread throughout East Asia and evolve into the written language that is still used in China today.

HISTORIANS DEBATE THE ISSUES **The Shang Dynasty: China's "Mother Culture"?** Until recently, the prevailing wisdom among historians—both Chinese and non-Chinese—was that the Yellow River Valley was the ancient heartland of Chinese civilization and that technological and cultural achievements gradually radiated from there to other areas in East Asia. Today, this **diffusion hypothesis**, as it is sometimes called, is no longer so widely accepted. The remains of early agricultural communities have now been unearthed in the Yangzi River Valley and along the southern coast, and a rich trove of bronze vessels has been discovered in grave sites in central Sichuan (suh–CHWAHN) Province. Such finds suggest that although the Yellow River civilization may have taken the lead in some areas, such as complex political organization and the development of writing, equally important advances, such as the development of wet rice agriculture, were already under way in other parts of China.

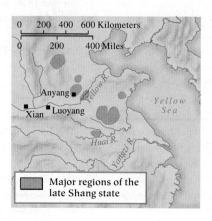

Map 3.2 Shang China

The Afterlife and Prized Possessions

Religion & Philosophy

THE EARLY CHINESE BELIEVED IN AN AFTERLIFE, and they filled their tombs with prized possessions from daily life. The tombs were most likely furnished and stocked with supplies—chairs, boats, chests, weapons, games, and dishes, among other items—so the spiritual body could continue its life despite the death of the physical body. In Image 3.2a, we see the remains of a chariot and horses in a burial pit in China's Hebei Province that dates from the early Zhou Dynasty. The tradition of providing items of daily use for the departed continues today in Chinese communities throughout Asia. The papier-mâché vehicle from a Chinese temple in Singapore in Image 3.2b will be burned so that it will ascend in smoke to the world of the spirits.

Q *How did Chinese beliefs about the afterlife compare with those discussed in other civilizations discussed in earlier chapters? What do the differences tell you about these societies? What do the items shown here have in common?*

Lowell Georgia/Corbis

3.2a

William J. Duiker

3.2b

3-2 THE ZHOU DYNASTY

Q **Focus Question:** What were the major tenets of Confucianism, Legalism, and Daoism, and to what degree do they compare with philosophical and intellectual trends elsewhere in the ancient world?

Around the mid-eleventh century B.C.E., the Shang Dynasty was overthrown by an aggressive young state called the Zhou (JOH), which was located to the west of the Shang capital, near the great bend of the Yellow River as it begins to flow directly eastward to the sea. According to tradition, the last Shang ruler was a tyrant who oppressed the people (Chinese sources assert that he was a degenerate who built "ponds of wine" and ordered the composing of lustful music that "ruined the morale of the nation"),[3] leading the ruler of the principality of Zhou to revolt and establish a new dynasty.

The Zhou located their capital in their home territory, near the present-day city of Xian. Later they established a second capital city at Luoyang (LWOH-yahng), farther to the east, to administer new territories captured from the Shang. This practice of having eastern and western capitals would endure off and on in China for nearly 2,000 years.

3-2a Political Structures

The Zhou Dynasty (ca. 1045–221 B.C.E.) adopted the political system of its predecessors with some changes. The Shang practice of dividing the kingdom into a number of territories governed by officials appointed by the king was continued under the Zhou. At the apex of the government hierarchy was the Zhou king, who was served by a bureaucracy of growing size and complexity. It now included several ministries responsible for rites, education, law, and public works. Beyond the capital, the Zhou kingdom was divided into many principalities governed by members of the hereditary aristocracy appointed by the king and at least theoretically subordinate to his authority.

COMPARATIVE ESSAY

The Use of Metals

Science & Technology Around 6000 B.C.E., people in western Asia discovered how to use metals. They soon realized the advantage of metal instead of stone for both tools and weapons. Metal could be shaped more precisely, allowing artisans to make more refined tools and weapons with sharper edges and more regular shapes. Copper, silver, and gold, which were commonly found in their elemental forms, were the first metals to be used. These were relatively soft and could be easily pounded into different shapes. But an important step was taken when people discovered that a rock that contained metal could be heated to liquefy the metal (a process called *smelting*). The liquid metal could then be poured into molds of clay or stone to make precisely shaped tools and weapons.

Copper was the first metal to be used in making tools. The first known copper smelting furnace, dated to 3800 B.C.E., was found in the Sinai. Within the next centuries, artisans in western Asia discovered that tin could be added to copper to make bronze. Bronze has a lower melting point, which makes it easier to cast, but it is also a harder metal than copper and corrodes less. The widespread use of bronze that ensued has led historians to speak of the period from around 3000 to 1200 B.C.E. as the Bronze Age, although this is somewhat misleading in that many peoples continued to use stone tools and weapons even after bronze became available.

But there were limitations to the use of bronze. Tin was not as readily available as copper, so bronze tools and weapons were expensive. After 1200 B.C.E., bronze was increasingly replaced by iron, which was probably first used around 1500 B.C.E. in western Asia, where the Hittites made weapons from it. Between 1500 and 600 B.C.E., ironmaking spread across Europe, North Africa, and Asia. Bronze continued to be used, but mostly for jewelry and other domestic purposes. Iron was used to make tools and weapons with sharp edges. Because iron weapons were cheaper than bronze ones, more warriors could be armed, and wars could be fought on a larger scale.

The Chinese were slower than some of their contemporaries in the ancient world to master the use of metals—entering the Bronze Age only at the end

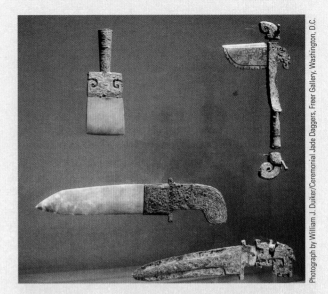

3.3 Shang Dynasty Ceremonial Jade and Bronze Daggers. These ceremonial weapons found in a tomb dating back to the Shang dynasty are among the earliest examples of metalwork in ancient China.

of the third millennium B.C.E. But they were quick to excel in bronze technology, and by 1400 B.C.E. Chinese metalworkers were making beautiful bronze ritual objects with a high degree of technological expertise. Eventually, they also took the lead in iron technology as well. Iron was handled differently from bronze: it was heated until it could be beaten into a desired shape. Each hammering made the metal stronger. This "wrought iron," as it was called, was typical of iron manufacturing in the West until the late Middle Ages. In China, however, the use of heat-resistant clay in the walls of blast furnaces raised temperatures to 1537° Celsius, enabling artisans to liquefy iron as early as the fourth century B.C.E. so that it too could be cast in molds to produce high-quality weapons and farming tools. Europeans would not develop such blast furnaces until the fifteenth century C.E.

 What were the advantages of making objects out of bronze versus iron in the ancient world? Which metal ultimately triumphed in China?

The Mandate of Heaven

Politics & Government   **WHEN THE RULERS OF THE RISING STATE OF ZHOU** overthrew the last king of the Shang Dynasty in the middle of the eleventh century B.C.E., they declared the founding of a new dynasty with its capital located near the Yellow River in central China. To justify their action, they issued an official decree asserting that the mandate of heaven—according to which each ruling family was anointed by heaven, provisional on its ability to govern by virtue and wisdom—had been passed from one dynastic family to another, as the Shang had previously replaced their predecessors, the Xia.

Such, at any rate, is the historical account presented in the ancient Chinese classic known as the *Book of History* (*Shujing*), a collection of sayings and documents compiled sometime during the Zhou dynasty (1045–221 B.C.E.). The concept of the Mandate of Heaven gradually evolved into an essential element in Chinese political culture over the next two millennia.

The *Book of History*

Oh! God dwelling in the great heavens has changed his decree respecting his great son and the great dynasty of Yin [Shang]. Our king has received that decree. Unbounded is the happiness connected with it, and unbounded is the anxiety. Oh! How can he be other than reverent?

When Heaven rejected and made an end of the decree in favor of the great dynasty of Yin, there were many of its former wise kings in Heaven. The king, however, who had succeeded to them, the last of his race, from the time of his entering into their appointment, proceeded in such a way as to keep the wise in obscurity and the vicious in office. The poor people in such a case, carrying their children and leading their wives, made their moan to Heaven. They even fled, but were apprehended again. Oh! Heaven had compassion on the people of the four quarters; its favoring decree lighted on our earnest founders. Let the king sedulously cultivate the virtue of reverence.

Examining the men of antiquity, there was Yu, founder of the Hsia [Xia] dynasty. Heaven guided his mind, allowed his descendants to succeed him, and protected them. He acquainted himself with Heaven, and was obedient to it. But in process of time the decree in his favor fell to the ground. So also is it now when we examine the case of Yin. There was the same guiding of its founder T'ang, who corrected the errors of Hsia, and whose descendants enjoyed the protection of Heaven. He also acquainted himself with Heaven, and was obedient to it. But now the decree in favor of him has fallen to the ground. Our king has now come to the throne in his youth. Let him not slight the aged and experienced, for it may be said of them that they have studied the virtuous conduct of the ancients and have matured their counsels in the sight of Heaven.

Oh! Although the king is young, yet he is the eldest son of Heaven. Let him effect a great harmony with the lower people and that will be the blessing of the present time. Let not the king presume to be remiss in this but continually regard and stand in awe of the perilous uncertainty of the people's attachment.

Let the king come here as the vice-regent of God and undertake the duties of government in this center of the land. Tan said, "Now that this great city has been built, from henceforth he may be the mate of great Heaven, and reverently sacrifice to the spirits above and below; henceforth he may from this central spot administer successful government" Thus shall the king enjoy the favoring regard of Heaven all complete, and the government of the people will now be prosperous.

 How would you compare the advice in this statement with that provided by the author of the Arthasastra in Chapter 2 (see Section 2-2b)? Are there any key differences?

Source: Clae Waltham, *Shu Ching: Book of History: A Modernized Edition of the Translation of James Legge* (Chicago: Henry Regnery Co. 1971), pp. 162–164.

The Mandate of Heaven But, according to Chinese historical tradition, the Zhou kings also introduced some innovations. The *Rites of Zhou*, one of the oldest surviving documents on statecraft,[4] declared that the Zhou Dynasty ruled China because it possessed the **Mandate of Heaven**. According to this concept, heaven (now increasingly viewed at court as an impersonal law of nature rather than as an anthropomorphic deity) maintained order in the universe through the Zhou king, who thus ruled as a representative of heaven but not as a divine being. The king, who was selected to rule because of his talent and virtue, was responsible for governing the people with compassion and efficiency (see Historical Voices, "The Mandate of Heaven," above). It was his duty to appease the gods in order to protect the people from natural calamities or bad harvests. But if the king failed to rule effectively, he could be overthrown and replaced by a new ruler— theoretically at least. As already noted, this idea was used to justify the Zhou conquest of the Shang. Eventually, through the writings of the great Chinese philosopher Mencius (370–290 B.C.E.), the concept of the heavenly mandate would become a cardinal principle of Chinese statecraft.

By the sixth century B.C.E., the Zhou Dynasty began to decline. As the power of the central government waned, bitter internal rivalries arose among various principalities where governing officials had made their positions hereditary at the expense of the king. As the power of these officials grew, they began to regulate the local economy and seek reliable sources of revenue for their expanding armies, such as a uniform tax system and government monopolies on key commodities such as salt and iron. Eventually, the Zhou rulers had lost all pretense of authority, and China was divided into a cauldron of squabbling states, an era known to Chinese historians as the "Period of the Warring States" (see "3-3 The First Chinese Empire: The Qin Dynasty").

3-2b Economy and Society

During the Zhou Dynasty, the essential characteristics of Chinese economic and social institutions began to take shape. The pattern of land ownership that had existed under the Shang remained in operation: the peasants worked on lands owned by their lord but also had land of their own to cultivate for their own use. The practice was called the **well-field system** because the Chinese character for well (井) resembles a simplified picture of the division of the farmland into nine separate segments. Each peasant family tilled an outer plot for its own use and then joined with other families to work the inner one for the hereditary lord. How widely this system was used is unclear, but it represented an ideal described by Confucian scholars of a later day. As the following passage from the *Book of Songs* indicates, life for the average farmer was not easy. The "big rat" is probably the government or a lord who has imposed high taxes on the peasants.

> Big rat, big rat
> Do not eat my millet!
> Three years I have served you,
> But you will not care for me.
> I am going to leave you
> And go to that happy land;
> Happy land, happy land,
> Where I will find my place.[5]

Trade and manufacturing were carried out by merchants and artisans who lived in walled towns under the direct control of the local lord. Merchants did not operate independently but were considered the property of the local lord and on occasion could even be bought and sold like chattels. A class of slaves—most of whom were probably prisoners of war captured during conflicts with neighboring principalities—performed a variety of menial tasks and perhaps worked on local irrigation projects. The period of the later Zhou, from the sixth to the third centuries B.C.E., was an era of significant economic growth and technological innovation, especially in agriculture. During that time, large-scale water-control projects were undertaken to regulate the flow of rivers and distribute water evenly to the fields, as well as to construct canals to facilitate the transport of goods from one region to another (see Comparative Illustration, "Early Agricultural Technology," p. 63). One irrigation project in south China served an area populated by as many as 5 million people and is still in use today.

Food production was also stimulated by many advances in farm technology. By the mid-sixth century B.C.E., the introduction of iron had led to the development of iron plowshares, which permitted deep plowing for the first time. Other innovations dating from the later Zhou were the use of natural fertilizer, the collar harness, and the technique of leaving land fallow to preserve or replenish nutrients in the soil. By the late Zhou Dynasty, the cultivation of wet rice had become one of the prime sources of food in China. Although rice was difficult and time-consuming to produce, it replaced other grain crops in areas with a warm climate because of its good taste, relative ease of preparation, and high nutritional value.

The advances in agriculture, which enabled the population of China to rise as high as 20 million people during the late Zhou era, were undoubtedly a major factor in the growth of commerce and manufacturing. During the late Zhou, economic wealth began to replace noble birth as the prime source of power and influence. Utensils made of iron became more common, and trade developed in a variety of useful commodities, including cloth, salt, and various manufactured goods. Silk, which had been cultivated since as early as the Shang Dynasty, became a highly desirable luxury product, as did jade, blocks of which were mined in the mountains of Tibet as early as the sixth millennium B.C.E.

With the development of trade and manufacturing, China began to move toward a money economy. The first form of money, as in much of the rest of the world, may have been cowries or other seashells (the Chinese character for goods or property contains the ideographic symbol for "shell":貝), but by the Zhou Dynasty, people were using pieces of iron shaped like a knife or round coins with a hole in the middle so that they could be carried in strings of a thousand. Most ordinary Chinese, however, simply

Early Agricultural Technology

Science & Technology **FOR CENTURIES, FARMERS AROUND THE GLOBE** have adopted various techniques to guarantee the flow of adequate amounts of water for their crops. One of the most effective ways to irrigate fields in hilly regions is to construct terraces to channel the flow of water from higher elevations. Shown in Image 3.4a is a hillside terrace near the Yellow River in northern China, an area where dry crops such as oats and millet have been cultivated since the sixth millennium B.C.E. Image 3.4b shows a terraced hillside in the southwestern corner of the Arabian Peninsula. Excavations show that despite dry conditions through much of the peninsula, terraced agriculture has been practiced in mountainous parts of the region for as long as 5,000 years.

 In what other areas of the Middle East is irrigated agriculture practiced?

William J. Duiker

3.4a

William J. Duiker

3.4b

used a system of barter. Taxes, rents, and even the salaries of government officials were normally paid in grain.

3-2c The Hundred Schools of Ancient Philosophy

In China, as in other great river valley societies, the birth of civilization was accompanied by the emergence of an organized effort to comprehend the nature of the cosmos and the role of human beings within it. Speculation over such questions culminated at the end of the Zhou era in the "hundred schools" of ancient philosophy, a wide-ranging debate over the nature of human beings, society, and the universe.

Early Beliefs The first hint of religious belief in ancient China comes from relics found in royal tombs of Neolithic times. The Shang had begun to believe in the existence of one transcendent god, known as Shang Di, who presided over all the forces of nature. As time went on, this "transcendent god" evolved from a vaguely anthropomorphic deity to a somewhat more impersonal symbol of universal order known as Heaven (Tian). There was also much speculation among Chinese intellectuals about the nature of the cosmic order. One of the earliest ideas was that the universe was divided into two primary forces of good and evil, light and dark, male and female, represented symbolically by the sun (*yang*) and the moon (*yin*). According to this theory, life was a dynamic process of interaction between the forces of yang and yin, and one led inexorably to the other and back again. Early Chinese could only attempt to understand the process and perhaps to have some minimal effect on its operation. One of the most famous manuals used for this purpose was the *Yi Jing,* known in English as the *Book of Changes*.

Confucianism   Such efforts to divine the mysterious purposes of heaven notwithstanding, Chinese thinking about metaphysical reality also contained a strain of pragmatism that is readily apparent in the ideas of the great philosopher Confucius (from the Latin version of Kongfuzi, or "Master Kong"). Confucius was born in the state of Lu, in the modern province of Shandong (SHAHN-doong), in 551 B.C.E. After reaching maturity, he apparently hoped to find employment as a political adviser in one of the principalities into which China was divided at that time, but he had little success in finding a patron. Nevertheless, he won over many followers, and his ideas, as drawn together by them in the *Analects* and other works attributed to him, made an indelible mark on the history of political and social thought.

In conversations with his disciples contained in the *Analects,* Confucius adopted a detached and almost skeptical view of heaven. He believed it was useless to speculate about metaphysical questions. Better by far to assume that there was a rational order to the universe and concentrate one's attention on ordering the affairs of this world (see Historical Voices, "The Wit and Wisdom of Confucius," p. 65).

Confucius's interest in philosophy, then, was essentially political and ethical. The universe was constructed in such a way that if human beings could act harmoniously in accordance with its purposes, their own affairs would prosper. Much of his concern was with human behavior. The key to proper behavior was to behave in accordance with the **Dao** (DOW), or the Way. Confucius assumed that all human beings had their own Dao, depending on their individual role in life, and it was their duty to follow it. Even the ruler had his own Dao, and he ignored it at his peril, for to do so could mean the loss of the Mandate of Heaven. The idea of the Dao is reminiscent of the concept of Dharma in ancient India and played a similar role in governing the affairs of society.

Two elements in the Confucian interpretation of the Dao are particularly worthy of mention. The first is the concept of duty. All individuals were responsible for subordinating their own interests and aspirations to the broader needs of the family and the community. Confucius assumed that if each individual sought to fulfill his or her assigned destiny, then the affairs of society as a whole would prosper as well. In this respect, it was important for the ruler to set a good example. If he followed his "kingly way," the beneficial effects would radiate throughout society.

The second key element is the idea of humanity, which is sometimes translated as "human-heartedness." This concept involves a sense of compassion and empathy for others. It is similar in some ways to Christian concepts, but with a subtle twist. Where Christian teachings call on human beings to "behave toward others as you would have them behave toward you," the Confucian maxim is put in a different way: "Do not do unto others what you would not wish done to yourself." To many Chinese, this attitude symbolizes an element of tolerance in the Chinese character that has not always been practiced in other societies.

But perhaps Confucius's most striking idea was that the government should be open to all men of superior quality, and not limited to those of noble birth. He undoubtedly had himself in mind as one of those "superior" men, but the rapacity of the hereditary lords must have added strength to his convictions. The concept of rule by merit was, of course, not an unfamiliar idea in the China of his day; the *Rites of Zhou* had clearly stated that the king earned the right to rule because of his talent and virtue, rather than as the result of noble birth. In practice, however, aristocratic privilege must often have opened the doors to political influence, and many of Confucius's contemporaries must have regarded his appeal for government by talent as both exciting and dangerous.

Confucius's ideas were passed on to later generations through the *Analects* as well as through other writings attributed to him, all of which strongly influenced Chinese political thinkers of the late Zhou period, a time when the existing system was in disarray and open to serious question. But as with most great thinkers, Confucius's ideas were sufficiently ambiguous to be interpreted in contradictory ways. Thinkers such as philosopher Mencius (370–290 B.C.E.), stressed the humanistic side of Confucian ideas, arguing that human beings were by nature good and hence could be taught their civic responsibilities by example. Mencius also stressed that the ruler had a duty to govern with compassion. Other thinkers, however, rejected Mencius's rosy view of human nature and argued for a different approach. The ambiguity over this issue would resonate through the Chinese political debate for centuries (see Opposing Viewpoints, "A Debate over Good and Evil," p. 66).

Legalism   One school of thought that challenged Confucian views during the hundred schools era in ancient China was the philosophy of **Legalism**. Taking issue with the view of Mencius that human nature was essentially good, the Legalists argued that human beings were by nature evil and would follow the correct path only if coerced by harsh laws and stiff punishments. These thinkers were referred to as the School of Law because they rejected the Confucian view that government by "superior men" could solve society's problems and argued instead

The Wit and Wisdom of Confucius

Religion & Philosophy

THE *ANALECTS* (*LUN YU*), a collection of sayings supposedly uttered by the ancient Chinese philosopher Confucius and drawn up after his death by his disciples, is considered to be a primary source for the master's ideas and thought. The degree to which the collection provides an accurate account of his remarks on various subjects has long been a matter of debate among specialists. Some scholars argue that the sayings in the *Analects* reflect the views of his followers two centuries after his death in the fifth century B.C.E. more than they do those of Confucius himself.

Whatever the truth of this contention, the sayings in the *Analects* have provided moral and philosophical guidance to countless generations of Chinese over the centuries, and have thus played a major role in shaping the lives and culture of the Chinese people.

The Confucian *Analects*

On Human Nature

17.2 By their nature, men are quite similar; in practice, they become far apart.

17.3 Only the wisest and the most ignorant of men cannot be changed.

16.9 Confucius said: Those born with innate knowledge are the highest of men; those who become learned are next in line; those who study but fail to learn follow; those who are ignorant yet do not study are the lowest of men.

On Morality

4.5 All men desire wealth and honor. But unless they can be achieved by virtuous means, they should not be sought after.

4.16 The moral man seeks righteousness; the immoral man seeks profit.

6.28 The virtuous man thinks of the needs of others before those of his own; he seeks to benefit others before himself.

15.23 Tzu Kung [one of the Master's disciples] asked if there was one word that could be applied as a standard for virtuous behavior. Confucius replied: It is reciprocity; do not do unto others what you would not wish done to yourself.

On Filial Piety

2.5 [Asked about filial piety] Confucius replied: It consists in not being disobedient; when they are alive, parents should be served according to the rules of propriety; after their death, they should be buried correctly and sacrifices should be carried out in a proper manner.

4.18 Confucius said: When serving one's parents, it is permissible to remonstrate with them, but in a respectful manner; if they do not agree, one should not oppose their wishes and even accept punishment without complaint.

On Education

2.15 Study without thought is a waste of time; thought without study is dangerous.

8.12 It is rare to find a man who has studied for three years without making progress.

On Government

2.3 If the government seeks to rule by decrees and the threat of punishment, the people will have no sense of shame; but if they are governed by virtue and a sense of propriety, they will feel shame and seek to behave correctly.

13.6 If its conduct is correct, a government can succeed without issuing directives; if not, directives will not be obeyed.

12.7 Confucius said: Without the confidence of the people, government cannot succeed.

On Religion

13.3 With regard to what he does not know, the superior man reserves judgment.

7.20 The Master did not comment on the supernatural, on feats of strength, on disorder, and on the spirits.

6.20 To meet one's human obligations, to respect the spirits but maintain distance from them, such indeed may be called wisdom.

11.11 [Asked about serving the spirits of the departed], Confucius replied: If you are unable to serve men, how can you serve the spirits? If you do not understand life, how can you understand death?

Q *Confucius is viewed by some observers as a reformer, and by others as a conservative. Based on the information available to you in this chapter, how would you classify his ideas, as expressed in the* Analects?

Source: *The Four Books: Confucian Analects,* by James Legge (Hong Kong: The International Publication Society, n.d.). Translation by William J. Duiker and 2011 William J. Duiker.

A Debate over Good and Evil

Religion & Philosophy

DURING THE LATTER PART OF THE ZHOU DYNASTY, one major preoccupation of Chinese philosophers was determining the essential qualities of human nature. In the *Analects,* Confucius was cited as asserting that humans' moral instincts were essentially neutral at birth; their minds must be cultivated to bring out the potential goodness therein. In later years, the master's disciples elaborated on this issue. The great humanitarian philosopher Mencius maintained that human nature was essentially good. But his rival Xunzi (SHYOON-zuh) took the opposite tack, arguing that evil was inherent in human nature and could be eradicated only by rigorous training at the hands of an instructor. Later, Xunzi's views would be adopted by the Legalist philosophers of the Qin Dynasty, although his belief in the efficacy of education earned him a place in the community of Confucian scholars.

The Book of Mencius

Mencius said, . . . "The goodness of human nature is like the downward course of water. There is no human being lacking in the tendency to do good, just as there is no water lacking in the tendency to flow downward. . . .

"All human beings have a mind that cannot bear to see the sufferings of others. . . .

"Here is why. . . . Now, if anyone were suddenly to see a child about to fall into a well, his mind would always be filled with alarm, distress, pity, and compassion. That he would react accordingly is not because he would use the opportunity to ingratiate himself with the child's parents, nor because he would seek commendation from neighbors and friends, nor because he would hate the adverse reputation. From this it may be seen that one who lacks a mind that feels pity and compassion would not be human; one who lacks a mind that feels shame and aversion would not be human; one who lacks a mind that feels modesty and compliance would not be human; and one who lacks a mind that knows right and wrong would not be human.

"The mind's feeling of pity and compassion is the beginning of humaneness; the mind's feeling of shame and aversion is the beginning of lightness; the mind's feeling of modesty and compliance is the beginning of propriety; and the mind's sense of right and wrong is the beginning of wisdom."

The Book of Xunzi

Human nature is evil; its goodness derives from conscious activity. Now it is human nature to be born with a fondness for profit. Indulging this leads to contention and strife, and the sense of modesty and yielding with which one was born disappears. One is born with feelings of envy and hate, and, by indulging these, one is led into banditry and theft, so that the sense of loyalty and good faith with which he was born disappears. One is born . . . with a fondness for beautiful sights and sounds, and by indulging these, one is led to licentiousness and chaos, so that the sense of ritual, rightness, refinement, and principle with which one was born is lost. Hence, following human nature and indulging human emotions will inevitably lead to contention and strife, causing one to rebel against one's proper duty, reduce principle to chaos, and revert to violence. Therefore, one must be transformed by the example of a teacher and guided by the way of ritual and right before one will attain modesty and yielding, accord with refinement and ritual and return to order. From this perspective it is apparent that human nature is evil and that its goodness is the result of conscious activity.

Mencius said, "Now human nature is good, and [when it is not] this is always a result of having lost or destroyed one's nature." I say that he was mistaken to take such a view. Now, it is human nature that, as soon as a person is born, he departs from his original substance and from his rational disposition so that he must inevitably lose and destroy them. Seen in this way, it is apparent that human nature is evil.

 What arguments do these two Confucian thinkers advance to support their point of view about the essential elements of human nature? In your view, which argument is more persuasive?

Source: Excerpt from William Theodore de Bary and Irene Bloom, *Sources of Chinese Tradition,* Vol. I, 2nd ed. (New York, 1999). Copyright © 1999 by Columbia University Press.

The Daoist Answer to Confucianism

Religion & Philosophy

THE *DAO DE JING* (*THE WAY OF THE TAO*) is the great classic of philosophical Daoism (Taoism). It has traditionally been attributed to the legendary Chinese philosopher Laozi (Old Master), but recently discovered ancient texts suggest that it was probably written sometime during the era of Confucius. This opening passage illustrates two of the key ideas that characterize Daoist belief: it is impossible to define the nature of the universe, and "inaction" (not Confucian action) is the key to ordering the affairs of human beings.

The Way of the Tao

The Tao that can be told of is not the eternal Tao;
The name that can be named is not the eternal name.
The Nameless is the origin of Heaven and Earth;
The Named is the mother of all things.
Therefore let there always be nonbeing, so we may see their
　　subtlety.
And let there always be being, so we may see their outcome.
The two are the same,
But after they are produced, they have different names.
They both may be called deep and profound.
Deeper and more profound,
The door of all subtleties!
When the people of the world all know beauty as beauty,

There arises the recognition of ugliness.
When they all know the good as good,
There arises the recognition of evil.
Therefore:
Being and nonbeing produce each other;
Difficult and easy complete each other;
Long and short contrast each other;
High and low distinguish each other;
Sound and voice harmonize each other;
Front and behind accompany each other.
Therefore the sage manages affairs without action
And spreads doctrines without words.
All things arise, and he does not turn away from them.
He produces them but does not take possession of them.
He acts but does not rely on his own ability.
He accomplishes his task but does not claim credit for it.
It is precisely because he does not claim credit that his
　　accomplishment remains with him.

 What is Laozi, the presumed author of this document, trying to express about the basic nature of the universe? Based on the Confucian Analects and The Way of the Tao, how do you think the Chinese attempted to understand the order of nature through their philosophies?

Source: From *The Way of Lao Tzu* (Tao-te Ching), by Wing-Tsit Chan, trans. Copyright © 1963 by Macmillan College Publishing Company, Inc.

for a system of impersonal laws that would achieve the same purpose.

The Legalists also disagreed with the Confucian belief that the universe has a moral core. They therefore believed that only firm action by the state could bring about social order. Fear of harsh punishment, more than the promise of material reward, could best motivate the common people to serve the interests of the ruler. Because human nature was essentially corrupt, officials could not be trusted to carry out their duties in a fair and evenhanded manner, and only a strong ruler could create an orderly society. All human actions should be directed to the effort to create a strong and prosperous state subject to his will.

Daoism One of the most popular alternatives to **Confucianism** was the philosophy of **Daoism** (DOW-iz-uhm) (frequently spelled Taoism). According to Chinese tradition, the Daoist school was founded by a contemporary

of Confucius popularly known as Laozi (LOW ["ow" as in "how"]dzuh), or the Old Master. Obtaining a clear understanding of the original concepts of Daoism is difficult because its primary document, a short treatise known as the *Dao De Jing* (DOW deh JING) (sometimes translated as *The Way of the Tao*), is an inscrutable book whose interpretation has baffled scholars for centuries (see Historical Voices, "The Daoist Answer to Confucianism," above). The opening line, for example, explains less what the Dao is than what it is not: "The Tao [Way] that can be told of is not the eternal Tao. The name that can be named is not the eternal name."

At first glance, the basic concepts of Daoism appear to resemble those of its rival, Confucianism. Daoism does not anguish over the underlying meaning of the cosmos but instead attempts to set forth proper forms of behavior for human beings here on Earth. In most other respects, however, Daoism presents a view of life and its ultimate

Experience an interactive version of this period in MINDTAP

3.5 Laozi and Confucius. Little is known about the life of Laozi (shown on the left in the illustration), and it is unlikely that he and Confucius ever met. According to tradition, though, the two held a face-to-face meeting. The alleged discussion must have been interesting, for their views about the nature of reality were diametrically opposed. Nevertheless, the Chinese have managed to preserve both traditions, perhaps a reflection of the dualities represented in the Chinese approach to life. A similar duality existed among Platonists and Aristotelians in ancient Greece (see Chapter 4).

Topham/The Image Works

debate over the ultimate meaning of life was less important than the daily struggle for survival. Even among the elites, interest in the occult and in astrology was high, and magico-religious ideas coexisted with interest in natural science and humanistic philosophy throughout the ancient period.

For most Chinese, Heaven was not a vague, impersonal law of nature, as it was for many Confucian and Daoist intellectuals. Instead, it was a terrain peopled with innumerable gods and spirits of nature, both good and evil, who existed in trees, mountains, and streams as well as in heavenly bodies. Farmers, for example, called on divine intervention to guarantee a good harvest. Other gods were responsible for the safety of fishermen, transportation workers, or prospective mothers.

Another aspect of popular religion was the belief that the spirits of deceased human beings lived in the atmosphere for a time before ascending to heaven or descending to hell. During that period, surviving family members had to care for the spirits through proper ritual or they would become evil spirits and haunt the survivors. From this conviction comes the concept of the **veneration of ancestors** (mistakenly known in the West as "ancestor worship") and the practice of burning replicas of physical objects to accompany the departed on their journey to the next world.

meaning that is almost diametrically opposed to that of Confucianism. Where Confucian doctrine asserts that it is the duty of human beings to work hard to improve life here on Earth, Daoists contend that the true way to interpret the will of heaven is not action but inaction (wu wei). The best way to act in harmony with the universal order is to act spontaneously and let nature take its course. Such a message could be highly appealing to people who were uncomfortable with the somewhat rigid flavor of the Confucian work ethic and preferred a more individualistic approach.

Daoism achieved considerable popularity in the waning years of the Zhou Dynasty. It was especially popular among intellectuals, who may have found it appealing as an escapist antidote in a world characterized by growing disorder.

Popular Religion Daoism also played a second role as a loose framework for popular spiritualistic and animistic beliefs among ordinary Chinese. Popular Daoism was less a philosophy than a religion; it comprised a variety of rituals and forms of behavior that were commonly regarded as a means of achieving heavenly salvation or even a state of immortality on Earth. Daoist sorcerers practiced various types of exercises for training the mind and body in the hope of achieving power, sexual prowess, and long life.

The philosophical forms of Confucianism and Daoism did not provide much in the way of concrete significance to the mass of the population, for whom intellectual

3-3 THE FIRST CHINESE EMPIRE: THE QIN DYNASTY

Focus Question: How did the First Emperor of the Qin Dynasty transform the political, social, and economic institutions of early China?

During the last two centuries of the Zhou Dynasty, the authority of the king became increasingly nominal, and several of the small principalities into which the Zhou kingdom had been divided began to evolve into powerful states that presented a potential challenge to the Zhou ruler himself. Chief among these were Qu (CHOO) in the central Yangzi Valley, Wu (WOO) in the Yangzi Delta, and Yue (yoo-EH) along the southeastern coast. At first, their mutual rivalries were in check, but by the late fifth century B.C.E., competition intensified into civil war, giving birth to the

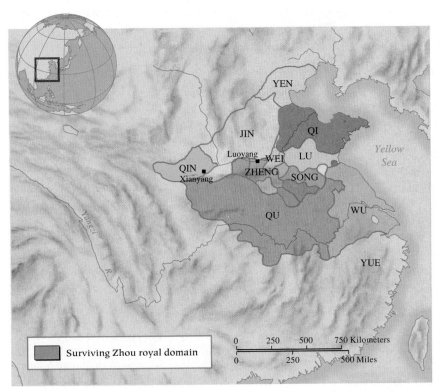

Map 3.3 China During the Warring States Period. From the fifth to the third centuries B.C.E., China was locked in an era of civil strife known as the Warring States Period. This map shows the Zhou Dynasty capital at Luoyang, along with the major states that were squabbling for precedence in the region.

Q *Why did most of the early states emerge in areas adjacent to China's two major river systems, the Yellow and the Yangzi?*

so-called Warring States Period. Powerful principalities vied with each other for preeminence and largely ignored the now purely titular authority of the Zhou court (see Map 3.3). New forms of warfare emerged with the invention of iron weapons and the introduction of foot soldiers and cavalry armed with powerful crossbows. Cities that erected high walls as protection found that their opponents countered by developing new techniques for siege warfare.

By the mid-fourth century B.C.E., the relatively young state of Qin (CHIN), located in the original homeland of the Zhou, had emerged as a key player in these conflicts by adopting many reforms in agriculture, government administration, military organization, and fiscal policy. As a result of policies put into effect by

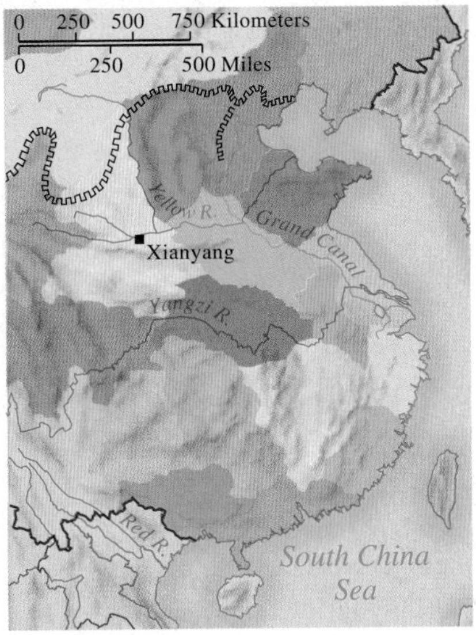

Map 3.4 The Qin Empire, 221–206 B.C.E.

the adviser Shang Yang (SHAHNG yahng) in the mid-fourth century B.C.E., Qin society was ruled with ruthless efficiency.

Benefiting from a strong defensive position in the mountains to the west of the great bend of the Yellow River, as well as from their control of the rich Sichuan plains, the Qin gradually subdued their main rivals through conquest or diplomatic maneuvering. In 221 B.C.E., the Qin ruler declared the establishment of a new dynasty, the first truly unified government in Chinese history.

One primary reason for the triumph of the Qin was probably the character of the first Qin ruler, known to history as Qin Shi Huang-di (see the chapter introduction), or the First Emperor of Qin. A man of forceful personality and immense ambition, Qin Shi Huang-di had ascended to the throne of Qin in 246 B.C.E. at age thirteen. Described by the famous Han Dynasty historian Sima Qian (SUH-mah chee-AHN) as having "the chest of a bird of prey, the voice of a jackal, and the heart of a tiger," the new king found the Legalist views of his adviser Li Su (lee SUH) all too appealing. In 221 B.C.E., Qin Shi Huang-di defeated the last of his rivals and founded a new dynasty with himself as emperor (see Map 3.4).

3-3a Political Structures

The Qin Dynasty transformed Chinese politics. Philosophical doctrines that had proliferated during the late Zhou period were prohibited, and Legalism was adopted as the official ideology. Those who opposed the policies of the new regime were punished and sometimes executed, and books presenting ideas contrary to the official orthodoxy were publicly put to the torch, perhaps the first example of book burning in history (see Historical Voices, "Memorandum on the Burning of Books," p. 70).

Memorandum on the Burning of Books

Politics & Government **LI SU,** who is quoted in the following passage, was a chief minister of the First Emperor of Qin. An exponent of Legalism, Li Su hoped to eliminate all rival theories of government. His recommendation to the emperor on how to accomplish this was recorded by Han Dynasty historian Sima Qian. The emperor approved the proposal and ordered all books contrary to the spirit of Legalist ideology to be destroyed on pain of death. Fortunately, some texts were preserved by being hidden or even memorized by their owners and were thus available to later generations. For centuries afterward, the First Emperor of Qin and his minister were singled out for criticism because of their intolerance and their effort to control the minds of their subjects. Totalitarianism, it seems, is not a modern concept.

Sima Qian, *Historical Records*

In antiquity all under Heaven was divided and in chaos, and nobody was capable of bringing unity to the rest, and it was for this reason that the feudal lords became active together. In their utterances they all spoke of the past in order to injure the present, and they made a display of empty verbiage in order to throw the truth into confusion. People approved what they had learnt in private in order to reject what their superiors laid down. Now Your Majesty has unified and taken possession of all under Heaven. You have distinguish white from black and fixed a single focus of adulation. But those who have studied privately in fact collaborate with each other to reject the regulations laid down by law and teaching; and when they hear orders promulgated, each criticizes them in accordance with his private studies. Indoors they mentally reject them, and outdoors they make criticisms in the byways. To reject their sovereign they consider a source of fame, disagreement they regard as noble, and they encourage all the orders to fabricate slander. If such things are not prohibited then above the sovereign's power will decline, and below factions will form. To prohibit this would be expedient.

Your servant requests that all who possess literature such as *the Songs*, *the Documents*, and the sayings of the hundred schools should get rid of it without penalty. If they have not got rid of it a full thirty days after the order has reached them, they should be branded and sent to do forced labour on the walls. There should be exemption for books concerned with medicine, pharmacy, divination by tortoise-shell . . . , the sowing of crops, and the planting of trees. If there are those who wish to study, they should take the law officers as their teachers.

 Why did the Legalist thinker Li Su believe that his proposal to destroy dangerous ideas was justified? Are there examples of similar thinking in our own time? Are there occasions when it might be permissible to outlaw unpopular ideas?

Source: R. Dawson (tr.), *Sima Qian: Historical Records* (Oxford: Oxford University Press, 1994), pp. 30–31.

Legalistic theory gave birth to several new administrative and political practices, some of which would survive the Qin and serve as a model for future dynasties. Unlike the Zhou, the Qin was a highly centralized state. The central bureaucracy was divided into three primary ministries: a civil authority, a military authority, and a censorate, whose inspectors surveyed the efficiency of officials throughout the system. This would later become standard administrative procedure for future Chinese dynasties. Below the central government were two levels of administration: provinces and counties. Unlike the Zhou system, officials at these levels did not inherit their positions but were appointed by the court and were subject to dismissal at the emperor's whim.

3-3b Society and the Economy

Qin Shi Huang-di, who had a passion for centralization, unified the system of weights and measures, standardized the monetary system and the written forms of Chinese characters, and ordered the construction of a system of roads extending throughout the empire. He also attempted to eliminate the remaining powers of the landed aristocrats and divided their estates among the peasants, who were now taxed directly by the state. He thus eliminated potential rivals and secured tax revenues for the central government. Members of the aristocratic clans were required to live in the capital city at Xianyang (shi-AHN-yahng), just north of modern Xian, so that the court could monitor their activities. Such a system may not necessarily have been advantageous to the peasants, however, because the central government could now collect taxes more effectively and mobilize the peasants for military service and for various public works projects. The Qin Dynasty was equally unsympathetic to the merchants, whom it viewed as parasites. Private commercial activities were severely restricted and heavily taxed, and many vital forms of commerce and manufacturing, including mining, wine making, and the distribution of salt, became government monopolies.

3-3c Beyond the Frontier: The Nomadic Peoples and the Great Wall

Qin Shi Huang-di was equally aggressive in foreign affairs. His armies continued the gradual advance to the south that had taken place during the final years of the Zhou Dynasty, extending the border of China to the edge of the Red River in modern Vietnam. To supply the Qin armies operating in the area, a canal was dug to provide direct inland navigation from the Yangzi River in central China to what is now the modern city of Guangzhou (gwahng-JOE) (Canton) in the south.

The main area of concern for the Qin emperor, however, was in the north, where a nomadic people known as the Xiongnu (SHYAHNG-noo), who may have been related to the Huns (see Chapter 5), had become increasingly active in the Gobi Desert. During the early first millennium B.C.E., the climate in the area was somewhat milder and moister than it is today, and parts of the region were heavily forested. The local population probably lived by hunting and fishing, practicing limited forms of agriculture, or herding animals such as cattle or sheep.

As the climate gradually became drier, however, people were forced to rely increasingly on animal husbandry as a means of livelihood. Their response was to master the art of riding on horseback and to adopt a nomadic life. Organized loosely into lineage communities, they ranged far and wide in search of pasture for their herds of cattle, goats, or sheep. As they moved seasonally from one pasture to another, they often traveled several hundred miles carrying their goods and their *yurts*, circular felt tents.

But the new way of life presented its own challenges. Increased food production led to a growing population, which in times of drought outstripped the available resources. As rival groups competed for the best pastures, territorial warfare—now carried on by armed warriors on horseback—became commonplace throughout the entire frontier region from the Pacific Ocean to central Asia.

By the end of the third century B.C.E., the Xiongnu posed a serious threat to the security of China's northern frontier, and many Chinese principalities in the area began to build walls of tamped earth or stones to keep them out. But warriors on horseback possessed significant advantages over the infantry of the Chinese. Qin Shi Huang-di's answer to the problem was to introduce archers mounted on sturdy horses imported from Central Asia into his military units stationed in the north to counter nomad attacks. He also strengthened the system of walls that had already been erected under the Zhou, while adding fortifications at strategic points to keep the marauders out.

Today, of course, we know Qin Shi Huang-di's project as the Great Wall, which extends nearly 4,000 miles from the sandy wastes of Central Asia to the sea. Parts are constructed of granite blocks, and its top is wide enough to serve as a roadway for horse-drawn chariots. Although the wall that appears in most photographs today was built 1,500 years after the Qin (see Chapter 10), some of the walls built by the Qin are still standing. Their construction was a massive project that required the efforts of thousands of laborers, many of whom met their deaths there and, according to legend, are now buried within the wall (see the illustrations entitled "The Great Walls of China" in Chapter 10).

The Fall of the Qin The Legalist system put in place by the Qin was designed to achieve maximum efficiency as well as total security for the state. It did neither. Qin Shi Huang-di was apparently aware of the dangers of factions within the imperial family and established a class of **eunuchs** (males whose testicles have been removed) who served as personal attendants for himself and female members of the royal family. The original idea may have been to restrict the influence of male courtiers, and the eunuch system later became a standard feature of the Chinese imperial system. But as confidential advisers to the royal family, eunuchs were in a position of influence, and the rivalry between the "inner" imperial court and the "outer" court of bureaucratic officials led to tensions that persisted until the end of the imperial system.

By ruthlessly gathering control over the empire into his own hands, Qin Shi Huang-di had hoped to establish a rule that, in the words of the contemporary historian Sima Qian, "would be enjoyed by his sons for ten thousand generations." In fact, his centralizing zeal alienated many key groups. Landed aristocrats and Confucian intellectuals, as well as the common people, groaned under the censorship of thought and speech, harsh taxes, and forced labor projects. "He killed men," recounted the historian, "as though he thought he could never finish, he punished men as though he were afraid he would never get around to them all, and the whole world revolted against him."[6]

CHRONOLOGY	Ancient China
Xia Dynasty	?–ca. 1570 B.C.E.
Shang Dynasty	ca. 1570–ca. 1045 B.C.E.
Zhou Dynasty	ca. 1045–221 B.C.E.
Life of Confucius	551–479 B.C.E.
Warring States Period	403–221 B.C.E.
Life of Mencius	370–290 B.C.E.
Qin Dynasty	221–206 B.C.E.
Life of the First Emperor of Qin	259–210 B.C.E.
The Han Dynasty	202 B.C.E.–221 C.E.

Shortly after the emperor died in 210 B.C.E., the dynasty quickly descended into factional rivalry, and four years later it was overthrown.

3-4 THE GLORIOUS HAN DYNASTY

 Focus Question: Why and to what degree did the Han Dynasty turn to Confucianism as an ideology of the state, and how were the Old Master's precepts affected by the process?

The fall of the Qin Dynasty in 206 B.C.E. was followed by a brief period of civil strife as aspiring successors competed for hegemony. Out of this conflict emerged one of the greatest and most durable dynasties in Chinese history— the Han (HAHN). The Han Dynasty would later become so closely identified with the advance of Chinese civilization that even today the Chinese sometimes refer to themselves as "people of Han" and to their language as the "language of Han."

The founder of the Han Dynasty was Liu Bang (lyoo BAHNG), a commoner of peasant origin who would be known historically by his imperial title of Han Gaozu (HAHN gow-dzoo), or Exalted Emperor of Han. Under his and his successors' strong rule, the new dynasty quickly moved to consolidate its control over the empire and promote the welfare of its subjects. Efficient and benevolent, at least by the standards of the time, Gaozu maintained the centralized political institutions of the Qin but abandoned its harsh Legalistic approach to law enforcement. Han rulers discovered in Confucian principles a useful foundation for the creation of a new state philosophy. Confucianism, supplemented by elements from the surviving classics of the hundred schools period, began to take on the character of an official ideology.

3-4a Confucianism and the State

Although it took awhile to accomplish, Confucian doctrine was integrated with Legalist institutions to create a system generally known as **State Confucianism**. At first, founding emperor Han Gaozu departed from the Qin policy of centralized rule by rewarding some of his key allies with vast fiefdoms, restricting his own territory to lands around the new capital of Chang-an (CHENG-AHN). But chronic unrest throughout the countryside eventually forced a change in policy. By the mid-second century B.C.E., the influence of unruly aristocratic forces had been curbed, and once again power was concentrated at the imperial court.

The Han rulers then sought to restore key components of the Qin system of centralized rule. For example, they borrowed the tripartite division of the central government into civilian and military authorities and a censorate. The administration was headed by a Grand Council that included representatives from all three segments of government. The Han also retained the system of local government, dividing the empire into provinces and districts.

Finally, the Han sought to apply the Qin system of selecting government officials on the basis of merit rather than birth. Shortly after founding the new dynasty, Emperor Gaozu decreed that local officials would be asked to recommend promising candidates for public service. In 165 B.C.E., the first known **civil service examination** was administered to candidates for positions in the bureaucracy. Shortly after, an academy was established to train candidates. The first candidates were almost all from aristocratic or other wealthy families, and the bureaucracy itself was still dominated by the traditional hereditary elites. Still, the principle of selecting officials on the basis of talent had been established and would eventually become standard practice. By the end of the first century B.C.E., as many as 30,000 students were enrolled at the academy.

Driven by a policy that applied tax incentives to promote large families, the population of the empire increased rapidly—by some estimates rising from some 20 million to more than 60 million at the height of the dynasty— creating the need for a large and efficient bureaucracy to maintain the state in proper working order. Unfortunately, the Han were unable to resolve other problems left over from the past. Despite their efforts, factionalism at court remained a serious problem. At the same time, the Han rulers were never able to restrain the great aristocratic families, who continued to play a dominant role in political and economic affairs. The failure to curb the power of the wealthy clans eventually became a major factor in the collapse of the dynasty.

3-4b The Economy

Han rulers unwittingly contributed to their own problems by adopting fiscal policies that led eventually to greater concentration of land in the hands of the wealthy. They were aware that a free peasantry paying taxes directly to the state would both limit the wealth and power of the great noble families and increase the state's revenues. But they had difficulty in preventing the recurrence of the economic inequities that had characterized the last years of the Zhou. Land taxes were not especially high but had to be paid in cash rather than in grain to make collection easier. In years of bad harvests, poor farmers were unable to pay their taxes and were forced to sell their land and become tenant farmers, paying rents of up to half the annual harvest. Although food production increased steadily because of the application of natural fertilizer and the use of the iron tools that brought new lands under the plow, the trebling of the population under the early Han eventually reduced the average size of a family farm to about one acre per person, barely enough for survival.

Manufacturing and Trade   Although such economic problems contributed to the eventual downfall of the dynasty, in general the period of the early Han was one of unparalleled productivity and prosperity, marked by a major expansion of trade, both domestic and foreign. This was not necessarily the result of official encouragement because the Han were as suspicious of private merchants as their predecessors had been and levied stiff taxes on trade in an effort to limit commercial activities. Merchants were also subject to severe social constraints. Disqualified from seeking office and restricted in their place of residence, they were generally viewed as parasites who provided little true value to Chinese society.

The state directed much trade and manufacturing; it produced weapons, for example, and operated shipyards, granaries, and mines. The system of roads was expanded and modernized, and new bridges, rest houses, and post stations for changing horses were added. Unlike the Romans (see Chapter 5), the Chinese relied on waterways for the bulk of their transportation needs. To supplement the numerous major rivers crisscrossing the densely populated heartland, new canals were dug to facilitate the moving of goods from one end of the vast empire to the other.

New technology contributed to the economic prosperity of the Han era. Following the initiatives adopted under the Qin, the currency was further standardized for use throughout the empire, and significant progress was achieved in such areas as textile manufacturing, water mills (chain pumps with wooden pellets appeared in the

3.6 Making Paper. One of China's most important contributions to the world was the invention of paper during the Han Dynasty. Although the first known use of paper for writing dates back to the first century B.C.E., paper was also used for clothing, wrapping materials, military armor, and toilet tissue. It was even suggested to a prince in 93 B.C.E. that he use a paper handkerchief. Paper was made by pounding fibers of hemp and linen. Then the crushed fibers were placed on a flat meshed surface and soaked in a large vat. After the residue dried, it was peeled away as a sheet of paper, seen piled at the right in this eighteenth-century painting.

first century B.C.E.), and iron casting. Improvements in ironworking led to the production of steel a few centuries later. Paper was invented during the first century C.E., and the development of the rudder and fore-and-aft rigging permitted ships to sail into the wind for the first time. Thus equipped, Chinese merchants ships carrying heavy cargoes could sail throughout the islands of Southeast Asia and into the Indian Ocean.

3-4c Imperial Expansion and the Origins of the Silk Road

The Han emperors continued the process of territorial expansion and consolidation that had begun under the Zhou and the Qin. Early Han rulers successfully completed the assimilation into the empire of the regions south of the Yangzi River, including what is known today as northern Vietnam. Han armies also marched westward as far as the Caspian Sea, pacifying nomadic peoples and extending China's boundary far into Central Asia (see Map 3.5).

The latter project was originally planned as a means of fending off pressure from the Xiongnu peoples, who periodically threatened Chinese lands from their base north of the Great Wall. In 138 B.C.E., Emperor Wudi dispatched the courtier Zhang Qian (JANG chee-AHN) on a mission westward into Central Asia to seek alliances with other states to counter the common menace. Although he failed in

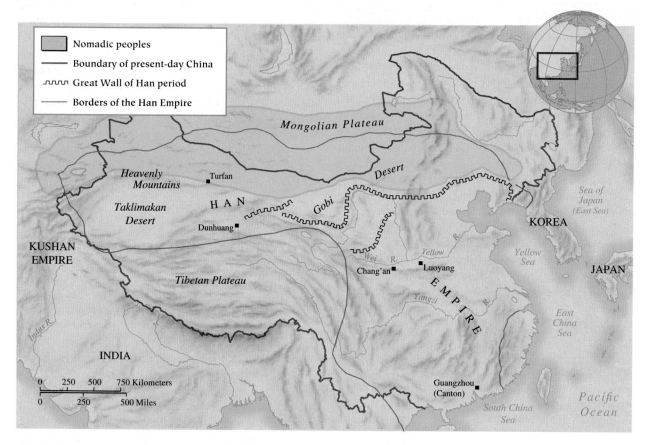

Map 3.5 The Han Empire. This map shows the territory under the control of the Han Empire at its greatest extent during the first century B.C.E. Note the Great Wall's placement relative to nomadic peoples.

Q *How did the expansion of Han rule to the west parallel the Silk Road?*

his assigned task, Zhang Qian returned home with ample information about conditions in Central Asia, enabling the Han government to establish the first Chinese military presence in the Taklimakan (tah-kluh-muh-KAHN) Desert and the Tian Shan (TEE-en SHAN) (Heavenly) Mountains. Eventually, this area would become known to the Chinese people as Xinjiang (SHIN-jyahng), or "New Region."

Chinese commercial exchanges with peoples in Central Asia now began to expand dramatically. Eastward into China came grapes, precious metals, glass objects, and horses from Persia and Central Asia. Horses were of particular significance because Chinese military strategists had learned of the importance of cavalry in their battles against the Xiongnu and sought the sturdy Ferghana horses of Bactria to increase their own military effectiveness. In return, China exported goods, especially silk, to countries to the west.

Silk, a filament recovered from the cocoons of silkworms, had been produced in China since the fourth millennium B.C.E. Eventually, knowledge of the wonder product reached the outside world, and Chinese silk exports began to rise dramatically. By the second century B.C.E., the first items made from silk reached the Mediterranean Sea, stimulating the first significant contacts between China and Rome (see Chapter 5). The bulk of the trade went overland through Central Asia (thus earning this route its modern name, the Silk Road), although significant exchanges also took place via the maritime route (see Chapter 9).

The silk trade also stimulated an increase in mutual curiosity between China and other civilizations farther to the west. Roman authors such as Pliny the Elder and the geographer Strabo (who speculated that silk was produced from the leaves of a "silk tree") wrote of a strange land called "Seres" beyond the rising sun, while Chinese sources mentioned the empire of "Great Qin" at the far end of the Silk Road to the west. Of more immediate consequence was the increased communication that took place with societies in the South Asian subcontinent. One of the most important consequences was the introduction

3.7 Terra Cotta Horse and Rider. This clay sculpture is a striking example of Han Dynasty artistry. Although the Chinese had domesticated the smaller Mongolian pony as early as 2000 B.C.E., not until the end of the first millennium B.C.E. did the Chinese acquire horses as a result of military expeditions into central Asia. Often they were acquired in exchange for silk, an item much prized by peoples living throughout the region. Admired for their power and grace, horses made of terra cotta or bronze were often placed in Qin or Han tombs.

of Buddhism from India. In the first century C.E., a new salvationist faith appeared on the horizon as merchants from Central Asia brought Buddhist teachings to China for the first time. At first, its influence was limited because no Buddhist text was translated into Chinese until the fifth century C.E. But the terrain was ripe for the introduction of a new religion into China, and the first Chinese monks departed for India shortly after the end of the Han Dynasty (see Chapter 10).

3-4d The Decline and Fall of the Han

By the end of the first century B.C.E., the Han empire had been crumbling for decades. As frivolous or depraved rulers amused themselves with the pleasures of court life, the power and influence of the central government began to wane, and the great noble families filled the vacuum, amassing vast landed estates and transforming free farmers into tenants. In 9 C.E., the reformist official Wang Mang (Wahng MAHNG), who was troubled by the plight of the

peasants, seized power from the Han court and declared the foundation of the Xin (SHIN) (New) Dynasty. Wang Mang tried to confiscate the great estates, restore the ancient well-field system, and abolish slavery. In so doing, however, he alienated powerful interests, who conspired to overthrow him. In 23 C.E., beset by administrative chaos and a collapse of the frontier defenses, Wang Mang was killed in a coup d'etat.

For a time, strong leadership revived some of the glory of the early Han (Chinese historians refer to the period after the Wang Mang revolt as the Later Han Dynasty). The court sought to reduce land taxes and carry out land-resettlement programs. The growing popularity of nutritious crops such as rice, wheat, and soybeans, along with the introduction of new crops such as alfalfa and grapes, helped boost food production. But the great landed families' firm grip on land and power continued. Weak rulers were isolated within their imperial chambers and dominated by eunuchs and other powerful court insiders. Official corruption and the concentration of land in the hands of the wealthy led once again to widespread peasant unrest.

In the meantime, skirmishes with the Xiongnu tribes in the north continued. In part, the conflict focused on control over the area between the grazing lands and farming areas in northern China. But trade disputes were also involved because silk and other commodities from China were in great demand by pastoral communities, and conflict over availability and price often led to conflict. After their attempts to reach a negotiated settlement failed, Han rulers—tired of paying tribute to maintain peace—returned to a policy of military force. Professional armies were recruited from among minority peoples along the periphery of the empire, but they proved to be unreliable in both performance and loyalty. As a result, raids on Chinese territory continued intermittently up to the end of the dynasty, sometimes reaching almost to the gates of the capital city.

Buffeted by insurmountable problems within and without, by the end of the second century C.E. the dynasty had entered a period of inexorable decline. The population of the empire shrank to fewer than 20 million from its peak of 60 million at the first census taken in 2 C.E., and the dynasty was brought to an end when power was seized by Cao Cao (TSOW tsow), a general known to later generations as one of the main characters in the famous Chinese epic *The Romance of the Three Kingdoms*. But Cao Cao was unable to consolidate his power, and China entered a period of almost constant anarchy and internal division, compounded by invasions of northern nomadic peoples. The country would not be reunified until the beginning of the seventh century, 400 years later.

3-5 DAILY LIFE IN ANCIENT CHINA

 Focus Question: What were the key aspects of social and economic life in early China, and how did they compare with conditions elsewhere in the ancient world?

Few social institutions have been as closely identified with China as the family. As in most agricultural civilizations, the family served as the basic economic and social unit in society. In traditional China, however, it took on an almost sacred quality as a microcosm of the entire social order.

3-5a The Role of the Family

In Neolithic times, the farm village, organized around the clan, was the basic social unit in China, at least in the core region of the Yellow River Valley. Even then, however, the smaller family unit was becoming more important. At the Banpo archaeological site in central China, the remains of a Neolithic village dating back several thousand years contain the foundations of what appear to be several small nuclear family dwellings, in addition to the communal longhouse, all built as early as the end of the second millennium B.C.E. The concept of family was especially important to the nobility, who attached considerable significance to the ritual veneration of their immediate ancestors.

During the Zhou Dynasty, the family took on increasing importance, in part because of the need for cooperation in agriculture. The cultivation of rice, which had become the primary crop along the Yangzi River and in the provinces to the south, is highly labor intensive. The seedlings must be planted in several inches of water in a nursery bed and then transferred individually to the paddy beds, which must be irrigated constantly (see the illustration "Rice Culture in Southeast Asia" in Chapter 9). During the harvest, the stalks must be cut and the kernels carefully separated from the stalks and husks. As a result, children—and the labor they supplied—were considered essential to the survival of the family, not only during their youthful years but also later when sons were expected to provide for their parents. Loyalty to family members came to be considered even more important than allegiance to the broader community or the state.

At the crux of the concept of family was the idea of **filial piety**, which called on all members to subordinate their personal needs and desires to the patriarchal head of the family. More broadly, it created a hierarchical system in which every family member had his or her appropriate place. All Chinese learned the **five relationships** that were the key to a proper social order. The son was subordinate to his father, the wife to her husband, and the younger brother to his older brother, and all were subject to their king. The final relationship was the proper one between friend and friend. Only if all members of the family and the community as a whole behaved in a properly filial manner would society function effectively.

A stable family system based on obedient and hardworking members can serve as a bulwark for an efficient government, but putting loyalty to the family and the clan over loyalty to the state can also present a threat to a centralizing monarch. For that reason, the Qin Dynasty attempted to destroy the clan system in China and assert the primacy of the state. Legalists even imposed heavy taxes on any family with more than two adult sons in order to break down the family concept.

But the efforts of the Qin to eradicate or at least reduce the importance of the family system ran against tradition and the dynamics of the Chinese economy, and under the Han Dynasty, which succeeded the Qin in 202 B.C.E., the family system revived and increased in importance. With official encouragement, the family began to take on the character that it would possess until our own day.

3-5b Lifestyles

We know much more about the lifestyle of the elites than that of the common people in ancient China. The first houses were probably constructed of wooden planks, or of wattle and thatch, but later Chinese mastered the art of building in tile and brick. By the first millennium B.C.E., most public buildings and the houses of the wealthy were probably constructed in this manner. By Han times, most Chinese probably lived in simple houses of mud, wooden planks, or brick with thatch or occasionally tile roofs. But in some areas, especially the regions of northern China with loess (LESS) soil, cave dwelling remained common down to modern times.

Chinese houses in ancient times usually had little furniture; most people squatted or sat with their legs spread out on the packed mud floor. Chairs were apparently not introduced until the sixth or seventh century C.E. Clothing was simple, consisting of cotton trousers and shirts in the summer and wool or burlap in the winter.

The staple foods in the north were dry grain crops such as millet, barley, and wheat; rice predominated in the south. Other common foods were wheat, barley, soybeans, mustard greens, and bamboo shoots. Archaeologists have discovered the remains of millet noodles dating back to 2000 B.C. In early times, most foods were often consumed in the form of porridge, but by the Zhou Dynasty, stir-frying in a wok was becoming common. When possible, the Chinese family would vary its diet of grain foods with vegetables, fruit (including pears, peaches, apricots, and plums), and fish or meat; but for most families, such additions to the daily plate of rice, millet, or soybeans were a rare luxury.

Chinese legend hints that tea—a plant originally found in upland regions in southern China and Southeast Asia—was introduced by the mythical emperor Shen Nong. In fact, however, tea drinking did not become widespread in China until around 500 C.E. By then it was lauded for its medicinal qualities and its capacity to soothe the spirit. Alcohol in the form of ale was drunk at least by the higher classes; by the early Zhou era, alcoholic consumption had already begun to inspire official concern. For the poorer classes, alcohol in any form was probably a rare luxury.

3-5c Cities

Under the Qin and the Han, cities began to take on the importance they would hold through later Chinese history. Urban centers were divided into neighborhoods—perhaps a forerunner of the grid pattern used in later imperial cities—as a means of facilitating control over the population. Cities became the cultural hubs of Chinese society, although their residents made up only a tiny proportion of the total population. In the crowded streets, nobles sought to avoid rubbing shoulders with commoners, while merchants, workers, wandering gangs, and prostitutes imitated the mannerisms of the elite.

3-5d The Humble Estate: Women in Ancient China

Male dominance was a key element in the social system of ancient China. As in many traditional societies, the male was considered of transcendent importance because of his role as food procurer or, in the case of farming communities, food producer. In ancient China, men worked in the fields, and women raised children and took care of the home. These different roles based on gender go back to prehistoric times and are embedded in Chinese creation myths. According to legend, Fu Xi's wife Nu Wa (noo WAH) assisted her husband in organizing society by establishing the institution of marriage and the family. Yet Nu Wa was not just a household drudge. After Fu Xi's death, she became China's first female sovereign.

During ancient times, apparently women normally did not occupy formal positions of authority, but they often became a force in politics, especially at court, where wives of the ruler or other female members of the royal family were often influential in palace intrigues.

The nature of gender relationships was also graphically demonstrated in the Chinese written language. The character for man (男) combines the symbols for strength and rice field, while the character for woman (女) represents a person in a posture of deference and respect. The character for peace (安) is a woman under a roof. A wife is symbolized by a woman with a broom. Male chauvinism has deep linguistic roots in China.

Confucian thought, although not denigrating the importance of women as mothers and homemakers, accepted the dual roles of men and women in Chinese society. Men governed society. They carried on family ritual through the veneration of ancestors. They were the warriors, scholars, and ministers. Their dominant role was firmly enshrined in the legal system. Men were permitted to have more than one wife and to divorce a spouse who did not produce a male child. Women were denied the right to own property, and there was no dowry system in ancient China that would have provided the wife with a degree of financial security from her husband and his family. As the third-century C.E., poet Fu Xuan (foo SHWAHN), a woman, lamented:

> How sad it is to be a woman
> Nothing on earth is held so cheap.
> No one is glad when a girl is born.
> By her the family sets no store.
> No one cries when she leaves her home
> Sudden as clouds when the rain stops.[7]

3-6 CHINESE CULTURE

 Focus Questions: What were the chief characteristics of the Chinese arts and writing system? How did they differ from those used in Egypt and Mesopotamia?

In civilizations located in relatively arid areas such as the Middle East, artifacts have been preserved from the ravages of time. In more humid regions, such as China and South Asia, the cultural residue left by the civilizations of antiquity has been adversely affected by climate.

As a result, relatively little remains of the cultural achievements of the prehistoric Chinese aside from Neolithic pottery and the relics found at gravesites dating from the early second millennium B.C.E. In the 1970s, a rich trove from the time of the Qin Empire was unearthed near the tomb of Qin Shi Huang-di near Xian in central China and at Han tombs nearby. More recently, ancient texts recorded on bamboo slips and discovered at burial sites in Central China have provided scholars with fascinating new insights into the nature of debates over political and philosophical issues during the latter part of the fourth century B.C.E.

3-6a Metalwork and Sculpture

Discoveries at archaeological sites indicate that ancient China was a society rich in cultural achievement. Handmade pottery dates back at least to the sixth millennium B.C.E. and pottery found at Neolithic sites such as Longshan and Yangshao exhibits a freshness and vitality of form and design, and ornaments such as rings and beads show a strong aesthetic sense.

Bronze Casting The pace of Chinese cultural development began to quicken during the Shang Dynasty, which ruled in northern China from the sixteenth to the eleventh century B.C.E. By that time, objects cast in bronze with an astonishing degree of delicacy began to appear. Various bronze vessels were produced for use in preparing and serving food and drink in the royal ancestral rites. Eventually such vessels were used for decoration or for dining at court.

The method of casting used was one reason for the extraordinary quality of Shang bronze work. Bronze workers in most ancient civilizations used the lost-wax method in which a model was first made in wax. After a clay mold had been formed around it, the model was heated so that the wax would melt away, and the empty space was filled with molten metal. In China, clay molds composed of several sections were tightly fitted together before liquid bronze was introduced. This technique, which had evolved from ceramic techniques used during the Neolithic period, enabled artisans to apply designs directly to molds and thus contributed to the clarity of line and rich surface decoration of the Shang bronzes.

Bronze casting became a large-scale business, and more than 10,000 vessels of an incredible variety of form and design survive today. Factories were located not only in the Yellow River Valley but also in Sichuan Province, in southern China. The art of bronze working continued into the Zhou Dynasty, but the quality and originality declined. The Shang bronzes remain the pinnacle of creative art in ancient China.

One reason for the decline of bronze casting in China was the rise in popularity of iron. Ironmaking developed in China around the ninth or eighth century B.C.E., much later than in the Middle East, where it had been mastered almost a millennium earlier. Once familiar with the process, however, the Chinese quickly moved to the forefront. Ironworkers in Europe and the Middle East, lacking the technology to achieve the high temperatures necessary to melt iron ore for casting, were forced to work with wrought iron, a cumbersome and expensive process. By the fourth century B.C.E., the Chinese had invented the blast furnace, powered by a worker operating a bellows. They were, therefore, able to manufacture cast iron ritual vessels and agricultural tools centuries before an equivalent technology appeared in the West.

Another reason for the deterioration of the bronze-casting tradition was the development of cheaper materials such as lacquerware and ceramics. Lacquer was made from resins obtained from the juice of sumac trees native to the region and had been produced since Neolithic times; by the second century B.C.E., it had become a popular method of applying a hard coating to objects made of wood or fabric. Pottery, too, had existed since early times, but technological advances led to the production of a high-quality form of pottery covered with a brown or gray-green glaze, the latter known popularly as *celadon*. By the end of the

3.8 A Shang Wine Vessel. Used initially as food containers in royal ceremonial rites during the Shang Dynasty, Chinese bronzes were the product of an advanced technology unmatched by any contemporary civilization. This wine vessel displays a deep green patina as well as a monster motif, complete with large globular eyes, nostrils, and fangs, typical of many Shang bronzes. Known as the *taotie* (TOW-tee-YU H ["ow" as in "how"]), this fanciful beast is normally presented in silhouette as two dragons face to face so that each side forms half of the mask. Although the taotie presumably served as a guardian force against evil spirits, scholars are still not aware of its exact significance for early Chinese peoples.

first millennium B.C.E., both lacquerware and pottery had replaced bronze in popularity, much as plastic goods have replaced more expensive materials in our own time.

The First Emperor's Tomb

In a remarkable discovery in 1974, farmers digging a well some thirty-five miles east of Xian unearthed many terra cotta figures in an underground pit around one mile east of the burial mound of the First Emperor of Qin. Chinese archaeologists sent to work at the site discovered a vast terra cotta army that they believed was a re-creation of Qin Shi Huang-di's imperial guard and meant to accompany the emperor on his journey to the next world.

One of the astounding features of the terra cotta army is its size. The army is enclosed in four massive pits that were originally encased in a wooden framework, which has since disintegrated. More than 1,000 figures have been unearthed in the first pit, along with horses, wooden chariots, and 7,000 bronze weapons. Archaeologists estimate that there are more than 6,000 figures in that pit alone.

Equally impressive is the quality of the work. Slightly larger than life size, the figures were molded of finely textured clay and then fired and painted. The detail on the uniforms is realistic and sophisticated, but the most striking feature is the individuality of the facial features of the soldiers. Apparently, ten different head shapes were used

and were then modeled further by hand to reflect the variety of ethnic groups and personality types in the army.

The emperor's mausoleum has not yet been unearthed, but it is enclosed in a mound nearly 250 feet high and is surrounded by a rectangular wall nearly four miles around. According to the Han historian Sima Qian, the ceiling is a replica of the heavens, and the floor contains a relief model of the entire Qin kingdom, with rivers flowing in mercury. According to tradition, traps were set within the mausoleum to prevent intruders, and the workers applying the final touches were buried alive in the tomb with its secrets.

3-6b Language and Literature

Precisely when writing developed in China cannot be determined, but certainly by Shang times, as the oracle bones demonstrate, the Chinese had developed a simple but functional script. Like many other languages of antiquity, it was primarily ideographic and pictographic in form. Symbols, usually called *characters*, were created to represent an idea or to form a picture of the object to be represented. For example, the Chinese characters for mountain (山), the sun (日), and the moon (月) were meant to represent the objects themselves. Other characters, such as "big" (大) (a man with his arms outstretched), represent an idea. The character "east" (東) symbolizes the sun coming up behind the trees.

3.9 The tomb of Qin Shi Huang-di. The First Emperor of Qin ordered the construction of an elaborate mausoleum, an underground palace complex protected by an army of terra cotta soldiers and horses to accompany him on his journey to the afterlife. This massive formation of 6,000 life-sized armed soldiers, discovered accidentally by farmers in 1974, reflects Qin Shi Huang-di's grandeur and power.

William J. Duiker

Martin Puddy/Asia Images/Getty Images

Each character, of course, would be given a sound by the speaker when pronounced. In other cultures, this process led to the abandonment of the system of ideographs and the adoption of a written language based on phonetic symbols. The Chinese language, however, has never entirely abandoned its original ideographic format, although the phonetic element has developed into a significant part of the individual character. In that sense, the Chinese written language is virtually unique in the world today.

One reason why the Chinese language retained its ideographic quality was the fact that although most languages and dialects spoken in China are derived from a parent Sinitic prototype, they differ dramatically in pronunciation, as well as in vocabulary and syntax. The Chinese answer to this problem was to give all the spoken languages the same writing system. Although any character might be pronounced differently in different regions of China, that character would be written the same way (after the standardization undertaken under the Qin) no matter where it was written. This system of written characters could be read by educated Chinese from one end of the country to the other. It became the language of the bureaucracy and the vehicle for the transmission of Chinese culture to all Chinese from the Great Wall to the southern border and even beyond.

The earliest extant form of Chinese literature dates from the Zhou Dynasty. It was written on silk or strips of bamboo and consisted primarily of historical records such as the *Rites of Zhou*, philosophical treatises such as the *Analects* and *The Way of the Tao,* and poetry, as recorded in *The Book of Songs* and *The Song of the South.* In later years when Confucian principles had been elevated to a state ideology, the key works identified with the Confucian school were integrated into a set of so-called Confucian Classics. These works became required reading for generations of Chinese schoolchildren and introduced them to the forms of behavior that would be expected of them as adults.

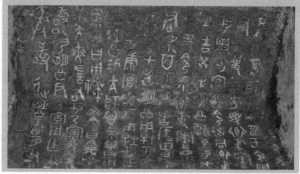

Photograph by William J. Duiker/Freer Gallery of Art, Washington, D.C.

3.10 **Ancient Chinese Writing.** Although the origins of the Chinese writing system remain shrouded in mystery, the first extant texts that can be clearly deciphered date from the late Shang Dynasty and were inscribed on tortoise shells and chicken bones. Eventually, however, characters became increasingly stylized and began to be engraved on metal objects. The text shown here was engraved on a bronze bowl that was commonly used for ritual purposes and dates back to the early Zhou era. The text itself describes the results of an administrative meeting that took place at the royal court in the city of Chengzhou.

CHAPTER SUMMARY

Of the great classical civilizations discussed in Part I of this book, China was the last to come into full flower. By the time the Shang Dynasty began to emerge as an organized state, the societies in Mesopotamia and the Nile Valley had already reached advanced levels of civilization.

Unfortunately, not enough is known about the early stages of these civilizations to allow us to determine why some developed earlier than others, but one likely reason for China's comparatively late arrival was that it was virtually isolated from other emerging centers of culture elsewhere in the world and thus was compelled to develop essentially on its own. Only at the end of the first millennium B.C.E. did China come into regular contact with other civilizations in South Asia, the Middle East, and the Mediterranean.

Once embarked on its own path toward the creation of a complex society, however, China achieved results that were in all respects the equal of its counterparts else-where. By the rise of the first unified empire in the late third century B.C.E., the state extended from the edge of the Gobi Desert in the north to the subtropical regions near the borders of modern Vietnam in the south. Chinese philosophers had engaged in debate over intricate questions relating to human nature and the state of the universe, and China's artistic and technological achievements—especially in terms of bronze casting and the terra cotta figures entombed in Qin Shi Huang-di's mausoleum—were unsurpassed throughout the world.

Meanwhile, another great civilization was beginning to take form on the northern shores of the Mediterranean Sea. Unlike China and the other ancient societies discussed thus far, this new civilization in Europe was based as much on trade as on agriculture. Yet the political and cultural achievements of ancient Greece were the equal of any of the great human experiments that had preceded it, and soon this civilization began to exert a significant impact on the rest of the ancient world.

REFLECTION QUESTIONS

Q What were some of the key contributions in political structures, social organization, and culture that the Shang Dynasty bequeathed to its successor, the Zhou Dynasty? Does the Shang deserve to be called the "mother culture" of China?

Q What appears to be the justification for the types of political and social institutions established during the Qin Dynasty?

Q What contributions did the ancient Chinese people make in the field of metallurgy? How do their achievements compare with developments in ancient Egypt and the Middle East?

CHAPTER TIMELINE

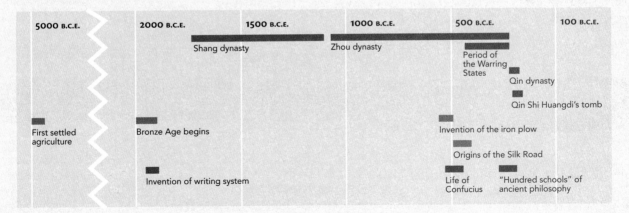

| 5000 B.C.E. | 2000 B.C.E. | 1500 B.C.E. | 1000 B.C.E. | 500 B.C.E. | 100 B.C.E. |

Shang dynasty

Zhou dynasty

Period of the Warring States

Qin dynasty

Qin Shi Huangdi's tomb

First settled agriculture

Bronze Age begins

Invention of the iron plow

Origins of the Silk Road

Invention of writing system

Life of Confucius

"Hundred schools" of ancient philosophy

CHAPTER NOTES

1. Book of Changes, quoted in Chang Chi-yun, *Chinese History of Fifty Centuries,* vol. 1, *Ancient Times* (Taipei, 1962), pp. 15, 31, and 65.
2. Ibid., p. 381.
3. Quoted in E. N. Anderson, *The Food of China* (New Haven, Conn., 1988), p. 21.
4. According to Chinese tradition, the *Rites of Zhou* was written by the duke of Zhou himself near the time of the founding of the Zhou Dynasty. Modern historians, however, believe that it was written much later, perhaps as late as the fourth century B.C.E. Recently discovered ancient texts suggest that the issue of royal succession attracted considerable interest among Chinese political thinkers at this time, with some recommending the idea that a sage ruler should abdicate his authority to a virtuous successor rather than to a member of his own family. For further information, see Sarah Allan, *Buried Ideas: Legends of Abdication and Ideal Government in Early Chinese Bamboo-Slip Manuscripts* (Albany, NY, 2015).
5. From the *Book of Songs,* quoted in S. de Grazia, ed., *Masters of Chinese Political Thought: From the Beginnings to the Han Dynasty* (New York, 1973), pp. 40–41.
6. B. Watson, *Records of the Grand Historian of China* (New York, 1961), vol. 2, pp. 32, 53.
7. A. Waley, ed., *Chinese Poems* (London, 1983), p. xx

MINDTAP
From Cengage

MindTap® is a fully online, highly personalized learning experience built upon Cengage Learning content. MindTap combines student learning tools—readings, multimedia, activities, and assessments—into a singular Learning Path that guides students through the course and helps students develop the critical thinking, analysis, and communication skills that are essential to academic and professional success.

Chapter Outline and Focus Questions

4.1 A bust of Pericles

Critical Thinking

Q *In what ways did the culture of the Hellenistic period differ from that of the classical period, and what do those differences suggest about society in the two periods?*

Connections to Today

Q *What are the similarities and differences between ancient Athenian democracy and modern democracy in the United States?*

DURING THE ERA OF CIVIL WAR in China known as the Warring States Period, a civil war also erupted on the northern shores of the Mediterranean Sea. In 431 B.C.E., two strikingly different Greek city-states—Athens and Sparta—fought for domination of the Greek world. The people of Athens felt secure behind their walls, and in the first winter of the war, they held a public funeral to honor those who had died in battle. On the day of the ceremony, the citizens of Athens joined in a procession, with the relatives of the dead wailing for their loved ones. As was the custom in Athens, one leading citizen was asked to address the crowd, and on this day it was Pericles who spoke to the people. He talked about the greatness of Athens and reminded the Athenians of the strength of their political system: "Our constitution," he said, "is called a democracy because power is in the hands not of a minority but of the whole people. When it is a question of settling private disputes, everyone is equal before the law. Just as our political life is free and open, so is our day-to-day life in our relations with each other. . . . Here each individual is interested not only in his own affairs but in the affairs of the state as well."

Experience an interactive version of this period in MINDTAP

In this famous funeral oration, Pericles gave voice to the ideal of democracy and the importance of the individual, ideals that were quite different from those of some other ancient societies, in which the individual was subordinated to a larger order based on obedience to an exalted ruler. The Greeks asked basic questions about human life: What is the nature of the universe? What is the purpose of human existence? What is our relationship to divine forces? What constitutes a community? What constitutes a state? What is truth, and how do we realize it? The Greeks not only provided answers to these questions but also created a system of logical, analytical thought to examine them. Their answers and their system of rational thought laid the intellectual foundation of Western civilization's understanding of the human condition.

The remarkable story of ancient Greek civilization begins with the arrival of the Greeks around 1900 B.C.E. By the eighth century B.C.E., the characteristic institution of ancient Greek life, the *polis*, or city-state, had emerged. Greek civilization flourished and reached its height in the classical era of the fifth century B.C.E., but the inability of the Greek states to end their fratricidal warfare eventually left them vulnerable to Philip II, the Macedonian king, and helped bring an end to the era of independent Greek city-states.

Although the city-states were never the same after their defeat by the Macedonian monarch, this defeat did not end the influence of the Greeks. Philip's son Alexander led the Macedonians and Greeks on a spectacular conquest of the Persian Empire and opened the door to the spread of Greek culture throughout the Middle East.

4-1 EARLY GREECE

Focus Questions: How did the geography of Greece affect Greek history? Who was Homer, and why was his work used as the basis for Greek education?

Geography played an important role in Greek history. Compared to Mesopotamia and Egypt, Greece occupied a small area, a mountainous peninsula that encompassed only 45,000 square miles of territory, approximately the size of the state of Louisiana. The mountains and the sea were especially significant. Much of Greece consists of small plains and river valleys surrounded by mountain ranges 8,000 to 10,000 feet high. The

mountains isolated Greeks from one another, causing Greek communities to follow their own separate paths and develop their own ways of life. Over a period of time, these communities became so fiercely attached to their independence that they were only too willing to fight one another to gain advantage. No doubt the small size of these independent Greek communities fostered participation in political affairs and unique cultural expressions, but the rivalry among them also led to the internecine warfare that ultimately devastated Greek society.

The sea also influenced Greek society. Greece had a long seacoast that was dotted with bays and inlets that provided numerous harbors. The Greeks also inhabited many islands to the west, south, and particularly the east of the Greek mainland. It is no accident that the Greeks became seafarers who sailed out into the Aegean and Mediterranean Seas to make contact with the outside world and later to establish colonies that would spread Greek civilization throughout the Mediterranean region.

Greek topography helped determine the major territories into which Greece was ultimately divided (see Map 4.1). South of the Gulf of Corinth was the Peloponnesus (pell-uh-puh-NEE-suss), virtually an island connected to the mainland by a narrow isthmus. Consisting mostly of hills, mountains, and small valleys, the Peloponnesus was the location of Sparta. Northeast of the Peloponnesus was the Attic Peninsula (or Attica), the site of Athens, hemmed in by mountains to the north and west and surrounded by the sea to the south and east. Northwest of Attica was Boeotia (bee-OH-shuh) in central Greece, with its chief city of Thebes (THEEBZ). To the north of Boeotia was Thessaly, which contained the largest plains and became a great producer of grain and horses. To the north of Thessaly lay Macedonia, which was not of much importance in Greek history until 338 B.C.E. when the Macedonian king conquered the Greeks.

4-1a Minoan Crete

The earliest civilization in the Aegean region emerged on the large island of Crete, southeast of the Greek mainland. A Bronze Age civilization that used metals, especially bronze, in making weapons had been established there by 2800 B.C.E. This civilization was discovered at the turn of the twentieth century by English archaeologist Arthur Evans, who named it "Minoan" (mih-NOH-uhn) after Minos (MY-nuss), a legendary king of Crete. In language and religion, the Minoans were not Greek, but they did have some influence on the peoples of the Greek mainland (see Map 4.2).

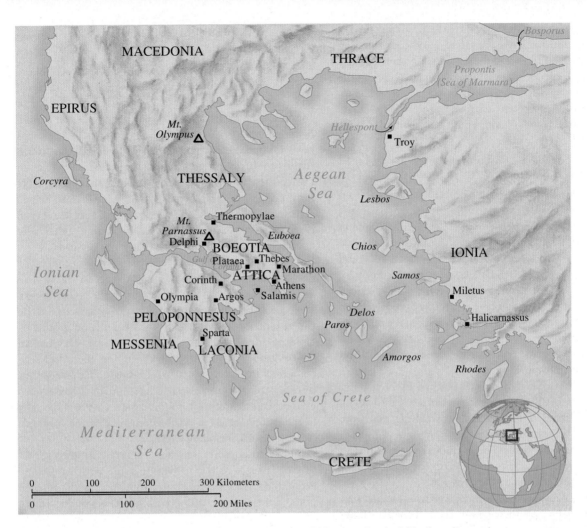

 Map 4.1 Ancient Greece (ca. 750–338 B.C.E.). Between 750 and 500 B.C.E., Greek civilization witnessed the emergence of the city-state as the central institution in Greek life and the Greeks' colonization of the Mediterranean and Black Seas. Classical Greece lasted from around 500 to 338 B.C.E. and encompassed the high points of Greek civilization in the arts, science, philosophy, and politics, as well as the Persian wars and the Peloponnesian War.

Q *How does the geography of Greece help explain the rise and development of the Greek city-state?*

Evans's excavations on Crete at the beginning of the twentieth century unearthed an enormous palace complex at Knossus (NOSS-suss), near modern Iráklion (ir-RAK-lee-on; also spelled Heracleion). The remains revealed a prosperous culture with Knossus as the apparent center of a far-ranging "sea empire" based on trade.

The Minoan civilization reached its height between 2000 and 1450 B.C.E. The palace at Knossus, the royal seat of the kings, was an elaborate structure that

Map 4.2 Minoan Crete and Mycenaean Greece

included numerous private living rooms for the royal family and workshops for making decorated vases, ivory figurines, and jewelry. The complex even had bathrooms with elaborate drains like those found at Mohenjo-daro in India. The rooms were decorated with brightly colored frescoes showing sporting events and nature scenes.

The centers of Minoan civilization on Crete eventually suffered a collapse. Some historians once believed that a tsunami triggered by a powerful volcanic eruption on the island of Thera was responsible for destroying towns and ships on the north coast of Crete, but the latest dating of that eruption places it in the seventeenth century B.C.E. Alternative evidence shows that mainland Greeks—the Mycenaeans—invaded and pillaged many centers, including Knossus, which was destroyed around 1400 B.C.E. However, Knossus was soon rebuilt and made the chief administrative center on Crete for the Mycenaeans.

4-1b The First Greek State: Mycenae

The term *Mycenaean* (my-suh-NEE-uhn) is derived from Mycenae (my-SEE-nee), a remarkable fortified site excavated by amateur German archaeologist Heinrich Schliemann (HYN-rikh SHLEE-mahn) starting in 1870. Mycenae was one center in a civilization that flourished between 1600 and 1100 B.C.E. The Mycenaean Greeks were part of the Indo-European family of peoples (see Chapter 1) who spread from their original location into southern and western Europe, India, and Persia. One group entered the territory of Greece from the north around 1900 B.C.E. and eventually managed to gain control of the Greek mainland and develop a civilization.

Mycenaean civilization, which reached its high point between 1400 and 1200 B.C.E., consisted of several powerful monarchies based in fortified palace complexes that were built on hills and surrounded by gigantic stone walls such as those found at Mycenae. These various centers of power probably formed a loose confederacy of independent states, with Mycenae being the strongest.

The Mycenaeans were above all a warrior people who prided themselves on their heroic deeds in battle. Some scholars believe that the Mycenaeans spread outward and conquered Crete. The most famous of all their supposed military adventures has come down to us in the epic poetry of Homer (see "Homer" in the section titled "The Greeks in a Dark Age"). Did the Mycenaean Greeks, led by King Agamemnon of Mycenae, sack the city of Troy on the northwestern coast of Asia Minor around 1250 B.C.E.? Scholars have debated this question ever since Schliemann's excavations began. Some believe that Homer's account does have a basis in fact, although little archeological evidence actually supports it.

By the late thirteenth century B.C.E., Mycenaean Greece was showing signs of serious trouble because of two causes—earthquakes and attacks. Earthquakes caused widespread damage, as did attacks from without. Mycenae itself was torched around 1190 B.C.E., and other Mycenaean centers show a similar pattern of destruction as new waves of Greek-speaking invaders moved into Greece from the north. By 1100 B.C.E., Mycenaean culture was coming to an end, and the Greek world was entering a new period of considerable insecurity.

4-1c The Greeks in a "Dark Age" (ca. 1100 – ca. 750 B.C.E.)

After the collapse of Mycenaean civilization, Greece entered a difficult period in which population declined and food production dropped. Because of the difficult conditions and our lack of knowledge about the period, historians refer to it as the "Dark Age," but many historians now view it more as a period of transition from the Bronze Age to the Iron Age in Greece. Iron replaced bronze in the construction of weapons, making them affordable for more people. And farming tools made of iron helped reverse the decline in food production and lead to a revival of farming by 850 B.C.E. At the same time, other new developments were forming the basis for a revived Greece.

During this transitional period, large numbers of Greeks left the mainland and migrated across the Aegean Sea to various islands and especially to the southwestern shore of Asia Minor, a strip of territory that came to be called Ionia (y-OH-nee-uh). Two other major groups of Greeks settled in established parts of Greece. The Aeolian (ee-OH-lee-uhn) Greeks of northern and central Greece colonized the large island of Lesbos and the adjacent territory of the mainland. The Dorians (DOR-ee-unz) established themselves in southwestern Greece, especially in the Peloponnesus, as well as on some of the southern Aegean islands, including Crete.

Other important activities occurred in this period as well. Greece saw a revival of some trade and some economic activity besides agriculture. In addition, at some point in the eighth century B.C.E., the Greeks adopted the Phoenician alphabet to give themselves a new system of writing. And near the end of this period appeared the work of Homer, who has come to be viewed as one of the greatest poets of all time.

Homer The first great epics of early Greece, the *Iliad* and the *Odyssey*, were based on stories that had been passed down from generation to generation. It is generally assumed that early in the eighth century B.C.E. Homer made use of these oral traditions to compose the *Iliad*, his epic poem of the Trojan War. The war was sparked by Paris, a prince of Troy, who kidnapped Helen, wife of the king of the Greek state of Sparta, outraging the Greeks. Under the leadership of the Spartan king's brother, Agamemnon of Mycenae, the Greeks attacked Troy. After ten years of combat, the Greeks finally sacked the city. The *Iliad* is not so much the story of the war itself, however, as it is the tale of the Greek hero Achilles (uh-KIL-eez) and how the "wrath of Achilles" led to disaster. The *Odyssey*, Homer's other masterpiece, is an epic romance that recounts the journeys of another Greek hero, Odysseus (oh-DISS-ee-uss), from the fall

HISTORICAL VOICES

Homer's Ideal of Excellence

Family & Society   THE *ILIAD* AND THE *ODYSSEY*, which the Greeks believed were written by Homer, were used as basic texts for the education of Greeks for hundreds of years during antiquity. This passage from the *Iliad*, describing the encounter between Hector, prince of Troy, and his wife, Andromache (an-DRAH-muh-kee), illustrates the Greek ideal of gaining honor through combat. At the end of the passage, Homer also reveals what became the Greek attitude toward women: they are supposed to spin and weave and take care of their households and children.

Homer, *Iliad*

Hector looked at his son and smiled, but said nothing. Andromache, bursting into tears, went up to him and put her hand in his. "Hector," she said, "you are possessed. This bravery of yours will be your end. You do not think of your little boy or your unhappy wife, whom you will make a widow soon. Some day the Achaeans [Greeks] are bound to kill you in a massed attack. And when I lose you I might as well be dead. . . . I have no father, no mother, now. . . . I had seven brothers too at home. In one day all of them went down to Hades' House. The great Achilles of the swift feet killed them all. . . .

"So you, Hector, are father and mother and brother to me, as well as my beloved husband. Have pity on me now; stay here on the tower; and do not make your boy an orphan and your wife a widow. . . ."

"All that, my dear," said the great Hector of the glittering helmet, "is surely my concern. But if I hid myself like a coward and refused to fight, I could never face the Trojans and the Trojan ladies in their trailing gowns. Besides, it would go against the grain, for I have trained myself always, like a good soldier, to take my place in the front line and win glory for my father and myself. . . ."

As he finished, glorious Hector held out his arms to take his boy. . . . Then he kissed his son, dandled him in his arms, and prayed to Zeus and the other gods: "Zeus, and you other gods, grant that this boy of mine may be, like me, preeminent in Troy; as strong and brave as I; a mighty king of Ilium. May people say, when he comes back from battle, 'Here is a better man than his father.' Let him bring home the bloodstained armor of the enemy he has killed, and make his mother happy."

Hector handed the boy to his wife, who took him to her fragrant breast. She was smiling through her tears, and when her husband saw this he was moved. He stroked her with his hand and said, "My dear, I beg you not to be too much distressed. No one is going to send me down to Hades before my proper time. But Fate is a thing that no man born of woman, coward or hero, can escape. Go home now, and attend to your own work, the loom and the spindle, and see that the maidservants get on with theirs. War is men's business; and this war is the business of every man in Ilium, myself above all."

 What important ideals for Greek men and women are revealed in this passage from the Iliad*? How do the women's ideals compare with those for ancient Indian and Chinese women?*

Source: The *Iliad* by Homer, trans. E. V. Rieu (London: Penguin Classics, 1950; revised translation, 2003).

---

of Troy until his eventual return to his wife, Penelope, twenty years later.

The Greeks regarded the *Iliad* and the *Odyssey* as authentic history as recorded by one poet, Homer. They gave the Greeks an idealized past, somewhat like the concept of the golden age in ancient China, with a legendary age of heroes, and the story came to be used as standard texts for the education of generations of Greek males. As one Athenian stated, "My father was anxious to see me develop into a good man . . . and as a means to this end he compelled me to memorize all of Homer."[1] The values Homer inculcated were essentially the aristocratic values of courage and honor (see Historical Voices, "Homer's Ideal of Excellence," above). It was important to strive for the excellence befitting a hero, which the Greeks called *arete*. In the warrior-aristocrat world of Homer, arete is won in a struggle or contest. Through his willingness to fight, the hero protects his family and friends, preserves his own and his family's honor, and earns his reputation. In the Homeric world, aristocratic women, too, were expected to pursue excellence. Penelope, for example, the wife of Odysseus, remains faithful to her husband and displays great courage and intelligence in preserving their household during her husband's long absence.

Experience an interactive version of this period in ⟲ MINDTAP

To later generations of Greeks, these heroic values formed the core of aristocratic virtue, a fact that explains the tremendous popularity of Homer as an educational tool. Homer gave to the Greeks a universally accepted model of heroism, honor, and nobility. But in time, as a new world of city-states emerged in Greece, new values of cooperation and community also transformed what the Greeks learned from Homer.

4-2 THE WORLD OF THE GREEK CITY-STATES (ca. 750 – ca. 500 B.C.E.)

 Focus Question: What were the chief features of the *polis,* or city-state, and how did the city-states of Athens and Sparta differ?

In the eighth century B.C.E., Greek civilization burst forth with new energies, beginning the period that historians have called the Archaic Age of Greece. Two major developments stand out in this era: the evolution of the city-state, or what the Greeks called a *polis* (plural, *poleis),* as the central institution in Greek life and the movement of people from the Greek states into lands bordering the Mediterranean and Black Seas.

4-2a The Polis

The Greek polis (plural, *poleis*) developed slowly, but by the eighth century B.C.E. it had emerged as a unique and fundamental institution in Greek society. In a physical sense, the polis encompassed a town, city, or even a village and its surrounding countryside. But each had a central place where the citizens of the polis could assemble for political, social, and religious activities. In some poleis, this central meeting point was a hill, like the Acropolis (uh-KRAH-puh-liss) at Athens, which could serve as a place of refuge during an attack and later, at some sites, came to be the religious center on which temples and public monuments were erected. Below the acropolis would be an *agora* (AG-er-ah), an open space or plaza that served both as a market and as a place where citizens could assemble.

Poleis varied greatly in size from a few square miles to a few hundred square miles. They also varied in population. Athens had a population of around 250,000 by the fifth century B.C.E. But most poleis were much smaller, consisting of only a few hundred to several thousand people.

Although our word *politics* is derived from the Greek term *polis,* the polis itself was much more than just a political institution. It was a community of citizens in which all political, economic, social, cultural, and religious activities were focused. As a community, the polis consisted of citizens with political rights (adult males), citizens with no political rights (women and children), and noncitizens (slaves and resident aliens). All citizens of a polis possessed fundamental rights, but these rights were coupled with responsibilities. Greek philosopher Aristotle argued that the citizen did not just belong to himself: "We must rather regard every citizen as belonging to the state." The unity of citizens was important and often meant that states would take an active role in directing the patterns of life. This idea of citizenship created a Greek society that was quite different from the societies of the despotic states we have examined and was an important element in the Greeks' contribution to Western civilization.

A New Military System: The Greek Way of War   As the polis developed, so did a new military system. In earlier times, wars in Greece had been fought by aristocratic cavalry soldiers—nobles on horseback. These aristocrats, who were large landowners, also dominated the political life of their poleis. By 700 B.C.E., however, a new military order came into being that was based on **hoplites** (HAHP-lyts), heavily armed infantrymen who wore bronze or leather helmets, breastplates, and greaves (shin guards). Each carried a round shield, a short sword, and a nine-foot-long thrusting spear. Hoplites advanced into battle as a unit, forming a **phalanx** (a rectangular formation) in tight order, usually eight ranks deep. As long as the hoplites kept their order, were not outflanked, and did not break, they either secured victory or at the least suffered no harm. The phalanx was easily routed, however, if it broke its order. Thus, the safety of the phalanx depended on the solidarity and discipline of its members. As one seventh-century B.C.E. poet observed, a good hoplite was a "short man firmly placed upon his legs, with a courageous heart, not to be uprooted from the spot where he plants his legs."[2] (See Image 4.2.)

The hoplite force had political as well as military repercussions. The aristocratic cavalry was now outdated. Because each hoplite provided his own armor, men of property, both aristocrats and small farmers, made up the new phalanx. Those who could become hoplites and fight for the state could also challenge aristocratic control. Thus, the development of the hoplite and phalanx became an important factor in the rise of democracy in Greece.

4-2b Greek Expansion and the Growth of Trade

Between 750 and 550 B.C.E., large numbers of Greeks from different city-states left their homelands to settle in distant lands. The growing gulf between rich and poor, overpopulation, and the development of trade

4.2 The hoplite forces. The Greek hoplites were infantrymen equipped with large round shields and long thrusting spears. In battle, they advanced in tight phalanx formation and were dangerous opponents as long as the formation remained unbroken. This vase painting of the seventh century B.C.E. shows two groups of hoplite warriors engaged in battle. The piper on the left is leading another line of soldiers preparing to enter the fray.

were all factors that led to the establishment of colonies. Each colony was founded as a polis and was usually independent of the mother polis (the *metropolis*) that had established it.

In the western Mediterranean, new Greek settlements were established along the coastline of southern Italy, southern France, eastern Spain, and northern Africa west of Egypt. To the north, some Greek states set up colonies in Thrace, where they sought good farmland to grow grains. Others also settled along the shores of the Black Sea and secured the approaches to it with cities on the Hellespont and Bosporus, most notably Byzantium, site of the later Constantinople (Istanbul). In establishing these settlements, the Greeks spread aspects of their culture throughout the Mediterranean basin. Moreover, colonization helped the Greeks foster a greater sense of Greek identity. Before the eighth century, Greek communities were mostly isolated from one another, leaving many neighboring states on unfriendly terms. Once Greeks from different communities went abroad and found peoples with different languages and customs, they became more aware of their own linguistic and cultural

similarities, thus aiding in the development of a common Greek identity.

Expansion abroad also led to increased trade and industry. The Greeks on the mainland sent their pottery, wine, and olive oil to the colonized areas. In return, they received grains and metals from the west and fish, timber, wheat, metals, and slaves from the Black Sea region. In many poleis, the expansion of trade and industry created a new group of rich men who perceived that the decisions of the polis could affect their businesses. They now desired new political privileges but found them impossible to gain because of the power of the ruling aristocrats. This desire for change soon led to political crises in many Greek states.

4-2c Tyranny in the Greek Polis

The aspirations of the new industrial and commercial groups laid the groundwork for the rise of **tyrants** in the seventh and sixth centuries B.C.E. They were not necessarily oppressive or wicked, as the modern English word *tyrant* connotes. Greek tyrants were rulers who came to power in an unconstitutional way; a tyrant was not subject

Many tyrants were actually aristocrats who ̇e control of ruling aristocratic factions in their ̇upport for the tyrants, however, came from the ̇ho had made their money in trade and industry, ̇m poor peasants, who were becoming increasingly indebted to landholding aristocrats. Both groups were opposed to the domination of political power by aristocratic **oligarchies** (*oligarchy* means "rule by the few").

Once in power, the tyrants built new marketplaces, temples, and walls that not only glorified their cities but also enhanced their own popularity. Tyrants also favored the interests of merchants and traders. Despite these achievements, however, **tyranny** was largely extinguished by the end of the sixth century B.C.E. Greeks believed in the rule of law, and tyranny made a mockery of that ideal.

Although tyranny did not last, it played a significant role in the evolution of Greek history by ending the rule of narrow aristocratic oligarchies. Once the tyrants were eliminated, the door was open to the participation of new and more people in governing the affairs of the community. Although this trend culminated in the development of democracy in some communities, in other states expanded oligarchies of one kind or another managed to remain in power. Greek states exhibited considerable variety in their governmental structures; this can perhaps best be seen by examining the two most famous and most powerful Greek city-states, Sparta and Athens.

4-2d Sparta

Located in the southeastern Peloponnesus, Sparta was like other Greek states in facing the need for more land. Instead of sending its people out to found new colonies, however, the Spartans conquered the neighboring Laconians and later, beginning around 730 B.C.E., undertook the conquest of neighboring Messenia despite its larger size and population. Messenia possessed a large, fertile plain ideal for growing grain. After its conquest in the seventh century B.C.E., the Messenians, like the Laconians earlier, were reduced to serfdom—they were known as *helots* (HEL-uts), a name derived from a Greek word for "capture"—and forced to work for the Spartans. But the helots drastically outnumbered the Spartan citizens—perhaps as much as ten to one—and constantly threatened to revolt. To ensure control over them, the Spartans made a conscious decision to create a military state.

The New Sparta   Between 800 and 600 B.C.E., the Spartans instituted a series of reforms that are associated with the name of the lawgiver Lycurgus (ly-KUR-guss) (see Historical Voices, "The Lycurgan Reforms," p. 91). Although historians are not sure whether Lycurgus really existed, there is no doubt about the result of the reforms that were made: the lives of Spartans were now rigidly organized and tightly controlled (to this day, the word *spartan* means "highly self-disciplined"). Boys were taken from their mothers at the age of seven and put under the control of the state. They lived in military-style barracks, where they were subjected to harsh discipline to make them tough and given an education that stressed military training and obedience to authority. At age twenty, Spartan males were enrolled in the army for regular military service. Although allowed to marry, they continued to live in the barracks and ate all their meals in public dining halls with fellow soldiers. Meals were simple; the famous Spartan black broth consisted of a piece of pork boiled in blood, salt, and vinegar, causing a visitor who ate in a public mess to remark that he now understood why Spartans were not afraid to die. At age thirty, Spartan males were allowed to vote in the assembly and live at home, but they remained in military service until age sixty.

While their husbands remained in military barracks, Spartan women lived at home. Because of this separation, they had considerable freedom of movement. Permitted to own and inherit land, Spartan women had greater power in the household than was common elsewhere in Greece and could even supervise large estates. They were encouraged to exercise and remain fit to bear and raise healthy children. Like the men, Spartan women engaged in athletic exercises in the nude. Many Spartan women upheld the strict Spartan values, expecting their husbands and sons to be brave in war. The story is told that as a Spartan mother was burying her son, an old woman came up to her and said, "You poor woman, what a misfortune." "No," replied the mother, "because I bore him so that he might die for Sparta and that is what has happened, as I wished."[3]

The Spartan State   The so-called Lycurgan reforms also reorganized the Spartan government, creating an oligarchy. Two kings were primarily responsible for military affairs and served as the leaders of the Spartan army on its campaigns. A group of five men known as the *ephors* (EFF-urz) were elected each year and were responsible for the education of youth and the conduct of all citizens. A council of elders composed of the two kings and twenty-eight male citizens over age sixty decided on the issues that would be presented to an assembly. This assembly of all-male citizens did not debate but only voted on the issues put before it by the council of elders.

To make their new military state secure, the Spartans deliberately turned their backs on the outside world. Foreigners were discouraged from visiting Sparta because they might bring in new ideas. Nor were Spartans, except for military reasons, allowed to travel abroad, where they might pick up new ideas dangerous to the stability of the state. Likewise, Spartan citizens were discouraged from studying philosophy, literature, the arts, or any other

The Lycurgan Reforms

Family & Society

TO MAINTAIN THEIR CONTROL OVER THE HELOTS, the Spartans instituted the reforms that created their military state. In this account of the lawgiver Lycurgus, Greek historian Plutarch discusses the effect of these reforms on the treatment and education of boys.

Plutarch, *Lycurgus*

Lycurgus was of another mind; he would not have masters bought out of the market for his young Spartans, . . . nor was it lawful, indeed, for the father himself to breed up the children after his own fancy; but as soon as they were seven years old they were to be enrolled in certain companies and classes, where they all lived under the same order and discipline, doing their exercises and taking their play together. Of these, he who showed the most conduct and courage was made captain; they had their eyes always upon him, obeyed his orders, and underwent patiently whatsoever punishment he inflicted; so that the whole course of their education was one continued exercise of a ready and perfect obedience. The old men, too, were spectators of their performances, and often raised quarrels and disputes among them, to have a good opportunity of finding out their different characters, and of seeing which would be valiant, which a coward, when they should come to more dangerous encounters. Reading and writing they gave them, just enough to serve their turn; their chief care was to make them good subjects, and to teach them to endure pain and conquer in battle. To this end, as they grew in years, their discipline was proportionately increased; their heads were close-clipped, they were accustomed to go barefoot, and for the most part to play naked.

After they were twelve years old, they were no longer allowed to wear any undergarments; they had one coat to serve them a year; their bodies were hard and dry, with but little acquaintance of baths and unguents; these human indulgences they were allowed only on some few particular days in the year. They lodged together in little bands upon beds made of the rushes which grew by the banks of the river Eurotas, which they were to break off with their hands with a knife; if it were winter, they mingled some thistle down with their rushes, which it was thought had the property of giving warmth. By the time they were come to this age there was not any of the more hopeful boys who had not a lover to bear him company. The old men, too, had an eye upon them, coming often to the grounds to hear and see them contend either in wit or strength with one another, and this as seriously . . . as if they were their fathers, their tutors, or their magistrates; so that there scarcely was any time or place without someone present to put them in mind of their duty, and punish them if they had neglected it.

[Spartan boys were also encouraged to steal their food.] They stole, too, all other meat they could lay their hands on, looking out and watching all opportunities, when people were asleep or more careless than usual. If they were caught, they were not only punished with whipping, but hunger, too, being reduced to their ordinary allowance, which was but very slender, and so contrived on purpose, that they might set about to help themselves, and be forced to exercise their energy and address. This was the principal design of their hard fare.

 What does this passage from Plutarch's account of Lycurgus reveal about the nature of the Spartan state? Why would the entire program have been distasteful to the Athenians?

Source: Plutarch, *The Lives of the Noble Grecians and Romans*, translated by John Dryden, and revised by Arthur Hugh Clough. (New York: Modern Library, 1992).

subject that might encourage new thoughts. The art of war was the Spartan ideal, and all other arts were frowned on.

4-2e Athens

By 700 B.C.E., Athens had established a unified polis on the peninsula of Attica. Although early Athens had been ruled by a monarchy, it had fallen under the control of its aristocrats by the seventh century B.C.E. They possessed the best land and controlled political life by means of a council of nobles who were assisted by a board of nine officials called *archons*. Although there was an assembly of full citizens, it possessed few powers.

Near the end of the seventh century B.C.E., Athens faced political turmoil because of serious economic problems. Increasing numbers of Athenian farmers found themselves sold into slavery when they were unable to repay loans they had obtained from their aristocratic neighbors, pledging themselves as collateral. Repeatedly, there were cries to cancel the debts and give land to the poor.

In 594 B.C.E., the ruling Athenian aristocrats responded to this crisis by giving full power to make changes to Solon (SOH-lun), a reform-minded aristocrat. Solon canceled all land debts, outlawed new loans based on humans as collateral, and freed people who had fallen into slavery for debts. He refused, however, to carry out land redistribution. Thus, Solon's reforms, though popular, did not truly solve Athens's problems. Aristocratic factions continued to vie for power, and poor peasants could not get land. Internal strife finally led to the very institution Solon had hoped to avoid—tyranny. Pisistratus (puh-SIS-truh-tuss), an aristocrat, seized power in 560 B.C.E. Pursuing a foreign policy that aided Athenian trade, Pisistratus remained popular with the mercantile and industrial classes. But the Athenians rebelled against his son and ended the tyranny in 510 B.C.E. When the aristocrats attempted to reestablish an aristocratic oligarchy, Cleisthenes (KLYSS-thuh-neez), another aristocratic reformer, opposed their plan and, with the backing of the Athenian people, gained the upper hand in 508 B.C.E.

Cleisthenes created the Council of Five Hundred to supervise foreign affairs and the treasury and propose laws that would be voted on by the assembly. The Athenian assembly, composed of all male citizens, was given final authority on the passing of laws after free and open debate. Because the assembly of citizens now had the central role in the Athenian political system, the reforms of Cleisthenes created the foundations for Athenian democracy.

4-3 THE HIGH POINT OF GREEK CIVILIZATION: CLASSICAL GREECE

 Focus Questions: What did the Greeks mean by *democracy*, and in what ways was the Athenian political system a democracy? What effect did the two great conflicts of the fifth century—the Persian wars and the Peloponnesian War—have on Greek civilization?

Classical Greece is the name given to the period of Greek history from around 500 B.C.E. to the conquest of Greece by the Macedonian king Philip II in 338 B.C.E. Many of the cultural contributions of the Greeks

occurred during this period. The age began with a mighty confrontation between the Greek states and the mammoth Persian Empire.

4-3a The Challenge of Persia

As the Greeks spread throughout the Mediterranean, they came into contact with the Persian Empire to the east. The Greeks were still divided into independent city-states, but the growing Persian threat would serve to deepen an increased sense of Greek cultural identity. The Ionian Greek cities in western Asia Minor had already fallen subject to the Persian Empire by the mid-sixth century B.C.E. An unsuccessful revolt by the Ionian cities in 499 B.C.E., assisted by the Athenians, led the Persian ruler Darius (duh-RY-uss) to seek revenge by attacking the mainland Greeks. In 490 B.C.E., the Persians landed an army on the plain of Marathon, only twenty-six miles from Athens. The Athenians and their allies were clearly outnumbered, but the Greek hoplites charged across the plain of Marathon and crushed the Persian forces. The Persians did not mount another attack against mainland Greece for ten years. A Persian victory might well have cut short the Athenian experiment with democracy.

Xerxes (ZURK-seez), the new Persian monarch after the death of Darius in 486 B.C.E., vowed revenge and planned to invade Greece. In preparation for the attack, some of the Greek states formed a defensive league under Spartan leadership. In the meantime, the Athenians had acquired a new leader, Themistocles (thuh-MISS-tuh-kleez), who persuaded his fellow citizens to pursue a new military policy by developing a navy. By the time of the Persian invasion in 480 B.C.E., the Athenians had produced a fleet of some 200 vessels.

Xerxes led a massive invasion force into Greece: close to 150,000 troops, almost 700 naval ships, and hundreds of supply ships to keep the large army fed. The Greeks tried to delay the Persians at the pass of Thermopylae (thur-MAHP-uh-lee) along the main road into central Greece. A Greek force numbering close to 9,000 men—under the leadership of a Spartan king and his contingent of 300 Spartans—held off the Persian army for several days. The Spartan troops were especially brave. When told that Persian arrows would darken the sky in battle, one Spartan warrior supposedly responded: "That is good news. We will fight in the shade!" Unfortunately for the Greeks, a traitor told the Persians how to use a mountain path that would allow them to outflank the Greek force. The Spartans fought to the last man.

The Athenians, now threatened by the onslaught of the Persian forces, abandoned their city. While the Persians sacked and burned Athens, the Greek fleet remained offshore near the island of Salamis (SAH-luh-miss) and challenged the Persian navy. Although the Greeks were outnumbered, they managed to outmaneuver the Persian fleet and utterly defeated it. A few months later, early in 479 B.C.E., the Greeks formed the largest Greek army seen up to that time and decisively defeated the Persian army at Plataea (pluh-TEE-uh) northwest of Attica. The Greeks had won the war and were now free to pursue their own destiny.

4-3b The Growth of an Athenian Empire in the Age of Pericles

After the defeat of the Persians, Athens took over the leadership of the Greek world by forming a defensive alliance against the Persians called the Delian League in the winter of 478–477 B.C.E. The league had its main headquarters on the island of Delos, but its chief officials, including the treasurers and commanders of the fleet, were Athenian. Under the leadership of the Athenians, the Delian League pursued the attack against the Persian Empire and liberated virtually every Greek state in the Aegean from Persian control. In 454 B.C.E., the Athenians moved the treasury of the league from Delos to Athens. By controlling the Delian League, Athens had created an empire.

At home, Athenians favored the new imperial policy, especially after 461 B.C.E., when politics came to be dominated by a political faction led by a young aristocrat named Pericles (PER-i-kleez). Under Pericles, who remained a leading figure in Athenian politics for more than three decades, Athens embarked on a policy of expanding democracy at home and its new empire abroad. This period of Athenian and Greek history, which historians have subsequently labeled the Age of Pericles, witnessed the height of Athenian power and the culmination of its brilliance as a civilization.

During the Age of Pericles, the Athenians became deeply attached to their democratic system. The sovereignty of the people was embodied in the assembly, which consisted of all male citizens over eighteen years of age. In the fifth century B.C.E., that was probably a group of around 43,000. Not all attended, however, and the number present at the meetings, which were held every ten days on a hillside east of the Acropolis, seldom reached 6,000. The assembly passed all laws and made final decisions on war and foreign policy.

Routine administration of public affairs was handled by a large body of city magistrates, who were usually chosen by lot without regard to class and typically served only one-year terms. This meant that many male citizens held public office at some time in their lives. A board of ten officials known as generals—strategoi (strah-tay-GOH-ee)—was elected by public vote to guide affairs of state, although

their power depended on the respect they had attained. Generals were usually wealthy aristocrats, even though the people were free to select otherwise. The generals could be reelected, enabling individual leaders to play an important political role. Pericles's frequent reelection (fifteen times) as one of the ten generals made him one of the leading politicians between 461 and 429 B.C.E.

The Athenians came to call their form of government *democracy*. Power was in the hands of the people; male citizens voted in the assemblies and served as jurors in the courts. Lower-class citizens were now eligible for public offices formerly closed to them. Pericles expanded democracy and also introduced state pay for officeholders, including the widely held jury duty. This meant that even poor citizens could afford to participate in public affairs and hold public office. Nevertheless, although the Athenians developed a system of government that was unique in its time in which citizens had equal rights and the people were the government, aristocrats continued to hold the most important offices, and many people—including women, slaves, and foreigners residing in Athens—were not given the same political rights.

Under Pericles, Athens became the leading center of Greek culture. The Persians had destroyed much of the city during the Persian wars, but Pericles used the money from the treasury of the Delian League to set in motion a massive rebuilding program. New temples and statues soon made the greatness of Athens more visible. Art, architecture, and philosophy flourished, and Pericles proudly boasted that Athens had become the "school of Greece." But the achievements of Athens alarmed the other Greek states, especially Sparta, and soon all Greece was confronting a new war.

4-3c The Great Peloponnesian War and the Decline of the Greek States

During the forty years after the defeat of the Persians, the Greek world came to be divided into two major camps: Sparta and its supporters and the Athenian maritime empire. Sparta and its allies feared the growing Athenian Empire. Then, too, Athens and Sparta had created two decidedly different kinds of societies, and neither state was able to tolerate the other's system. A series of disputes finally led to the outbreak of war in 431 B.C.E. (see Map 4.3).

At the beginning of the war, both sides believed they had winning strategies. The Athenians planned to remain behind the protective walls of Athens while the overseas empire and the navy would keep them supplied. Pericles knew that the Spartans and their allies could beat the Athenians in open battles, which was the chief aim of the Spartan strategy. The Spartans and their allies

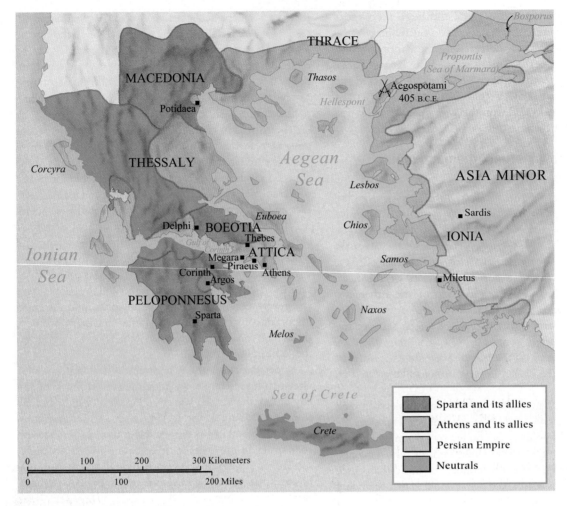

Map 4.3 The Great Peloponnesian War (431–404 B.C.E.)

attacked Athens, hoping that the Athenians would send out their army to fight beyond the walls. But Pericles was convinced that Athens was secure behind its walls and stayed put.

In the second year of the war, however, plague devastated the crowded city of Athens and wiped out possibly one-third of the population. Pericles himself died the following year (429 B.C.E.), a severe loss to Athens. Despite the losses from the plague, the Athenians fought on in a struggle that dragged on for twenty-seven years. A final crushing blow came in 405 B.C.E. when the Athenian fleet was destroyed at Aegospotami (ee-guh-SPOT-uh-my) on the Hellespont. Athens was besieged and surrendered in 404 B.C.E. Its walls were torn down, the navy was disbanded, and the Athenian Empire was no more. The great war was finally over.

The Great Peloponnesian War weakened the major Greek states and led to new alliances among them. The next seventy years of Greek history are a sorry tale of efforts by Sparta, Athens, and new Greek power Thebes to dominate Greek affairs. In continuing their petty wars, the Greeks remained oblivious to the growing power of Macedonia to their north.

4-3d The Culture of Classical Greece

Classical Greece was a period of remarkable intellectual and cultural growth throughout the Greek world, and Periclean Athens was the most important center of classical Greek culture.

The Writing of History History as we know it—the systematic analysis of past events—was introduced to the Western world by the Greeks. Herodotus (huh-ROD-uh-tuss) (ca. 484 – ca. 425 B.C.E.) wrote *History of the Persian Wars*, which is commonly regarded as the first real history in

Western civilization. The central theme of Herodotus's work was the conflict between the Greeks and the Persians, which he viewed as a struggle between freedom and despotism.

Thucydides (thoo-SID-uh-deez) (ca. 460 – ca. 400 B.C.E.) was a better historian by far; indeed, he is considered the greatest historian of the ancient world. In his *History of the Peloponnesian War*, Thucydides examined the causes of the Peloponnesian War in a clear and objective fashion, placing much emphasis on accuracy and the precision of his facts. Thucydides also provided remarkable insight into the human condition. He believed that political situations recur in similar fashion and that the study of history is therefore of great value in understanding the present.

Greek Drama
Drama as we know it in Western culture originated with the Greeks. Plays were presented in outdoor theaters as part of religious festivals and followed a fairly stable form. Three male actors wore masks and acted all the parts. An all-male chorus spoke lines that explained and commented on the action.

The first Greek dramas were tragedies, plays based on the suffering of a hero and usually ending in disaster. Greek tragedies were sometimes presented in a trilogy (a set of three plays) built around a common theme. The only complete trilogy we possess, called the *Oresteia* (uh-res-TY-uh), was composed by Aeschylus (ESS-kuh-luss) (525–456 B.C.E.), the first tragedian whose plays are known to us. Two other great fifth-century Athenian playwrights were Sophocles (SAHF-uh-kleez) (ca. 496–406 B.C.E.) and Euripides (yoo-RIP-uh-deez) (ca. 485–406 B.C.E.). Greek tragedies dealt with universal themes still relevant to our day. They probed such issues as the nature of good and evil, the rights of the individual, the nature of divine forces, and the essence of human beings. Over and over, the tragic lesson was repeated: humans were free and yet could operate only within limitations imposed by the gods. Striving to do one's best may not always lead to success in human terms but is nevertheless always a worthy endeavor. Greek pride in human accomplishment and independence was real. As the chorus chanted in Sophocles's *Antigone* (an-TIG-uh-nee), "Is there anything more wonderful on Earth, our marvelous planet, than the miracle of man?"[4]

Greek comedy developed later. The plays of Aristophanes (ar-is-STAH-fuh-neez) (ca. 450 – ca. 385 B.C.E.), who used both grotesque masks and obscene jokes to entertain the Athenian audience, are examples of Old Comedy. But comedy in Athens was also more clearly political than tragedy and was used to attack or savagely satirize both politicians and intellectuals. Of special importance was Aristophanes' opposition to the Peloponnesian War.

The Arts: The Classical Ideal
The artistic standards established by the Greeks of the classical period largely dominated the arts of the Western world until the nineteenth and twentieth centuries. Classical Greek art was concerned with expressing eternally true ideals. Its subject matter was basically the human being as harmoniously expressed as an object of great beauty. The classical style—based on the ideals of reason, moderation, symmetry, balance, and harmony in all things—was meant to civilize the emotions.

In architecture, the most important form was the temple dedicated to a god or goddess. At the center of Greek temples were walled rooms that housed the statues of deities and treasuries where gifts to the gods and goddesses were safeguarded. These central rooms were surrounded by a screen of columns that made Greek temples open structures rather than closed ones. The columns were originally made of wood but were changed to marble in the fifth century B.C.E.

Some of the finest examples of Greek classical architecture were built in fifth-century Athens. The most famous building was the Parthenon, which was built between 447 and 432 B.C.E. and now considered the greatest example of the classical Greek temple (see Image 4.3).

Adam Crowley/Photodisc/Getty Images

4.3 The Parthenon. The arts in classical Greece were designed to express the eternal ideals of reason, moderation, symmetry, balance, and harmony. In architecture, the most important form was the temple, and the greatest example is the Parthenon, built in Athens between 447 and 432 B.C.E. Located on the Acropolis, the Parthenon was dedicated to Athena, the patron goddess of Athens, but it also served as a shining example of the power and wealth of the Athenian Empire.

Consecrated to Athena, the patron goddess of Athens, the Parthenon was also dedicated to the glory of the city-state and its inhabitants. The structure typifies the principles of classical architecture: calmness, clarity, and the avoidance of superfluous detail.

Greek sculpture also developed a classical style. Statues of the male nude, the favorite subject of Greek sculptors, exhibited relaxed attitudes; their faces were self-assured, their bodies flexible and smoothly muscled. Although the figures possessed natural features that made them lifelike, Greek sculptors sought to achieve not realism but a standard of ideal beauty. Polyclitus (pahl-ee-KLY-tuss), a fifth-century sculptor, wrote a treatise (now lost) on proportion that he illustrated in a work known as the *Doryphoros* (doh-RIF-uh-rohss) (see Image 4.4). His theory maintained that the use of ideal proportions, based on mathematical ratios found in nature, could produce an ideal human form, beautiful in its perfected and refined features. This search for ideal beauty was the dominant feature of the classical standard in sculpture.

The Greek Love of Wisdom Athens became the foremost intellectual and artistic center in classical Greece. Its reputation was perhaps strongest of all in philosophy, a Greek term that originally meant "love of wisdom." Socrates, Plato, and Aristotle raised basic questions that have been debated for more than 2,000 years; they are, for the most part, the very same philosophical questions we wrestle with today (see Comparative Essay, "The Axial Age," p. 97, and Image 4.5).

Socrates (SAHK-ruh-teez) (469–399 B.C.E.) left no writings, but we know about him from his pupils. Socrates was a stonemason whose true love was philosophy. He taught many pupils, although not for pay, because he believed that the goal of education was solely to improve the individual. His approach, still known as the **Socratic method**, employs a question-and-answer technique to lead pupils to see things for themselves using their own reason. Socrates believed that all knowledge is within each person; only critical examination was needed to call it forth. This was the real task of philosophy, because "the unexamined life is not worth living."

Socrates questioned authority, and this soon led him into trouble. Athens had had a tradition of free thought and inquiry, but its defeat in the Peloponnesian War had created an environment intolerant of open debate. Socrates was accused of corrupting the youth of Athens by his teaching. An Athenian jury convicted him and sentenced him to death.

One of Socrates's disciples was Plato (PLAY-toh) (ca. 429–347 B.C.E.), considered by many the greatest

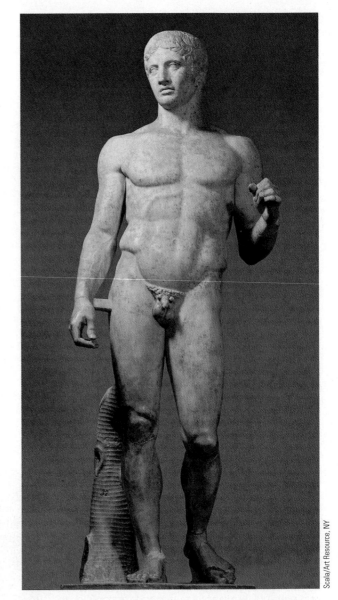

4.4 Doryphoros. This statue, known as the *Doryphoros*, or spear carrier, is by Polyclitus, a fifth-century B.C.E. sculptor who believed it illustrated the ideal proportions of the human figure. Classical Greek sculpture moved away from the stiffness of earlier figures but retained the young male nude as the favorite subject. The statues became more lifelike, with relaxed poses and flexible, smooth-muscled bodies. The aim of sculpture, however, was not simply realism but the expression of ideal beauty.

philosopher of Western civilization. Unlike his master Socrates, who wrote nothing, Plato wrote a great deal. He was fascinated with the question of reality: how do we know what is real? According to Plato, a higher world of eternal, unchanging Ideas or Forms has always existed. To know these Forms is to know truth. These ideal Forms constitute reality and can be apprehended only by a

The Axial Age

Art & Ideas By the fourth century B.C.E., important regional civilizations existed in China, India, Southwest Asia, and the Mediterranean basin. During their formative periods between 700 and 300 B.C.E., all were characterized by the emergence of religious and philosophical thinkers who established ideas—or "axes"—that remained the basis for religions and philosophical thought in those societies for hundreds of years. Consequently, some historians have referred to the period when these ideas developed as the "Axial Age."

By the seventh century B.C.E., concepts of monotheism had developed in Persia through the teachings of Zoroaster and in Canaan through the Hebrew prophets. In Judaism, the Hebrews developed a world religion that influenced the later religions of Christianity and Islam. During the fifth and fourth centuries B.C.E. in Greece, philosophers Socrates, Plato, and Aristotle not only proposed philosophical and political ideas crucial to the Greek world and later Western civilization but also conceived of a rational method of inquiry that became important to modern science.

During the sixth century B.C.E., two major schools of thought—Confucianism and Daoism—emerged in China. Both sought to spell out the principles that would create a stable order in society. Although their views of reality were diametrically opposed, both came to have an impact on Chinese civilization that lasted into the twentieth century.

Two of the world's greatest religions, Hinduism and Buddhism, began in India during the Axial Age. Hinduism was an outgrowth of the religious beliefs of the Aryan peoples who settled in India. These ideas were expressed in the sacred texts known as the Vedas and in the Upanishads, which were commentaries on the Vedas compiled in the sixth century B.C.E. With its belief in reincarnation, Hinduism provided justification for India's rigid class system. Buddhism was the product of one man, Siddhartha Gautama, known as the Buddha, who lived in the sixth century B.C.E. The Buddha's simple message of achieving wisdom created a new spiritual philosophy

Erich Lessing/Art Resource, NY

4.5 Philosophers in the Axial Age. This mosaic from the Roman city of Pompeii depicts a gathering of Greek philosophers at the school of Plato.

that would rival Hinduism. Although a product of India, Buddhism also spread to other parts of the world.

Although these philosophies and religions developed in different areas of the world, they had features in common. Like the Chinese philosophers Confucius and Lao Tzu, the Greek philosophers Plato and Aristotle had different points of view about the nature of reality. Thinkers in India and China also developed rational methods of inquiry similar to those of Plato and Aristotle. And regardless of their origins, when we speak of Judaism, Hinduism, Buddhism, Confucianism, Daoism, or Greek philosophical thought, we realize that the ideas of the Axial Age not only spread around the world at different times but also remain an integral part of our world today.

 What do historians mean when they speak of the Axial Age? What do you think could explain the emergence of similar ideas in different parts of the world during this period?

trained mind, which, of course, is the goal of philosophy. The objects that we perceive with our senses are simply reflections of the ideal Forms. They are shadows; reality is in the Forms themselves.

Plato's ideas of government were set out in a dialogue titled *The Republic*. Based on his experience in Athens, Plato had come to distrust the workings of democracy. Individuals could not attain an ethical life unless they lived in a just and rational state. Plato constructed an ideal state in which the population was divided into three basic groups. At the top was an upper class of philosopher-kings: "Unless . . . political power and philosophy meet together . . . there can be no rest from troubles . for states, nor yet, as I believe, for all mankind."[5] The second group consisted of the courageous— the warriors who protected the society. All the rest made up the masses, essentially people driven not by wisdom or courage but by desire. They would be the producers of society—the artisans, tradespeople, and farmers. Contrary to common Greek custom, Plato also believed that men and women should have the same education and equal access to all positions.

Plato established a school at Athens known as the Academy. One of his pupils was Aristotle (AR-iss-tot-ul) (384–322 B.C.E.), who did not accept Plato's theory of ideal Forms. Instead, he believed that by examining individual objects, we can perceive their form and arrive at universal principles, but these principles do not exist as a separate higher world of reality beyond material things; rather they are a part of things themselves. Aristotle's interests, then, lay in analyzing and classifying things based on thorough research and investigation. His interests were wide-ranging, and he wrote treatises on an enormous number of subjects: ethics, logic, politics, poetry, astronomy, geology, biology, and physics.

Like Plato, Aristotle wished for an effective form of government that would rationally direct human affairs. For his *Politics,* he examined the constitutions of 158 states and identified three good forms of government: monarchy, aristocracy, and constitutional government. He favored constitutional government as the best form for most people.

Aristotle's philosophical and political ideas played an enormous role in the development of Western thought during the Middle Ages (see Chapter 12). So did his ideas on women. Aristotle maintained that women were biologically inferior to men: "A woman is, as it were, an infertile male. She is female in fact on account of a kind of inadequacy." Therefore, according to Aristotle, women must be subordinated to men, not only in the community but also in marriage: "The association between husband and wife is clearly an aristocracy. The man rules by virtue of merit, and in the sphere that is his by right; but he hands over to his wife such matters as are suitable for her."[6]

4-3e Greek Religion

Greek religion played an important role in Greek society and was intricately connected to every aspect of daily life; it was both social and practical. Public festivals originated from religious practices and served specific functions: boys were prepared to be warriors, girls to be mothers. Because religion was related to every aspect of life, citizens had to have a proper attitude toward the gods. Religion was a civic cult necessary for the well-being of the state. Temples dedicated to a god or goddess were the major buildings of Greek society.

The poetry of Homer gave an account of the gods that provided Greek religion with a definite structure. Over a period of time, most Greeks came to accept a basic polytheistic religion with twelve chief gods and goddesses who supposedly lived on Mount Olympus, the highest mountain in Greece. Among the twelve were Zeus (ZOOSS), the chief deity and father of the gods; Athena, goddess of wisdom and crafts; Apollo, god of the sun and poetry; Aphrodite (af-ruh-DAHY-tee), goddess of love; and Poseidon (poh-SAHYD-n), brother of Zeus and god of the seas and earthquakes.

Because the Greeks wanted the gods to look favorably on their activities, ritual assumed enormous proportions in Greek religion. Prayers were often combined with gifts to the gods based on the principle "I give so that you, the gods, will give in return." Ritual meant sacrifices, whether of animals or agricultural products. Animal sacrifices were burned on an altar in front of a temple or on a small altar in front of a home.

Festivals also developed as a way to honor the gods and goddesses. Some of these (the Panhellenic celebrations) came to have significance for all Greeks and were held at special locations, such as those dedicated to the worship of Zeus at Olympia or to Apollo at Delphi. The great festivals featured numerous events in honor of the gods, including athletic competitions to which all Greeks were invited.

According to tradition, such games were first conducted at the Olympic festival in 776 B.C.E. and then held every four years thereafter to honor Zeus. Initially, the Olympic contests consisted of foot races and wrestling, but later boxing, javelin throwing, and various other contests were added. Competitions were always between individuals, not groups, and were not without danger to the participants. Athletes competed in the nude, and rules were rather relaxed. Wrestlers, for example, were allowed to gouge eyes and even pick up their opponents and bring them down head first onto a hard surface. Some athletes were killed during the games. Given the hatred that often existed between city-states in ancient Greece, their deaths were not always accidental.

The Olympic games, combined with other all-Greek athletic games, served a valuable role. The system of Greek poleis had led to separation and individual goals. But participation in these games also caused Greeks to become more aware of a wider sense of community as Greeks. By the sixth century, this led to an emerging sense of Greekness. And as we have seen, the later threat from the Persians would serve to solidify this growing cultural identity.

The Greek Olympic games came to an end in 393 C.E. when a Christian Roman emperor banned them as pagan exercises. Fifteen hundred years later, the games were revived through the efforts of a French baron, Pierre de Coubertin (PYAYR duh koo-ber-TANH). In 1896, the first modern Olympic games were held in Athens, Greece.

As another practical side of Greek religion, Greeks wanted to know the will of the gods. To do so, they made use of the oracle, a sacred shrine dedicated to a god or goddess who revealed the future. The most famous was the oracle of Apollo at Delphi (DEL-fy), located on the side of Mount Parnassus (par-NASS-suss), overlooking the Gulf of Corinth. At Delphi, a priestess listened to questions while in a state of ecstasy that was believed to be induced by Apollo. Her responses were interpreted by the priests and given in verse form to the person asking questions. Representatives of states and individuals traveled to Delphi to consult the oracle of Apollo. Responses were often enigmatic and at times even politically motivated. Croesus (KREE-suss), the king of Lydia in Asia Minor who was known for his incredible wealth, sent messengers to the oracle at Delphi, asking whether he should go to war with the Persians. The oracle replied that if Croesus attacked the Persians, he would destroy a mighty empire. Overjoyed to hear these words, Croesus made war on the Persians but was crushed. A mighty empire was indeed destroyed—his own.

4-3f Daily Life in Classical Athens

Above all, the polis was a male community: only adult male citizens took part in public life. In Athens, this meant the exclusion of women, slaves, and foreign residents, or roughly 85 percent of the population of Attica. There were probably 150,000 citizens in Athens, of whom some 43,000 were adult males who exercised political power. Resident foreigners numbered around 35,000 and received the protection of the laws but were subject to some of the responsibilities of citizens, including military service and the funding of festivals. The remaining social group, the slaves, numbered around 100,000. Most slaves in Athens worked in the home as cooks and maids or worked in the fields. Some were owned by the state and worked on public construction projects.

The Athenian economy was largely based on agriculture and trade. Athenians grew grains, vegetables, and fruit for local consumption. Grapes and olives were cultivated for wine and olive oil, which were used locally and exported. The Athenians also raised sheep and goats for wool and dairy products. Because of the size of the population and the lack of abundant fertile land, Athens had to import 50 to 80 percent of its grain, a staple in the Athenian diet. Trade was thus critical to the Athenian economy.

Family and Relationships The family was a central institution in ancient Athens. It was composed of husband, wife, and children (a nuclear family), although other dependent relatives and slaves were regarded as part of the family economic unit. The family's primary social function was to produce new citizens.

Adult female citizens could participate in most religious cults and festivals but were otherwise excluded from public life. They could not own property beyond personal items and always had male guardians. An Athenian woman was expected to be a good wife. Her foremost obligation was to bear children, especially male children who would preserve the family line. A wife was also to take care of her family and her house, either doing the household work herself or supervising the slaves who did the actual work (see Opposing Viewpoints, "Women in Athens and Sparta," p. 100).

Male homosexuality was also a prominent feature of Athenian life. The Greek homosexual ideal was a relationship between a mature man and a young male. Although the relationship was frequently physical, the Greeks also viewed it as educational. The older male (the "lover") won the love of his "beloved" through his value as a teacher and the devotion he demonstrated in training his charge. In a sense, this love relationship was seen as a way of initiating young males into the male world of political and military dominance. The Greeks did not feel that the coexistence of homosexual and heterosexual predilections created any special problems for individuals or their society.

Women in Athens and Sparta

Family & Society

IN CLASSICAL ATHENS, a woman's place was in the home. In the first selection, from a dialogue on estate management, Xenophon (ZEN-uh-fuhn) relates the instructions of an Athenian to his new wife. Although women in Sparta had the same responsibilities as women in Athens, they assumed somewhat different roles as a result of the Spartan lifestyle. The second, third, and fourth selections are taken from accounts by three ancient Greek writers and demonstrate these differences.

Xenophon, *Oeconomicus*

[Ischomachus addresses his new wife:] For it seems to me, dear, that the gods with great discernment have coupled together male and female, as they are called, chiefly in order that they may form a perfect partnership in mutual service. For, in the first place that the various species of living creatures may not fail, they are joined in wedlock for the production of children. Secondly, offspring to support them in old age is provided by this union, to human beings, at any rate. Thirdly, human beings live not in the open air, like beasts, but obviously need shelter. Nevertheless, those who mean to win stores to fill the covered place, have need of someone to work at the open-air occupations; since plowing, sowing, planting and grazing are all such open-air employments; and these supply the needful food. . . . For he made the man's body and mind more capable of enduring cold and heat, and journeys and campaigns; and therefore imposed on him the outdoor tasks. To the woman, since he had made her body less capable of such endurance, I take it that God has assigned the indoor tasks. And knowing that he had created in the woman and had imposed on her the nourishment of the infants, he meted out to her a larger portion of affection for new-born babes than to the man. . . .

Your duty will be to remain indoors and send out those servants whose work is outside, and superintend those who are to work indoors, and to receive the incomings, and distribute so much of them as must be spent, and watch over so much as is to be kept in store, and take care that the sum laid by for a year be not spent in a month. And when wool is brought to you, you must see that cloaks are made for those that want them. You must see too that the dry corn [grain] is in good condition for making food. One of the duties that fall to you, however,

will perhaps seem rather thankless: you will have to see that any servant who is ill is cared for.

Xenophon, *Constitution of the Spartans*

First, to begin at the beginning, I will start with the begetting of children. Elsewhere those girls who are going to have children and are considered to have been well brought up are nourished with the plainest diet which is practicable and the smallest amount of luxury good possible; wine is certainly not allowed them at all, or only if well diluted. Just as the majority of craftsmen are sedentary, the other Greeks expect their girls to sit quietly and work wool. But how can one expect girls brought up like this to give birth to healthy babies? Lycurgus [see below and next page] considered slave girls quite adequate to produce clothing, and thought that for free women the most important job was to bear children. In the first place, therefore, he prescribed physical training for the female sex no less than for the male; and next, just as for men, he arranged competitions of racing and strength for women also, thinking that if both parents were strong their children would be more robust.

Aristotle, *Politics*

Now, this license of the [Spartan] women, from the earliest times, was to be expected. For the men were absent from home for long periods of time on military expeditions, fighting [in wars] . . . And nearly two-fifths of the whole country is in the hands of women, both because there have been numerous heiresses, and because large dowries are customary. And yet it would have been better to have regulated them, and given none at all or small or even moderate ones. But at present it is possible for a man to give an inheritance to whomever he chooses.

Plutarch, *Lycurgus*

Because Lycurgus regarded education as the most important and finest duty of the legislator, he began at the earliest stage by looking at matters relating to marriages and births. . . . For he exercised the girls' bodies with races and wrestling and discus and javelin throwing, so that the embryos formed in them would have a strong start in strong bodies and develop better, and they would undergo their pregnancies with vigor and would cope well and easily with childbirth. He got rid of daintiness and sheltered upbringing and effeminacy of all kinds, by accustoming the girls no less than the young men to walking naked in processions and dancing and singing at certain festivals, when young men were present and watching. . . . The nudity of the girls had nothing disgraceful in it for modesty was present and immorality absent, but rather it made them accustomed to simplicity and enthusiastic as to physical fitness, and gave the female sex a taste of noble spirit, inasmuch as they too had a share in valor and ambition.

Sources: From *Ancient Greece: Social and Historical Documents from Archaic Times to the Death of Socrates*, edited by Matthew Dillon and Lynda Garland. London: Routledge, 1994, pp. 393–95. Copyright © 1994 Matthew and Lynda Garland. From Aristotle, *A Treatise on Government*, trans. William Ellis (J. M. Dent & Sons Ltd.: London, 1912), p. 1270a. From *Ideal Commonwealths: Plutarch's Lycurgus*, ed. Henry Morley, 5th ed. (George Rutledge and Sons, Limited, London, 1890).

 In what ways were the lifestyles of Athenian and Spartan women the same? In what ways were they different? How did the Athenian and Spartan views of the world shape their conceptions of gender and gender roles, and why were those conceptions different?

4-4 THE RISE OF MACEDONIA AND THE CONQUESTS OF ALEXANDER

 Focus Question: How was Alexander the Great able to amass his empire, and what was his legacy?

While the Greek city-states were continuing to fight each other, to their north a new and ultimately powerful kingdom was emerging in its own right. To the Greeks, the Macedonians were little more than barbarians, a mostly rural folk organized into tribes rather than city-states. Not until the end of the fifth century B.C.E. did Macedonia emerge as an important kingdom. But when Philip II (359–336 B.C.E.) came to the throne, he built an efficient army and turned Macedonia into the strongest power in the Greek world—one that was soon drawn into the conflicts among the Greeks.

The Athenians at last took notice of the new contender. Fear of Philip led them to ally with several other Greek states and confront the Macedonians at the Battle of Chaeronea (ker-uh-NEE-uh), near Thebes, in 338 B.C.E. The Macedonian army crushed the Greeks, and Philip quickly gained control of all Greece, bringing an end to the freedom of the Greek city-states. He insisted that the Greek states form a league and then cooperate with him in a war against Persia. Before Philip could undertake his invasion of Asia, however, he was assassinated, leaving the task to his son Alexander.

4-4a Alexander the Great

Alexander was only twenty when he became king of Macedonia. In many ways, he had been prepared to rule by his father, who had taken Alexander along on military campaigns and had given him control of the cavalry at the important Battle of Chaeronea. After his father's

assassination, Alexander moved quickly to assert his authority, securing the Macedonian frontiers and quashing a rebellion in Greece. He then turned to his father's dream, the invasion of the Persian Empire. (See Image 4.6.)

4.6 Alexander the Great. This marble head of Alexander the Great was made in the second or first century B.C.E. The long hair and tilt of his head reflect the description of Alexander in the literary sources of the time. Alexander claimed to be descended from Heracles, a Greek hero worshiped as a god, and when he proclaimed himself pharaoh of Egypt, he gained recognition as a living deity. It is reported that one statue, now lost, showed Alexander gazing at Zeus. At the base of the statue were the words "I place the earth under my sway; you, O Zeus, keep Olympus."

Alexander's Conquests There is no doubt that Alexander was taking a chance in attacking Persia, which was still a strong state. In the spring of 334 B.C.E., Alexander entered Asia Minor with an army of some 37,000 men. Approximately half were Macedonians, the rest Greeks and other allies. The cavalry, which would play an important role as a strike force, numbered around 5,000. By the following spring, the entire western half of Asia Minor was in Alexander's hands (see Map 4.4). Meanwhile, the Persian king, Darius III, mobilized his forces to stop Alexander's army, but the subsequent Battle of Issus (ISS-uss) in 333 B.C.E. resulted in yet another Macedonian success. Alexander then turned south, and by the winter of 332 B.C.E., Syria, Palestine, and Egypt were under his control.

In 331 B.C.E., Alexander turned east and fought a decisive battle with the Persians at Gaugamela (gaw-guh-MEE-luh) northwest of Babylon. After his victory, Alexander entered Babylon and then proceeded to the Persian capitals at Susa and Persepolis, where he acquired the Persian treasuries and took possession of vast quantities of gold and silver. By 330 B.C.E., Alexander was again on the march, pursuing Darius. After Darius was killed by one of his own men, Alexander took the title and office of the Great King of the Persians. Over the next three years, he traveled east and northeast as far as modern Pakistan. By the summer of 327 B.C.E., he had entered India, which at that time was divided into several warring states. In 326 B.C.E., Alexander and his armies arrived in the plains of northwestern India. At the Battle of the Hydaspes River, Alexander won a brutally fought battle. When Alexander made clear his determination to march east to conquer more of India, his soldiers, weary of campaigning year after year, mutinied and refused to go further. Alexander returned to Babylon, where he planned more campaigns. But in June 323 B.C.E., weakened by wounds, fever, and probably excessive alcohol consumption, he died at age thirty-two (see Film & History, *Alexander*, p. 103).

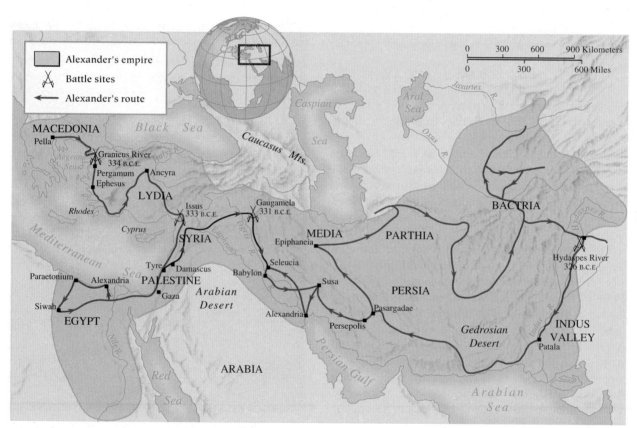

Map 4.4 The conquests of Alexander the Great. In just twelve years, Alexander the Great conquered vast territories. Dominating lands from west of the Nile to east of the Indus, he brought the Persian Empire, Egypt, and much of the Middle East under his control and laid the foundations for the Hellenistic world.

Q *Approximately how far did Alexander and his troops travel during those twelve years, and what kinds of terrain did they encounter on their journey?*

CHRONOLOGY	The Rise of Macedonia and the Conquests of Alexander
Reign of Philip II	359–336 B.C.E.
Battle of Chaeronea; conquest of Greece	338 B.C.E.
Reign of Alexander the Great	336–323 B.C.E.
Alexander's invasion of Asia	334 B.C.E.
Battle of Gaugamela	331 B.C.E.
Fall of Persepolis	330 B.C.E.
Alexander's entry into India	327 B.C.E.
Death of Alexander	323 B.C.E.

HISTORIANS DEBATE The Legacy: Was Alexander Great?

Alexander is one of the most puzzling significant figures in history (see Historical Voices, "The Character of Alexander," p. 104). Historians relying on the same sources draw strikingly different pictures of him. For some, his military abilities, extensive conquests, and creation of a new empire alone justify calling him Alexander the Great. Other historians also praise Alexander's love of Greek culture and his intellectual brilliance, especially in matters of warfare. In the lands that he conquered, Alexander attempted to fuse the Macedonians, Greeks, and Persians into a new ruling class. Did he do this because he was an idealistic visionary who believed in an ideal of universal humanity as some suggest? Or was he merely trying to bolster his power and create an autocratic monarchy?

Those historians who see Alexander as aspiring to autocratic monarchy present a decidedly different portrait of him as a ruthless Machiavellian. One has titled his biography *Alexander the Great Failure*. These critics ask whether a man who slaughtered indigenous peoples, who risked the lives of his solders for his own selfish reasons, whose fierce temper led him to kill his friends, and whose neglect of administrative duties weakened his own kingdom can really be called great.

But how did Alexander view himself? We know that he sought to imitate Achilles, the warrior-hero of Homer's *Iliad*. Alexander kept a copy of the *Iliad*—and a dagger—under his pillow. He also claimed to be descended from Heracles, the Greek hero who came to be worshiped as a god.

Regardless of his ideals, motives, or views about himself, one fact stands out: Alexander ushered in a new age, the Hellenistic era. The word *Hellenistic* is derived from a Greek word meaning "to imitate Greeks." It is an appropriate way, then, to describe an age that saw the extension of the Greek language and ideas to the non-Greek world of the Middle East. Alexander's destruction of the Persian monarchy opened up opportunities for Greek engineers, intellectuals, merchants, administrators, and soldiers. Those who followed Alexander and his successors participated in a new political unity based on the principle of monarchy. His vision of empire no doubt inspired the Romans, who were, of course, Alexander's real heirs.

But Alexander also left a cultural legacy. As a result of his conquests, Greek language, art, architecture, and literature spread throughout the Middle East. The urban centers of the Hellenistic Age, many founded by Alexander and his successors, became springboards for the diffusion of Greek culture. Even as the Greeks spread their culture in the east, they were themselves inevitably influenced by eastern ways. Thus, Alexander's legacy included one of the basic characteristics of the Hellenistic world: the clash and fusion of different cultures.

The Character of Alexander

Family & Society ARRIAN (ca. 86 – ca. 160 c.e.) was a Greek historian and Roman citizen in Bithynia. He wrote the *Anabasis of Alexander*, a historical account of Alexander's military campaigns. In this excerpt from the work, he discusses the character of Alexander. He was obviously an admirer of the great conqueror.

Arrian, *The Anabasis of Alexander*

Alexander . . . lived thirty-two years, and had reached the eighth month of his thirty-third year. He had reigned twelve years and these eight months. He was very handsome in person, and much devoted to exertion. He was very active in mind, very heroic in courage, very tenacious of honor, exceedingly fond of incurring danger, and strictly observant of his duty to the gods. In regard to the pleasures of the body, he had perfect self-control; and of those of the mind, praise was the only one of which he was insatiable. . . . In marshaling, equipping, and ruling an army, he was exceedingly skillful. He was very renowned for rousing the courage of his soldiers, filling them with hopes of success, and dispelling their fear in the midst of danger by his own freedom from fear. Therefore, even what he had to in uncertainty of the result, he did with greatest boldness. . . .

That Alexander should have committed errors in conduct from impetuosity or from wrath, and that he should have been induced to act like the Persian monarchs to an immoderate degree, I do not think remarkable, if we fairly consider both his youth and his uninterrupted career of good fortune. . . . However, I am certain that Alexander was the only one of the ancient kings who, from nobility of character, repented of the errors which he had committed . . . I do not think that even Alexander's tracing his origin to a god was a great error on his part, if it was not perhaps merely a device to induce his subjects to show him reverence. . . . His adoption of the Persian mode of dressing also seems to me to have been a political device in regard to the foreigners, that the king might not appear altogether alien to them; and in regard to the Macedonians, to show them that he had a refuge from their rashness of temper and insolence. . . . Aristobulus also asserts that Alexander used to have long drinking parties, not for the purpose of enjoying the wine, as he was not a great wine-drinker, but in order to exhibit his sociability and friendly feeling to his companions.

Whoever, therefore, reproaches Alexander as a bad man, let him do so; but let him first not only bring before his mind all his actions deserving reproach, but also gather into one view all his deeds of every kind. Then, indeed, let him reflect . . . who that man was whom he reproaches as bad, and to what a height of human success he attained, becoming without any dispute a king of both continents and reaching every place by his fame. . . . For my own part, I think there was at that time no race of men, no city, or even a single individual to whom Alexander's name and fame had not penetrated. For this reason it seems to me that a hero, totally unlike any other human being, could not have been born without the agency of the gods. . . .

 What is Arrian's opinion of Alexander? Why do you think he was so praiseworthy of Alexander's character?

Source: Hutton Webster, *Readings in Ancient History* (Boston: D.C. Heath, 1913) pp. 152–153; pick up from World History, 9th ed., Chapter 4

4-5 THE WORLD OF THE HELLENISTIC KINGDOMS

 Focus Question: How did the political and social institutions of the Hellenistic world differ from those of classical Greece?

The united empire that Alexander created by his conquests crumbled after his death. All too soon, Macedonian military leaders were engaged in a struggle for power, and by 300 b.c.e. four major Hellenistic kingdoms had emerged as the successors to Alexander (see Map 4.5): Macedonia under the Antigonid (an-TIG-uh-nid) dynasty, Syria and the east under the Seleucids (suh-LOO-sids), the Attalid (AT-uh-lid) kingdom of Pergamum (PURR-guh-mum) in western Asia Minor, and Egypt under the Ptolemies (TAHL-uh-meez). All were eventually conquered by the Romans.

4-5a Political Institutions and the Role of Cities

Although Alexander had apparently planned to fuse Greeks and easterners—he used Persians as administrators,

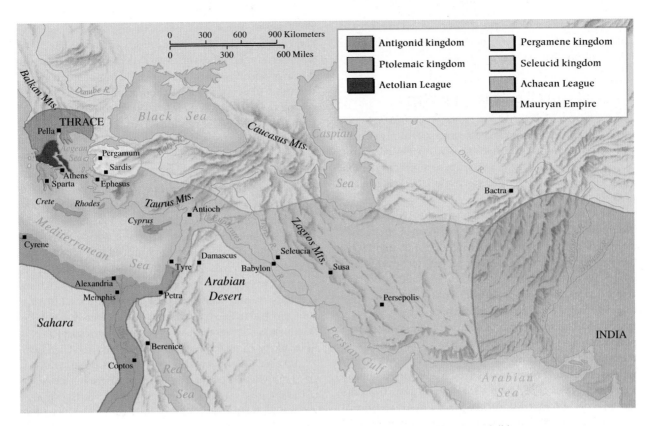

Map 4.5 The world of the Hellenistic kingdoms. Alexander died unexpectedly at the age of thirty-two and did not designate a successor. After his death, his generals struggled for power, eventually establishing four monarchies that spread Hellenistic culture and fostered trade and economic development.

 Which kingdom encompassed most of the old Persian Empire?

encouraged his soldiers to marry easterners, and did so himself—Hellenistic monarchs who succeeded him relied primarily on Greeks and Macedonians to form the new ruling class. Even those easterners who did advance to important administrative posts had learned Greek (all government business was transacted in Greek). This often required alienation from one's own culture. Some were willing to do so because Greekness meant power, giving incentive to local people to become Hellenized in a cultural sense. The policy of excluding non-Greeks from leadership positions was due not to the incompetence of the natives but to the determination of the Greek ruling class to maintain its privileged position. It was the Greco-Macedonian ruling class that provided the only unity in the Hellenistic world.

Alexander had founded new cities and military settlements, and Hellenistic kings did likewise. The new population centers varied considerably in size and importance. Military settlements were meant to maintain order and might consist of only a few hundred men strongly dependent on the king. But there were also new

independent cities with thousands of people. Alexandria in Egypt was the largest city in the Mediterranean region by the first century B.C.E.

Hellenistic rulers encouraged a massive spread of Greek colonists to the Middle East. Greeks and Macedonians provided not only recruits for the army but also a pool of civilian administrators and workers who contributed to economic development. Even architects, engineers, dramatists, and actors were in demand in the new Greek cities. Many Greeks and Macedonians were quick to see the advantages of moving to the new urban centers and gladly sought their fortunes in the Middle East. The Greek cities of the Hellenistic era were the chief agents in the spread of Greek culture in the Middle East—as far, in fact, as modern Afghanistan and India.

The Greeks' belief in their own cultural superiority provided an easy excuse for their political dominance of the eastern cities. But Greek control of the new cities was also necessary because the kings frequently used the cities as instruments of government and so could rule considerable territory without an extensive bureaucracy. At the same time, for security reasons, the Greeks needed the support of the kings. After all, the Hellenistic cities were islands of Greek culture in a sea of non-Greeks.

4-5b Culture in the Hellenistic World

Although the Hellenistic kingdoms encompassed vast territories and many diverse peoples, the diffusion of Greek culture throughout the Hellenistic world provided a sense of unity. The Hellenistic era was a period of considerable accomplishment in many areas, especially science and philosophy.

The founding of new cities and the rebuilding of old ones provided numerous opportunities for Greek architects and sculptors. The Hellenistic monarchs were particularly eager to spend their money to beautify and adorn the cities within their states. The buildings of the Greek homeland—gymnasiums, baths, theaters, and temples—lined the streets of these cities.

Both Hellenistic monarchs and rich citizens patronized sculptors. Hellenistic sculptors traveled throughout this world, attracted by the material rewards offered by wealthy patrons. These sculptors maintained the technical skill of the classical period, but they moved away from the idealism of fifth-century classicism to a more emotional and realistic art that is evident in numerous statues of old women, drunk people, and little children at play. Hellenistic artistic styles even affected artists in India (see Comparative Illustration, "Hellenistic Sculpture and a Greek-Style Buddha," p. 107).

A Golden Age of Science The Hellenistic era witnessed a more conscious separation of science from philosophy. In classical Greece, what we would now call the physical and life sciences had been divisions of philosophical inquiry. In the Hellenistic Age, the sciences tended to be studied in their own right.

By far the most famous scientist of the Hellenistic period was Archimedes (ahr-kuh-MEE-deez) (287–212 B.C.E.). Archimedes was especially important for his work on the geometry of spheres and cylinders and for establishing the value of the mathematical constant pi. Archimedes was also a practical inventor. He may have devised the so-called Archimedean screw used to pump water out of mines and to lift irrigation water. During the Roman siege of his native city of Syracuse in what is now Sicily, he constructed many devices to thwart the attackers. Archimedes's accomplishments inspired a wealth of semilegendary stories. Supposedly, he discovered specific gravity by observing the water he displaced in his bath and became so excited by his realization that he jumped out of the water and ran home naked, shouting, "Eureka!" ("I have found it").

Philosophy While Alexandria became the renowned cultural center of the Hellenistic world, Athens remained the prime center for philosophy. After Alexander the Great, the home of Socrates, Plato, and Aristotle continued to attract the most illustrious philosophers from the Greek world who chose to establish their schools there. New schools of philosophical thought reinforced Athens's reputation as a philosophical center.

Epicurus (ep-i-KYOOR-uss) (341–270 B.C.E.), the founder of **Epicureanism** (ep-i-kyoo-REE-uh-niz-uhm), established a school in Athens near the end of the fourth century B.C.E. Epicurus believed that human beings were free to follow self-interest as a basic motivating force. Happiness was the goal of life, and the means to achieve it was the pursuit of pleasure, the only true good. But the pursuit of pleasure was not meant in a physical, hedonistic sense (as our word *epicurean* has come to mean) but rather referred to freedom from emotional turmoil and worry. To achieve this kind of pleasure, one had to free oneself from public affairs and politics. But this was not a renunciation of all social life; to Epicurus, a life could be complete only when it was based on friendship.

Another school of thought was **Stoicism** (STOH-i-siz-uhm), which became the most popular philosophy of the Hellenistic world and later flourished in the Roman Empire as well. It was the product of a teacher named Zeno (ZEE-noh) (335-263 B.C.E.), who came to Athens and began to teach in a public colonnade known as the Painted Portico (the *Stoa Poikile*—hence the name *Stoicism*). Like Epicureanism, Stoicism was concerned with how individuals find happiness. But Stoics took a radically different approach to the problem. To them, happiness—the supreme good—could be found only by living in harmony with the divine will, by which people gained inner peace. Life's problems could not disturb these people, and they could bear whatever life offered (hence our word *stoic*). Unlike Epicureans, Stoics did not believe in the need to separate themselves from the world and politics. Public service was regarded as noble, and the real Stoic was a good citizen and could even be a good government official.

Both Epicureanism and Stoicism focused primarily on human happiness, and their popularity would suggest a fundamental change in the Greek lifestyle. In the classical Greek world, the happiness of individuals and the meaning of life were closely associated with the life of the polis. A person found fulfillment in the community. In the Hellenistic kingdoms, the sense that one could find fulfillment through life in the polis had weakened. People sought new philosophies that offered personal happiness, and in the cosmopolitan world of the Hellenistic states, with their mixtures of peoples, a new openness to thoughts of universality could also emerge. For some people, Stoicism embodied this larger sense of community.

Hellenistic Sculpture and a Greek-Style Buddha

Art & Ideas

A GREEK TERRA COTTA STATUETTE of a draped young woman made as a tomb offering near Thebes, dates to probably around 300 B.C.E. (Image 4.7a). The incursion of Alexander into western India left Greek cultural influences there. During the first century B.C.E., Indian sculptors in Gandhara, which today is part of Pakistan, began to make statues of the Buddha in a style that combined Indian and Hellenistic artistic traditions, as in the stone sculpture of the Buddha on the right (Image 4.7b). Note the wavy hair topped by a bun tied with a ribbon, also a feature of earlier statues of Greek deities. This Buddha is also wearing a Greek-style toga.

Q *How do you explain the influence of Hellenistic styles in India? What can you conclude from this example about the impact of conquerors on conquered people?*

© Gianni Dagli Orti/The Art Archive at Art Resource, NY

© Borromeo/Art Resource, NY

4.7a　　　　　　　4.7b

CHAPTER SUMMARY

Unlike the great centralized empires of the Persians and the Chinese, ancient Greece consisted of a large number of small, independent city-states. The most famous were Sparta, a militaristic polis ruled by an oligarchy, and Athens, which became known for its democratic institutions even though slaves and women had no political rights. Despite the small size of their city-states, the ancient Greeks created a civilization that was the fountainhead of Western culture. Socrates, Plato, and Aristotle established the foundations of Western philosophy. Western literary forms are largely derived from Greek poetry and drama. Greek notions of harmony, proportion, and beauty have remained the touchstones for all subsequent Western art.

A rational method of inquiry—critically important to modern science—was conceived in ancient Greece. Many political terms are Greek in origin, and so too are concepts of

the rights and duties of citizenship, especially as they were conceived in Athens, the first great democracy the world had seen. Especially during the classical era of the fifth century B.C.E., a century that began with the Persian wars, the Greeks raised and debated the fundamental questions about the purpose of human existence, the structure of human society, and the nature of the universe that have concerned thinkers ever since.

But the growth of an Athenian empire in that same century led to a mighty conflict with Sparta—the Great Peloponnesian War—that resulted in the weakening of the Greek city-states and opened the door to an invasion by Philip II of Macedonia that put an end to their freedom in 338 B.C.E. But Greek culture did not die, and a new age known as the *Hellenistic era* eventually came into being.

That era began with the conquest of the Persian Empire by Alexander the Great, the young successor to his father, Philip II. Though a great military leader, Alexander was not a good political administrator. He failed to establish any definite structure for the empire he had conquered, and

four Hellenistic kingdoms eventually emerged as his successors. The society that developed within those kingdoms is known as *Hellenistic,* meaning Greek-like or in imitation of the Greeks. The Greek language became the dominant one as Greek ideas became influential. Greek merchants, artists, philosophers, and soldiers found opportunities and rewards throughout the Near East, now a world of kingdoms rather than independent city-states.

The Hellenistic period was, in its own way, a vibrant one. New cities arose and flourished. New philosophical doctrines—such as Epicureanism and Stoicism—captured the minds of many. Significant achievements occurred in science, and Greek culture spread throughout the Near East and made an impact wherever it was carried. Although the Hellenistic era achieved a degree of political stability, signs of decline were beginning to multiply by the late third century B.C.E., and the growing power of Rome eventually endangered the Hellenistic world.

REFLECTION QUESTIONS

Q Compare Greek civilization with the early civilizations developed in India and China. What are the differences and similarities, and how do you explain them?

Q The classical age in Greece is known for its literary, artistic, and intellectual achievements. What basic characteristics of Greek culture are reflected in the major

achievements of the Greeks in history, drama, the arts, and philosophy? What universal human concerns did these same achievements reflect?

Q What were the main achievements of the Hellenistic kingdoms, and why did they fail to bring any lasting order to the lands of the Near East?

CHAPTER TIMELINE

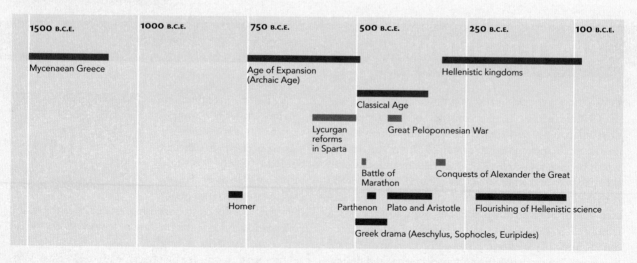

CHAPTER NOTES

1. Xenophon, *Symposium,* trans. O. J. Todd (Harmondsworth, England, 1946), 3:5.
2. Quoted in T. R. Martin, *Ancient Greece* (New Haven, Conn., 1996), p. 62.
3. The words from Plutarch are quoted in E. Fantham et al., *Women in the Classical World* (New York, 1994), p. 64.
4. Sophocles, *Antigone,* trans. D. Taylor (London: 1986), p. 146.
5. Plato, *The Republic,* trans. F. M. Cornford (New York, 1945), pp. 178–179.
6. Quotations from Aristotle are in S. Blundell, *Women in Ancient Greece* (London, 1995), pp. 106, 186.

MINDTAP
From Cengage

MindTap® is a fully online, highly personalized learning experience built upon Cengage Learning content. MindTap combines student learning tools—readings, multimedia, activities, and assessments—into a singular Learning Path that guides students through the course and helps students develop the critical thinking, analysis, and communication skills that are essential to academic and professional success.

Chapter Outline and Focus Questions

Critical Thinking

Q *Compare and contrast the Roman Empire and Han Chinese Empire in regard to dynastic rule, bureaucratic government, trade, the military, and imperial expansion.*

Connections to Today

Q *What lessons does the fall of the Roman republic offer to the United States today?*

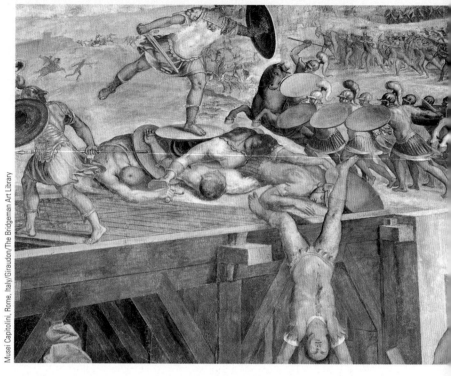

Musei Capitolini, Rome, Italy/Giraudon/The Bridgeman Art Library

5.1 Horatius defending the bridge. Event as envisioned by Tommaso Laureti, a sixteenth-century Italian painter

AT THE BEGINNING of the first millennium C.E., almost 50 percent of the world's population lived in one of two mighty world empires—the Han and Roman Empires. They were the largest political entities the world had yet seen. The Han Empire (see Chapter 3) extended from Central Asia to the Pacific Ocean; the Roman Empire encompassed the lands around the Mediterranean, parts of the Middle East, and western and central Europe. Although there were no diplomatic contacts between the two civilizations, the two great empires were linked commercially.

Roman history is the remarkable story of how a group of Latin-speaking people who established a small community on a plain called *Latium* in central Italy went on to conquer all of Italy and then the entire Mediterranean world. Why were the Romans able to do this? Scholars do not really have all the answers, but the Romans had their own explanation.

Early Roman history is filled with legendary tales of the heroes who made Rome great. One of the best known is the story of Horatius at the bridge.

Threatened by attack from neighboring Etruscans, Roman farmers abandoned their fields and moved into the city, where they would be protected by the walls. One weak point in the Roman defenses, however, was a wooden bridge over the Tiber River. Horatius was on guard at the bridge when a sudden assault by the Etruscans caused many Roman troops to throw down their weapons and flee. Horatius urged them to make a stand at the bridge; when they hesitated, he told them to destroy the bridge behind him while he held the Etruscans back. Astonished at the sight of a single defender, the confused Etruscans threw their spears at Horatius, who caught them on his shield and barred the way. By the time the Etruscans were about to overwhelm the lone defender, the Roman soldiers had brought down the bridge. Horatius then dived, fully armed, into the water and swam safely to the other side through a hail of arrows. Rome had been saved by the courageous act of a Roman who knew his duty and was determined to carry it out. Courage, duty, determination—these qualities would serve the many Romans who believed that it was their divine mission to rule nations and peoples. As one writer proclaimed: "By heaven's will, my Rome shall be capital of the world."

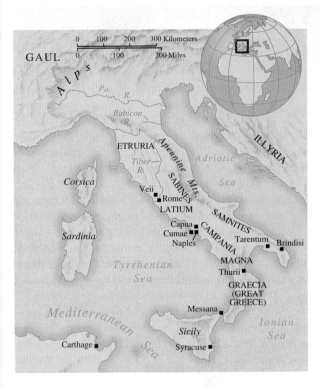

Map 5.1 Ancient Italy. Ancient Italy was home to several groups. Both the Etruscans in the north and the Greeks in the south had a major influence on the development of Rome.

 Once Rome conquered the Etruscans and other local groups, what aspects of the Italian peninsula helped make it defensible against outside enemies?

5-1 EARLY ROME AND THE REPUBLIC

 Focus Questions: What policies and institutions help explain the Romans' success in conquering Italy? How did Rome achieve its empire from 264 to 133 B.C.E., and what problems did Rome face as a result of its growing empire?

Italy is a peninsula extending 750 miles from north to south (see Map 5.1). It is relatively narrow, however, averaging some 120 miles across. The Apennine Mountains form a ridge down the middle of Italy that divides west from east. Nevertheless, Italy has some fairly large fertile plains that are ideal for farming. Most important are the Po River Valley in the north; the plain of Latium (LAY-shee-um), on which Rome was located; and Campania (kahm-PAH-nyuh or kam-PAY-nyuh) to the south of Latium. To the east of the Italian peninsula is the Adriatic Sea and to the west the Tyrrhenian

(ti-REE-nee-uhn) Sea, bounded by the large islands of Corsica and Sardinia. Sicily lies just west of the "toe" of the boot-shaped Italian peninsula.

Geography affected Roman history to a great degree. Although the Apennines bisected Italy, they were less rugged than the mountain ranges of Greece and did not divide the peninsula into many small isolated communities. Italy also possessed considerably more productive agricultural land than Greece, which enabled it to support a large population. Rome's location was favorable from a geographic point of view. Located eighteen miles inland on the Tiber River, Rome had access to the sea and yet was far enough inland to be safe from pirates. Built on seven hills, it was easily defended.

Moreover, the Italian peninsula juts into the Mediterranean, making Italy an important crossroads between the western and eastern ends of the sea. Once Rome had unified Italy, involvement in Mediterranean affairs was natural. After the Romans had conquered their Mediterranean empire, governing it was made easier by Italy's central location.

5-1a Early Rome

To provide a noble ancestry for their city, the Romans created two significant legends. One was the story of Aeneas, the son of the goddess Venus and a mortal man, He was a Trojan hero fighting the Greeks, who escaped from the sacking of Troy, and eventually made his way to Italy. According to one version of the legend, he founded the city of Rome. The legend reflects the desire of the Romans to connect Roman history to Greek history, and especially Greece's heroic age, an indication of the strong impact Greek culture made on the Romans.

The other legend is the story of Romulus and Remus, the twin sons of the god Mars, whose mother was punished for losing her virginity by Amulius, who had become king of Alba Longa by overthrowing her father. Her boys were set adrift on the Tiber River in a reed basket. They were found by a she-wolf who suckled them, and they were then raised by a shepherd's family. When the boys were grown men, they were told of their origins and avenged their mother and grandfather by killing Amulius and founding the city of Rome. According to the legend, Romulus founded a new city on the Palatine Hill in 753 B.C.E., killed his brother in an argument, and then became the first king of Rome.

Of course, the Romans invented these stories to provide a noble ancestry for their city. Archaeologists have found, however, that by the eighth century B.C.E., a village of huts had been built on the tops of Rome's hills. The early Romans, basically a pastoral people, spoke Latin, which, like Greek, belongs to the Indo-European family of languages (see Table 1.2 in Chapter 1). The Roman historical tradition also maintained that early Rome (753–509 B.C.E.) had been under the control of seven kings and that two of the last three had been Etruscans (i-TRUSS- kunz), people who lived north of Rome in Etruria. Historians believe that the king list may have some historical accuracy. What is certain is that Rome did fall under the influence of the Etruscans for around 100 years during the period of the kings and that by the beginning of the sixth century B.C.E., Rome began to emerge as a city under Etruscan influence. The Etruscans were responsible for an outstanding building program. They constructed the first roadbed of the chief street through Rome, the Sacred Way, before 575 B.C.E. and oversaw the development of temples, markets, shops, streets, and houses. By 509 B.C.E., supposedly when the monarchy was overthrown and a republican form of government was established, a new Rome had emerged, essentially a result of the fusion of Etruscan and native Roman elements.

5-1b The Roman Republic

The transition from monarchy to a republican government was not easy. Rome felt threatened by enemies from every direction. To meet these threats, it embarked on a military course that led to the conquest of the entire Italian peninsula.

The Roman Conquest of Italy   At the beginning of the republic, Rome was surrounded by enemies, including the Latin communities on the plain of Latium. If we are to believe Livy (LIV-ee), one of the chief ancient sources for the history of the early Roman republic, Rome was engaged in almost continuous warfare with these enemies for the next 100 years. In his account, Livy provided a detailed narrative of Roman efforts. Many of his stories were legendary in character; writing in the first century B.C.E., he used his stories to teach Romans the moral values and virtues that had made Rome great. As seen in the story of Cincinnatus, these included tenacity, duty, courage, and especially discipline (see Historical Voices, "Cincinnatus Saves Rome," p. 113).

By 338 B.C.E., Rome had crushed the Latin states in Latium. During the next fifty years, the Romans waged a successful struggle with hill peoples from central Italy and then came into direct contact with the Greek communities. Greeks had arrived on the Italian peninsula in large numbers during the age of Greek colonization (750–550 B.C.E.; see Chapter 4). Initially, they settled in southern Italy and then crept around the coast and up the peninsula. The Greeks had much influence on Rome. They cultivated olives and grapes, passed on their alphabet, and provided artistic and cultural models through their sculpture, architecture, and literature. By 267 B.C.E., the Romans had completed the conquest of southern Italy by defeating the Greek cities. After crushing the remaining Etruscan states to the north in 264 B.C.E., Rome had conquered most of Italy.

To rule Italy, the Romans had created the Roman Confederation in 338 B.C.E. Under this system, Rome allowed some peoples—especially the Latins—to have full Roman citizenship. Most of the remaining communities were made allies. They remained free to run their own local affairs but were required to provide soldiers for Rome. Moreover, the Romans made it clear that loyal allies could improve their status and even aspire to becoming Roman citizens. The Romans had found a way to give conquered peoples a stake in Rome's success.

In the course of their expansion throughout Italy, the Romans had pursued consistent policies that help explain their success. The Romans were superb diplomats who excelled in making the correct diplomatic decisions. In addition, the Romans were not only good soldiers but also persistent ones. The loss of an army or a fleet did not cause them to quit but spurred them on to build new armies and new fleets. And by granting citizenship to conquered peoples, Rome had achieved the ability to

Cincinnatus Saves Rome: A Roman Morality Tale

Politics & Government

THERE IS PERHAPS NO BETTER ACCOUNT of how the virtues of duty and simplicity enabled good Roman citizens to prevail during the travails of the fifth century B.C.E. than Livy's account of Cincinnatus (sin-suh-NAT-uss). He was chosen dictator, supposedly in 457 B.C.E., to defend Rome against the attacks of the Aequi (EE-kwy). The position of dictator was a temporary expedient used only in emergencies; the consuls would resign, and a leader with unlimited power would be appointed for a limited period (usually six months). In this account, Cincinnatus did his duty, defeated the Aequi, and returned to his simple farm in just fifteen days.

Livy, *The Early History of Rome*

The city was thrown into a state of turmoil, and the general alarm was as great as if Rome herself were surrounded. . . . [The] situation evidently called for a dictator, and, with no dissentient voice, Lucius Quinctius Cincinnatus was named for the post.

Now I would solicit the particular attention of those numerous people who imagine that money is everything in this world, and that rank and ability are inseparable from wealth: let them observe that Cincinnatus, the one man in whom Rome reposed all her hope of survival, was at that moment working a little three-acre farm . . . west of the Tiber, just opposite the spot where the shipyards are today. A mission from the city found him at work on his land—digging a ditch, maybe, or plowing. Greetings were exchanged, and he was asked—with a prayer for divine blessing on himself and his country—to put on his toga and hear the Senate's instructions. This naturally surprised him, and, asking if all were well, he told his wife Racilia to run to their cottage and fetch his toga. The toga was brought, and wiping the grimy sweat from his hands and face he put it on; at once the envoys from the city saluted him, with congratulations, as Dictator, invited him to enter Rome, and informed him of the terrible danger of Municius's army. A state vessel was waiting for him on the river, and on the city bank he was welcomed by his three sons who had come to meet him, then by other kinsmen and friends, and finally by nearly the whole body of senators. Closely attended by all these people and preceded by his lictors he was then escorted to his residence through streets lined with great crowds of common folk who, be it said, were by no means so pleased to see the new Dictator, as they thought his power excessive and dreaded the way in which he was likely to use it.

[Cincinnatus proceeds to raise an army, march out, and defeat the Aequi.]

In Rome the Senate was convened by Quintus Fabius the City Prefect, and a decree was passed inviting Cincinnatus to enter in triumph with his troops. The chariot he rode in was preceded by the enemy commanders and the military standards, and followed by his army loaded with its spoils. . . . Cincinnatus finally resigned after holding office for fifteen days, having originally accepted it for a period of six months.

 What values did Livy emphasize in his account of Cincinnatus? How important were those values to Rome's success? Why did Livy say he wrote his history? As a writer in the Augustan Age, would he have pleased or displeased Augustus by writing a history with such a purpose?

Source: Livy, *The Early History of Rome*, trans. A. de Selincourt (London: Penguin Classics, 1960).

---

raise new armies following defeats. Finally, the Romans had a practical sense of strategy. As they conquered, they established colonies—fortified towns—at strategic locations throughout Italy. By building roads to these settlements and connecting them, the Romans created an impressive communications and military network that enabled them to rule effectively and efficiently (see Map 5.2). By insisting on military service from new citizens and the allies in the Roman Confederation, Rome essentially mobilized the entire military manpower of all Italy for its wars.

The Roman State   After the overthrow of the monarchy, Roman nobles were eager to maintain their position of power, so they established a republican form of government. The chief executive officers of the Roman republic were the **consuls** (KAHN-sulls) and **praetors** (PREE-turs). Two consuls were chosen annually to administer the government and lead the Roman army into battle. The office of praetor was created in 366 B.C.E. The praetor was in charge of civil law (law as it applied to Roman citizens), but he could also lead armies and govern Rome when the consuls were away from the city. As the Romans' territory expanded, they added another praetor to judge cases in which one or both people were noncitizens. The Roman state also had many administrative officials who handled specialized duties, such as the administration of financial affairs and the supervision of the public games of Rome.

The Roman **senate** came to hold an especially important position in the Roman republic. The senate or council of elders was a select group of some 300 men who served for life. The senate could only advise the magistrates, but this advice was not taken lightly and by the third century B.C.E. had virtually the force of law.

The Roman republic also had several popular assemblies. By far the most important was the **centuriate assembly**. Organized by classes based on wealth, it was structured in such a way that the wealthiest citizens always had a majority. This assembly elected the chief magistrates and passed laws. Another assembly, the **council of the plebs**, came into being in 471 B.C.E. as a result of the struggle of the orders.

This struggle arose from the most noticeable element in the social organization of early Rome: the division into two groups, **patricians** and **plebeians**. The patricians were descendants of the original senators appointed during the period of the kings and great landowners, who constituted the aristocratic governing class. Only they could be consuls, magistrates, and senators. The plebeians constituted the considerably larger group of nonpatrician large landowners, less wealthy landholders, artisans, merchants, and small farmers. Although they, too, were citizens, they did not have the same rights as the patricians. Both patricians and plebeians could vote, but only the patricians could be elected to governmental offices. Both had the right to make legal contracts and marriages, but intermarriage between patricians and plebeians was forbidden. At the beginning of the fifth century B.C.E., the plebeians began to seek both political and social equality with the patricians.

The struggle between the patricians and plebeians dragged on for hundreds of years, but the plebeians ultimately were successful. The council of the plebs, a popular assembly for plebeians only, was created in 471 B.C.E., and new officials, known as **tribunes of the plebs**, were given the power to protect plebeians against arrest

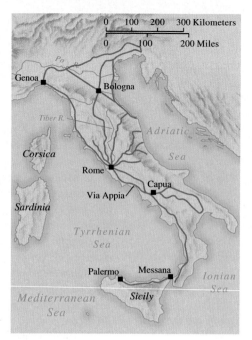

Map 5.2 Roman roads in Italy

by patrician magistrates. A new law allowed marriages between patricians and plebeians, and in the fourth century B.C.E. plebeians were permitted to become consuls. Finally, in 287 B.C.E., the council of the plebs received the right to pass laws for all Romans.

The struggle between the patricians and plebeians, then, had a significant impact on the development of the Roman state. Plebeians could now hold the highest offices of state, they could intermarry with patricians, and they could pass laws binding on the entire Roman community. Theoretically, by 287 B.C.E., all Roman citizens were equal under the law, and all could strive for political office. But in reality, as a result of the right of intermarriage, a select number of patrician and plebeian families formed a new senatorial aristocracy that came to dominate the political offices. The Roman republic had not become a democracy.

5-1c The Roman Conquest of the Mediterranean (264–133 B.C.E.)

After their conquest of the Italian peninsula, the Romans found themselves face to face with a formidable Mediterranean power: Carthage (KAHR-thij). Founded around 800 B.C.E. on the coast of North Africa by Phoenicians, Carthage had flourished and assembled an enormous empire in the western Mediterranean. By the third century B.C.E., the Carthaginian Empire included the coast of northern Africa, southern Spain, Sardinia, Corsica, and western Sicily. The presence of Carthaginians in Sicily, so close to the Italian coast, made the Romans apprehensive. In 264 B.C.E., the two powers began a lengthy struggle for control of the western Mediterranean (see Map 5.3).

In the First Punic (PYOO-nik) War (the Latin word for Phoenician was *Punicus*), the Romans resolved to conquer Sicily. The Romans—a land power—realized they could not win the war without a navy and promptly developed a substantial naval fleet. After a long struggle, a Roman fleet defeated the Carthaginian navy off Sicily, and the war quickly came to an end. In 241 B.C.E., Carthage gave up all rights to Sicily and had to pay an indemnity. Sicily became the first Roman province.

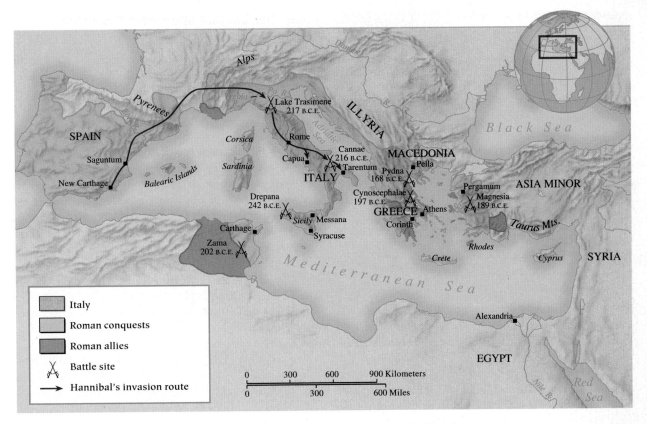

Map 5.3 Roman conquests in the Mediterranean, 264–133 B.C.E. Beginning with the Punic Wars, Rome expanded its holdings, first in the western Mediterranean at the expense of Carthage and later in Greece and western Asia Minor.

Q *What aspects of Mediterranean geography, combined with the territorial holdings and aspirations of Rome and the Carthaginians, made the Punic Wars more likely?*

Carthage vowed revenge and extended its domains in Spain to compensate for the territory lost to Rome. When the Romans encouraged one of Carthage's Spanish allies to revolt against Carthage, Hannibal (HAN-uh-bul), the greatest of the Carthaginian generals, struck back, beginning the Second Punic War (218–201 B.C.E.).

This time, the Carthaginian strategy aimed to take the war home to the Romans and defeat them in their own backyard. Hannibal crossed the Alps with an army of 30,000 to 40,000 men and inflicted a series of defeats on the Romans. At Cannae (KAH-nee) in 216 B.C.E., the Romans lost an army of almost 40,000 men. Rome seemed on the brink of disaster but refused to give up, raised yet another army, and began to reconquer some of the Italian cities that had gone over to Hannibal's side. The Romans also sent troops to Spain, and by 206 B.C.E. Spain was freed of the Carthaginians.

The Romans then took the war directly to Carthage, forcing the Carthaginians to recall Hannibal from Italy. At the Battle of Zama (ZAH-muh) in 202 B.C.E., the Romans

crushed Hannibal's forces, and the war was over. By the peace treaty signed in 201 B.C.E., Carthage lost Spain, which became another Roman province. Rome had become the dominant power in the western Mediterranean.

Fifty years later, the Romans fought their third and final struggle with Carthage. In 146 B.C.E., Carthage was destroyed. For ten days, Roman soldiers burned and pulled down all of the city's buildings. The inhabitants—50,000 men, women, and children—were sold into slavery. The territory of Carthage became a Roman province called Africa.

During its struggle with Carthage, Rome also had problems with the Hellenistic states in the eastern Mediterranean, so after defeating Carthage, Rome turned its attention there. In 148 B.C.E., Macedonia was made a Roman province, and two years later, Greece was placed under the control of the Roman governor of Macedonia. In 133 B.C.E., the king of Pergamum deeded his kingdom to Rome, giving Rome its first province in Asia. Rome was now master of the Mediterranean Sea.

CHRONOLOGY	The Roman Conquest of Italy and the Mediterranean
Conquest of Latium completed	340 B.C.E.
Creation of the Roman Confederation	338 B.C.E.
First Punic War	264–241 B.C.E.
Second Punic War	218–201 B.C.E.
Battle of Cannae	216 B.C.E.
Roman seizure of Spain	206 B.C.E.
Battle of Zama	202 B.C.E.
Third Punic War	149–146 B.C.E.
Macedonia made a Roman province	148 B.C.E.
Destruction of Carthage	146 B.C.E.
Kingdom of Pergamum to Rome	133 B.C.E.

The Nature of Roman Imperialism Rome's empire was built in three stages: the conquest of Italy, the conflict with Carthage and expansion into the western Mediterranean, and the involvement with and domination of the Hellenistic kingdoms in the eastern Mediterranean. The Romans did not possess a master plan for the creation of an empire. Much of their expansion was opportunistic; once involved in a situation that threatened their security, the Romans did not hesitate to act. And the more they expanded, the more threats to their security appeared on the horizon, involving them in yet more conflicts. Indeed, the Romans liked to portray themselves as declaring war only for defensive reasons or to protect allies. That is only part of the story, however. It is likely, as some historians have suggested, that at some point a group of Roman aristocratic leaders emerged who favored expansion both for the glory it offered and for the economic benefits it provided. Certainly, by the second century B.C.E., aristocratic senators perceived new opportunities for lucrative foreign commands, enormous spoils of war, and an abundant supply of slave labor for their growing landed estates.

At the same time, the Roman political system encouraged an imperialistic policy. There was an intense competition between families for the consulship (as we have seen, there were only two per year). Moreover, many Romans believed in outdoing the deeds of their ancestors. The combination of these factors helped lead upper-class Romans to seek glory and power by winning wars abroad.

By the second century B.C.E., as the destruction of Carthage indicates, Roman imperialism had become more arrogant and brutal as well. Rome's foreign success also had enormous repercussions for the internal development of the Roman republic.

5-1d The Decline and Fall of the Roman Republic (133–31 B.C.E.)

By the middle of the second century B.C.E., Roman domination of the Mediterranean Sea was complete. Yet the process of creating an empire had weakened the internal stability of Rome, leading to a series of crises that plagued the empire for the next hundred years.

Growing Unrest and a New Role for the Roman Army By the second century B.C.E., the senate had become the effective governing body of the Roman state. It comprised 300 men drawn primarily from the landed aristocracy; they remained senators for life and held the chief magistracies of the republic. The senate directed the wars of the third and second centuries and took control of both foreign and domestic policy, including financial affairs.

Of course, these aristocrats formed only a tiny minority of the Roman people. The backbone of the Roman state had traditionally been the small farmers. But over time, many small farmers had found themselves unable to compete with large, wealthy landowners and had lost their lands. By taking over state-owned land and by buying out small peasant owners, these landed aristocrats had amassed large estates called *latifundia* (lat-i-FOON-dee-uh) that used slave labor. Thus, the rise of the latifundia contributed to a decline in the number of small citizen farmers who were available for military service. Moreover, many of these small farmers drifted to the cities, especially Rome, forming a large class of landless poor.

Some aristocrats tried to remedy this growing economic and social crisis. Two brothers, Tiberius and Gaius Gracchus (ty-BEER-ee-uss and GY-uss GRAK-us), came to believe that the underlying cause of Rome's problems was the decline of the small farmer. To help the landless poor, they bypassed the senate by having the council of the plebs pass land reform bills that called for the government to reclaim public land held by large landowners and to distribute it to landless Romans. Many senators, themselves large landowners whose estates included large areas of public land, were furious. A group of senators took the law into their own hands and murdered Tiberius in 133 B.C.E. Twelve years later, Gaius suffered the same fate. The attempts of the Gracchus brothers to bring reforms had opened the door to further violence. Changes in the Roman army soon brought even worse problems.

In the closing years of the second century B.C.E., a Roman general named Marius (MAR-ee-uss) began to recruit his armies in a new way. The Roman army had traditionally been a conscript army of small farmers who were landholders, but Marius recruited landless volunteers from both the urban and rural poor. These volunteers swore an oath of loyalty to their general, not the senate, and thus formed a professional army no longer subject to the state. Moreover, to recruit these men, generals would promise them land, but then the generals would have to play politics to get laws passed that would provide the land promised to their veterans. Marius had created a new system of military recruitment that placed much power in the hands of the individual generals.

The Collapse of the Republic   The first century B.C.E. was characterized by two important features: the jostling for dominance of several powerful individuals and the civil wars generated by their conflicts. Three individuals came to hold enormous military and political power—Crassus (KRASS-uss), Pompey (PAHM-pee), and Julius Caesar. Crassus was known as the richest man in Rome and led a successful military command against a major slave rebellion. Pompey had returned from a successful military command in Spain in 71 B.C.E. and had been hailed as a military hero. Julius Caesar also had a military command in Spain. In 60 B.C.E., Caesar joined with Crassus and Pompey to form a coalition that historians call the First Triumvirate (*triumvirate* means "three-man rule").

The combined wealth and influence of these three men was enormous, enabling them to dominate the political scene and achieve their basic aims: Pompey received a command in Spain, Crassus a command in Syria, and Caesar a special military command in Gaul (modern France). When Crassus was killed in battle in 53 B.C.E., his death left two powerful men with armies in direct competition. Caesar had conquered all of Gaul and gained fame, wealth, and military experience as well as an army of seasoned veterans who were loyal to him. When leading senators endorsed Pompey as the less harmful to their cause and voted for Caesar to lay down his command and return as a private citizen to Rome, Caesar refused. He chose to keep his army and moved into Italy illegally by crossing the Rubicon, the river that formed the southern boundary of his province. Caesar marched on Rome and defeated the forces of Pompey and his allies. Caesar was now in complete control of the Roman government.

Caesar was officially made **dictator** in 47 B.C.E. and three years later was named dictator for life. Realizing the need for reforms, he gave land to the poor and increased the senate to 900 members. He also reformed the calendar by introducing the Egyptian solar year of 365 days (with later changes in 1582, it became the basis of our own calendar). Caesar planned much more in the way of building projects and military adventures in the east, but in 44 B.C.E., a group of leading senators assassinated him.

A few years after Caesar's death, two men had divided the Roman world between them: Octavian (ahk-TAY-vee-un), Caesar's grandnephew and adopted son, took the western portion; Antony, Caesar's ally and assistant, the eastern half. But the empire of the Romans, large as it was, was still too small for two masters, and Octavian and Antony eventually came into conflict. Antony allied himself closely with the Egyptian queen Cleopatra VII. At the Battle of Actium in Greece in 31 B.C.E., Octavian's forces smashed the army and navy of Antony and Cleopatra, who both fled to Egypt, where they committed suicide a year later. Octavian, at age thirty-two, stood supreme over the Roman world. The civil wars had ended. And so had the republic.

5-2 THE ROMAN EMPIRE AT ITS HEIGHT

Focus Question: What were the chief features of the Roman Empire at its height in the second century C.E.?

With the victories of Octavian, peace finally settled over the Roman world. Although civil conflict still erupted occasionally, the new imperial state constructed by Octavian experienced remarkable stability for the next 200 years. The Romans imposed their peace on the largest empire established in antiquity.

5-2a The Age of Augustus (31 B.C.E.–14 C.E.)

In 27 B.C.E., Octavian proclaimed the "restoration of the republic." He understood that only traditional republican forms would satisfy the senatorial aristocracy. At the same time, Octavian was aware that the republic could not be fully restored. Although he gave some power to the senate, Octavian in reality became the first Roman emperor. The senate awarded him the title of Augustus, "the revered one," a fitting title in view of his power and one that had previously been reserved for gods. Augustus proved highly popular, but the chief source of his power was his continuing control of the army. The senate gave Augustus the title of *imperator* (im-puh-RAH-tur) (our word *emperor*), or commander in chief.

Why had Augustus succeeded in establishing a new order where Julius Caesar, his adoptive father, had failed? Caesar had defined himself as a dictator for life, thus raising suspicion among the Romans that he planned to become a king, a position they strongly disliked. Many Romans believed that Caesar had been justly killed as a tyrant. Augustus was careful to present himself as an ordinary citizen and to exercise power by holding the traditional offices of the Roman republic (see Image 5.2).

5.2 Augustus. Octavian, Caesar's adopted son, emerged victorious from the civil conflict that rocked the republic after Caesar's assassination. The senate awarded him the title of *Augustus*. This marble statue from Prima Porta, an idealized portrait, is based on Greek rather Roman models. The statue was meant to be a propaganda piece depicting a youthful general addressing his troops. At the bottom stands Cupid, the son of Venus, goddess of love, meant to be a reminder that the Julians, Caesar's family, claimed descent from Venus and that the ruler thus had a divine background.

Augustus maintained a standing army of twenty-eight legions—some 150,000 men (a legion was a military unit of around 5,000 troops). Only Roman citizens could be legionaries, but subject peoples could serve as auxiliary forces, which numbered around 130,000 under Augustus. Augustus was also responsible for setting up a **praetorian guard** of roughly 9,000 men who had the important task of guarding the emperor.

While claiming to have restored the republic, Augustus inaugurated a new system for governing the provinces. Under the republic, the senate had appointed the governors of the provinces. Now certain provinces were given to

the emperor, who assigned deputies known as legates to govern them. The senate continued to name the governors of the remaining provinces, but the authority of Augustus enabled him to overrule the senatorial governors and establish a uniform imperial policy (see Historical Voices, "The Achievements of Augustus," p. 119).

Augustus also stabilized the frontiers of the Roman Empire. He conquered the central and maritime Alps and then expanded Roman control of the Balkan Peninsula up to the Danube River. His attempt to conquer Germany failed when three Roman legions led by a general named Varus were massacred in 9 C.E. by a coalition of German tribes. His defeats in Germany not only taught Augustus that Rome's power was not unlimited but also devastated him; for months, he would beat his head on a door, shouting "Varus, give me back my legions!"

Augustus died in 14 C.E. after dominating the Roman world for forty-five years. He had created a new order while placating the old by restoring traditional values. By the time of his death, his new order was so well established that few Romans agitated for an alternative. Indeed, as the Roman historian Tacitus (TASS-i-tuss) pointed out, "Practically no one had ever seen truly Republican government. . . . Political equality was a thing of the past; all eyes watched for imperial commands."[1]

5-2b The Early Empire (14–180 C.E.)

There was no serious opposition to Augustus's choice of his stepson Tiberius (ty-BEER-ee-uss) as his successor. By his actions, Augustus established the Julio-Claudian Dynasty; the next four successors of Augustus were related to his family or that of his wife, Livia.

Several major tendencies emerged during the reigns of the Julio-Claudians (14–68 C.E.). In general, more and more of the responsibilities that Augustus had given to the senate tended to be taken over by the emperors, who also instituted an imperial bureaucracy staffed by talented freedmen to run the government on a daily basis. As the Julio-Claudian successors of Augustus acted more openly as real rulers rather than as "first citizens of the state," the opportunity for arbitrary and corrupt acts also increased. Nero (NEE-roh) (54–68 C.E.), for example, freely eliminated people he wanted out of the way, including his own mother, whose murder he arranged. Without troops, the senators proved unable to oppose these excesses, but the Roman legions finally revolted. Abandoned by his guards, Nero chose to commit suicide by stabbing himself in the throat after uttering his final words, "What an artist the world is losing in me!"

The Five Good Emperors (96–180 C.E.) Many historians see the **Pax Romana** (PAKS *or* PAHKS ro-MAH-nuh)

The Achievements of Augustus

Politics & Government

THIS EXCERPT IS TAKEN FROM A TEXT written by Augustus and inscribed on a bronze tablet in Rome. Copies of the text in stone were displayed in many provincial capitals. Called "the most famous ancient inscription," the *Res Gestae* of Augustus summarizes his accomplishments in three major areas: his offices, his private expenditures on behalf of the state, and his exploits in war and peace. Though factual in approach, it is a highly subjective account.

Augustus, *Res Gestae*

The following is a copy of the accomplishments of the deified Augustus by which he brought the whole world under the empire of the Roman people, and of the moneys expended by him on the state and the Roman people as inscribed on two bronze pillars set up in Rome.

1. At the age of nineteen, on my own initiative and at my own expense, I raised an army by means of which I liberated the Republic, which was oppressed by the tyranny of a faction [Mark Antony and his supporters]. . . .

2. Those who assassinated my father [Julius Caesar, his adoptive father] I drove into exile, avenging their crime by due process of law; and afterwards when they waged war against the state, I conquered them twice on the battlefield.

3. I waged many wars throughout the whole world by land and by sea, both civil and foreign, and when victorious I spared all citizens who sought pardon. . . .

5. The dictatorship offered to me . . . by the people and the senate, both in my absence and in my presence, I refused to accept. . . .

17. Four times I came to the assistance of the treasury with my own money, transferring to those in charge of the treasury 150,000,000 sesterces. And in the consulship of Marcus Lepidus and Lucius Arruntius I transferred out of my own patrimony 170,000,000 sesterces to the soldiers' bonus fund, which was established on my advice for the purpose of providing bonuses for soldiers who had completed twenty or more years of service. . . .

25. I brought peace to the sea by suppressing the pirates. In that war I turned over to their masters for punishment nearly 30,000 slaves who had run away from their owners and taken up arms against the state. . . .

26. I extended the frontiers of all the provinces of the Roman people on whose boundaries were peoples not subject to our empire. . . .

27. I added Egypt to the empire of the Roman people. . . .

35. When I held my thirteenth consulship, the senate, the equestrian order, and the entire Roman people gave me the title of "father of the country" and decreed that this title should be inscribed in the vestibule of my house, in the Julian senate house, and in the Augustan Forum. . . . At the time I wrote this document I was in my seventy-sixth year.

 What were the achievements of Augustus? To what extent did these accomplishments create the "job" of being emperor? In what sense could this document be called a piece of propaganda?

Source: N. Lewis and M. Renhold. *Roman Civilization*, vol. I (New York: Columbia University Press, 1955).

(the Roman peace) and the prosperity it engendered as the chief benefits of Roman rule during the first and second centuries C.E. These benefits were especially noticeable during the reigns of the five so-called **good emperors**. These rulers treated the ruling classes with respect, maintained peace in the empire, and supported generally beneficial domestic policies. Though absolute monarchs, they were known for their tolerance and diplomacy. By adopting capable men as their sons and successors, the first four of these emperors reduced the chances of succession problems.

Under the five good emperors, the powers of the emperor continued to expand at the expense of the senate. Increasingly, imperial officials appointed and directed by the emperor took over the running of the government. The good emperors also extended the scope of imperial administration to areas previously untouched by the imperial government. Trajan (TRAY-jun) (98–117 C.E.) implemented an alimentary program that provided state funds to assist poor parents in raising and educating their children. The good emperors were widely praised for their extensive building programs. Trajan and Hadrian

(HAY-dree-un) (117–138 C.E.) were especially active in constructing public works—aqueducts, bridges, roads, and harbor facilities—throughout the provinces and in Rome.

Although we think of the Pax Romana as a time of peace and orderly government, there were rebellions against Roman rule. Revolts of Jews in Egypt and North Africa during the reign of Trajan in 115 C.E. were crushed. In 60 or 61 C.E., there occurred the revolt of Boudica, the British queen of the Iceni tribe. She led an attack against Roman rule that burned and destroyed several cities before Roman forces won out. Rebellions against Roman rule were crushed without mercy, leading one Scottish chieftain to say (according to the Roman author Tacitus) when he was rousing his troops to fight the Romans, "To robbery, slaughter, plunder, they give the lying name of empire; they make a desert and call it peace." Obviously, Roman imperialism had a negative as well as positive side.

Frontiers and the Provinces Although Trajan extended Roman rule into Dacia (modern Romania), Mesopotamia, and the Sinai peninsula (see Map 5.4), his successors recognized that the empire was overextended and returned to Augustus's policy of defensive imperialism. Hadrian withdrew Roman forces from much of Mesopotamia. Although he retained Dacia and Arabia, he went on the defensive in his frontier policy by reinforcing the fortifications along a line connecting the Rhine and Danube Rivers and building a defensive wall 80 miles long across northern Britain to keep the Scots out of Roman Britain. By the end of the second century, the Roman forces were established in permanent bases behind the frontiers.

At its height in the second century C.E., the Roman Empire was one of the greatest states the world had seen. It covered roughly 3.5 million square miles and had a population, like that of Han China, estimated at more

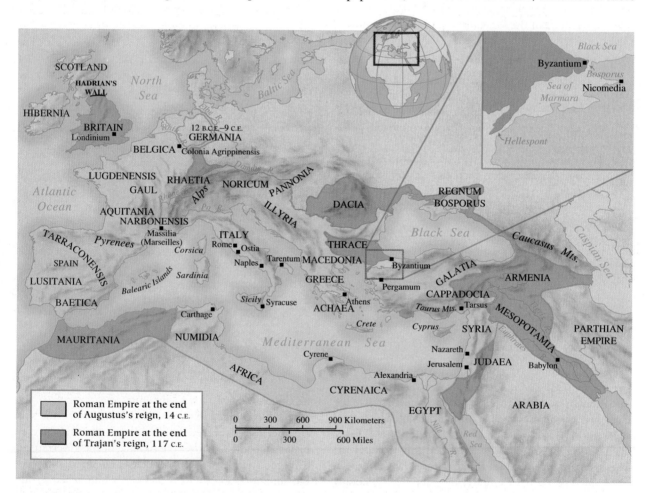

Map 5.4 The Roman Empire from Augustus through Trajan (14–117 C.E.). Augustus and later emperors continued the expansion of the Roman Empire, adding more resources but also increasing the tasks of administration and keeping the peace. Compare this map with Map 5.3.

Q *Which of Trajan's acquisitions were relinquished during Hadrian's reign?*

than 50 million. Whereas the emperors and the imperial administration provided a degree of unity, considerable leeway was given to local customs, and the privileges of Roman citizenship were extended to many people throughout the empire. In 212 C.E., the emperor Caracalla (kar-uh-KAL-uh) completed the process by giving Roman citizenship to every free inhabitant of the empire. Latin was the language of the western part of the empire, and Greek was used in the east. Roman culture spread to all parts of the empire and freely mixed with Greek culture, creating what has been called Greco-Roman civilization.

The administration and cultural life of the Roman Empire depended greatly on cities and towns. A provincial governor's staff was not large, so it was left to local city officials to act as Roman agents in carrying out many government functions, especially those related to taxes. Most towns and cities were not large by modern standards. The largest was Rome, but there were also large cities in the east: Alexandria in Egypt numbered more than 300,000 inhabitants. In the west, cities were usually small, with only a few thousand inhabitants. Cities were important in what some have called the process of romanization, or the spread of Roman culture, law, and the Latin language. Cities also often resembled one another with their temples, markets, amphitheaters, and other public buildings.

HISTORIANS DEBATE 5-2c **What Was Romanization?**

Romanization is a controversial term. An earlier generation of historians used the term to describe a process of transformation in which the Roman governors of provinces imposed the Romans' "civilized" ways on conquered peoples. Many historians today reject that model and argue that becoming Roman—in adopting Roman architecture, food, clothing, language and religious policy—was a process initiated by local elites themselves. They adopted the trappings of Roman civilization because being Roman was a means to power. Thus, the elites of the western provinces followed a policy, as one historian has stated, of "self-romanization."

The eastern part of the empire presented a different picture. The Greek language was dominant and the pre-Roman, Hellenistic culture survived. Instead of self-romanization, some historians use the term *culture of classicism* to refer to ways in the east. At the same time, although Roman and Greek culture spread to all parts of the empire, local languages persisted and many of the empire's residents spoke neither Latin nor Greek.

Prosperity in the Early Empire The internal peace of the Early Empire resulted in considerable prosperity and unprecedented levels of trade. Merchants from all over the empire came to the chief Italian ports of Puteoli on the Bay of Naples and Ostia at the mouth of the Tiber River. Long-distance trade beyond the Roman frontiers also developed, aided by economic expansion in both the Roman and Chinese Empires. Although both empires built roads chiefly for military purposes, the roads also came to facilitate trade. Moreover, by creating large empires, the Romans and Chinese not only established internal stability but also pacified bordering territories, thus reducing the threat that bandits posed to traders. As a result, merchants developed a network of trade routes that brought these two great empires into commercial contact.

Most important was the overland Silk Road, a regular caravan route between West and East (see Chapter 3). Silk, a filament recovered from the cocoons of silkworms, had been produced in China since the fourth millennium B.C.E. By the second century B.C.E., the first clothing made from silk reached the Mediterranean Sea, stimulating the contacts between China and the Roman Empire. The bulk of the trade went overland through Central Asia (thus earning this route its modern name, the Silk Road). By the first century C.E., large quantities of silk were being delivered to markets in Rome through the Silk Road trade. Silk became a craze among Roman elites, leading Roman scholar Pliny the Elder to remark that the Roman treasury was being depleted because wealthy Roman women were purchasing so much silk clothing.

The silk trade also stimulated a degree of mutual curiosity between the two great empires but not much mutual knowledge. Roman geographer Strabo wrote of a strange land called "Seres" far to the east, whereas Chinese sources mentioned the empire of "Great Qin" at the far end of the Silk Road to the west. There was little personal or diplomatic contacts between the two civilizations, but Chinese sources do reveal that a delegation from emperor Marcus Aurelius arrived in China in 166 C.E. and that a Roman merchant made it to the court of Emperor Wu in 226 C.E. Nevertheless, for the first time a commercial relationship linked two great empires at either extreme of the Eurasian supercontinent.

After the takeover of Egypt in the first century C.E., Roman merchants also began an active trade with India, from where they received precious pearls as well as pepper and other spices used in the banquets of the wealthy. The Romans even established a trading post in southern India where their merchants built warehouses and docks.

Increased trade helped stimulate manufacturing. The cities of the east still produced the items made in Hellenistic times. The first two centuries of the empire also witnessed the high point of industrial development in Italy. Some industries became concentrated in certain areas such as bronze work in Capua. Other industries, such as brickmaking, were pursued in rural areas as by-products of large landed estates.

Despite the profits from trade and commerce, agriculture remained the chief pursuit of most people and the underlying basis of Roman prosperity. Although the large latifundia still dominated agriculture, especially in southern and central Italy, small peasant farms continued to flourish, particularly in Etruria and the Po River Valley. Large estates depended on slaves for the raising of sheep and cattle, but some were also worked by free tenant farmers who paid rent in labor, produce, or sometimes cash.

Despite the prosperity of the Roman world, an enormous gulf existed between rich and poor. The development of towns and cities, so important to the creation of any civilization, is based largely on the agricultural surpluses of the countryside. In ancient times, the surplus produced by each farmer was relatively small. Therefore, the upper classes and urban populations had to be supported by the labor of a large number of agricultural producers, who never found it easy to produce much more than they needed for themselves. In lean years, when there were no surpluses, the townspeople often took what they wanted, leaving little for the peasants.

5-2d Culture and Society in the Roman World

One of the notable characteristics of Roman culture and society is the influence of the Greeks. Greek ambassadors, merchants, and artists traveled to Rome and spread Greek thought and practices. After their conquest of the Hellenistic kingdoms, Roman generals shipped Greek manuscripts and artworks back to Rome. Multitudes of educated Greek slaves labored in Roman households. Rich Romans hired Greek tutors and sent their sons to Athens to study. As Roman poet Horace (HOR-uss) said, "Captive Greece took captive her rude conqueror." Greek thought captivated less sophisticated Roman minds, and the Romans became willing transmitters of Greek culture.

Roman Literature The high point of Latin literature was reached in the age of Augustus, which is often called the "golden age of Latin literature." The most distinguished poet of the Augustan Age was Virgil (VUR-jul) (70–19 B.C.E.). The son of a small landholder in northern Italy, he welcomed the rule of Augustus and wrote his greatest work in the emperor's honor. Virgil's masterpiece was the *Aeneid* (ih-NEE-id), an epic poem clearly intended to rival the work of Homer. The connection between Troy and Rome is made in the poem when Aeneas (ih-NEE-uss), a hero of Troy, survives the destruction of that city and eventually settles in Latium—establishing a link between Roman civilization and Greek history. Aeneas is portrayed as the ideal Roman—his virtues are duty, piety, and faithfulness. Virgil's overall purpose was to show that Aeneas had fulfilled his mission to establish

the Romans in Italy and thereby start Rome on its divine mission to rule the world.

> Let others fashion from bronze more lifelike, breathing images—
> For so they shall—and evoke living faces from marble; Others excel as orators, others track with their instruments
> The planets circling in heaven and predict when stars will appear.
> But, Romans, never forget that government is your medium!
> Be this your art—to practice men in the habit of peace, Generosity to the conquered, and firmness against aggressors.[2]

As Virgil expressed it, ruling was Rome's gift.

Roman Art The Romans were also dependent on the Greeks for artistic inspiration. The Romans developed a taste for Greek statues, which they placed not only in public buildings but also in their private houses. The Romans' own portrait sculpture was characterized by an intense realism that included even unpleasant physical details. Wall paintings and frescoes in the homes of the rich realistically depicted landscapes, portraits, and scenes from mythological stories.

The Romans excelled in architecture, a highly practical art. Although they continued to adapt Greek styles and made use of colonnades and rectangular structures, the Romans were also innovative. They made considerable use of curvilinear forms: the arch, vault, and dome. The Romans were also the first people in antiquity to use concrete on a massive scale. They constructed huge buildings—public baths, such as those of Caracalla, and amphitheaters capable of seating 50,000 spectators. Their engineering skills were also put to use in constructing roads, aqueducts, and bridges: a network of 50,000 miles of roads linked all parts of the empire; in Rome, almost a dozen aqueducts kept the population of 1 million supplied with water.

Roman Law One of Rome's chief gifts to the Mediterranean world then and to later generations was its system of law. Rome's first code of laws was the Twelve Tables of 450 B.C.E., but that was designed for a simple farming society and proved inadequate for later needs. So, from the Twelve Tables, the Romans developed a system of civil law that applied to all Roman citizens. As Rome expanded, problems arose between citizens and noncitizens and also among noncitizen residents of the empire. Although some of the rules of civil law could be used in these cases, special rules were often needed. These rules gave rise to what was known as the *law of nations*, defined as the part of the law that applied to both Romans and foreigners. Under the influence of Stoicism, the Romans came to identify their law of nations with **natural law**, a

5.3 The Pantheon. Shown here is the Pantheon, one of Rome's greatest buildings. Constructed of brick, six kinds of concrete, and marble, it is a stunning example of the Romans' engineering skills. The outside porch of the Pantheon contains eighteen Corinthian columns made of granite, but it is the inside of the temple that amazes onlookers. The interior is a large circular space topped by a huge dome. A hole in the center of the roof is the only source of light. The dome was built up layer by layer from concrete and weighed 10 million pounds. The walls holding the dome are almost 20 feet thick.

set of universal laws based on reason. This enabled them to establish standards of justice that applied to all people.

These standards of justice included principles that we would immediately recognize. A person was regarded as innocent until proved otherwise. People accused of wrongdoing were allowed to defend themselves before a judge. A judge, in turn, was expected to weigh evidence carefully before arriving at a decision. These principles lived on long after the fall of the Roman Empire.

The Roman Family At the heart of the Roman social structure stood the family, which was headed by the *paterfamilias* (pay-tur-fuh-MEE-lee-uss)—the dominant male. The household also included the wife, sons with their wives and children, unmarried daughters, and slaves. Like the Greeks, Roman males believed that females needed male guardians. The paterfamilias exercised that authority; on his death, sons or nearest male relatives assumed the role of guardians.

Fathers arranged the marriages of their daughters. In the republic, women married "with legal control" passing from father to husband. By the mid-first century B.C.E., the dominant practice had changed to "without legal control," which meant that married daughters officially remained within the father's legal power. Because the fathers of most married women died sooner or later, not being in the "legal control" of a husband made possible independent

property rights that forceful women could translate into considerable power within the household and outside it.

Some parents in upper-class families provided education for their daughters by hiring private tutors or sending them to primary schools. At the age when boys were entering secondary schools, however, girls were pushed into marriage. The legal minimum age for marriage was twelve, although fourteen was a more common age in practice (for males, the legal minimum age was fourteen, and most men married later). Although some Roman doctors warned that early pregnancies could be dangerous for young girls, early marriages persisted because women died at a relatively young age. A good example is Tullia, Cicero's beloved daughter. She was married at sixteen, widowed at twenty-two, remarried one year later, divorced at twenty-eight, remarried at twenty-nine, and divorced at thirty-three. She died at thirty-four, which was not unusually young for women in Roman society.

By the second century C.E., significant changes were occurring in the Roman family. The paterfamilias no longer had absolute authority over his children; he could no longer sell his children into slavery or have them put to death. Moreover, the husband's absolute authority over his wife also disappeared, and by the late second century, upper-class Roman women had considerable freedom and independence (see Opposing Viewpoints, "Women in the Roman and Han Empires," p. 124). They

Women in the Roman and Han Empires

Family & Society

THE FOLLOWING TWO EXCERPTS below are taken from the works of writers in two of the ancient world's great empires: one is a male philosopher living in the Roman Empire, and the other is a female writer in Han China. Gaius Musonius Rufus was a philosopher who taught Stoicism in Rome in the first century c.e. His students wrote down some of his philosophical opinions. The excerpt here is taken from his thoughts on whether women should study philosophy. Ban Zhao was a well-educated woman from a prominent aristocratic family. She wrote *Admonitions for Women* as a guide for upper-class women in the proper performance of their wifely duties.

Gaius Musonius Rufus, "That Women Too Should Study Philosophy"

When he was asked whether women ought to study philosophy, he began to answer. . . . Women have received from the gods the same ability to reason that men have. . . . Likewise women have the same senses as men, sight, hearing, smell, and the rest. . . . Since that is so, why is it appropriate for men to seek out and examine how they might live well, that is, to practice philosophy, but not women? . . .

Let us consider in detail the qualities that a woman who seeks to be good must possess, for it will be apparent that she could acquire each of these qualities from the practice of philosophy.

In the first place a woman must run her household and pick out what is beneficial for her home and take charge of the household slaves. . . . Next a woman must be chaste, and capable of keeping herself free from illegal love affairs, . . . and not enjoy quarrels, not be extravagant or occupied with her appearance . . . she must control anger, and not be overcome by grief, and be stronger than every kind of emotion. . . .

[When asked if sons and daughters should be given the same education, he replied,] There are not different sets of virtues for men and women. First, men and women both need to be sensible. . . . Second, both need to live just lives. . . . Third, a wife ought to be chaste, and so should a husband. . . .

Well, then, suppose someone says, "Do you think that men ought to learn spinning like women and that women ought to practice gymnastics like men?" No, that is not what I suggest. I say that because in the case of the human race, the males are naturally stronger, and the women weaker, appropriate work ought to be assigned to each, and the heavier task be given to the stronger, and the lighter to the weaker. For this reason, spinning is more appropriate work for women than for men, and household management. Gymnastics are more appropriate for men than for women, and outdoor work likewise. . . . Some tasks are more appropriate for one nature, others for the other. For that reason some jobs are called men's work, and others women's. . . .

Without philosophy no man and no woman either can be well educated. I do not mean to say that women need to have clarity with or facility in argument, because they will use philosophy as women use it. . . . My point is that women ought to be good and noble in their characters, and that philosophy is no other than the training for that nobility.

Ban Zhao, *Admonitions for Women*

Let a woman modestly yield to others; let her respect others, let her put others first, herself last. Should she do something good, let her not mention it; should she do something bad, let her not deny it. Let her bear contempt; let her even endure when others speak or do evil to her. . . .

Let a woman retire late to bed, but rise early to her duties; let her not dread tasks by day or night. Let her not refuse to perform domestic duties whether easy or difficult. That which must be done, let her finish completely, tidily and systematically. . . .

Let a woman be composed in demeanor and upright in bearing in the service of her husband. Let her live in purity and quietness and keep watch over herself. Let her not love gossip and silly laughter. Let her cleanse, purify and arrange in order the wine and the food for the offerings to the ancestors. . . .

Now examine the gentlemen of the present age. They only know that wives must be controlled and that the husband's authority must be maintained. They therefore teach their boys to read books and study histories. . . . Yet only to teach men and not to teach women—is this not ignoring the reciprocal relation between them? . . .

In womanly behavior there are four things . . . womanly virtue, womanly speech, womanly appearance, and womanly work.

To guard carefully her chastity, to control circumspectly her behavior, in every motion to exhibit modesty, . . . : this may be called womanly virtue.

To choose her words with care, to avoid vulgar language, to speak at appropriate times, and not to be offensive to others may be called womanly speech.

To wash and scrub dirt and grime, to keep clothes and ornaments fresh and clean, to wash the head and bathe the body regularly, . . . may be called womanly appearance.

With wholehearted devotion to sew and weave, not to love gossip and silly laughter, to prepare the wine and food for serving guests may be called womanly work.

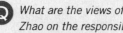 *What are the views of Gaius Musonius Rufus and Ban Zhao on the responsibilities of a woman? In what ways do they agree? In what ways do they disagree? How do you explain the differences? From your point of view, what are the strengths and weaknesses in each argument?*

Sources: M. R. Lefkowitz and M. B. Fant, eds. *Women's Life in Greece and Rome: A Source Book in Translation,* 2nd ed. (Baltimore: Johns Hopkins University Press, 1992), pp. 50–54; W. T. DeBary and I. Bloom *Sources of Chinese Tradition,* 2nd ed. (New York: Columbia University Press, 1999), pp. 821–824.

had acquired the right to own, inherit, and dispose of property. Women still could not participate in politics, but the early empire saw several important women who influenced politics through their husbands or sons. Remember, however, that the advantages of upper-class women were not necessarily true of women's experiences overall. Like the Greeks, the Romans adhered to the belief that a woman's place was in the home, and her role was to perform the domestic tasks crucial to the home. In other words, a Roman woman should be a "good wife" and a "good mother."

Slaves and their Masters Although slavery was a common institution throughout the ancient world, no people possessed more slaves or relied so much on slave labor as the Romans eventually did. Slaves were used in many ways in Roman society. The rich owned the most and the best. In the late Roman republic, it became a badge of prestige to be attended by many slaves. Greek slaves were in much demand as tutors, musicians, doctors, and artists. Roman businessmen would employ them as shop assistants or craftspeople. Slaves were also used as farm laborers; huge gangs of slaves worked the large landed estates under pitiful conditions. Many slaves of all nationalities were used as menial household workers such as cooks, waiters, cleaners, and gardeners. Contractors used slave labor to build roads, aqueducts, and other public structures.

The treatment of Roman slaves varied. There are numerous instances of humane treatment by masters and even reports of slaves protecting their owners from danger out of gratitude and esteem. But slaves were also subject to severe punishments, torture, abuse, and hard labor that drove some to run away despite stringent laws against aiding a runaway slave. Some slaves revolted against their owners and even murdered them, causing some Romans to live in unspoken fear of their slaves.

Near the end of the second century B.C.E., large-scale slave revolts occurred in Sicily, where enormous gangs of slaves were subjected to horrible working conditions on large landed estates. The most famous uprising on the Italian peninsula occurred in 73 B.C.E. Led by a gladiator named Spartacus (SPAR-tuh-kuss), the revolt broke out in southern Italy and involved seventy thousand slaves. Spartacus managed to defeat several Roman armies before being trapped and killed in southern Italy in 71 B.C.E. Six thousand of his followers were crucified, the traditional form of execution for slaves.

Imperial Rome At the center of the colossal Roman Empire was the ancient city of Rome. Truly a capital city, Rome had the largest population of any city in the empire, close to 1 million by the time of Augustus. Only Chang'an, the imperial capital of the Han Empire in China, had a comparable population during this time.

Both food and entertainment were provided on a grand scale for Roman inhabitants. Poet Juvenal (JOO-vuh-nul) said of the Roman masses: "But nowadays, with no vote to sell, their motto is 'Couldn't care less.' Time was when their plebiscite elected generals, heads of state, commanders of legions: but now they've pulled in their horns, there's only two things that concern them: Bread and Circuses."[3] The emperor and other state officials provided public spectacles as part of the great religious festivals celebrated by the state. Most famous were the gladiatorial shows, which took place in amphitheaters. Perhaps the most famous was the amphitheater known as the Colosseum, constructed in Rome to seat 50,000 spectators. In most cities and towns, amphitheaters were the biggest buildings, rivaled only by the circuses (arenas) for races and the public baths.

Gladiatorial games were held from dawn to dusk (see Film & History, *Gladiator*, p. 126). Contests to the death between trained fighters formed the central focus

of these games, but the games included other forms of entertainment as well. Criminals of all ages and both genders were sent into the arena without weapons to face certain death from wild animals who would tear them to pieces. Numerous types of animal contests were also held: wild beasts against each other, such as bears against buffaloes; staged hunts with men shooting safely from behind iron bars; and gladiators in the arena with bulls, tigers, and lions. It is recorded that 5,000 animals were killed in one day of games when Emperor Titus inaugurated the Colosseum in 80 C.E.

5-3 CRISIS AND THE LATE EMPIRE

Q **Focus Questions:** What reforms did Diocletian and Constantine institute, and to what extent were the reforms successful? What role did the Germanic tribes play in the Late Roman Empire?

During the reign of Marcus Aurelius, the last of the five good emperors, several natural catastrophes struck Rome. To many Romans, these natural disasters seemed to portend an ominous future for Rome. New problems arose soon after the death of Marcus Aurelius in 180 C.E.

5-3a Crises in the Third Century

In the course of the third century, the Roman Empire nearly collapsed. Military monarchy under the Severan rulers (193–235 C.E.), which restored order after a series of civil wars, was followed by military anarchy. For the next forty-nine years, the Roman imperial throne was occupied by anyone who had the military strength to seize it—a total of twenty-two emperors, only two of whom did not meet a violent death. At the same time, the empire was beset by a series of invasions, no doubt exacerbated by the civil wars. In the east, the Sassanian (suh-SAN-ee-an) Persians made inroads into Roman territory. Germanic tribes also poured into the empire. Not until the end of the third century were most of the boundaries restored.

Invasions, civil wars, and plague created new problems for the Roman Empire in the third century. There was a noticeable decline in trade and small industry, and the labor shortage caused by a plague affected both military recruiting and the economy. Farm production deteriorated significantly as fields were ravaged by invaders or, even more often, by the defending Roman armies. The monetary system began to collapse as a result of debased coinage and inflation. Armies were needed more than ever, but financial strains made it difficult to pay and enlist more soldiers. By the mid-third century, the state had to hire Germans to fight under Roman commanders.

5-3b The Late Roman Empire

At the end of the third and the beginning of the fourth century, the Roman Empire gained a new lease on life through the efforts of two strong emperors, Diocletian (dy-uh-KLEE-shun) and Constantine (KAHN-stun-teen). Their rule transformed the empire into a new state, the so-called Late Empire, distinguished by a new governmental structure, a rigid economic and social system, and a new state religion—Christianity (see "Transformation of the Roman World: The Development of Christianity" later in this chapter).

The Reforms of Diocletian and Constantine Both Diocletian (284–305 C.E.) and Constantine (306–337 C.E.) extended imperial control by strengthening and expanding the administrative bureaucracies of the Roman Empire. A hierarchy of officials exercised control at various levels of government. The army was enlarged, and mobile units were set up that could be quickly moved to support frontier troops when the borders were threatened.

Constantine's biggest project was the construction of a new capital city in the east on the site of the Greek city of Byzantium on the shores of the Bosporus. Eventually renamed Constantinople (modern Istanbul), the city was developed for defensive reasons and had an excellent strategic location. Calling it his "New Rome," Constantine endowed the city with a forum, large palaces, and a vast amphitheater.

The political and military reforms of Diocletian and Constantine also greatly enlarged two institutions—the army and the civil service—that drained most of the public funds.

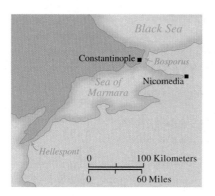

Map 5.5 Location of Constantinople, the "New Rome"

Though more revenues were needed to pay for the army and bureaucracy, the population was not growing, so the tax base could not be expanded. To ensure the tax base and keep the empire going despite the shortage of labor, the emperors issued edicts that forced people to remain in their designated vocations. Basic jobs such as bakers and shippers became hereditary. The fortunes of free tenant farmers also declined. Soon they found themselves bound to the land by large landowners who took advantage of depressed agricultural conditions to enlarge their landed estates.

The End of the Western Empire Constantine had reunited the Roman Empire and restored a semblance of order. After his death, however, the empire continued to divide into western and eastern parts, which would become two virtually independent states by 395 C.E. In the course of the fifth century, the empire in the east remained intact under the Roman emperor in Constantinople, but the empire in the west disintegrated as more and more Germans moved in and challenged Roman authority.

Although the Romans had established a series of political frontiers along the Rhine and Danube Rivers, Romans and Germans often came into contact across these boundaries. Until the fourth century, the empire had proved capable of absorbing these people without harm to its political structure. In the late fourth century, however, the Germanic tribes came under new pressure when the Huns, a fierce tribe of nomads from the steppes of Asia who may have been related to the Xiongnu (SHYAHNG-noo), the invaders of the Han Empire in China, moved into the Black Sea region, possibly attracted by the riches of the empire to the south. Among the groups displaced by the Huns were the Visigoths (VIZ-uh-gahthz), who moved south and west, crossed the Danube River into Roman territory, and settled down as Roman allies. But the Visigoths soon revolted, and the Roman attempt to stop them at Adrianople led to a crushing defeat for [...]

Increasing numbers of [...] now crossed the frontiers. In [...] the Visigoths sacked Rome. Vandals poured into southern Spain and Africa, and Visigoths into Spain and Gaul. The Vandals crossed into Italy from North Africa and ravaged Rome again in 455. By the middle of the fifth century, the western provinces of the Roman Empire had been taken over by Germanic peoples who were in the process of setting up independent kingdoms. At the same time, a semblance of imperial authority remained in Rome, although the real power behind the throne tended to rest in the hands of important military officials known as *masters of the soldiers*. These military commanders controlled the government and dominated the imperial court. In 476, Odoacer (oh-doh-AY-sur), a new master of the soldiers, himself of German origin, deposed the Roman emperor, the boy Romulus Augustulus (RAHM-yuh-lus ow-GOOS-chuh-luss). To many historians, the deposition of Romulus signaled the end of the Roman Empire in the west. Of course, this is only a symbolic date because much of direct imperial rule had already been lost in the course of the fifth century.

HISTORIANS DEBATE **5-3c What Caused the Fall of the Western Roman Empire?**

The end of the Roman Empire in the west has given rise to numerous theories that attempt to provide a single, all-encompassing reason for the "decline and fall of the Roman Empire." These include the following: Christianity's emphasis on a spiritual kingdom undermined Roman military virtues and patriotism; traditional Roman values declined as non-Italians gained prominence in the empire; lead poisoning caused by water pipes and cups made of lead resulted in a mental decline; plague decimated the population; Rome failed to advance technologically because of slavery; and Rome was unable to achieve a workable political system. Each theory may have an element of truth, but all of them have been challenged. History is an intricate web of relationships, causes, and effects. No single explanation will ever suffice to explain historical events. One thing is clear, however. Weakened by a shortage of manpower, the Roman army in the west was simply not able to fend off the hordes of people moving into Italy and Gaul. In contrast, the Eastern Roman Empire, which would survive for another 1,000 years, remained largely free from invasion.

5-4 TRANSFORMATION OF THE ROMAN WORLD: THE DEVELOPMENT OF CHRISTIANITY

 Focus Question: What characteristics of Christianity enabled it to grow and ultimately triumph as the official religion of the Roman Empire?

The rise of Christianity marked a fundamental break with the dominant values of the Greco-Roman world. To understand the rise of Christianity, we must first examine both the religious environment of the Roman world and the Jewish background from which Christianity emerged.

The Roman state religion focused on the worship of a pantheon of Greco-Roman gods and goddesses, including Juno, the patron goddess of women; Minerva, the goddess of craftspeople; Mars, the god of war; and Jupiter Optimus Maximus (JOO-puh-tur AHP-tuh-muss MAK-suh-muss) ("best and greatest"), who became the patron deity of Rome and assumed a central place in the religious life of the city. The Romans believed that the observance of proper ritual by state priests brought them into a right relationship with the gods, thereby guaranteeing security, peace, and prosperity. They also believed their success in creating an empire confirmed they enjoyed the favor of the gods. As the first-century B.C.E. politician Cicero claimed, "We have overcome all the nations of the world because we have realized that the world is directed and governed by the gods."[4]

The polytheistic Romans were extremely tolerant of other religions. They allowed the worship of native gods and goddesses throughout their provinces and even adopted some local deities. In addition, beginning with Augustus, emperors were often officially made gods by the Roman senate, thus bolstering support for the emperors (see the already noted Comparative Essay "Rulers and Gods").

As the Romans expanded into the eastern Mediterranean, they came into contact with the various peoples of the east, including the Jews. Roman involvement with the Jews began in 63 B.C.E., and by 6 C.E. Judaea (which embraced the old Israelite kingdom of Judah) had been made a province and placed under the direction of a Roman procurator. But unrest continued, augmented by divisions among the Jews themselves. One group, the Essenes, awaited a messiah who would save Israel from oppression, usher in the kingdom of God, and establish paradise on Earth. Another group, the Zealots, were militant extremists who advocated the violent overthrow of Roman rule. A Jewish revolt in 66 C.E. was crushed by the Romans four years later. The Jewish Temple in Jerusalem was destroyed, and Roman power once more stood supreme in Judaea.

Another Jewish revolt against Roman rule occurred in 132 C.E. when emperor Hadrian attempted to set up a new Roman colony on the site of Jerusalem. Although Jewish forces under the leadership of Simon bar Kokhba, who was viewed by many Jews as a messiah, were initially successful, the Roman legions gradually wore down the Jewish forces and captured Jerusalem in 135. Judaea, now renamed Syria-Palaestina, was a wasteland, and Jews were forbidden to enter Jerusalem. Driven by their religious uniqueness, the Jews had tried and failed to maintain an independent state. Another Jewish state would not arise until after World War II with the creation of modern Israel.

5-4a The Origins of Christianity

Jesus of Nazareth (ca. 6 B.C.E. – ca. 29 C.E.) was a Palestinian Jew who grew up in Galilee, an important center of the militant Zealots. Jesus's message was simple. He reassured his fellow Jews that he did not plan to undermine their traditional religion. What was important was not strict adherence to the letter of the law but the transformation of the inner person: "So in everything, do to others what you would have them do to you, for this sums up the Law and the Prophets."[5] God's command was simply to love God and one another: "Love the Lord your God with all your heart and with all your soul and with all your mind and with all your strength. The second is this: Love your neighbor as yourself."[6] In the Sermon on the Mount, Jesus presented ethical concepts—humility, charity, and brotherly love—that would form the basis of the value system of medieval Western civilization.

To the Roman authorities of Palestine, however, Jesus was a potential revolutionary who might transform Jewish expectations of a messianic kingdom into a revolt against Rome. Therefore, he found himself denounced on many sides, and the procurator Pontius Pilate ordered his crucifixion. But that did not solve the problem. A few loyal followers of Jesus spread the story that Jesus had overcome death, been resurrected, and then ascended into heaven. The belief in Jesus's resurrection became an important tenet of Christian doctrine. Jesus was now hailed as "the anointed one" (*Christus* in Greek), the messiah who would return and usher in the kingdom of God on earth.

Rulers and Gods

Religion & Philosophy

All of the world's earliest civilizations believed in a close relationship between rulers and gods. In Egypt, pharaohs were considered gods whose role was to maintain the order and harmony of the universe in their own kingdom. In the words of an Egyptian hymn, "What is the king of Upper and Lower Egypt? He is a god by whose dealings one lives, the father and mother of all men, alone by himself, without an equal." In Mesopotamia, India, and China, rulers were thought to rule with divine assistance. Kings were often believed to derive their power from the gods and to be the agents or representatives of the gods. In ancient India, rulers claimed to be representatives of the gods because they were descended from Manu, the first man who had been made a king by Brahman, the supreme god. Many Romans certainly believed that their success in creating an empire was a visible sign of divine favor.

This supposed connection to the gods also caused rulers to seek divine aid in the affairs of this world. This led to the art of divination, or an organized method of discovering the intentions of the gods. In Mesopotamian and Roman society, one form of divination involved the examination of the livers of sacrificed animals; features seen in the livers were interpreted to foretell events to come. The Chinese used oracle bones to receive advice from supernatural forces that were beyond the power of human beings. Questions to the gods were scratched on turtle shells or animal bones, which were then exposed to fire. Shamans then interpreted the meaning of the resulting cracks on the surface of the shells or bones as messages from supernatural forces. The Greeks divined the will of the gods by use of the oracle, a priestess in a sacred shrine dedicated to a god or goddess who revealed the future in response to a question.

Underlying all of these divinatory practices was a belief in a supernatural universe—a world inhabited by divine forces on which humans depended for their well-being. Not until the Scientific Revolution of the modern world did many people begin to believe in a natural world that was not governed by spiritual forces.

Q *What role did spiritual forces play in early civilizations?*

Fitzwilliam Museum, University of Cambridge, UK/The Bridgeman Art Library

5.4 Vishnu. Brahman the Creator, Shiva the Destroyer, and Vishnu the Preserver are the three chief Hindu gods of India. Vishnu is known as the Preserver because he mediates between Brahman and Shiva and thus maintains the stability of the universe.

Christianity began, then, as a religious movement within Judaism and was viewed that way by Roman authorities for many decades. However, one prominent figure in early Christianity—Paul of Tarsus (ca. 5 – ca. 67 C.E.)—believed that the message of Jesus should be preached not only to Jews but also to gentiles (non-Jews). Paul taught that Jesus was the savior, the son of God, who had come to Earth to save all humans, who were sinners as a result of Adam's sin of disobedience against God. By his death, Jesus had atoned for the sins of all humans and made possible their reconciliation with God and hence their salvation. By accepting Jesus as their savior, they too could be saved.

5-4b The Spread of Christianity

Christianity spread slowly at first. Although the teachings of early Christianity were mostly disseminated by the preaching of convinced Christians, written materials also appeared. Among them were a series of epistles (letters) written by Paul, outlining Christian beliefs for different Christian communities. Some of Jesus's disciples may also have preserved some of the sayings of the master in writing and would have passed on personal memories that became the basis of the written *Gospels*—the "good news" concerning Jesus—which by the end of the first century C.E. had become the authoritative record of Jesus's life and teachings and formed the core of the New Testament.

5.5 Jesus and his apostles. Pictured is a fourth-century ce fresco from a Roman catacomb depicting Jesus and his apostles. Catacombs were underground cemeteries where early Christians buried their dead. Christian tradition holds that in times of imperial repression, Christians withdrew to the catacombs to pray and hide.

Although Jerusalem was the first center of Christianity, its destruction by the Romans in 70 C.E. dispersed the Christians and left individual Christian churches with considerable independence. By 100, Christian churches had been established in most of the major cities of the east and in some places in the western part of the empire. Many early Christians came from the ranks of Hellenized Jews and the Greek-speaking populations of the east. But in the second and third centuries, an increasing number of followers came from Latin-speaking peoples.

Initially, the Romans did not pay much attention to the Christians, whom they regarded as simply another Jewish sect. As time passed, however, the Roman attitude toward Christianity began to change. The Romans tolerated other religions as long as they did not threaten public order or public morals. But because Christians refused to worship the state gods and emperors, many Romans came to view them as harmful to the Roman state. Nevertheless, Roman persecution of Christians in the first and second centuries was only sporadic and local, never systematic. In the second century, Christians were largely ignored as harmless (see Historical Voices, "Roman Authorities on Christianity," p. 131). By the end of the reigns of the five good emperors, Christians still represented a small minority, but one of considerable strength.

5-4c The Triumph of Christianity

Christianity grew slowly in the first century, took root in the second, and had spread widely by the third. Why was Christianity able to attract so many followers? First, the Christian message had much to offer the Roman world. The promise of salvation, made possible by Jesus's death and supposed resurrection, made a resounding impact on a world full of suffering and injustice. Christianity seemed to imbue life with a meaning and purpose beyond the simple material things of everyday reality. Second, Christianity seemed familiar. It was regarded as simply another of the mystery religions, common in the Hellenistic east, that offered immortality as the result of the sacrificial death of a savior god. At the same time, it offered more than the other mystery religions did. Jesus had been a human figure, not a mythological one, and people found it easier to relate to him.

Christianity also proved attractive to all classes. The promise of eternal life was for all—rich, poor, aristocrats, slaves, men, and women. Christianity emphasized a sense of spiritual equality for all people. Many women, in fact, found that Christianity offered them new roles and new forms of companionship with other women. Christian women fostered the new religion in their homes and preached their convictions to other people in their towns and villages. Many also died for their faith. Perpetua, for example, was an aristocratic woman who converted to Christianity. Her pagan family begged her to renounce her new faith, but she refused. Arrested by Roman authorities, she chose instead to die for her faith and was one of a group of Christians who were slaughtered by wild beasts in the arena at Carthage on March 7, 203 C.E.

Moreover, the sporadic persecution of Christians by the Romans in the first and second centuries not only did little to stop the growth of Christianity but also served to strengthen it as an institution in the second and third centuries by causing it to become more organized. Crucial to this change was the emerging role of the bishops, who began to assume more control over church communities. The Christian church was creating a well-defined hierarchical structure in which the bishops and clergy were salaried officers separate from the laity or regular church members.

HISTORICAL VOICES

Roman Authorities on Christianity

 AT FIRST, ROMAN AUTHORITIES were uncertain how to deal with Christians. In the second century, Christians were often viewed as harmless and yet were subject to persecution if they persisted in their beliefs. The first selection—an exchange between Pliny the Younger and Emperor Trajan—illustrates this approach. Pliny, the governor of the province of Bithynia in northwestern Asia Minor, wrote to the emperor for advice about how to handle people accused of being Christians. Trajan's response reflects the general attitude toward Christians taken by emperors in the second century.

An Exchange Between Pliny and Trajan

Pliny to Trajan

It is my custom to refer all my difficulties to you, Sir, for no one is better able to resolve my doubts and to inform my ignorance.

I have never been present at an examination of Christians. Consequently, I do not know the nature of the extent of the punishments usually meted out to them, nor the grounds for starting an investigation and how far it should be pressed. . . .

For the moment this is the line I have taken with all persons brought before me on the charge of being Christians. I have asked them in person if they are Christians, and if they admit it, I repeat the question a second and third time, with a warning of the punishment awaiting them. If they persist, I order them to be led away for execution. . . .

Now that I have begun to deal with this problem, as so often happens, the charges are becoming more widespread and increasing in variety. An anonymous pamphlet has been circulated which contains the names of a number of accused persons. . . .

I have therefore postponed any further examination and hastened to consult you. The question seems to me to be worthy of your consideration, especially in view of the number of persons endangered; for a great many individuals of every age and class, both men and women, are being brought to trial, and this is likely to continue. It is not only the towns, but villages and rural districts too which are infected through contact with this wretched cult. I think though that it is still possible for it to be checked and directed to better ends, for there is no doubt that people have begun to throng the temples which had been almost entirely deserted for a long time.

Trajan to Pliny

You have followed the right course of procedure, my dear Pliny, in your examination of the cases of persons charged with being Christians, for it is impossible to lay down a general rule to a fixed formula. These people must not be hunted out; if they are brought before you and the charge against them is proved, they must be punished, but in the case of anyone who denies that he is a Christian, and makes it clear that he is not by offering prayers to our gods, he is to be pardoned as a result of his repentance however suspect his past conduct may be. But pamphlets circulated anonymously must play no part in any accusation. They create the worst sort of precedent and are quite out of keeping with the spirit of our age.

 What were Pliny's personal opinions of Christians? Why was he willing to execute them? What was Trajan's response, and what were its consequences for the Christians?

Source: *From Readings in Ancient History*, Hutton Webster (D.C. Heath and Co.: Boston 1919), p. 250.

As the Christian church became more organized, some emperors in the third century responded with more systematic persecutions, but their efforts failed. The last great persecution occurred at the beginning of the fourth century, but Christianity had by then become too strong to be eradicated by force. After Constantine became the first Christian emperor, Christianity flourished. Although Constantine was not baptized until the end of his life, in 313 C.E. he issued the Edict of Milan officially tolerating Christianity. Under Theodosius (thee-uh-DOH-shuss) the Great (378–395 C.E.), it was made the official religion of the Roman Empire. In less than four centuries, Christianity had triumphed.

Emperors, West and East

Politics & Government **TWO GREAT EMPIRES** with strong central governments dominated much of the ancient world—the Roman Empire in the West and the Han Empire in the East. Shown here are two emperors from these empires. The Roman emperor Hadrian (Image 5.6a), who ruled from 117 to 138 C.E., was the third of the five good emperors. He had been adopted by Emperor Trajan to serve as his successor. Hadrian was a strong and intelligent ruler who took his responsibilities seriously. Between 121 and 132, he visited all of the provinces in the empire. Liu Bang (lyoo BAHNG) (Image 5.6b) came from the peasant class,

5.6b

5.6a

but through his military prowess, he defeated all rivals in the civil wars that followed the death of the First Emperor of Qin. Liu Bang, who is known historically by his title of Han Gaozu (HAHN gow-DZOO), was the first emperor of the Han Dynasty, which ruled China for 400 years. He won the support of his subjects by reducing their tax burden. He was also responsible for bringing China back under central control but was killed in a frontier battle in 195 B.C.E.

 What similarities do you see in the lives of these two rulers?

5-5 A COMPARISON OF THE ROMAN AND HAN EMPIRES

 Focus Question: In what ways were the Roman Empire and the Han Chinese Empire similar, and in what ways were they different?

At the beginning of the first millennium C.E., two great empires—the Roman Empire in the West and the Han Empire in the East—dominated large areas of the world. Although there was little contact between them, the two empires exhibited some remarkable similarities. Both lasted for centuries, and both were extremely successful in establishing centralized control (see Comparative Illustration, "Emperors, West and East"). Both built elaborate systems of roads in order to rule efficiently and relied on provincial officials—especially towns and cities—for local administration. In both empires, settled conditions led to a high level of agricultural production that sustained large populations, estimated at between 50 and 60 million in each empire. Although both empires expanded into areas with different languages, ethnic groups, and ways of life, they managed to extend their legal and political institutions, their technical skills, and their languages throughout their empires. In this way, they integrated local communities into a common political and cultural framework.

The Roman and Han Empires also had similar social and economic structures. The family stood at the heart of the social structure, and the male head of the family was all-powerful. The family also inculcated the values that helped make the empires strong—duty, courage, obedience, and discipline. The wealth of both societies also depended on agriculture. Although a free peasantry provided a backbone of strength and stability in each empire, wealthy landowners were able to gradually convert free peasants into tenant farmers and thereby ultimately undermine the power of the imperial governments.

Of course, there were also significant differences. The empires came into existence in different ways. Han China inherited an ideal of imperial culture on which to build. The Romans, on the other hand, began with a small city-state ruled collectively by its prominent citizens. As the Romans expanded throughout Italy and the Mediterranean, they eventually created a single imperial state.

Economic and social differences are also apparent. Merchants were more highly regarded and allowed more freedom in Rome than they were in China. One key reason for this difference is that whereas many inhabitants of the Roman Empire depended to a considerable degree on commerce to obtain such staples as wheat, olives, wine, cloth, and timber, the vast majority of Chinese were subsistence farmers whose needs—when they were supplied—could normally be met by the local environment. As a result, there was less social mobility in China than in Rome, and many Chinese peasants spent their entire lives without venturing far beyond their village gates.

Another difference is that over the 400 years of the empires' existence, Chinese imperial authority was far more stable. With a more cohesive territory and a strong dynastic principle, Chinese rulers could easily pass on their authority to other family members. In contrast, political instability was a chronic problem in the Roman Empire, at least in some periods. Although Roman emperors were accorded divine status by the Roman senate after death, accession to the Roman imperial throne depended less on solid dynastic principles and more on pure military force.

Despite the differences, one major inescapable similarity remains: both empires eventually faced overwhelming problems. They suffered from overexpansion and fortified their long borders with walls, forts, and military garrisons to guard against invasions of nomadic peoples. Both empires were periodically beset by invasions of these peoples: the Han Dynasty was weakened by the incursions of the Xiongnu, and the Western Roman Empire eventually collapsed in the face of incursions by the Germanic peoples. Yet, although the Han Dynasty collapsed, the Chinese imperial tradition, along with the class structure and set of values that sustained that tradition, survived, and the Chinese Empire, under new dynasties, continued into the twentieth century as a single political entity. In stark contrast, the Roman Empire collapsed and lived on only as an idea.

CHAPTER SUMMARY

Sometime in the eighth century B.C.E., a group of Latin-speaking people built a small community called Rome on the Tiber River in Italy. Between 509 and 264 B.C.E., this  city expanded and brought almost all of Italy under its control. During this time of conquest, Rome also developed the political institutions of a republic ruled by an aristocratic oligarchy. Between 264 and 133 B.C.E., Rome expanded to the west and east and became master of the Mediterranean Sea and its surrounding territories, creating one of the largest empires in antiquity. In the second century B.C.E., the conservative and traditional values of Rome declined as affluence and individualism increased. After 133 B.C.E., Rome's republican institutions proved inadequate for the task of ruling an empire, and after a series of bloody civil wars, Augustus created a new order that established a Roman imperial state.

The Roman Empire experienced a lengthy period of peace and prosperity between 14 C.E. and 180 C.E. During this Pax Romana, trade flourished and the provinces were governed efficiently. In the course of the third century, however, the empire came near to collapse because of invasions,

civil wars, and economic decline. At the same time, a new religion—Christianity—was spreading throughout the empire and slowly gaining acceptance. The response to the crises of the third century and the rise of Christianity gradually brought a transformation of the Roman Empire in the fourth and fifth centuries. Although the emperors Diocletian and Constantine brought new life to the so-called Late Empire, their efforts only shored up the empire temporarily. Beginning in 395, the empire divided into western and eastern parts, and in 476 the Roman Empire in the west came to an end.

Although the Roman Empire in the west collapsed and lived on only as an idea, Roman achievements were bequeathed to the future. The Romance languages of today (French, Italian, Spanish, Portuguese, and Romanian) are based on Latin. Western practices of impartial justice and trial by jury owe much to Roman law. As great builders, the Romans left monuments to

their skills throughout Europe, some of which, such as aqueducts and roads, are still in use today. Aspects of Roman administrative practices survived in the Western world for centuries. The Romans also preserved the intellectual heritage of the Greco-Roman world of antiquity. Nevertheless, although many aspects of the Roman world would continue, the heirs of Rome went on to create new civilizations—European, Islamic, and Byzantine—that would mark yet another stage in the development of human societies.

The Han Dynasty also created one of the greatest empires in antiquity. Like the Roman Empire, the Han Empire left a rich legacy to its successors. The Confucian institutions and principles enshrined during the long years of Han rule survived several centuries of internal division and eventually reemerged as the governing doctrine of later Chinese empires down to the twentieth century.

REFLECTION QUESTIONS

Q Was the fall of the Roman republic the result of systemic institutional weaknesses or the personal ambitions of generals and politicians? Explain your answer.

Q In what ways was the rule of the Roman emperors in the first and second centuries C.E. an improvement over

the republic of the first century B.C.E.? In what ways was their rule not an improvement over the last century of the republic?

Q In what ways were the Roman and Han Chinese imperial systems of government alike? In what ways were they different?

CHAPTER TIMELINE

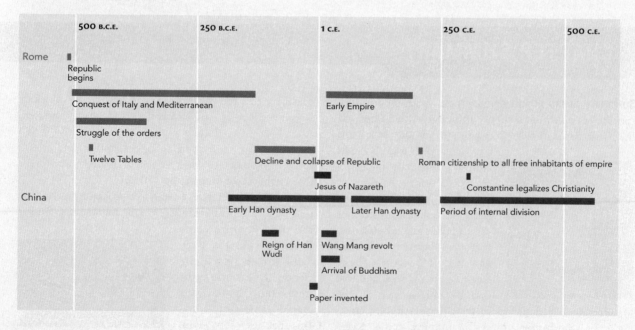

CHAPTER NOTES

1. Tacitus, *The Annals of Imperial Rome,* trans. M. Grant (Harmondsworth, England, 1964), p. 31.
2. Virgil, *The Aeneid,* trans. C. Day Lewis (Garden City, N.Y., 1952), p. 154.
3. Juvenal, *The Sixteen Satires,* trans. P. Green (New York, 1967), sat. 10, p. 207.
4. Quoted in C. Starr, *Past and Future in Ancient History* (Lanham, Md., 1987), pp. 38–39.
5. Matthew 7:12.
6. Mark 12:30–31.

MINDTAP
From Cengage

MindTap® is a fully online, highly personalized learning experience built upon Cengage Learning content. MindTap combines student learning tools—readings, multimedia, activities, and assessments—into a singular Learning Path that guides students through the course and helps students develop the critical thinking, analysis, and communication skills that are essential to academic and professional success.

PART II

NEW PATTERNS OF CIVILIZATION (500–1500 C.E.)

BY THE BEGINNING of the first millennium C.E., the great states of the ancient world were in decline; some were even at the point of collapse. On the ruins of these ancient empires, new patterns of civilization began to take shape between 400 and 1500 C.E. In some cases, these new societies were built on the political and cultural foundations laid down by their predecessors. The Tang Dynasty in China and the Guptas in India both looked back to the ancient period to provide an ideological model for their own time. The Byzantine Empire carried on parts of the classical Greek tradition while also adopting the powerful creed of Christianity from the Roman Empire. In other cases, new states incorporated elements of the former classical civilizations while heading in markedly different directions; the Arabic states in the Middle East and the new European civilization of the Middle Ages are good examples.

During this period, many significant forces were at work in human society. The accoutrements of a technologically advanced society gradually spread from the heartland regions of the Middle East, the Mediterranean basin, the South Asian subcontinent, and China into new areas of the world—sub-Saharan Africa, central and western Europe, Southeast Asia, and even the islands of Japan off the eastern edge of the Eurasian landmass. Across the oceans, unique but advanced civilizations began to take shape in isolation in the Americas. In the meantime, the vast migration of peoples continued, leading not only to bitter conflicts but also to increased interchanges of technology and ideas. The result was the transformation of separate and distinct cultures and civilizations into an increasingly complex and vast world system embracing not only technology and trade but also ideas and religious beliefs.

As had been the case during antiquity, the Middle East was at the heart of this activity. The Arab Empire, which took shape after the death of Muhammad in the early seventh century, brought a measure of stability and provided the key link in the revived trade routes through the region. Muslim traders—both Arab and Berber—opened contacts with West African societies south of the Sahara, while ships manned by Arab and South Asian sailors followed the monsoon winds eastward as far as the Spice Islands in Southeast Asia. Merchants from Central Asia carried goods back and forth along the Silk Road between the Middle East and China. For the next several hundred years, the great cities of the Middle East—Mecca, Damascus, and Baghdad—became among the wealthiest in the known world.

Islam's contributions to the human experience during this period were cultural and technological as well as economic. Muslim philosophers preserved the works of the ancient Greeks for posterity, Muslim scientists and mathematicians made new discoveries about the nature of the universe and the human body, and Arab cartographers and historians mapped the known world and speculated about the fundamental forces in human society.

But the Middle East was not the only or even the primary contributor to the spread of civilization during

From *Al Maqamat* (The Meetings) by Al-Hariri. c.1240 (gouache on paper). Al-Wasiti, Yahya ibn Mahmud (13th Century)/Bibliotheque Nationale, Paris, France/Bridgeman Images.

II.1 Abu Zayd and Al-Harith Question Villagers.

this period. Although the Arab Empire became the linchpin of trade between the Mediterranean and eastern and southern Asia, a new center of primary importance in world trade was emerging in East Asia and focused on China. China had been a major participant in regional trade during the Han Dynasty when its silks were already being transported to Rome via Central Asia, but its role had declined after the fall of the Han. Now, with the rise of the great Tang and Song Dynasties, China reemerged as a major commercial power in East Asia, trading by sea with societies throughout southern and eastern Asia and by land with the nomadic peoples of Central Asia. Like the Middle East, China was also a prime source of new technology. From China came paper, printing, the compass, and gunpowder. The double-hulled Chinese junks that entered the Indian Ocean during the Ming Dynasty were slow and cumbersome but extremely seaworthy and capable of carrying substantial quantities of goods over long distances. Many inventions arrived in Europe by way of India or the Middle East, and their Chinese origins were therefore unknown in the West.

Increasing trade on a regional or global basis also led to the exchange of ideas. Buddhism was brought to China by merchants, and Islam first arrived in sub-Saharan Africa

and Southeast Asia in the same manner. Merchants were not the only means by which religious and cultural ideas spread, however. Sometimes migration, conquest, or relatively peaceful processes played a part. The case of the Bantu-speaking peoples in Central Africa is apparently an example of peaceful expansion; and although Islam sometimes followed the path of Arab warriors, they did not always impose their religion by force on local populations. In some instances, as with the Mongols, the conquerors made no effort to convert others to their own religions. By contrast, Christian monks, motivated by missionary fervor, sought to convert many of the peoples of central and eastern Europe. Roman Catholic missionaries brought Latin Christianity to the Germanic and western Slavic peoples, and monks from the Byzantine Empire introduced the southern and eastern Slavic populations to Eastern Orthodox Christianity.

Another characteristic of the period between 500 and 1500 C.E. was the almost constant migration of nomadic and seminomadic peoples. Dynamic forces in the Gobi Desert, central Asia, the Arabian Peninsula, and central Africa provoked vast numbers of peoples to abandon their homelands and seek their livelihood elsewhere. Sometimes the migration was peaceful and had few disruptive consequences. Often, however, migration produced violent conflict and sometimes invasion and subjugation. As had been the case during antiquity, the most active source of migrants was Central Asia. The region later gave birth to the fearsome Mongols, whose armies advanced to the gates of central Europe and conquered China in the thirteenth century. Wherever they went, they left a train of enormous destruction and loss of life. Inadvertently, the Mongols were also the source of a new wave of epidemics that swept through much of Europe and the Middle East in the fourteenth century. The spread of the plague—known at the time as the Black Death—took much of the population of Europe to an early grave.

But there was another side to this era of widespread human migration. Even the invasions of the Mongols—the "scourge of God" as Europeans of the thirteenth and fourteenth centuries called them—eventually had constructive as well as destructive consequences. After their initial conquests, the Mongols provided an avenue for the peaceful exchange of goods and ideas throughout the most extensive empire (known as the *Pax Mongolica*) the world had yet seen. The world would never be the same again.

Chapter Outline and Focus Questions

6-1 *The Peopling of the Americas*

Q Who were the first Americans, and when and how did they come?

6-2 *Early Civilizations in Mesoamerica*

Q What were the main characteristics of religious belief in early Mesoamerica, and how did they compare with belief systems in the ancient empires discussed in Part I of this book?

6-3 *Peoples and Societies in Early North America*

Q What were the main characteristics of the first human societies in North America, and how did they resemble and differ from their counterparts in Mesoamerica?

6-4 *The First Civilizations in South America*

Q What role did the environment play in the evolution of societies in South America?

6.1 Warriors Raid a Village to Capture Prisoners for The Ritual of Sacrifice.

Sef/Art Resource, NY

Critical Thinking

Q *In what ways were the early civilizations in the Americas similar to those discussed in Part I, and in what ways were they unique?*

Connections to Today

Q *Do the environmental problems encountered by pre-Columbian societies in the Americas have relevance today? Why or why not?*

IN THE SUMMER OF 2001, a powerful hurricane swept through Central America, destroying houses and flooding villages all along the Caribbean coast of Belize and Guatemala. Farther inland, at the archaeological site of Dos Pilas (dohs PEE-las), the hurricane uncovered new evidence concerning a series of dramatic events that took place nearly 1,500 years earlier. Beneath a tree uprooted by the storm, archaeologists discovered a block of stones containing hieroglyphics that described a brutal war between two powerful city-states of the area, a conflict that ultimately contributed to the decline and fall of Maya civilization, perhaps the most advanced society then in existence throughout Central America.

Maya civilization, the origins of which can be traced back to around 500 B.C.E., was not as old as some of its counterparts that we have discussed in Part I of this book. But it was the most recent version of a whole series of human societies that had emerged throughout the Western Hemisphere as early as the third millennium B.C.E. Although these early societies are not yet as well known as those of ancient Egypt, Mesopotamia, and India, evidence is accumulating that advanced civilizations had existed in the Americas thousands of years before the arrival of the Spanish conquistadors led by Hernando Cortés in 1519. Because the arrival of the Spanish led to both the rapid decline of the traditional cultures in the Western Hemisphere and an early stage in the dramatic expansion of European power throughout the world, those events that were initiated by the arrival of the conquistadors will be treated in a later chapter (see Chapter 14).

6-1 THE PEOPLING OF THE AMERICAS

 Focus Question: Who were the first Americans, and when and how did they come?

The Maya (MY-uh) were only the latest in a series of sophisticated societies that had sprung up at various locations in North and South America since human beings first crossed the Bering Strait several millennia earlier. Most of these early peoples, today often referred to as **Amerindians**, lived by hunting and fishing or by food gathering. But eventually organized societies based on the cultivation of agriculture began to take root in Central and South America. One key area of development was on the plateau of central Mexico. Another was in the lowland regions along the Gulf of Mexico and extending into modern Guatemala. A third was in the central Andes adjacent to the Pacific coast of South America. Others were just beginning to emerge in the vast Amazon River basin and in the river valleys and Great Plains of North America.

For thousands of years, these societies developed in isolation from their counterparts elsewhere in the world. This lack of contact with other human beings deprived them of access to technological and cultural developments taking place in Africa, Asia, and Europe. They did not benefit from the presence of the horse, which had died out in the Americas thousands of years previously. Nor did they know of the wheel, and their written languages were rudimentary compared to equivalents in complex civilizations in other parts of the globe. Still, in other respects, their cultural achievements were the equal of those realized elsewhere. When the first European explorers arrived in the Americas at the turn of the sixteenth century, they described much that they observed in glowing terms.

6-1a The First Americans

Just when the first human beings arrived in the Western Hemisphere has long been a matter of dispute. In the centuries following the voyages of Christopher Columbus, speculation centered on the possibility that the first settlers to reach the American continents had crossed the Atlantic

Ocean. Were they the lost tribes of Israel? Were they Phoenician seafarers from Carthage? Were they refugees from the legendary lost continent of Atlantis? In all cases, the assumption was that they were relatively recent arrivals.

By the mid-nineteenth century, a new theory developed. It proposed that the peopling of America had taken place much earlier as a result of the migration of small communities across the Bering Strait at a time when the area was a land bridge uniting the continents of Asia and North America. Recent evidence, including numerous physical similarities between most early Americans and contemporary peoples living in northeastern Asia, has confirmed this hypothesis. The debate on when the migrations began continues, however. Archaeologist Louis Leakey (LEE-kee), one of the pioneers in the search for the origins of humankind in Africa, suggested that the first hominids may have arrived in America as long as 100,000 years ago. Most scholars today, however, suggest that the first Americans were members of *Homo sapiens sapiens* who crossed from Asia via the Bering Strait by foot sometime between 15,000 and 10,000 years ago. Some of them were probably hunters in pursuit of herds of bison and caribou that moved into the area in search of grazing land at the end of the last ice age. Others may have followed a maritime route (sometimes dubbed "the kelp highway") down the western coast of the Americas, supporting themselves by fishing and feeding on other organisms floating in the sea.

Whatever their origins, these first Americans were food gatherers and hunters who lived in small nomadic communities close to their food supplies. As they spread throughout the Western Hemisphere, they gradually mastered the art of agriculture. Beans and squash seeds have been found at sites that date back at least 10,000 years. The cultivation of maize (corn), and perhaps other crops as well, appears to have been under way quite early in the lowland regions of modern-day Mexico. There, in the region that archaeologists call **Mesoamerica**, one of the first civilizations in the Western Hemisphere began to appear.

6-2 EARLY CIVILIZATIONS IN MESOAMERICA

 Focus Question: What were the main characteristics of religious belief in early Mesoamerica, and how did they compare with belief systems in the ancient empires discussed in Part I of this book?

The first signs of civilization in Mesoamerica appeared at the end of the second millennium B.C.E. with the emergence of what is called *Olmec* (AHL-mek *or* OHL-mek)

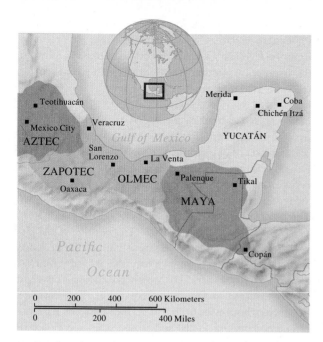

Map 6.1 **Early Mesoamerica.** Mesoamerica was home to some of the first civilizations in the Western Hemisphere. This map shows the major urban settlements in the region.

 What types of ecological areas were most associated with Olmec, Maya, and Aztec cultures?

made from the sap of a local rubber tree, thus providing the name *Olmec:* "people of the land of rubber."

Trade between the Olmecs and their neighbors was apparently quite extensive, and rubber was one of the products most desired by peoples in nearby regions. It was used not only for the manufacture of balls but also for rubber bands and footwear because the Olmec had learned how to mix the raw latex (the sap of the rubber tree) with other ingredients to make it more supple.

Eventually, Olmec civilization began to decline, and it apparently collapsed around the fourth century B.C.E. During its heyday, however, it extended from Mexico City to El Salvador and perhaps to the shores of the Pacific Ocean.

6-2b The Zapotecs

Parallel developments were occurring at Monte Albán (MON-tee ahl-BAHN), on a hillside overlooking the modern city of Oaxaca (wah-HAH-kuh) in central Mexico. Around the middle of the first millennium B.C.E., the Zapotec (zah-puh-TEK) peoples created an extensive civilization that flourished for several hundred years in the highlands. Like the Olmec sites, Monte Albán contains several temples and pyramids, but they are located in much more awesome surroundings on a massive stone terrace atop a 1,200-foot-high mountain overlooking the Oaxaca Valley. The majority of the population, estimated at around 20,000, dwelled on terraces cut into the sides of the mountain, which is known to local residents as Danibaan, or "sacred mountain."

6-2c Teotihuacán: America's First Metropolis

The first major metropolis in Mesoamerica was the city of Teotihuacan (tay-oh-tee-hwah-KAHN), capital of an early state some thirty miles northeast of Mexico City that arose around the third century B.C.E. and flourished for nearly a millennium until it collapsed under mysterious circumstances around 800 C.E. Along the main thoroughfare were temples and palaces, all dominated by the massive Pyramid of the Sun (see the Comparative Illustration, "The Pyramid," p. 141), under which archaeologists have discovered the remains of sacrificial victims who were probably put to death during the dedication of the structure. In the vicinity are the remains of a large market where goods from distant regions as well as agricultural produce grown by local farmers were exchanged. The products traded included cacao, rubber, feathers, and various types of vegetables and meat. Pulque (POOL-kay), a liquor extracted from the agave (uh-GAH-vee) plant, was used in religious ceremonies. An obsidian mine nearby may explain the location of the city; obsidian is a volcanic

culture in the hot, swampy lowlands along the coast of the Gulf of Mexico south of Veracruz (see Map 6.1).

6-2a The Olmecs: In the Land of Rubber

Olmec civilization was characterized by intensive agriculture along the muddy riverbanks in the area and by the carving of stone ornaments, tools, and monuments at sites such as San Lorenzo and La Venta. The site at La Venta contains a ceremonial precinct with a thirty-foot-high earthen pyramid, the largest of its date in all Mesoamerica. The Olmec peoples organized a widespread trading network, carried on religious rituals, and devised a system of hieroglyphs that has yet to be deciphered but is similar in some respects to later Maya writing (see "Maya Hieroglyphs and Calendars" later in this chapter) and may be the ancestor of the first true writing systems in the Western Hemisphere.

Olmec society apparently consisted of several classes, including a class of skilled artisans who carved many massive stone heads, some more than ten feet high. The Olmec peoples supported themselves primarily by cultivating crops such as corn and beans, but they also fished and hunted. The Olmecs apparently played a ceremonial game on a stone ball court, a ritual that would later be widely practiced throughout the region (see section 6-2d, "The Maya," p. 142). The ball was

The Pyramid

Religion & Philosophy **THE BUILDING OF MONUMENTAL STRUCTURES** known as *pyramids* was characteristic of several civilizations that arose in antiquity. The pyramid symbolized the link between the world of human beings and the realm of deities and was often used to house the tomb of a deceased ruler. Shown here are two prominent examples. Image 6.2a shows the pyramids of Giza, Egypt, built in the third millennium B.C.E. and located near the modern city of Cairo. Image 6.2b shows the Pyramid of the Sun at Teotihuacán, erected in central Mexico in the fifth century C.E. Similar structures of various sizes were built throughout the Western Hemisphere. The concept of the pyramid was also widely applied in parts of Asia. Scholars still debate the technical aspects of constructing such pyramids.

Q *How do the pyramids erected in the Western Hemisphere compare with similar structures in other parts of the world? What were their symbolic meanings to the builders?*

6.2a

6.2b

glass that was prized in Mesoamerica for use in tools, mirrors, and the blades of sacrificial knives.

Most of the city consisted of one-story stucco apartment compounds; some were as large as 35,000 square feet, which was sufficient to house more than 100 people. Each apartment was divided into several rooms, and the compounds were covered by flat roofs made of wooden beams, poles, and stucco. The compounds were separated by wide streets laid out on a rectangular grid and were entered through narrow alleys.

Living in the fertile Valley of Mexico, an upland plateau surrounded by magnificent snow-capped mountains, the inhabitants of Teotihuacán probably obtained the bulk of their wealth from agriculture. At that time, the valley floor was filled with swampy lakes containing the water runoff from the surrounding mountains. The combination

of fertile soil and adequate water combined to make the valley one of the richest farming areas in Mesoamerica.

Sometime during the eighth century C.E., perhaps because of drought or overcultivation of the land, the wealth and power of the city began to decline. The next two centuries were a time of troubles throughout the region as principalities fought over limited farmland. The problem was later compounded when peoples from surrounding areas, attracted by the rich farmlands, migrated into the Valley of Mexico and began to compete for territory with the small city-states already established there. As the local population expanded, farmers began to engage in more intensive agriculture. They drained the lakes to build **chinampas** (chee-NAM-pahs), swampy islands crisscrossed by canals that provided water for their crops and easy transportation to local markets for their excess produce.

6-2d The Maya

Far to the east of the Valley of Mexico, another major civilization had arisen in what is now the state of Guatemala and the Yucatán Peninsula. This was the civilization of the Maya, which was older than and just as sophisticated as the society at Teotihuacán.

Origins When human beings first inhabited the Yucatán Peninsula is not known, but peoples contemporaneous with the Olmecs were already cultivating such crops as corn, yams, and manioc in the area during the first millennium B.C.E. As the population increased, an early civilization began to emerge along the Pacific coast directly to the south of the peninsula and in the highlands of modern Guatemala. Contacts were already established with the Olmecs to the west.

Because the area was a source for cacao trees and obsidian, the inhabitants soon developed relations with other early civilizations in the region. Cacao trees (whose name derives from the Maya word *kakaw*) were the source of chocolate, which had been drunk as a beverage by the upper classes as early as the second millennium B.C.E. Cocoa beans, the fruit of the cacao tree, were used as currency in markets throughout the region.

As the population in the area increased, the inhabitants began to migrate into the central Yucatán Peninsula and farther to the north. The overcrowding forced farmers in the lowland areas to shift from slash-and-burn cultivation to swamp agriculture of the type practiced in the lake region of the Valley of Mexico. By the middle of the first millennium C.E., the entire area was honeycombed with a patchwork of small city-states competing for land and resources. The largest urban centers such as Tikal (tee-KAHL) may have had 100,000 inhabitants at their height and displayed a level of technological and cultural achievement that was unsurpassed in the region. By the end of the third century C.E., Maya civilization had begun to enter its classical phase.

Political Structures The power of Maya rulers was impressive. One of the monarchs at Copán (koh-PAHN)—known to scholars as "18 Rabbit" from the hieroglyphs

Polychrome "waisted" cylindrical vase with "Palace Scene"/WERNER FORMAN ARCHIVE/Bridgeman Images

6.3 Chocolate: Sacred Drink of Mesoamerica. The Maya recorded religious rites, as well as scenes of daily life, on polychrome clay vessels. Used in ritual ceremonies dedicated to their deities, these vessels contained a foamy chocolate beverage called *kakaw*, from which we derive the word *cacao*, the tree that produces the cocoa beans from which chocolate is made. After the Maya civilization declined, chocolate (*xocoatl*, or "bitter water," in the Aztec language) continued to be used as a sacred beverage by other Mesoamerican peoples. In this image, a Maya palace servant is apparently preparing cups of the heavenly nectar to use in a religious ceremony in one of the Maya city-states.

composing his name—ordered the construction of a grand palace requiring more than 30,000 person-days of labor. Gathered around the ruler was a class of aristocrats whose wealth was probably based on the ownership of land farmed by their poorer relatives. Eventually, many of the nobles became priests or scribes at the royal court or adopted honored professions as sculptors or painters. As the society's wealth grew, so did the role of artisans and traders, who began to form a small middle class.

The majority of the population on the peninsula (estimated at roughly 3 million at the height of Maya prosperity), however, were farmers. They lived on their chinampa plots or on terraced hills in the highlands. Houses were built of adobe and thatch and probably resembled the houses of the majority of the population in the area today. There was a fairly clear-cut division of labor along gender lines. The men were responsible for fighting and hunting, the women for homemaking and the preparation of cornmeal, the staple food of much of the population.

Some noblewomen, however, seem to have played important roles in both political and religious life. In the seventh century C.E., for example, Pacal (pa-KAL) became king of Palenque (pah-LEN-kay), one of the most powerful of the Maya city-states, through the royal line of his mother and grandmother, thereby breaking the patrilineal descent twice. His mother ruled Palenque for three years and was the power behind the throne for her son's first twenty-five years of rule. Pacal legitimized his kingship by transforming his mother into a divine representation of the "first mother" goddess (for a picture of Pacal's death mask, see Image 6.9, "Jade and gold funeral masks," p. 154).

Scholars once believed that the Maya were a peaceful people who rarely engaged in violence. Now, however, it is thought that rivalry among Maya city-states was endemic and often involved bloody clashes. Scenes from paintings and rock carvings depict a society preoccupied with war and the seizure of captives for sacrifice. The conflict mentioned at the beginning of this chapter is but one example. During the seventh century C.E., two powerful city-states, Tikal and Calakmul (kah-lahk-MOOL), competed for dominance throughout the region, setting up puppet regimes and waging bloody wars that wavered back and forth for years but ultimately resulted in the total destruction of Calakmul at the end of the century.

Maya Religion Maya religion was polytheistic. Although the names were different, Maya gods shared many of the characteristics of deities of nearby cultures. The supreme god was named Itzámna (eet-SAHM-nuh) ("Lizard House").

6.4 A Maya Bloodletting Ceremony. The Maya elite drew blood at various ritual ceremonies. Here we see Lady Xok, the wife of a king of Yaxchilian, passing a rope pierced with thorns along her tongue in a bloodletting ritual. Above her, the king holds a flaming torch. This vivid scene from an eighth-century C.E. palace lintel demonstrates the excellence of Maya stone sculpture as well as the sophisticated weaving techniques shown in the queen's elegant gown.

Viewed as the creator of all things, he was credited with bringing maize, cacao, medicine, and writing to the Maya people.

Deities were ranked in order of importance and had human characteristics as in ancient Greece and India. Some, like the jaguar god of night, were evil rather than good. Some scholars believe that many of the nature deities may have been viewed as manifestations of one supreme godhead (see Historical Voices, "The Creation of the World," p. 144). As at Teotihuacán, human sacrifice (normally by decapitation) was practiced to propitiate the heavenly forces.

The Creation of the World: A Maya View

Religion & Philosophy **POPUL VUH** (puh-PUL VOO), a sacred work of the ancient Maya, is an account of Maya history and religious beliefs. No written version in the original Maya script is extant, but shortly after the Spanish conquest it was written down, apparently from memory, in Quiché (kee–CHAY) (the spoken language of the Maya) using Latin script. This version was later translated into Spanish. The following excerpt from the opening lines of Popul Vuh recounts the Maya myth of the creation.

Popul Vuh: The Sacred Book of the Maya

This is the account of how all was in suspense, all calm, in silence; all motionless, still, and the expanse of the sky was empty.

This is the first account, the first narrative. There was neither man, nor animal, birds, fishes, crabs, trees, stones, caves, ravines, grasses, nor forests; there was only the sky.

The surface of the earth had not appeared. There was only the calm sea and the great expanse of the sky.

There was nothing brought together, nothing which could make a noise, nor anything which might move, or tremble, or could make noise in the sky.

There was nothing standing; only the calm water, the placid sea, alone and tranquil. Nothing existed.

There was only immobility and silence in the darkness, in the night. Only the Creator, the Maker, Tepeu, Gucumatz, the Forefathers, were in the water surrounded with light. They were hidden under green and blue feathers, and were therefore called Gucumatz. By nature they were great sages and great thinkers. In this manner the sky existed and also the Heart of Heaven, which is the name of God and thus He is called.

Then came the word. Tepeu and Gucumatz came together in the darkness, in the night, and Tepeu and Gucumatz talked together. They talked then, discussing and deliberating; they agreed, they united their words and their thoughts.

Then while they meditated, it became clear to them that when dawn would break, man must appear. Then they planned the creation, and the growth of the trees and the thickets and the birth of life and the creation of man. Thus it was arranged in the darkness and in the night by the Heart of Heaven who is called Huracan.

The first is called Caculha Huracan. The second is Chipi-Caculha. The third is Raxa-Caculha. And these three are the Heart of Heaven.

So it was that they made perfect the work, when they did it after thinking and meditating upon it.

 What similarities and differences do you see between this account of the beginning of the world and those of other ancient civilizations?

Source: From Popul-Vuh, *The Sacred Book of the Ancient Quiche Maya,* translated by Adrian Recinos. Copyright © 1950 by the University of Oklahoma Press.

Maya cities were built around a ceremonial core dominated by a central pyramid surmounted by a shrine to the gods. Nearby were other temples, palaces, and a sacred ball court. Like many of their modern counterparts, Maya cities suffered from urban sprawl, with separate suburbs for the poor and the middle class.

The ball court was a rectangular space surrounded by vertical walls with metal rings through which the contestants attempted to drive a hard rubber ball. Although the rules of the game are imperfectly understood, it apparently had religious significance, and the vanquished players were sacrificed in ceremonies held after the close of the game. Most players were men, although there may have been some women's teams. Similar courts have been found at sites throughout Central and South America, with the earliest near Veracruz dating back to around 1500 B.C.E.

Maya Hieroglyphs and Calendars The Maya writing system developed during the mid-first millennium B.C.E. and was based on hieroglyphs that remained undeciphered until scholars recognized that symbols appearing in many passages represented dates in the Maya calendar. This elaborate calendar, which measures time back to a particular date in August 3114 B.C.E., required a sophisticated understanding of astronomical events and mathematics to compile. Starting with these known symbols as a foundation, modern scholars have gradually deciphered the script. Like the scripts of the Sumerians and ancient Egyptians, the Maya hieroglyphs were both ideographic and phonetic and were becoming more phonetic as time passed (see Image 1.5 in Chapter 1).

The responsibility for compiling official records in the Maya city-states was given to a class of scribes who wrote on deerskin or strips of tree bark. Unfortunately, virtually all such records have fallen victim to the ravages of a humid climate or were deliberately destroyed by Spanish missionaries after their arrival in the sixteenth century. As one Spanish bishop remarked at the time, "We found a large number of books in these characters and, as they contained nothing in which there were not to be seen superstition and lies of the devil, we burned them all, which they regretted to an amazing degree, and which caused them much affliction."[1]

As a result, almost the only surviving written records dating from the classical Maya era are those that were carved in stone. One of the most important repositories of Maya hieroglyphs is at Palenque, an archaeological site deep in the jungles in the neck of the Mexican peninsula, considerably to the west of the Yucatán (see Map 6.2). In a chamber located under the Temple of Inscriptions, archaeologists discovered a royal tomb and a massive limestone slab covered with hieroglyphs. By deciphering the message on the slab, archaeologists for the first time identified a historical figure in Maya history. He was the ruler named Pacal, known from his glyph as "The Shield"; Pacal ordered the construction of the Temple of Inscriptions in the mid-seventh century, and it was his body that was buried in the tomb at the foot of the staircase leading down into the crypt.

As befits their intense interest in the passage of time, the Maya also had a sophisticated knowledge of astronomy and kept voluminous records of the movements of the heavenly bodies. There were practical reasons for their concern. The arrival of the planet Venus in the evening sky, for example, was a traditional time to prepare for war. The Maya also devised the so-called Long Count, a system of calculating time based on a lunar calendar that called for the end of the current cycle of 5,200 years in the year 2012 of the Western solar-based Gregorian calendar.

HISTORIANS DEBATE 6-2e **Why Did The Maya Decline?**

Sometime in the eighth or ninth century, the classical Maya civilization in the central Yucatán Peninsula began to decline. At Copán, for example, it ended abruptly in 822 C.E. when work on various stone sculptures ordered by the ruler suddenly ceased. The end of Palenque soon followed, and the city of Tikal was abandoned by 870 C.E. Whether the decline was caused by overuse of the land, incessant warfare, internal revolt, or a natural disaster such as a volcanic eruption is a question that has puzzled archaeologists for decades. Recent evidence supports the theory that overcultivation of the land because of a growing population gradually reduced crop yields. A long drought that began in the seventh century and lasted

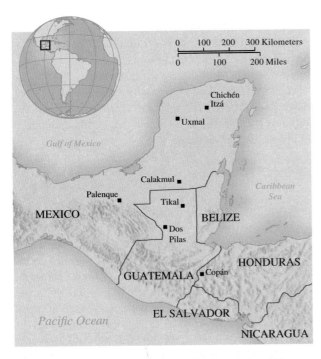

Map 6.2 The Maya Heartland. During the classical era, Maya civilization was centered on modern-day Guatemala and the lower Yucatán Peninsula. After the ninth century, new centers of power like Chichán Itzá and Uxmal began to emerge farther north.

Q *What factors appear to have brought an end to classical Maya civilization?*

William J. Duiker

6.5 Maya Temple at Tikal. This eighth-century temple, peering over the treetops of a jungle at Tikal, represents the zenith of the engineering and artistry of the Maya peoples. Erected to house the body of a ruler, such pyramidal tombs contained elaborate works of jade jewelry, polychrome ceramics, and intricate bone carvings depicting the ruler's life and various deities. This temple dominates a great plaza that is surrounded by a royal palace and various religious structures.

The Legend of the Feathered Serpent

Religion & Culture

THE MYTHICAL FIGURE KNOWN AS QUETZALCOATL permeates the religious belief of Mesoamerican peoples from the first century C.E. city of Teotihuacan to the Aztecs. Half human, half deity, he is usually portrayed as a feathered serpent, and is identified variously as the god of the Wind, of the Dawn, and of Learning and the Arts. In Mayan and Aztec literature, as a youth he took on his familiar mask to hide his ugliness. Later, his exploits run through the narrative of Mesoamerican history, from the abandonment of Teotihuacan in the eighth century C.E. to the Toltec conquest of the northern Yucatan many years later. Becoming ashamed after misbehaving in a drunken stupor, he immolated himself on the coast of Yucatan and merged his identity with Venus, the Dawn Star. The excerpts here are from the Codex Chimalpopoca, originally recited verbally by Aztec priests and then written down in Spanish in 1570. The first segment describes his adornment by a feather wizard, and the second portrays his self-immolation and transformation into the Dawn Star.

From the Codex Chimalpopoca

And so then Coyotlinahual the feather-artist fashioned them; first he made Quetzalcoatl's plumed headdress, then his turquoise inlay mask. He took red with which to paint his mouth; he took yellow with which to stripe his face. Next he prepared his serpent teeth, then his beard of cotinga and roseate spoonbill feathers across his lower face.

And so he arrayed him in his attire and he was Quetzalcoatl. Then he handed him the mirror, and when he looked on himself he was very pleased with what he saw. Then Quetzalcoatl abandoned forthwith the place where he was guarded. . . .

And it was again on the day 1 Reed, it is recounted, it is said, when he arrived at Teoapan Illhuicaatenco, "Along the divine water, At the shore of heavenly water." Then he halted and stood; he wept, took up his vestments and adorned himself in his insignia, his turquoise mask, etc.

And when he was fully adorned then with his own hand he set himself on fire, he offered himself up in flame.

So the place where Quetzalcoatl went to immolate himself came to be called Tlatlayan, "Place of the Burning."

And it is said that even as he burned, his ashes emerged and arose: and there appeared, before the sight of everyone, all the birds of great value when emerged and rose into the sky. They saw the roseate spoonbill, the cotinga, the trogon, the heron, the yellow parrot, the scarlet macaw, the white-bellied parrot, and every other bird of precious plumage.

And when the ashes were extinguished, then arose his heart, the quetzal bird itself; they saw it. And so they knew he had entered the sky within the sky.

The old ones used to say he was transformed to the dawn start; thus it is said that when Quetzalcoatl died this star appeared, and so he is named Tlahuizcalpanteuctli, "Lord of the Dawn House."

Source: Roberta H. and Peter T. Markman, *The Flayed God* (San Francisco: Harper Colllins, 1992), pp. 369–377, translated by Willard Gingerich as reproduced in Miguel Léon-Portilla and Earl Shorris, *In the Language of Kings: An Anthology of Mesoamerican Literature* (New York, W.W. Norton, 2001), pp. 188–191.

several hundred years may have played a major role, although overuse of the land because of growing population density was probably also a factor. In general, though, as arable land and water became increasingly scarce, conflict among the various ministates in the region may have intensified, accelerating the process leading to a final collapse.

Whatever the case, cities like Tikal and Palenque were abandoned to the jungles. In their place, newer urban centers in the northern part of the peninsula like Uxmal (oosh-MAHL) and Chichén Itzá (chee-CHEN eet-SAH), continued to prosper, although the level of cultural achievement in this postclassical era did not match that of previous years. According to local history, this latter area was taken over by peoples known as the Toltecs (TOHL-teks), led by a man known as Kukulcan (koo-kul-KAHN), who migrated to the peninsula from Teotihuacán in central Mexico sometime in the tenth century. Some scholars believe this flight was associated with the legend of the departure from that city of Quetzalcoatl (KWET-sul-koh-AHT-ul), a deity in the form of a feathered serpent who promised that he would someday return to reclaim his homeland (see Historical Voices, "The Land of the Feathered Serpent"). The Toltecs apparently controlled the upper peninsula from their capital at Chichén Itzá for several centuries, but this area was less fertile and more susceptible to drought than the earlier regions of Maya settlement, and eventually the Toltecs too declined. By the early sixteenth century, the area was divided into many small principalities, and the cities, including Uxmal and Chichén Itzá, had been abandoned.

6-2f The Aztecs

Among the groups moving into the Valley of Mexico after the fall of Teotihuacán were the Mexica (meh-SHEE-kuh). No one knows their origins, although folk legend held that their original homeland was an island in a lake called Aztlán (az-TLAHN). From that legendary homeland comes the name *Aztec*, by which they are known to the modern world. Sometime during the early twelfth century, the Aztecs left their original habitat and, carrying an image of their patron deity, Huitzilopochtli (WEET-see-loh-POHSHT-lee), began a lengthy migration that climaxed with their arrival in the Valley of Mexico more than 100 years later.

Less sophisticated than many of their neighbors, the Aztecs were at first forced to seek alliances with stronger city-states. They were excellent warriors, however, and soon used their prowess to become the leading city-state in the lake region, just like Sparta in ancient Greece and the state of Qin in China's Zhou Dynasty. Establishing their capital at Tenochtitlán (teh-nahch-teet-LAHN) on an island in the middle of Lake Texcoco (tess-KOH-koh), they set out to bring the entire region under their domination (see Map 6.3).

For the remainder of the fifteenth century, the Aztecs consolidated their control over much of what is modern Mexico from the Atlantic to the Pacific Ocean and as far south as the Guatemalan border. The new kingdom was not a centralized state but a collection of semiautonomous territories. To provide a unifying focus for the kingdom, the Aztecs promoted their patron god, Huitzilopochtli, as the guiding deity of the entire population, which now numbered several million.

Politics Like all great empires in ancient times, the Aztec state was authoritarian. Power was vested in the monarch, whose authority had both a divine and a secular character. The Aztec ruler claimed descent from the gods and served as an intermediary between the material and the metaphysical worlds. Unlike many of his counterparts in other ancient civilizations, however, the monarch did not obtain his position by a rigid law of succession. On the death of the ruler, his successor was selected from within the royal family by a small group of senior officials, who were also members of the family and were therefore eligible for the position. Once placed on the throne, the Aztec ruler was advised by a small council of lords headed by a prime minister who served as the chief executive of the government and a bureaucracy. Beyond the capital, the power of the central government was limited. Rulers

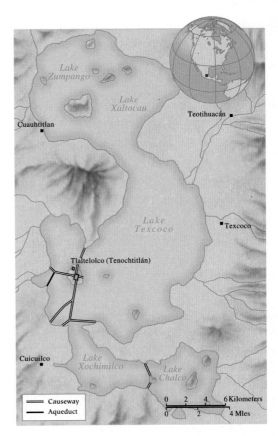

Map 6.3 The Valley of Mexico Under Aztec Rule. The Aztecs were one of the most advanced peoples in pre-Columbian Central America. The capital at Tenochtitlan—Tlaltelolco (tuh-lahl-teh-LOH-koh)—was located at the site of modern-day Mexico City. Of the five lakes shown here, only Lake Texcoco remains today.

 What was the significance of Tenochtitlán's location?

of territories subject to the Aztecs were allowed considerable autonomy in return for paying tribute to the central government in the form of goods or captives. The most important government officials in the provinces were the tax collectors who collected the tribute. Tax collectors used the threat of military action against those who failed to carry out their tribute obligations and therefore were understandably not popular with the taxpayers; according to one contemporary Spanish observer, these officials often "robbed them of all they possessed."[2]

Social Structures Positions in the government bureaucracy were the exclusive privilege of the hereditary nobility, all of whom traced their lineage to the founding family of the Aztec clan. Male children in noble families were sent to temple schools, where they were exposed to a harsh regimen of manual labor, military training, and memorization of information about Aztec society

Arrival of human beings in America	At least 15,000 years ago
Agriculture first practiced	ca. 8000 B.C.E.
Rise of Olmec culture	ca. 1200 B.C.E.
End of Olmec era	ca. 400 B.C.E.
Teotihuacán civilization	ca. 300 B.C.E.–800 C.E.
Origins of Maya civilization	First millennium C.E.
Classical era of Maya culture	300–900 C.E.
Tikal abandoned	870 C.E.
Migration of Mexica to Valley of Mexico	Late 1100s
Kingdom of the Aztecs	1300s–1400s

and religion. On reaching adulthood, they would select a career in the military service, the government bureaucracy, or the priesthood.

The remainder of the population consisted of commoners, indentured workers, and slaves. Most indentured workers were landless laborers who contracted to work on the nobles' estates, and slaves served in the households of the wealthy. Slavery was not an inherited status, and the children of slaves were considered free citizens.

The vast majority of the population were commoners. All commoners were members of large kinship groups called *calpullis* (kal-PUL-eez). Each calpulli, many of which consisted of as many as 1,000 members, was headed by an elected chief who ran its day-to-day affairs and served as an intermediary with the central government. Each calpulli was responsible for providing taxes (usually in the form of goods) and conscript labor to the state.

Each calpulli also maintained its own temples and schools and administered the land held by the community. Farmland within the calpulli was held in common and could not be sold, although it could be inherited within the family. In the cities, each calpulli occupied a separate neighborhood, where its members often performed a particular function such as metalworking, stonecutting, weaving, carpentry, or commerce. Apparently, a large proportion of the population engaged in some form of trade, at least in the densely populated Valley of Mexico, where an estimated half of the people lived in an urban environment. Many farmers brought their goods to the markets via the canals and sold them directly to retailers (see Historical Voices, "Markets and Merchandise in Aztec Mexico," p. 149).

Gender roles within the family were rigidly stratified. Male children were trained for war and were expected to serve in the army on reaching adulthood. Women were expected to work in the home, weave textiles, and raise children, although like their brothers they were permitted to enter the priesthood. As in most traditional societies, chastity and obedience were desirable female characteristics. Although women in Aztec society enjoyed more legal rights than women in some traditional Old World civilizations, they were still not equal to men. Women were permitted to own and inherit property and to enter into contracts. Marriage was usually monogamous, although noble families sometimes practiced **polygyny** (the state or practice of having more than one wife at a time). As in most societies at the time, parents usually selected their child's spouse, often for purposes of political or social advancement.

Aztec cosmology was based on a belief in the existence of two worlds, the material and the divine. Earth was the material world and took the form of a flat disk surrounded by water on all sides. The divine world, which consisted of both heaven and hell, was the abode of the gods. Human beings could aspire to a form of heavenly salvation but first had to pass through a transitional stage, somewhat like Christian purgatory, before reaching their final destination, where the soul was finally freed from the body. To prepare for the final day of judgment, as well as to help them engage in proper behavior through life, all citizens underwent religious training at temple schools during adolescence and took part in various rituals throughout their lives. The most devout were encouraged to study for the priesthood. Once accepted, they served at temples ranging from local branches at the calpulli level to the highest shrines in the ceremonial precinct at Tenochtitlán. In some respects, however, Aztec society may have been undergoing a process of secularization. By late Aztec times, athletic contests at the ball court had apparently lost some of their religious significance. Gambling was increasingly common, and wagering over the results of the matches was widespread. One province reportedly sent 16,000 rubber balls to the capital city of Tenochtitlán as annual tribute to the royal court.

Aztec religion contained a distinct element of fatalism that was inherent in the creation myth, which described an unceasing struggle between the forces of good and evil throughout the universe. This struggle had led to the creation and destruction of four worlds or suns. The world was now living in the time of the fifth sun. But that world, too, was destined to end with the destruction of Earth and all that is within it:

Even jade is shattered,
Even gold is crushed,
Even quetzal plumes are torn. . . .
One does not live forever on this earth:
We endure only for an instant! [3]

Markets and Merchandise in Aztec Mexico

Interaction & Exchange

ONE OF OUR MOST VALUABLE DESCRIPTIONS OF AZTEC CIVILIZATION is *The Conquest of New Spain,* written by Bernal Díaz, a Spaniard who visited Mexico in 1519. In the following passage, Díaz describes the great market at Tenochtitlán.

Bernal Díaz, *The Conquest of New Spain*

Let us begin with the dealers in gold, silver, and precious stones, feathers, cloaks, and embroidered goods, and male and female slaves who are also sold there. They bring as many slaves to be sold in that market as the Portuguese bring Negroes from Guinea. Some are brought there attached to long poles by means of collars round their necks to prevent them from escaping, but others are left loose. Next there were those who sold coarser cloth, and cotton goods and fabrics made of twisted thread, and there were chocolate merchants with their chocolate. In this way you could see every kind of merchandise to be found anywhere in New Spain, laid out in the same way as goods are laid out in my own district of Medina del Campo, a center for fairs, where each line of stalls has its own particular sort. So it was in this great market. There were those who sold sisal cloth and ropes and the sandals they wear on their feet, which are made from the same plant. All these were kept in one part of the market, in the place assigned to them, and in another part were skins of tigers and lions, otters, jackals, and deer, badgers, mountain cats, and other wild animals, some tanned and some untanned, and other classes of merchandise.

There were sellers of kidney beans and sage and other vegetables and herbs in another place, and in yet another they were selling fowls, and birds with great dewlaps, also rabbits, hares, deer, young ducks, little dogs, and other such creatures. Then there were the fruiterers; and the women who sold cooked food, flour and honey cake, and tripe, had their part of the market. Then came pottery of all kinds, from big water jars to little jugs, displayed in its own place, also honey, honey paste, and other sweets like nougat. Elsewhere they sold timber too, boards, cradles, beams, blocks, and benches, all in a quarter of their own.

Then there were the sellers of pitch pine for torches, and other things of that kind, and I must also mention, with all apologies, that they sold many canoe loads of human excrement, which they kept in the creeks near the market. This was for the manufacture of salt and the curing of skins, which they say cannot be done without it. I know that many gentlemen will laugh at this, but I assure them it is true. I may add that on all the roads they have shelters made of reeds or straw or grass so that they can retire when they wish to do so, and purge their bowels unseen by passersby, and also in order that their excrement shall not be lost.

 Which of the items offered for sale in this account might also have been available in a market in Asia, Africa, or Europe? What types of goods mentioned here appear to be unique to the Americas?

Source: From *The Conquest of New Spain* by Bernal Díaz. Copyright © 1975. (Harmondsworth: Penguin), pp. 232–233.

To postpone the day of reckoning, the Aztecs practiced human sacrifice. The Aztecs believed that appeasing the sun god Huitzilopochtli with sacrifices could delay the final destruction of their world. Victims were prepared for the ceremony through elaborate rituals and then brought to the holy shrine, where their hearts were ripped out of their chests and presented to the gods as a holy offering. It was an honor to be chosen for sacrifice, and captives were often used as sacrificial victims because they represented valor, the trait the Aztecs prized most.

Like the art of the Olmecs, most Aztec architecture, art, and sculpture had religious significance. At the center of the capital city of Tenochtitlán was the sacred precinct, which was dominated by the massive pyramid dedicated to Huitzilopochtli and the rain god Tlaloc. The entire pyramid was covered with brightly colored paintings and sculptures.

Although little Aztec painting and sculpture survive, they were evidently of high quality. Artisans worked with stone and with soft metals such as gold and silver, which they cast using the lost-wax technique. They did not have the knowledge for making implements in bronze or iron, however. Stoneworking consisted primarily of representations of the gods and bas-reliefs depicting religious ceremonies. Among the most famous is the massive disk called the Stone of the Fifth Sun, which was carved for use at the central pyramid at Tenochtitlán.

Werner Forman/Art Resource, NY

6.6 The Stone of the Fifth Sun. This basalt disk, which weighs 26 tons, recorded the Aztec view of the cosmos. It portrays the perpetual struggle between forces of good and evil in the universe; in the center is an intimidating image of the sun god clutching human hearts with his talons. Having previously traversed the creation and destruction of four worlds, the Aztecs believed they were living in the world of the fifth and final sun—hence this stone carving, which was found in the central pyramid at Tenochtitlán.

The Aztecs had devised a form of writing based on hieroglyphs that represented an object or a concept. The symbols had no phonetic significance and did not constitute a writing system as such but could give the sense of a message and were probably used by civilian or religious officials as notes or memorandums for their orations. A trained class of scribes carefully painted the notes on paper made from the inner bark of fig trees. Unfortunately, many of these notes were destroyed by the Spaniards as part of their effort to eradicate all aspects of Aztec religion and culture.

6-3 PEOPLES AND SOCIETIES IN EARLY NORTH AMERICA

Q Focus Question: What were the main characteristics of the first human societies in North America, and how did they resemble or differ from their counterparts in Mesoamerica?

To the north of the great civilizations in ancient Mesoamerica lay the vast continent of North America, where other communities of Amerindians were also beginning to master the art of agriculture and building

organized societies. From early times, many of these peoples maintained active contacts with other human societies to the south, and in many ways their culture bore some resemblance to the advanced civilizations in Mesoamerica, but geographical and climatic differences resulted in the creation of societies that differed in vital respects.

Although human beings had occupied much of the continent of North America during the early phases of human settlement, the switch to farming as a means of survival did not occur until the third millennium B.C.E. at the earliest and much later in most areas of the continent. Until that time, most Amerindian communities lived by hunting, fishing, or foraging. As the supply of large animals began to diminish, they turned to smaller game and to fishing and foraging for wild plants, fruits, and nuts.

6-3a The Eastern Woodlands

It was probably during the third millennium B.C.E. that peoples in the Eastern Woodlands (the land in eastern North America from the Great Lakes to the Gulf of Mexico) began to cultivate indigenous plants for food in a systematic way. As wild game and food became scarce, some communities began to place more emphasis on cultivating crops. This shift first occurred in the Mississippi River Valley from what are now Ohio, Indiana, and Illinois down to the Gulf of Mexico. Among the most commonly cultivated crops were maize, squash, beans, and various grasses.

As the area's population increased, people began to congregate in villages, and sedentary communities began to develop in the alluvial lowlands, where the soil could be cultivated for many years at a time because of the nutrients deposited by the river water.

Village councils were established to adjudicate disputes, and in a few cases several villages banded together under the authority of a local chieftain. Urban centers began to appear, some of them inhabited by 10,000 people or more. At the same time, regional trade increased. The people of the **Hopewell culture** in Ohio ranged from the shores of Lake Superior to the Appalachian Mountains and the Gulf of Mexico in search of metals, shells, obsidian, and manufactured items to support their economic needs and religious beliefs.

6-3b Cahokia

At the site of Cahokia near the modern city of East Saint Louis, Illinois, archaeologists found a burial mound more than 98 feet high with a base larger than that of the Great Pyramid at Giza in Egypt. A hundred smaller mounds were also found in the vicinity. The town itself, which covered almost 300 acres and was surrounded by a wooden stockade, was apparently the administrative capital of much of the surrounding territory until its decline in the 1200s. With a population of more than 20,000, it was possibly the largest city in North America until Philadelphia surpassed that number in the early nineteenth century. Cahokia carried on extensive trade with other communities throughout the region, and there are some signs of regular contacts with the civilizations in Mesoamerica such as the presence of ball courts in the Central American style. But wars were not uncommon, leading the Iroquois, who inhabited much of the modern states of Pennsylvania and New York, as well as parts of southern Canada, to create a tribal alliance called the League of Iroquois.

6-3c The Ancient Pueblo Peoples

West of the Mississippi River basin, most Amerindian peoples lived by hunting or food gathering. During the first millennium C.E., knowledge of agriculture gradually spread up the rivers to the Great Plains, and farming was practiced as far west as southwestern Colorado, where an agricultural community was established in an area extending from northern New Mexico and Arizona to southwestern Colorado and parts of southern Utah. Although they apparently never invented the wheel or used beasts of burden, these Ancient Pueblo peoples (formerly known by the Navajo name *Anasazi*, or "alien ancient ones") created a system of roads that facilitated an extensive exchange of technology, products, and ideas throughout the region. By the ninth century, they had mastered the art of irrigation, which allowed them to expand their productive efforts to squash and beans, and they had established an important urban center at Chaco Canyon in southern New Mexico, where they built a walled city with dozens of three-story adobe communal houses, today called *pueblos*, with timbered roofs. Community religious functions were carried out in two large circular chambers called *kivas* (KEE-vuhs). Clothing was made from hides or cotton cloth. At its height, **Pueblo Bonito** contained hundreds of compounds housing several thousand residents.

In the mid-twelfth century, the Ancient Pueblo peoples moved north to Mesa Verde in southwestern Colorado. At first, they settled on top of the mesa, where maize had been cultivated since as early as the seventh century C.E., but eventually—for reasons that are still unclear—they migrated onto the cliffs of surrounding canyons.

Sometime during the late thirteenth century, however, Mesa Verde was also abandoned, and the inhabitants migrated southward. Their descendants, the Zuni and the Hopi, now occupy pueblos in central Arizona and New Mexico (thus leading them to adopt their new name). For years, archaeologists surmised that a severe drought was the cause of the migration, but new evidence has raised doubts that decreasing rainfall by itself was a sufficient explanation. An increase in internecine warfare, perhaps brought about by climatic changes, may also have played a role in the decision to relocate. Perhaps migrants from the south arrived in the area, provoking bitter rivalries with Ancient Pueblo society. In any event, with increasing aridity and the importation of the horse by the Spanish

William J. Duiker

6.7 Cliff Palace at Mesa Verde. Mesa Verde is one of the best-developed sites of the Ancient Pueblo peoples in southwestern North America. At one time they were farmers who tilled the soil atop the mesas, but eventually they were forced to build their settlements in more protected locations. At Cliff Palace, shown here, adobe houses were hidden on the perpendicular face of the mesa. Access was achieved only by a perilous descent via indented finger- and toeholds on the rock face.

in the sixteenth century, hunting revived, and mounted nomads like the Apache and the Navajo came to dominate much of the Southwest. Before their relocation, however, the Pueblo Bonito peoples clearly maintained commercial contacts with their counterparts in Mexico and even as far south as the Pacific Coast of South America. Jars containing the residue of fermented chocolate have been found in the area, suggesting that trade with peoples in Mesoamerica, where cacao trees were cultivated, was common.

6-4 THE FIRST CIVILIZATIONS IN SOUTH AMERICA

 Focus Question: What role did the environment play in the evolution of societies in South America?

South America is a vast continent characterized by extremes in climate and geography. The north is dominated by the mighty Amazon River, which flows through dense tropical rain forests carrying the largest flow of water of any river system in the world (see Map 6.4). Farther to the south, the forests are replaced by prairies and steppes stretching westward to the Andes, which extend the entire length of the continent from the northern Isthmus of Panama to the southern Strait of Magellan. The western slopes of the Andes along the Pacific coast are some of the driest desert regions in the world.

South America has been inhabited by human beings for more than 12,000 years. Wall paintings discovered at the "cavern of the painted rock" in the Amazon region suggest that Stone Age peoples were living in the area at least 11,000 years ago. Early peoples were hunters, fishers, and food gatherers, but there are indications that irrigated farming was practiced in the northern fringe of the Andes as early as 2000 B.C.E. Other farming communities of similar age have been discovered in the Amazon River Valley and on the western slopes of the Andes, where evidence of terraced agriculture dates back 5,000 years.

6-4a Caral

The first complex societies had begun to emerge in the coastal regions of modern-day Peru and Ecuador by the early third millennium B.C.E. Some settlements were located along the coast, but the remnants of farming communities watered by canals have also been found in

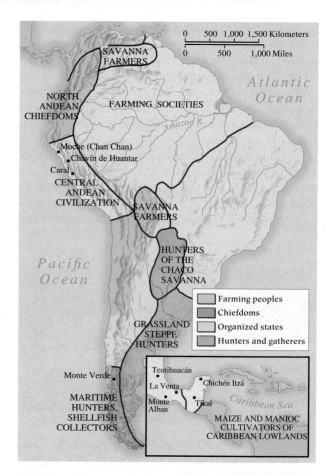

Map 6.4 Early Peoples and Cultures of Central and South America. This map shows regions of early human settlements in Central and South America. Urban conglomerations appear in Mesoamerica (see inset) and along the western coast of South America.

 Why do you think urban centers appeared in these areas?

the valleys of the rivers flowing down to the sea from the Andes Mountains. Fish and agricultural products were traded to inland peoples for wool and salt. The most developed of such centers was at Caral, a highly publicized site located fourteen miles inland from the coast, where the remnants of a 4,500-year-old city sit on the crest of a 60-foot-high pyramid. The inhabitants farmed squash, corn, beans, and tomatoes and also provided cotton to fishing communities along the coast, who used it to make fishnets. Land was divided in a manner similar to the well-field system in ancient China (see Chapter 3). Similar communities are located at nearby sites along the Supe River, which flows from the nearby mountains to the Pacific Ocean nearby.

This early culture, which reached its height during the first millennium B.C.E. near the modern city of Chavín de

Huantar (chah-VEEN day HWAHN-tahr), was marked by the presence of impressive ceremonial precincts dominated by the familiar pyramids—known as *huacas*—and a system of canals that channeled water throughout the otherwise arid surrounding region. Evidence of metallurgy has also been found, with objects made of copper and gold. Another impressive technological achievement was the building in 300 B.C.E. of the first solar observatory in the Americas in the form of thirteen stone towers on a hillside north of Lima, Peru. There are even signs of a rudimentary writing system (see "Inka Culture" later in this chapter).

6-4b Moche

Chavín society had broken down by 200 B.C.E., but early in the first millennium C.E. another advanced civilization appeared in the valley of the Moche River some 200 miles north of the complex at Caral. It occupied an area of more than 2,500 square miles, and its capital city was large enough to contain more than 15,000 people and was dominated by two massive adobe pyramids, each nearly 100 feet high. The larger one, known today as the Pyramid of the Sun, covered a total of fifteen acres. The smaller structure, known as the Pyramid of the Moon, was adorned with painted murals depicting battles, ritual sacrifices, and various local deities.

Artifacts found at Moche (moh-CHAY), especially the metalwork and stone and ceramic figures, exhibit a high quality of artisanship. They were imitated at river valley sites throughout the surrounding area, which suggests that the authority of the Moche rulers may have extended as far as 400 miles along the coast. The artifacts also indicate that the people at Moche, like those in Central America, were preoccupied with warfare. Paintings and pottery as well as other artifacts in stone, metal, and ceramics frequently portray warriors, prisoners, and sacrificial victims. The Moche were also fascinated by the heavens, and much of their art consisted of celestial symbols and astronomical constellations.

Environmental Problems The Moche River Valley is extremely arid, normally receiving less than an inch of rain annually. The peoples in the area compensated by building a sophisticated irrigation system to carry water from the river to the parched fields. By the eighth century C.E., the civilization was in a state of collapse, the irrigation canals had been abandoned, and the remaining population had left the area and moved farther inland or suffered from severe malnutrition.

What happened to bring Moche culture to this untimely end? Archaeologists speculate that environmental

CHRONOLOGY	Early South America
First human settlements in South America	10,500 B.C.E.
Agriculture first practiced	ca. 3200 B.C.E.
Founding of Caral	ca. 2500 B.C.E.
Chavin style	First millennium B.C.E.
Moche civilization	ca. 150–800 C.E.
Wari culture	ca. 500–1000 C.E.
Civilization of Chimor	ca. 1100–1450
Inka takeover in central Andes	1400s

disruptions in the sixth and seventh centuries, perhaps brought on by changes in the temperature of the Pacific Ocean known as **El Niño**, led to alternating periods of drought and flooding of coastal regions, which caused the irrigated fields to silt up (see Comparative Essay, "History and the Environment," p. 154). The warm water created by El Niño conditions also killed local marine life, severely damaging the local fishing industry.

6-4c Wari and Chimor

A few hundred miles to the south of Moche, a people known as the Wari (WAH-ree) culture began to expand from their former home in the Andes foothills and established communities along the coast in the vicinity of modern Lima, Peru. As the state of Moche declined, the Wari gradually spread northward in the eighth century and began to occupy many of the urban sites in the Moche Valley. According to some scholars, they may even have made use of the Moche's sacred buildings and appropriated their religious symbolism. In the process, the Wari created the most extensive land empire yet seen in South America. In the end, however, they too succumbed to the challenge posed by unstable environmental conditions.

Around 1100, a new power, the kingdom of Chimor (chee-MAWR), with its capital at Chan Chan (CHAHN CHAHN) at the mouth of the Moche River, emerged in the area. Built almost entirely of adobe, the city of Chan Chan housed an estimated 30,000 residents in an area of more than twelve square miles that included many palace compounds surrounded by walls nearly thirty feet high. One compound contained an intricate labyrinth that wound its way progressively inward until it ended in a central chamber, probably occupied by the ruler. Like the Moche before them, the people of Chimor relied on irrigation to funnel the water from the river into their fields.

History and the Environment

Earth & Environment

Ai Apaec was the founding deity of the Moche peoples. His abode was on Cerro Blanco, the mountain that today towers over the ruins of the Moche capital city on the coast of northern Peru. In times of drought or flood, Ai Apaec presided in spirit over sacrificial ceremonies held at the nearby Pyramid of the Moon to beseech the heavenly forces in the mountain to provide precious water to the parched fields below. In the end, Ai Apaec's labors were in vain because the Moche civilization was eventually brought to an end by a series of disastrous droughts and floods—through what is known as the El Niño effect—in the eighth century C.E. Moche was by no means the only civilization to be brought down by dramatic changes in the natural environment. Climatic change or natural disaster almost certainly led to the decline and fall of the Indus Valley civilization and the Maya city-states in Mesoamerica. A lengthy drought may have fatally damaged the wheat-growing regions in North Africa and contributed to the collapse of the Roman Empire itself.

Sometimes the problems may have been self-inflicted, as in the case of Mesopotamia and the Maya, where overuse of land may have led to erosion or leached nutrients from the soil. Whatever the case, historians have become increasingly aware that climatic change or environmental conditions may have been a contributing factor in the fate of several of the great civilizations throughout the ancient world, including Medieval Europe and the Tang Dynasty in China. In the case of the Moche, massive flooding brought about by the El Niño effect (environmental conditions triggered by changes in water temperature in the Pacific Ocean) led to the collapse of a great civilization.

Climatic changes, of course, have not always been detrimental to the health and prosperity of human beings. A warming trend that took place at the end of the last ice age eventually made much of the world more habitable for farming peoples around 10,000 years ago. The effects of El Niño may be beneficial to people living in some areas of the world and disastrous to others. But human misuse of land and water resources is always dangerous to settled societies, especially those living in fragile environments.

 Many ancient civilizations throughout the world were weakened or destroyed by changes taking place in the environment. What are some examples in the pre-Columbian Americas?

Photograph by William J. Duiker.

6.8 Ai Apaec: The Decapitator God

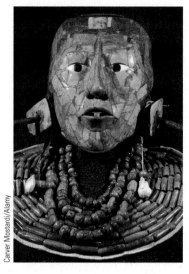

6.9 Jade and Gold Funeral Masks Early civilizations in the Americas, as elsewhere, often placed precious artifacts in the royal tombs of their deceased rulers. The jade and gold mined in Mesoamerica and the continent of South America were transformed into stunning burial masks, as seen here. The jade funeral mask of Lord Pacal (left), a seventh-century ruler of Palenque, was placed in his tomb in the hope that its spiritual energy would propel Pacal into the afterlife, thereby merging him with the divine in the Mayan cosmos. The hammered gold mask from the Chimor culture (right), successors to the Moche civilization in what is present-day Peru, is reminiscent of the famous death mask found at Mycenae, in central Greece (see Chapter 4).

An elaborate system of canals brought the water through hundreds of miles of hilly terrain to the fields near the coast. Nevertheless, by the fifteenth century, Chimor also had disappeared, a victim of floods and a series of earthquakes that destroyed the intricate irrigation system that had been the basis of its survival.

These early civilizations in the Andes were by no means isolated from other societies in the region. As early as 2000 B.C.E., local peoples had been venturing into the Pacific Ocean on wind-powered rafts constructed of woven reeds or balsa wood. By the late first millennium C.E., seafarers from the coast of Ecuador had established a vast trading network that extended southward to central Peru and as far north as western Mexico more than 2,000 miles away. Items transported included jewelry, beads, and metal goods. In all likelihood, technological exchanges were an important by-product of the relationship.

Transportation by land was more difficult. Although roads were constructed to facilitate communication between communities, the forbidding character of the terrain in the mountains was a serious obstacle, and the only draft animal on the entire continent was the llama, which is considerably less hardy than the cattle, horses, and water buffalo used in much of Asia. Such problems undoubtedly hampered the development of regular contacts with distant societies in the Americas, as well as the exchange of goods and ideas

that had lubricated the rise of civilizations from China to the Mediterranean Sea.

6-4d The Inka

The Chimor kingdom was eventually succeeded in the late fifteenth century by an invading force from the mountains far to the south. In the late fourteenth century, the Inka were a small community in the area of Cuzco (KOOS-koh), a city 10,000 feet high in the mountains of southern Peru. In the 1440s, however, under the leadership of their powerful ruler Pachakuti (pah-chah-KOO-tee) (sometimes called Pachacutec, or "he who transforms the world"), the Inka peoples launched a campaign of conquest that eventually brought the entire region under their authority. Under Pachakuti and his immediate successors, Topa Inka (TOH-puh INK-uh) and Huayna Inka (WY-nuh INK-uh) (the word *Inka* means "ruler"), the boundaries of the empire were extended as far as Ecuador, central Chile, and the edge of the Amazon basin.

The Four Quarters: Inka Politics and Society Pachakuti created a highly centralized state (see Map 6.5). With a stunning concern for mathematical precision, he divided his empire—which comprised more than 20,000 square miles and was called Tahuantinsuyu (tuh-HWAHN-tin-SOO-yoo)

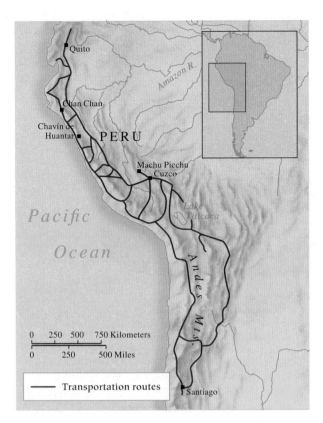

Map 6.5 The Inka Empire Around 1500 C.E. The Inka were the last civilization to flourish in South America before the arrival of the Spanish. The impressive system of roads constructed to facilitate communication shows the extent of Inka control throughout the Andes.

Q *What made the extent of the Inka Empire such a remarkable achievement?*

covered from top to bottom with plates and slabs of gold."[4] Equally impressive are the ruins of the abandoned city of Machu Picchu (MAH-choo PEE-choo), built on a lofty hill-top far above the Urubamba River.

Another major construction project was a system of 24,800 miles of highways and roads that extended for more than 3,000 miles from the border of modern Colombia to a point south of modern Santiago, Chile. Two major road-ways extended in a north–south direction, one through the Andes and the other along the coast, with connecting routes between them. Rest houses and storage depots were placed along the roads. Suspension bridges made of braided fiber and fastened to stone abutments on opposite banks were built over ravines and waterways. Use of the highways was restricted to official and military purposes. Trained runners carried messages rapidly from one way station to another, enabling information to travel as many as 140 miles in a single day. Parts of the road are still in use.

In rural areas, the population lived mainly by farming. In the mountains, the most common form was terraced agriculture with irrigation systems that carried precise amounts of water into the fields, which were planted with maize, potatoes, and other crops. The plots were tilled by collective labor regulated by the state. Like other aspects

or "the world of the four quarters"—into provinces and districts. Each province contained around 10,000 residents (at least in theory) and was ruled by a governor related to the royal family. Excess inhabitants were transferred to other locations. The capital of Cuzco was divided into four quarters, or residential areas, and the social status and economic functions of the residents of each quarter were rigidly defined.

The state was built on forced labor. Often entire communities of workers were moved from one part of the country to another to open virgin lands or engage in massive construction projects. Under Pachakuti, the capital of Cuzco was transformed from a city of mud and thatch into an imposing metropolis of stone. The walls, built of close-fitting stones without the use of mortar, were a wonder to early European visitors. The most impressive structure in the city was a temple dedicated to the sun. According to a Spanish observer, "All four walls of the temple were

6.10 Machu Picchu. Situated in the Andes in modern Peru, Machu Picchu reflects the glory of Inka civilization. To farm such rugged terrain, the Inka constructed terraces and stone aqueducts. To span vast ravines, they built suspension bridges of braided fiber and fastened them to stone abutments on the opposite banks. The most revered of the many temples and stone altars at Machu Picchu was the thronelike "hitching post of the sun," so called because of its close proximity to the sun god.

Virgins with Red Cheeks

Family & Society

A LETTER FROM A PERUVIAN CHIEF to King Philip III of Spain written 400 years ago gives us a firsthand account of the nature of traditional Inka society. The purpose of author Huaman Poma was both to justify the history and culture of the Inka peoples and record their sufferings under Spanish domination. In his letter, Poma describes Inka daily life from birth to death in minute detail. He explains the different tasks assigned to men and women, beginning with their early education. Whereas boys were taught to watch the flocks and trap animals, girls were taught to dye, spin, and weave cloth and perform other domestic chores. Most interesting, perhaps, was the emphasis that the Inka placed on virginity, as described in the selection presented here. The Inka's tradition of temple virgins is reminiscent of similar practices in ancient Rome, where young girls from noble families were chosen as priestesses to tend the sacred fire in the Temple of Vesta for thirty years. If one lost her virginity, she was condemned to be buried alive in an underground chamber.

Huaman Poma, *Letter to a King*

During the time of the Inkas, certain women, who were called *accla* or "the chosen," were destined for lifelong virginity. Mostly they were confined in houses and they belonged to one of two main categories, namely sacred virgins and common virgins.

The so-called "virgins with red cheeks" entered upon their duties at the age of twenty and were dedicated to the service of the Sun, the Moon, and the Day-Star. In their whole life they were never allowed to speak to a man.

The virgins of the Inka's own shrine of Huanacauri were known for their beauty as well as their chastity. The other principal shrines had similar girls in attendance. At the less important shrines there were the older virgins who occupied themselves with spinning and weaving the silklike clothes worn by their idols. There was a still lower class of virgins, over forty years of age and no longer very beautiful, who performed unimportant religious duties and worked in the fields or as ordinary seamstresses.

Daughters of noble families who had grown into old maids were adept at making girdles, headbands, string bags, and similar articles in the intervals of their pious observances.

Girls who had musical talent were selected to sing or play the flute and drum at Court, weddings and other ceremonies, and all the innumerable festivals of the Inka year.

There was yet another class of *accla* or "chosen," only some of whom kept their virginity and others not. These were the Inka's beautiful attendants and concubines, who were drawn from noble families and lived in his palaces. They made clothing for him out of material finer than taffeta or silk. They also prepared a maize spirit of extraordinary richness, which was matured for an entire month, and they cooked delicious dishes for the Inka. They also lay with him, but never with any other man.

In this passage, one of the chief duties of a woman in Inka society was to spin and weave. In what other traditional societies was textile making a woman's work? Why do you think this was the case?

Source: From *Letter to a King* by Guaman Poma de Ayala. Translated and edited by Christopher Dilke. Published by E. P. Dutton, New York, 1978.

of Inka society, marriage was strictly regulated, and men and women were required to select a marriage partner from within the immediate tribal group. For women, there was only one escape from a life of domestic servitude. Fortunate maidens were selected to serve as "chosen virgins" in temples throughout the country (see Historical Voices, "Virgins with Red Cheeks," above). Noblewomen were eligible to compete for service in the Temple of the Sun at Cuzco, whereas commoners might hope to serve in

temples in the provincial capitals. Punishment for breaking the vow of chastity was harsh, and few women evidently took the risk.

Inka Culture Like many other civilizations in pre-Columbian Latin America, the Inka state was built on war. Soldiers for the 200,000-man Inka army, the largest and best armed in the region, were raised by universal male conscription. Military units were moved rapidly

6.11 The Quipu. Not having a writing system, the Inka tallied the various data of their kingdom on strands of knotted yarn. Highly skilled and esteemed, official secretaries recorded population census data, crop and household inventories, government inspector reports, crime investigations, taxes, legal decisions and contracts, and all the official statistics of the realm by an intricate system of tying knots on a circular grouping of strings of yarn. Meaning was achieved by varying the colors and numbers of knots on each string. The use of knotted yarn as a means of recording data was apparently not unique to the Inka.

The Inka had no writing system but kept records using a system of knotted strings called *quipu* (KEE-poo), that were maintained by professionally trained officials and were able to record all types of numerical data. What could not be recorded that way was committed to memory and then recited when needed. The practice was apparently not invented by the Inka. Fragments of quipu have been found at Caral and dated as approximately 5,000 years ago. Nor apparently was the experiment limited to the Americas. A passage in the Chinese classic *The Way of the Tao* declares, "Let the people revert to communication by knotted cords."

As in the case of the Aztecs and the Maya, the lack of a fully developed writing system did not prevent the Inka from realizing a high level of cultural achievement. Most of what survives was recorded by the Spanish and consists of entertainment for the elites. The Inka had a highly developed tradition of court theater, including both tragic and comic works. There was also some poetry composed in blank verse and often accompanied by music played on reed instruments. Inka architecture, as exemplified by massive stone structures at Cuzco and the breathtaking mountaintop palace at Machu Picchu, was stunning.

6-4e Stateless Societies in South America

East of the Andes Mountains in South America, other Amerindian societies were beginning to make the transition to agriculture. Perhaps the most prominent were the Arawak (AR-uh-wahk), a people living along the Orinoco River in modern Venezuela. Having begun to cultivate manioc (a tuber used today in the manufacture of tapioca) along the banks of the river, they gradually migrated down to the coast and then proceeded to move eastward along the northern coast of the continent. Some occupied the islands of the Caribbean Sea. In their new island habitat, they lived by a mixture of fishing, hunting, and cultivating maize, beans, manioc, and squash, as well as other crops such as peanuts, peppers, and pineapples. As the population increased, a pattern of political organization above the village level appeared, along with recognizable social classes headed by a chieftain whose authority included control over the economy. Some urban centers contained ball courts, suggesting the possibility of contacts with Mesoamerica.

Eventually, new peoples from South America began to migrate into the islands of the Caribbean. Known as Caribs, they tended to be more warlike than their predecessors and often drove the previous arrivals to seek refuge on islands farther to the north. A Carib community

along the highway system and were housed in the rest houses along the roadside. Because the Inka had no wheeled vehicles, supplies were carried on the backs of llamas. Once an area was placed under Inka authority, the local inhabitants were instructed in the Quechua (KEH-chuh-wuh) language, which became the lingua franca of the state, and were introduced to the state religion. Like most other faiths in the Western Hemisphere, the Inka religion was polytheistic, with separate deities for the heavens and Earth, and it relied on human sacrifice to appease the gods and win their support. Pachamama, the "mother of the earth," was common to all religions throughout the Andes.

survives today on the island of Dominica, in the Lesser Antilles, although many current inhabitants in the islands are undoubtedly at least partly of Carib or Arawak ancestry.

In most such societies, where clear-cut class stratifications had not yet taken place, men and women were considered of equal status. Men were responsible for hunting, warfare, and dealing with outsiders, whereas women were accountable for the crops, food distribution, maintaining the household, and bearing and raising children. Their roles were complementary and were often viewed as a divine division of labor. In such cases, women in the stateless societies of North America held positions of greater respect than their counterparts in the river valley civilizations of Africa and Asia.

Although the Arawak and the Carib peoples eventually left their original homeland in the northern sections of South America, others remained. Small groups of hunter-gatherers continue today to live in virtual isolation throughout the vast Amazon River basin. Although conditions along the Amazon and its tributaries often appear to impose limits on the forms of economic and cultural activity practiced by local inhabitants, this was apparently not always the case. One of the most intriguing puzzles in pre-Columbian South American archaeology is the recently discovered evidence of substantial human activity that took place in the Amazon River Valley. Scholars had long been skeptical that advanced societies could take shape in the region because the soil lacked adequate nutrients to support a large population. Recent archaeological evidence, however, suggests that in areas where decaying organic matter produces a rich soil suitable for farming—such as the region near the modern river port of Santarem—large agricultural societies may once have existed. More information about this previously unknown society must await further archaeological evidence.

CHAPTER SUMMARY

The first human beings did not arrive in the Americas until quite late in the prehistorical period. For the next several millennia, their descendants were forced to respond to the challenges of the environment in total isolation from other parts of the world. Nevertheless, around 5000 B.C.E., farming settlements began to appear in river valleys and upland areas in both Central and South America. Not long afterward—as measured in historical time—organized communities embarked on the long march toward creating advanced technological societies. Although the total number of people living in the Americas is a matter of debate, estimates range from 10 million to as many as 90 million people.

Perhaps the most striking fact about developments in the Western Hemisphere is how closely the process paralleled those of other civilizations. Irrigated agriculture, long-distance trade, urbanization, and the development of a writing system were all hallmarks of the emergence of advanced societies of the classic type.

Some of the parallels, of course, were less appealing. States in the Western Hemisphere were every bit as addicted to warfare as their counterparts elsewhere. The widespread use of human sacrifice is reminiscent of similar practices in other ancient societies such as India and Shang China. Not much is yet known about relations between men and women in the Americas, but it appears that gender roles were as sharply delineated there as in much of Asia and the Mediterranean world.

In some respects, the societies that emerged in the Americas were not as advanced technologically as their counterparts elsewhere. They were not familiar with the process of smelting iron, for example, and had not yet invented wheeled vehicles. Their writing systems were still in their infancy. Several possible reasons have been advanced to explain this technological gap. Geographic isolation—not only from people of other continents but also, in some cases, from each other—deprived them of the benefits of the diffusion of ideas that had enabled other societies to learn from their neighbors. Contacts among societies in the Americas were made much more difficult because of the topography and the diversity of the environment.

In some ways, too, they were not as blessed by nature. As sociologist Jared Diamond has pointed out, the Americas did not possess many indigenous varieties of edible grasses that could encourage hunter-gatherers to take up farming. Nor were there abundant large mammals that could easily be domesticated for food and transport (horses had disappeared from the Western Hemisphere before the arrival of *Homo sapiens sapiens* at the end of the last ice age). Not until the arrival of Europeans did such familiar attributes of civilization become widely available for human use in the Americas.[5]

These disadvantages can help explain some of the problems that the early peoples of the Americas encountered in their efforts to master their environments. Note that the spread of agriculture and increasing urbanization had already begun to produce a rising incidence of infectious diseases. It is also significant that in the Americas, as elsewhere, many of the first civilizations formed by the human species appear to have been brought to an end as much by environmental changes and disease as by war. In the next chapter, we shall return to Asia, where new civilizations were in the process of replacing the ancient empires.

REFLECTION QUESTIONS

Q How did geographic and climatic factors affect the rise and fall of early societies in the Americas? Were similar factors at work among contemporary societies in other parts of the world?

Q What are some of the reasons advanced for the collapse of Maya civilization in the late first millennium C.E.? Which do archaeologists find the most persuasive?

Q What common features linked the emerging societies in the Americas during the pre-Columbian period? Does it appear that technological and cultural achievements passed from one society to another as frequently as in other parts of the world?

CHAPTER TIMELINE

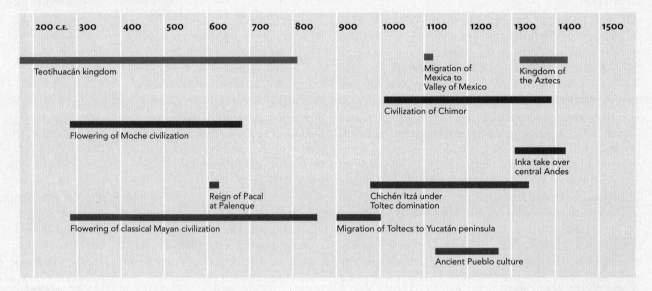

CHAPTER NOTES

1. Quoted in S. Morley and G. W. Brainerd, *The Ancient Maya* (Stanford, Calif., 1983), p. 513.
2. B. Díaz, *The Conquest of New Spain* (Harmondsworth, England, 1975), p. 210.
3. Quoted in M. D. Coe, D. Snow, and E. P. Benson, *Atlas of Ancient America* (New York, 1988), p. 149.
4. G. de la Vega (El Inca), *Royal Commentaries of the Incas and General History of Peru,* pt. 1, trans. H. V. Livermore (Austin, Tex., 1966), p. 180.
5. J. Diamond, *Guns, Germs, and Steel: The Fates of Human Societies* (New York, 1997), pp. 187–188.

MINDTAP
From Cengage

MindTap® is a fully online, highly personalized learning experience built upon Cengage Learning content. MindTap combines student learning tools—readings, multimedia, activities, and assessments—into a singular Learning Path that guides students through the course and helps students develop the critical thinking, analysis, and communication skills that are essential to academic and professional success.

CHAPTER 7

FERMENT IN THE MIDDLE EAST: THE RISE OF ISLAM

Chapter Outline and Focus Questions

7.1 Muhammad Rises to Heaven

Critical Thinking

Q *In what ways did the arrival of Islam change or maintain the political, social, and cultural conditions that had existed in the area before Muhammad?*

Connections to Today

Q *Do the tactics and the motives that led to the crusades provide any lessons for the conduct of foreign policy by the United States and its allies in the Middle East today? If so, what are those lessons?*

IN THE YEAR 570 c.e., in the Arabian city of Mecca, a child named Muhammad (moh-HAM-id *or* muh-HAHM-ud) was born whose life would change the course of world history. The son of a merchant, Muhammad grew to maturity in a time of transition. The Roman Empire, which had once been able to impose its hegemony over the Middle East, was only a distant memory. The region was now divided into many squabbling states, and the people adhered to many different faiths.

Concerned about the corrupt and decadent society of his day, Muhammad took to wandering in the hills outside Mecca, where on one occasion, he experienced visions that he was convinced had been inspired by Allah (AH-lah). Eventually, they would be transcribed into the Qur'an (kuh-RAN or kuh-RAHN)—the holy book of Islam—and provide inspiration to millions of people throughout the world. According to popular belief, Muhammad, mounted on his faithful steed Buraq and accompanied by the angel Gabriel, embarked on a mystical "night journey" to heaven, where Allah introduced him to paradise and hell so that on his return to Earth he could instruct the faithful on their prospects in the next world (see the chapter-opening illustration).

Within a few decades after Muhammad's death, the Middle East was united once again. As Arab armies under the command of Muhammad's followers swept through the Middle East to the gates of India and the shores of the Mediterranean Sea, Arab beliefs and customs, as reflected through the prism of Muhammad's teachings, transformed the societies and cultures of the peoples living in the new empire. Although the distinctive political and cultural forces that had long characterized the region eventually began to reassert themselves, conditions in all areas affected by these events would never be the same again.

7-1 THE RISE OF ISLAM

Focus Question: What were the main tenets of Islam, and how does the religion compare with Judaism and Christianity?

The Arabs are a Semitic-speaking people of southwestern Asia who have a long history. They were mentioned in Greek sources of the fifth century B.C.E. and even earlier in the Old Testament. The Greek historian Herodotus had applied the name Arab to the entire peninsula, calling it Arabia. In 106 B.C.E., the Romans extended their authority to the Arabian Peninsula, transforming it into a province of their growing empire.

During Roman times, the region was inhabited primarily by **Bedouin** (BED-oo-un *or* BED-wuhn) Arabs, nomadic peoples who came originally from the northern part of the peninsula. Bedouin society was organized on a tribal basis. The ruling member of the tribe was called the *sheikh* (SHAYK *or* SHEEK) and was selected from one of the leading families by a council of elders called the *majlis* (MAHJ-liss). The sheikh ruled the tribe with the consent of the council. Each tribe was autonomous but felt a general sense of allegiance to the larger unity of all the clans in the region. In early times, the

Bedouins had supported themselves primarily by sheep-herding or by raiding passing caravans, but after the domestication of the camel during the second millennium B.C.E., they began to participate in the caravan trade themselves and became major carriers of goods between the Persian Gulf and the Mediterranean Sea.

The Arabs of pre-Islamic times were polytheistic, with a supreme god known as *Allah* presiding over a community of spirits. It was a communal faith involving all members of the tribe and without a priesthood. Spirits were believed to inhabit natural objects such as trees, rivers, and mountains, and the supreme deity was symbolized by a sacred stone. Each tribe possessed its own stone but by Muhammad's time, a massive black meteorite housed in a central shrine called the Ka'ba (KAH-buh) in the commercial city of Mecca had come to possess especially sacred qualities.

In the fifth and sixth centuries C.E., the economic importance of the Arabian Peninsula began to increase. As a result of political disorder in Mesopotamia—a consequence of constant wars between the Eastern Roman (Byzantine) and Persian Empires—and in Egypt, the trade routes that ran directly across the arid peninsula or down the Red Sea became increasingly risky. A third route, which passed from the Mediterranean through Mecca to Yemen and then by ship across the Indian Ocean, became more popular. The communities in that part of the peninsula benefited from the change and took a larger share of the caravan

7.2 The Ka'aba in Mecca. The shrine containing a black meteorite in the Arabian city of Mecca—the Ka'aba—is the most sacred site of the Islamic faith. Wherever Muslims pray, they are instructed to face Mecca; each thus becomes a spoke of the Ka'aba, the holy center of the wheel of Islam. All Muslims are encouraged to visit the Ka'aba, which is now dwarfed by skyscrapers erected to provide temporary housing for the faithful, at least once in their lifetime if they are able to do so. Called the *hajj*, this pilgrimage to Mecca represents the ultimate in spiritual fulfillment for every Muslim.

trade—much of it in spices—between the Mediterranean and the countries on the other side of the Indian Ocean. As a consequence, relations between the Bedouins of the desert and the increasingly wealthy merchant class of the towns began to become strained.

7-1a The Role of Muhammad

Into this world came Muhammad (also known as Mohammed), a man whose spiritual visions unified the Arab world (see Map 7.1) with a speed no one would have suspected possible. Born in Mecca to a merchant family and orphaned at age six, Muhammad (570–632 C.E.) grew up to become a caravan manager and eventually married a rich widow, Khadija (kah-DEE-juh), who was also his employer.

A member of the local Hashemite (HASH-uh-myt) clan of the Quraysh (koo-RYSH) tribe, he lived in Mecca as a merchant for several years but, according to tradition, was troubled by the growing gap between the Bedouin values of honesty and generosity and the acquisitive behavior of the affluent commercial elites in the city. Deeply concerned, he began to retreat to the nearby hills to meditate in isolation. There he encountered the angel Gabriel, who commanded him to preach the revelations that he would be given.

Muhammad was apparently acquainted with Jewish and Christian beliefs and came to believe that even though Allah had already revealed himself in part through Moses and Jesus—and thus through the Hebraic and Christian traditions—the final revelations were now being given to him. Out of his revelations, which were eventually dictated to scribes, came the Qur'an ("recitation"; also spelled *Koran*), the holy scriptures of Islam (*Islam* means "submission," implying submission to the will of Allah). The Qur'an contained the guidelines by which followers of Allah, known as Muslims (practitioners of Islam), were to live. Like the Christians and the Jews, Muslims (also known as Moslems) were a "people of the Book," believers in a faith based on scripture.

After returning home, Muhammad set out to comply with Gabriel's command by preaching to the residents of Mecca about his revelations. At first, many were convinced that he was a madman or a charlatan. Others were undoubtedly concerned that his vigorous attacks on traditional beliefs and the corrupt society around him could severely shake the social and political order. After three years of proselytizing, he had only thirty followers.

Discouraged—perhaps by the systematic persecution of his followers, which was reportedly undertaken

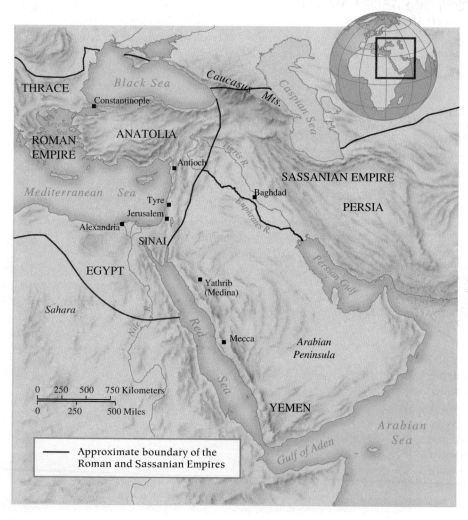

Map 7.1 The Middle East in the Time of Muhammad. When Islam began to spread throughout the Middle East in the early seventh century, the dominant states in the region were the Eastern Roman Empire in the eastern Mediterranean and the Sassanian Empire in Persia.

Q *What were the major territorial divisions existing at the time and the key sites connected to the rise of Islam?*

with a brutality reminiscent of the cruelties suffered by early Christians—in 622 C.E. Muhammad and his closest supporters (mostly from his own Hashemite clan) left the city and retreated north to the rival city of Yathrib, later renamed Medina (muh-DEE-nuh), or "city of the Prophet." That flight, known in history as the **Hegira** (huh-JY-ruh or HEH-juh-ruh) (*Hijrah*), marks the first date on the official calendar of Islam. At Medina, Muhammad failed in his original purpose of converting the Jewish community in Medina to his beliefs, but he was successful in winning support from many residents of the city as well as from Bedouins in the surrounding countryside. From this mixture, he formed the first Muslim community—the *umma* (UM-mah). Returning to his birthplace at the head of a considerable military force, Muhammad conquered Mecca and converted the townspeople to the new faith. In 630, he made a symbolic visit to the Ka'aba, where he declared it a sacred shrine of Islam and ordered the destruction of the idols of the traditional faith. Two years later, Muhammad died, just as Islam was beginning to spread throughout the peninsula (see Film & History, *The Message*).

To what degree this traditional account of the early years of Islam stands up to historical analysis is a matter of debate. As with the founding of many other major religions, verifiable evidence to corroborate received beliefs is sparse. As a result, the circumstances surrounding the life of Muhammad and his role in founding the religion of Islam remain speculative. To complicate matters, the earliest versions of the Qur'an available today do not contain the diacritical marks that modern Arabic uses to clarify meaning, thus leaving much of the sacred text ambiguous and open to varying interpretations.

7-1b The Teachings of Muhammad

Like Christianity and Judaism, Islam is monotheistic. Allah is the all-powerful being who created the universe and everything in it. Islam is also concerned with salvation and offers the hope of an afterlife. Those who hope to achieve it must subject themselves to the will of Allah. Unlike Christianity, Islam makes no claim to the divinity of its founder. Like Abraham, Moses, and other figures of the Old Testament, Muhammad was a prophet—but he was also a man like other men. According to the Qur'an, because earlier prophets had corrupted his revelations, Allah sent his complete revelation through Muhammad.

At the heart of Islam is the Qur'an, with its basic message that there is no God but Allah and Muhammad is his prophet. Consisting of 114 *suras* (SUR-uhz) (chapters) drawn together by a committee established after Muhammad's death, the Qur'an is not only the sacred book of Islam but also an ethical guidebook and a code of law and political theory combined.

As it evolved, Islam developed several fundamental tenets. At its heart was the need to obey the will of Allah. This meant following a basic ethical code consisting of what are popularly termed the **Five Pillars of Islam**: belief in Allah and Muhammad as his prophet; standard prayer five times a day and public prayer on Friday at midday to worship Allah; observation of the holy month of **Ramadan** (RAH-muh-dan), including fasting from dawn to sunset; if possible, making a pilgrimage to Mecca at least once in one's lifetime; and giving alms, or *zakat* (zuh-KAHT), to the poor and unfortunate. The faithful who observed the law were guaranteed a place in an eternal paradise (a vision of a luxurious and cool garden shared by some versions of Eastern Christianity) with the sensuous delights so obviously lacking in the midst of the Arabian desert.

Islam was not just a set of religious beliefs but a way of life. After the death of Muhammad, Muslim scholars, known as the *ulama* (OO-luh-mahor or oo-LAH-muh), drew up a law code called the *shari'a* (shah-REE-uh) to provide believers with a set of prescriptions to regulate their daily lives. Much of the shari'a was drawn from existing legal regulations or from the *Hadith* (hah-DEETH), a collection

▣ FILM & HISTORY

The Message

John Bryson/Time Life Pictures/Getty Images

Few films about the prophet Muhammad and the early years of Islam have appeared in the English language. *The Message*, also known as *Muhammad: Messenger of God* (1976), was designed by Syrian-American filmmaker Moustapha Akka to fill that gap. The film emphasizes factual accuracy rather than glitz and therefore lacks some of the emotional punch of some familiar biblical epics, but it is beautifully produced and includes several swashbuckling battle scenes. Because of the Muslim stricture against showing the face of Muhammad, he does not appear on screen and is represented by only his voice.

Q *Why do Muslims object to the portrayal of the Prophet Muhammad in works of art?*

MINDTAP See full-length Film & History feature in MindTap.
From Cengage

"Draw Their Veils over Their Bosoms"

Religion & Philosophy

BEFORE THE ISLAMIC ERA, many upper-class women greeted men on the street, entertained their husbands' friends at home, went on pilgrimages to Mecca, and even accompanied their husbands to battle. Such women were neither veiled nor secluded. Muhammad, however, specified that his own wives, who (according to the Qur'an) were "not like any other women," should be modestly attired and should be addressed by men from behind a curtain. Over the centuries, Muslim theologians, fearful that female sexuality could threaten the established order, interpreted Muhammad's "modest attire" and his reference to curtains to mean that all Muslim women should remain in segregated seclusion and conceal their bodies. In fact, one strict scholar in fourteenth-century Cairo went so far as to prescribe that ideally a woman should leave her home only three times in her life: on entering her husband's home after marriage, after the death of her parents, and after her own death.

In traditional Islamic societies, veiling and seclusion were more prevalent among urban women than among their rural counterparts. The latter, who worked in the fields and rarely saw people outside their extended family, were less restricted. In this excerpt from the Qur'an, women are instructed to "guard their modesty" and "draw veils over their bosoms." Nowhere in the Qur'an, however, does it stipulate that women should be sequestered or covered from head to toe.

Source: The Holy Quran, 24:32.

Qur'an, Chapter 24: "The Light"

And say to the believing women
That they should lower
Their gaze and guard
Their modesty: that they
Should not display their
Beauty and ornaments except
What [must ordinarily] appear
Thereof: that they should
Draw their veils over
Their bosoms and not display
Their beauty except
To their husbands, their fathers,
Their husbands' fathers, their sons,
Their husbands' sons,
Their brothers or their brothers' sons,
Or their sisters' sons,
Or their women, or the slaves
Whom their right hands
Possess, or male servants
Free of physical needs,
Or small children who
Have no sense of the shame
Of sex; and that they
Should not strike their feet
In order to draw attention
To their hidden ornaments.

 How does the role of women in Islam compare with what we have seen in other traditional societies such as India, China, and the Americas?

---

of the sayings of the prophet that was used to supplement the revelations contained in the holy scriptures.

Believers were subject to strict behavioral requirements. In addition to being commanded to follow the Five Pillars, Muslims were forbidden to gamble, eat pork, drink alcoholic beverages, and engage in dishonest behavior. Sexual mores were also strict. Contacts between unmarried men and women were discouraged, and ideally marriages were to be arranged by the parents. In accordance with Bedouin custom, polygyny was permitted, but Muhammad attempted to limit the practice by restricting males to four wives (see Historical Voices, "Draw Their Veils over Their Bosoms").

7-2 THE ARAB EMPIRE AND ITS SUCCESSORS

 Focus Question: Why did the Arabs undergo such a rapid expansion in the seventh and eighth centuries, and why were they so successful in creating an empire?

The death of Muhammad presented his followers with a dilemma. Although Muhammad had not claimed divine qualities, Muslims saw no separation between political and religious authority. Submission to the will of Allah meant submission to his prophet, Muhammad. According to the Qur'an, "Whoso obeyeth the messenger obeyeth Allah."[1] Muhammad's charismatic authority and political skills had been at the heart of his success. But Muslims have never agreed as to whether he named a successor, and although he had several daughters, he left no sons. In the male-oriented society of his day, who would lead the community of the faithful?

Shortly after Muhammad's death, several of his closest followers selected Abu Bakr (ah-boo BAHK-ur), a wealthy merchant from Medina who was Muhammad's father-in-law and one of his first supporters, as caliph (KAY-liff) (*khalifa*, literally "successor"). The caliph was the temporal leader of the Islamic community and was also considered in general terms to be a religious leader, or **imam** (ih-MAHM). Under Abu Bakr's prudent leadership, the movement succeeded in suppressing factional tendencies among some of the Bedouin tribes in the peninsula and began to direct its attention to wider fields. Muhammad had used the Arabic tribal custom of the *razzia* (RAZZ-ee-uh), or raid, in the struggle against his enemies. Now his successors turned to the same custom to expand the authority of the movement.

When historians of the Middle East today discuss the expansion of Islam after the death of Muhammad, the Arabic term *jihad* (jee-HAHD) is often used to describe the process. The word appears in the Qur'an on several occasions, and it appears to have had multiple meanings, much as the word *crusade* does in English. Sometimes jihad is used in the sense of "striving in the way of the Lord," as a means of exhorting believers to struggle against the evil within themselves. In other cases, however, it has been translated as "holy war," justifying hostile action against the enemies of Islam. In that sense, the word can be used to describe the expansion of the world of Islam into the realm of the unbelievers (see Historical Voices, "The Spread of the Muslim Faith," p. 168). Many of today's Islamic terrorist movements clearly view *jihad* in the latter sense, an interpretation to which many other Muslims vigorously object. Because the word is so heavily laden with emotional connotations, it clearly should be used sparingly and with care.

7-2a Creation of an Empire

Once the Arabs had become unified under Muhammad's successor, they began directing the energy they formerly directed against each other outward against neighboring peoples. The Byzantine and Sassanian (suh-SAY-nee-uhn) Empires were the first to feel the strength of the newly united Arabs, now aroused to a peak of zeal by their common faith. In 636 c.e., the Muslims defeated the Byzantine army at the Yarmuk (yahr-MOOK) River, north of the Dead Sea. Four years later, they took possession of the Byzantine

province of Syria. To the east, the Arabs defeated a Persian force in 637 and then went on to conquer the entire empire of the Sassanians by 650. In the meantime, Egypt and other areas of North Africa were also brought under Arab authority (see Chapter 8).

7-2b What Was the Secret of Arab Success?

What accounts for this rapid expansion of the Arabs after the rise of Islam in the early seventh century? Historians have proposed various explanations ranging from a prolonged drought on the Arabian Peninsula to the use of the Arabian camel as an instrument of war and to the desire of Islam's leaders to channel the energies of their new converts. Others have suggested that the Byzantine Empire had been weakened by a plague epidemic that had not affected the desert regions farther to the east. Still another hypothesis is that the expansion was deliberately planned by the ruling elites in Mecca to extend their trade routes and bring surplus-producing regions under their control. Whatever the case, Islam's ability to unify the Bedouin peoples certainly played a role. Although the Arab triumph was made substantially easier by the ongoing conflict between the Byzantine and Persian Empires, which had weakened both powers, the strength and mobility of the Bedouin armies with their much-vaunted cavalry should not be overlooked. Led by a series of brilliant generals, the Arabs assembled a large, highly motivated army whose valor was enhanced

William J. Duiker

7.3 The Camel: Islam's Secret Weapon. The one-humped Arabian camel, technically known as the *dromedary*, was first domesticated in the Horn of Africa about 5,000 years ago. By the beginning of the first millennium b.c.e., it was introduced in the Middle East, where it became popular as a beast of burden and—after the rise of Islam—as an instrument of war, where its adaptability to desert conditions made it superior to the horse. Even today, camels are prized throughout the region, where fleet-footed varieties like the one shown here command high prices for their prowess on the race track.

The Spread of the Muslim Faith

Religion & Philosophy | **LIKE CHRISTIANITY, ISLAM IS NOT AN EXCLUSIVE RELIGION** intended solely for members of a particular social or ethnic group; it is universalist in form, with all humans eligible to join the ranks of the believers. As a result, the sacred books of both religions—the Bible and the Qur'an—contain passages that encourage the spread of faith by whatever means are necessary and appropriate. In this selection from the Qur'an, Muslims are called on to take part in the proselytizing effort, sometimes known in Arabic as *jihad*. Although the vast majority of Muslims today believe that conversion to Islam should take place only by peaceful means, militants cite this passage from Chapter 47 as justification for their decision to make war on "unbelievers."

The Qur'an, Chapter 47: "Muhammad, Revealed at Medina"

Allah will bring to nothing the deeds of those who disbelieve and debar others from His path. As for the faithful who do good works and believe in what is revealed to Muhammad—which is the truth from their Lord—He will forgive them their sins and ennoble their state.

This, because the unbelievers follow falsehood, while the faithful follow the truth from their Lord. Thus Allah coins their sayings for mankind.

When you meet the unbelievers in the battlefield strike off their heads and, when you have laid them low, bind your captives firmly. Then grant them their freedom or take ransom from them, until War shall lay down her armour.

Thus shall you so. Had Allah willed, He could Himself have punished them; but He has ordained it thus that He might test you, the one by the other.

As for those who are slain in the cause of Allah, He will not allow their works to perish. He will vouchsafe them guidance and ennoble their state; He will admit them to the Paradise He has made known to them.

Believers, if you help Allah, Allah will help you and make you strong. But the unbelievers shall be consigned to perdition. He will bring their deeds to nothing. Because they opposed His revelations, He will frustrate their works.

Have they never journeyed through the land and seen what was the end of those who have gone before them? Allah destroyed them utterly. A similar fate awaits the unbelievers because Allah is the protector of the faithful; because the unbelievers have no protector.

Allah will admit those who embrace the true faith and do good works to gardens watered by running streams. The unbelievers take their fill of pleasure and eat as the beasts eat: but Hell shall be their home. . . .

This is the Paradise which the righteous have been promised. There shall flow in it rivers of unpolluted water, and rivers of milk forever fresh; rivers of delectable wine and rivers of clearest honey. They shall eat therein of every fruit and receive forgiveness from their Lord. Is this like the lot of those who shall abide in Hell forever and drink scalding water which will tear their bowels? . . .

Know that there is no god but Allah. Implore Him to forgive your sins and to forgive the true believers, men and women. Allah knows your busy haunts and resting places.

 According to this passage, what is the fate of those who adhere to the teachings of the Prophet Muhammad? How should unbelievers be treated?

Source: From The Koran, trans. N. J. Dawood (Penguin Classics, 1956, 5th rev. ed. 1990). Copyright © N. J. Dawood.

by the belief that Muslim warriors who died in battle were guaranteed a place in paradise. This is clearly a case where the multitudes had been inspired by a message and were prepared to carry that message to the ends of Earth.

Once the armies had prevailed, Arab civilian administration of the conquered areas was applied. Although hostile sources traditionally portrayed the takeover in violent terms, many historians today adopt a more nuanced approach, pointing out that Arab policy varied from place to place. In some cases, pressure was applied on nonbelievers to convert to Islam. In others, the decision was left to the individual in accordance with the maxim in the Qur'an that "there shall be no compulsion in religion."[2] Those who chose not to convert were required only to submit to Muslim rule and pay a head tax in return for exemption from military service, which was required of all Muslim males. Under such conditions, the local populations often welcomed Arab rule as preferable to Byzantine rule or that of the Sassanian Dynasty in Persia. Furthermore, the simple and direct character of the new religion, as well as its egalitarian qualities (all people were viewed as equal in the eyes of Allah), were undoubtedly attractive to peoples throughout the region.

7-2c The Rise of the Umayyads

The main challenge to the growing empire came from within. Some of Muhammad's followers had not agreed with the selection of Abu Bakr as the first caliph and promoted the candidacy of Ali, Muhammad's cousin and son-in-law, as an alternative. Ali's claim was ignored by other leaders, however, and after Abu Bakr's death, the office was passed to Umar (oo-MAR), another of Muhammad's followers. In 656 C.E., Umar's successor, Uthman (ooth-MAHN), was assassinated, and Ali, who fortuitously happened to be in Medina at that time, was finally selected for the position. But according to tradition, Ali's rivals were convinced that he had been implicated in the death of his predecessor, and a factional struggle broke out within the Muslim leadership. In 661, Ali himself was assassinated, and Mu'awiya (moo-AH-wee-yuh), the governor of Syria and one of Ali's chief rivals, replaced him in office. Mu'awiya thereupon made the caliphate hereditary in his own family, the Umayyads (oo-MY-ads), a branch of the Quraysh clan. The new caliphate

(KAY-luh-fayt), with its capital at Damascus, remained in power for nearly a century.

The factional struggle within Islam did not bring an end to Arab expansion. At the beginning of the eighth century, new attacks were launched at both the western and the eastern ends of the Mediterranean world (see Map 7.2). Arab armies advanced across North Africa, displacing Byzantine rule and conquering the Berbers, a primarily pastoral people living along the Mediterranean coast and in the mountains in the interior. Muslim fleets seized several islands in the eastern Mediterranean. Then around 710 C.E., Arab forces, supplemented by Berber allies under their commander, Tariq (tuh-REEK), crossed the Strait of Gibraltar and occupied southern Spain. The Visigothic kingdom, already weakened by internecine warfare, quickly collapsed. By 725, most of the Iberian Peninsula had become a Muslim state with its center in Andalusia (anduh-LOO-zhuh). Seven years later, an Arab force, making a foray into southern France, was defeated by the army

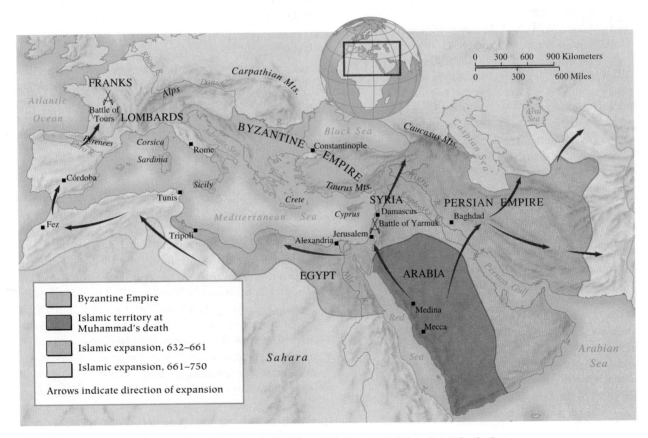

Map 7.2 The Expansion of Islam. This map shows the expansion of the Islamic faith from its origins in the Arabian Peninsula. Muhammad's followers carried the religion as far west as Spain and southern France and eastward to India and Southeast Asia.

Q *In which of these areas is the Muslim faith still the dominant religion?*

of Charles Martel between Tours (TOOR) and Poitiers (pwah-TYAY). For the first time, Arab horsemen had met their match in the form of a disciplined force of Frankish infantry. Some historians think that internal exhaustion would have forced the invaders to retreat even without their defeat at the hands of the Franks. In any event, the Battle of Tours (or Poitiers) would be the high-water mark of Arab expansion in Europe.

In the meantime, in 717 C.E. another Muslim force had launched an attack on Constantinople with the hope of destroying the Byzantine Empire. But the Byzantines' use of Greek fire, a petroleum-based compound containing quicklime and sulfur, destroyed the Muslim fleet, thereby saving the empire and indirectly Christian Europe because the fall of Constantinople would have opened the door to an Arab invasion of eastern Europe. The Byzantine Empire and Islam now established an uneasy frontier in southern Asia Minor.

Arab power also extended to the east, consolidating Islamic rule in Mesopotamia and Persia, and northward into Central Asia. But factional disputes continued to plague the empire. Many Muslims of non-Arab extraction resented the favoritism shown by local administrators to Arabs. In some cases, resentment led to revolt, as in the soggy marshlands at the head of the Persian Gulf, where Ali's second son, Hussein, disputed the legitimacy of the Umayyads and incited his supporters—to be known in the future as **Shi'ites** (SHEE-yts) (from the Arabic phrase *shi'at Ali*, "partisans of Ali")—to rise up against Umayyad rule in 680 C.E.. Although Hussein's forces were defeated and Hussein himself died in the battle, a schism between Shi'ite and **Sunni** (SOON-nee) (usually translated as "orthodox") Muslims had been created that continues to this day.

Umayyad rule created resentment, not only in Mesopotamia but also in Persia, where Arab migrants began to replace local aristocrats in positions of influence, as well as in North Africa, where Berber resistance continued, especially in the mountainous areas south of the coastal plains. According to critics, the Umayyads may have contributed to their own demise by their decadent behavior. One caliph allegedly swam in a pool of wine and then imbibed enough of the contents to lower the level significantly. Finally, in 750 C.E., a revolt led by Abu al-Abbas (ah-boo al-ah-BUSS), a descendant of Muhammad's uncle, led to the overthrow of the Umayyads and the establishment of the Abbasid (uh-BAH-sid or AB-uh-sid) Dynasty (750–1258) in what is now Iraq.

7-2d The Abbasids

The Abbasid caliphs brought political, economic, and cultural change to the world of Islam. While seeking to implant their own version of religious orthodoxy, to be known as *Sunni*, or "the law," they opened schools—known as **madrasas**—to popularize their teachings. They also tried to break down the distinctions between Arab and non-Arab Muslims. All Muslims were now allowed to hold both civil and military offices. This change helped open Islamic culture to the influences of the occupied civilizations. Many Arabs now began to intermarry with the peoples they had conquered. In many parts of the Islamic world, notably North Africa and the eastern Mediterranean, most Muslim converts began to consider themselves Arabs. In 762, the Abbasids built a new capital city at Baghdad on the Tigris River far to the east of the Umayyad capital at Damascus. The new capital was strategically positioned to take advantage of river traffic to the Persian Gulf and also lay astride the caravan route from the Mediterranean to Central Asia. The move eastward allowed Persian influence to come to the fore, encouraging a new cultural orientation. Under the Abbasids, judges, merchants, and government officials, rather than warriors, were viewed as the ideal citizens.

Abbasid Rule The new Abbasid caliphate experienced a period of splendid rule well into the ninth century. Best known of the caliphs of the time was Harun al-Rashid (hah-ROON al-rah-SHEED) (r. 786–809 C.E.), or Harun "the Upright," whose reign is often described as the golden age of the Abbasid caliphate. His son al-Ma'mun (al-muh-MOON) (r. 813–833 C.E.) was a patron of learning who founded an astronomical observatory and established a foundation for undertaking translations of classical Greek works (see "Philosophy and Science" later in this chapter). This was also a period of growing economic prosperity. The Arabs had conquered many of the richest provinces of the Roman Empire and now controlled the routes to the east (see Map 7.3). Baghdad became the center of an enormous commercial market that extended into Europe, Central Asia, and Africa, greatly adding to the wealth of the Islamic world and promoting an exchange of culture, ideas, and technology from one end of the known world to the other. Paper was introduced from China and eventually passed on to North Africa and Europe. Crops from India and Southeast Asia such as rice, sugar, sorghum, and cotton moved toward the west, while glass, wine, and indigo dye were introduced into China. Under the Abbasids, the caliphs became more regal. More temporal than spiritual leaders, described by such august phrases as the "caliph of God," they ruled by autocratic means, hardly distinguishable from the kings and emperors in neighboring states.

As the caliph took on more of the trappings of a hereditary autocrat, the bureaucracy assisting him in administering the expanding empire grew more complex as well. The caliph was advised by a council called a *diwan* (di-WAHN) and headed by a prime minister known as a **vizier** (veh-ZEER)

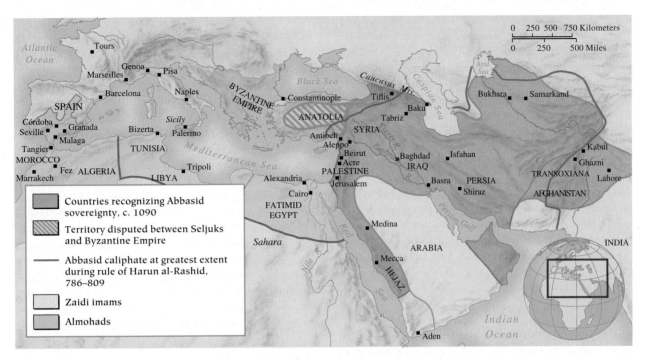

Map 7.3 The Abbasid Caliphate at the Height of its Power. The Abbasids arose in the eighth century as the defenders of the Muslim faith and established their capital at Baghdad. With its prowess as a trading state, the caliphate was the most powerful and extensive state in the region for several centuries. The "Zaidi imams" indicated on the map were a group of dissident Shi'ites who established an independent kingdom on the southern tip of the Arabian Peninsula.

 Which of the major urban centers shown on this map were under the influence of Islam?

(*wazir*). The caliph did not attend meetings of the diwan in the normal manner but sat behind a screen and then communicated his divine will to the vizier. Some historians have ascribed the change in the caliphate to Persian influence, which permeated the empire after the capital was moved to Baghdad. Persian influence was indeed strong (the mother of the caliph al-Ma'mun, for example, was a Persian), but the increase in pomp and circumstance was more likely a natural consequence of the growing power and prosperity of the empire.

Instability and Division Nevertheless, an element of instability lurked beneath the surface. The lack of spiritual authority may have weakened the caliphate in competition with its potential rivals, and disputes over the succession were common. At Harun's death, the rivalry between his two sons, Amin and al-Ma'mun, led to civil war and the destruction of Baghdad. As described by al-Mas'udi (al-muh-SOO-dee), a tenth-century Muslim historian, "Mansions were destroyed, most remarkable monuments obliterated; prices soared. . . . Brother turned his sword against brother, son against father, as some fought for Amin, others for Ma'mun. Houses and palaces fueled the flames; property was put to the sack."[3]

Wealth contributed to financial corruption. By awarding important positions to court favorites, the Abbasid caliphs began to undermine the foundations of their own power and eventually became mere figureheads. Under Harun al-Rashid, members of his Hashemite clan received large pensions from the state treasury, and his wife, Zubaida (zoo-BY-duh), reportedly spent huge sums shopping while on a pilgrimage to Mecca. One powerful family, the Barmakids, amassed vast wealth and power until Harun al-Rashid eliminated the entire clan in a fit of jealousy.

The life of luxury enjoyed by the caliph and other political and economic elites in Baghdad seemingly undermined the stern fiber of Arab society as well as the strict moral code of Islam. Strictures against sexual promiscuity were widely ignored, and caliphs were rumored to maintain thousands of concubines in their harems. Divorce was common, homosexuality was widely practiced, and alcohol was consumed in public despite Islamic law's prohibition against imbibing spirits. The process of disintegration was accelerated by changes that were taking place within the armed forces and the bureaucracy of the empire. Given the shortage of qualified Arabs for key positions in the army and the administration, the caliphate began to recruit officials from among the non-Arab peoples in the empire such as Persians and Turks from Central Asia. These people gradually became a dominant force in the army and administration.

Environmental problems added to the regime's difficulties. The Tigris and Euphrates river system, lifeblood of Mesopotamia for three millennia, was beginning to silt up. Bureaucratic inertia now made things worse, as many of the country's canals became virtually unusable, leading to widespread food shortages.

The fragmentation of the Islamic empire accelerated in the tenth century. Morocco became independent, and in 973 c.e. a new Shi'ite dynasty under the Fatimids (FAT-uh-mids) was established in Egypt with its capital at Cairo. With increasing disarray in the empire, the Islamic world was held together only by the common commitment to the Qur'an and the use of the Arabic language as the prevailing means of communication.

7-2e The Seljuk Turks

In the eleventh century, the Abbasid caliphate faced yet another serious threat in the form of the Seljuk (SEL-jook) Turks, a nomadic people from Central Asia who had converted to Islam. They flourished as military mercenaries for the Abbasid caliphate, where they were known for their ability as mounted archers. Moving gradually into Iran and Armenia as the Abbasids weakened, the Seljuk Turks grew in number until by the eleventh century they were able to occupy the eastern provinces of the Abbasid Empire. In 1055, a Turkish leader captured Baghdad and assumed command of the empire with the title of **sultan** (SUL-tun) ("holder of power"). Although the Abbasid caliph remained the chief representative of Sunni religious authority, the real military and political power of the state was in the hands of the Seljuk Turks. The latter did not establish their headquarters in Baghdad, which now entered a period of decline. Baghdad would revive, but it would no longer be the "gift of God" of Harun al-Rashid.

By the last quarter of the eleventh century, the Seljuks were exerting military pressure on Egypt and the Byzantine Empire. In 1071, when the Byzantines foolishly challenged the Turks, their army was routed at Manzikert (MANZ-ih-kurt) near Lake Van in eastern Turkey, and the victors took over most of the Anatolian Peninsula (see Map 7.4). In dire straits, the Byzantine Empire turned to the west for help, setting in motion the papal pleas that led to the **crusades** (see the next section).

In Europe, and undoubtedly within the Muslim world itself, the arrival of the Turks was regarded as a disaster. The Turks were viewed as barbarians who destroyed civilizations and oppressed populations. In fact, in many respects, Turkish rule in the Middle East was probably beneficial. Converted to Islam, the Turkish rulers temporarily brought an end to the fraternal squabbles between Sunni and Shi'ite Muslims while supporting the Sunnis. They put their energies into revitalizing Islamic law and institutions and provided much-needed political stability to the empire, which helped restore its former prosperity. Under Seljuk rule, Muslims began to organize themselves into autonomous brotherhoods, whose relatively tolerant practices characterized Islamic religious attitudes until the end of the nineteenth century, when increased competition with Europe led to confrontation with the West.

Seljuk political domination over the old Abbasid Empire, however, provoked resentment on the part of many Persian Shi'ites, who viewed the Turks as usurping foreigners who had betrayed the true faith of Islam. Among the regime's most feared enemies was Hasan al-Sabahh (hah-SAHN al-SAH-bah), a Cairo-trained Persian who formed a rebel group popularly known as "assassins" (guardians), who for several decades terrorized government officials and other leading political and religious figures from their

7.4 The Great Mosque of Samarra. The ninth-century mosque of Samarra, located north of Baghdad in present-day Iraq, was for centuries the largest mosque in the Islamic world. Rising from the center of the city of Samarra, the capital of the Abbasids for more than half a century and one of the largest medieval cities of its time, the imposing tower shown here is 156 feet in height. Its circular ramp may have inspired medieval artists in Europe as they imagined the ancient cultures of Mesopotamia. Although the mosque is in ruins today, its spiral tower still signals the presence of Islam to the faithful across the broad valley of the Tigris and Euphrates Rivers.

© Josef Polleross/The Image Works

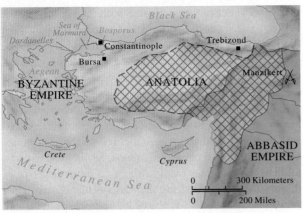

Frontier between the Byzantine and Abbasid
empires, c. 930

Areas of Anatolia occupied by the Abbasids in 1070

Areas of Anatolia occupied by the Seljuk Turks
in the early thirteenth century

Map 7.4 The Turkish Occupation of Anatolia. This map shows
the expansion of the Seljuk Turks into the Anatolian Peninsula
in the eleventh and twelfth centuries. Later, another group
of Turkish-speaking peoples, the Ottoman Turks, would move
into the area, establishing their capital at Bursa in 1335 and
eventually at Constantinople in 1453 (see Chapter 16).

 *What role did the expansion of the Seljuk Turks play in
the origin of the crusades?*

base in the mountains south of the Caspian Sea. Like their
modern-day equivalents in the terrorist organization known
as al-Qaeda, Sabahh's followers were highly motivated and
were adept at infiltrating the enemy's camp to carry out their
clandestine activities. The organization was finally eliminated
by the invading Mongols in the thirteenth century.

7-2f The Crusades

Just before the end of the eleventh century, the Byzantine
emperor Alexius I desperately asked for assistance from
other Christian states in Europe to protect his empire
against the invading Seljuk Turks. As part of his appeal, he
said that the Muslims were desecrating Christian shrines
in the Holy Land and molesting Christian pilgrims en
route to the shrines. In actuality, the Muslims had never
threatened the shrines or cut off Christian access to them.
But tension between Christendom and Islam was on the
rise, and the Byzantine emperor's appeal received a ready
response in Europe. Beginning in 1096 and continuing into
the thirteenth century, a series of Christian incursions on
Islamic territories known as the *crusades* brought the Holy
Land and adjacent areas on the Mediterranean coast from
Antioch to the Sinai Peninsula under Christian rule (see

Chapter 12). In 1099, the armies of the First Crusade succeeded in capturing Jerusalem after a long siege.

At first, Muslim rulers in the area were taken aback by
the invading crusaders, whose armored cavalry presented
a new challenge to local warriors, and their response was
ineffectual. The Seljuk Turks by that time were preoccupied with events taking place farther to the east and took
no action themselves. But in 1169, Sunni Muslims under
the leadership of Saladin (SAL-uh-din) (Salah al-Din), vizier
to the last Fatimid caliph, brought an end to the Fatimid
Dynasty in Egypt. Proclaiming himself sultan, Saladin
succeeded in establishing his control over both Egypt and
Syria, thereby confronting the Christian states in the area
with united Muslim power on two fronts. In 1187, Saladin's
army invaded the kingdom of Jerusalem and destroyed the
Christian forces concentrated there. Further operations
reduced Christian occupation in the area to a handful of
fortresses along the northern coast. Unlike the Christians
of the First Crusade, who had slaughtered much of the
population of Jerusalem when they captured the city,
Saladin did not permit a massacre of the civilian population and even tolerated the continuation of Christian
religious services in conquered territories. For a time,
Christian occupation forces even carried on a lively trade
relationship with Muslim communities in the region.

The Christians returned for another try a few years after
the fall of Jerusalem, but the campaign succeeded only in
securing some of the coastal cities. Although the Christians
would retain a toehold on the coast for much of the thirteenth century (Acre, their last stronghold, fell to the
Muslims in 1291), they were no longer a significant force
in Middle Eastern affairs. In retrospect, the crusades had
only minimal importance in the history of the Middle East,
although they may have served to unite the forces of Islam
against the foreign invaders, thus creating a residue of distrust toward Christians that continues to resonate through
the Islamic world today. Far more important in their impact
were the Mongols, a pastoral people who swept out of
the Gobi Desert in the early thirteenth century to seize
control over much of the known world (see Chapter 10).
Beginning with the advances of Genghis Khan (JING-uss
or GENG-uss KAHN) in northern China, Mongol armies
later spread across Central Asia. In 1258, under the leadership of Hulegu (HOO-lay-goo), brother of the more famous
Khubilai Khan (KOO-bluh KAHN), they seized Persia and
Mesopotamia, bringing an end to the caliphate at Baghdad.

7-2g The Mongols

Unlike the Seljuk Turks, the Mongols were not Muslims,
and they found it difficult to adapt to the settled conditions
they found in the major cities in the Middle East. Their
treatment of the local population in conquered territories

was often brutal and destructive to the economy. Cities were razed to the ground, and dams and other irrigation works were destroyed, reducing prosperous agricultural societies to the point of mass starvation. The Mongols advanced as far as the Red Sea, but their attempt to seize Egypt failed in part because of the effective resistance posed by the Mamluks (MAM-looks) (or Mamelukes, a military class originally composed of Turkish slaves), who had recently overthrown the administration set up by Saladin and seized power for themselves. Eventually, the Mongol rulers in the Middle East began to take on the coloration of the peoples they had conquered. Mongol elites converted to Islam, Persian influence became predominant at court, and the cities began to be rebuilt. By the fourteenth century, the Mongol Empire began to split into separate kingdoms and then to disintegrate. In the meantime, however, the old Islamic empire originally established by the Arabs in the seventh and eighth centuries had come to an end. The new center of Islamic civilization was in Cairo, which was now about to promote a renaissance in Muslim culture under the sponsorship of the Mamluks.

To the north, another new force began to appear on the horizon with the rise of the Ottoman Turks on the Anatolian Peninsula. In 1453, Ottoman Sultan Mehmet II seized Constantinople and brought an end to the Byzantine Empire. Then the Ottomans began to turn their attention to the rest of the Middle East (see Chapter 16).

7-2h Andalusia: A Muslim Outpost in Europe

After the decline of Baghdad, perhaps the brightest star in the Muslim firmament was in Spain, where a member of the Umayyad Dynasty had managed to establish himself after his family's rule in the Middle East had been overthrown in 750 C.E. Abd al-Rathman (AHB-d al-rahkh-MAHN) escaped the carnage in Damascus and made his way to Spain, where Muslim power had recently replaced that of the Visigoths. By 756, he had legitimized his authority in southern Spain—known to the Arabs as *al-Andaluz* and to Europeans as *Andalusia*—and took the title of *emir* (EH-meer) (commander), with his capital at Córdoba (KOR-duh-buh). There he and his successors sought to build a vibrant new center for Islamic culture in the region. With the primacy of Baghdad now at an end, Andalusian rulers established a new caliphate in 929.

Now that the seizure of Crete, Sardinia, Sicily, and the Balearic Islands had turned the Mediterranean Sea into a Muslim lake, Andalusia became part of a vast trade network that stretched all the way from the Strait of Gibraltar to the Red Sea and beyond. Valuable new agricultural products, including cotton, sugar, olives, wheat, citrus, and the date palm, were introduced to the Iberian Peninsula.

Andalusia also flourished as an artistic and intellectual center. The court gave active support to writers and artists, creating a brilliant culture focused on the emergence of three world-class cities—Córdoba, Seville, and Toledo. Intellectual leaders arrived in the area from all parts of the Islamic world, bringing their knowledge of medicine, astronomy, mathematics, and philosophy. With the establishment of a paper factory near Valencia, the means of disseminating such information dramatically improved, and the libraries of Andalusia became the wonder of their time (see "Philosophy and Science" later in this chapter).

One major reason for the rise of Andalusia as a hub of artistic and intellectual activity was the atmosphere of tolerance in social relations fostered by the state. Although Islam was firmly established as the official faith and non-Muslims were encouraged to convert as a means of furthering their careers, the policy of *convivéncia* (con-vee-VEN-cee-uh) (commingling) provided an environment for many Christians and Jews to maintain their religious beliefs and even obtain favors from the court.

A Time of Troubles Unfortunately, the primacy of Andalusia as a cultural center was short lived. By the end of the tenth century, factionalism was beginning to undermine the foundations of the emirate. In 1009, the royal palace at Córdoba was totally destroyed in a civil war. Twenty-two years later, the caliphate itself disappeared as the emirate dissolved into a patchwork of city-states.

In the meantime, the Christian kingdoms that had managed to establish themselves in the north of the Iberian Peninsula were consolidating their position and beginning to expand southward. In 1085, Alfonso VI, the Christian king of Castile, seized Toledo, one of Andalusia's main intellectual centers. The new rulers continued to foster the artistic and intellectual activities of their predecessors. To recoup their recent losses, the Muslim rulers in Seville called on fellow Muslims, the Almoravids (al-MOR-uh-vids)—a Berber dynasty in Morocco—to assist in halting the Christian advance. Berber mercenaries defeated Castilian forces at

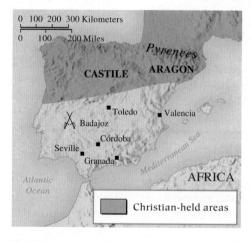

0 100 200 300 Kilometers
0 100 200 Miles

Pyrenees
CASTILE ARAGON
Toledo Valencia
Badajoz
Córdoba
Seville
Granada
Atlantic Ocean
Mediterranean Sea
AFRICA

Christian-held areas

Map 7.5 Spain in the Eleventh Century

Badajoz (bah-duh-HOHZ) in 1086 but then stayed in the area to establish their own rule over the remaining Muslim-held areas in southern Spain.

A warrior culture with no tolerance for heterodox ideas, the Almoravids quickly brought an end to the era of religious tolerance and intellectual achievement. But the presence of Andalusia's new warlike rulers was unable to stem the Christian advance. In 1215, Pope Innocent III called for a new crusade to destroy Muslim rule in southern Spain. Over the next 200 years, Christian armies advanced relentlessly southward, seizing the cities of Seville and Córdoba. Only a single redoubt of Abd al-Rathman's glorious achievement remained: the remote mountain city of Granada (greh-NAH-duh), with its imposing hilltop fortress, the Alhambra (al-HAM-bruh).

HISTORIANS DEBATE   7-2i Moorish Spain: An Era of "Cultural Tolerance"?

In standard interpretations of European history, Western historians have usually described the *reconquista* (ray-con-KEES-tuh) (reconquest) of southern Spain by the Christian kingdoms in the north as a positive development that freed the Spanish people from centuries of oppressive Muslim rule. In recent years, however, it has become fashionable to point to the Moorish era in Spain (the term *Moors* is often used to refer to the Muslims in Spain) as a period of "cultural tolerance," a time of diversity that was followed by the bloody era of the Spanish Inquisition when the Catholic church

7.5 The Alhambra in Granada. Islamic civilization reached its zenith with the fourteenth-century castle known as the *Alhambra*, in southern Spain. Sitting high above the city of Granada, the castle is forbidding from the exterior, but behind its walls lies a magical world. The Lion Court in the ruler's private quarters is world renowned for its marble fountain supported by carved lions and its reflecting pool surrounded with elegant columns and carvings. Like the Hindus in India, the Muslims of the Middle East and Spain lived in a hot, dry climate, making water a highly prized commodity both literally and psychologically.

Clarie L. Duiker

CHRONOLOGY	Islam: The First Millennium	
Life of Muhammad	570–632 C.E.
Flight to Medina	622
Conquest of Mecca	630
Defeat of Persians	650
Election of Ali to caliphate	656
Muslim entry into Spain	ca. 710
Abbasid caliphate	750–1258
Construction of city of Baghdad	762
Reign of Harun al-Rashid	786–809
Umayyad caliphate in Spain	929–1031
Founding of Fatimid Dynasty in Egypt	973
Capture of Baghdad by Seljuk Turks	1055
Seizure of Anatolia by Seljuk Turks	1071
First Crusade	1096
Saladin destroys Fatimid kingdom	1169
Mongols seize Baghdad	1258
Ottoman Turks capture Constantinople	1453

persecuted Muslims, Jews, and Christian heretics for their refusal to accept the true faith. This interpretation has been especially popular since the terrorist attacks in September 2001, as revisionist scholars seek to present a favorable image of Islam to counter the popular perception that all Muslims are sympathetic to terrorism against the West.

Some historians, however, argue that this portrayal of the Moorish era as a period of "cultural tolerance" overstates the case. They point out that even under the relatively benign rule of Abd al-Rathman, true religious tolerance was never achieved and that, in any event, any such era came to an end with the arrival of the Almoravids and the Almohads (AL-moh-hads), a Berber dynasty that supplanted the Almoravids in Andalusia in the twelfth century. For historian J. S. Elliot, the era was, at best, one of "cultural interaction," which was eventually followed by a hardening of attitudes on both sides of the cultural spectrum. If there was an era of religious diversity in Spain under Muslim rule, it was all too brief.

7-3 ISLAMIC CIVILIZATION

Focus Question: What were the main features of Islamic society and culture during its era of early growth?

To be a Muslim is not simply to worship Allah but to live according to his law as revealed in the Qur'an, which is

Experience an interactive version of this period in ⁚᛫ MINDTAP

Sage Advice from Father to Son

Politics & Government **TAHIR IBN HUSAYN** (tah-HEER IB-un HOO-sayn) was born into an aristocratic family in Central Asia and became a key political adviser to al-Ma'mun, the Abbasid caliph of Baghdad in the early ninth century. Appointed in 821 C.E. to a senior position in Khurusan (kor-uh-SAHN), a district near the city of Herat in what is today Afghanistan, he wrote the following letter to his son, giving advice on how to wield authority most effectively. The letter so impressed al-Ma'mun that he had it widely distributed throughout his bureaucracy.

Letter of Tahir ibn Husayn

Look carefully into the matter of the land-tax which the subjects have an obligation to pay. . . . Divide it among the taxpayers with justice and fairness with equal treatment for all. Do not remove any part of the obligation to pay the tax from any noble person just because of his nobility or any rich person because of his richness or from any of your secretaries or personal retainers. Do not require from anyone more than he can bear, or exact more than the usual rate. . . .

[The ruler should also devote himself] to looking after the affairs of the poor and destitute, those who are unable to bring their complaints of ill-treatment to you personally and those of wretched estate who do not know how to set about claiming their rights. . . . Turn your attention to those who have suffered injuries and their orphans and widows and provide them with allowances from the state treasury, following the example of the Commander of the Faithful, may God exalt him, in showing compassion for them and giving them financial support, so that God may thereby bring some alleviation into their daily lives and by means of it bring you the spiritual food of His blessing and an increase of His favor. Give pensions from the state treasury to the blind, and give higher allowances to those who know of the Qur'an, or most of it by heart. Set up hospices where sick Muslims can find shelter, and appoint custodians for these places who will treat the patients with kindness and physicians who will cure their illnesses. . . .

Keep an eye on the officials at your court and on your secretaries. Give them each a fixed time each day when they can bring you their official correspondence and any documents requiring the ruler's signature. They can let you know about the needs of the various officials and about all the affairs of the provinces you rule over. Then devote all your faculties, ears, eyes, understanding and intellect, to the business they set before you: consider it and think about it repeatedly. Finally take those actions which seem to be in accordance with good judgment and justice.

 How does Tahir's advice compare with that given in the political treatise Arthasastra *discussed in Chapter 2? Would Tahir's letter provide an effective model for political leadership today?*

Source: H. Keller (ed.), *Ibn Abi Tahir Kitab Baghdad* (Leipzig, 1908), cited in H. Kennedy, *When Baghdad Ruled the Muslim World: The Rise and Fall of Islam's Greatest Dynasty* (Cambridge, MA, 2004), pp. 204–205.

viewed as fundamental and immutable doctrine that is not to be revised by human beings.

As Allah has decreed, so must humans behave. Therefore, Islamic doctrine must be consulted to determine questions of politics, economic behavior, civil and criminal law, and social ethics. In Islamic society, there is no demarcation between church and state, between the sacred and the secular.

7-3a Political Structures

For early converts, establishing political institutions and practices that conformed to Islamic doctrine was a daunting task. In the first place, the will of Allah, as revealed to his prophet, was not precise about the relationship between religious and political authority, simply decreeing that human beings should "conduct their affairs by mutual consent." On a more practical plane, establishing political institutions for a large and multicultural empire presented a challenge for the Arabs, whose own political structures were relatively rudimentary and relevant only to small pastoral communities (see Historical Voices, "Sage Advice from Father to Son").

During Muhammad's life, the problem could be avoided because he was generally accepted as both the religious and the political leader of the Islamic community—the umma. His death, however, raised the question of how a successor should be chosen and what authority that person should have. As we have seen, Muhammad's immediate successors were called *caliphs*. Their authority was purely temporal, although they were also considered in general terms to be religious leaders holding the title of *imam*. At first, each caliph was selected informally by leading members of the umma. Soon succession became hereditary in the Umayyad clan, but their authority was still limited, at least in theory, by the idea that they should consult with other leaders. Under the Abbasids, as we saw earlier, the caliphs took on more of the trappings of kingship and became more autocratic.

7-3b The Wealth of Araby: Trade and Cities in the Middle East

Overall, as we have noted, this era was probably one of the most prosperous periods in the history of the Middle East. Trade flourished not only in the Islamic world but also with China (now in a period of efflorescence during the era of the Tang and the Song Dynasties—see Chapter 10), the Byzantine Empire, and trading societies in Southeast Asia (see Chapter 9). Trade goods were carried both by ship and by the "fleets of the desert," the camel caravans that traversed the arid land from Morocco in the far west to the countries beyond the Caspian Sea. From West Africa came gold and slaves; from China, silk and porcelain; from East Africa, gold, ivory, and rhinoceros horn; and from the lands of South Asia, sandalwood, cotton, wheat, sugar, and spices. Within the empire, Egypt contributed grain; Iraq, linens, dates, and precious stones; Spain, leather goods, olives, and wine; and western India, various textile goods. The exchange of goods was facilitated by the development of banking and the use of currency and letters of credit (see Comparative Essay, "Trade and Civilization," p. 178).

One key reason for the Arab Empire's emergence as a major participant in the regional trade network was its success in mastering the latest in naval technology. Arab ships known as *dhow*—with hulls of teakwood and lateen sails appropriate for the sailing conditions in the Indian Ocean—were guided to their destinations by the astrolabe (an invention of the Greeks) and the compass (invented in China). Soon Muslim fleets were a familiar feature in the sea-lanes from the western Mediterranean to the coast of southern China (for an illustration of such ships, see Chapter 8).

Under these conditions, urban areas flourished. While the Abbasids were in power, Baghdad was probably the greatest city in the empire, but after the rise of the Fatimids in Egypt, the focus of trade shifted to Cairo, which traveler Leo Africanus described as "one of the greatest and most famous cities in all the whole world, filled with stately and admirable palaces and colleges, and most sumptuous temples."[4] In the cities, the inhabitants were generally segregated by religion, with Muslims, Jews, and Christians living in separate neighborhoods. But all were equally subject to the most common threats to urban life—fire, flood, and disease.

The most impressive urban buildings were usually the palace for the caliph or the local governor and the great mosque. Houses were often constructed of stone or brick around a timber frame. The larger houses were often built around an interior courtyard, where the residents could retreat from the dust, noise, and heat of the city streets. The houses of the wealthy were often multistoried, with balconies and windows covered with latticework to provide privacy for those inside. The poor in both urban and rural areas lived in simpler houses composed of clay or unfired bricks, and the Bedouins lived in tents that could be dismantled and moved according to their needs.

Although the Arab Empire was more urbanized than most other areas of the known world at the time, the bulk of the population continued to live in the countryside and support themselves by farming or herding animals. In river valleys such as the Tigris, the Euphrates, and the Nile, the majority of the farmers were probably independent peasants, but eventually some concentration of land in the hands of wealthy owners began to take place. Some lands were owned by the state or the court and were cultivated by slave labor, but plantation agriculture was not as common as it would be later in many areas of the world.

Eating habits varied in accordance with economic standing and religious preference. Muslims did not eat pork, but those who could afford it often served other meats such as mutton, lamb, poultry, or fish. Fruit, spices, and various sweets were delicacies. The poor were generally forced to survive on boiled millet or peas with an occasional lump of meat or fat. Bread—white or whole meal—could be found on tables throughout the region except in the deserts, where boiled grain was the staple food.

7-3c Islamic Society

In some ways, Arab society was probably one of the most egalitarian of its time. Both the principles of Islam, which held that all were equal in the eyes of Allah, and the importance of trade to the prosperity of the society as a whole probably contributed to this egalitarianism. Although there was a fairly well-defined upper class consisting of the ruling families, senior officials, tribal elites, and the wealthiest merchants, there was no hereditary nobility as in many contemporary societies, and the merchants enjoyed a degree of respect that they did not receive in Europe, China, or India.

Not all benefited from the high degree of social mobility in the Islamic world, however. Slavery was widespread.

Trade and Civilization

Interaction & Exchange In 2002, archaeologists unearthed the site of an ancient Egyptian port city on the shores of the Red Sea. Established sometime during the first millennium bce, the city of Berenike (ber-eh-NEE-kay) linked the Nile River Valley with ports as far away as the island of Java in Southeast Asia. The discovery of Berenike is only the latest piece of evidence confirming the importance of interregional trade since the beginning of the historical era. The exchange of goods between far-flung societies became a powerful engine behind the rise of advanced civilizations throughout the ancient world. Raw materials such as copper, tin, and obsidian; items of daily necessity including salt, fish, and other foodstuffs; and luxury goods such as gold, silk, and precious stones passed from one end of the Eurasian supercontinent to the other, across the desert from the Mediterranean Sea to sub-Saharan Africa, and throughout much of the Americas. Less well known but also important was the maritime trade that stretched from the Mediterranean across the Indian Ocean to port cities on the distant coasts of Southeast and East Asia.

During the first millennium C.E., the level of interdependence among human societies intensified as three major trade routes—across the Indian Ocean, along the Silk Road, and by caravan across the Sahara—created the framework for a single system of trade. The new global network was informational as well as commercial, transmitting technology and ideas, such as the emerging religions of Buddhism, Christianity, and Islam, to new destinations.

There was a close relationship between missionary activities and trade. Buddhist merchants brought the teachings of Siddhartha Gautama to China, and Muslim traders carried Muhammad's words to Southeast Asia and sub-Saharan Africa. Indian traders carried Hindu beliefs and political institutions to Southeast Asia.

What caused the rapid expansion of trade during this period? One key factor was the introduction of technology that facilitated transportation. The development of the compass, improved techniques in mapmaking and shipbuilding, and greater knowledge of wind patterns all contributed to the expansion of maritime trade. Caravan trade, once carried by wheeled chariots or on the backs of oxen, now used the camel as the preferred beast of burden through the deserts of Africa, Central Asia, and the Middle East.

Another reason for the expansion of commerce during this period was the appearance of several multinational empires that created zones of stability and affluence in key areas of the Eurasian landmass. Most important were

7.6 The Dhow: Workhorse of the Indian Ocean The word *dhow* is a generic term for various types of sailing ships found in the Arabian Sea or along the east coast of Africa. Dhows have been the classic vessels for transporting goods in the Indian Ocean for more than two millennia. Their lateen sails and narrow hulls composed of teak planking make them ideal for catching the monsoon winds that blow seasonally across the ocean between the Asian landmass and the coast of East Africa. This medieval painting by an unknown artist is somewhat stylized, but the resemblance to modern-day vessels is clear, although many of the latter are motorized and thus no longer subject to the whims of the yearly monsoon winds. Wind-powered vessels of this type, however, remain common throughout the region.

the emergence of the Abbasid Empire in the Middle East and the prosperity of China during the Tang and Song Dynasties (see Chapter 10). The Mongol invasions in the thirteenth century temporarily disrupted the process but then established a new era of stability that fostered long-distance trade throughout the world.

The importance of interregional trade as a crucial factor in promoting the growth of human civilizations can be highlighted by comparing the social, cultural, and technological achievements of active trading states with those of communities that have traditionally been cut off from contacts with the outside world. We shall encounter many of these communities in later chapters. Even in the Western Hemisphere, where regional trade linked societies from the Great Plains of North America to the Andes in present-day Peru, geographic barriers limited the exchange of inventions and ideas, putting these societies at a distinct disadvantage when the first contacts with peoples across the oceans occurred at the beginning of the modern era.

 What were the chief factors that led to the expansion of interregional trade during the first millennium C.E.? How did the growth of international trade contacts affect other aspects of society?

Because a Muslim could not be enslaved, the supply came from sub-Saharan Africa or from non-Islamic populations elsewhere in Asia or in Europe. Most slaves were employed in the army (which was sometimes a road to power, as in the case of the Mamluks) or as domestic servants, who were sometimes permitted to purchase their freedom. The slaves who worked the large estates experienced the worst living conditions and rose in revolt on several occasions.

The Islamic principle of human equality also fell short in the treatment of women. Although the Qur'an instructed men to treat women with respect, and women did have the right to own and inherit property, in general the male was dominant in Muslim society. Polygyny was permitted, and the right of divorce was in practice restricted to the husband, although some schools of legal thought permitted women to stipulate that their husband could have only one wife or to seek a separation in certain specific circumstances. Adultery and homosexuality were stringently forbidden (although such prohibitions were frequently ignored in practice), and custom required that women be cloistered in their homes and prohibited from social contacts with males outside their own family. A prominent example of this custom was the *harem*, introduced at the Abbasid court during the reign of Harun al-Rashid. Members of the royal harem were drawn from non-Muslim female populations throughout the empire. In accordance with the reference in the Qur'an requiring women to "guard their modesty," the practice of covering the face and body of women whenever they appeared in public prevailed in many Muslim societies. For example, in the picture from a cultural display in the Persian Gulf state of Oman shown here, the bride covers her face during a traditional wedding ceremony.

7-3d The Culture of Islam

The Arabs were heirs to many elements of the remaining Greco-Roman culture of the Roman Empire, and they assimilated Byzantine and Persian culture just as readily. In the eighth and ninth centuries, numerous Greek, Syrian, and Persian scientific and philosophical works were translated into Arabic and eventually found their way to Europe. As the chief language in the southern Mediterranean and the Middle East, Arabic became an international language. Later, Persian and Turkish also came to be important in administration and culture.

The spread of Islam led to the emergence of a new culture throughout the Arab Empire. This was true in all fields of endeavor from literature to art and architecture. But pre-Islamic traditions were not extinguished and frequently combined with Muslim motifs, resulting in creative works of great imagination and originality.

Philosophy and Science During the centuries following the rise of the Arab Empire, it was the Islamic world that was most responsible for preserving and spreading the scientific and philosophical achievements of ancient civilizations. At a time when ancient Greek philosophy was largely unknown in Europe, key works by Aristotle, Plato, and other Greek philosophers were translated into Arabic and stored in a "house of wisdom" in Baghdad, where they were read and studied by Muslim scholars. Eventually, many of these works were translated into Latin and were taken to Europe, where they exercised a profound influence on the later course of Christianity and Western philosophy.

The process began in the sixth century C.E. when the devout Byzantine ruler Justinian (see Chapter 13) shut down the Platonic Academy in Athens, declaring that it promoted heretical ideas. Many of the scholars at the academy fled to Baghdad, where their ideas and the classical texts they brought with them soon aroused local interest and were translated into Persian or Arabic. Later such works were supplemented by acquisitions in Constantinople and possibly also from the famous library at Alexandria.

The academies where the translations were carried out—often by families specializing in the task—were not true universities like those that would later appear in Europe. Instead, they were private operations working under the sponsorship of a great patron, many of whom were highly cultivated Persians living in Baghdad or other major cities. Dissemination of the translated works was

7.7 A Marriage Ceremony. In much of the Middle East, women were expected to avoid contact with males outside the bounds of the family. On those occasions when a public appearance was required, custom decreed that women should cover their bodies and faces in accordance with the stipulations of the Qur'an. In this cultural display of a wedding ceremony at the Khasab Museum in Khasab, Oman, the bride wears a mask to hide her face from the direct view of those in attendance.

Photo by William J. Duiker. From the Khasab Museum in Khasab, Oman.

stimulated by the arrival of paper in the Middle East from Buddhist pilgrims from China passing along the Silk Road. Paper was much cheaper to manufacture than papyrus, and by the end of the eighth century, the first paper factories were up and running in Baghdad. Libraries and booksellers soon appeared.

What motives inspired this ambitious literary preservation project? At the outset, it may have simply been an effort to provide philosophical confirmation for existing religious beliefs as derived from the Qur'an. Eventually, however, more adventurous minds began to use the classical texts not only to seek greater knowledge of the divine will but also to obtain a better understanding of the laws of nature.

Such was the case with physician and intellectual Ibn Sina (IB-un SEE-nuh) (980–1037), known in the West as Avicenna (av-i-SENN-uh). A native of the Central Asian city of Balkh, in his own philosophical writings, he cited Aristotle to the effect that the world operated not only at the will of Allah but also by its own natural laws, laws that could be ascertained by human reason. Such ideas eventually aroused the ire of traditional Muslim scholars, and although works by such ancient writers as Euclid, Ptolemy, and Archimedes continued to be translated, the influence of Greek philosophy and science began to wane in Baghdad by the end of the eleventh century and did not recover.

By then, however, interest in classical Greek ideas had spread to Spain. Philosophers such as Averroës (uh-VERR-oh-eez), whose Arabic name was Ibn Rushd (IB-un RUSH-ed or IB-un RUSHT), and Maimonides (my-MAH-nuh-deez) (Musa Ibn Maymun), a Jew who often wrote in Arabic, undertook their own translations and wrote in support of Avicenna's defense of the role of human reason. Both were born in Córdoba in the early twelfth century but were persecuted for their ideas by the Almohads, a Berber dynasty that had supplanted Almoravid authority in Andalusia, and both men ended their days in exile in North Africa.

Although Islamic scholars are justly praised for preserving much of classical Greek knowledge, which eventually made its way into Europe, they also made considerable advances of their own. Nowhere is this more evident than in mathematics and the natural sciences. Islamic scholars adopted and passed on the numerical system of India, including the use of zero, and a ninth-century Persian mathematician founded the mathematical discipline of algebra (al-jabr, "the reduction"). Simplified "Arabic" numerals had begun to replace cumbersome Roman numerals in Italy by the thirteenth century.

In astronomy, Muslims set up an observatory at Baghdad to study the position of the stars. They were aware that Earth is round and in the ninth century produced a world map based on the tradition of the Greco-Roman astronomer Ptolemy (see Comparative Illustration, "A Twelfth-Century Map of the World," p. 181). Aided by the astrolabe, an instrument designed to enable sailors to track their position by means of the stars, Muslim fleets and caravans opened up new trade routes connecting the Islamic world with other civilizations, and Muslim travelers such as al-Mas'udi and Ibn Battuta (IB-un ba-TOO-tuh) wrote accurate descriptions of political and social conditions throughout the Middle East.

Muslim scholars also made many new discoveries in optics and chemistry and, with the assistance of texts on anatomy by ancient Greek physician Galen (GAY-lun) (ca. 129 – ca. 200 C.E.), developed medicine as a distinct field of scientific inquiry. Avicenna compiled a medical

Topkapi Palace Museum, Istanbul, Turkey//The Bridgeman Art Library International

7.8 Preserving the Wisdom of the Greeks. After the fall of the Roman Empire, the philosophical works of ancient Greece were virtually forgotten in Europe or were banned as heretical by the Byzantine Empire. It was thanks to Muslim scholars, who located copies at the magnificent library in Alexandria, Egypt, that many classical Greek writings survived. Here young Muslim scholars are being trained in the Greek language so that they can translate classical Greek writings into Arabic. Later the texts were translated back into Western languages and served as the catalyst for an intellectual revival in medieval and Renaissance Europe.

A Twelfth-Century Map of the World

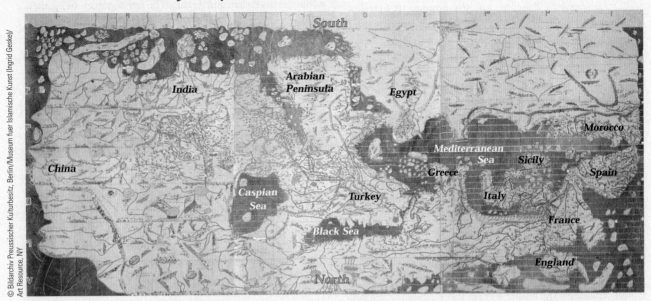

© Bildarchiv Preussischer Kulturbesitz, Berlin/Museum fuer Islamische Kunst (Ingrid Geske)/ Art Resource, NY

7.9a

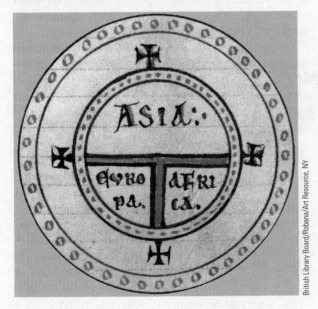

British Library Board/Robana/Art Resource, NY

7.9b

Religion & Philosophy

TWELFTH-CENTURY MUSLIM GEOGRAPHER AL-IDRISI (al-ih-DREE-see) received his education in the Spanish city of Córdoba while it was under Islamic rule. Later he served at the court of the Norman king of Sicily, Roger II, where he created an atlas of the world based on Arab and European sources. In Muslim practice at the time, north and south were inverted from modern practice. Al-Idrisi's map, shown in Image 7.9a, depicts the world as it was known at that time, stretching from the Iberian Peninsula on the right to the civilization of China on the far left. It is also a testimonial to the vast extension of the power and influence of Islam in the five centuries since the death of Muhammad in 632 C.E. Maps drawn by al-Idrisi's European contemporaries were still highly stylized, with the Christian holy city of Jerusalem placed at the center of the world, as in the map shown in Image 7.9b.

Q *How much of the world shown on al-Idrisi's map had been explored by Muslim fleets?*

encyclopedia that, among other things, emphasized the contagious nature of certain diseases and showed how they could be spread by contaminated water supplies. After its translation into Latin, Avicenna's work became a basic medical textbook for medieval European university students.

Although the spurt of interest in classical philosophy and science throughout the Muslim world ultimately proved abortive, it had played an important role in preserving the wisdom of the Greeks, which eventually made its way to Europe through Spain, where it aroused the interest of late

Experience an interactive version of this period in ⠿ MINDTAP medieval Christian clerics and thence opened the door to the emergence of the modern world (see Chapter 12).

Islamic Literature   The tradition of Arabic poetry was well established by the time of Muhammad. It extolled Bedouin tribal life, courage in battle, hunting, sports, and respect for the animals of the desert, especially the camel. Because the Arabic language did not possess a written script until the fourth century C.E., poetry was originally passed on by memory. Later, in the eighth and ninth centuries, it was compiled in anthologies.

Pre-Muslim Persia also boasted a long literary tradition, most of it oral and written down in later centuries in the Arabic alphabet. Lacking the desert tradition of the Arabs, Persian writers focused on legends of past kings, Zoroastrian religious themes, romances, fables, and folktales. The transcendent literary monument of early Persian literature is *The Book of Lords*, an early-sixth-century compilation of poetry about Persian myths and legendary heroes.

Islam brought major changes to the culture of the Middle East, not least to literature. Muslims regarded the Qur'an as their greatest literary work, but pre-Islamic traditions continued to influence writers throughout the region. *The Book of Kings*, a ten-volume epic poem by Persian poet Ferdowzi (fur-DOW-see) (940–1020), is one of the greatest achievements of Persian literature, tracing the history of the country from legendary times to the arrival of Islam.

Sadi (sah-DEE) (1210–1292), considered the Persian Shakespeare, remains to this day the favorite author of Iran. His *Rose Garden* is a collection of entertaining stories written in prose sprinkled with verse. He is also renowned for his sonnet-like love poems, which set a model for generations to come.

In the West, the most famous works of Middle Eastern literature are undoubtedly the *Rubaiyat* (ROO-by-yaht) of Omar Khayyam (OH-mar ky-YAHM) and *Tales from 1001 Nights* (also called *The Arabian Nights*). Paradoxically, these two works are not as popular with Middle Eastern readers. Both, in fact, were freely translated into Western languages for nineteenth-century European readers, who developed a taste for stories set in exotic foreign places—a classic example of the tendency of Western observers to regard the customs and cultures of non-Western societies as strange or exotic. Even today Omar Khayyam's poetry, which reflects an attitude of skepticism about the impermanence of life and the impossibility of knowing God, continues to appeal to many modern readers in the West: "We come from dust, and with the wind are gone . . . / Drink wine by moonlight, darling, for the moon / Will shine long after this, and find us not."[5]

Like Omar Khayyam's verse, *The Arabian Nights* was loosely translated into European languages and adapted to Western tastes. A composite of folktales, fables, and romances of Indian and indigenous origin, the stories interweave the natural with the supernatural. The earliest stories were told orally and were later transcribed, with many later additions in Persian and Arabic. The famous story of Aladdin and the Magic Lamp, for example, was an eighteenth-century addition. Nevertheless, *The Arabian Nights* has entertained readers for centuries, allowing them to enter a land of wish fulfillment through extraordinary plots, sensuality, comic and tragic situations, and a cast of unforgettable characters.

Some Arabic and Persian literature reflected the deep spiritual and ethical concerns of the Qur'an. Many writers, however, carried Islamic thought in novel directions. The thirteenth-century poet Rumi (ROO-mee), for example, embraced **Sufism** (SOO-fiz-uhm), a form of religious belief that called for a mystical relationship between Allah and human beings. Converted to Sufism by a wandering dervish (dervishes, from the word for "poor" in Persian, sought to achieve a mystical union with Allah through dancing and chanting in an ecstatic trance), Rumi abandoned orthodox Islam to embrace God directly through ecstatic love. Realizing that love transcends intellect, he sought to reach God through a trance attained by the whirling dance of the dervish, set to mesmerizing music. As he twirled, the poet extemporized some of the most passionate lyrical verse ever conceived. His faith and art remain an important force in Islamic society today.

The Islamic world also made a major contribution to historical writing, another discipline that was stimulated by the introduction of paper manufacturing. The first great Islamic historian was al-Mas'udi. Born in Baghdad in 896 C.E., he wrote about both the Muslim and the non-Muslim world, traveling widely in the process. His *Meadows of Gold* is the source of much of our knowledge about the golden age of the Abbasid caliphate. Translations of his work reveal a wide-ranging mind and a keen intellect combined with a human touch that practitioners of the art in our century might find reason to emulate. Equaling al-Mas'udi in talent and reputation was fourteenth-century historian Ibn Khaldun (IB-un kal-DOON). Combining scholarship with government service, Ibn Khaldun was one of the first historians to attempt a philosophy of history (see Historical Voices, "Ibn Khaldun: Islam's Greatest Historian," p. 183).

Islamic Art and Architecture   The art of Islam is a blend of Arab, Turkish, and Persian traditions. Although local influences can be discerned in various parts of the Arab Empire, for centuries Islamic art remained remarkably coherent over a wide area, perhaps because the Arabs, with their new religion and their writing system, served as a unifying force.

Ibn Khaldun: Islam's Greatest Historian

Art & Ideas

IBN KHALDUN (1332–1406), born of an official family in Tunis, is generally recognized as the greatest of Muslim historians. Many years spent in the cosmopolitan city of Granada exposed him to ancient Greek science and philosophy, and a lifetime of travel and service in official capacities familiarized him with political conditions in the real world. His most famous work, the *Muqaddimah* (*Introduction*), has been widely praised for its striking modern sensitivity to the role of climate and geography on historical events. In this introductory passage, the author presents his interpretation of the primary tasks of the historian. It is well worth reading by practitioners of the craft today.

From the *Muqaddimah*

It should be known that history is a discipline that has a great number of approaches. Its useful aspects are very many. Its goal is distinguished.

History makes us acquainted with the conditions of past nations as they are reflected in their national character. It makes us acquainted with the biographies of the prophets and with the dynasties and policies of rulers. Whoever so desires may thus achieve the useful result of being able to imitate historical examples in religious and worldly matters.

The (writing of history) requires numerous sources and much varied knowledge. It also requires a good speculative mind and thoroughness, which lead the historian to the truth and keep him from slips and errors. If he trusts historical information in its plain transmitted form and has no clear knowledge of the principles resulting from custom, the fundamental facts of politics, the nature of civilization, or the conditions governing human social organization, and if, furthermore, he does not evaluate remote or ancient material through comparison with near or contemporary material, he often cannot avoid stumbling and slipping and deviating from the path of truth. Historians, Qur'an commentators and leading transmitters have committed frequent errors in the stories and events they reported. They accepted them in the plain transmitted form, without regard for its value. They did not check them with the principles underlying such historical situations, nor did they compare them with similar material. Also, they did not probe with the yardstick of philosophy, with the help of knowledge of the nature of things, or with the help of speculation and historical insight. Therefore, they strayed from the truth and found themselves lost in the desert of baseless assumptions and errors.

This is especially the case with figures, either of sums of money or of soldiers, whenever they occur in stories. They offer good opportunity for false information and constitute a vehicle for nonsensical statements. They must be controlled and checked with the help of known fundamental facts.

Source: Ibn Khaldun, *The Muqaddimah: An Introduction to History* (trans. Franz Rosenthal), Princeton University Press, classics edition 2015.

The ultimate expression of Islamic art is to be found in magnificent architectural monuments beginning in the late seventh century. The first great example is the Dome of the Rock, which was built in 691 C.E. to proclaim the spiritual and political legitimacy of the new religion to the ancient world. Set in the sacred heart of Jerusalem on Muhammad's holy rock and touching both the Western Wall of the Jews and the oldest Christian church, the Dome of the Rock remains one of the most revered Islamic monuments. The second is the great mosque at Córdoba, in southern Spain, originally built in the ninth century on top of an earlier Visigothic church. Its interior is one of the wonders of the world of art.

As was once the case with churches in early Christendom, the mosque is often the most dominant architectural structure in Muslim cities and towns. At first, desert Arabs, whether nomads or conquering armies, prayed in an open court, shaded along the *qibla* (KIB-luh) (the wall facing the holy city of Mecca) by a thatched roof supported by rows of palm trunks. As Islam became better established, enormous mosques were constructed, but they were still modeled on the open court, which would be surrounded on all four sides with pillars supporting a wooden roof over the prayer area facing the qibla wall. One of the most impressive was the famous ninth-century mosque at Córdoba in southern Spain, which is still in remarkable condition. Its 514 columns supporting double-horseshoe arches transform this architectural wonder into a unique forest of trees pointing upward, contributing to a light and airy effect. The unparalleled sumptuousness and elegance make the Córdoba mosque one of the wonders of world art (see Image 7.10, "The Recycled Mosque," p. 184).

Because the Muslim religion combines spiritual and political power in one, palaces also reflected the glory of

7.10 The Recycled Mosque. The great mosque at Córdoba was erected on the site of a Christian church built by the Visigoths. Earlier the same site had been dedicated to the Roman god Janus. In the eighth century, the Muslims incorporated parts of the Visigothic church into their new mosque, aggrandizing it over the centuries. After the Muslims were driven from Spain, the mosque reverted to Christianity, and in 1523, a soaring cathedral sprouted from its spine. Inside, the mosque and the cathedral seem to blend well aesthetically, a prototype for harmonious religious coexistence. In the interior, a series of arched columns provide the entire structure with an effect of mass as well as lightness. Throughout history, societies have all too often destroyed past architectural wonders, robbing older marble glories to erect new marvels. It is rare and wonderful that the great mosque has survived as a testimonial to the continuing struggle to achieve religious tolerance.

Islam. Beginning in the eighth century with the spectacular castles of Syria, the rulers constructed large brick domiciles reminiscent of Roman design with protective walls, gates, and baths. With a central courtyard surrounded by two-story arcades and massive gate towers, they resembled fortresses as much as palaces. Characteristic of such "desert palaces" was the gallery over the entrance gate, with holes through which boiling oil could be poured down on the heads of attacking forces. Unfortunately, none of these structures has survived.

The ultimate remaining Islamic palace is the fourteenth-century Alhambra in Spain. The extensive succession of courtyards, rooms, gardens, and fountains created a fairy-tale castle perched high above the city of Granada. Every inch of surface is decorated in intricate floral and semi-abstract patterns; much of the decoration is done in carved plasterwork so fine that it resembles lace. The Lion Court in the center of the harem is world renowned for its lion fountain and surrounding arcade with elegant columns and carvings.

Painting has been less prized in Muslim societies. Because representation of the Prophet Muhammad has traditionally been strongly discouraged in painting or in any other art form, Muslim artists have generally avoided painting scenes that related to human subjects. For a time, representational painting was common among Persian court painters, but in recent times the practice has been discouraged, and Muslim artists have responded by developing a sense of rhythm and abstraction that

7.11 The Qur'an as Sculptured Design. Muslim sculptors and artists, reflecting the official view that any visual representation of the Prophet Muhammad was blasphemous, turned to geometric patterns, as well as flowers and animals, as a means of fulfilling their creative urge. The predominant motif, however, was the reproduction of Qur'anic verses in Arabic script. Calligraphy, which was almost as important in the Middle East as it was in traditional China, used Arabic script to decorate all of the Islamic arts from painting to pottery, tile and ironwork, and wall decorations such as this carved plaster panel in a courtyard of the Alhambra palace in Spain. Because a recitation from the Qur'an was an important component of the daily devotional activities for all practicing Muslims, elaborate scriptural panels such as this one perfectly blended the spiritual and the artistic realms.

has found expression in the use of repetitive geometric ornamentation.

One consequence of this tradition is reflected in the production of carpets and other textiles. Since antiquity, one of the primary occupations of women has been the spinning and weaving cloth to make clothing and other useful items for their families. In the Middle East, this skill reached an apogee in the art of the knotted woolen rug. Originating in the pre-Muslim era, rugs were initially used to insulate stone palaces against the cold as well as to warm shepherds' tents. Eventually, they were applied to religious purposes because of the religious requirement that every practicing Muslim pray five times a day on clean ground. Small rugs served as prayer mats for individual use, whereas larger and more elaborate ones were given by rulers as rewards for political favors. Bedouins in the Arabian desert covered their sandy floors with rugs to create a cozy environment in their tents.

In villages throughout the Middle East, the art of rug weaving was passed down from mother to daughter over the centuries. By age six, girls would begin their first rug, and their slender fingers would be producing fine carpets before they reached adolescence. Skilled artisanship represented an extra enticement to prospective bridegrooms, and rugs often became an important part of a woman's dowry to her future husband. Reflecting common practice, most decorations on rugs, as in all forms of Islamic art, consisted of Arabic script and natural plant and figurative motifs. Repeated continuously in naturalistic or semiabstract geometrical patterns called *arabesques*, these decorations completely covered the surface and left no area undecorated.

CHAPTER SUMMARY

After the collapse of Roman power in the west, the Eastern Roman Empire, centered in Constantinople, continued to dominate much of the eastern Mediterranean and eventually emerged as the unique Christian civilization known as the Byzantine Empire, which flourished for hundreds of years (see Chapter 13). The seventh century, however, saw the emergence of a new force—Islam—that blossomed in the Arabian Peninsula and spread rapidly throughout the Middle East. In the eyes of some Europeans during the Middle Ages, the Arab Empire was a malevolent force that posed a serious threat to the security of Christianity. Their fears were not entirely misplaced, for within half a century after the death of Islam's founder, Muhammad, Arab armies overran Christian states in North Africa and the Iberian Peninsula, and Turkish Muslims moved eastward onto the fringes of the Indian subcontinent.

But although the teachings of Muhammad brought war and conquest to much of the known world, they also brought hope and a sense of political and economic stability to peoples throughout the region. Thus, for many people in the medieval Mediterranean world, the arrival of Islam was a welcome event. Islam brought a code of law and a written language to societies that had previously lacked them. Finally, by creating a revitalized trade network stretching from West Africa to East Asia, it established a vehicle for the exchange of technology and ideas that brought untold wealth to thousands and a better life to millions.

Like other empires in the region, the Arab Empire did not last. It fell victim to a combination of internal and external pressures, and it was no more than a memory by the end of the thirteenth century. But it left a powerful legacy in Islam, which remains one of the great religions of the world. In succeeding centuries, Islam began to penetrate into new areas beyond the edge of the Sahara and across the Indian Ocean into the islands of the Indonesian Archipelago.

REFLECTION QUESTIONS

Q By what process was Arab power expanded throughout the Middle East and North Africa in the years after Muhammad's death? What was the impact of that expansion on the subject peoples?

Q What role did the Abbasid Empire play in promoting the establishment of a trade network extending from East Asia to the Mediterranean Sea and beyond? Is it reasonable to say that the Muslim world was the linchpin of global trade during this period?

Q What circumstances do some historians refer to when they say that the Muslim governments in Spain provided an example of religious tolerance?

Experience an interactive version of this period in ⠿ MINDTAP

CHAPTER TIMELINE

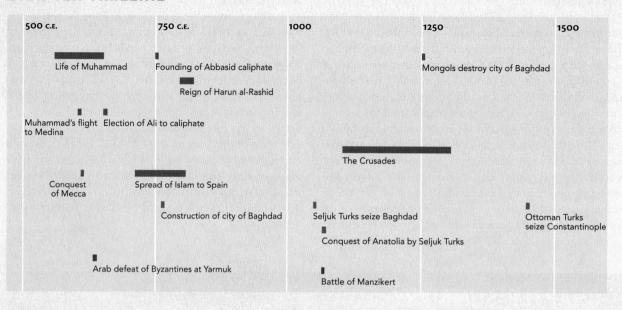

500 C.E.	750 C.E.	1000	1250	1500

Life of Muhammad

Founding of Abbasid caliphate

Reign of Harun al-Rashid

Mongols destroy city of Baghdad

Muhammad's flight to Medina Election of Ali to caliphate

The Crusades

Conquest of Mecca

Spread of Islam to Spain

Construction of city of Baghdad

Seljuk Turks seize Baghdad

Conquest of Anatolia by Seljuk Turks

Ottoman Turks seize Constantinople

Arab defeat of Byzantines at Yarmuk

Battle of Manzikert

CHAPTER NOTES

1. M. M. Pickthall, trans., *The Meaning of the Glorious Koran* (New York, 1953), p. 89.
2. Quoted in T. W. Lippman, *Understanding Islam: An Introduction to the Moslem World* (New York, 1982), p. 118.
3. Al-Mas'udi, *The Meadows of Gold: The Abbasids*, ed. P. Lunde and C. Stone (London, 1989), p. 151.
4. L. Africanus, *The History and Description of Africa and of the Notable Things Therein Contained* (New York, n.d.), pp. 820–821.
5. E. Yarshater, ed., *Persian Literature* (Albany, N.Y., 1988), pp. 154–159.

MINDTAP
From Cengage

MindTap® is a fully online, highly personalized learning experience built upon Cengage Learning content. MindTap combines student learning tools—readings, multimedia, activities, and assessments—into a singular Learning Path that guides students through the course and helps students develop the critical thinking, analysis, and communication skills that are essential to academic and professional success.

Chapter Outline and Focus Questions

8-1 *The Emergence of Civilization*

Q How did the advent of farming and pastoralism affect the various peoples of Africa? How did the consequences of the agricultural revolution in Africa compare with its consequences in Eurasia and America?

8-2 *The Coming of Islam*

Q What effects did the coming of Islam have on African religion, society, political structures, trade, and culture?

8-3 *States and Noncentralized Societies in Central and Southern Africa*

Q What role did migrations play in the evolution of early African societies? How did the impact of these migrations compare with similar population movements elsewhere?

8-4 *African Society*

Q What role did lineage groups, women, and slavery play in African societies? In what ways did African societies in various parts of the continent differ? What accounted for these differences?

8-5 *African Culture*

Q What are some of the chief characteristics of African sculpture and carvings, music, and architecture, and what purpose did these forms of creative expression serve in African society?

Nick Greaves/Alamy

8.1 The Temple at Great Zimbabwe

Critical Thinking

Q *In what parts of Africa did the first states and city-states emerge? What conditions led to their appearance?*

Connections to Today

Q *How does the discussion in the Comparative Essay "The Migration of Peoples" in this chapter relate to migratory movements of people around the world today? Is large-scale migration a natural process? If so, should it be allowed to run its course, or should it be restricted in some ways?*

IN 1871, GERMAN EXPLORER KARL MAUCH began to search southern Africa's central plateau for the colossal stone ruins of a legendary lost civilization. In late August, he found what he had been looking for. According to his diary,

> Presently I stood before it and beheld a wall of a height of about 20 feet of granite bricks. Very close by there was a place where a kind of footpath led over rubble

into the interior. Following this path I stumbled over masses of rubble and parts of walls and dense thickets. I stopped in front of a towerlike structure. Altogether it rose to a height of about 30 feet.

Mauch was convinced that "a civilized nation must once have lived here." Like many other nineteenth-century Europeans, however, Mauch was equally convinced that the Africans who had lived there could never have built such splendid structures as the ones he had found at Great Zimbabwe (zim-BAHB-way). To Mauch and other archaeologists, Great Zimbabwe must have been the work of "a northern race closely akin to the Phoenician and Egyptian." Not until the twentieth century did Europeans overcome their prejudices and finally admit that Africans south of Egypt had also developed advanced civilizations with spectacular achievements.

The continent of Africa has played a central role in the long evolution of humankind. It was in Africa that the first hominids appeared more than 3 million years ago. It was probably in Africa that the immediate ancestors of modern human beings—*Homo sapiens*—emerged for the first time. The domestication of animals and perhaps the initial stages of the agricultural revolution may have occurred first in Africa. Certainly, one of the first states appeared in Africa in the form of the kingdom of pharaohs in the Nile Valley in the northeastern corner of the continent.

In more recent times, the peoples of Africa appeared to many outside observers to be relatively isolated from the momentous events taking place in many other areas of the world, leaving them behind in the steady progression of human societies to more complex forms of civilization. To the degree that this was the case, it may have been above all a product of geography.

The landmass of Africa is so vast and its topography so diverse that communications within the continent and between Africans and peoples living elsewhere in the world have often been more difficult than in many neighboring regions. As a consequence, although some parts of the continent were directly exposed to the currents of change sweeping across Eurasia and were influenced by them to varying degrees, other regions were virtually isolated from the "great tradition" cultures discussed in Part I of this book and, like the cultures of the Americas, developed in their own directions, rendering generalizations about Africa difficult, if not impossible, to make.

8-1 THE EMERGENCE OF CIVILIZATION

Focus Questions: How did the advent of farming and pastoralism affect the various peoples of Africa? How did the consequences of the agricultural revolution in Africa compare with its consequences in Eurasia and America?

After Asia, Africa is the largest of the continents (see Map 8.1). It stretches nearly 5,000 miles from the Cape of Good Hope in the south to the Mediterranean in the north and extends a similar distance from Cape Verde (VURD) on the west coast to the Horn of Africa on the Indian Ocean.

8-1a The Land

Africa is as physically diverse as it is vast. The northern coast is washed by the Mediterranean Sea and is mountainous for much of its length. South of the mountains lies the greatest desert on Earth, the Sahara, which stretches from the Atlantic Ocean to the Indian Ocean. To the east is the Nile River, heart of the ancient Egyptian civilization. Beyond that lies the Red Sea, which separates Africa from Asia.

The Sahara acts as a great divide separating the northern coast from the rest of the continent. Africa south of the Sahara contains many major regions. In the west is the so-called hump of Africa, which juts like a massive shoulder into the Atlantic Ocean. Here the Sahara gradually gives way to grasslands in the interior and then to tropical rain forests along the coast. This region is dominated by the Niger River; rich in natural resources, it was the home of many ancient civilizations.

Far to the east, bordering the Indian Ocean, is a decidedly different terrain of snowcapped mountains, upland plateaus, grasslands, and lakes. Here, in the East African Rift Valley in the lake district of modern Kenya, early hominids began their long trek toward civilization several million years ago.

Directly to the west lies the Congo basin, with its rain forests watered by the mighty Congo River. The forests of equatorial Africa then fade gradually into the hills, plateaus, and deserts of the south. This rich land contains some of the most valuable mineral resources known today.

8-1b The First Farmers

When exactly agriculture was first practiced on the continent of Africa is not known. Until recently, historians

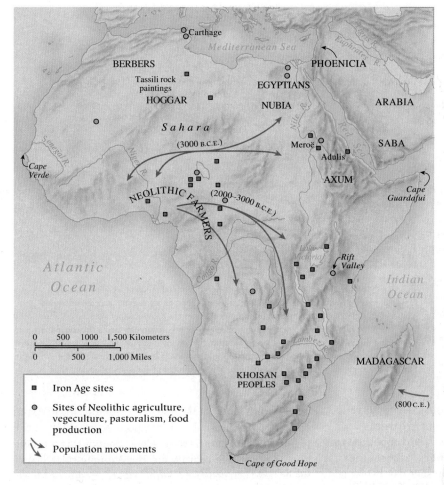

Map 8.1 Ancient Africa. Modern human beings, the primate species known as *Homo sapiens,* first evolved on the continent of Africa. Some key sites of early human settlement are shown on this map.

Q *What are the main river systems on the continent of Africa?*

Eventually, the practice of agriculture began to spread westward across the Sahara. At that time, the world's climate was much cooler and wetter than it is today, but a warm, humid climate prevailed in parts of the Sahara, creating lakes and ponds, as well as vast grasslands (known as *savannas*) replete with game. Hence, indigenous peoples in the area were able to provide for themselves by hunting, food gathering, and fishing. By the seventh and sixth millennia B.C.E., however, conditions were becoming increasingly arid, forcing them to find new means of support. Rock paintings found in what are today some of the most inhabitable parts of the region (see Image 8.4 that accompanies the Comparative Essay "The Migration of Peoples," p. 192) show that by the fourth millennium B.C.E. fishing and pastoralism in the heart of the Sahara were being supplemented by the limited cultivation of grain crops, including a drought-resistant form of dry rice.

Thus, the peoples of northern Africa, from Nubia westward into the heart of the Sahara, were among the earliest in the world to adopt settled agriculture as a means of subsistence. Shards of pottery found at archaeological sites in the area suggest that they were also among the first to manufacture clay pots. By 5000 B.C.E., they were cultivating cotton plants and manufacturing textiles.

After 4000 B.C.E., as the desiccation (drying up) of the Sahara intensified, many local inhabitants migrated eastward toward the Nile River and southward into the grasslands. As a result, farming began to spread into the savannas on the southern fringes of the desert and eventually into the tropical forest areas to the south. In the meantime, the foundation was being laid for the emergence of an advanced civilization in Egypt along the banks of the Nile River (see Chapter 1).

8-1c Axum and Meroë

To the south of Egypt in Nubia, the kingdom of Kush had emerged as a major trading state by the end of the second millennium B.C.E. (see Chapter 1). Kush adopted many of

assumed that crops were first cultivated in the Lower Nile Valley (the northern part near the Mediterranean) some 7,000 or 8,000 years ago, when wheat and barley were introduced, possibly from the Middle East. Eventually, as explained in Chapter 1, this area gave rise to the civilization of ancient Egypt.

Recent evidence, however, suggests that this hypothesis may need some revision. South of Egypt, near the junction of the White Nile and the Blue Nile, is an area historically known as Nubia (see Chapter 1). By the ninth millennium B.C.E., peoples living in this area began to domesticate animals, first wild cattle and then sheep and goats, which had apparently originated in the Middle East. In areas where the climate permitted, they supplemented their diet by gathering wild grains and soon learned how to cultivate grains such as sorghum and millet while also growing gourds and melons.

its political institutions and much of its culture from the kingdom of the pharaohs farther to the north and—at a time of Egyptian weakness in the eighth century B.C.E.—even managed to seize the city of Memphis and much of the Nile River Delta. Eventually, however, the Kushite rulers were driven out of Lower Egypt and forced to retreat back to their original habitat in Nubia, where a new capital was established at Meroë (MER-oh-ee or MER-uh-wee) near the Sixth Cataract in the great bend of the Nile River.

The new capital was located near extensive iron deposits; once smelting techniques were developed, iron evidently provided the basis for much of the area's growing prosperity. Meroë eventually became a major trading hub for iron goods and other manufactures for the entire region. The prosperity of the area is attested to by the remnants of several pyramids that are similar in design but smaller in size than their Egyptian counterparts and still constructed to serve as tombs for the deceased rulers of the ruling dynasty.

By the third century C.E., however, a competitor to Meroë began to arise a few hundred miles to the southeast in the mountainous highlands of present-day Ethiopia. The founders of Axum (AHK-soom) claimed descent from migrants to Africa from the kingdom of Saba (SAH-buh) (also known as Sheba) across the Red Sea on the southern tip of the Arabian Peninsula. During antiquity, Saba was a major trading state, serving as a transit point for goods carried from South Asia to the Mediterranean basin. Biblical sources credited the "queen of Sheba" with vast wealth. In fact, much of that wealth had originated much farther to the east and passed through Saba en route to the Mediterranean. Whether migrants from Saba were responsible for founding Axum is sheer conjecture, but a similarity in architectural styles suggests that some form of relationship probably existed between the two states.

After Saba declined, Axum survived for centuries. Like Saba, Axum owed much of its prosperity to its location on the trade route between India and the Mediterranean, and ships from Egypt stopped regularly at the port of Adulis (a-DOO-luss) on the Red Sea. Axum exported ivory, frankincense, myrrh, and slaves, and its primary imports were textiles, metal goods, wine, and olive oil. For a time, Axum competed for control of the ivory trade with the

8.2 The Pyramids at Meroë. The kingdom of Kush borrowed much of its culture from the Egyptian Empire to the north while placing its own imprint on all imports. Kushite rulers, for example, modeled their political institutions after those of the pharaohs, but governmental authority was somewhat more centralized, and monarchical power was apparently limited by the influence of priests and the local aristocracy. The pyramids at Meroë, on the banks of the Nile River, are another example. Younger, smaller, unpointed at the top, and more standardized in size and shape than their famous counterparts at Giza, they remain a dramatic reminder of the glory of ancient Kush.

Jack Jackson/Robert Harding Picture Library Ltd/Alamy

neighboring state of Meroë, and hunters from Axum armed with imported iron weapons scoured the entire region for elephants. Probably as a result of this competition, in the fourth century C.E. the Axumite ruler, claiming he had been provoked, launched an invasion of Meroë and conquered it, creating an empire that, in the view of some contemporaries, rivaled those of Rome and Persia (see Map 8.2).

Perhaps the most distinctive feature of Axumite civilization was its religion. Originally, the rulers of Axum followed the religion of Saba, but in the fourth century C.E., they adopted the Egyptian form of Christianity—often called **Coptic** (KAHP-tik) from the local language of the day. Later, Axum (now renamed Ethiopia) would be identified by some Europeans as the "hermit kingdom" and the home of Prester John, a legendary Christian king of East Africa.

8-1d The Sahara and Its Environs

Meroë and Axum were part of the ancient trading network that extended from the shores of the Mediterranean to the Indian Ocean and were affected in various ways by the cross-cultural contacts that took place throughout that region. Elsewhere in Africa, somewhat different patterns prevailed with variation from area to area depending on the geography and climate.

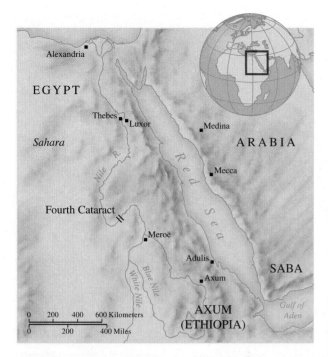

Map 8.2 Ancient Ethiopia and Nubia. The first civilizations to appear on the African continent emerged in the Nile River Valley. Early in the first century C.E., the state of Axum emerged in what today is the state of Ethiopia.

Q *Where were the major urban settlements in the region as shown on this map?*

Historians do not know when goods first began to be exchanged across the Sahara in a north–south direction, but during the first millennium B.C.E. the commercial center of Carthage on the Mediterranean had become a focal point of the trans-Saharan trade. The **Berbers**, an ethnic group indigenous to western parts of North Africa (see Chapter 7), served as intermediaries, carrying food products and manufactured goods from Carthage across the desert and exchanging them for salt, gold and copper, skins, various agricultural products, and perhaps slaves. The introduction of the camel provided a major stimulus to the trans-Saharan trade. With its ability to store considerable amounts of food and water, the camel was far better equipped to handle the arduous conditions of the desert than the ox and the donkey used previously.

This trade initiated a process of cultural exchange that would exert a significant impact on the peoples of tropical Africa. Among other things, it may have spread the knowledge of ironworking south of the desert. Whether the technique was brought to the area from Meroë or by Berber traders from Carthage or, as some historians believe, was developed independently, the **Nok** (NAHK) **culture** in northern Nigeria eventually became one of the

8.3 Nok Pottery Head. The Nok peoples of the Niger River are the oldest known culture in West Africa to have created sculptures. This terra cotta head is typical of Nok culture sculptures produced between 500 B.C.E. and 200 C.E. Discovered by accident in the twentieth century by tin miners, these heads feature perforated eyes set in triangles or circles, stylized eyebrows, open thick lips, broad noses with wide nostrils, and large ears. Perhaps the large facial openings permitted the hot air to escape as the heads were fired. Although the function of these statues is not known for certain, they were likely connected with religious rituals or devotion to ancestors.

most active ironworking societies in Africa. Excavations have unearthed numerous terra cotta and metal figures, as well as stone and iron farm implements, dating back as far as 500 B.C.E. The remains of smelting furnaces confirm that the iron was produced locally.

The Garamantes   Not all the peoples involved in the carrying trade across the Sahara were nomadic. Recent exploratory work in the Libyan Desert has revealed the existence of an ancient kingdom that transported goods between societies along the Mediterranean Sea and sub-Saharan West Africa for more than 1,000 years. The Garamantes (gar-uh-MAN-teez), as they were known to the Romans, carried salt, glass, metal, olive oil, and wine southward in return for gold, slaves, and various tropical products. To provide food for their communities in the heart of the desert, they constructed a complex irrigation system consisting of several thousand miles of underground channels. The technique is reminiscent of similar systems in Persia and Central Asia. Scholars believe that the kingdom

The Migration of Peoples

Interaction & Exchange Some 50,000 years ago, a small band of *Homo sapiens sapiens* crossed the Sinai Peninsula from Africa and began to spread out across the Eurasian supercontinent. Thus began a migration of peoples that continued with accelerating speed throughout the ancient era and beyond. By 40,000 B.C.E., their descendants had spread across Eurasia as far as China and eastern Siberia and had even settled the distant continent of Australia.

Who were these peoples, and what provoked their decision to change their habitat? Undoubtedly, the first migrants were foragers or hunters in search of wild game, but with the advent of agriculture and the domestication of animals around 12,000 years ago, other peoples began to migrate vast distances in search of fertile lands for farming and pasture.

The ever-changing climate was undoubtedly a major factor driving the process. In the fourth millennium B.C.E., the drying up of rich pasturelands in the Sahara forced the local inhabitants to migrate eastward toward the Nile River Valley and the grasslands of East Africa. At about the same time, Indo-European–speaking farming peoples left the region of the Black Sea and moved gradually into central Europe in search of new farmlands. They were eventually followed by nomadic groups from Central Asia who began to occupy lands along the frontiers of the Roman Empire as other bands of nomads threatened the plains of northern China from the Gobi Desert. In the meantime, Bantu-speaking farmers migrated from the Niger River eastward to the Swahili coast and southward into the rain forests of Central Africa and beyond. Similar movements took place in Southeast Asia and the Americas.

This steady flow of migrating peoples often had a destabilizing effect on sedentary societies in their path. Nomadic incursions were a constant menace to the security of China, Egypt, and the Roman Empire and ultimately brought them to an end. But this vast movement of peoples often had beneficial effects as well, spreading new technologies and means of livelihood. Although some migrants like the Huns came for plunder and left havoc in their wake, other groups like the Celtic peoples and the Bantu interacted with previous inhabitants and apparently prospered in their new environment.

Erich Lessing/Art Resource, NY

8.4 **Rock Paintings of the Sahara.** Even before the Egyptians built their pyramids at Giza, other peoples far to the west in the vast wastes of the Sahara were creating their own art forms. These rock paintings, some of which date back to the fourth millennium B.C.E., are reminiscent of similar examples from Europe, Asia, and Australia and provide a valuable record of a society that supported itself by a combination of farming, hunting, and herding animals. After the introduction of the horse around 1200 B.C.E., subsequent rock paintings depicted chariots and horseback riding. Eventually, camels began to appear in the paintings, a consequence of the increasing desiccation of the Sahara.

The most famous of all nomadic invasions represents a case in point. In the thirteenth century C.E., the Mongols left their homeland in the Gobi Desert and advanced westward into the Russian steppes and southward into China and Central Asia, leaving death and devastation in their wake. At the height of their empire, the Mongols controlled virtually all of Eurasia except its western and southern fringes, thus creating a zone of stability stretching from China to the shores of the Mediterranean in which a global trade and informational network could thrive.

 What have been some of the key reasons for the migration of large numbers of people throughout human history? Is the process still under way in our own day?

declined as a result of the fall of the Roman Empire and the drying up of the desert.

8-1e East Africa

South of Axum, along the shores of the Indian Ocean and in the inland plateau that stretches from the mountains of Ethiopia through the lake district of Central Africa, lived a mixture of peoples, some living by hunting and food gathering and others following pastoral pursuits.

Beginning in the third millennium B.C.E., farming peoples speaking dialects of the Bantu (BAN-too) family of languages began to migrate from their original homeland in what today is Nigeria (see Comparative Essay, "The Migration of Peoples," p. 192). By the early centuries C.E., they reached East Africa, where they may have been responsible for introducing the widespread cultivation of crops and knowledge of ironworking to much of that region, although there are signs of limited iron smelting in the area before their arrival.

The Bantu settled in rural communities based on subsistence farming. The primary crops were millet and sorghum, along with yams, melons, and beans. The land was often tilled with both stone and iron tools—the latter were usually manufactured in a local smelter. Some people kept domestic animals such as cattle, sheep, goats, or chickens or supplemented their diets by hunting and food gathering. Because the population was minimal and an ample supply of cultivable land was available, most settlements were relatively small; each village formed a self-sufficient political and economic entity.

As early as the era of the New Kingdom in the second millennium B.C.E., Egyptian ships plied the waters off the East African coast in search of gold, ivory, palm oil, and perhaps slaves. By the first century C.E., the region was an established part of a trading network that included the Mediterranean and the Red Sea. In that century, a Greek seafarer from Alexandria wrote an account of his travels down the coast from Cape Guardafui at the tip of the Horn of Africa (see Map 8.1) to the Strait of Madagascar thousands of miles to the south. Called the *Periplus* (PER-ih-pluss), this work provides descriptions of the peoples and settlements along the African coast and the trade goods they supplied.

According to the *Periplus,* the port of Rhapta (RAHP-tuh) (possibly modern Dar es Salaam) was a commercial metropolis, exporting ivory, rhinoceros horn, and tortoiseshell and importing glass, wine, grain, and metal goods such as weapons and tools. The identity of the peoples taking part in this trade is not clear, but the area was probably inhabited primarily by various local peoples supplemented by a small number of immigrants from the Arabian Peninsula. Out of this mixture would eventually emerge a cosmopolitan **Swahili** (swah-HEE-lee) culture (see "East Africa: The Land

of the Zanj" later in this chapter) that continues to exist in coastal areas today. Beyond Rhapta was "unexplored ocean."

Trade across the Indian Ocean and down the coast of East Africa was facilitated by the monsoon winds, and it would gradually become one of the most lucrative sources of commercial profit in the ancient and medieval worlds. Traders eventually came by sea from as far away as China and mainland Southeast Asia (see Historical Voices, "A Chinese View of Africa," p. 194). Early in the first millennium C.E., Malay (muh-LAY *or* MAY-lay) peoples bringing cinnamon to the Middle East from the Indonesian archipelago began to cross the Indian Ocean directly and landed on the southeastern coast of Africa. Eventually, a Malay settlement was established on the island of Madagascar, where the population is still of mixed Malay–African origin.

8-2 THE COMING OF ISLAM

 Focus Questions: What effects did the coming of Islam have on African religion, society, political structures, trade, and culture?

As described in Chapter 7, the rise of Islam during the first half of the seventh century C.E. had ramifications far beyond the Arabian Peninsula. Arab armies swept across North Africa, incorporating it into the Arab Empire and isolating the Christian state of Axum to the south. Although East Africa and West Africa south of the Sahara were not occupied by the Arab forces, Islam began to penetrate these areas as well.

8-2a African Religious Beliefs Before Islam

When Islam arrived, most societies in Africa already had well-developed systems of religious beliefs. Like other aspects of life, early African religious beliefs varied considerably, but certain characteristics appear to have been shared throughout much of the continent. One common feature was **pantheism**, belief in a single creator god from whom all things came. Sometimes the creator god was accompanied by a whole pantheon of lesser deities. The Ashanti (uh-SHAN-tee *or* uh-SHAHN-tee) people of Ghana (GAH-nuh) in West Africa believed in a supreme being called Nyame (NY-AH-may), whose sons were lesser gods. Each son served a different purpose: one was the rainmaker, another was the compassionate, and a third was responsible for the sunshine. This heavenly hierarchy paralleled earthly arrangements: worship of Nyame was the exclusive preserve of the king through his priests; lesser officials and the common people worshiped Nyame's sons, who might intercede with their father on behalf of ordinary Africans.

A Chinese View of Africa

Interaction & Exchange

THIS PASSAGE FROM A THIRTEENTH-CENTURY TREATISE ON GEOGRAPHY describes various aspects of life along the eastern coast of Africa in what is now Somalia, including the urban architecture. The author, Chau Ju-kua (zhow RU-gwah), was an inspector of foreign trade in the city of Quanzhou (CHWAHN-JOE) (sometimes called Zayton) on the southern coast of China. His account was compiled from reports of seafarers. Note the varied uses that local people make of a whale carcass.

Chau Ju-kua on East Africa

The inhabitants of the Chung-li country [the Somali coast] go bareheaded and barefooted; they wrap themselves in cotton stuffs, but they dare not wear jackets, for the wearing of jackets and turbans is a privilege reserved to the ministers and the king's courtiers. The king lives in a brick house covered with glazed tiles, but the people live in huts made of palm leaves and covered with grass-thatched roofs. Their daily food consists of baked flour cakes, sheep's and camel's milk. There are great numbers of cattle, sheep, and camels. . . .

There are many sorcerers among them who are able to change themselves into birds, beasts, or aquatic animals, and by these means keep the ignorant people in a state of terror. If some of them in trading with some foreign ship have a quarrel, the sorcerers pronounce a charm over the ship so that it can neither go forward nor backward, and they only release the ship when it has settled the dispute. The government has formally forbidden this practice.

When one of the inhabitants dies, and they are about to bury him in his coffin, his kinsfolk from near and far come to condole. Each person, flourishing a sword in his hand, goes in and asks the mourners the cause of the person's death. If he was killed by the hand of man, each one says, we will revenge him on the murderer with these swords. Should the mourners reply that he was not killed by any one, but that he came to his end by the will of Heaven, they throw away their swords and break into violent wailing.

Every year there are driven on the coast a great many dead fish measuring two hundred feet in length and twenty feet through the body. The people do not eat the flesh of these fish, but they cut out their brains, marrow, and eyes, from which they get oil. They mix this oil with lime to caulk their boats, and use it also in lamps. The poor people use the ribs of these fish to make rafters, the backbones for door leaves, and they cut off vertebrae to make mortars with.

 What does this passage offer in terms of information about housing and consumption habits in East Africa?

Source: *Chau Ju-Kua: His Work on the Chinese and Arab Trade in the Twelfth and Thirteenth Centuries, entitled Chu-fan-chi,* translated from the Chinese and annotated by Friedrich Hirth and W. W. Rockhill (St. Petersburg: Printing Office of the Imperial Academy of Sciences, Vass. Ostr., Kinth Liao, 12.1911), pp. 130–131.

Belief in an afterlife was closely connected to the importance of ancestors and the **lineage group** or clan. Each lineage (LIN-nee-ij) group could trace itself back to a founding ancestor or group of ancestors. These ancestral souls would not be extinguished as long as the lineage group continued to perform rituals in their name. The rituals could also benefit the lineage group on Earth because the ancestral souls, being closer to the gods, had the power to influence the lives of their descendants for good or evil.

Such beliefs were challenged but not always replaced in those parts of

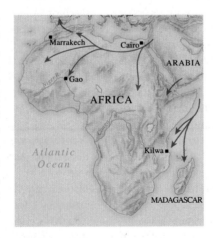

Map 8.3 The Spread of Islam in Africa

the continent affected by the arrival of Islam. In some ways, the tenets of Islam were in conflict with traditional beliefs and customs. Although the concept of a single transcendent deity did not always present a problem, Islam's rejection of spirit worship and a priestly class sometimes ran counter to local beliefs and was often ignored in practice. Similarly, as various Muslim travelers observed, Islam's insistence on the separation of men and women contrasted with the relatively informal relationships that prevailed in many African societies and was probably slow to take root. In the long run, imported ideas were synthesized with indigenous beliefs to create a unique brand of Africanized Islam.

8-2b The Arabs in North Africa

In 641, Arab forces advanced into Egypt, seized the Nile River Delta, and brought two centuries of Byzantine rule to an end. To guard against attacks from the Byzantine fleet, they eventually built a new capital at Cairo, inland from the previous Byzantine capital of Alexandria, and began to consolidate their control over the entire region.

The Arab conquerors were probably welcomed by many, if not the majority, of the local inhabitants. Although Egypt had been a thriving commercial center under the Byzantines, the average Egyptian had not shared in this prosperity. Tax rates were generally high, and Christians were subjected to periodic persecution by the Byzantines, who viewed the local Coptic faith and other sects in the area as heresies. Although the new rulers continued to obtain much of their revenue from taxing the local farming population, tax rates were generally lower than they had been under the corrupt Byzantine government, and conversion to Islam brought exemption from taxation. During the next generations, many Egyptians converted to the Muslim faith, but Islam did not move into the Upper Nile Valley until several hundred years later. As Islam spread southward, it was adopted by many lowland peoples, but it had less success in the mountains of Ethiopia, where Coptic Christianity continued to win adherents (see the next section).

In the meantime, Arab rule was gradually being extended westward along the Mediterranean coast. When the Romans conquered Carthage in 146 B.C.E., they called their new province Africa, thus introducing a name that would eventually be applied to the entire continent. After the fall of the Roman Empire, much of the area reverted to the control of local Berber chieftains, but the Byzantines captured Carthage in the mid-sixth century C.E. In 690, the city was seized by the Arabs, who then began to extend their control over the entire area, which they called *al-Maghrib* (al-MAH-greb) ("the west").

At first, the local Berber peoples—who were tough fighters—resisted their new conquerors and limited Arab rule to the towns and lowland coastal areas. But Arab persistence eventually paid off; by the early eighth century, the entire North African coast was under Muslim rule. The Arabs were now poised to cross the Strait of Gibraltar and expand into southern Europe and push south beyond the fringes of the Sahara.

8-2c The Kingdom of Ethiopia: A Christian Island in a Muslim Sea

By the end of the sixth century C.E., the kingdom of Axum, long a dominant force in the trade network through the Red Sea, was in a state of decline. Overexploitation of farmland had played a role in its decline, as had a shift in trade routes away from the Red Sea to the Arabian Peninsula and Persian Gulf. By the beginning of the ninth century, the capital had been moved farther into the mountainous interior, and Axum was gradually transformed from a maritime power into a landlocked agricultural society.

The rise of Islam on the Arabian Peninsula hastened this process, with the Arab world increasingly serving as the focus of the regional trade passing through the area. By the eighth century, several Muslim trading states had been established on the African coast of the Red Sea. At first, relations between Christian Axum and its Muslim neighbors were relatively peaceful as the larger and more powerful Axumite kingdom attempted with some success to compel the coastal Islamic states to accept a tributary relationship. The area became a prime source for ivory, gold, resins such as frankincense and myrrh, and slaves, the

CHRONOLOGY	Early Africa
Origins of agriculture in Africa	ca. 9000–5000 B.C.E.
Desiccation of the Sahara begins	ca. 7000–5000 B.C.E.
Kingdom of Kush in Nubia	ca. 1070–350 B.C.E.
Iron Age begins	ca. Sixth century B.C.E.
Beginning of trans-Saharan trade	ca. First millennium B.C.E.
Rise of Meroë	ca. 300 B.C.E.
Rise of Axum	First century C.E.
Arrival of Malays on Madagascar	Second century C.E.
Arrival of Bantu in East Africa	Early centuries C.E.
Conquest of Meroë by Axum	Fourth century C.E.
Origins of Ghana	Fifth century C.E.
Arab takeover of Lower Nile Valley	641 C.E.
Development of Swahili culture	ca. First millennium C.E.
Spread of Islam across North Africa	Seventh century C.E.
Spread of Islam in Horn of Africa	Ninth century C.E.
Decline of Ghana	Twelfth century C.E.
Kingdom of Zimbabwe	ca. 1100 – ca. 1450
Establishment of Zagwe Dynasty in Ethiopia	ca. 1150
Rise of Mali	ca. 1250

Beware the Troglodytes!

Family & Society

IN AFRICA, AS ELSEWHERE, relations between pastoral peoples and settled populations living in cities or in crowded river valleys were frequently marked by distrust and conflict. Such was certainly the case in the city of Meroë in the upper Nile Valley, where the residents viewed the nomadic peoples in the surrounding hills and deserts with a mixture of curiosity and foreboding. In the following selection, the second century B.C.E. Greek historian Agatharchides (a-ga-THAR-kuh-deez) describes the so-called Troglodyte (TRAH-gluh-dyt) people living in the mountains east of the Nile River.

On the Erythraean Sea

Now, the Troglodytes are called "Nomads" by the Greeks and live a wandering life supported by their herds in groups ruled by tyrants. Together with their children they have their women in common except for the one belonging to the tyrant. Against a person who has sexual relations with her the chief levies as a fine a specified number of sheep.

This is their way of life. When it is winter in their country—this is at the time of the Etesian winds—and the god inundates their land with heavy rains, they draw their sustenance from blood and milk, which they mix together and stir in jars which have been slightly heated. When summer comes, however, they live in the marshlands, fighting among themselves over the pasture. They eat those of their animals that are old and sick after they have been slaughtered by butchers whom they call "Unclean."

For armament the tribe of Troglodytes called Megabari have circular shields made of raw ox-hide and clubs tipped with iron knobs, but the others have bows and spears.

They do not fight with each other, as the Greeks do, over land or some other pretext but over the pasturage as it sprouts up at various times. In their feuds, they first pelt each other with stones until some are wounded. Then for the remainder of the battle they resort to a contest of bows and arrows. In a short time many die as they shoot accurately because of their practice in this pursuit and their aiming at a target bare of defensive weapons. The older women, however, put an end to the battle by rushing in between them and meeting with respect. For it is their custom not to strike these women on any account so that immediately upon their appearance the men cease shooting.

They do not, he says, sleep as do other men. They possess a large number of animals which accompany them, and they ring cowbells from the horns of all the males in order that their sound might drive off wild beasts. At nightfall, they collect their herds into byres and cover these with hurdles made from palm branches. Their women and children mount up on one of these. The men, however, light fires in a circle and sing additional tales and thus ward off sleep, since in many situations discipline imposed by nature is able to conquer nature.

 Does the author of this passage describe the customs of the Troglodytes in an impartial manner or do you detect a subtle attitude of disapproval or condescension?

Source: Agatharchides of Cnidus, *On the Erythraen Sea*, trans. S. Burstein (London, 1989), fragments 62–64, as cited in S. Burstein (ed.), *Ancient African Civilizations: Kush and Axum* (Princeton, 1998), pp. 47–50.

latter seized from restive nomadic peoples living in the Amharic (am-HAR-ik) plateau beyond its southern border (see Historical Voices, "Beware the Troglodytes!" above).

Beginning in the twelfth century, however, relations between Axum and its neighbors deteriorated as the Muslim states along the coast began to move inland to gain control over the growing trade in slaves and ivory. Axum underwent significant internal change during this period. The Zagwe (ZAH-gweh)

Map 8.4 The Swahili Coast

Dynasty, which seized control of the country in the mid-twelfth century, centralized the government and extended the Christian faith throughout the kingdom, which was now known as Ethiopia. Military commanders and officials with ties to the royal court established vast landed estates to facilitate the collection of taxes from the local population, while Christian missionaries established monasteries and churches to propagate the faith in outlying areas. Close relations were reestablished with leaders of the

Coptic Church in Egypt and with Christian officials in the Holy Land. This process was continued by the Solomonids (sah-luh-MAHN-ids), who succeeded the Zagwe Dynasty in 1270. By the early fifteenth century, the state had become more deeply involved in an expanding conflict with the Muslim state of Adal (a-DAHL) to the east, a conflict that lasted more than a century and gradually took on the characteristics of a holy war.

8-2d East Africa: The Land of the Zanj

The rise of Islam also had a lasting impact on the coast of East Africa, which the Greeks had called Azania and the Arabs called Zanj (ZANJ), referring to the "burnt skin" of the indigenous population. According to Swahili oral traditions, during the seventh and eighth centuries peoples from the Arabian Peninsula and the Persian Gulf began to settle at ports along the coast and on the small islands offshore. Then, in the middle of the tenth century, a Persian from the city of Shiraz (shi-RAHZ) sailed to the area with his six sons. As his small fleet stopped along the coast, each son disembarked on one of the coastal islands and founded a small community. These settlements eventually grew into important commercial centers, including Mombasa (mahm-BAH-suh), Pemba (PEM-buh), Zanzibar (ZAN-zi-bar) (literally, "the coast of the Zanj"), and Kilwa (KIL-wuh). Although this oral tradition undoubtedly underestimates the role played by the indigenous population in the emergence of the region as a major participant in the trade network centered on the Indian Ocean, it probably also reflects the degree to which African merchants—who often served as middlemen between the peoples of the interior and the traders arriving from ports all around the Indian Ocean—saw themselves as part of an important commercial network.

By the tenth century, a string of trading ports stretched from Mogadishu (moh-guh-DEE-shoo) (today the capital of Somalia) in the north to Kilwa (south of present-day Dar es Salaam) in the south. Kilwa became especially important because it was near the southern limit for a ship hoping to complete the round-trip journey in a single season. Goods such as ivory, gold, and rhinoceros horn were exported across the Indian Ocean to countries as far away as China; imports included iron goods, glassware, Indian textiles, and Chinese porcelain. Profits could be considerable, as

evidenced by the merchants' lavish stone palaces, some of which still stand in Mombasa and Zanzibar. Though now in ruins, Kilwa was one of the most magnificent cities of its day. The fourteenth-century Arab traveler Ibn Battuta (IB-un ba-TOO-tuh) described it as "amongst the most beautiful of cities and most elegantly built. All of it is of wood, and the ceilings of its houses are of *al-dis* [reeds]."[1] Particularly impressive was the Husini Kubwa (hoo-SEE-nee KOOB-wuh), a massive palace with vaulted roofs capped with domes and elaborate stone carvings that surrounded an inner courtyard. Conditions for ordinary townspeople and the residents of smaller towns were not so luxurious, but nevertheless affluent urban residents lived in spacious stone buildings, with indoor plumbing and consumer goods imported from as far away as China and southern Europe.

Most of the coastal states were self-governing, although sometimes several towns were grouped together under a single dominant authority. Government revenue came primarily from taxes imposed on commerce. Some trade went on between these coastal city-states and the peoples of the interior, who provided gold and iron, ivory, and various agricultural goods and animal products in return for textiles, manufactured articles, and weapons. Relations with domestic suppliers apparently varied, and the coastal merchants sometimes resorted to force to obtain goods from the inland peoples. A Portuguese visitor recounted that "the men [of Mombasa] are oft-times at war and but seldom at peace with those of the mainland, and they carry on trade with them, bringing thence great store of honey, wax, and ivory."[2]

Xinhua/Alamy

8.5 The Great Mosque of Kilwa. The city of Kilwa, located on an island south of the present-day city of Dar es Salaam, was a long-time major center of Muslim culture along the coast of East Africa, and its mosque was one of the most impressive stone structures on the entire African continent. Today the city has been abandoned, but the ruins of its mosque serve as a testimonial to the renowned achievements of Swahili civilization, which was vividly described by such tireless Muslim travelers as al-Mas'udi and Ibn Battuta.

By the twelfth and thirteenth centuries, a cosmopolitan culture, eventually known as Swahili from the Arabic *sahel* (sah-HEL) meaning "coast" (thus, "peoples of the coast"), began to emerge throughout the coastal area. Intermarriage between the small number of immigrants and the local population was common, leading to the emergence of a ruling class, some of whom were of mixed heritage and could trace their genealogy to Arab or Persian ancestors. By this time, too, many members of the ruling class had converted to Islam. Middle Eastern urban architectural styles and other aspects of Arab culture were implanted within a society still predominantly African. Arabic words and phrases were combined with Bantu grammatical structures to form a distinct language also known as Swahili that is the national language of Kenya and Tanzania today.

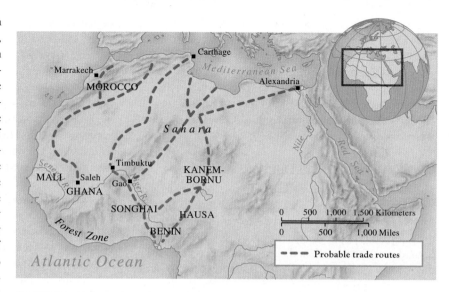

Map 8.5 Trans-Saharan Trade Routes. Trade across the Sahara began during the first millennium B.C.E. With the arrival of the camel from the Middle East, trade expanded dramatically.

Q *What were the major cities involved in the trade, as shown on this map?*

8-2e The States of West Africa

During the eighth century, merchants from the Maghrib began to carry Muslim beliefs to the savannas south of the Sahara. At first, conversion took place on an individual basis rather than through official encouragement. The first rulers to convert to Islam were the royal family of Gao (GAH-oh) at the end of the tenth century. Five hundred years later, most of the population in the grasslands south of the Sahara had accepted Islam.

The expansion of Islam into West Africa had a major impact on the political system. By introducing Arabic as the first written language in the region and Muslim law codes and administrative practices from the Middle East, Islam provided local rulers with the tools to increase their authority and the efficiency of their governments. Moreover, as Islam gradually spread throughout the region, a common religion united previously diverse peoples into a more coherent community.

When Islam arrived in the grasslands south of the Sahara, the region was beginning to undergo significant political and social change. Several major trading states were in the making, and they eventually transformed the Sahara into a leading avenue of world trade crisscrossed by caravan routes leading to the Atlantic Ocean, the Mediterranean, and the Red Sea (see Map 8.5).

Ghana The first of these great commercial states was Ghana, which emerged in the fifth century C.E. in the Upper Niger Valley, a grassland region between the Sahara and the tropical forests along the West African coast. (The modern state of Ghana, which takes its name from this early trading society, is located in the forest region to the south.) The majority of the people in the area were farmers living in villages under local chieftains; as climatic conditions in the region gradually improved, these local communities were united to form the kingdom of Ghana. Although the people of the region had traditionally lived from agriculture, gold became a primary reason for Ghana's growing importance. The heartland of the state was located near one of the richest gold-producing areas in Africa. Ghanaian merchants transported the gold to Morocco, whence it was distributed throughout the known world, a trade that had apparently begun in ancient times according to Greek historian Herodotus.[3]

Eventually, other exports from Ghana found their way to the bazaars of the Mediterranean coast and beyond—ivory, ostrich feathers, hides, leather goods, and ultimately slaves. The origins of the slave trade in the area probably go back to the first millennium B.C.E. when Berber tribesmen seized African villagers in the regions south of the Sahara and sold them to buyers in Europe and the Middle East. In return, Ghana imported metal goods (especially weapons), textiles, horses, and salt.

Much of the trade across the desert was still conducted by the nomadic Berbers, but by the eighth and ninth centuries much of this trade was conducted by Muslim

Royalty and Religion in Ghana

Religion & Philosophy

AFTER ITS FIRST APPEARANCE IN WEST AFRICA in the decades following the death of Muhammad, Islam competed with native African religions for followers. Eventually, several local rulers converted to the Muslim faith. This passage by Arab geographer al-Bakri (al-BAHK-ree) reflects religious tolerance in the state of Ghana during the eleventh century under a non-Muslim ruler with many Muslim subjects.

Al-Bakri's Description of Royalty in Ghana

The king's residence comprises a palace and conical huts, the whole surrounded by a fence like a wall. Around the royal town are huts and groves of thorn trees where live the magicians who control their religious rites. These groves, where they keep their idols and bury their kings, are protected by guards who permit no one to enter or find out what goes on in them.

None of those who belong to the imperial religion may wear tailored garments except the king himself and the heir presumptive, his sister's son. The rest of the people wear wrappers of cotton, silk or brocade according to their means. Most of the men shave their beards and the women

their heads. The king adorns himself with female ornaments around the neck and arms. On his head he wears gold-embroidered caps covered with turbans of finest cotton. He gives audience to the people for the redressing of grievances in a hut around which are placed [ten] horses covered in golden cloth. Behind him stand [ten] slaves carrying shields and swords mounted with gold. On his right are the sons of vassal kings, their heads plaited with gold and wearing costly garments. On the ground around him are seated his ministers, whilst the governor of the city sits before him. On guard at the door are dogs of fine pedigree, wearing collars adorned with gold and silver. The royal audience is announced by the beating of a drum, called daba, made out of a long piece of hollowed-out wood. When the people have gathered, his coreligionists draw near upon their knees sprinkling dust upon their heads as a sign of respect, whilst the Muslims clap hands as their form of greeting.

 Why might an African ruler find it advantageous to adopt the Muslim faith? What kinds of changes would the adoption of Islam entail for the peoples living in West Africa?

Source: Adapted from translation quoted in J. S. Trimingham, *A History of Islam and West Africa*, copyright 1970 by Oxford University Press.

merchants in Ghana, who purchased tropical products such as bananas, kola nuts, and palm oil from the forest states along the Atlantic coast (using iron and copper cash or cowrie shells as the primary means of exchange) and then sold them to Berbers, who carried them across the desert to the Moroccan city of Marrakech (mar-uh-KESH). The merchants who carried on this trade often became quite wealthy and lived in splendor in cities like Saleh (SAH-leh), the capital of Ghana. So did the king, of course, who taxed the merchants as well as the farmers and the producers.

Like his West African counterparts, the king of Ghana ruled by divine right and was assisted by a hereditary aristocracy composed of the leading members of the prominent clans, who also served as district chiefs responsible for maintaining law and order and collecting taxes. The king

William J. Duiker

8.6 The Great Gate at Marrakech. The Moroccan city of Marrakech, founded in the ninth century C.E., was a major northern terminus of the trans-Saharan trade and one of the chief commercial centers in premodern Africa. Widely praised by such famous travelers as Ibn Battuta, the city was an architectural marvel in that all of its major public buildings were constructed of red sandstone. Shown here is the city's great gate through which camel caravans passed en route to and from the vast desert. In the Berber language, *Marrakech* means "pass without making a noise," a necessity for caravan traders who had to be alert to the danger of thieves in the vicinity.

was responsible for maintaining the security of his kingdom, serving as an intermediary with local deities, and adjudicating disputes. The kings of Ghana did not convert to Islam themselves, although they welcomed Muslim merchants and apparently did not discourage their subjects from adopting the new faith (see Historical Voices, "Royalty and Religion in Ghana," p. 199).

Mali The state of Ghana flourished for several hundred years, but by the twelfth century, it had begun to decline, weakened by ruinous wars with Berber tribesmen. It collapsed at the end of the century. In its place rose several new trading societies, including large territorial empires such as Mali (MAHL-ee) in the west and Kanem-Bornu (KAH-nuhm-BOR-noo) toward the east, and small commercial city-states such as the Hausa (HOW-suh) states in what is today northern Nigeria (see Map 8.6).

The greatest of the empires that emerged after the destruction of Ghana was Mali. Extending from the Atlantic coast inland as far as the trading cities of Timbuktu (tim-buk-TOO) and Gao on the Niger River, Mali built its wealth and power on the gold trade. But the heartland of Mali was situated south of the Sahara in the savannas, where sufficient moisture enabled farmers to grow such crops as sorghum, millet, and rice. The farmers lived in villages ruled by a local chieftain, called a *mansa* (MAHN-suh), who served as both religious and administrative leader and was responsible for forwarding tax revenues from the village to higher levels of government.

The primary wealth of the country was accumulated in the cities. Here lived the merchants, who were mostly of local origin although many were now practicing Muslims. Commercial activities were taxed but were apparently so lucrative that both merchants and kings prospered. One of the most powerful kings of Mali was Mansa Musa (MAHN–suh MOO-suh) (r. 1312–1337), whose primary contribution to his people was probably not economic prosperity but the Muslim faith. Mansa Musa strongly encouraged the building of mosques and

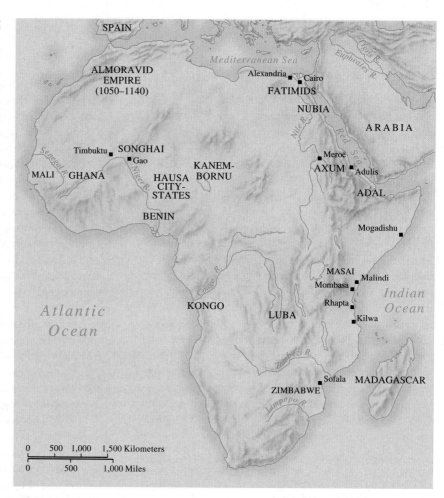

Map 8.6 The Emergence of States in Africa. By the end of the first millennium C.E., organized states had begun to appear in various parts of Africa.

Ⓠ *Why did organized states appear in these particular areas and not in other places in Africa?*

the study of the Qur'an in his kingdom and imported scholars and books to introduce his subjects to the message of Allah. One visitor from Europe, writing in the late fifteenth century, reported that in Timbuktu "are a great store of doctors, judges, priests, and other learned men, that are bountifully maintained at the king's cost and charges. And hither are brought divers manuscripts of written books out of Barbary [North Africa] which are sold for more money than any other merchandise."[4]

The city of Timbuktu ("well of Bouctu," in memory of a Taureg woman who lived in the area) was founded in 1100 C.E. as a seasonal camp for caravan traders on the Niger River. Under Mansa Musa and his successors, the city gradually emerged as a major intellectual and cultural center in West Africa and the site of schools of law, literature, and the sciences.

British Library, London//HIP/Art Resource, NY

8.7 Mansa Musa. King of the West African state of Mali, Mansa Musa was one of the richest and most powerful rulers of his day. During a famous pilgrimage to Mecca, he arrived in Cairo with a hundred camels laden with gold and gave away so much gold that its value depreciated there for several years. To promote the Islamic faith in his country, he bought homes in Cairo and Mecca to house pilgrims en route to the holy shrine, and he brought back to Mali a renowned Arab architect to build mosques in the trading centers of Gao and Timbuktu. His fame spread to Europe as well as evidenced by this Spanish map of 1375, which depicts Mansa Musa seated on his throne in Mali, holding an impressive gold nugget.

8-3 STATES AND NONCENTRALIZED SOCIETIES IN CENTRAL AND SOUTHERN AFRICA

Q Focus Questions: What role did migrations play in the evolution of early African societies? How did the impact of these migrations compare with similar population movements elsewhere?

In the southern half of the African continent, from the great basin of the Congo River to the Cape of Good Hope, states formed somewhat more slowly than in the north. Until the eleventh century C.E., most people in this region lived in what are sometimes called **noncentralized societies** that are characterized by autonomous villages organized by clans and ruled by local chieftains or clan heads. Beginning in the eleventh century, in some parts of southern Africa, these independent villages gradually began to consolidate. Out of these groupings came the first states.

8-3a The Congo River Valley

One area where this process occurred was the Congo River Valley, where the combination of fertile land and nearby

deposits of copper and iron enabled the inhabitants to enjoy an agricultural surplus and engage in regional commerce. Two new states in particular underwent this transition. Sometime during the fourteenth century, the kingdom of Luba (LOOB-uh) was founded in the center of the continent in a rich agricultural and fishing area near the shores of Lake Kisale (kee-SAHL-eh). Luba had a relatively centralized government in which the king appointed provincial governors who were responsible for collecting tribute from the village chiefs. At about the same time, the kingdom of Kongo was formed just south of the mouth of the Congo River on the Atlantic coast.

These new states were primarily agricultural, although both Luba and Kongo had thriving manufacturing sectors and were active in the growing exchange of goods throughout the region. With the passage of time, both began to expand southward to absorb the mixed farming and pastoral peoples in the area of modern Angola. In the drier grasslands to the south, other small communities continued to support themselves by herding, hunting, or food gathering. We know little about these peoples, however, because they possessed no writing system and had few visitors. A Portuguese sailor who encountered them in the late sixteenth century reported, "These people are herdsmen and cultivators. . . . Their main crop is millet, which they grind between two stones or in wooden mortars to make flour. . . . Their wealth consists mainly in their huge number of dehorned cows. . . . They live together in small villages, in houses made of reed mats, which do not keep out the rain."[5]

8-3b Zimbabwe

Farther to the east, the situation was somewhat different. In the grasslands immediately to the south of the Zambezi (zam-BEE-zee) River, a mixed economy of farming, cattle herding, and commercial pursuits had begun to develop during the early centuries of the first millennium C.E. Characteristically, villages in this area were constructed inside walled enclosures to protect livestock at night. The most famous of these communities was Zimbabwe, which was located on the plateau of the same name between the Zambezi and Limpopo (lim-POH-poh) Rivers. From the twelfth century to the middle of the fifteenth century, Zimbabwe was the most powerful and most prosperous state in the region and played a major role in the gold trade with the Swahili trading communities on the eastern coast.

The ruins of Zimbabwe's capital, known as Great Zimbabwe (the term *Zimbabwe* means "stone house" in the Bantu language), provide a vivid illustration of the kingdom's power and influence. Strategically situated between substantial gold reserves to the west and a small river leading to the coast, Great Zimbabwe was well placed to benefit from the expansion of trade between the coast and the interior. The town sits on a hill overlooking the river and is surrounded by stone walls that enclosed an area large enough to hold more than 10,000 residents. The houses of the wealthy were built of cement on stone foundations, but those of the common people were of dried mud with thatched roofs. In the valley below is the royal palace surrounded by a thirty-foot-high stone wall (see Image 8.1, p. 187). Artifacts found at the site include household implements and ornaments made of gold and copper, as well as jewelry and even porcelain imported from China.

Most of the royal wealth probably came from two sources: the ownership of cattle and the king's ability to levy heavy taxes on the gold that passed through the kingdom en route to the coast. By the middle of the fifteenth century, however, the city was apparently abandoned, possibly because of environmental damage caused by overgrazing.

8-3c Southern Africa

South of the East African plateau and the Congo basin is a vast land of hills, grasslands, and arid desert stretching almost to the Cape of Good Hope at the tip of the continent. As Bantu-speaking farmers spread southward during the final centuries of the first millennium B.C.E., they began to encounter Neolithic peoples in the area who still lived primarily by hunting and foraging.

Two such peoples were the Khoi (KOI) and the San (SAHN), whose language, known as Khoisan (KOI-sahn), is distinguished by the use of "clicking" sounds. The Khoi were herders, whereas the San were hunter-gatherers who lived in small family communities of twenty to twenty-five members throughout southern Africa from Namibia in the west to the Drakensberg Mountains near the southeastern coast. Some of these peoples were probably absorbed into what became a dominantly Bantu-speaking pastoral and agricultural society that spread throughout the region, and others may have been driven into less hospitable desert regions farther to the west.

HISTORIANS DEBATE 8-3d Africa: A Continent Without History?

Until the second half of the twentieth century, the prevailing view among Western historians was that Africa was a continent without history, a land of scattered villages long isolated from the main currents of world affairs. But in the decades after World War II, a new generation of historians trained in African studies, spurred on in part by the appearance in 1959 of Basil Davidson's path-breaking work, *Lost Cities of Africa*, began to contest that view. Their studies have demonstrated that throughout history many African societies were not only actively in contact with peoples beyond their shores but also created several advanced civilizations of their own.

Although the paucity of written sources continues to present a challenge, historians are using other sources with increasing success to throw light on the African historical experience. African peoples were at the forefront of the agricultural revolution in the ninth and eighth millennia B.C.E.; although parts of the continent remained isolated from the main currents of world history, as early as the first millennium C.E. several African societies began to play an active role in the expanding global trade network that stretched from the Mediterranean Sea deep into the Sahara. Another major commercial trade route ran from the Arabian Peninsula down the coast of East Africa along the shores of the Indian Ocean. Thus, it is becoming increasingly clear that from the dawn of history the peoples of Africa have made a significant contribution to the human experience.

8-4 AFRICAN SOCIETY

 Focus Questions: What role did lineage groups, women, and slavery play in African societies? In what ways did African societies in various parts of the continent differ? What accounted for these differences?

Drawing generalizations about social organization, cultural development, and daily life in traditional Africa is difficult because of the extreme diversity of the continent and its inhabitants. One-quarter of all the languages in the world are spoken in Africa, and five of the major language families are found there. Ethnic divisions are equally pronounced. Because many of these languages did not have a system of writing until fairly recently, historians must rely on accounts of the occasional visitor such as al-Mas'udi and famous fourteenth-century chronicler Ibn Battuta. Such travelers, however, were mostly in contact with the wealthy and the powerful, leaving us to speculate about what life was like for ordinary Africans during this early period.

8-4a Urban Life

African towns often began as fortified walled villages and gradually evolved into larger communities serving several purposes. Here, of course, was the center of government as well as teeming markets filled with goods from distant regions. Here also were artisans skilled in metalworking or woodworking, pottery making, and other crafts. Unlike rural areas, where a village was usually composed of a single lineage group or clan, towns drew their residents from several clans, although individual clans usually lived in their own compounds and were governed by their own clan heads.

In the states of West Africa, the focal point of the major towns was the royal precinct. The relationship between the ruler and the merchant class differed from the situation in most Asian societies, where the royal family and the aristocracy were largely isolated from the remainder of the population. In Africa, the chasm between the king and the common people was not so great. Often the ruler would hold an audience to allow people to voice their complaints or to welcome visitors from foreign countries. In the city-states of the East African coast, the rulers were often wealthy merchants who, as in the town of Kilwa, "did not possess more country than the city itself."[6]

This is not to say that the king was not elevated above all others in status. In wealthier states, the walls of the audience chamber would be covered with sheets of beaten silver and gold, and the king would be surrounded by hundreds of armed soldiers and some of his trusted advisers. Nevertheless, the symbiotic relationship between the ruler and merchant class served to reduce the gap between the king and his subjects. The relationship was mutually beneficial because the merchants received honors and favors from the palace while the king's coffers were filled with taxes paid by the merchants. Certainly, it was to the king's benefit to maintain law and order in his domain so that the merchants could ply their trade. As Ibn Battuta observed, among the good qualities of the states of West Africa was the prevalence of peace in the region. "The traveler may proceed alone among them," he remarked, "without the least fear of a thief or robber."[7]

8-4b Village Life

The vast majority of Africans lived in small rural villages. Their identities were established by their membership in a nuclear family and a lineage group. At the basic level was the nuclear family composed of parents and preadult children; sometimes it included an elderly grandparent and perhaps other family dependents. They lived in small round huts constructed of packed mud and topped with a conical thatch roof. In most African societies, these nuclear family units would in turn be combined into larger kinship communities known as *households* or *lineage groups*.

The lineage group was similar in many respects to the clan in China or the class system in India: it was normally based on kinship ties, although sometimes outsiders such as neighbors or other dependents may have been admitted to membership. Throughout the precolonial era, lineages served, in the words of one historian, as the "basic building blocks" of African society. The authority of the leading members of the lineage group was substantial. As in China, the elders had considerable power over the economic functions of the other people in the group, which provided mutual support for all members.

A village would usually be composed of a single lineage group, although some communities may have consisted of several unrelated families. At the head of the village was the familiar "big man," who was often assisted by a

Photograph by Yvonne V. Duiker

8.8 Home Sweet Home: A Traditional House in South Africa. The conical mud-and-thatch hut is a familiar site throughout much of rural Africa today. Built of widely available local materials, such one-room dwellings are generally inexpensive and easy to build, and they have been a common form of housing on the continent for thousands of years. In this Xhosa village in South Africa, some of the local residents live in modern houses in a nearby town but maintain such traditional huts like the one shown here to perform their ancestral ceremonies. According to villagers, the design of the conical shape is meant to keep out evil spirits.

council of representatives of the various households in the community. Often the "big man" was believed to possess supernatural powers; as the village grew in size and power, he might eventually be transformed into a local chieftain or monarch.

8-4c The Role of Women

Although generalizations are risky, we can say that women were usually subordinate to men in Africa, as in most early societies. In some cases, they were valued for the work they could do or for their role in increasing the size of the lineage group. Polygyny was not uncommon, particularly in Muslim societies. Women often worked in the fields while the men of the village tended the cattle or went on hunting expeditions. In some communities, the women specialized in commercial activities. In one area in southern Africa, young girls were sent into the mines to extract gold because of their smaller physiques.

But there were some key differences between the role of women in Africa and elsewhere. In many African societies, lineage was **matrilinear** rather than **patrilinear**. As Ibn Battuta observed during his travels in West Africa, "[T]he sister's son always succeeds to property in preference to the son."[8] He said he had never encountered this custom before except among the unbelievers of the Malabar coast in India. Women were often permitted to inherit property, and the husband was often expected to move into his wife's house.

Relations between men and women were also sometimes more relaxed than in China or India, with none of the taboos characteristic of those societies. Again, in the words of Ibn Battuta, himself a Muslim:

> As to their women, they are not shy with regards to the men, nor do they veil themselves from them, although they constantly accompany them at prayers. . . . It is a custom among them, that many may have a mistress, . . . who may come and associate with him, even in the presence of her own husband and of his wife. In like manner, a man will enter his own house, and see the friend of his wife with her alone, and talking with her, without the least emotion or attempt to disturb them; he will only come in and sit down on one side, till the man goes.

When Ibn Battuta asked an African acquaintance about these customs, the latter responded, "Women's companionship with men in our country is honorable and takes place in a good way: there is no suspicion about it. They are not like the women in your country." Ibn Battuta noted his astonishment at such a "thoughtless" answer and did not accept further invitations to visit his friend's house.[9]

Such informal attitudes toward the relationship between the sexes were not found everywhere in Africa and were probably curtailed as many Africans converted to Islam (see Historical Voices, "Women and Islam in North Africa," p. 205). But it is a testimony to the tenacity of traditional customs that the relatively puritanical views about the role of women in society brought by Muslims from the Middle East made little impression even among Muslim families in West Africa.

8-4d Slavery

African slavery is often associated with the period after 1500. Indeed, the slave trade did reach enormous proportions in the seventeenth and eighteenth centuries when European slave ships transported millions of unfortunate victims abroad to Europe or the Americas (see Chapter 14).

Slavery did not originate with the coming of the Europeans, however. It had been practiced in Africa since ancient times and probably originated with prisoners of war who were forced into perpetual servitude. Slavery was common in ancient Egypt and became especially prevalent during the New Kingdom, when slaving expeditions brought back thousands of captives from the Upper Nile to be used in labor gangs, for tribute, and even as human sacrifices.

Slavery persisted during the early period of state building, in the first and early second millennia C.E. Berber tribes may have regularly raided agricultural communities south of the Sahara for captives, who were then transported northward and eventually sold throughout the Mediterranean. Some were enrolled as soldiers, whereas others, often women, were used as domestic servants in the homes of the wealthy. The use of captives for forced labor or exchange was apparently also common in African societies farther to the south and along the eastern coast.

Life was difficult for the average slave. The least fortunate were probably those who worked on plantations owned by the royal family or other wealthy landowners. Those pressed into service as soldiers were sometimes more fortunate because in Muslim societies in the Middle East they might at some point win their freedom. Many slaves were employed in the royal household or as domestic servants in private homes. In general, these slaves probably had the most tolerable existence. Although they ordinarily were not permitted to purchase their freedom, their living conditions were often decent and sometimes practically indistinguishable from those of the free individuals in the household. In some societies in North Africa, slaves reportedly made up as much as 75 percent of the entire population. Elsewhere the percentage was much lower, in some cases less than 10 percent.

Women and Islam in North Africa

Family & Society   **IN MUSLIM SOCIETIES IN NORTH AFRICA,** as elsewhere, women were required to cover their bodies to avoid tempting men, but Islam's puritanical insistence on the separation of the sexes did not accord with the relatively informal relationships that prevailed in many African societies. In this excerpt from *The History and Description of Africa*, Leo Africanus describes the customs along the Mediterranean coast of Africa. A resident of Spain of Muslim parentage who was captured by Christian corsairs in 1518 and later served under Pope Leo X, Leo Africanus undertook many visits to Africa.

Leo Africanus, *The History and Description of Africa*

Their women (according to the guise of that country) go very gorgeously attired: they wear linen gowns dyed black, with exceeding wide sleeves, over which sometimes they cast a mantle of the same color or of blue, the corners of which mantle are very [attractively] fastened about their shoulders with a fine silver clasp. Likewise they have rings hanging at their ears, which for the most part are made of silver; they wear many rings also upon their fingers. Moreover they usually wear about their thighs and ankles certain scarfs and rings, after the fashion of the Africans. They cover their faces with certain masks having only two holes for the eyes to peep out at. If any man chance to meet with them, they presently hide their faces, passing by him with silence, except it be some of their allies or kinsfolks; for unto them they always [uncover] their faces, neither is there any use of the said mask so long as they be in presence. These Arabians when they travel any journey (as they oftentimes do) they set their women upon certain saddles made handsomely of wicker for the same purpose, and fastened to their camel backs, neither be they anything too wide, but fit only for a woman to sit in. When they go to the wars each man carries his wife with him, to the end that she may cheer up her good man, and give him encouragement. Their damsels which are unmarried do usually paint their faces, breasts, arms, hands, and fingers with a kind of counterfeit color: which is accounted a most decent custom among them.

 Which of the practices described here are dictated by the social regulations of Islam? Does the author approve of the behavior of African women as described in this passage?

Source: From *The History and Description of Africa*, by Leo Africanus (New York: Burt Franklin), pp. 158–159.

8-5 AFRICAN CULTURE

 Focus Question: What are some of the chief characteristics of African sculpture and carvings, music, and architecture, and what purpose did these forms of creative expression serve in African society?

In early Africa, as in much of the rest of the world at the time, creative expression—whether in the form of painting, literature, or music—was above all a means of serving religion and the social order. To the uninitiated, a wooden mask or the bronze and iron statuary of southern Nigeria may simply appear to be a work of art, to the artist it was often a means of expressing religious convictions and common concerns. Some African historians reject the use of the term *art* to describe such artifacts because they were produced for spiritual or moral rather than aesthetic purposes.

8-5a Painting and Sculpture

The earliest extant art forms in Africa are rock paintings. The most famous examples are in the Tassili Mountains in the central Sahara, where the earliest paintings may date back as far as 5000 B.C.E., though the majority are a millennium or so younger. Some of the later paintings depict the two-horse chariots used to transport goods before the introduction of the camel. Rock paintings are also found elsewhere in the continent, including the Nile Valley and eastern and southern Africa. Those of the San peoples of southern Africa are especially interesting for their illustrations of ritual ceremonies in which village shamans induce rain, propitiate the spirits, or cure illnesses.

More familiar, perhaps, are African wood carvings and sculpture. Mentioned in the account of the traveler Ibn Battuta as early as the fourteenth century, these remarkable statues, masks, and headdresses were carved from living trees after the artist had made a sacrifice to the tree's spirit. Costumed singers and dancers wore these masks and headdresses in performances in honor of the various spirits, revealing the identification and intimate connection of the African with the natural world. The "Fang" masks of Equatorial Africa, for example, were used both for initiation ceremonies as well as for entertainment on festive occasions. Masks decorated in white clay were meant to convey the embodied spirits of the deceased so as to protect the village from evil forces.

In the thirteenth and fourteenth centuries C.E., metalworkers at Ife (EE-fay) in what is now southern Nigeria produced handsome bronze and iron statues using the lost-wax method, in which melted wax is replaced in a mold by molten metal. The Ife sculptures may in turn have influenced artists in Benin (bay-NEEN) in West Africa who produced equally impressive works in bronze during the same period. The Benin sculptures include bronze heads, relief plaques depicting life at court, ornaments, and figures of various animals.

Westerners once regarded African wood carvings and metal sculpture as a form of "primitive art," but the label is not appropriate. The metal sculpture of Benin, for example, is highly sophisticated, and some of the best works are considered masterpieces. Such artistic works were often created by artisans in the employ of the royal court.

8-5b Music

Like sculpture and wood carving, African music and dance often served a religious function. With their characteristic heavy rhythmic beat, dances were a means of communicating with the spirits, and the frenzied movements that are often identified with African dance were intended to represent the spirits acting through humans.

African music during the traditional period varied to some degree from one society to another. A wide variety of instruments were used, including drums and other percussion instruments, xylophones, bells, horns, and flutes, and stringed instruments such as the fiddle, harp, and zither. Still, the music throughout the continent had sufficient common characteristics to justify a few generalizations. In the first place, a strong rhythmic pattern was an important feature of most African music, although the desired effect was achieved through a wide variety of means, including gourds, pots, bells, sticks beaten together, and hand clapping, as well as drums.

Another important feature was the integration of voice and instrument into a total musical experience. Musical instruments and the human voice were often woven together to tell a story, and instruments such as the famous "talking drum" were frequently used to represent the voice. Choral music and individual voices were used in a pattern of repetition and variation that is sometimes

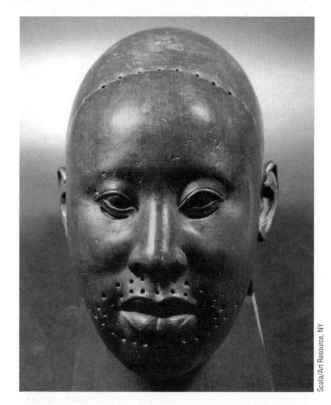

Scala/Art Resource, NY

8.9 African Metalwork. The rulers of emerging West African states frequently commissioned royal artifacts to adorn their palaces and promote their grandeur. Elaborate stools, weaponry, shields, and sculpted heads of members of the royal family served to commemorate the ruler's reign and preserve his memory for later generations. This regal thirteenth-century brass head attests to the technical excellence and sophistication of Ife metalworkers. The small holes along the scalp and the mouth permitted either hair, a veil, or a crown to be attached to the head, which itself was often attached to a wooden mannequin dressed in elaborate robes for display during memorial services.

known as *call and response*. Through this technique, the audience participated in the music by uttering a single phrase over and over as a choral response to the changing call sung by the soloist. Sometimes instrumental music achieved a similar result.

Much music was produced in the context of such social rituals as weddings and funerals, religious ceremonies, and official inaugurations. Music could also educate by passing on to young people information about the history and social traditions of the community. In the absence of written languages in sub-Saharan Africa (except for the Arabic script used in Muslim societies in East and West Africa), music served as the primary means of transmitting folk legends and religious traditions from generation to generation. Oral tradition, which was usually undertaken by a priestly class or a specialized class of storytellers, served a similar function.

8-5c Architecture

No aspect of African artistic creativity is more varied than architecture. From the pyramids along the Nile to the ruins of Great Zimbabwe south of the Zambezi River, from the Moorish palaces at Zanzibar to the turreted mud mosques of West Africa, African architecture shows a striking diversity of approach and technique that is unmatched in other areas of creative endeavor.

The kingdom of Axum was especially noteworthy in developing its own architectural traditions. Most distinctive were the carved stone pillars known as *stelae* (STEE-lee) that were used to mark the tombs of dead kings. Some stood as high as 100 feet (see Comparative Illustration, "The Stele," p. 208). The advent of Christianity eventually affected Axumite architecture. During the Zagwe Dynasty in the twelfth and thirteenth centuries C.E., churches carved out of solid rock were constructed throughout the country (see Comparative Illustration, "Rock Architecture," p. 224 in Chapter 9). The earliest may have been built in the eighth century C.E. Stylistically, they combined indigenous techniques inherited from the pre-Christian period with elements borrowed from Christian churches in the Holy Land.

In West Africa, buildings constructed in stone were apparently a rarity until the emergence of states during the first millennium ce. At that time, both the royal palace and other buildings of civic importance were often built of stone or cement, whereas the houses of the majority of the population continued to be constructed of dried mud. On his visit to the state of Guinea on the West African coast, sixteenth-century traveler Leo Africanus noted that the houses of the ruler and other elites were built of chalk with roofs of straw. Even then, however, well into the state-building period, mosques were often built of mud.

Along the east coast, the architecture of the elite tended to reflect Middle Eastern styles. In the coastal towns and islands from Mogadishu to Kilwa, the houses of the wealthy were built of stone and reflected Arabic influence. As elsewhere, the common people lived in huts of mud, thatch, or palm leaves. Mosques were built of stone.

The most famous stone buildings in sub-Saharan Africa are those at Great Zimbabwe. Constructed of carefully cut stones that were set in place without mortar, the great wall and the public buildings at Great Zimbabwe are an impressive monument to the architectural creativity of the peoples of the region.

8-5d Literature

Literature in the sense of written works did not exist in sub-Saharan Africa during the early traditional period, except in regions where Islam had brought the Arabic script from the Middle East. But African societies compensated for the absence of a written language with a rich tradition of oral lore. The **bard**, or professional storyteller, was an ancient African institution by which history was transmitted orally from generation to generation. In many West African societies, bards were highly esteemed and served as counselors to kings as well as protectors of local tradition. Bards were revered for their oratory and singing skills, phenomenal memory, and astute interpretation of history. As one African scholar wrote, the death of a bard was equivalent to the burning of a library.

Bards served several necessary functions in society. They were chroniclers of history, preservers of social customs and proper conduct, and entertainers who possessed a monopoly over the playing of the musical instruments that accompanied their narratives. Because of their unique position above normal society, bards often played the role of mediator between hostile families or clans in a community. They were also credited with possessing occult powers and could read divinations and issue blessings and curses. Traditionally, bards also served as advisers to the king, sometimes inciting a ruler to action (such as going to battle) through the passion of their poetry. When captured by the enemy, bards were often treated with respect and released or compelled to serve the victor with their art.

One of the most famous West African epics is *The Epic of Son-Jara*, which was passed down orally by bards for more than 700 years. It relates the heroic exploits of Son-Jara (sun-GAR-uh) (also known as *Sunjata* or *Sundiata*), the founder and ruler (r. 1230–1255) of Mali's empire. Although Mansa Musa is famous throughout the world because of his flamboyant pilgrimage to Mecca in the fourteenth century, Son-Jara is more celebrated in West Africa because of the dynamic and unbroken oral traditions of the West African peoples.

Like the bards, women were appreciated for their storytelling talents, as well as for their role as purveyors of the moral values and religious beliefs of African societies. In societies that lacked a written tradition, women represented the glue that held the community together. Through the recitation of fables, proverbs, poems, and songs, mothers conditioned the communal bonding and moral fiber of succeeding generations in a way that was rarely encountered in the patriarchal societies of Europe, eastern and southern Asia, and the Middle East. Such activities not only were vital aspects of education in traditional Africa but also offered a welcome respite from the drudgery of everyday life and a spark to develop the imagination and artistic awareness of the young. Renowned for its many proverbs, Africa also offers the following: "A good story is like a garden carried in the pocket."

The Stele

Art & Ideas

A STELE IS A STONE SLAB OR PILLAR that is usually decorated or inscribed and placed upright. Stelae were often used to commemorate the accomplishments of a ruler or significant figure. Image 8.10a shows the tallest of the Axum stelae still standing in present-day Ethiopia. The stone stelae in Axum in the fourth century B.C.E. marked the location of royal tombs with inscriptions commemorating the glories of the kings. An earlier famous stele, Image 8.10b, is the obelisk at Luxor in southern Egypt. A similar kind of stone pillar, Image 8.10c, was erected in India during the reign of Ashoka in the third century B.C.E. (see Chapter 2) to commemorate events in the life of the Buddha. Archaeologists have also found stelae in ancient China, Greece, and Mexico.

 Why do you think the stele was so widely used during early times as a symbol of royal power?

8.10a

Werner Forman/Art Resource, NY

8.10b

William J. Duiker

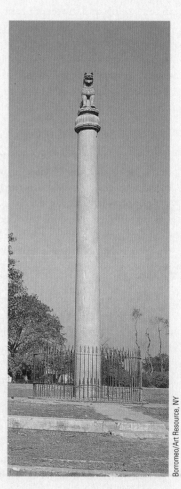

8.10c

Borromeo/Art Resource, NY

CHAPTER SUMMARY

Thanks to the dedicated work of a generation of archaeologists, anthropologists, and historians, we now have a much better understanding of the evolution of human societies in Africa than we did a few decades ago. Intensive efforts by archaeologists have demonstrated beyond reasonable doubt that the first hominids lived there. Recently discovered evidence suggests that farming may have been practiced in Africa more than 11,000 years ago.

Less is known about more recent African history, partly because of the paucity of written records. Still, historians have established that the first civilizations had begun to take shape in sub-Saharan Africa by the first millennium C.E., and the continent as a whole was an active participant in the emerging regional and global trade with the Mediterranean world and across the Indian Ocean.

Thus, the peoples of Africa were not as isolated from the main currents of human history as was once assumed. Although the state-building process in sub-Saharan Africa was still in its early stages compared with the ancient civilizations of India, China, and Mesopotamia, in many respects these new states were as impressive and sophisticated as their counterparts elsewhere in the world.

In the fifteenth century, a new factor was added to the equation. Urged on by the tireless efforts of Prince Henry the Navigator, Portuguese fleets began to probe southward along the coast of West Africa. At first, their sponsors were in search of gold and slaves, but at the end of the century, Vasco da Gama's voyage around the Cape of Good Hope signaled Portugal's determination to dominate the commerce of the Indian Ocean in the future. The new situation posed a challenge to the peoples of Africa, whose nascent states and technology would be severely tested by the rapacious demands of the Europeans.

REFLECTION QUESTIONS

Q Where and under what conditions was agriculture first practiced on the continent of Africa? What effect did the advent of farming have on the formation of human communities there?

Q Although geographic barriers posed a challenge for African peoples in establishing communications with societies beyond their shores, by the end of the first millennium C.E. the continent had become an active player in the global trade network. What areas of Africa took part in this commercial expansion, and what products were exchanged?

Q The migration of the Bantu-speaking peoples was one of the most extensive population movements in world history. Trace the Bantu migration from its point of origin and discuss how it affected the later history of the continent.

CHAPTER TIMELINE

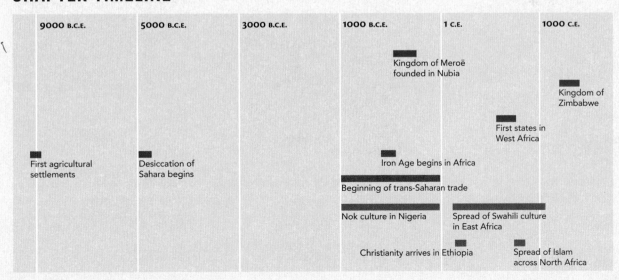

9000 B.C.E.	5000 B.C.E.	3000 B.C.E.	1000 B.C.E.	1 C.E.	1000 C.E.

Kingdom of Meroë founded in Nubia

Kingdom of Zimbabwe

First states in West Africa

First agricultural settlements

Desiccation of Sahara begins

Iron Age begins in Africa

Beginning of trans-Saharan trade

Nok culture in Nigeria

Spread of Swahili culture in East Africa

Christianity arrives in Ethiopia

Spread of Islam across North Africa

CHAPTER NOTES

1. S. Hamdun and N. King, eds., *Ihn Battuta in Africa* (London, 1975), p. 19.
2. D. Barbosa, *The Book of Duarte Barbosa* (Nedeln, Liechtenstein, 1967), p. 28.
3. Herodotus, The Histories, trans. A. de Selincourt (Baltimore, 1964), p. 307.
4. Quoted in M. Shinnie, *Ancient African Kingdoms* (London, 1965), p. 60.
5. C. R. Boxer, ed., *The Tragic History of the Sea, 1589–1622* (Cambridge, 1959), p. 121–122.
6. Quoted in D. Nurse and T. Spear, *The Swahili: Reconstructing the History and Language of an African Society 800–1500* (Philadelphia, 1985), p. 84.
7. S. Lee (tr. and ed.), *The Travels of Ibn Battuta in the Near East, Asia and Africa, 1325–1354* (Mineola, N.Y., 2004), p. 240.
8. Ibid., p. 234.
9. Ibid., pp. 28–30.

MINDTAP
From Cengage

MindTap® is a fully online, highly personalized learning experience built upon Cengage Learning content. MindTap combines student learning tools—readings, multimedia, activities, and assessments—into a singular Learning Path that guides students through the course and helps students develop the critical thinking, analysis, and communication skills that are essential to academic and professional success.

CHAPTER 9

THE EXPANSION OF CIVILIZATION IN SOUTH AND SOUTHEAST ASIA

Chapter Outline and Focus Questions

Thomas J. Abercrombie/National Geographic Creative

9.1 One of Two Massive Carved Statues of the Buddha Formerly at Bamiyan

Critical Thinking

Q *New religions had a significant impact on the social and cultural life of peoples living in southern Asia during the period covered in this chapter. What factors caused the spread of these religions in the first place? What changes occurred as a result of the introduction of these new faiths? Were the religions themselves affected by their spread into new regions of Asia?*

Connections to Today

Q *What does the Comparative Essay titled "Caste, Class, and Family" tell us about the role that nuclear and joint families tend to play in human societies? Do the examples cited provide any lessons for the present day?*

WHILE TRAVELING FROM HIS NATIVE CHINA to India along the Silk Road in the early fifth century C.E., Buddhist monk Fa Xian (fah SHEE-ahn) stopped en route at a town called Bamiyan (BAH-mee-ahn), a rest stop located deep in the mountains of what today is Afghanistan. At that time, Bamiyan was a major center of Buddhist studies, with dozens of temples and monasteries filled with students, all overlooked by two giant standing statues of the Buddha hewn directly out of the side of a massive cliff. Fa Xian was thrilled at the sight. "The law of Buddha," he remarked with satisfaction in his account of the experience, "is progressing and flourishing." He then continued southward to India, where he spent several years visiting Buddhists throughout the country. Because little of the period's literature survives, Fa Xian's observations are a valuable resource for our knowledge of the daily lives of the Indian people.

The India that Fa Xian visited was no longer the unified land it had been under the Mauryan (MOWR-yun) Dynasty. After the overthrow of the Mauryas in the early second century B.C.E., the subcontinent was divided into many separate kingdoms and principalities. The dominant force in the north was the Kushan (KOO-shan) state, which was established by Indo-European–speaking peoples who had migrated into the area from what is now China's Xinjiang (SHIN-jyahng) Province (see Chapter 3). The Kushans settled in the mountains north of the Indus River, where they formed a kingdom with its capital at Bactria, not far from modern Kabul (KAH-bul). Over the next two centuries, the Kushans expanded their supremacy along the Indus River and into the central Ganges Valley.

Meanwhile, to the south several kingdoms arose among the Dravidian-speaking peoples of the Deccan Plateau, which had been only partly under Mauryan rule. The most famous of these kingdoms was Chola (CHOH-luh) (sometimes spelled Cola) on the southeastern coast. Chola developed into a major trading power and sent merchant fleets eastward across the Bay of Bengal (ben-GAHL), where they introduced Indian culture as well as Indian goods to the peoples of Southeast Asia.

9-1 THE SILK ROAD

 Focus Question: What were some of the chief destinations along the Silk Road, and what kinds of products and ideas traveled along the route?

Shortly after the fall of the Mauryas, the Kushan kingdom became the dominant political force in northern India after the fall of the Mauryas partly because it sat astride the main trade routes across the northern half of the subcontinent

and was able to thrive on the commerce that passed through the area (see Map 9.1). Before the Kushans migrated southward, they had already begun to engage in the silk trade with China from their base at Khotan (koh-THAN) on the southern route through the Taklimakan (tah-kluh-muh-KAHN) Desert. Although most of the trade was local, some goods were transported all the way to the Mediterranean, where the rise of the Roman Empire created an expanded market for products such as raw silk and precious stones. Much of this trade was transported along the route now known as the Silk Road, one segment of which passed through the mountains northwest of India. From there, goods were shipped to Rome through the Persian Gulf or the Red Sea.

Trade between India and Europe had begun even before the rise of the Roman Empire, but it expanded rapidly in the first century C.E. when sailors mastered the pattern of the monsoon winds in the Indian Ocean (blowing from the southwest in the summer and the northeast in the winter). Commerce between the Mediterranean

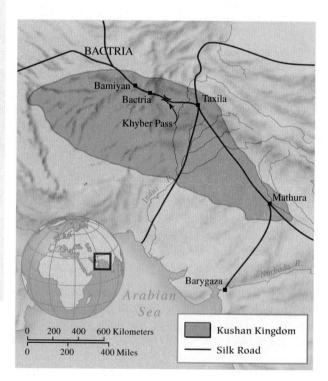

Map 9.1 The Kushan Kingdom and the Silk Road. After the collapse of the Mauryan Empire, a new state formed by recent migrants from the north arose north of the Indus River Valley. For the next four centuries, the Kushan kingdom played a major role in regional trade via the Silk Road until it declined in the third century C.E.

 What were the major products shipped along the Silk Road? Which countries beyond the borders of this map took an active part in trade along the Silk Road?

A Portrait of Medieval India

Interaction & Exchange

MUCH OF WHAT WE KNOW ABOUT LIFE in medieval India comes from the accounts of Chinese missionaries who visited the subcontinent in search of documents recording the teachings of the Buddha. Here Buddhist monk Fa Xian, who spent several years there in the fifth century C.E., reports on conditions in the kingdom of Mathura (MAH-too-ruh) (Mo-tu-lo), a vassal state in western India that was part of the Gupta Empire. Although he could not have been pleased that the Gupta monarchs in India had adopted the Hindu faith, Fa Xian found that the people were contented and prosperous except for the untouchables, whom he called *Chandalas.*

Fa Xian, *The Travels of Fa Xian*

Going southeast from this somewhat less than 80 *jojanas,* we passed very many temples one after another, with some myriad of priests in them. Having passed these places, we arrived at a certain country. This country is called Mo-tu-lo. Once more we followed the Puna River. On the sides of the river, both right and left, are twenty *sangharamas,* with perhaps 3,000 priests. The law of Buddha is progressing and flourishing. Beyond the deserts are the countries of western India. The kings of these countries are all firm believers in the law of Buddha. They remove their caps of state when they make offerings to the priests. The members of the royal household and the chief ministers personally direct the food giving; when the distribution of food is over, they spread a carpet on the ground opposite the chief seat (the president's seat) and sit down before it. They dare not sit on couches in the presence of the priests. The rules relating to the alms-giving of kings have been handed down from the time of Buddha till now. Southward from this is the so-called middle country (Madhyadesa). The climate of this country is warm and equable, without frost or snow. The people are very well off, without poll tax or official restrictions. Only those who till the royal lands return a portion of profit of the land. If they desire to go, they go; if they like to stop, they stop. The kings govern without corporal punishment; criminals are fined, according to circumstances, lightly or heavily. Even in cases of repeated rebellion they only cut off the right hand. The king's personal attendants, who guard him on the right and left, have fixed salaries. Throughout the country the people kill no living thing nor drink wine, nor do they eat garlic or onions, with the exception of Chandalas only. The Chandalas are named "evil men" and dwell apart from others; if they enter a town or market, they sound a piece of wood in order to separate themselves; then men, knowing who they are, avoid coming in contact with them. In this country they do not keep swine nor fowls, and do not deal in cattle; they have no shambles [slaughterhouses] or wine shops in their marketplaces. In selling they use cowrie shells. The Chandalas only hunt and sell flesh.

 To what degree do the practices described here conform to the principles established by Siddhartha Gautama in his teachings? Would political advisers such as Kautilya and Chinese philosopher Mencius have approved of the governmental policies?

Source: "Fu-kwo-ki," in Hiuen Tsang, Si-Yu Ki: *Buddhist Records of the Western World,* translated by Samuel Beal (London: Routledge and Kegan Paul). Used with permission. (London: Trubner & Co., 1886).

and the Indian Ocean, as described in the *Periplus* (PER-ihpluss), a first-century C.E. account by a Greek participant, was extensive and often profitable, and it resulted in the establishment of several small trading settlements along the Indian coast. Rome imported ivory, indigo, textiles, precious stones, and pepper from India and silk from China. The Romans sometimes paid cash for these goods but also exported silver, wine, perfume, slaves, and glass and cloth from Egypt. Overall, Rome appears to have imported much more than it sold to the Far East.

The Silk Road was a conduit for technology and ideas as well as material goods. The first Indian monks to visit China may have traveled over the road during the second century C.E. By the time of Fa Xian, Buddhist monks from China were arriving in increasing numbers to visit holy sites in India. The exchange of visits not only enriched the study of Buddhism in the two countries but also led to a fruitful exchange of ideas and technological advances in astronomy, mathematics, and linguistics. According to one scholar, the importation of Buddhist writings from India encouraged the development of printing in China, and the Chinese also obtained lessons in health care from monks returned from the Asian subcontinent.

Indeed, the emergence of the Kushan kingdom as a major commercial power was a result not only of its role as an intermediary in the Rome–China trade but also to

Experience an interactive version of this period in MINDTAP

the rising popularity of Buddhism. During the second century C.E., Kanishka (kuh-NISH-kuh), the greatest of the Kushan monarchs, began to patronize Buddhism. Under Kanishka and his successors, an intimate and mutually beneficial relationship was established between Buddhist monasteries and the local merchant community in thriving urban centers like Taxila (tak-SUH-luh) and Varanasi (vah-RAH-nah-see). Merchants were eager to build stupas and donate money to monasteries in return for social prestige and the implied promise of a better life in this world or the hereafter.

For their part, the wealthy monasteries ceased to be simple communities where monks could find a refuge from the material cares of the world; instead they became major consumers of luxury goods provided by their affluent patrons. Monasteries and their inhabitants became increasingly involved in the economic life of society, and Buddhist architecture began to be richly decorated with precious stones and glass purchased from local merchants or imported from abroad. The process was strikingly similar to the changes that would later occur in the Christian church in medieval Europe.

It was from the Kushan kingdom that Buddhism began its long journey across Central Asia to China and other societies in eastern Asia. As interregional trade increased, merchants and missionaries flowed from Bactria over the routes snaking through the mountains toward the northeast. At various stopping points on the trail, pilgrims erected statues and decorated mountain caves with magnificent frescoes depicting the life of the Buddha and his message to his followers. One of the most prominent of these centers was at Bamiyan, not far from modern-day Kabul, where believers carved two mammoth statues of the Buddha out of a sheer sandstone cliff. According to the Chinese pilgrim Fa Xian (see Historical Voices, "A Portrait of Medieval India," p. 213), more than 1,000 monks were attending a religious ceremony at the site when he visited the area in 400 C.E.

9-2 INDIA AFTER THE MAURYAS

 Focus Question: How did Buddhism change in the centuries after Siddhartha Gautama's death, and why did the religion ultimately decline in popularity in India?

Weakened by wars with Persia and the collapse of the Han Dynasty in China, the Kushan kingdom came to an end under uncertain conditions sometime in the third century C.E. In 320, a new state was established in the central Ganges Valley by a local raja named Chandragupta (chun-druh-GOOP-tuh) (no relation to Chandragupta Maurya, the founder of the Mauryan Dynasty). Chandragupta (r. 320 – ca. 335) located his capital at Pataliputra (pah-tah-lee-POO-truh), the site of the now-decaying palace of the Mauryas. Under his successor Samudragupta (suh-moo-druh-GOOP-tuh) (r. ca. 335–375), the territory under Gupta (GOOP-tuh) rule was extended into surrounding areas, and eventually the new kingdom became the dominant political force throughout northern India. It also established a loose suzerainty over the state of Pallava (pah-LAH-vuh) to the south, thus becoming the greatest state in the subcontinent since the decline of the Mauryan Empire. Under a succession of powerful, efficient, and highly cultured monarchs, notably Samudragupta and Chandragupta II (r. 375–415), India enjoyed a new "classical age" of civilization (see Map 9.2).

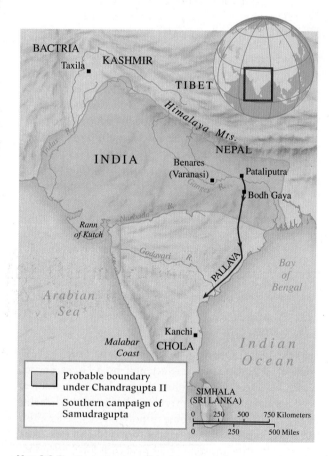

Map 9.2 The Gupta Empire. This map shows the extent of the Gupta Empire, the only major state to arise in the Indian subcontinent during the first millennium C.E. The arrow indicates the military campaign into southern India led by King Samudragupta.

 How did the Gupta Empire differ in territorial extent from its great predecessor, the Mauryan Empire?

9-2a The Gupta Dynasty: A New Golden Age?

Historians of India have traditionally viewed the Gupta era as a time of prosperity and thriving commerce with China, Southeast Asia, and the Mediterranean. Great cities rose along the main trade routes throughout the subcontinent, notable for their temples and Buddhist monasteries as well as their economic prosperity. Religious exchanges also prospered as pilgrims from across India and as far away as China came to visit the major religious centers.

As with the Mauryas, much of the trade in the Gupta Empire was managed or regulated by the government. The Guptas owned mines and vast crown lands and earned massive profits from their commercial dealings. But there was also a large private sector dominated by great *jati* (caste) guilds that monopolized key sectors of the economy. A money economy had probably been in operation since the second century B.C.E. when copper and gold coins had been introduced from the Middle East. This, in turn, led to the development of banking. Nevertheless, there are indications that the circulation of coins was limited and that cowrie shells continued to be used for local trade. Chinese missionary Xuan Zang (SHOO-wen ZAHNG), who visited India in the first half of the seventh century, remarked that most commercial transactions were conducted by barter.[1]

But the good fortunes of the Guptas proved to be relatively short-lived. Beginning in the late fifth century C.E., incursions by nomadic warriors from the northwest gradually reduced the power of the empire. Soon northern India was once more divided into myriad small kingdoms engaged in seemingly constant conflict. In the south, however, emerging states like Chola and Pallava prospered from their advantageous position athwart the regional trade network stretching from the Red Sea eastward into Southeast Asia.

9-2b The Transformation of Buddhism

Chinese pilgrims who traveled to India during the Gupta era encountered a Buddhism that had changed in many ways since the time of Siddhartha Gautama. They also found a doctrine that was beginning to decline in popularity in the face of the rise of Hinduism, as the Brahmanical religious beliefs of the Aryan people would eventually be called.

The transformation in Buddhism had come about partly because the earliest written sources were transcribed two centuries after Siddhartha's death and partly because his message was reinterpreted as it became part of people's everyday lives. Abstract concepts of a nirvana that cannot be described began to be replaced, at least in the popular mind, with more concrete visions of heavenly salvation, and Siddhartha was increasingly regarded as a divinity rather than as a sage. As a sign of that transformation, the face of the Buddha began to be displayed in sacred sculptures, along with clear suggestions that, like Jesus, he was of divine birth. The Buddha's teachings that all four classes were equal gave way to the familiar Brahmanical conviction that some people, by reason of previous reincarnations, were closer to nirvana than others.

Theravada These developments led to a split in the movement. Purists emphasized what they insisted were the original teachings of the Buddha, describing themselves as the school of **Theravada** (thay-ruh-VAH-duh), or "the teachings of the elders." Followers of Theravada considered Buddhism a way of life, not a salvationist creed. Theravada stressed the importance of strict attention to personal behavior and the quest for understanding as a means of release from the wheel of life.

Mahayana In the meantime, another interpretation of Buddhist doctrine was emerging in the northwest. Here Buddhist believers, perhaps hoping to compete with other salvationist faiths circulating in the region, began to promote the view that nirvana could be achieved through devotion and not just through painstaking attention to one's behavior. According to advocates of this school, eventually to be known as **Mahayana** (mah-huh-YAH-nuh) ("greater vehicle"), Theravada teachings were too demanding or too strict for ordinary people to follow and therefore favored the wealthy, who were more apt to have the time and resources to spend weeks or months away from their everyday occupations. Mahayana Buddhists referred to their rivals as **Hinayana** (hee-nuh-YAH-nuh), or "lesser vehicle," because in Theravada fewer would reach enlightenment. Mahayana thus attempted to provide hope for the masses in their efforts to reach nirvana; to the followers of Theravada, however, it did so at the expense of insisting on proper behavior.

CHRONOLOGY	Medieval India
Kushan kingdom	ca. 150 B.C.E. – ca. 200 C.E.
Gupta Dynasty	320–600s
Chandragupta I	r. 320 – ca. 335
Samudragupta	r. ca. 335–375
Chandragupta II	r. 375–415
Arrival of Fa Xian in India	ca. 406
Cave temples at Ajanta	Fifth century
Travels of Xuan Zang in India	630–643
Conquest of Sind by Arab armies	ca. 711
Mahmud of Ghazni	r. 997–1030
Delhi sultanate	1206–1527
Invasion of Tamerlane	1398

To advocates of the Mahayana school, salvation could also come from the intercession of a **bodhisattva** (boh-duh-SUT-vuh) ("he who possesses the essence of Buddhahood"). According to Mahayana beliefs, some individuals who had achieved *bodhi* and were thus eligible to enter the state of nirvana after death chose instead, because of their great compassion, to remain on Earth in spirit form to help all human beings achieve release from the life cycle. Followers of Theravada, who believed the concept of bodhisattva applied only to Siddhartha Gautama himself, denounced such ideas as "the teaching of demons." But to their proponents, such ideas extended the hope of salvation to the masses. Mahayana Buddhists revered the saintly individuals who, according to tradition, had become bodhisattvas at death and erected temples in their honor where the local population could pray and render offerings.

A final distinguishing characteristic of Mahayana Buddhism was its reinterpretation of Buddhism as a religion rather than a philosophy. Although Mahayana had philosophical aspects, many of its adherents regarded the Buddha as a divine figure, and an elaborate Buddhist

cosmology developed. Nirvana was not a form of extinction but a true heaven.

Under Kushan rule, Mahayana achieved considerable popularity in northern India, but in the end neither Mahayana nor Theravada was able to retain its popularity in Indian society. By the seventh century C.E., the Buddhist faith had declined rapidly on the subcontinent, although Theravada retained its foothold in Sri Lanka and across the Bay of Bengal in Southeast Asia, where it has remained an influential force to this time (see Map 9.3). Mahayana prospered in the northwest for centuries, but eventually it was supplanted by a revived Hinduism and later by a new arrival, Islam. But Mahayana too would find better fortunes abroad as it was carried over the Silk Road or by sea to China and then to Korea and Japan (see Chapters 10 and 11).

9-2c The Decline of Buddhism in India

Why was Buddhism unable to retain its popularity in its native India even though it became a major force elsewhere in Asia? Some have speculated that in denying

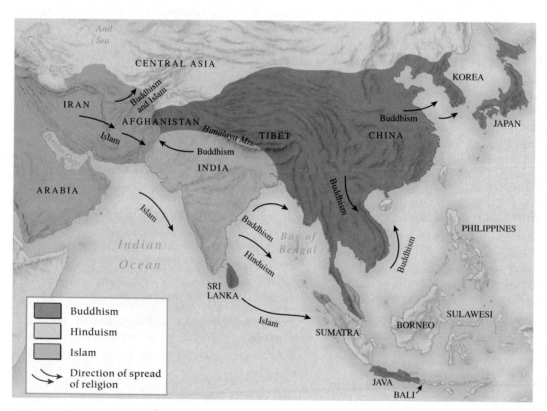

Map 9.3 The Spread of Religions in Southern and Eastern Asia, 600–1400 C.E. Between 600 and 1400 C.E., three of the world's great religions—Buddhism, Hinduism, and Islam—continued to spread from their original sources to different parts of southern and eastern Asia.

Q *Which religion had the greatest impact? How might the existence of major trade routes help explain the spread of these religions?*

The Education of a Brahmin

Religion & Philosophy ALTHOUGH SEVENTH-CENTURY CHINESE TRAVELER XUAN ZANG was a Buddhist, he faithfully recorded his impressions of the Hindu religion in his memoirs. Here he describes the education of a brahmin, the highest class in Indian society. Brahmin youths were educated at what were called *ashramas* (ash-RAHM-uhz), where they received instruction in medicine, science, astronomy, and the Vedas. Their Buddhist counterparts were taught at monasteries, including a famous one at Sarnath, where Siddhartha gave his first sermon.

Xuan Zang, *Records of Western Countries*

The Brahmans study the four *Veda Sastras*. The first is called *Shau* [longevity]; it relates to the preservation of life and the regulation of the natural condition. The second is called *Sse* [sacrifice]; it relates to the [rules of] sacrifice and prayer. The third is called *Ping* [peace or regulation]; it relates to decorum, casting of lots, military affairs, and army regulations. The fourth is called *Shue* [secret mysteries]; it relates to various branches of science, incantations, medicine.

The teachers [of these works] must themselves have closely studied the deep and secret principles they contain, and penetrated to their remotest meaning. They then explain their general sense, and guide their pupils in understanding the words that are difficult. They urge them on and skillfully conduct them. They add luster to their poor knowledge, and stimulate the desponding. If they find that their pupils are satisfied with their acquirements, and so wish to escape to attend to their worldly duties, then they use means to keep them in their power. When they have finished their education, and have attained thirty years of age, then their character is formed and their knowledge ripe. When they have secured an occupation they first of all thank their master for his attention. There are some, deeply versed in antiquity, who devote themselves to elegant studies, and live apart from the world, and retain the simplicity of their character. These rise above mundane presents, and are as insensible to renown as to the contempt of the world. Their name having spread afar, the rulers appreciate them highly, but are unable to draw them to the court. The chief of the country honors them on account of their [mental] gifts, and the people exalt their fame and render them universal homage. . . . They search for wisdom, relying on their own resources. Although they are possessed of large wealth, yet they will wander here and there to seek their subsistence. There are others who, whilst attaching value to letters, will yet without shame consume their fortunes in wandering about for pleasure, neglecting their duties. They squander their substance in costly food and clothing. Having no virtuous principle, and no desire to study, they are brought to disgrace, and their infamy is widely circulated.

 How do the educational practices described here compare with the training provided to young men in other traditional societies in Europe, Asia, and the Americas? What, if anything, was distinctive about the educational system in India?

Source: From Hiuen Tsang, *Si-Yu Ki: Buddhist Records of the Western World*, translated by Samuel Beal (London: Trubner & Co., 1886).

the existence of the soul, Buddhism ran counter to traditional Indian belief. Perhaps, too, one of Buddhism's strengths was also a weakness. In rejecting the class divisions that defined the Indian way of life, Buddhism appealed to those very groups that lacked an accepted place in Indian society—the untouchables, for example. At the same time, it represented a threat to those with a higher status. Moreover, by emphasizing the responsibility of each person to seek an individual path to nirvana, Buddhism undermined the strong social bonds of the Indian class system.

Perhaps a final factor in the decline of Buddhism was the rise of Hinduism. In its early development, Brahmanism had been highly elitist (see Historical Voices, "The Education of a Brahmin," above). Observance of court ritual was not only a monopoly of the brahmin class but also the major route to individual salvation—asceticism—was hardly realistic for the average Indian. In the centuries after the fall of the Mauryas, however, a growing emphasis on devotion—*bhakti* (BAHK-tee)—as a means of religious observance brought the possibility of improving one's karma by means of ritual acts within the reach of

Experience an interactive version of this period in **MINDTAP**

Indians of all classes. It seems likely that Hindu devotionalism rose precisely to combat the inroads of Buddhism and reduce the latter's appeal among the Indian population. The Chinese Buddhist missionary Fa Xian, who visited India in the mid-Gupta era, reported that mutual hostility between the Buddhists and the brahmins was quite strong:

> Leaving the southern gate of the capital city, on the east side of the road is a place where Buddha once dwelt. Whilst here he bit [a piece from] the willow stick and fixed it in the earth; immediately it grew up seven feet high, neither more nor less. The unbelievers and Brahmans, filled with jealousy, cut it down and scattered the leaves far and wide, but yet it always sprang up again in the same place as before.[2]

For awhile, Buddhism was probably able to stave off the Hindu challenge with its own salvationist creed of Mahayana, which also emphasized the role of devotion, but Buddhism's days as a dominant faith in the subcontinent were numbered. By the eighth century C.E., Hindu missionaries spread throughout southern India, where their presence was spearheaded by new temples honoring Shiva in Kanchipuram (KAHN-chee-pur-rum, today Kanchi), the site of a famous Buddhist monastery, and at Mamallapuram (muh-MAH-luh-poor-um) (see Image 9.2).

9.2 Mamallapuram Shore Temple. Mamallapuram ("The City of the Great Warrior") was so named by one of the powerful kings of the Pallavan kingdom on the eastern coast of south India. From this port, ships embarked on naval expeditions to Sri Lanka and far-off destinations in Southeast Asia. Although the site was originally identified with the Hindu deity Vishnu, in the eighth century C.E. a Pallavan monarch built this shore temple in honor of Vishnu's rival deity, Shiva. It stands as a visual confirmation of the revival of the Hindu faith in southern India at the time. Centuries of wind and rain have eroded the ornate carvings that originally covered the large granite blocks.

William J. Duiker

HISTORIANS DEBATE **9-2d When Did the Indians Become Hindus?**

When did Brahmanism—the faith brought to India by the Aryan peoples in the second millennium B.C.E.—evolve into Hinduism, the religion practiced by the majority of the Indian people today? That question has aroused considerable interest among historians of India in recent years. Of course, there is no single precise answer because the issue is partly a matter of definition and the transition was undoubtedly gradual.

Some observers point to the advent of Muslim rule in the northern parts of the subcontinent in the late first millennium C.E. (see Section 9-3, The Arrival of Islam), when the indigenous people, labeled "Hindus" by the new arrivals, began to develop a greater sense of their distinct ethnic and cultural identity. Others point to the colonial era when British policies reinforced an Indian sense of being "the Other," provoking them to rise to the defense of their cultural and historical heritage.

But perhaps the most decisive transition took place during the first millennium C.E. when the Brahmanical emphasis on court sacrifice and asceticism was gradually replaced by a more populist tradition focused on personal worship known as *puja* (POO-juh) and the achievement of individual goals. In that interpretation, the change to a faith more accessible to the masses may initially have been stimulated by the egalitarian tendencies of early Buddhism. In any event, by the end of the first millennium C.E., the religious faith originally known as Brahmanism had fought off the challenges of alternative belief systems while transforming itself into the religion of the majority of the Indian people.

What were the primary characteristics of this new popular religion? In addition to the familiar trinity of gods, all of whom had consorts with readily identifiable roles and personalities, the Hindu pantheon was now inhabited by countless minor deities such as Ganesha (see Image 9.3), each again with his or her own specific function. The rich variety and earthy character of many of these deities is somewhat misleading, however, for Hindus regard the multitude of gods simply as different manifestations of one ultimate reality. The various deities also provide a way for ordinary Indians to personify their religious feelings. Even though some individuals continued to express their piety through the practice of asceticism, most sought to satisfy their own individual religious needs through devotion, which they expressed through ritual ceremonies and

9.3 Ganesha: The God of Good Fortune. One of the best examples of a popular deity in Hindu religious belief is Ganesha, described in Indian literature as a son of the deity Shiva who was accidentally beheaded by his father in a fit of anger. When Shiva repented of his action, he provided his son with the head of an elephant. Beginning in the fourth and fifth centuries C.E., Ganesha became a popular subject of devotion, especially in the state of Maharashtra and the city of Bombay (today Mumbai), where a religious holiday is annually celebrated in his name. Even today, Ganesha is widely revered as the god of good fortune, as well as a patron of the arts and sciences, and his image is regularly approached by wives hoping to give birth to a child.

offerings at a temple. Such offerings were not only a way of seeking salvation but also a means of satisfying all the aspirations of daily life.

9-3 THE ARRIVAL OF ISLAM

 Focus Question: How did Islam arrive in the Indian subcontinent, and why were Muslim peoples able to establish states there?

While India was still undergoing a transition after the collapse of the Gupta Empire, the new and dynamic force of Islam was arising in the Arabian Peninsula. Although Arab merchants had been active along the Indian coasts for

centuries, Arab armies did not reach India until the early eighth century. When Indian pirates attacked Arab shipping near the delta of the Indus River, the Muslim ruler in Mesopotamia demanded an apology from the ruler of Sind (SINNED), a Hindu state in the Indus Valley. When the latter refused, Muslim forces conquered lower Sind in 711 C.E. and then moved northward into the Punjab (pun-JAHB), bringing Arab rule into the frontier regions of the subcontinent for the first time.

9-3a The Empire of Mahmud of Ghazni

For the next three centuries, Islam made no further advances into India. But a second phase began at the end of the tenth century with the rise of the state of Ghazni (GAHZ-nee) in the area of the old Kushan kingdom. The new kingdom was founded in 962 C.E. when Turkic-speaking slaves seized power from the Samanids, a Persian dynasty. When the founder of the new state died in 997, his brilliant and ambitious son, Mahmud (MAHKH-mood) of Ghazni (r. 997–1030), succeeded him. Through sporadic forays against neighboring Hindu kingdoms to the southeast, Mahmud was able to extend his rule throughout the Upper Indus Valley and as far south as the Indian Ocean (see Map 9.4). In wealth and cultural brilliance, his court at Ghazni rivaled that of the Abbasid Dynasty in neighboring Baghdad. But Mahmud was not universally admired. Describing his conquests in northwestern India, the contemporary historian al-Biruni (al-buh-ROO-nee) wrote:

> Mahmud utterly ruined the prosperity of the country, and performed wonderful exploits by which the Hindus became like atoms scattered in all directions, and like a tale of old in the mouth of the people. Their scattered remains cherish, of course, the most inveterate aversion towards all Muslims.[3]

Resistance against the advances of Mahmud and his successors into northern India was led by the Rajputs (RAHJ-pootz), aristocratic Hindu clans who were probably descended from tribal groups that had penetrated into northwestern India from Central Asia in earlier centuries. The Rajputs possessed a strong military tradition and fought bravely, but their military tactics, based on infantry supported by elephants, were no match for the fearsome cavalry of the invaders, whose ability to strike with lightning speed contrasted sharply with the slow-footed forces of their adversaries. Although the power of Ghazni declined after Mahmud's death, a successor state in the area resumed the advance in the late twelfth century; by 1200, Muslim power, in the form of a new Delhi (DEL-ee) sultanate, had been extended over the entire plain of northern India (see Image 9.4).

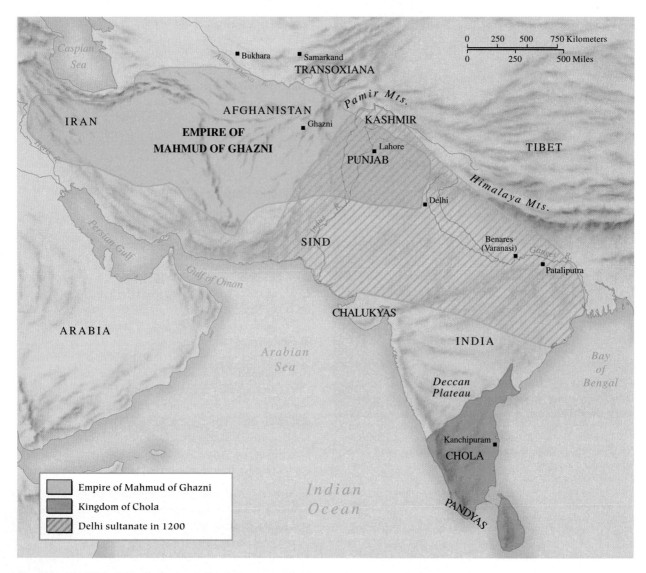

Map 9.4 India, 1000–1200. Beginning in the tenth century, Turkic-speaking peoples invaded northwestern India and introduced Islam to the peoples in the area. Most famous was the empire of Mahmud of Ghazni.

Q *Locate the major trade routes passing through the area. What geographic features explain the location of those routes?*

9-3b The Delhi Sultanate

South of the Ganges River Valley, Muslim influence spread more slowly and had little immediate impact. Muslim traders made some converts along the western coast of India, and Muslim rulers launched occasional forays into the Deccan Plateau, but at first they had little success, even though the area was divided among several warring kingdoms, including the Cholas along the eastern coast and the Pandyas (PUHN-dee-ahz) far to the south.

One reason the Delhi sultanate failed to take advantage of the disarray of its rivals was the threat posed by the Mongols on the northwestern frontier (see Chapter 10). Mongol armies unleashed by great tribal warrior Genghis Khan occupied Baghdad and destroyed the Abbasid caliphate in the 1250s, while other forces occupied the Punjab around Lahore (luh-HOR), from which they threatened Delhi on several occasions. For the next half century, the attention of the sultanate was focused on the Mongols.

That threat finally declined in the early fourteenth century with the gradual breakup of the Mongol Empire. A new Islamic state also emerged as the Tughluq (tug-LUK) Dynasty (1320–1413) extended its power into the Deccan Plateau. In praise of his sovereign, the Tughluq monarch

some contemporary historians, as many as 100,000 Hindu prisoners were massacred before the gates of the city. Such was India's first encounter with Tamerlane (TAM-ur-layn).

9-3c Tamerlane

Tamerlane (ca. 1330s–1405), also known as Timur-i-lang (Timur the Lame), was the ruler of a Mongol khanate based in Samarkand (SAM-ur-kand) to the north of the Pamir (pah-MEER) Mountains. His kingdom had been founded on the ruins of the Mongol Empire, which had begun to disintegrate as a result of succession struggles in the thirteenth century. Of mixed Turko–Mongolian heritage and the son of a local aristocrat, Tamerlane seized power in Samarkand in 1369 and immediately launched a program of conquest. During the 1380s, he brought the entire region east of the Caspian Sea under his authority and then conquered Baghdad and occupied Mesopotamia (see Map 9.5). After his brief foray into northern India, he turned to the west and raided the Anatolian Peninsula. Defeating the army of the Ottoman Turks, he advanced almost as far as the Bosporus before withdrawing. "The last of the great nomadic conquerors," as one recent historian described him, died in 1405 in the midst of a final military campaign (see Image 9.5).

The passing of Tamerlane removed a major menace from the diverse states of the Indian subcontinent. But the respite from external challenge was not long. By the end of the fifteenth century, two new challenges had appeared from

9.4 The Kutub Minar. To commemorate their victory in 1192, the Muslim conquerors of northern India constructed a magnificent mosque on the site of Delhi's largest Hindu temple. Much of the material for the mosque came from twenty-seven local Hindu and Jain shrines. Adjacent to the mosque soars the Kutub Minar (KUH-tub mee-NAHR), symbol of the new conquering faith. Originally 238 feet high, the tower's inscription proclaimed its mission to cast the long shadow of Allah over the realm of the Hindus.

9.5 Samarkand, Gem of the Empire. The city of Samarkand has a long history. Originating during the first millennium B.C.E. as a caravan stop on the Silk Road, it was occupied by Alexander the Great, the Abbasids, and the Mongols before becoming the capital of Tamerlane's expanding empire. Tamerlane expended great sums in creating a city worthy of his imperial ambitions. Shown here is the great square known as the Registan. Site of a mosque, a library, and a Muslim university, all built in the exuberant Persian style, Samarkand was the jumping-off point for trade with China far to the east.

Ala-ud-din (uh-LAH-ud-DEEN), the poet Amir Khusrau (ah-MEER KOOS-roh) exclaimed:

> *Happy be Hindustan, with its splendor of religion,*
> *Where Islamic law enjoys perfect honor and dignity;*
> *In learning Delhi now rivals Bukhara;*
> *Islam has been made manifest by the rulers.*
> *From Ghazni to the very shore of the ocean*
> *You see Islam in its glory.*[4]

Such happiness was not destined to endure, however. During the latter half of the fourteenth century, the Tughluq Dynasty gradually fell into decline. In 1398, a new military force crossed the Indus River from the northwest, raided the capital of Delhi, and then withdrew. According to

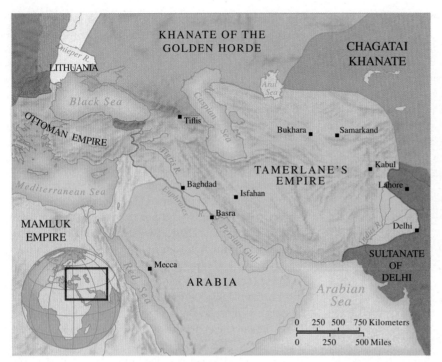

Map 9.5 The Empire of Tamerlane. In the fourteenth century, Tamerlane, a feared conqueror of Mongolian extraction, established a brief empire in Central Asia with his capital at Samarkand.

 Which of the states shown in this map were part of Muslim civilization?

beyond the horizon: the Mughals, a newly emerging nomadic power beyond the Khyber Pass in the north, and Portuguese traders who arrived by sea from the eastern coast of Africa in search of gold and spices. Both, in different ways, would exert a major impact on the later course of Indian civilization.

9-4 SOCIETY AND CULTURE

Focus Questions: What impact did Muslim rule have on Indian society? What are some of the most important cultural achievements of Indian civilization in the era between the Mauryas and the Mughals?

The establishment of Muslim rule over the northern parts of the subcontinent had a significant impact on the society and culture of the Indian people.

9-4a Religion

Like their counterparts in other areas that came under Islamic rule, some Muslim rulers in India were relatively tolerant of other faiths and used peaceful means, if any, to encourage nonbelievers to convert to Islam. Even the more enlightened, however, could be fierce when their religious zeal was aroused. One ruler, on being informed that a Hindu fair had been held near Delhi, ordered the promoters of the event put to death. Hindu temples were razed, and mosques were erected in their place. Eventually, however, most Muslim rulers realized that not all nonbelievers could be converted and recognized the necessity of accepting what to them were alien and repugnant religions. Although Hindu religious practices were generally tolerated, all non-Muslims were compelled to pay a tax to the state. Some probably converted to Islam to avoid the tax, but they were then expected to make the traditional charitable contribution required of Muslims in all Islamic societies.

Over time, millions of Indians did turn to the Muslim faith. Some were individuals or groups in the employ of the Muslim ruling class such as government officials, artisans, or merchants catering to the needs of the court. But many others were probably peasants from the *sudra* class or even untouchables who found in the egalitarian message of Islam a way of removing the stigma of low-class status in the Hindu social hierarchy.

Seldom have two major religions been so strikingly different. Whereas Hinduism tolerated a belief in the existence of several deities (although admittedly they were all considered by some to be manifestations of one supreme god), Islam was uncompromisingly monotheistic. Whereas Hinduism was hierarchical, Islam was egalitarian. Whereas Hinduism featured a priestly class to serve as an intermediary with the ultimate force of the universe, Islam permitted no one to come between believers and their god. Such differences contributed to the mutual hostility that developed between the adherents of the two faiths in the Indian subcontinent, but more mundane issues—such as the Muslim habit of eating beef and the idolatry and sexual frankness in Hindu art—were probably a greater source of antagonism at the popular level.

In other cases, the two peoples borrowed from each other. Some Muslim rulers found the Indian idea of divine kingship appealing. In their turn, Hindu rajas learned by bitter experience the superiority of cavalry mounted on horses instead of elephants, the primary assault weapon in early India.

Some upper-class Hindu males were attracted to the Muslim tradition of *purdah* (PUR-duh or POOR-duh) and began to keep their women in seclusion (termed locally "behind the curtain") from everyday society. All in all, however, Muslim rule probably did not have a significant impact on the lives of most Indian women). *Purdah* was more commonly practiced by the higher classes than by the lower classes. Though it was probably of little consolation, gender relations in poor and lower-class families were relatively egalitarian, with men and women working together on press gangs or in the fields. Muslim customs apparently had little effect on the Hindu tradition of *sati* (suh-TEE). In fact, in many respects, Muslim women had more rights than their Hindu counterparts. They had more property rights than Hindu women and were legally permitted to divorce under certain conditions and to remarry after the death of their husbands. The primary role for Indian women in general, however, was to produce children. Sons were preferred over daughters, not only because they alone could conduct ancestral rites, but also because a daughter was a financial liability. A father had to provide a costly dowry for a daughter when she married, yet after the wedding she would transfer her labor assets to her husband's family. Still, women held a place with men in the Indian religious pantheon. The Hindu female deity known as Devi (DAY-vee) was celebrated by both men and women as the source of cosmic power, a bestower of wishes, and a symbol of fertility.

Overall, the Muslims continued to view themselves as foreign conquerors and generally maintained a strict separation between the Muslim ruling class and the mass of the Hindu population. Although a few Hindus rose to important positions in the local bureaucracy, most high posts in the central government and the provinces were reserved for Muslims.

An exception to this separation was the religion of the Sikhs (SEEKS *or* see-ihks) ("disciples"). Founded by the guru Nanak (NAH-nuhk) in the early sixteenth century in the Punjab, **Sikhism** attempted to integrate the best of the two faiths in a single religion. Sikhism originated in the devotionalist movement in Hinduism, which taught that God was the single true reality. All else is illusion. But Nanak rejected the Hindu tradition of asceticism and mortification of the flesh and, like Muhammad, taught his disciples to participate in the world. Sikhism achieved considerable popularity in northwestern India, where Islam and Hinduism confronted each other directly, and it eventually evolved into a militant faith that fiercely protected its adherents against its two larger rivals. In the end, Sikhism failed to reconcile Hinduism and Islam but did provide an alternative to them.

One complication for both Muslims and Hindus as they tried to come to terms with their mixed society was the problem of class and caste (see Comparative Essay, "Caste, Class, and Family," p. 224). Could non-Hindus form castes, and if so, how were they related to the Hindu castes? The problem was resolved in a pragmatic manner that probably followed an earlier tradition of assimilating non-Hindu tribal groups into the system. Members of the Turkic ruling groups formed social groups that were roughly equivalent to the Hindu brahmin or kshatriya class. Ordinary Indians who converted to Islam also formed Muslim castes, although at a lower level on the social scale. Many who did so were probably artisans who converted en masse to obtain the privileges that conversion could bring. In the south, where Muslim rule was restricted to certain limited areas, the class and caste system was essentially unaffected. One European visitor in the early sixteenth century reported that in Malabar (MAL-uh-bar), along the southwestern coast, there were separate castes for fishing, pottery making, weaving, carpentry and metalworking, salt mining, sorcery, and labor on the plantations. There were separate castes for doing the laundry, one for the elite and the other for the common people.

9-4b Economy and Daily Life

India's landed and commercial elites lived in the cities, often in conditions of considerable opulence. The rulers, of course, possessed the most wealth. One maharaja of a relatively small state in southern India, for example, had more than 100,000 soldiers in his pay along with 900 elephants and 20,000 horses. Another maintained 1,000 high-class women to serve as sweepers of his palace. Each carried a broom and a brass basin containing a mixture of cow dung and water and followed him from one house to another, plastering the path where he was to tread. Most urban dwellers, of course, did not live in such style, although, according to the Chinese Buddhist missionary Xuan Zang, many lived their lives in relative comfort:

> Their houses are surrounded by low walls, and form the suburbs. The earth being soft and muddy, the walls of the towns are mostly built of brick or tiles. The towers on the walls are constructed of wood or bamboo; the houses have balconies and belvederes, which are made of wood, with a coating of lime or mortar, and covered with tiles. The different buildings have the same form as those in China; rushes, or dry branches, or tiles, or boards are used for covering them. The walls are covered with lime and mud, mixed with cow's dung for purity. At different seasons they scatter flowers about. Such are some of their different customs.[5]

Caste, Class, and Family

Family & Society

Why have men and women played such different roles throughout human history? Why have some societies historically adopted the nuclear family, whereas others preferred the joint family or the clan? Such questions are controversial and often arouse vigorous debate, yet they are crucial to our understanding of the human experience.

As we know, the first human beings practiced foraging and hunting, living in small bands composed of one or more lineage groups and moving from place to place in search of sustenance. Individual members of the community were assigned different economic and social roles—usually with men as the hunters and women as the food gatherers—but such roles were not rigidly defined. The concept of private property did not exist, and all members shared the goods possessed by the community according to need.

The agricultural revolution brought about dramatic changes in human social organizations. Although women as food gatherers may have been the first farmers, men—now increasingly deprived of their traditional role as hunters—began to replace them in the fields. As communities gradually adopted a sedentary lifestyle, women were increasingly assigned to domestic tasks in the home while raising the children. As farming communities grew in size and prosperity, vocational specialization and the concept of private property appeared, leading to the family as a legal entity and the emergence of a class system composed of elites, commoners, and slaves. Women were deemed inferior to men and placed in a subordinate status.

This trend toward job specialization and a rigid class system was less developed in pastoral societies, some of which still practiced a nomadic lifestyle and shared communal goods on a roughly equal basis within the community. Even within sedentary societies, there was considerable variety in the nature of social organizations. In some areas, the nuclear family consisted of parents and their dependent children. Other societies, however, adopted (either in theory or in practice) the idea of the joint family (ideally consisting of three generations of a family living under one roof) and sometimes even went a step further, linking several families under the larger grouping of the caste or the clan. Prominent examples of the latter tendency include India and China, although the degree to which reality conformed to these concepts is a matter of debate.

Such large social organizations, where they occurred, often established a rigid hierarchy of status within the community, including the subordination of women. At the same time, they sometimes played a useful role in society, providing a safety net or a ladder of upward mobility for disadvantaged members of the group, as well as a source of stability in societies where legitimate and effective authority at the central level was lacking.

 What were some of the unique aspects of community and family life in traditional India? What do you think accounts for these unique characteristics?

9.6 The Good Life. On the walls of the Buddhist temple of Borobudur are a series of bas-reliefs in stone depicting the path to enlightenment. The lower levels depict the pleasures of the material world. Shown here is a woman of leisure, assisted by her maidservants, at her toilette.

Agriculture The majority of India's population (estimated at slightly more than 100 million in the first millennium C.E.), however, lived on the land. Most were peasants who tilled small plots with a wooden plow pulled by oxen and paid a percentage of the harvest to their landlord. The landlord, in turn, forwarded part of the payment to the local ruler. In effect, the landlord functioned as a tax collector for the king, who retained ultimate ownership of all farmland in his domain. At best, most peasants lived at the subsistence level. At worst, they were forced into debt and fell victim to moneylenders who charged exorbitant rates of interest.

In the north and in the upland regions of the Deccan Plateau, the primary grain crops were wheat and barley. In the Ganges Valley and the southern coastal plains, the main crop was rice. Vegetables were grown everywhere, and southern India produced many spices, fruits, sugarcane, and cotton. Sugarcane was first cultivated in the Indonesian Archipelago, while the cotton plant apparently originated in the Indus River Valley and spread from there. Spices such as cinnamon, pepper, ginger, sandalwood, cardamom, and cumin were also major products.

Foreign Trade Since ancient times, the subcontinent had served as a major entrepôt for trade between the Middle East and the Pacific basin, as well as the source of other goods shipped throughout the known world. Although civil strife and piracy, heavy taxation of the business community by local rulers to finance their fratricidal wars, and increased customs duties between principalities may have contributed to a decline in internal trade, the level of foreign trade remained high, particularly in the kingdoms in the south and along the northwestern coast, which were located along the traditional trade routes to Southeast Asia, the Middle East, and the Mediterranean Sea.

Throughout this period, cotton goods and spices represented the most important export products. Although the knowledge of sugar and cotton products was carried westward by the Arabs, India remained the primary producer of cotton goods into the nineteenth century. Much of this foreign trade was carried on by wealthy Hindu castes with close ties to the royal courts. But there were other participants as well, including such non-Hindu minorities as the Muslims, Jews from the Middle East, the Parsis (PAR-seez), and the Jain community. The Parsis, expatriates from Persia who practiced the Zoroastrian religion, dominated banking and the textile industry in the cities bordering the large salt marsh called the Rann of Kutch (RUN of KUTCH). Later they would become a major economic force in the modern city of Mumbai (Bombay). The Jains became prominent in trade and manufacturing even though their faith emphasized simplicity and the rejection of materialism.

According to early European travelers, merchants often lived quite well. One Portuguese observer described the "Moorish" population in Bengal as follows:

> They have girdles of cloth, and over them silk scarves; they carry in their girdles daggers garnished with silver and gold, according to the rank of the person who carries them; on their fingers many rings set with rich jewels, and cotton turbans on their heads. They are luxurious, eat well and spend freely, and have many other extravagances as well. They bathe often in great tanks which they have in their houses. Everyone has three or four wives or as many as he can maintain. They keep them carefully shut up, and treat them very well, giving them great store of gold, silver and apparel of fine silk.[6]

HISTORIANS DEBATE ### 9-4c The Indian Economy: Promise Unfulfilled?

Outside these relatively small, specialized trading communities, most manufacturing and commerce were in the hands of petty traders and artisans, who were generally limited to local markets. This failure to build on the promise of antiquity has led some historians to ask why India did not produce an expansion of commerce and growth of cities similar to the developments that began in Europe during the High Middle Ages or even in China during the Song Dynasty (see Chapter 10). Some have pointed to the traditionally low status of artisans and merchants in Indian society as symbolized by the comment in the *Arthasastra* that merchants were "thieves that are not called by the name of thief."[7]

More important, perhaps, was the state monopoly on foreign trade in many areas of the country, as well as the impact of the class and caste system, which limited the ability of entrepreneurs to expand their activities and have dealings with other members of the commercial and manufacturing community. Successful artisans, for example, normally could not set up as merchants to market their products, nor could merchants compete for buyers outside their normal area of operations. The complex interlocking relationships among the various classes in a given region were a powerful factor inhibiting the development of a thriving commercial sector in medieval India.

Science and Technology Still, Indian thinkers during this period played an important role in promoting knowledge of the sciences throughout the Eurasian world. The fifth-century astronomer Aryabhata (AHR-yuh-BAH-tuh), for example, accurately calculated the value of pi and measured the length of the solar year

Rock Architecture

Art & Ideas

AS WE HAVE SEEN, ONE OF THE EARLIEST FORMS of religious architecture in India was the rock temple (see Chapter 2). One of the most famous examples is the eighth-century temple at Ellora (e-LAWR-uh), in central India, shown in Image 9.7a. Named after Shiva's holy mountain in the Himalayas, the temple is approximately the size of the Parthenon in Athens but was literally carved out of a hillside, with its exquisite sculptures open to the sky. This form of architecture also found expression in parts of Africa. In 1200 C.E., Christian monks in Ethiopia began to carve a remarkable series of eleven churches out of solid volcanic rock, shown in Image 9.7b. After a forty-foot trench was formed by removing the bedrock, the central block of stone was hewed into the shape of a Greek cross; then it was hollowed out and decorated. These churches, which are still in use today, testify to the fervor of Ethiopian Christianity, which plays a major role in preserving the country's cultural and national identity.

Q *Why do you think some early cultures made frequent use of the concept of rock architecture, while others did not? Why do you think the process was discontinued?*

9.7a

Yvonne V. Duiker

9.7b

Werner Forman/Art Resource, NY

at slightly more than 365 days. Indian writings on astronomy, mathematics, and medicine were influential elsewhere in the region, while—as noted in Chapter 7—the Indian system of numbers, including the concept of zero, was introduced into the Middle East and ultimately replaced the Roman numerals then in use in medieval Europe.

9-4d The Wonder of Indian Culture

The era between the Mauryas and the Mughals in India was a period of cultural evolution as Indian writers and artists built on the literary and artistic achievements of their predecessors. This is not to say that Indian culture rested on its ancient laurels. To the contrary, this was an era of tremendous innovation in all fields of creative endeavor.

Art and Architecture At the end of antiquity and continuing into the first millennium C.E., the primary forms of religious architecture were the Buddhist cave temples and monasteries. These richly decorated caves and temples hewn out of rock remain today among the most impressive achievements of Indian art and architecture. Two of the finest examples are at Ajanta and Ellora in the Deccan Plateau, both of which at various times served the needs of both the Buddhist and Hindu faithful (see Comparative Illustration, "Rock Architecture," above).

The caves at Ajanta (uh-JAHN-tuh) date from the fifth century and consist of ornate pillars, beamed ceilings, and statues of Buddha and bodhisattvas. Several served as monasteries, which had been transformed from simple holes in a wall to large complexes with living apartments, halls, and shrines to the Buddha. The inner surfaces of many of these caves were painted in vivid colors and often portrayed scenes from daily life or descriptions from the life of the Buddha.

By the eighth century, Indian architects began to build their Hindu temples exclusively above ground. Each temple consisted of a central shrine surmounted by a sizable tower, a hall for worshipers, a vestibule, and a porch, all set in a rectangular courtyard that might also contain other minor shrines. Some were so ornate that the sculpture began to dominate the structure itself. The eighth-century shore temple at Mamallapuram (see Image 9.2) is one of the earliest surviving such structures on the subcontinent, but the greatest example of medieval Hindu temple art is probably Khajuraho (khah-joo-RAH-hoh). All of the towers are buttressed at various levels on the sides, giving the whole a sense of unity and creating a vertical movement similar to Mount Kailasa (ky-LAH-suh) in the Himalayas, a site sacred to Hindus. Everywhere the viewer is entertained by voluptuous temple dancers bringing life to the massive structures. One is removing a thorn from her foot, another is applying eye makeup, and yet another is wringing out her hair.

William J. Duiker

9.8 **The Beauty of Sigiriya.** Closely linked to Indian art and culture are a series of surviving paintings at the sixth-century rock fortress at Sigiriya on the island of Sri Lanka. Portraits of dancers and serving girls from the king's harem were painted high up along the cliff wall. Many of these paintings dealt with secular subjects, and therefore were destroyed by Buddhist monks when they returned to the area after the king's death. Thankfully, a few of these graceful, languid maidens—such as the one shown here—were left unharmed to captivate viewers over the centuries.

Literature During this period, Indian authors produced a prodigious number of written works, both religious and secular. Indian religious poetry was written in Sanskrit as well as the languages of southern India. As Hinduism was transformed from a contemplative to a more devotional religion, its poetry became more ardent and erotic and prompted a sense of divine ecstasy. Much of the religious verse extolled the lives and heroic acts of Shiva, Vishnu, Rama, and Krishna by repeating the same themes over and over, which is also a characteristic of Indian art.

The great secular literature of traditional India was also written in Sanskrit in the form of poetry, drama, and prose. One of India's most famous authors, Kalidasa (kah-lee-DAH-suh), lived during the Gupta Dynasty. Although little is known of him, including the dates of his birth and death, he probably wrote for the court of Chandragupta II (r. 375–415 C.E.). Even today Kalidasa's hundred-verse poem, *The Cloud Messenger,*

remains one of the most popular Sanskrit poems. In addition to poetry, Kalidasa wrote three plays, all dramatic romances that blend the erotic with the heroic and the comic. *Shakuntala,* perhaps the best-known play in Indian literature, tells the story of a king who falls in love with the maiden Shakuntala. He asks her to marry him but is suddenly recalled to his kingdom before their wedding. Shakuntala, who is pregnant, goes to him, but the king has been cursed and no longer recognizes her. With the help of the gods, the king eventually recalls their love and is reunited with Shakuntala and their son.

Like poetry, prose developed in India from the Vedic period and was established by the sixth and seventh centuries C.E.—a full millennium before the novel developed in seventeenth-century Europe. One of the greatest masters of Sanskrit prose was Dandin (DUN-din), who lived during the seventh century. In *The Ten Princes,* he created a fantastic world that fuses history and fiction. His keen powers of observation, details of low life, and humor give his writing considerable vitality.

Music Indian music also developed during this era. Ancient Indian music had come from the chanting of the Vedic hymns and thus had a strong metaphysical and spiritual flavor. The actual physical vibrations of particular raga the same way twice. As with jazz music in the West, creativity rather than faithful reproduction is the primary concern.

9-5 THE GOLDEN REGION: EARLY SOUTHEAST ASIA

 Focus Question: What were the main characteristics of Southeast Asian social and economic life, culture, and religion before 1500 C.E.?

Between China and India lies the region that today is called *Southeast Asia*. It has two major components: a mainland region extending southward from the Chinese border to the tip of the Malay Peninsula and an extensive archipelago, most of which is part of present-day Indonesia and the Philippines. Travel among the islands and to regions to the west, north, and east was not difficult, so Southeast Asia has historically served as a vast land bridge for the movement of peoples between China, the Indian subcontinent, and the more than 25,000 islands of the South Pacific. The first arrivals probably appeared as long as 40,000 years ago as part of the initial exodus of *Homo sapiens* from Africa. The final destination for some of these peoples was Australia, where their descendants, known today as *Aborigines*, still live.

Mainland Southeast Asia consists of several north–south mountain ranges separated by river valleys that run in a southerly or southeasterly direction. Much of the population of the region consists of descendants of migrants who came down the valleys from China or Tibet centuries ago in search of new homelands. One of the earliest were **Malayo-Polynesian** (muh-LAY-oh-pah-leh-NEE-zhun) speakers who settled in the southern part of the mainland or on the islands to the south. Then came the Thai (TY) from southwestern China and the Burmese from the Tibetan highlands. Once in Southeast Asia, most of these migrants settled in the fertile deltas of the rivers—the Irrawaddy (ir-uh-WAH-dee) and the Salween (SAL-ween) in Burma, the Chao Phraya (chow PRY-uh) in Thailand, and the Red River and the Mekong (MAY-kahng) in Vietnam—or in lowland areas on the islands to the south.

Although the river valleys facilitated north–south travel on the Southeast Asian mainland, the mountains made movement between east and west relatively difficult. Consequently, the lowland peoples in the river valleys were often isolated from each other and had only limited contacts with upland peoples in the mountains. These geographic barriers may help explain why Southeast Asia is

9.9 Dancing Shiva. From the tenth to the twelfth centuries C.E., the southern kingdom of Chola excelled in the use of the lost-wax technique to make portable bronze statues of Hindu gods. Bathed, clothed, and decorated with flowers, these Chola bronzes were then paraded in religious ceremonies. One of the most numerous and iconic of these bronze deities was the dancing Shiva. As shown here, the statue portrays Shiva performing a cosmic dance in which he simultaneously creates and destroys the universe. While his upper right hand creates the cosmos, his upper left hand reduces it in flames. With his right foot, Shiva crushes the back of the dwarf of ignorance. Shiva's dancing statues visually convey to his followers the message of his power and compassion.

William J. Duiker

music (*nada*) were considered to be related to the spiritual world. An off-key or sloppy rendition of a sacred text could upset the harmony and balance of the entire universe.

In form, Indian classical music is based on a scale called a *raga* (RAH-guh). There are dozens, if not hundreds, of separate scales, which are grouped into separate categories depending on the time of day during which they are to be performed. The performers use a stringed instrument called a *sitar* (si-TAHR) and various types of wind instruments and drums. The performers select a basic raga and then are free to improvise the melodic structure and rhythm. A good performer never performs a

The Kingdom of Angkor

Interaction & Exchange **ANGKOR WAS THE GREATEST KINGDOM** of its time in Southeast Asia. This passage was written in the thirteenth century by Chinese customs inspector Chau Ju-kua (zhow RU-gwah) in the city of Quanzhou (CHWAHN-JOE) (sometimes called *Zaiton*) on the southern coast of China. His account, compiled from reports of seafarers, includes a brief description of the capital city, Angkor Thom, which is still one of the great archaeological sites of the region. Angkor was already in decline when Chau Ju-kua described the kingdom, and the capital was abandoned in 1432.

Chau Ju-kua, *Records of Foreign Nations*

The officials and the common people dwell in houses with sides of bamboo matting and thatched with reeds. Only the king resides in a palace of hewn stone. It has a granite lotus pond of extraordinary beauty with golden bridges, some three hundred odd feet long. The palace buildings are solidly built and richly ornamented. The throne on which the king sits is made of gharu wood and the seven precious substances; the dais is jewelled, with supports of veined wood [possibly ebony]; the screen [behind the throne] is of ivory.

When all the ministers of state have audience, they first make three full prostrations at the foot of the throne; they then kneel and remain thus, with hands crossed on their breasts, in a circle round the king, and discuss the affairs of state. When they have finished, they make another prostration and retire. . . .

[The people] are devout Buddhists. There are serving [in the temples] some three hundred foreign women; they dance and offer food to the Buddha. They are called *a-nan* or slave dancing girls.

As to their customs, lewdness is not considered criminal; theft is punished by cutting off a hand and a foot and by branding on the chest.

The incantations of the Buddhist and Taoist priests [of this country] have magical powers. Among the former those who wear yellow robes may marry, while those who dress in red lead ascetic lives in temples. The Taoists clothe themselves with leaves; they have a deity called P'o-to-li which they worship with great devotion.

[The people of this country] hold the right hand to be clean, the left unclean, so when they wish to mix their rice with any kind of meat broth, they use the right hand to do so and also to eat with.

The soil is rich and loamy; the fields have no bounds. Each one takes as much as he can cultivate. Rice and cereals are cheap; for every tael [1.3 ounces] of lead one can buy two bushels of rice.

The native products comprise elephants' tusks, the *chan* and *su* [varieties of gharu wood], good yellow wax, kingfisher's feathers, . . . resin, foreign oils, ginger peel, goldcolored incense, . . . raw silk and cotton fabrics.

The foreign traders offer in exchange for these gold, silver, porcelainware, sugar, preserves, and vinegar.

 Because of the paucity of written records about Angkor society, documents such as this one from a Chinese source are important for the knowledge they provide about local conditions. What does this excerpt tell us about the political system, religious beliefs, and land use in thirteenth-century Angkor?

Source: Excerpt from Chau Ju-kua: *His Work on the Chinese and Arab Trade in the Twelfth and Thirteenth Centuries*, entitled *Chu-fan-chi*, Friedrich Hirth and W. W. Rockhill, eds., copyright © 1966 by Paragon Reprint.

---

one of the few regions in Asia that was never unified under a single government.

9-5a Paddy Fields and Spices: The States of Southeast Asia

The first states of Southeast Asia began gradually to emerge in the first millennium C.E. and can be broadly divided between agricultural and trading societies. Whereas the trading societies were located on the trade routes that crisscrossed the region, the agricultural societies—notably,

Vietnam, Thailand, Angkor (AN-kor) in what is now Cambodia, and the Burmese state of Pagan (puh-GAHN)— were situated in fertile river deltas that were conducive to the development of a wet rice economy (see Map 9.6). Although all produced some goods for regional markets, these mainland societies were not situated in areas that naturally produced large quantities of export goods such as spices and other tropical products. As a result, they were not tempted to turn to commerce as the prime source of national income. The emerging societies on the Malay Peninsula and the Indonesian archipelago, on the other

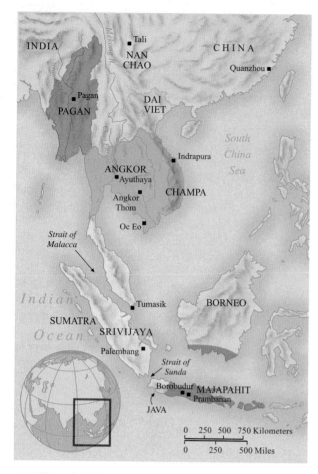

Map 9.6 Southeast Asia in the Thirteenth Century. This map shows the major states that arose in Southeast Asia after 1000 C.E. Some, like Angkor and Dai Viet, were predominantly agricultural. Others, like Srivijaya and Champa, were commercial.

 How did geography influence whether states were primarily agricultural or commercial?

hand, not only were rich in the highly desired spices and aromatic woods so fervently prized in regional markets but also located at the nexus of trade routes stretching between the South China Sea and the Indian Ocean. As a result, they soon became actively involved in the regional trade that passed between China and the Indian subcontinent.

The Mainland States The first major state in the region was the kingdom of Funan (FOO-nan), which arose in the fertile valley of the Lower Mekong River in the second century C.E. At that time, much of the regional trade between India and the South China Sea moved across the narrow neck of the Malay Peninsula. With access to copper, tin, and iron, as well as a variety of tropical agricultural products, Funan played an active role in this process. When trade began to pass through the Strait of Malacca

(muh-LAK-uh) in the fifth century, Funan declined and was eventually replaced by the great kingdom of Angkor.

Angkor was the most powerful state to emerge in mainland Southeast Asia before the sixteenth century (see Historical Voices, "The Kingdom of Angkor," p. 229). The remains of its capital city, Angkor Thom (AN-kor TOHM), give a sense of the magnificence of Angkor civilization. The city formed a square two miles on each side. Its massive stone walls were several feet thick and were surrounded by a moat. Four main gates led into the city, which at its height had a substantial population, much of it located in suburban areas outside the extensive city wall. The wealth of Angkor was based on both agriculture and trade, although it heavily depended on the cultivation of wet rice, which had been introduced to the Mekong River Valley from China in the third millennium B.C.E. Other products were honey, textiles, fish, and salt. By the fourteenth century, however, Angkor had begun to decline, a product of drought, incessant wars with its neighbors, and the silting of its irrigation system. In 1432, Angkor Thom was destroyed by the Thai, who had migrated into the region from southwestern China in the thirteenth century and established their capital at Ayuthaya (ah-yoo-TY-yuh) in lower Thailand in 1351.

As the Thai expanded southward, however, their main competition came from the west, where the Burmese peoples had formed their own agricultural society in the valleys of the Salween and Irrawaddy Rivers. Like the Thai, they were relatively recent arrivals in the area, having migrated southward from the highlands of Tibet beginning in the seventh century C.E. After subjugating weaker societies already living in the area, in the eleventh century they founded the first great Burmese state, the kingdom of Pagan. Like the Thai, they quickly converted to Buddhism and adopted Indian political institutions and culture. For awhile, they were a major force in the western part of Southeast Asia, but attacks from the Mongols in the late thirteenth century (see Chapter 10) weakened Pagan, and the resulting vacuum may have benefited the Thai as they moved into areas occupied by Burmese migrants in the Chao Phraya Valley.

The Malay World In the Malay Peninsula and the Indonesian Archipelago, a different pattern emerged. For centuries, this area had been linked to regional trade networks; as long-distance shipping gradually became more commonplace, much of its wealth came from the export of tropical products to China, India, and the Middle East. Because the river valleys in the archipelago were generally shorter, the emerging polities in the region tended to be smaller and more decentralized than on the mainland. Nevertheless, the Malay people living in the region were

William J. Duiker

9.10 Rice Culture in Southeast Asia. Rice was first cultivated in southern Asia 7,000 to 8,000 years ago. It is a labor-intensive crop that requires many workers to plant the seedlings and organize the distribution of water. Initially, the fields are flooded to facilitate the rooting of the rice seedlings and to add nutrients to the soil. In this photograph, workers are performing the backbreaking task of transplanting rice seedlings in a flooded field in modern Vietnam. The significance of rice in Southeast Asia is reflected in the fact that all cultures in the region have traditionally venerated its sacred nature by creating elaborate rituals in honor of the rice goddess. In Indonesia, the worship of Dewi Sri has long been essential to ensure a good harvest.

active seafarers, and as the trade networks expanded, the islands of the Indonesian Archipelago eventually gave rise to two of the region's most notable trading societies— Srivijaya (sree-vih-JAH-yuh) on the island of Sumatra, and the Javanese kingdom of Majapahit (mah-jah-PAH-hit). Both were based in large part on the spice trade.

As the wealth of China, the Arab Empire, and then of Europe increased, so did the demand for the products of Southeast Asia. Merchant fleets from China, India, and the Arabian Peninsula sailed to the Indonesian islands to buy cloves, pepper, nutmeg, cinnamon, precious woods, and other exotic products coveted by the wealthy. In the eighth century, Srivijaya, which had been established along the eastern coast of Sumatra around 670, became a powerful commercial state that dominated the trade route passing through the Strait of Malacca, at that time the most convenient route from East Asia into the Indian Ocean. The rulers of Srivijaya had helped bring the route to prominence by controlling the pirates who had previously preyed on shipping in the strait. Another inducement was Srivijaya's capital at Palembang (pah-lem-BAHNG), a deepwater port where sailors could wait out the change in the monsoon season before making their return voyage. In 1025, however, Chola, one of the kingdoms of southern India and a commercial rival of Srivijaya, inflicted a devastating defeat on the island kingdom. Although Srivijaya survived, it was unable to regain its former dominance, in part because the main trade route had shifted to the east through the Strait of Sunda (SOON-duh) and directly out into the Indian

Ocean. In the late thirteenth century, this shift in trade patterns led to the founding of a new kingdom of Majapahit on the island of Java. In the mid-fourteenth century, Majapahit succeeded in uniting most of the archipelago and perhaps even part of the Southeast Asian mainland under its rule.

The Role of China and India Given Southeast Asia's location between China and India, it is not surprising that both of these major civilizations influenced developments in the region. In 111 B.C.E., the young Vietnamese kingdom was conquered by the Han Dynasty and remained under Chinese control for more than a millennium (we will discuss these events in Chapter 10). Other parts of the region were exposed to varying degrees of Chinese influence, depending on the importance of their trade relations with the Celestial Empire.

For their part, the Indian states never exerted much political control over Southeast Asia, but their influence was pervasive nevertheless. The first contacts had taken place by the fourth century B.C.E. when Indian merchants began sailing to Southeast Asia; they were soon followed by Buddhist and Hindu missionaries. Indian influence can be seen in many aspects of Southeast Asian culture from political institutions to religion, architecture, language, and literature. Basing themselves on south Indian models, Southeast Asian rulers began to claim to possess special godlike qualities that set them apart from their subjects. In societies such as Angkor and Pagan, some division of the population into separate classes based on occupation and ethnic background (called *varna* in imitation of the Indian model) seems to have occurred, although with less rigidity than the Indian class system.

India also supplied Southeast Asians with a writing system. The societies of the region had no written scripts for their spoken languages before the arrival of the Indian merchants and missionaries. Indian phonetic symbols were borrowed and used to record the spoken language. Initially, Southeast Asian literature was written in the Indian Sanskrit but eventually came to be written in the local languages. Southeast Asian authors borrowed popular Indian themes such as stories from the Buddhist scriptures and tales from the *Ramayana*.

Local forms of cultural expression, however, were never totally abandoned. A popular form of entertainment among the common people, the *wayang kulit* (WAH-yahng KOO-lit), or shadow play, may have come originally from India or possibly China, but it became a distinctive art form

9.11 Angkor Wat. The Khmer (kuh-MEER) rulers of Angkor constructed many remarkable temples and palaces. Devised as either Hindu or Buddhist shrines, the temples also reflected the power and sanctity of the king. This twelfth-century temple known as Angkor Wat is renowned both for its spectacular architecture and the thousands of fine bas-reliefs relating Hindu legends and Khmer history. Most memorable are the heavenly dancing maidens and the royal processions with elephants and soldiers.

William J. Duiker

in Java and other islands of the Indonesian Archipelago. In a shadow play, flat leather puppets were manipulated behind an illuminated screen while the narrator recited tales from the Indian classics. The plays were often accompanied by a *gamelan* (GA-muh-lan), an orchestra composed primarily of percussion instruments such as gongs and drums that apparently originated in Java.

CHRONOLOGY	Early Southeast Asia
Chinese conquest of Vietnam	111 B.C.E.
Arrival of Burmese peoples	ca. Seventh century C.E.
Formation of Srivijaya	ca. 670
Construction of Borobudur	ca. Eighth century
Creation of Angkor kingdom	ca. Ninth century
Thai migrations into Southeast Asia	ca. Thirteenth century
Rise of Majapahit Empire	Late thirteenth century
Fall of Angkor kingdom	1432

9-5b Daily Life

Because of the diversity of ethnic backgrounds, religions, and cultures, making generalizations about daily life in Southeast Asia during the early historical period is as difficult as it is for Africa.

Social Structures In general, Southeast Asian societies were somewhat more egalitarian and less hierarchical than in neighboring regions, and the rigid social distinctions that prevailed in India were less deeply rooted. For example, although peoples in societies such as Angkor and Pagan were classified according to a variety of economic functions, the dividing lines between classes were not as rigid as they were in the Indian subcontinent.

Still, traditional societies in Southeast Asia, especially on the mainland, exhibited clearly hierarchical characteristics. At the top of the social ladder were the hereditary aristocrats, who monopolized both political power and economic wealth and enjoyed a borrowed aura of charisma by virtue of their proximity to the ruler. Some elites lived in the capital, which was the main source of power, wealth, and foreign influence in the country. Others lived outside the major cities, where they were responsible for maintaining public order and forwarding taxes to the central government. Some regional elites possessed family ties to the royal family, and others were local potentates who possessed their own power base and whose loyalty to the ruling dynasty was contingent on benefits received.

Below the elite classes lived the mass of the population—farmers, fishers, artisans, and merchants. In most mainland societies, the vast majority were probably rice farmers living at a bare subsistence level and paying rents or taxes to a landlord or a local ruler. Some were considered free subjects of the king, whereas others were indentured to a higher official with ties to the central government. Few of them were actively engaged in commerce except as consumers of various necessities.

In the Malay world, social relations were generally less formal. Most of the people in the region, whether engaged in farming, fishing, or handicrafts, lived in small *kampongs* (KAHM-pahngs) (Malay for "villages") in wooden houses built on stilts to avoid flooding during the monsoon season. Some farmers were probably sharecroppers who paid a part of their harvest to a landlord, but the tradition of free farming was strong. Unlike the situation in the mainland states, many were involved in growing or mining products for export such as tropical food products, precious woods, tin, and gems. Most regional trade was carried on by local merchants who purchased products from local growers and then transported them to the major port cities (see Historical Voices, "Chinese Traders in the Philippines," p. 234). During the early state-building era, roads were few and relatively primitive, so most of the trade was transported down rivers to the major ports along the coast. There the goods were loaded onto larger ships for delivery outside the region. Growers of export goods in areas near the coast were thus indirectly involved in the regional trade network but received few economic benefits from the relationship.

Women and the Family The women of Southeast Asia during this era have been described as the most fortunate in the world. Although most women worked side by side with men in the fields, Southeast Asian women also often actively engaged in trading activities just like their African counterparts. This not only led to a higher literacy rate among women than among men but also allowed them more financial independence than their counterparts in China and India, a fact that was noticed by Chinese traveler Zhou Daguan (JOE dah-GWAHN) at the end of the thirteenth century: "In Cambodia it is the women who take charge of trade. For this reason a Chinese arriving in the country loses no time in getting himself a mate, for he will find her commercial instincts a great asset."[8]

One reason for the enhanced status of women in traditional Southeast Asia is that the nuclear family was more common than the joint family system prevalent in China and the Indian subcontinent. Throughout the region, wealth in marriage was passed from the male to the female in contrast to the dowry system used in China and India. Most societies usually did not put a high value on virginity in brokering a marriage, and divorce proceedings could be initiated by either party. Still, most marriages were monogamous, and marital fidelity was taken seriously.

The relative availability of cultivable land in the region may help explain the absence of joint families. Joint families under patriarchal leadership tend to be found in areas where land is scarce and individual families must work together to conserve resources and maximize income. With the exception of a few crowded river valleys, few areas in Southeast Asia had a high population density. Throughout most of the area, water was plentiful, and the land was relatively fertile.

9-5c World of the Spirits: Religious Belief

Indian religions had a profound effect on Southeast Asia. Traditional religious beliefs in the region took the familiar form of spirit worship and animism that we have seen in other cultures. Southeast Asians believed that spirits dwelled in the mountains, rivers, streams, and other sacred places in their environment. Mountains were particularly sacred because they were considered to be the abode of ancestral spirits, the place to which the souls of all the departed would retire after death.

When Hindu and Buddhist ideas began to penetrate into mainland Southeast Asia early in the first millennium C.E., they exerted a strong appeal among local elites. The new doctrines not only offered a more convincing explanation of the nature of the cosmos but also provided local rulers with a means of enhancing their prestige and power and conferred an aura of legitimacy on their relations with their subjects. In Angkor, the king's duties included performing sacred rituals at Angkor Wat (AN-kor WHAT), the impressive mountain temple in the capital city; in time, the ritual became a state cult uniting Hindu gods with local nature deities and ancestral spirits in a complex pantheon.

This state cult, financed by the royal court, eventually led to the construction of temples throughout the country. Many of these temples housed thousands of priests and retainers and amassed great wealth, including vast estates farmed by local peasants. An estimated 300,000 priests may have lived in Angkor at the height of its power. This vast wealth, which was often exempt from taxes, may be one explanation for the gradual decline of Angkor in the thirteenth and fourteenth centuries.

Chinese Traders in the Philippines

Interaction & Exchange

FROM EARLY TIMES, the peoples living in the islands south of the East Asian mainland played an active role in the regional trade network between the Chinese coast and the Indian Ocean. This excerpt from a thirteenth-century Chinese account describes the nature of the commercial exchanges that took place between Chinese merchants and the indigenous population in the Philippine Islands. The author of the account, Chau Ju-kua, was a superintendent of trade in South China. His description of the indigenous peoples in the Philippines is one of the few sources on such communities before the arrival of European ships in the sixteenth century.

A Description of Barbarian Peoples

The country of Ma-i [Philippine Archipelago] is to the north of P'o-ni [Borneo]. Over a thousand families are settled together along both banks of a creek (or, gully). The natives cover themselves with a sheet of cotton cloth, or hide the lower part of the body with a loincloth.

There are bronze images of gods, of unknown origin, scattered about in the grassy wilderness. Pirates seldom come to this country.

When trading ships enter the anchorage, they stop in front of the officials' place, for that is the place for bartering of the country. After a ship has been boarded, the natives mix freely with the ship's folk. The chiefs are in the habit of using white umbrellas, for which reason the traders offer them as gifts.

The custom of the trade is for the savage traders to assemble in crowds and carry the goods away with them in baskets; and, even if one cannot at first know them, and can but slowly distinguish the men who remove the goods, there will yet be no loss. The savage traders will after this carry these goods on to other islands for barter, and, as a rule, it takes them as much as eight or nine months till they return, when they repay the traders on shipboard with what they have obtained (for the goods). Some, however, do not return within the proper term, for which reason vessels trading with Ma-i are the latest in reaching home. . . .

The products of the country consist of yellow wax, cotton, pearls, tortoise-shell, medicinal betel-nuts and yü-ta cloth [abaca textiles]; and (the foreign) traders barter for these porcelain, trade-gold, iron censers, lead, coloured glass beads, and iron needles. . . .

The San-sü (or "Three Islands"), belong to the Ma-i; their names are Kia-ma-yen [Calamián Island Group between Mindoro and Palawan], Pa-lau-yu [Palawan], and Pa-ki-nung [Busuanga Island, largest of the Calamián Islands], and each has its own tribes scattered over the islands. When ships arrive there, the natives come out to trade with them; the generic name (of these islands) is San-sü.

Their local customs are about the same as those of Ma-i. Each tribe consists of about a thousand families. The country contains many lofty ridges, and ranges of cliffs rise steep as the walls of a house.

The natives build wattled huts perched in lofty and dangerous spots, and since the hills contain no springs, the women may be seen carrying on their heads two or three jars one above the other in which they fetch water from the streams, and with their burdens mount the hills with the same ease as if they were walking on level ground. . . .

Whenever foreign traders arrive at any of the settlements, they live on board ship before venturing to go on shore, their ships being moored in mid-stream, announcing their presence to the natives by beating drums. Upon this the savage traders race for the ship in small boats, carrying cotton, yellow wax, native cloth, cocoanut-heart mats, which they offer for barter. If the prices (of goods they may wish to purchase) cannot be agreed upon, the chief of the (local) traders must go in person, in order to come to an understanding, which being reached the natives are offered presents of silk umbrellas, porcelain, and rattan baskets; but the foreigners still retain on board one or two (natives) as hostages. After that they go on shore to traffic, which being ended they return the hostages. A ship will not remain at anchor longer than three or four days, after which it proceeds to another place; for the savage settlements along the coast of San-sü are not connected by a common jurisdiction (i.e., are all independent).

 How does the trading process take place in this account? How does each side seek to guarantee satisfaction?

Source: From *Chau Ju-kua: His Work on the Chinese and Arab Trade in the Twelfth and Thirteenth Centuries, entitled Chu-fan-chi,* trans. F. Hirth and W. W. Rockhill (St. Petersburg: Printing Office of the Imperial Academy of Sciences, 1911), pp. 159–162.

Hindu and Buddhist missionaries from the Indian subcontinent penetrated into island Southeast Asia as well. Temple architecture reflecting Gupta or southern Indian styles began to appear in the Indonesian Archipelago during the first centuries C.E. Most famous is the Buddhist temple at Borobudur (boh-roh-buh-DOOR) in central Java. Begun in the late eighth century at the behest of a king of Sailendra (SY-len-druh), an agricultural kingdom in the area, Borobudur is a massive stupa with nine terraces surmounted by hollow bell-like towers containing representations of the Buddha in various stages of his existence and capped by a single stupa. Even today, the structure dominates the landscape for miles around.

Initially, the spread of Hindu and Buddhist doctrines took place primarily among the elite. Although the common people were expected to participate in the state cult and helped construct the temples, they retained their traditional beliefs in local deities and ancestral spirits. A major transformation began in the eleventh century, however, when Theravada Buddhism began to penetrate the kingdom of Pagan in mainland Southeast Asia from the island of Sri Lanka. From Pagan, it spread rapidly to other areas in Southeast Asia, where its appeal to the local population is reminiscent of the original attraction of Buddhist thought centuries earlier on the Indian subcontinent. By teaching that individuals could seek nirvana through their own actions rather than through the intercession of the ruler or a priest, Theravada was more accessible to the masses than the state cults promoted by the rulers. During the next centuries, Theravada gradually undermined the influence of state-supported religions and became the

9.12 The Temple of Borobudur. The colossal pyramid temple at Borobudur on the island of Java is one of the greatest Buddhist monuments in the world. Constructed in the eighth century C.E., it depicts the path to spiritual enlightenment in stone. Sculptures and relief portrayals of the life of the Buddha at the lower level depict the world of desire. At higher elevations, they give way to empty bell towers (see the inset) and culminate at the summit with an empty and closed stupa, signifying the state of nirvana. Shortly after it was built, Borobudur was abandoned when a new ruler switched his allegiance to Hinduism and ordered the erection of the Hindu temple of Prambanan nearby. Buried for a thousand years under volcanic ash and jungle, Borobudur was rediscovered in the nineteenth century and has recently been restored to its former splendor.

dominant faith in several mainland societies, including Burma, Thailand, Laos, and Cambodia.

Theravada did not penetrate far into the Malay Peninsula or the Indonesian island chain, however, perhaps because it entered Southeast Asia through Burma farther to the north. But the Malay world found its own popular alternative to state religions when Islam began to enter the area through the arrival of merchants from India and the Middle East in the thirteenth and fourteenth centuries. Because Muslim expansion into Southeast Asia took place for the most part after 1500, its emergence as a major force in the region will be discussed in a later chapter.

9-5d Expansion into the Pacific

One of the great maritime feats of human history was the penetration of the islands of the Pacific Ocean by Malayo-Polynesian–speaking peoples. By 2000 B.C.E., these seafarers had migrated as far as the Bismarck Archipelago northeast of the island of New Guinea, where they encountered Melanesian peoples whose ancestors had taken part in the first wave of human settlement into the region 30,000 years earlier.

From there, the Polynesian peoples—as they are now familiarly known—continued their explorations eastward in large sailing canoes up to 100 feet long that carried more than forty people and many of their food staples such as chickens, chili peppers, and a tuber called *taro*, the source of the Hawaiian dish poi. Stopping in Fiji, Samoa, and the Cook Islands during the first millennium C.E., their descendants pressed onward, eventually reaching Tahiti, Hawai'i, and even Easter Island, one of the most remote sites of human habitation in the world. Eventually, one group of Polynesians, now known as the Maori (MAU-ree), sailed southwestward from the island of Rarotonga and settled in New Zealand, around 1,000 miles from Australia's southeast coast. The final frontier of human settlement had been breached.

William J. Duiker

9.13 Giant Heads of Easter Island. When the Malayo-Polynesian–speaking peoples spread out from their homeland into the islands of the Pacific, they eventually settled in areas as distant as Hawaii and Easter Island. Some of these peoples first arrived on Easter Island in the fifth century C.E. and soon began to erect giant stone statues. It is thought that they were erected by rival chiefdoms for reasons of prestige. Some scholars estimate that the process of moving the statues from the quarry (shown here) by rolling them on a bed of rounded logs eventually devastated the forests and caused the total erosion of the landscape. As a result, almost the entire population was wiped out.

During the more than 1,500 years from the fall of the Mauryas to the rise of the Mughals, Indian civilization faced many severe challenges. One challenge was primarily external and took the form of a continuous threat from beyond the mountains in the northwest. As a result of the foreign conquest of northern India, Islam was introduced into the region. The new religion soon became a serious rival to traditional beliefs among the people of India. Another challenge had internal causes, stemming from the tradition of factionalism and internal rivalry that had marked relations within the aristocracy since the Aryan influx in the second millennium B.C.E. (see Chapter 2). Despite the abortive efforts of the Guptas, that tradition continued almost without interruption down to the founding of the Mughal Empire in the sixteenth century.

During the same period that Indian civilization faced these challenges at home, it was profoundly affecting the emerging states of Southeast Asia. Situated at the crossroads between two oceans and two great civilizations, Southeast Asia has long served as a bridge linking peoples and cultures, and as complex societies began to develop in the area, it is not surprising that they were strongly influenced by the older civilizations of neighboring China and India. At the same time, the Southeast Asian peoples put their own unique stamp on the ideas that they adopted and eventually rejected those that were inappropriate to local conditions.

The result was a region characterized by an almost unparalleled cultural richness and diversity, reflecting influences from as far away as the Middle East yet preserving indigenous elements that were deeply rooted in the local culture. Unfortunately, that very diversity posed potential problems for the peoples of Southeast Asia as they faced a new challenge from beyond the horizon. We shall deal with that challenge when we return to the region later in the book. In the meantime, we must turn our attention to the other major civilization that spread its shadow over the societies of southern Asia—China.

REFLECTION QUESTIONS

Q How does the religion known today as Hinduism compare in its essential respects with the Brahmanical faith from which it emerged in the first millennium C.E.? What may explain the differences?

Q The Indian social system has been characterized by the existence of extensive lineage groups—known as *jati*—that are larger than the traditional joint and nuclear families found in many other societies. What are the most prominent features of such lineage groups, and why have they endured for so long in Indian society?

Q Many of the states that were formed in Southeast Asia during the first millennium C.E. absorbed strong influences from merchants and missionaries arriving from India. What political, social, and religious characteristics of Indian civilization were adopted by the indigenous states in Southeast Asia, and how were they applied in their new environment?

CHAPTER TIMELINE

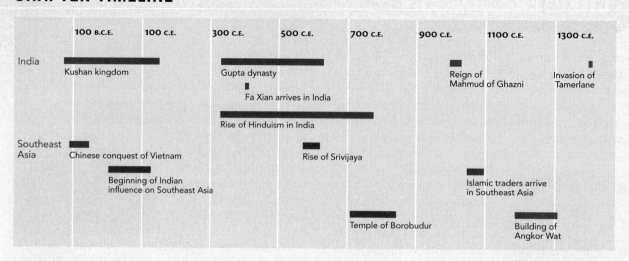

	100 B.C.E.	100 C.E.	300 C.E.	500 C.E.	700 C.E.	900 C.E.	1100 C.E.	1300 C.E.

India
Kushan kingdom
Gupta dynasty
Fa Xian arrives in India
Rise of Hinduism in India
Reign of Mahmud of Ghazni
Invasion of Tamerlane

Southeast Asia
Chinese conquest of Vietnam
Beginning of Indian influence on Southeast Asia
Rise of Srivijaya
Islamic traders arrive in Southeast Asia
Temple of Borobudur
Building of Angkor Wat

CHAPTER NOTES

1. Hiuen Tsiang, *Si-Yu-Ki: Buddhist Records of the Western World*, trans. S. Beal (London, 1982), pp. 89–90.
2. "Fo-Kwo-Ki" (Travels of Fa Xian), ch. 20, p. 43, in ibid.
3. E. C. Sachau, *Alberoni's India*, vol. 1 (London, 1914), p. 22.
4. Quoted in S. M. Ikram, *Muslim Civilization in India* (New York, 1964), p. 68.
5. Hiuen Tsiang, *Si-Yu-Ki*, pp. 73–74.
6. D. Barbosa, *The Book of Duarte Barbosa* (Nedeln, Liechtenstein, 1967), pp. 147–148.
7. Quoted in R. Lannoy, *The Speaking Tree: A Study of Indian Culture and Society* (London, 1971), p. 232.
8. Quoted in S. Hughes and B. Hughes, *Women in World History*, vol. 1 (Armonk, N.Y., 1995), p. 217.

MindTap® is a fully online, highly personalized learning experience built upon Cengage Learning content. MindTap combines student learning tools—readings, multimedia, activities, and assessments—into a singular Learning Path that guides students through the course and helps students develop the critical thinking, analysis, and communication skills that are essential to academic and professional success.

Chapter Outline and Focus Questions

Werner Forman/Art Resource, NY

10.1 Detail of a Chinese Scroll, "Going Up the River at the Spring Festival"

Critical Thinking

Q *The civilization of ancient China fell under the onslaught of nomadic invasions, as did some of its counterparts elsewhere in the world. But China, unlike other ancient empires, was later able to reconstitute itself on the same political and cultural foundations. How do you account for the difference?*

Connections to Today

Q *The Comparative Essay "The Spread of Technology" in this chapter suggests that active participation in the global trade network helped medieval societies compete more effectively in the international marketplace. Do you feel that this argument could be made about societies today?*

Experience an interactive version of this period in ⊹ MINDTAP

ON HIS FIRST VISIT to the city, the traveler was mightily impressed. Its streets were so straight and wide that he could see through the city from one end to the other. Along the wide boulevards were beautiful palaces and inns in great profusion. The city was laid out in squares like a chessboard, and within each square were spacious courts and gardens. Truly, said the visitor, this must be one of the largest and wealthiest cities on Earth—a city "planned out to a degree of precision and beauty impossible to describe."[1]

The visitor was Marco Polo (MAR-koh POH-loh), and the city was Khanbaliq (kahn-bah-LEEK) (later known as Beijing), capital of the Yuan (YOO-enn or YWAHN) Dynasty (1279–1368) and one of the great urban centers of the Chinese empire. Marco Polo was an Italian merchant who had traveled to China in the late thirteenth century and then served as an official at the court of Khubilai Khan (KOO-blah KAHN).

Polo's diary, published almost twenty years after his return to Italy, astonished readers with tales of this magnificent but unknown civilization far to the east. In fact, many of his European contemporaries were skeptical and suspected that he was a charlatan seeking to win fame and fortune with a fictional account of his travels to fantastic lands.

Readers of Marco Polo's memoirs in other parts of the world, however, undoubtedly would have found his account of the wonders of the East more credible because evidence of the greatness of the Chinese empire was all around them. Indeed, after the decline of the Abbasids in the eleventh and twelfth centuries, China had clearly emerged as the richest and most powerful empire on the Eurasian supercontinent.

10-1 CHINA'S GOLDEN AGE: THE SUI, THE TANG, AND THE SONG

 Focus Questions: What major changes in political structures and social and economic life occurred during the Sui, Tang, and Song Dynasties? To what degree do these changes compare with contemporary events in India and the Middle East?

After the collapse of the Han Dynasty at the beginning of the third century C.E., China fell into an extended period of division and civil war. Taking advantage of the absence of organized government in China, nomadic forces from the Gobi Desert penetrated south of the Great Wall and established their own rule over northern China. In the Yangzi Valley and farther to the south, native Chinese rule was

maintained, but the constant civil war and instability led later historians to refer to the period as the "era of the six dynasties."

10-1a A Time of Troubles: China after the Han

The collapse of the Han Empire was marked by the rise of several squabbling independent regimes throughout the region and had a marked effect on the Chinese psyche. The Confucian principles that emphasized hard work, subordination of the individual to community interests, and belief in the essentially rational order of the universe came under severe challenge, and many Chinese intellectuals began to reject the stuffy moralism and complacency of State Confucianism as they sought emotional satisfaction in hedonistic pursuits or philosophical Daoism.

But neither popular beliefs in the supernatural nor philosophical Daoism could satisfy deeper emotional needs or provide solace in time of sorrow or the hope of a better life in the hereafter. Instead, Buddhism filled that gap.

Buddhism was mainly brought to China in the first or second century C.E. by missionaries and merchants traveling over the Silk Road, and it soon began to make inroads among the local population. Conditions were especially conducive in the north, where the rulers of non-Chinese governments were receptive to the new doctrine. Although the intellectual hairsplitting that often accompanied discussion of the Buddha's message in India was somewhat esoteric for Chinese tastes, in the difficult years of the Han Dynasty's decline, Buddhist ideas—especially those of the Mahayana school—began to find adherents among intellectuals and ordinary people alike. As Buddhism increased in popularity, it was frequently attacked by supporters of Confucianism and Daoism for its foreign origins. But such sniping did not halt the progress of Buddhism, and eventually the new faith was assimilated into Chinese culture, assisted by the efforts of such tireless advocates as the missionaries Fa Xian (fah SHEE-ahn) and Xuan Zang (SHOO-wen ZAHNG) and the support of ruling elites in both northern and southern China (see "The Rise and Decline of Buddhism and Daoism" later in this chapter).

10-1b The Sui Dynasty

After nearly four centuries of internal division, China was unified once again in 581 C.E. when Yang Jian (yahng JEE-YEN), a member of a respected aristocratic family in northern China, founded a new dynasty known as the Sui (SWAY) (581–618). Yang Jian, who is also known by his reign title of Sui Wendi (SWAY wen-DEE), established his capital at the historic metropolis of Chang'an (CHENG-AHN) and began to extend his authority throughout the Chinese heartland (see Map 10.1).

Like many of his predecessors, the new emperor sought a unifying ideology to enhance the state's efficiency. Whereas Liu Bang, the founder of the Han Dynasty, had adopted Confucianism as the official doctrine to knit the empire together, Yang Jian turned to Daoism and Buddhism. He founded monasteries for both doctrines and appointed Buddhist monks to key positions as political advisers.

Yang Jian was a builder as well as a conqueror, ordering the construction of a new canal from the capital to the confluence of the Wei and Yellow Rivers nearly 100 miles to the east. His son, Sui Yangdi (SWAY yahng-DEE), continued the process, and the 1,400-mile-long Grand Canal linking the Yellow and Yangzi Rivers was essentially completed during his reign (see Image 10.2). The new canal facilitated the shipment of grain from the rice-rich southern provinces to the densely populated north and also served as an imperial highway for dispatching troops to troubled provinces.

Despite these achievements, the Sui Dynasty came to an end immediately after Sui Yangdi's death. The Sui

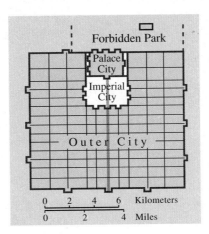

Map 10.1 Chang'an under the Sui and the Tang

emperor was a tyrannical ruler, and his expensive military campaigns aroused widespread unrest. After his return from a failed campaign against Korea in 618, the emperor was murdered in his palace. One of his generals, Li Yuan (lee YWAHN), took advantage of the ensuing instability and founded a new dynasty known as the Tang (TAHNG). Building on the successes of its predecessor, the Tang lasted for 300 years until 907.

10-1c The Tang Dynasty

After only a brief reign, the new ruler Li Yuan was elbowed aside by his son, who assumed the reign title *Tang Taizong* (tahng ty-ZOONG). Under his leadership, the Tang launched a program of internal renewal and external expansion that would make it one of the greatest Chinese dynasties (see Map 10.2). The northwest was pacified and given the name of Xinjiang (SHIN-jyahng), or "new region," sparking an increase in the traffic of goods and ideas across the region to the trading societies in Central Asia (see "The Silk Road" in section 10-1f, "The Economy"). After a long conflict with Tibet, Chinese control was also extended for the first time over that vast and desolate plateau. The southern provinces below the Yangzi were fully assimilated into the Chinese empire, and the imperial court established commercial and diplomatic relations with the states of Southeast Asia. With reason, China now claimed to be the foremost power in East Asia, and the Tang emperor demanded fealty from all his fellow rulers beyond the frontier. Korea accepted tribute status and attempted to adopt the Chinese model, and the Japanese dispatched official missions to China to learn more about its customs and institutions (see Chapter 11).

One key to the success of the Tang Dynasty in reuniting China after several centuries of internal division was the decision to revive many of the Confucian principles and practices that had been abandoned after the fall of the Han. Although the process took many years and did not reach its culmination until the advent of the Song Dynasty in the tenth century, Tang rulers began to draw on the principles of State Confucianism originally established during the Han as a means of centralizing power at court and weakening the power of the aristocrats (see section 10-1e "Political Structures: The Triumph of Confucianism").

The Controversial Empress Wu Perhaps the individual most responsible for this development was Wu Zhao (ca. 624–705 C.E.), also known as Wu Zetian, or simply

10.2 The Grand Canal. Built over centuries, the Grand Canal is one of the engineering wonders of the world and a crucial conduit for carrying goods between northern and southern China. In this stylized painting, "dragon boats" carry the emperor and his retinue on an inspection tour of the canal and its adjacent territories.

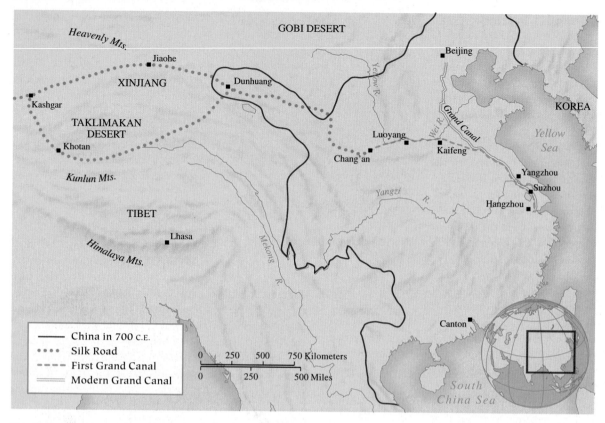

Map 10.2 China Under the Tang The era of the Tang Dynasty was one of the greatest periods in the long history of China. Tang influence spread from heartland China into neighboring regions, including Central and Southeast Asia.

Q *Why was the Grand Canal built, and what was its main function during this period?*

"Empress Wu." Selected by Emperor Tang Taizong as one of his many concubines, she rose from obscurity to a position of influence after his death in 649 C.E. and became the chief consort of his successor, Emperor Gaozong. At first she was content to exert her position at court discreetly, but when Gaozong became seriously ill in 660 she was able to win appointment as regent. After he died, she strengthened her hold on power and in 690 declared herself empress of China.

To bolster her claim to legitimacy as China's first female ruler, Empress Wu cited a Buddhist sutra to the effect that a woman would eventually rule the world after the death of Siddhartha Gautama. For her presumption, she has been vilified by generations of Chinese historians, but in recent years some scholars have claimed that she was actually a quite capable ruler who took measures to reform the agricultural system, undercut the power of the landed aristocracy, and strengthen the civil service system by selecting examination graduates for senior positions in government. Although few deny her ruthlessness in eliminating rivals, some modern historians contend that her actions laid the

groundwork for the "golden age" of Tang China that took root in the eighth century.

Under Empress Wu and her successors, the Tang achieved a flowering of culture. Historians have long held that the era represents the apogee of Chinese creativity in poetry and sculpture. One reason for this cultural explosion was the continuing influence of Buddhism, which affected art, literature, and philosophy as well as religion and politics). Monasteries sprang up throughout China, and (as under the Sui) Buddhist monks served as advisers at the imperial court. Even Empress Wu, whose policies generally reflected the growing influence of State Confucian ideology, was an avid supporter of Buddhism. The city of Chang'an once again became the seat of the empire. With a population estimated at nearly 2 million, it was possibly the greatest city in the world (see Comparative Illustration, "The Two Worlds of Tang China," p. 243).

But the Tang, like the Han, sowed the seeds of their own destruction. Tang rulers could not prevent the rise of internal forces that would ultimately weaken the dynasty and bring it to an end. Two familiar problems were court

The Two Worlds of Tang China

Religion & Philosophy

IN TANG DYNASTY CHINA, the arts often reflected influences from a wide variety of cultures. Image 10.3a shows an eighth-century wall painting from a cliffside cave at Dunhuang, a major rest stop on the Silk Road. The portrait of the Buddha clearly reflects Indian influence. Image 10.3b is a stone rubbing of Confucius based on a painting by the Tang Dynasty artist Wu Daozi (woo DOW-zuh) (ca. 685–758 C.E.). Although the original painting is not extant, this block print of a stone copy of Wu Daozi's work, showing Confucius in his flowing

robe, reflects the indigenous style for which the painter was famous. It became the iconic portrait of the Master for millions of later Chinese. The Chinese government recently commissioned a copy based on Wu's original painting to serve as the standard portrait of Confucius for people around the world.

 How do the two portraits shown here differ in the way their creators seek to present the character and the underlying philosophy of the Buddha and Confucius?

The Art Archive at Art Resource, NY

10.3a

William J. Duiker

10.3b

intrigues and official corruption. A prolonged drought may also have played a role in the dynasty's decline. In 755 C.E., rebellious forces briefly seized control of Chang'an itself. Although the revolt was eventually suppressed, the Tang never fully recovered. The loss of power by the central government led to increased influence by great landed families inside China and chronic instability along the northern and western frontiers, where local military commanders ruled virtually without central government interference. It was an eerie repetition of the final decades of the Han.

The end finally came in the early tenth century when border troubles with northern nomadic peoples called the Khitan (KEE-tan) caused the Tang to follow the classic Chinese strategy of "using a barbarian to oppose a barbarian" by allying with the Uighurs (WEE-gurz), a Turkic-speaking people who had taken over many of the caravan routes along the Silk Road. Yet another nomadic people called the Kirghiz (keer-GEEZ) defeated the Uighurs, however, and then turned on the Tang government in its moment of weakness and overthrew it.

10-1d The Song Dynasty

China slipped once again into chaos. This time, the period of foreign invasion and division was much shorter. In 960 C.E., a new dynasty known as the Song (SOONG) (960–1279) rose to power. From the start, however, the Song rulers encountered more problems in defending their territory than their predecessors. The founding emperor, Song Taizu (soong ty-DZOO), was unable to reconquer the northwestern part of the country from the nomadic Khitan peoples and therefore established his capital farther to the east at Kaifeng (KY-fuhng), where the Grand Canal intersected the Yellow River. Later, when pressures from the nomads in the north increased, the court was forced to move the capital even farther south to Hangzhou (HAHNG-joe), on the coast just south of the Yangzi River Delta; the dynasty that ruled from Hangzhou was known as the southern Song (1127–1279). Despite its political and military weaknesses, the dynasty nevertheless ruled during a period of economic expansion, prosperity, and cultural achievement and is therefore considered among the more successful Chinese dynasties. The empire's population, estimated at 40 million, was slightly higher than that of the continent of Europe.

The Song, however, were never able to surmount the external challenge from the north, and that failure eventually brought about the end of the dynasty. During its final decades, the Song rulers were forced to pay tribute to the Jurchen (roor-ZHEN) peoples from Manchuria (man-CHUR-ee-uh). In the early thirteenth century, the Song, ignoring precedent and the fate of the Tang, formed an alliance with the Mongols, a new and obscure nomadic people from the Gobi Desert. The decision proved disastrous. Within a few years, the Mongols had become a much more serious threat to China than the Jurchen. After defeating the Jurchen, the Mongols turned their attention to the south, advancing on Song territory from both the north and the west. By this time, the Song Empire had been weakened by internal factionalism and a loss of tax revenues. After a series of battles and sieges marked by the use of catapults and gunpowder, the Song were defeated, and the conquerors announced the creation of a new Yuan (Mongol) Dynasty. Ironically, the Mongols had first learned about gunpowder from the Chinese.

10-1e Political Structures: The Triumph of Confucianism

During the nearly 700 years from the Sui to the end of the Song, a mature political system based on principles originally established during the Qin and Han Dynasties gradually emerged in China. After the Tang Dynasty's brief flirtation with Buddhism, State Confucianism became the ideological cement that held the system together (see Opposing Viewpoints, "Confucianism and Its Enemies: An Ideological Dispute in Medieval China," p. 245). The development of this system took several centuries, and it did not reach its height until the period of the Song Dynasty.

Equal Opportunity in China: The Civil Service Examination At the apex of the government hierarchy was the **Grand Council** that was assisted by a secretariat and a chancellery; it included representatives from all three authorities—civil, military, and censorate. Under the Grand Council was the Department of State Affairs, which was composed of ministries responsible for justice, military affairs, personnel, public works, revenue, and rites (ritual).

The Tang Dynasty adopted the practice of selecting some officials through periodic civil service examinations. The effectiveness of this merit system was limited, however, because it was dominated by the great aristocratic clans that had mastered the technique of preparing candidates for the exams. According to one source, fully one-third of those who succeeded on the examinations during the Tang era came from the great families.

The Song were more successful at limiting aristocratic control over the bureaucracy, in part because the nobility had been weakened during the final years of the Tang Dynasty and the interregnum that followed its collapse. Song officials also sought to strengthen the power of the central administration by making the civil service examination system the primary route to an

Confucianism and Its Enemies: An Ideological Dispute in Medieval China

Religion & Philosophy

DURING THE INTERREGNUM between the fall of the Han Dynasty in 220 C.E. and the rise of the Tang 400 years later, Daoist critics lampooned the hypocrisy of the "Confucian gentleman" and the Master's emphasis on ritual and the maintenance of proper relations among individuals in society. In the first selection, a third-century Daoist launches an attack on the pompous and hypocritical Confucian gentleman who feigns high moral principles while secretly engaging in corrupt and licentious behavior.

By the eighth century, the tables had turned. In the second selection, Han Yu (hahn YOO) (768–824 C.E.), a key figure in the emergence of Neo-Confucian thought as the official ideology of the state, composes a memorial to the emperor containing a withering analysis of the dangers involved in allowing Daoist and Buddhist ideas to prosper among the common people. His tone is much more direct than that of most such memorials and probably reflects his confidence that the emperor would be receptive to his views.

Biography of a Great Man

What the world calls a gentleman [*chun-tzu*] is someone who is solely concerned with moral law [*fa*], and cultivates exclusively the rules of propriety [*li*]. His hand holds the emblem of jade [authority]; his foot follows the straight line of the rule. He likes to think that his actions set a permanent example; he likes to think that his words are everlasting models. In his youth, he has a reputation in the villages of his locality; in his later years, he is well known in the neighboring districts. Upward, he aspires to the dignity of the Three Dukes; downward, he does not disdain the post of governor of the nine provinces.

Have you ever seen the lice that inhabit a pair of trousers? They jump into the depths of the seams, hiding themselves in the cotton wadding, and believe they have a pleasant place to live. Walking, they do not risk going beyond the edge of the seam; moving, they are careful not to emerge from the trouser leg; and they think they have kept to the rules of etiquette. But when the trousers are ironed, the flames invade the hills, the fire spreads, the villages are set on fire and the towns burned down; then the lice that inhabit the trousers cannot escape.

What difference is there between the gentleman who lives within a narrow world and the lice that inhabit trouser legs?

Han Yu, *Memorial Discussing the Buddha's Bone*

I am of the opinion that Buddhism is nothing more than a religion of the outlying tribes. Since the Eastern Han it has made inroads into the heartland, but such a thing never existed in high antiquity. . . . [I]n those days the world enjoyed perfect peace; the common people were secure in their happiness and lived to ripe old age. Yet at this time there was no Buddhism in the heartland.

The Buddhist religion appeared only in the reign of Emperor Ming of the Han, and Emperor Ming sat on the throne for only eighteen years. After him, turmoil and destruction were continuous, and fate gave no long reigns. . . . Consideration of these cases leads us to understand that the Buddha does not merit devotion. . . .

When you first took the throne, Your Majesty did not permit people to take vows to become monks, nuns, or Daoist priests; you further did not permit the foundation of new monasteries and Daoist temples. . . . [H]ow can you give them free rein and make them prosper even more than before?

I recently heard that Your Majesty has commanded a group of monks to welcome the Buddha's bone in Fengxiang; then . . . it will be carried with ceremony into the palace precincts. . . . How could such a sagely and enlightened ruler as yourself bring himself to have faith in this sort of thing?

Nevertheless, the common people are foolish and ignorant, easy to lead into error and hard to enlighten. If Your Majesty behaves like this, they will assume that you serve the Buddha from genuine feeling. . . .

 How might the author of the first selection have responded to Han Yu's arguments? Which author appears to make the better case for his chosen ideological preference?

Source: Excerpt from ed. and translator, Stephen Owen, *An Anthology of Chinese Literature: Beginnings to 1911* (New York: W.W. Norton, 1996), pp. 598–601. From *Chinese Civilization and Bureaucracy*, by Etienne Balasz, p. 238. Copyright © 1964 by Yale University Press.

Arrival of Buddhism in China	ca. First century C.E.
Fall of the Han Dynasty	220 C.E.
Sui Dynasty	581–618
Tang Dynasty	618–907
Li Bo and Du Fu	700s
Song Dynasty	960–1279
Wang Anshi	1021–1086
Southern Song Dynasty	1127–1279
Mongol conquest of China	1279
Reign of Khubilai Khan	1260–1294
Fall of the Yuan Dynasty	1368
Ming Dynasty	1369–1644

official career (see Historical Voices, "Choosing the Best and Brightest," p. 247). To reduce the power of the noble families, relatives of individuals serving in the imperial court were prohibited from taking the examinations. But if the objective was to make the bureaucracy more subservient to the court, the Song rulers may have been disappointed. The rising professionalism and influence of the bureaucracy—which numbered about 20,000 with 10,000 in the imperial capital—sometimes enabled it to resist the whims of individual emperors.

Under the Song, the examination system attained the form it would have in later centuries. Three levels of examinations were administered. The first was a qualifying examination given annually at the provincial capital. Candidates who succeeded at this stage normally could only obtain positions at the local level. Candidates who wished to go on could take a second examination given at the capital every three years. Successful candidates could apply for an official position. Those who passed the final examination, which was given in the imperial palace once every three years, were eligible for high positions in the central bureaucracy or for appointments as district magistrates.

During the early Tang, the examinations included questions on Buddhist and Daoist topics, but by Song times the popularity of Buddhist and Daoist ideas had declined among the elite, and examinations were based entirely on the Confucian classics. Candidates were expected to memorize passages and be able to explain the moral lessons they contained. The system guaranteed that successful candidates would have received a full dose of Confucian political and social ethics. Many students complained about the rigors of memorization and the irrelevance of the process. Others brought crib notes into the examination hall (one enterprising candidate concealed an entire Confucian text

in the lining of his cloak). The Song authorities tried to open the system to provide an opportunity for the poor as well as the affluent, setting up training academies at the provincial and district levels. Without such academies, only individuals with access to family-run schools could have passed the examinations. Still, the majority of candidates came from the landed gentry, nonaristocratic landowners who controlled much of the wealth in the countryside. Because the gentry prized education and became the primary upholders of the Confucian tradition, they were often called the **scholar-gentry**.

Nor could the system guarantee an honest, efficient bureaucracy. Official arrogance, bureaucratic infighting, and corruption were as prevalent in medieval China as in bureaucracies the world over. Nepotism was a particular problem because many Chinese, following Confucius, held that filial duty transcended loyalty to the community.

Despite such weaknesses, the civil service examination system was an impressive achievement for its day and probably provided a more efficient government and more opportunity for upward mobility than existed in any other civilization of the time. Most Western governments, for example, did not begin to recruit officials on the basis of merit until the nineteenth century. Furthermore, by regulating the content of the examinations, the system helped provide China with a cultural uniformity lacking in empires elsewhere in Asia. At the base of the government pyramid was the district (or county) governed by a magistrate who was responsible for maintaining law and order and collecting taxes within his district, which could exceed 100,000 people. Below the district was the basic unit of Chinese government, the village. Villages were allowed to administer themselves, normally through a council of elders. The council, usually made up of the heads of influential families in the village, maintained the local irrigation and transportation network, adjudicated disputes, organized a militia, and assisted in collecting taxes (usually paid in grain).

10-1f The Economy

During the long period between the Sui and the Song, the Chinese economy, like the government, grew considerably in size and complexity. China was still an agricultural society, but commerce and manufacturing began to occupy a much larger percentage of the country's national product. The urban sector was becoming increasingly important, new social classes were beginning to appear, and the economic focus of the empire was beginning to shift from the Yellow River Valley in the north to the Yangzi River Valley in the center—a process that was encouraged both by the expansion of cultivation in the Yangzi Delta and by the control increasingly exerted over the north by nomadic peoples during the Song.

Choosing the Best and Brightest

Politics & Government   **WANG ANSHI** (WAHNG anh-SHEE) (1021–1086) was a prominent government official in Song Dynasty China. As a senior adviser at court, he sought to implement a series of reforms designed to improve the operations of the Chinese state and thus improve the well-being of the population. One key tenet of his program was to appoint honest and competent officials to key positions in the bureaucracy. In the great tradition of Chinese statecraft, Wang agreed with the proposition that it was good men, and not just laws, that created the best civil society. Current practice, however, placed primary emphasis on the ability of candidates to memorize passages from the ancient classics. In his view, it was more important for candidates to understand the general principles of governing and behavior; these principles could be gleaned from the writings of ancient times and did not need to be rotely memorized.

Memorial to Emperor Renzong (1058)

The most urgent need of the present time is to secure capable men. Only when we can produce a large number of capable men in the empire will it be possible to select a sufficient number of persons qualified to serve in the government. And only when we get capable men in the government will there be no difficulty in assessing what may be done, in view of the time and circumstances, and in consideration of the human distress that may be occasioned, gradually to change the decadent laws of the empire in order to approach the ideas of the ancient kings. The empire today is the same as the empire of the ancient kings. There were numerous capable men in their times. Why is there a dearth of such men today? It is because, as has been said, we do not train and cultivate men in the proper way. . . .

What is the way to select officials? The ancient kings selected men only from the local villages and through the local schools. The people were asked to recommend those they considered to be virtuous and able, sending up their nominations to the court, which investigated each one. Only if the men recommended proved truly virtuous and able would they be appointed to official posts commensurate with their individual virtue and ability. . . . Today, although we have schools in each prefecture and district, they amount to no more than school buildings. There are no officers of instruction and guidance; nothing is done to train and develop human talent. In recent years, teaching has been based on the essays required for the civil service examinations, but this kind of essay cannot be learned without resorting to extensive memorization and strenuous study, upon which students must spend their efforts the whole day long. Such proficiency as they attain is at best of no use in the government of the empire, and at most the empire can make no use of them. . . .

In addition, candidates are examined in such fields as the Nine Classics, the Five Classics, specialization [in one classic], and the study of law. The court has already become concerned over the uselessness of this type of knowledge and has stressed the need for an understanding of general principles [as set forth in the classics]. . . . When we consider the men selected through "understanding of the classics," however, it is still those who memorize, recite, and have some knowledge of literary composition who are able to pass the examination, while those who can apply them [the classics] to the government of the empire are not always brought in through this kind of selection.

 Does Wang Anshi cite examples from ancient times to strengthen his complaint about the current nature of training for a career in officialdom? Do his criticisms have relevance for our own day?

Source: From *Sources of Chinese Tradition*, Vol. 1, 2nd ed., by William Theodore de Bary and Irene Bloom, pgs. 612–616. Copyright © 1999 Columbia University Press. Reprinted with permission of the publisher.

Land Reform   The economic revival began shortly after the rise of the Tang. During the long period of internal division, land had become concentrated in the hands of aristocratic families, with most peasants reduced to serfdom or slavery. Under Empress Wu (see the previous section on her), the Tang Dynasty tried to reduce the power of the landed nobility and maximize tax revenues by adopting the ancient well-field system in which land was allocated to farmers for life in return for an annual tax payment and three weeks of conscript labor. Eventually, however, the rich and the politically influential, including some of the largest Buddhist monasteries, learned to manipulate the system and accumulated huge tracts of land. Finally, the government abandoned the effort to equalize landholdings and returned the land to private hands while attempting to prevent inequalities through the tax system. This approach resulted in more efficient production methods, but the growing population negated whatever gains had been made. The failure to resolve the land problem undoubtedly contributed to the fall of the Tang Dynasty in the early tenth century.

The Song tried to resolve the land problem by returning to the successful programs of the early Tang and reducing the power of the landed aristocrats. During the late eleventh century, Wang Anshi (WAHNG ahn-SHEE) (1021–1086), a reformist official, attempted to limit the size of landholdings through progressive land taxes and provided cheap credit to poor farmers to help them avoid bankruptcy. His reforms met with some success, but other developments probably contributed more to the general agricultural prosperity under the Song. These included the opening of new lands in the Yangzi River Valley, technological improvements such as the chain pump (a circular chain of square pallets on a treadmill that enabled farmers to lift water to a higher level), and the introduction of a quick-growing rice from Southeast Asia that allowed two crops to be produced each year. It was during the Song Dynasty that rice became the main food crop for the Chinese people.

An Increase in Manufacturing   Under the Tang and the Song, major changes also took place in the urban economy, which witnessed a significant increase in trade and manufacturing that was helped by several technological developments (see Comparative Essay, "The Spread of Technology," p. 249). During the Tang, the Chinese mastered the art of manufacturing steel by mixing cast iron and wrought iron. Blast furnaces were heated to a high temperature by burning coal. The resulting product was used for swords, sickles, and even suits of armor. By the eleventh century, more than 35,000 tons of steel were being produced annually. The introduction of cotton from southern Asia offered new opportunities in textile manufacturing. Gunpowder was invented by the Chinese during the late Tang Dynasty and was used primarily for explosives and as a primitive form of flamethrower; it reached the West via the Arabs in the twelfth century.

The Expansion of Commerce   The nature of trade was also changing. In the past, most long-distance trade had been undertaken by state monopoly; by the time of the Song, private commerce was being actively encouraged. Guilds began to appear, along with a new money economy. Paper currency began to be used in the eighth and ninth centuries and led to the development of banking as merchants found that strings of copper coins were too cumbersome for their

increasingly complex operations. Credit (at first called "flying money") also made its appearance during the Tang. The invention of the abacus, an early form of calculator, simplified the calculations needed for commercial transactions.

The Silk Road   Long-distance trade, both overland and by sea, expanded dramatically under the Tang Dynasty. Trade with countries and peoples to the west had been carried on for centuries (see Chapter 3), but it had declined between the fourth and sixth centuries C.E. as a result of the collapse of the Han and Roman Empires. It began to revive with the rise of the Tang and the simultaneous unification of much of the Middle East under the Arabs. During the Tang era, the route we call the Silk Road reached its zenith as Chinese military forts were established at strategic points along the edge of the Taklimakan Desert all the way to the borders of Central Asia. Along the Silk Road to China came raw hides, furs, and horses. Much of the trade was carried by the Turkic-speaking Uighurs or Iranian-speaking Sogdians (SAHG-dee-unz) from Central Asia. During the Tang, Uighur caravans of two-humped Bactrian camels carried goods between China and the countries of South Asia and the Middle East. Bolts of silk, a textile which was in great demand throughout the region, became a popular means of currency.

In actuality, the Silk Road was composed of several separate routes. The first to be used, probably because of the jade found in the mountains south of Khotan (koh-TAHN), ran along the southern rim of the Taklimakan (tah-kluh-muh-KAHN) Desert and thence through the Pamir (pah-MEER) Mountains into Bactria. The first Buddhist missionaries traveled this route from India to China. Eventually, however, this area began to dry up, and traders were forced to seek other routes. The route to the north of the Tian Shan (TEE-en SHAHN) (Heavenly Mountains) offered pastures where animals could graze, but the area was frequently infested by bandits, so most caravans followed the southern route, which passed along the northern fringes of the Taklimakan Desert to Kashgar (KASH-gahr) and down into northwestern India. Travelers avoided the direct route through the desert (in the Uighur language, the name means "go in and you won't come out") and trudged from oasis to oasis along the southern slopes of the Tian Shan (see Map 10.1 and Image 10.5).

The eastern terminus of the Silk Road was the city of Chang'an, perhaps the wealthiest city in the world during the Tang era. Its days as China's foremost metropolis were numbered, however. Chronic droughts throughout the region made it more and more difficult to supply the city with food, and the growing power of nomadic peoples in the hinterlands made the city increasingly vulnerable to attack. During the later Tang, the imperial court was periodically shifted to the old capital of Luoyang

The Spread of Technology

Science & Technology From the invention of stone tools and the discovery of fire to the introduction of agriculture and the writing system, mastery of technology has been a driving force in the history of human evolution. But why do some human societies appear to be much more advanced in their use of technology than others? People living on the island of New Guinea, for example, began cultivating local crops like taro and bananas as early as 10,000 years ago but never took the next steps toward creating a complex society until the arrival of Europeans many millennia later. Advanced societies had begun to emerge in the Western Hemisphere during the classical era, but none had discovered the use of the wheel or the smelting of metals for toolmaking. Writing was in its infancy there.

Technological advances appear to take place for two reasons: need and opportunity. Farming peoples throughout the world needed to control the flow of water, so in areas where water was scarce or unevenly distributed, they learned to practice irrigation to make resources available throughout the region. Peoples living in the Pacific Ocean learned how to read the stars and the ocean currents to navigate from island to island. Sometimes, however, opportunity strikes by accident (as in the legendary story of the Chinese princess who dropped a silkworm cocoon in her cup of hot tea, thereby initiating a series of discoveries that resulted in the manufacture of silk) or when new technology is introduced from a neighboring region (as when the discovery of tin in Anatolia launched the Bronze Age throughout the Middle East).

The most important factor enabling societies to keep abreast of the latest advances in technology, it would appear, is participation in the global trade and communications network. In this respect, the relative ease of communications between the Mediterranean Sea and the Indus River Valley represented a major advantage for the Abbasid Empire because the peoples living there had rapid access to all the resources and technological advances in that part of the world. China was more isolated from other major civilizations by distance, but with its size and high level of cultural achievement, it was almost a continent in itself and was able to communicate with countries to the west via the Silk Road and the South China Sea.

William J. Duiker

10.4 The First Paper Currency

Societies that were not linked to this vast network were at an enormous disadvantage in keeping up with new developments in technology. The peoples of New Guinea, at the far end of the Indonesian islands, had little or no contact with the outside world. In the Western Hemisphere, a trade network did begin to take shape between societies in the Andes and their counterparts in Mesoamerica. Because of difficulties in communication (see Chapter 6), contacts were more intermittent. As a result, technological developments taking place in distant Eurasia did not reach the Americas until the arrival of the conquistadors.

 In what ways did China contribute to the spread of technology and ideas throughout the world during the period from the Sui Dynasty to the beginning of the Ming Dynasty? How did China benefit from the process?

10.5 Tang Camel. During the Tang Dynasty, trade between China, India, and the Middle East along the famous Silk Road increased rapidly and introduced new Central Asian motifs to Chinese culture. As seen in this sturdy example, the Bactrian two-humped camel played a major role in carrying goods along the trade route because its ability to withstand long periods without water enabled it to survive the grueling trek across the Central Asian deserts. Created as tomb figures and therefore preserved for us today are numerous ceramic studies of horses and camels, along with officials, court ladies, and servants painted in brilliant gold, green, and blue lead glazes.

(LWOH-yahng). The Song Dynasty, a product of the steady drift of the national center of gravity toward the south, was forced to abandon Chang'an altogether.

The Maritime Route With the collapse of the Tang Dynasty in the tenth century, Chinese control over Xinjiang was disrupted, and the Silk Road became so hazardous that shipping goods by sea was seen as an appealing alternative. China had long been engaged in sea trade with other countries in the region, but much of the commerce was originally in the hands of Korean, Japanese, Southeast Asian, or Middle Eastern merchants. Under the Song, however, Chinese maritime activities were stimulated by the invention of the compass and technical improvements in shipbuilding such as the sternpost rudder. If Marco Polo's observations can be believed, by the thirteenth century

Chinese junks (a type of seagoing ship with square sails and a flat bottom) had multiple sails and were up to 2,000 tons in size, much larger than contemporary ships in the West. The Chinese governor of Canton (KAN-tahn) in the early twelfth century remarked,

> According to the government regulations concerning sea-going ships, the larger ones can carry several hundred men, and the smaller ones may have more than a hundred men on board. . . . The ship's pilots are acquainted with the configuration of the coasts; at night they steer by the stars, and in the daytime by the Sun. In dark weather they look at the south-pointing needle. They also use a line a hundred feet long with a hook at the end, which they let down to take samples of mud from the sea-bottom; by its appearance and smell they can determine their whereabouts.[2]

A wide variety of goods passed through Chinese ports. The Chinese exported tea, silk, and porcelain to the countries beyond the South China Sea and received exotic woods, precious stones, cotton from India, and various tropical spices in exchange. Silk was probably the most desirable commodity of trade because the quality of Chinese silk was generally recognized as far superior to that produced by other countries in the area. The major southern port was Canton, which was home to an estimated 100,000 merchants. Affluent Chinese, their appetite for material consumption stimulated by the affluence of much of the Tang and Song periods, were fascinated by the exotic goods shipped from the tropical lands of the South Seas and the flora and fauna of the desert that arrived via the Silk Road.

Some of this trade was a product of the tribute system. The Chinese viewed the outside world as they viewed their own society—as a hierarchy. Rulers of smaller countries along the periphery were viewed as "younger brothers" of the Chinese emperor and owed fealty to him. Foreign rulers who accepted the relationship were required to pay tribute and to promise not to harbor enemies of the Chinese Empire. In return, they obtained legitimacy and access to the vast Chinese market.

10-2 EXPLOSION IN CENTRAL ASIA: THE MONGOL EMPIRE

Focus Question: Why were the Mongols able to amass an empire, and what were the main characteristics of their rule in China?

The long era of indigenous Chinese rule came suddenly to an end with the emergence of the Mongols in the thirteenth century. The Mongols, who succeeded the Song as the rulers of China in 1279, rose to power in Asia with stunning rapidity. In the latter half of the twelfth century, the Mongols were a relatively obscure pastoral people in the region of modern Outer Mongolia. Like most of the nomadic groups in the region, they were organized loosely into clans and tribes and even lacked a common name for themselves. Rivalry among the various communities over pasture, livestock, and booty was intense and increased at the end of the twelfth century as a result of a growing population and the consequent overgrazing of pastures.

This challenge was met by Temuchin (TEM-yuh-jin) (or Temujin), who became the great Mongol chieftan Genghis Khan (also known as Chinggis Khan (GENG-uss or JING-uss KAHN) (ca. 1162–1227). When Temuchin was still a child, his father was murdered by a rival, and the boy was forced to seek refuge in the wilderness. Described as tall, adroit, and vigorous, young Temuchin gradually unified the Mongol tribes through his prowess and the power of his personality. In 1206, he was elected Genghis Khan ("universal ruler") at a massive tribal meeting in the Gobi Desert. From that time on, he devoted himself to military pursuits (see Image 10.6). "Man's highest joy," Genghis Khan reportedly remarked, "is in victory: to conquer one's enemies, to pursue them, to deprive

10.6 Genghis Khan. Founder of the Mongol Empire, Temuchin (later to be known as Genghis Khan) died in 1227, long before Mongol warriors defeated the armies of the Song and established the Yuan Dynasty in China in 1279. In this portrait by a Chinese court artist, the ruler appears in a stylized version, looking much like other Chinese emperors from the period. Painters in many societies used similar techniques to render their subjects in a manner more familiar to prospective observers.

© National Palace Museum, Taipei/The Bridgeman Art Library

them of their possessions, to make their beloved weep, to ride on their horses, and to embrace their wives and daughters."[3]

The army that Genghis Khan unleashed on the world was not exceptionally large—totaling fewer than 130,000 in 1227 at a time when the total Mongol population numbered between 1 million and 2 million. But their mastery of military tactics set the Mongols apart. Their tireless flying columns of mounted warriors surrounded their enemies and harassed them like cattle, luring them into pursuit and then ambushing them with flank attacks.

The Mongols first defeated tribal groups to their west and then turned their attention to the seminomadic non-Chinese kingdoms of northern China. There they discovered that their adversaries were armed with a weapon called a *firelance*, an early form of flamethrower that could spew out flames and projectiles a distance of thirty or forty yards. By the end of the thirteenth century, the firelance had evolved into the much more effective handgun and cannon. These inventions came too late to save China from the Mongols, however, and were transmitted to Europe by the early fourteenth century by foreigners employed by the Mongol rulers of China.

Some Mongol armies were engaged in the conquest of northern China, but others traveled farther afield and advanced as far as central Europe. Only the death of Genghis Khan in 1227 may have prevented an all-out Mongol attack on western Europe (see Historical Voices, "A Letter to the Pope," p. 252). In 1231, the Mongols attacked Persia and then defeated the Abbasids at Baghdad in 1258 (see Chapter 7). Mongol forces attacked the Song from the west in the 1260s and finally defeated the remnants of the Song navy in 1279 (see Map 10.3).

By then, the Mongol Empire was quite different from what it had been under its founder. Before Genghis Khan's conquests, the Mongols had been purely nomadic. They spent their winters in the southern plains, where they found pasture for their cattle, and traveled north in the summer. They lived in round, felt-covered tents called *yurts* that were lightly constructed so that they could be easily transported. For food, the Mongols depended on milk and meat from their herds and game from hunting.

To administer the new empire, Genghis Khan had set up a capital city at Karakorum (kah-rah-KOR-um), in present-day Outer Mongolia but prohibited his fellow Mongols from practicing sedentary occupations or living in cities. But under his successors, the Mongols began to adapt to their conquered areas. As one khan remarked, quoting his Chinese adviser, "Although you inherited the Chinese Empire on horseback, you cannot rule it from that position." Mongol aristocrats began to enter administrative positions, and commoners took up sedentary occupations as farmers or merchants.

A Letter to the Pope

Interaction & Exchange   **IN 1245, POPE INNOCENT IV** dispatched Franciscan friar John Plano Carpini to the Mongol headquarters at Karakorum to appeal to the great khan Kuyuk (koo-YOOK) to cease his attacks on Christians. After a considerable wait, Carpini was given the following reply, which could not have pleased the pope. The letter was discovered recently in the Vatican archives.

A Letter from Kuyuk Khan to Pope Innocent IV

By the power of the Eternal Heaven, We are the all-embracing Khan of all the Great Nations. It is our command:

This is a decree, sent to the great Pope that he may know and pay heed.

After holding counsel with the monarchs under your suzerainty, you have sent us an offer of subordination, which we have accepted from the hands of your envoy.

If you should act up to your word, then you, the great Pope, should come in person with the monarchs to pay us homage and we should thereupon instruct you concerning the commands of the Yasak.

Furthermore, you have said it would be well for us to become Christians. You write to me in person about this matter, and have addressed to me a request. This, your request, we cannot understand.

Furthermore, you have written me these words: "You have attacked all the territories of the Magyars and other Christians, at which I am astonished. Tell me, what was their crime?" These, your words, we likewise cannot understand. Jenghiz Khan and Ogatai Khakan revealed the commands of Heaven. But those whom you name would not believe the commands of Heaven. Those of whom you speak showed themselves highly presumptuous and slew our envoys. Therefore, in accordance with the commands of the Eternal Heaven the inhabitants of the aforesaid countries have been slain and annihilated. If not by the command of Heaven, how can anyone slay or conquer out of his own strength?

And when you say: "I am a Christian. I pray to God. I arraign and despise others," how do you know who is pleasing to God and to whom He allots His grace? How can you know it, that you speak such words?

Thanks to the power of the Eternal Heaven, all lands have been given to us from sunrise to sunset. How could anyone act other than in accordance with the commands of Heaven? Now your own upright heart must tell you: "We will become subject to you, and will place our powers at your disposal." You in person, at the head of the monarchs, all of you, without exception, must come to tender us service and pay us homage, then only will we recognize your submission. But if you do not obey the commands of Heaven, and run counter to our orders, we shall know that you are our foe.

That is what we have to tell you. If you fail to act in accordance therewith, how can we foresee what will happen to you? Heaven alone knows.

 Based on the account given here, what message was the pope seeking to convey to the great khan in Karakorum? What was the nature of the latter's reply?

Source: From Prawdin, Michael, *The Mongol Empire: Its Rise and Legacy* (Free Press, 1961), pp. 280–281.

The territorial nature of the empire also changed. Following tribal custom, at the death of the ruling khan, the territory was distributed among his heirs. The once-united empire of Genghis Khan was thus divided into several separate **khanates** (KHAH-nayts), each ruled by one of his sons by his principal wife. One son was awarded the khanate of Chaghadai (chag-huh-DY) in Central Asia with its capital at Samarkand; another ruled Persia from Baghdad; a third received the khanate of Kipchak (KIP-chahk), commonly known as the Golden Horde. But it was one of his grandsons, named Khubilai Khan (1215–1294), who completed the conquest of the Song and established a new Chinese dynasty called the Yuan (from a phrase in the *Book of Changes* referring to the "original creative force" of the universe). Khubilai moved the capital of China northward from Hangzhou to Khanbaliq ("city of the khan"), which was located on a major trunk route from the Great Wall to the plains of northern China (see Map 10.2). Later the city would be known by the Chinese name *Beijing* (bay-ZHING), or *Peking* (pee-KING) ("northern capital").

10-2a Mongol Rule in China

At first, China's new rulers exhibited impressive vitality. Under Khubilai Khan, the Yuan continued to flex their muscles by attempting to expand their empire. Mongol armies advanced into the Red River Valley and reconquered Vietnam, which had declared its independence after the fall of the Tang 300 years earlier. Mongol fleets were launched against Malay kingdoms in Java and Sumatra and also against Japan. Only the expedition against Vietnam succeeded, however, and even that success was temporary. The Vietnamese counterattacked and eventually drove the Mongols back across the border. The attempted conquest of Japan was even more disastrous. On one occasion, a massive storm destroyed the Mongol fleet, killing thousands (see Chapter 11).

The Mongols had more success in governing China. After a failed attempt to administer their conquest as they had ruled their own tribal society (some advisers reportedly even suggested that the plowed fields be transformed into pastures), Mongol rulers adapted to the Chinese political system and made use of local talents in the bureaucracy. The tripartite division of the administration into civilian, military, and censorate was retained, as were the six ministries. The civil service system, which had been abolished in the north in 1237 and in the south forty years later, was revived in the early fourteenth century. The state cult of Confucius was also restored, although Khubilai Khan himself remained a Buddhist (see Map 10.4).

But there were some key differences. Culturally, the Mongols were nothing like the Chinese and remained a separate class with their own laws. The highest positions in the bureaucracy were usually staffed by Mongols. Although some leading Mongols followed

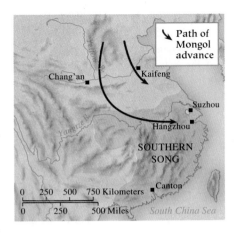

Map 10.3 The Mongol Conquest of China

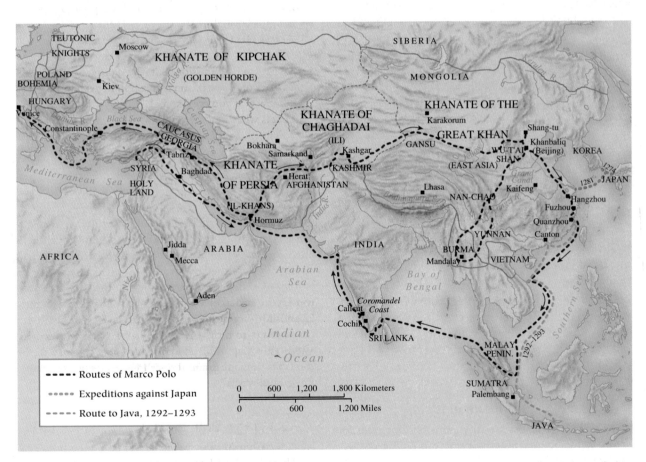

Map 10.4 Asia Under the Mongols. This map traces the expansion of Mongol power throughout Eurasia in the thirteenth century. After the death of Genghis Khan in 1227, the empire was divided into four separate khanates.

Q Why was the Mongol Empire divided into four separate khanates?

their ruler in converting to Buddhism, most commoners retained their traditional religion.

The Mongols' greatest achievement may have been the prosperity they fostered. They continued the relatively tolerant economic policies of the southern Song and brought much of the Eurasian landmass under a single rule; they also encouraged long-distance trade along the Silk Road, which was now dominated by Muslim merchants from Central Asia. To promote domestic commerce, the Grand Canal was extended from the Yellow River to the capital. Adjacent to the canal, a paved highway was constructed that extended all the way from the Song capital of Hangzhou to its Mongol counterpart at Khanbaliq.

The capital was a magnificent city. According to Italian merchant Marco Polo, who resided there during the reign of Khubilai Khan, it was twenty-four miles in diameter and surrounded by thick walls of earth penetrated by a dozen massive gates [see Film & History, *The Adventures of Marco Polo* (1938) and *Marco Polo* (2007)]. Polo was even more impressed by the old Song capital of Hangzhou, which he described as a noble city where the delights were so abundant that an inhabitant might "imagine himself in Paradise."[4]

The Yuan eventually fell victim to the same fate that had afflicted other powerful dynasties in China. Excessive spending on foreign campaigns, inadequate tax revenues, and factionalism and corruption at court and in the bureaucracy all contributed to the dynasty's demise. Khubilai Khan's successors lacked his administrative genius, and the Yuan Dynasty in China, like the Mongol khanates elsewhere in Central Asia, had fallen into a rapid decline by the middle of the fourteenth century.

The immediate instrument of Mongol defeat was Zhu Yuanzhang (JOO yoo-wen-JAHNG), the son of a poor peasant in the lower Yangzi Valley. After losing most of his family during a famine, Zhu became the leader of a band of bandits. In the 1360s, as unrest spread throughout the country, Zhu Yuanzhang defeated several rivals and put an end to the disintegrating Yuan regime, declaring the foundation of a new Ming (MING) ("bright") Dynasty (1369–1644).

10-2b The Mongols' Place in History

The Mongols were the last, and arguably the greatest, of the nomadic peoples who came out of the steppes of Central Asia, pillaging and conquering the territories of their adversaries. What caused this burst of energy, and why were the Mongols so much more successful

than their predecessors? Some historians have suggested that drought and overpopulation may have depleted the available pasture on the steppes. Others have cited the genius of Genghis Khan and his ability to arouse a sense of personal loyalty. Still others point to his reliance on the organizational unit known as the *ordos* (OR-dohz), described by historian Samuel Adshead as "a system of restructuring tribes into decimal units whose top level of leadership was organized on bureaucratic lines."[5] Although other nomadic peoples had also used the ordos, the Mongols applied it to create disciplined and highly effective military units. Once organized, the Mongols used their superior horsemanship and blitzkrieg tactics effectively while taking advantage of divisions within the enemy ranks and borrowing more advanced military technology.

Once in power, however, the Mongols' underlying weaknesses eventually proved fatal. The Mongols had difficulty making the transition from the nomadic life of the steppes to the sedentary life, and their unwieldy system of royal succession led to instability.

10-2c The Mongols: A Reputation Undeserved?

The era of Mongol expansion has usually been portrayed as a tragic period in human history. The Mongols' conquests resulted in widespread death and suffering throughout the world. Nations and empires were humbled, cities destroyed, and irrigations systems laid waste. Then, just when the ravages of the era appeared to come to an end, bubonic plague, probably carried by lice hidden in the saddlebags of Mongol horsemen, decimated the population of Europe and the Middle East (see Chapter 13). Some regions lost as much as one-third of their population to massacre or starvation.

Few modern historians would dispute the brutality that characterized Mongol expansion. But some now point out that beyond the legacy of death and destruction, the Mongols also brought an era of widespread peace known as the *Pax Mongolica* (PAKS *or* PAHKS mahn-GOH-lik-uh) to much of the Eurasian supercontinent and inaugurated what one scholar has described as "the idea of the unified conceptualization of the globe," creating a "basic information circuit" that spread commodities, ideas, and inventions from one end of the Eurasian supercontinent to the other. That being said, there is no denying that the Mongol invasions resulted in widespread suffering and misfortune. If there was a Mongol peace, it was, for many, the peace of death.

10-3 THE MING DYNASTY

Focus Questions: What were the chief initiatives taken by the early rulers of the Ming Dynasty to enhance the role of China in the world? Why did the imperial court order the famous voyages of Zheng He, and why were they discontinued?

The Ming inaugurated a new era of greatness in Chinese history. Under a series of strong rulers, China extended its rule into Mongolia and Central Asia. The Ming dispatched large fleets to far-flung areas of Asia and even briefly reconquered Vietnam. Along the northern frontier, the emperor Yongle (YOONG-luh) (r. 1402–1424) strengthened the Great Wall and pacified the nomadic tribespeople who had troubled China in previous centuries (see Comparative Illustration, "The Great Walls of China," p. 256). A tributary relationship was established with the Choson Dynasty in Korea. The internal achievements of the Ming were equally impressive. When they

replaced the Mongols in the fourteenth century, the Ming turned to traditional Confucian institutions as a means of ruling their vast empire. These included the six ministries at the apex of the bureaucracy, the use of civil service examinations to select members of the bureaucracy, and the division of the empire into provinces, districts, and counties.

The society that was governed by this vast hierarchy of officials was a far cry from the predominantly agrarian society that had been ruled by the Han. In the burgeoning cities near the coast and along the Yangzi River Valley, factories and workshops were vastly increasing the variety and output of their manufactured goods. The population had doubled, and new crops had been introduced, greatly expanding the empire's food output.

10-3a The Voyages of Zheng He

In 1405, in a splendid display of Chinese maritime might, Emperor Yongle sent a fleet of Chinese trading ships under eunuch admiral Zheng He (JEHNG-huh) through the Strait of Malacca and out into the Indian Ocean, where they stopped at ports throughout South Asia. The size of the fleet was impressive: it included nearly 28,000 sailors on 62 ships, some of them junks far larger than any other oceangoing vessels the world had yet seen (although the actual size of the largest ships is in dispute). During the next three decades, six other voyages of comparable size were launched, some of them extending their explorations as far west as the east coast of Africa. China seemed about to become a direct participant in the vast trade network that extended as far west as the Atlantic Ocean.

HISTORIANS DEBATE 10-3b Why Were Zheng He's Voyages Undertaken, and Why Were They Abandoned?

Why the expeditions were undertaken has been a matter of much debate. Some historians have pointed to Emperor Yongle's native curiosity and note that the voyages returned with not only goods but also a plethora of information about the outside world as well as with some items unknown in China (the emperor was especially intrigued by the giraffes and installed them in the imperial zoo, where they were identified by soothsayers with the advent of good government). Others argue that economic profit, or what in our day is called "power projection," was the main reason. In their view, the voyages were probably aimed at solidifying China's hegemonic role and the strengthening of its alliances with trading partners while simultaneously

The Great Walls of China

 Interaction & Exchange

ALTHOUGH THE GREAT WALL is popularly believed to be more than 2,000 years old, the part of the wall that is most frequently visited by tourists today was a reconstruction undertaken during the early Ming Dynasty to protect against invasion from the north. Part of that wall, which was built to protect the imperial capital of Beijing, is shown in Image 10.7a. The original walls stretched from the shores of the Pacific Ocean to the deserts of Central Asia and were often composed of loose stone, dirt, or piled rubble. The section shown in Image 10.7b is located north of the Turfan Depression in Xinjiang Province.

Q *What were the major reasons for building the Great Wall? To what degree was the wall successful in achieving these objectives?*

10.7a

10.7b

clearing the southern seas of pirates who preyed on merchant shipping throughout the region. Whatever the case, the voyages resulted in a dramatic increase in Chinese knowledge about the world and the nature of ocean travel. They also extended the power and prestige of the Chinese empire for the first time in history deep into the lands of Southeast Asia and out into the waters of the Indian Ocean beyond. In the process, they brought massive profits for their sponsors, some of whom were undoubtedly allies of Admiral Zheng He at court.

In 1433, shortly after the death of Emperor Yongle, the voyages were suddenly discontinued, never to be revived again. The reasons for this dramatic turnaround have long aroused curiosity among historians. Some have suggested that this turn inward may have been initiated, perhaps inadvertently by Yongle himself when he decided to move the imperial capital from Nanjing (nahn-JING) in central China, where the ships were built and the voyages launched, back to the old Mongol capital in Beijing, where official eyes were firmly focused on the rising threat from nomadic forces in the north. As a means of averting that threat, Yongle ordered the strengthening of sections of the Great Wall north of the new capital, along with the resettlement of thousands of families to the region from the fertile Yangzi Valley. Although the emperor may not have intended to divert the country from its contacts with the external world, the end result was a shift in the balance of power from central China, where it had been since the southern Song Dynasty, back to northern China, where it had originated and would remain for the rest of the Ming era. China would not look outward again for more than four centuries.

Some scholars seek other explanations for the dramatic shift in China's priorities. The voyages had undoubtedly aroused resentment among conservatives within the bureaucracy, some of whom viewed commercial activities with a characteristic measure of Confucian disdain. One disgruntled critic commented that an end to the voyages would provide the Chinese people with a respite "so that they can devote themselves to husbandry [agriculture] and schooling."

Others opt for a simpler explanation and argue that Ming officials may have concluded that when local rulers throughout the South Seas had been sufficiently intimidated to accept a tributary relationship with their "elder brother" in China, the voyages—which had been prohibitively expensive—were no longer necessary. Whatever the case, the decision had long-term consequences and affected China's relationships with the rest of Asia for several centuries.

10-4 IN SEARCH OF THE WAY

Focus Question: What roles did Buddhism, Daoism, and Neo-Confucianism play in Chinese intellectual life in the period between the Sui and Ming Dynasties?

By the time of the Sui Dynasty, Buddhism and Daoism had emerged as major rivals of Confucianism as the ruling ideology of the state. But during the last half of the Tang, Confucianism revived and once again became dominant at court, a position it would retain to the end of the dynastic period in the early twentieth century. Buddhist and Daoist beliefs, however, remained popular at the local level.

10-4a The Rise and Decline of Buddhism and Daoism

As noted previously, Buddhism arrived in China with travelers from India and found its first adherents within the merchant community and among intellectuals. During the chaotic centuries following the collapse of the Han Dynasty, Buddhism and Daoism appealed to those who were searching for more emotional and spiritual satisfaction than Confucianism could provide. Both faiths reached beyond the common people and found support among the ruling classes as well.

The Sinification of Buddhism As Buddhism attracted more followers, it began to take on Chinese characteristics and divided into many separate sects. Some, like the **Chan** (Zen in Japanese) sect, called for mind training and a strict regimen as a means of seeking enlightenment. Others like the **Pure Land** sect stressed the role of devotion, an approach that was more appealing to ordinary Chinese, who lacked the time and inclination for strict monastic discipline. Still others were mystical sects such as **Tantrism** (TUHN-tri-zum), which emphasized the importance of magical symbols and ritual. Some Buddhist groups, like their Daoist counterparts, had political objectives. The **White Lotus** sect founded in 1133 often adopted the form of a rebel movement, seeking political reform or the overthrow of a dynasty and forecasting a new era when a "savior Buddha" would come to earth to herald the advent of a new age. Most believers, however, assimilated Buddhism into their daily lives, where it joined Confucian ideology and spirit worship as an element in the highly eclectic and tolerant Chinese worldview.

The burgeoning popularity of Buddhism continued into the early years of the Tang Dynasty. Early Tang rulers lent their support to the Buddhist monasteries that had been established throughout the country. But ultimately, Buddhism and Daoism lost favor at court. Daoists and Confucianists made a point of criticizing the foreign origins of Buddhist doctrines, which one prominent Confucian scholar characterized as nothing but "silly relics" (see Opposing Viewpoints, "Confucianism and its Enemies: An Ideological Dispute in Medieval China," p. 245). But another reason for this change of heart may have been financial. The great Buddhist monasteries had accumulated thousands of acres of land and serfs that were exempt from paying taxes. As the state attempted to eliminate the great landholdings of the aristocracy, the large monasteries also attracted its attention. During the later Tang, countless temples and monasteries were destroyed, and more than 100,000 monks were compelled to leave the monasteries and return to secular life.

Buddhism Under Threat Yet there were probably deeper political and ideological reasons for the growing antagonism between Buddhism and the state. By preaching the illusory nature of the material world, Buddhism was denying the essence of Confucian teachings—the necessity for filial piety and hard work. By encouraging young Chinese to abandon their fields and seek wisdom in the monasteries, Buddhism was undermining the foundation stones of Chinese society—the family unit and the work ethic. Ultimately, Buddhism was incompatible with the activist element in Chinese society. In the competition with Confucianism for support by the state, Buddhism, like Daoism, was almost certain to lose.

10-4b Neo-Confucianism: The Investigation of Things

Into the vacuum left by the decline of Buddhism and Daoism stepped a revived Confucianism. Challenged by Buddhist and Daoist ideas about the nature of the universe, Confucian thinkers sought to flesh out the spare metaphysical structure of classical Confucian doctrine with a set of sophisticated theories about the nature of the cosmos and humans' place in it.

The fundamental purpose of **Neo-Confucianism**, as the newly revised doctrine was called, was to unite the metaphysical speculations of Buddhism and Daoism with the pragmatic Confucian approach to society. In response to Buddhism and Daoism, Neo-Confucianism maintained that the world is real, not illusory, and that fulfillment comes from participation, not withdrawal.

The primary contributor to this intellectual effort was philosopher Zhu Xi (JOO SHEE). Raised during the

10.8 Buddhist Sculpture at Longmen. The Silk Road was an avenue for ideas as well as trade. Over the centuries, Christian, Buddhist, and Muslim teachings came to China across the sandy wastes of the Taklimakan Desert. In the seventh century, Tang Emperor Gaozong (gow-ZOONG) commissioned this massive cliffside carving as part of a large complex of cave art devoted to the Buddha at Longmen (LAHNG-mun) in central China. Bold and grandiose in its construction, this towering statue of the Buddha, surrounded by temple guardians and bodhisattvas, reflects the glory of the Tang Dynasty.

southern Song era, Zhu Xi accepted the division of the world into a material world and a transcendent world, called the **Supreme Ultimate**, or *Tai Ji* (TY JEE), which was roughly equivalent to the Dao, or Way, in classical Confucian philosophy. To Zhu Xi, this Supreme Ultimate was a set of abstract principles governed by the law of yin and yang and the five elements.

Human beings served as a link between the two halves of this universe. Although human beings live in the material world, each individual has an identity that is linked with the Supreme Ultimate, and the goal of individual action is to transcend the material world in a Buddhist sense to achieve an essential identity with the Supreme Ultimate. According to Zhu Xi and his followers, this transcendence occurs through self-cultivation, which is achieved by the "investigation of things."

The School of Mind During the remainder of the Song Dynasty and into the early years of the Ming, Zhu Xi's ideas became the core of Confucian ideology and a favorite source of questions for the civil service examinations. But during the mid-Ming era, his ideas came under attack from a Confucian scholar named Wang Yangming (WAHNG yahng-MING). Wang and his supporters disagreed with Zhu Xi's focus on learning through an investigation of the outside world and asserted that the correct way to transcend the material world was through an understanding of self. According to this **School of Mind**, the mind and the universe were a single unit. Knowledge was thus intuitive rather than empirical and was obtained through internal self-searching rather than through an investigation of the outside world. The debate is reminiscent of a similar disagreement between followers of ancient Greek philosophers Plato and Aristotle. Plato had argued that all knowledge comes from within, whereas Aristotle argued that knowledge results from an examination of the external world. Wang Yangming's ideas attracted many followers during the Ming Dynasty, and the school briefly rivaled that of Zhu Xi in popularity. Nevertheless, it never won official acceptance, probably because it was too much like Buddhism in denying the importance of a life of participation and social action.

For the average Chinese, of course, an instinctive faith in the existence of household deities or nature spirits continued to take precedence over the intellectual ruminations of Buddhist monks or Confucian scholars. But a prevailing belief in the concept of karma and possible rebirth in a next life was one important legacy of the Buddhist connection, whereas a new manifestation of the Confucian concept of hierarchy was the village god—often believed to live in a prominent tree in the vicinity—who protected the community from wandering evil spirits.

10-5 CHANGING SOCIAL CONDITIONS IN TRADITIONAL CHINA

Focus Questions: In what ways did social conditions in China evolve during the period from the Tang to the Ming Dynasties? Do you see any parallel with similar events elsewhere in the world?

The political and economic changes that took place from the end of the Han to the rise of the Ming Dynasty affected Chinese society in several ways. For one thing, China had become much more complex. Whereas China had once been an almost exclusively rural society with a small urban class of merchants, artisans, and workers almost entirely dependent on the state, the cities had now grown into an important, if statistically still insignificant, part of the population. Urban life, too, had changed. Cities were no longer primarily administrative centers but now included a much broader mix of officials, merchants, artisans, peddlers, and entertainers. Unlike European cities during medieval times, however, Chinese cities did not possess special privileges that protected their residents from the rapacity of the central political authority.

In the countryside, equally significant changes were taking place as the relatively rigid demarcation between the landed aristocracy and the mass of the rural population gave way to a more complex mixture of landed gentry, free farmers, sharecroppers, and landless laborers. There was also a class of "base people"—actors, butchers, and prostitutes—who possessed only limited legal rights and were not permitted to occupy official permissions or take the civil service examination.

10-5a The Rise of the Gentry

Under the early Tang, powerful noble families not only possessed a significant part of the national wealth but also dominated high positions in the imperial government, just as they had at the end of the Han Dynasty 400 years earlier. Some Tang rulers, such as Empress Wu in the late seventh century, sought to limit the power of such great families by recruiting officials through the civil service examination system, but in the end it was the expansion of regional power—often under non-Chinese military governors—that sounded the death knell to the aristocratic system in the late Tang Dynasty.

During the Song Dynasty, the landed gentry emerged as the most influential force in Chinese society. From that time on, the scholar-gentry class—as it is often called—controlled much of the wealth in the rural areas and produced the majority of the candidates for the bureaucracy. By virtue of their possession of land and specialized knowledge of the Confucian classics, the scholar-gentry had replaced the aristocracy as the political and economic elite of Chinese society. Unlike the latter, however, they did not form an exclusive class separated by the accident of birth from the remainder of the population. Upward and downward mobility between the scholar-gentry and the remainder of the population was not uncommon and may have been a key factor in the stability and longevity of the system. A position in the bureaucracy opened the doors to wealth and prestige for the individual and his family, but it was no guarantee of long-term success, and the fortunes of individual families might experience a rapid rise and fall.

For affluent Chinese in this era, life offered many more pleasures than had been available to their forebears. As result of the increased contacts with the outside world first brought about under the Tang, the country was much more cosmopolitan than it had been in previous centuries. In the large commercial cities such as Chang'an, Hangzhou, and Guangzhou, merchants from Central Asia and the Middle East mingled with their Chinese counterparts, introducing their hosts to new forms of entertainment such as playing cards and chess (brought from India, although an early form had been invented in China during the Zhou Dynasty). There were also new forms of transportation such as the paddle-wheel boat and horseback riding (made possible by the introduction of the stirrup), better means of communication (block printing was first invented in the eighth century C.E.), and new tastes for the palate introduced from lands beyond the frontier. Tables and chairs as well as chopsticks (known in China as "fast ones") came into common usage in affluent homes during the Song era. Tea began to emerge as a popular drink and took on ritual significance among intellectuals, poets, and Buddhist monks, who believed that it could stimulate the brain cells and focus the mind. The turn inward that took place during the fifteenth century slowed down but did not end this process.

10-5b Village and Family

Despite the described changes, during the Ming Dynasty the vast majority of the Chinese people still lived off the land in villages ranging in size from a few dozen residents to several thousand. A farmer's life was bounded by his village. Although many communities were connected to the outside world by roads or rivers, the average Chinese citizen rarely left the confines of his native village except for an occasional visit to a nearby market town. This isolation was psychological as well as physical because most Chinese identified with their immediate environment and had difficulty envisioning themselves living beyond the bamboo hedges or mud walls that marked the limit of their horizon.

The family was an even more basic unit than the village for most Chinese. The ideal was the joint family with at least three generations under one roof. Because rice farming was heavily labor intensive, the tradition of the joint family was especially prevalent in the south. When a son married, he was expected to bring his new wife back to live in his parents' home. Often the parents added a new wing to the house for the new family. Women who did not marry remained in the home where they grew up.

Chinese village architecture reflected these traditions. Most family dwellings were simple, consisting of one or two rooms. They were usually constructed of dried mud, stone, or brick, depending on available materials and the family's prosperity. Roofs were of thatch or tile, and the floors were usually of packed dirt. Large houses were often built in a square around an inner courtyard, thus guaranteeing privacy from the outside world.

Within the family unit, the eldest male theoretically ruled as an autocrat. He was responsible for presiding over ancestral rites at an altar, usually in the main room of the house. He had traditional legal rights over his wife, and if she did not provide him with a male heir, he was permitted to take a second wife. In accordance with Confucian tradition, children were expected, above all, to obey their parents, who not only determined their children's careers but also selected their marriage partners. Filial piety was viewed as an absolute moral good that superseded virtually all other obligations.

10-5c The Role of Women

The tradition of male superiority continued from ancient times into the medieval era. Women were not permitted to take the civil service examinations and were discouraged from following any profession or occupation outside the home. Although many women—including the notorious Empress Wu—had achieved prominent positions in politics or the arts during the Tang Dynasty, the view that women's place was in the home achieved renewed emphasis during the southern Song, when Chinese social customs began to reflect a more rigid interpretation of Confucian orthodoxy. The wife had no recourse to divorce. As an old saying went, "Marry a chicken, follow the chicken; marry a dog, follow the dog." Wealthy Chinese males might keep concubines, who lived in a separate room in the house and sometimes competed with the legal wife for precedence. Female children were considered less desirable than males because they could not undertake heavy work in the fields or carry on the family traditions. Poor families often sold their daughters to wealthy villagers to serve as concubines; in times of famine, female infanticide was not uncommon, ensuring that there would be food for the remainder of the family.

A painful and degrading symbol of female inferiority was the tradition of **foot binding**, a technique that became popular during and after the Song Dynasty. The process of binding the feet of girls ages five to thirteen was excruciatingly painful because it bent and compressed the foot to half its normal size by imprisoning it in restrictive bandages. But the procedure was often performed by ambitious mothers intent on ensuring their daughters of the best possible prospects for marriage. Bound feet were considered to be sexually attractive and represented submissiveness and self-discipline, two attributes of the ideal Confucian wife. Beginning with the Song Dynasty, foot binding gradually became common for women of all social classes, although it was less common in southern China, where the cultivation of wet rice could not be carried out with bandaged feet; there it tended to be limited to the scholar-gentry.

As in most traditional societies, there were exceptions to the low status of women in Chinese society. Women had substantial property rights and retained control over their dowries even after divorce or the death of the husband. Wives were frequently an influential force within the home, often

10.9a

10.9 The Preparation of Silk. Since antiquity, the Chinese have fashioned textiles out of silk. The Shang Dynasty produced both hemp and silk cloth, whereas wool, cotton, and hemp were prominent in other parts of the world. Early Chinese dynasties used it for a variety of reasons: as clothing for elites, as currency along the Silk Road, and as a tax from peasants. Although much silk was produced in factories, it was also a cottage industry in the home, with women playing the primary role in the process. Shown here are two paintings from a Yuan Dynasty scroll portraying the various stages in the manufacture of silk yarn. In **10.9a**, women workers separate silk leaves. In **10.9b**, they feed leaves to the silkworms.

10.9b

handling the accounts and taking primary responsibility for raising the children. Some were actively involved in commerce, especially in the major cities, where they ran restaurants and guesthouses or served as owners or clerks of textile shops catering to female customers. Some were employed in silk factories or—as a thirteenth century scroll on the various stages of sericulture graphically demonstrates—even engaged in the production of woven silk in the home (see Image 10.9).

10-6 THE APOGEE OF CHINESE CULTURE

Q **Focus Question:** What were the main achievements in Chinese literature and art in the period between the Tang and Ming Dynasties, and what technological innovations and intellectual developments contributed to these achievements?

The period between the Tang and the Ming Dynasties was in many ways the great age of Chinese literature and art. Enriched by Buddhist and Daoist images and themes, Chinese poetry and painting reached the pinnacle of their creativity. Porcelain emerged as the highest form of Chinese ceramics, and sculpture flourished under the influence of styles imported from India and Central Asia.

10-6a Literature

The development of Chinese literature was stimulated by two technological innovations: the invention of paper during the Han Dynasty and the invention of woodblock printing during the Tang. No longer were written materials inscribed solely on strips of bamboo or silk scrolls. At first, paper was used primarily for clothing, wrapping material, toilet tissue, and even armor, but it was being used for writing as well by the first century B.C.E.

In the seventh century C.E., the Chinese developed the technique of carving an entire page of text into a wooden block, inking it, and then pressing it onto a sheet of paper. Ordinarily, a text was printed on a long sheet of paper like a scroll. Then the paper was folded and stitched together to form a book. The earliest printed book known today is a Buddhist text published in 868 C.E. that is more than sixteen feet long. Although the Chinese eventually developed movable type as well, block printing continued to be used until relatively modern times because of the large number of Chinese characters needed to produce a lengthy text.

Experience an interactive version of this period in MINDTAP

Two Tang Poets

Art & Ideas

LI BO WAS ONE OF THE GREAT POETS of the Tang Dynasty. The first selection here, "Quiet Night Thoughts," is probably the best known poem in China and has been memorized by schoolchildren for centuries. The second poem, "Drinking Alone in Moonlight," reflects the poet's carefree attitude toward life.

Du Fu, Li Bo's prime competitor as the greatest poet of the Tang Dynasty, was often the more reflective of the two. In "Spring Prospect," the poet has been imprisoned in the capital after a rebellion against the dynasty has left the city in ruins.

Li Bo, "Quiet Night Thoughts on a Quiet Night"

*Beside my bed the moon shines brightly
It almost looks like frost on the ground.
When I lift my head, I see the bright moon;
When I lower my head, I think of my old home.*

Li Bo, "Drinking Alone Beneath the Moon"

*A jug of wine among the flowers,
I drink alone—without friends or family.
I lift my cup to the bright moon.
With my shadow, we make a threesome.
But the moon is unable to drink,
And my shadow trails behind me.*

*So I join the moon and my shadow,
And we happily greet the end of spring.
I sing, and the moon sways to my song;
I dance, and my shadow trails behind.
When I'm sober we share our joys,
When I'm drunk, we go our separate ways:
Forever joined, we wander without care,
Until we meet in the Milky Way!*

Du Fu, "Spring Prospect"

*The city has fallen. Only the mountains and rivers have survived,
The grass and trees grow thickly to greet the spring.
Touched by the sight, even the flowers shed their tears;
Reluctant to leave, the birds are heavy of heart.
The beacon fires have been burning for three months;
A letter from home would be as precious as gold.
The hairs on my white head have grown so thin;
That they can barely hold a hairpin!*

 Historians often contrast these two famous poets in terms of their personalities and their approach to life. Can you see any differences in their points of view as conveyed in these short poems?

Source: Translation by William J. Duiker.

Even with printing, books remained too expensive for most Chinese, but they did help popularize all forms of literary writing among the educated elite.

Poetry   During the Tang and the Song dynasties, poetry was where most Chinese writers best expressed their literary talents. Chinese poems celebrated the beauty of nature, the changes of the seasons, and the joys of friendship; others expressed sadness at the brevity of life, old age, and parting. Love poems existed but were neither as intense as Western verse nor as sensual as Indian poetry.

Two eighth-century Tang poets, Li Bo (LEE BOH) and Du Fu (DOO FOO), symbolized the genius of the era. The two poets were a study in contrasts. Where Li Bo was a free spirit whose writing often centered on nature and shifted easily between moods of revelry and melancholy, Du Fu was a sober Confucian whose poems often dealt with historical or ethical issues. Many of his works reflect a concern with social injustice and the plight of the unfortunate

rarely found in the writings of his contemporaries (see Historical Voices, "Two Tang Poets," above).

Neither the poetry nor the prose of the great writers of the Tang and Song Dynasties, however, was written for or ever reached the majority of the Chinese population. Chinese peasants and artisans acquired their knowledge of Chinese history, Confucian moralisms, and even Buddhist scripture from a rich oral tradition passed down by storytellers, wandering minstrels, and itinerant monks.

The Chinese Novel   During the Yuan Dynasty, new forms of literary creativity, including popular theater and the novel, began to appear. One of the most famous novels was *Tale of the Marshes*, an often violent tale of bandit heroes who at the end of the northern Song banded together to oppose government taxes and official oppression. They stole from those in power to share with the poor. *Tale of the Marshes* is the first prose fiction that describes the daily ordeal of ordinary Chinese people in their own language.

10-6b Art

Although painting flourished in China under the Han and reached a level of artistic excellence under the Tang, little remains from those periods. From celebrated Tang Dynasty artist Wu Daozi, for example, little remains today except for copies of his paintings and rubbings (as seen in Image 10.3b). Many scroll paintings by artists of the Song and the Yuan Dynasties (or copies made my later admirers), however, have survived, and are considered the apogee of painting in traditional China.

Like literature, Chinese painting found inspiration in Buddhist and Daoist sources. Some of the best surviving examples of the Tang period are the Buddhist wall paintings in the caves at Dunhuang (doon-HWAHNG) in Central Asia. Like the few surviving Tang scroll paintings, these wall paintings display a love of color and refinement that are reminiscent of styles in India and Persia (see Comparative Illustration, "The Two Worlds of Tang China," p. 243).

Daoism ultimately had a greater influence than Buddhism on Chinese painting. From early times, Chinese artists retreated to the mountains to write and paint and find the Dao, or Way, in nature. In the fifth century, one Chinese painter who was too old to travel began to paint mountain scenes from memory and announced that depicting nature could function as a substitute for contemplating it. Painting, he said, could be the means of realizing the Dao. This explains in part the emphasis on nature in traditional Chinese painting. The word *landscape* in Chinese means "mountain-water," and the Daoist search for balance between Earth and water, hard and soft, yang and yin, is at play in the tradition of Chinese painting.

To represent nature, Chinese artists attempted to reveal the quintessential forms of the landscape. Rather than depicting a specific mountain, they tried to portray the idea of "mountain." Empty spaces were left in the paintings because, in the Daoist vision, one cannot know the whole truth. Daoist influence was also evident in the tendency to portray human beings as insignificant in the midst of nature. In contrast to Western art with its focus on the human body and personality, Chinese art presented people as tiny figures fishing in a small boat, meditating on a cliff, or wandering up a hillside trail, coexisting with but not dominating nature.

The Chinese displayed their paintings on long scrolls of silk or paper that were attached to a wooden cylindrical bar at the bottom. Varying in length from three to twenty feet, the paintings were unfolded slowly so that the eye could enjoy each segment, beginning at the bottom with water or a village and moving upward into the hills to the mountain peaks and the sky.

By the tenth century, Chinese painters began to eliminate color from their paintings, preferring to capture the distilled essence of a landscape in washes of black ink on white silk. Borrowing from calligraphy, now a sophisticated

Private Collection/The Bridgeman Art Library

10.10 Willows and Distant Mountains. In contrast to the focus on the human personality that is found in Western art, traditional Chinese painting often presented people as the insignificant figures coexisting within the totality of nature. Ma Yuan (1190–1235), who was descended from a family of painters, continued this long tradition of "mountain-water" landscapes in the painting shown here. Although they are dwarfed by the immensity of the surrounding mountains, these five tiny figures seem in harmony with nature as they go about their daily lives.

and revered art, they emphasized the brush stroke and created black-and-white landscapes characterized by a gravity of mood and dominated by overpowering mountains.

Second only to painting in creativity was the field of ceramics, notably the manufacture of porcelain. Made of fine clay baked at unusually high temperatures in a kiln, porcelain was first produced during the period after the fall of the Han and became popular during the Tang era. During the Song, porcelain came into its own. The translucence of Chinese porcelain represented the final product of a technique that did not reach Europe until the eighteenth century.

CHAPTER SUMMARY

Traditionally, Chinese historians believed that Chinese history tended to be cyclical and driven by the dynamic interplay of the forces of good and evil, yang and yin, growth and decay. Beyond the forces of conflict and change lay the essential continuity of Chinese history based on timeless principles established by Confucius and other thinkers during the Zhou dynasty in antiquity. This view of the underlying forces of Chinese history was long accepted as valid by historians in the West and led many to assert that Chinese history was unique and could not be placed in a European or universal framework. Whereas Western history was linear, leading steadily away from the past, China's always returned to its moorings and was rooted in the values and institutions of antiquity.

In recent years, however, this traditional view of a changeless China has come under increasing challenge from historians who see patterns of change that made the China of the late fifteenth century a far different place from the country that had existed at the rise of the Tang Dynasty in 600. To these scholars, China had passed through its own version of the "middle ages" and was on the verge of beginning a linear evolution into a posttraditional society.

As we have seen, China at the beginning of the Ming Dynasty had advanced in many ways since the end of the great Han Dynasty more than 1,000 years earlier. The industrial and commercial sector had grown considerably in size, complexity, and technological capacity; in the countryside, the concentration of political and economic power in the hands of the aristocracy had been replaced by a more stable and more equitable mixture of landed gentry, freehold farmers, and sharecroppers. The civil service provided an avenue of upward mobility that was unavailable elsewhere in the world, and the state tolerated a diversity of beliefs that responded to the emotional needs and preferences of the Chinese people. In many respects, China's achievements were unsurpassed throughout the world and marked a major advance beyond the world of antiquity.

Yet there were also key similarities between the China of the Ming and the China of late antiquity. Ming China was still a predominantly agrarian society, and wealth was based primarily on the ownership of land. Commercial activities flourished but remained under a high level of government regulation and by no means represented a major proportion of the national income. China also remained a relatively centralized empire based on an official ideology that stressed the virtue of hard work, social conformity, and hierarchy.

Thus, the significant change that China experienced during its medieval era can probably be best described as change within continuity, an evolutionary working out of trends that had first become visible during the Han Dynasty or even earlier. The result was a civilization that was the envy of its neighbors and of the world. It also influenced other states in the region, including Japan, Korea, and Vietnam. It is to these societies along the Chinese rimlands that we next turn.

REFLECTION QUESTIONS

Q Why is the Tang Dynasty often described as the greatest and most glorious era in Chinese history, and do you think that its reputation is justified?

Q What impact did the era of Mongol rule have on societies that were affected by it? Do you agree that some of the consequences ultimately had beneficial effects on world history? If so, why?

Q What are the arguments on both sides of the debate over whether Chinese society underwent fundamental changes during the period discussed in this chapter? Which arguments do you find more persuasive, and why?

CHAPTER TIMELINE

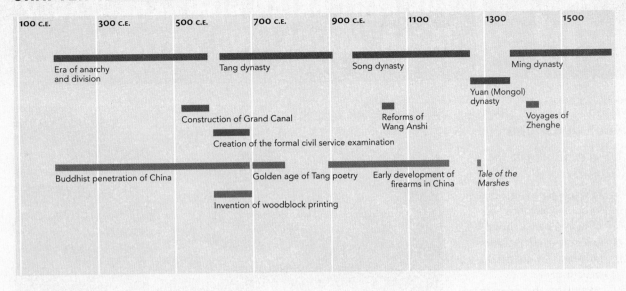

| 100 C.E. | 300 C.E. | 500 C.E. | 700 C.E. | 900 C.E. | 1100 | 1300 | 1500 |

Era of anarchy and division

Tang dynasty

Song dynasty

Ming dynasty

Yuan (Mongol) dynasty

Construction of Grand Canal

Reforms of Wang Anshi

Voyages of Zhenghe

Creation of the formal civil service examination

Buddhist penetration of China

Golden age of Tang poetry

Early development of firearms in China

Tale of the Marshes

Invention of woodblock printing

CHAPTER NOTES

1. *The Travels of Marco Polo* (New York, n.d.), pp. 128, 179.
2. Chu-yu, *P'ing-chow Table Talks,* quoted in R. Temple, *The Genius of China: 3,000 Years of Science, Discovery, and Invention* (New York, 1986), p. 150.
3. Quoted in J. K. Fairbank, E. O. Reischauer, and A. M. Craig, *East Asia: Tradition and Transformation* (Boston, 1973), p. 164.
4. *The Travels of Marco Polo* (New York, n.d.), p. 229.
5. S. A. M. Adshead, *China in World History* (New York, 2000), p. 132.

MINDTAP
From Cengage

MindTap® is a fully online, highly personalized learning experience built upon Cengage Learning content. MindTap combines student learning tools—readings, multimedia, activities, and assessments—into a singular Learning Path that guides students through the course and helps students develop the critical thinking, analysis, and communication skills that are essential to academic and professional success.

Chapter Outline and Focus Questions

11-1 Japan: Land of the Rising Sun

Q How did Japan's geographic location affect the course of early Japanese history, and how did the location influence the political structures and social institutions that arose there?

11-2 Korea: Bridge to the East

Q What were the main characteristics of economic and social life in early Korea?

11-3 Vietnam: The Smaller Dragon

Q What were the main developments in Vietnamese history before 1500? Why were the Vietnamese able to restore their national independence after a millennium of Chinese rule?

11.1 **The Jade Mountain Temple on Returned Sword Lake, Hanoi**

William J. Duiker

Critical Thinking

Q *How did Chinese civilization influence the societies that arose in Japan, Korea, and Vietnam during their early histories?*

Connections to Today

Q *The fact that Japan is an island nation has had a significant effect on how the Japanese people see their role in the world. How do you think the fact that the United States is a continental nation affects the attitude of the American people in today's world?*

A SMALL BODY OF WATER in the heart of the Vietnamese national capital of Hanoi (ha-NOY) is known affectionately to local city dwellers as Returned Sword Lake. The lake owes its name to a legend that Le Loi (LAY LOY), founder of the later Le (LAY) Dynasty in the fifteenth century, drew a magic sword from the lake that enabled him to achieve a great victory over Chinese occupation forces. Thus, to many Vietnamese the lake symbolizes their nation's historical resistance to domination by its powerful northern neighbor.

Ironically, however, a temple that was later erected on an island in the middle of the lake reflects—by its clear affinity with Chinese architectural counterparts— the strong influence that China continued to exert on traditional Vietnamese culture. After Le Loi's victory, according to the legend, the sword was returned to the water, and the Vietnamese ruler accepted a tributary relationship to his "elder brother," the Chinese emperor in Beijing. China's philosophy, political institutions, and social mores served as hallmarks for the Vietnamese people down to the early years of the twentieth century. That is why for centuries Vietnam was known as "the smaller dragon."

The legend of Returned Sword Lake provides us with a useful reminder about China's historic relations with some of the smaller states on its periphery, not only with Vietnam but also with other agricultural societies such as Japan and Korea. As the most technologically advanced society in East Asia in ancient times, China traditionally exerted a high degree of political, social, and cultural influence throughout the region. On some occasions, strong rulers in China actually sought to absorb these peripheral societies into the powerful embrace of the Chinese Empire. Ultimately, however, all three societies were able to retain their separate political and cultural identities while still carrying the imprint of several centuries of borrowing from China. In this chapter, we will take a closer look at these emerging societies along the Chinese rimlands and consider how their cultural achievements reflected or contrasted with those of the Chinese Empire.

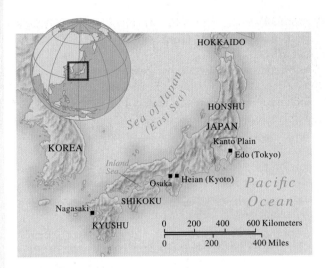

Map 11.1 Early Japan. This map shows key cities in Japan during the early development of the Japanese state.

 Where was the original heartland of Japanese civilization on the main island of Honshu?

11-1 JAPAN: LAND OF THE RISING SUN

 Focus Question: How did Japan's geographic location affect the course of early Japanese history, and how did the location influence the political structures and social institutions that arose there?

Geography accounts for some of the historical differences between Chinese and Japanese society. Whereas China is a continental civilization, Japan is an island country. It consists of four main islands (see Map 11.1): Hokkaido (hoh-KY-doh) in the north, the main island of Honshu (HAHN-shoo) in the center, and the two smaller islands of Kyushu (KYOO-shoo) and Shikoku (shee-KOH-koo) in the southwest. Its total land area is about 146,000 square miles, about the size of the state of Montana. Japan's main islands are at approximately the same latitude as the eastern seaboard of the United States and so are also blessed with a temperate climate. It is slightly warmer on the east coast, which is washed by the Pacific current that sweeps up from the south, and it has several natural harbors that provide protection from the winds and high waves of the Pacific Ocean. As a consequence, in recent times most Japanese people have tended to live along the east coast, especially in the flat plains surrounding the cities of Tokyo

(TOH-kee-oh), Osaka (oh-SAH-kuh), and Kyoto (KYOH-toh). In these favorable environmental conditions, Japanese farmers have been able to harvest two crops of rice annually since early times.

By no means, however, is Japan an agricultural paradise. Like China, much of the country is mountainous, so only about 20 percent of the total land area is suitable for cultivation. These mountains are of volcanic origin because the Japanese islands are located at the juncture of the Asian and Pacific tectonic plates. This location is both an advantage and a disadvantage. Volcanic soils are extremely fertile, which helps explain the exceptionally high productivity of Japanese farmers. At the same time, the area is prone to earthquakes, such as the famous earthquake of 1923, which destroyed almost the entire city of Tokyo, and the massive earthquake just offshore in 2011 that triggered a devastating tsunami along the east coast of northern Honshu Island.

The fact that Japan is an island country has had a significant impact on Japanese history. As we have seen, the continental character of Chinese civilization, with its constant threat of invasion from the north, had many consequences for Chinese history. One effect was to make the Chinese more sensitive to the preservation of their culture from destruction at the hands of non-Chinese invaders. As one fourth-century C.E. Chinese ruler remarked when he was forced to move his capital southward under pressure from nomadic incursions, "The King takes All Under Heaven as his home."[1] Proud of their considerable cultural achievements and their dominant position throughout the region, the Chinese have traditionally been reluctant to dilute the purity of their culture with foreign innovations. Culture more than race is a determinant of the Chinese sense of identity.

By contrast, the island character of Japan probably had the effect of strengthening the Japanese sense of ethnic and cultural distinctiveness. Although the Japanese view of themselves as the most ethnically homogeneous people in East Asia may not be entirely accurate (modern Japanese probably represent a mix of peoples, much like their neighbors on the continent), their sense of racial and cultural homogeneity has enabled them to import ideas from abroad without worrying that the borrowings will destroy the uniqueness of their own culture.

11-1a A Gift from the Gods: Prehistoric Japan

According to an ancient legend recorded in historical chronicles written in the eighth century C.E., the islands of Japan were formed as a result of the marriage of the god Izanagi (ee-zah-NAH-gee) and the goddess Izanami (ee-zah-NAH-mee). After giving birth to Japan, Izanami gave birth to a sun goddess whose name was Amaterasu (ah-mah-teh-RAH-soo). A descendant of Amaterasu later descended to Earth and became founder of the Japanese nation. This Japanese creation myth is reminiscent of similar beliefs in other ancient societies, which often saw themselves as the product of a union of deities. What is interesting about the Japanese version is that it has survived into modern times as an explanation for the uniqueness of the Japanese people and the divinity of the Japanese emperor, who is still believed by some Japanese to be a direct descendant of the sun goddess Amaterasu. Modern scholars have a more prosaic explanation for the origins of Japanese civilization. According to archaeological evidence, the Japanese islands have been occupied by human beings for at least 100,000 years. The earliest known Neolithic inhabitants are called the Jomon (JOH-mahn) people from the cord pattern of their pottery; they lived in the islands as early as 8000 B.C.E. They lived by hunting, fishing, and food gathering and probably had not mastered the techniques of agriculture.

Agriculture probably first appeared in Japan sometime during the first millennium B.C.E., although some archaeologists believe that the Jomon people had already learned how to cultivate some food crops considerably earlier. Around 800 B.C.E., rice cultivation was introduced, possibly by immigrants from the mainland by way of the Korean Peninsula. Until recently, historians believed that these immigrants drove out the existing inhabitants of the area and gave rise to the emerging Yayoi (yah-YOH-ee) culture (named for the site near Tokyo where pottery from the period was found). Now historians think that Yayoi culture was a product of a mixture between the Jomon people and

the new arrivals. In any event, it seems clear that the Yayoi peoples were the ancestors of the vast majority of present-day Japanese.

At first, the Yayoi lived primarily on the southern island of Kyushu, but eventually they migrated northward onto the main island of Honshu, assimilating with the previous inhabitants of the area, some of whose descendants, the Ainu (Y-nyoo), still live in the northern islands. Finally, in the first centuries C.E., the Yayoi settled in the Yamato (YAH-mah-toh) Plain in the vicinity of the modern cities of Osaka and Kyoto. Japanese legend recounts the story of a "divine warrior," Jimmu (JIH-moo), who led his people eastward from the island of Kyushu to establish a kingdom in the Yamato Plain.

In central Honshu, the Yayoi set up a tribal society based on clans called *uji* (oo-JEE). Each uji was ruled by a hereditary chieftain who provided protection to the local population in return for a proportion of the annual harvest. The population was divided between a small aristocratic class and the majority of the population, which was composed of rice farmers, artisans, and other household servants of the aristocrats. Yayoi society was highly decentralized, although eventually the chieftain of the dominant clan in the Yamato region, who claimed to be descended from the sun goddess Amaterasu, achieved a kind of titular primacy. There is no evidence, however, of a central ruler equivalent in power to the Chinese rulers of the Shang and Zhou eras.

11-1b The Rise of the Japanese State

Although the inhabitants of the Japanese islands had been aware of China for centuries, they paid relatively little attention to their more advanced neighbor until the early seventh century, when the rise of the centralized and expansionistic Tang Dynasty presented a challenge. When the Tang began to meddle in the affairs of the Korean Peninsula, Yamato rulers attempted to deal with this potential threat in two ways. First, they sought alliances with the remaining Korean states. Second, they attempted to centralize their authority so that they could mount a more effective resistance in the event of a Chinese invasion. The key figure in this effort was Shotoku Taishi (shoh-TOH-koo ty-EE-shee) (572–622), a leading aristocrat in one of the dominant clans in the Yamato region. Prince Shotoku sent missions to the Tang capital of Chang'an to learn about the political institutions already in use in the relatively centralized Tang kingdom.

Emulating the Chinese Model Shotoku Taishi then launched a series of reforms to create a new system based roughly on the Chinese model. In the so-called seventeen-article constitution, he called for the creation

The Longhouse

Science & Technology

MANY EARLY PEOPLES BUILT LONGHOUSES of wood and thatch to store their goods and carry on community activities. Many such structures were erected on heavy pilings to protect the interior from floods, insects, and wild animals. Image 11.2a shows a model of a sixth-century C.E. warehouse in Osaka, Japan. The original was apparently used by local residents to store grain and other foodstuffs. Image 11.2b shows a reconstruction of a similar structure built originally by Vikings in Denmark. The longhouses in Image 11.2c are still occupied by families living on Nias, a small island off the coast of Sumatra. The outer walls were built to resemble the hulls of Dutch galleons that plied the seas near Nias during the seventeenth and eighteenth centuries.

Q *The longhouse served as a communal structure in many human communities in early times. What types of structures serve communities in modern societies?*

11.2b

11.2a

11.2c

of a centralized government under a supreme ruler and a merit system for selecting and ranking public officials (see Historical Voices, "The Seventeen-Article Constitution," p. 270). His objective was to limit the powers of the hereditary nobility and enhance the prestige and authority of the Yamato ruler, who claimed divine status and was now emerging as the symbol of the supposedly unique character of the Japanese nation.

After Shotoku Taishi's death in 622, his successors continued to introduce reforms to make the government more efficient. In the series of **Taika reforms**—*taika* (TY-kuh) means "great change"—that began in the mid-seventh century, the Grand Council of State was established to preside over a cabinet of eight ministries. To the traditional six ministries of Tang China were added ministers representing the central secretariat and the imperial household. The islands of Japan were divided into administrative districts on the Chinese pattern. The rural village, composed ideally of fifty households, was the basic unit of government. The village chief was responsible for "the

Experience an interactive version of this period in ⫚ MINDTAP

The Seventeen-Article Constitution

Politics & Government THE FOLLOWING EXCERPT from the *Nihon Shoki* (nee-HAHN SHO H-kee) (*Chronicles of Japan*) is a passage from the seventeen-article constitution promulgated in 604 C.E. Although the opening section reflects Chinese influence in its emphasis on social harmony, there is also a strong focus on obedience and hierarchy. The constitution was put into practice during the reign of the famous Prince Shotoku.

The Chronicles of Japan

Summer, 4th month, 3rd day [12th year of Empress Suiko, 604 C.E.]. The Crown Prince personally drafted and promulgated a constitution consisting of seventeen articles, which are as follows:

I. Harmony is to be cherished, and opposition for opposition's sake must be avoided as a matter of principle. Men are often influenced by partisan feelings, except a few sagacious ones. Hence there are some who disobey their lords and fathers, or who dispute with their neighboring villages. If those above are harmonious and those below are cordial, their discussion will be guided by a spirit of conciliation, and reason shall naturally prevail. There will be nothing that cannot be accomplished.

II. With all our heart, revere the three treasures. The three treasures, consisting of Buddha, the Doctrine, and the Monastic Order, are the final refuge of the four generated beings, and are the supreme objects of worship in all countries. Can any man in any age ever fail to respect these teachings? Few men are utterly devoid of goodness, and men can be taught to follow the teachings. Unless they take refuge in the three treasures, there is no way of rectifying their misdeeds.

III. When an imperial command is given, obey it with reverence. The sovereign is likened to heaven, and his subjects are likened to earth. With heaven providing the cover and earth supporting it, the four seasons proceed in orderly fashion, giving sustenance to all that which is in nature. If earth attempts to overtake the functions of heaven, it destroys everything. . . . If there is no reverence shown to the imperial command, ruin will automatically result. . . .

IV. Every man must be given his clearly delineated responsibility. If a wise man is entrusted with office, the sound of praise arises. If a wicked man holds office, disturbances become frequent. . . . In all things, great or small, find the right man, and the country will be well governed. . . . In this manner, the state will be lasting and its sacerdotal functions will be free from danger.

Q *What are the key components in this first constitution in the history of Japan? To what degree do its provisions conform to Chinese Confucian principles?*

Source: Excerpt from *Sources of Japanese History*, David Lu, ed. (New York: McGraw-Hill, 1974), I, p. 7.

maintenance of the household registers, the assigning of the sowing of crops and the cultivation of mulberry trees, the prevention of offenses, and the requisitioning of taxes and forced labor." A law code was introduced, and a new tax system was established; now all farmland technically belonged to the state, so taxes were paid directly to the central government rather than through the local nobility, as had previously been the case.

As a result of their new acquaintance with China, the Japanese also developed a strong interest in Buddhism. Some of the first Japanese to travel to China during this period were Buddhist pilgrims hoping to learn more about the exciting new doctrine and take home scriptures. By the seventh century C.E., Buddhism had become quite popular among the aristocrats, who endowed wealthy monasteries that became active in Japanese politics. At first, the new faith did not penetrate to the masses, but eventually popular sects such as the Pure Land sect, an import from China, won many adherents among the common people.

The Nara Period Such efforts to build a new state modeled roughly after the Tang state were initially successful. After Shotoku Taishi's death in 622, political influence fell into the hands of the powerful Fujiwara (foo-jee-WAH-rah) clan, which managed to marry into the ruling family and continue the reforms Shotoku had begun. In 710, a new capital, laid out on a grid similar to the great Tang city of Chang'an, was established at Nara (NAH-rah) on the eastern edge of the Yamato Plain. The Yamato ruler began to use the title "son of Heaven" in the Chinese fashion. Unlike the case in China, however, the concept of the Mandate of Heaven did not apply. In deference to the belief in the Yamato family's divine character, the mandate to rule remained in perpetuity in the imperial house. It was apparently at this time that the Yamato also began to refer to their country as Japan ("Sun's origin") when dealing with the Tang court. Eventually the new name replaced the Tang's previous use of the term *Wa*, or "dwarf country," to refer to the peoples of Japan.

Had these reforms succeeded, Japan might have followed the Chinese pattern and developed a centralized bureaucratic government. But as time passed, the central government proved unable to curb the power of the aristocracy. Unlike in Tang China, the civil service examinations in Japan were not open to all but were restricted to individuals of noble birth. Leading officials were awarded large tracts of land and, like the powerful Buddhist monasteries, were able to keep the taxes from the lands for themselves. Increasingly starved for revenue, the central government steadily lost power and influence. There would be no empire in Japan similar to that created by the Tang Dynasty in China.

Map 11.2 The Yamato Plain

The Heian Period The influence of powerful Buddhist monasteries in the city of Nara soon became oppressive, and in 794 the emperor moved the capital to his family's original power base at nearby Heian (hay-AHN) on the site of present-day Kyoto. The new capital was laid out in the now familiar Chang'an checkerboard pattern but on a larger scale than at Nara. Increasingly self-confident, the rulers ceased to emulate the Tang and sent no more missions to Chang'an. The influence of Buddhism was restricted by prohibiting the establishment of monasteries inside the new capital. At Heian, the emperor—as the head of the royal line descended from the sun goddess was now officially styled—continued to rule in name, but actual power was in the hands of the Fujiwara clan, which had managed through intermarriage to link its fortunes closely with the imperial family. A senior member of the clan began to serve as regent (in practice, the chief executive of the government) for the emperor.

What was occurring was a return to the decentralization that had existed before Shotoku Taishi. The central government's attempts to impose taxes directly on the rice lands failed, and rural areas came under the control of powerful families whose wealth was based on the ownership of tax-exempt farmland called *shoen* (SHOH-en). To avoid paying taxes, peasants would often surrender their lands to a local aristocrat, who would then allow the peasants to cultivate the lands in return for the payment of rent. To obtain protection from government officials, these local aristocrats might grant title of their lands to a more powerful aristocrat with influence at court. In return, these individuals would receive inheritable rights to a portion of the income from the estate (see Comparative Essay, "Feudal Orders Around the World," p. 272).

With the decline of central power at Heian, local aristocrats tended to take justice into their own hands and increasingly used military force to protect their interests. A new class of military retainers called the **samurai** (SAM-uh-ry) emerged whose purpose was to protect the security and property of their patrons. The samurai lived a life of simplicity and self-sacrifice and were

11.3 A Worship Hall in Nara. Buddhist temple compounds in Japan traditionally offered visitors an escape from the tensions of the outside world. The temple site normally included an entrance gate, a central courtyard, a worship hall, a pagoda, and a cloister, as well as support buildings for the monks. The pagoda, a multitiered tower, harbored a sacred relic of the Buddha and served as the East Asian version of the Indian stupa. The worship hall corresponded to the Vedic carved chapel. Here we see the Todaiji (toh-DY-jee) worship hall in Nara. Originally constructed in the mid-eighth century C.E., it is reputed to be the largest wooden structure in the world and is the centerpiece of a vast temple complex on the outskirts of the old capital city.

William J. Duiker

Feudal Orders Around the World

Politics & Government The word *feudalism* usually conjures up images of European knights on horseback clad in armor and wielding a sword and lance. Between 800 and 1500, however, a form of social organization that modern historians have called *feudalism* developed in different parts of the world. By *feudalism*, these historians mean a decentralized political order in which local lords owed loyalty and provided military service to a king or more powerful lord. In Europe, a feudal order based on lords and vassals arose between 800 and 900 and flourished for the next 400 years.

In Japan, a feudal order much like that found in Europe developed between 800 and 1500. By the end of the ninth century, powerful nobles in the countryside, while owing a loose loyalty to the Japanese emperor, began to exercise political and legal power in their own extensive lands. To protect their property and security, these nobles retained samurai, warriors who owed loyalty to the nobles and provided military service for them. Like knights in Europe, the samurai followed a warrior code and fought on horseback while clad in armor. They carried a sword and bow and arrow, however, rather than a sword and lance.

In some respects, the political relationships among the Indian states beginning in the fifth century also took on the character of the feudal order that emerged in Europe in the Middle Ages. Like medieval European lords, local Indian rajas were technically vassals of the king; unlike in European feudalism, the relationship was not a contractual one. Still, the Indian model became highly complex, with "inner" and "outer" vassals, depending on their physical or political proximity to the king, and "greater" or "lesser" vassals, depending on their power and influence. As in Europe, the vassals themselves often had vassals.

In the Valley of Mexico, between 1300 and 1500 the Aztecs developed a political system that bore some similarities to the Japanese, Indian, and European feudal orders. Although the Aztec king was a powerful, authoritarian ruler, the local rulers of lands outside the capital city were allowed considerable freedom. Nevertheless, they paid tribute to the king and also provided him with military forces. Unlike the knights and samurai of Europe and Japan, however, Aztec warriors were armed with sharp knives made of stone and spears of wood fitted with razor-sharp blades cut from stone.

 What were the key characteristics of the political order we know as feudalism? To what degree did Japanese feudalism exhibit these characteristics?

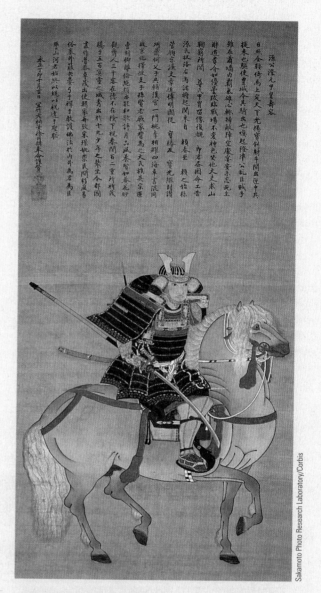

Sakamoto Photo Research Laboratory/Corbis

11.4 Samurai. During the Kamakura period, painters began to depict the adventures of the new warrior class. Here is an imposing mounted samurai warrior, the Japanese equivalent of the medieval knight in fief-holding Europe. Like his European counterpart, the samurai was supposed to live by a strict moral code and maintain unquestioning loyalty to his liege lord. Above all, a samurai's life was one of simplicity and self-sacrifice.

Japan's Warrior Class

Politics & Government

THE SAMURAI WAS THE JAPANESE EQUIVALENT of the medieval European knight. Like the knights, the samurai fought on horseback and were expected to adhere to a strict moral code. Although this selection comes from a document dating only to the 1500s, a distinct mounted warrior class had already begun to emerge in Japan as early as the tenth century. This passage shows the importance of hierarchy and duty in a society influenced by the doctrine of Confucius.

The Way of the Samurai

The master once said: . . . Generation after generation men have taken their livelihood from tilling the soil, or devised and manufactured tools, or produced profit from mutual trade, so that people's needs were satisfied. Thus, the occupations of farmer, artisan, and merchant necessarily grew up as complementary to one another. However, the samurai eats food without growing it, uses utensils without manufacturing them, and profits without buying or selling. . . . The samurai is one who does not cultivate, does not manufacture, and does not engage in trade, but it cannot be that he has no function at all as a samurai. . . .

If one deeply fixes [one's] attention on what I have said and examines closely one's own function, it will become clear what the business of the samurai is. The business of the samurai consists in reflecting on his own station in life, in discharging loyal service to his master if he has one, in deepening his fidelity in associations with friends, and, with due consideration of his own position, in devoting himself to duty above all. . . . The samurai dispenses with the business of the farmer, artisan, and merchant and confines himself to practicing this Way; should there be someone in the three classes of the common people who transgresses against these moral principles, the samurai summarily punishes him and thus upholds proper moral principles in the land. . . . Outwardly he stands in physical readiness for any call to service, and inwardly he strives to fulfill the Way of the lord and subject, friend and friend, father and son, older and younger brother, and husband and wife. Within his heart he keeps to the ways of peace, but without he keeps his weapons ready for use. The three classes of the common people make him their teacher and respect him. By following his teachings, they are enabled to understand what is fundamental and what is secondary.

Herein lies the Way of the samurai, the means by which he earns his clothing, food, and shelter; and by which his heart is put at ease, and he is enabled to pay back at length his obligation to his lord and the kindness of his parents. Were there no such duty, it would be as though one were to steal the kindness of one's parents, greedily devour the income of one's master, and make one's whole life a career of robbery and brigandage. This would be very grievous.

 In what ways were the duties and characteristics of a samurai similar to those of a Brahmin in India or a Confucian "gentleman" in China? What might account for the similarities and differences?

Source: From *Sources of Japanese Tradition* by William Theodore de Bary, Carol Gluck, and Arthur E. Tiedemann. Copyright © 2005 by Columbia University Press. Reprinted with permission of the publisher.

---

expected to maintain an intense and unquestioning loyalty to their lord. Bonds of loyalty were also quite strong among members of the samurai class, and homosexuality was common. Like the knights of medieval Europe, the samurai fought on horseback (although, as noted in the Comparative Essay, samurai carried swords and bows and arrows rather than lances and shields) and were supposed to live by a strict warrior code, known in Japan as **Bushido** (BOO-shee-doh), or "way of the warrior" (see Historical Voices, "Japan's Warrior Class," above). As time went on, they became a major force and almost a surrogate government in much of the Japanese countryside.

The Kamakura Shogunate and After By the end of the twelfth century, as rivalries among noble families led to almost constant civil war, centralizing forces once again asserted themselves. This time the instrument was a powerful noble from a warrior clan named Minamoto Yoritomo (mee-nah-MOH-toh yoh-ree-TOH-moh) (1142–1199), who defeated several rivals and set up his power base on the Kamakura (kah-mah-KOO-rah) Peninsula, south of the modern city of Tokyo. To strengthen the state, he created a more centralized government—the **bakufu** (buh-KOO-foo or bah-KOO-fuh) or "tent government"—under a powerful military leader known as the **shogun** (SHOH-gun)

Experience an interactive version of this period in ⁙ MINDTAP (general). The shogun attempted to increase the powers of the central government while reducing rival aristocratic clans to vassal status. In this **shogunate system**, the emperor was the titular authority while the shogun exercised actual power, the political system prevailing in Japan until the second half of the nineteenth century.

The shogunate (SHOH-gun-ut *or* SHOH-gun-ayt) system worked effectively, and it was fortunate that it did, because during the next century, Japan faced the most serious challenge it had yet confronted. The Mongols, who had destroyed the Song Dynasty in China, were now attempting to assert their hegemony throughout all of Asia (see Chapter 10). In 1266, Emperor Khubilai Khan demanded tribute from Japan. When the Japanese refused, he invaded with an army of more than 30,000 troops. Bad weather and difficult conditions forced a retreat, but the Mongols tried again in 1281. An army nearly 150,000 strong landed on the northern coast of Kyushu. The Japanese were able to contain them for two months until virtually the entire Mongol fleet was destroyed by a massive typhoon—a "divine wind," or *kamikaze* (kah-mi-KAH-zee). Japan would not face a foreign invader again until American forces landed on the Japanese islands in the summer of 1945.

The resistance to the Mongols had put a heavy strain on the system, however, and in 1333, the Kamakura Shogunate was overthrown by a coalition of powerful clans. A new shogun supplied by the Ashikaga (ah-shee-KAH-guh) family arose in Kyoto and attempted to continue the shogunate system. But the Ashikaga were unable to restore the centralized power of their predecessors. With the central government reduced to a shell, the power of local landed aristocracy increased to an unprecedented degree. Heads of great noble families, now called **daimyo** (DYM-yoh) ("great names"), controlled vast landed estates that owed no taxes to the government or to the court in Kyoto. As clan rivalries continued, the daimyo relied increasingly on samurai for protection, and political power came into the hands of a loose coalition of noble families.

By the end of the fifteenth century, Japan was again close to anarchy. A disastrous civil conflict known as the Onin War (1467–1477) led to the virtual destruction of the capital city of Kyoto and the disintegration of the shogunate. With the disappearance of any central authority, powerful aristocrats in rural areas now seized total control over large territories and ruled as independent great lords. Territorial rivalries and claims of precedence led to almost constant warfare in this period of "warring states," as it is called (in obvious parallel with a similar era during the Zhou Dynasty in China). The trend back toward central authority did not begin until the last quarter of the sixteenth century.

HISTORIANS DEBATE 11-1c **Was Japan a Feudal Society?**

That question has aroused vigorous debate among historians in recent years. Few would dispute that political,

11.5 The Burning of the Palace. The Kamakura era is represented in this action-packed thirteenth-century scene from the *Scroll of the Heiji Period*, which depicts the burning of a retired emperor's palace in the middle of the night. Servants and ladies of the court flee the massive flames; confusion and violence reign. The determined faces of the samurai warriors only add to the ferocity of the attack.

Museum of Fine Arts, Boston/Werner Forman/Art Resource, NY

social, and economic conditions in Japan were similar in a number of respects to those in medieval Europe, to which the term was first applied (see Comparative Essay, "Feudal Orders Around the World," p. 272, and Chapter 12). But some European historians worry that the term *feudalism* has been overused. They argue that it should be narrowly defined and based on conditions that existed in Europe during a specific time period.

For the student of world history, the term obviously has some comparative value in that the broad conditions that are normally considered characteristic of a feudal society can be found in many areas around the world. Still, remember that, under the surface, there were often profound differences between one "feudal" society and another.

With that in mind, the term can be a highly useful teaching tool for world historians.

11-1d Economic and Social Structures

From the time the Yayoi culture was first established on the Japanese islands, Japan was a predominantly agrarian society. Although Japan lacked the spacious valleys and deltas of the river valley societies, its inhabitants were able to take advantage of their limited amount of tillable land and plentiful rainfall to create a society based on the cultivation of wet rice.

Trade and Manufacturing As in China, commerce in Japan was slow to develop as an independent segment of the economy. During ancient times, each uji contained a local artisan class, composed of weavers, carpenters, and ironworkers, but trade was essentially local and regulated by local clan leaders. With the rise of the Yamato state, a money economy gradually began to develop, but most trade was still conducted through barter until the twelfth century, when metal coins introduced from China became

more popular. During the Kamakura period, foreign trade and manufacturing made their appearance with the emergence of such industries as paper, iron casting, and porcelain. Japan exported raw materials, paintings, swords, and other manufactured items to China and Korea in return for silk, porcelain, books, and copper cash. Some Japanese traders were so aggressive in pressing their interests that authorities in China and Korea attempted to limit the number of Japanese commercial missions that could visit each year.

Significantly, manufacturing and commerce developed rapidly during the more decentralized period of the Ashikaga Shogunate and the era of the warring states, perhaps because of the rapid growth in the wealth and autonomy of local daimyo families. Market towns began to appear operating on a full money economy, and local manufacturers formed guilds to protect their mutual interests. Sometimes local peasants would sell products at the markets made in their homes such as clothing made of silk or hemp, household items, or food products. In general, however, trade and manufacturing remained under the control of the local daimyo, who would often provide tax breaks to local guilds in return for other benefits. Although Japan remained a primarily agricultural society, it was on the verge of a major advance in manufacturing.

Daily Life One of the first descriptions of the life of the Japanese people comes from a Chinese dynastic history from the third century C.E. It describes lords and peasants living in an agricultural society that was based on the cultivation of wet rice. Laws had been enacted to punish offenders, local trade was conducted in markets, and government granaries stored the grain that was paid as taxes.

Life for the common people probably changed little over the next several hundred years. Most were peasants who worked on land owned by their lords or, in some cases, by the state or by Buddhist monasteries. Local officials, who were often well-to-do farmers, were responsible for organizing collective labor services and collecting tax grain from the peasants and in turn were exempt from such obligations themselves.

In theory, peasants were free to dispose of their harvest as they saw fit after paying their tax quota, but in practical terms their freedom was limited. Those unable to pay the tax sank to the level of **genin** (GAY-nin), or landless laborers, who could be bought and sold by their proprietors like slaves along with the land on which they worked. Some fled to escape such a fate and attempted to survive by clearing plots of land in the mountains or by becoming bandits.

In addition to the genin, the bottom of the social scale was occupied by the **eta** (AY-tuh), a class of hereditary slaves who were responsible for what were considered degrading occupations such as curing leather and burying the dead. The origins of the eta are not entirely clear, but they probably were descendants of prisoners of war, criminals, or mountain dwellers who were not related to the dominant Yamato peoples.

Daily life for ordinary people in early Japan resembled that of their counterparts throughout much of Asia. The vast majority lived in small villages, several of which normally made up a single shoen. Housing was simple. Most people lived in small two-room houses of timber, mud, or thatch, with dirt floors covered by straw or woven mats—the origin, perhaps, of the well-known *tatami* (tuh-TAH-mee), or woven-mat floor, of more modern times. Their diet consisted of rice (if some was left after the payment of the grain tax), wild grasses, millet, roots, and some fish and birds. Life must have been difficult at best; as one eighth-century poet lamented:

> Here I lie on straw
> Spread on bare earth,
> With my parents at my pillow,
> My wife and children at my feet,
> All huddled in grief and tears.
> No fire sends up smoke
> At the cooking place,
> And in the cauldron
> A spider spins its web.²

The Role of Women Evidence about the relations between men and women in early Japan presents a mixed picture (see Film & History, *Rashomon*). The Chinese dynastic history reports that "in their meetings and daily living, there is no distinction between . . . men and women." It notes that a woman "adept in the ways of shamanism" had briefly ruled Japan in the third century C.E. But it also remarks that polygyny was common, with nobles normally having four or five wives and commoners two or three.³ An eighth-century law code guaranteed the inheritance rights of women, and wives abandoned by their husbands were permitted to obtain a divorce and remarry. A husband could divorce his wife if she did not produce a male child, committed adultery, disobeyed her parents-in-law, talked too much, engaged in theft, was jealous, or had a serious illness.

When Buddhism was introduced, women were initially relegated to a subordinate position in the new faith. Although they were permitted to take up monastic life—often a widow entered a monastery on the death of her husband—they were not permitted to visit Buddhist holy

⊡ FILM & HISTORY

Rashomon

The film *Rashomon* (1950), directed by the celebrated filmmaker Akira Kurosawa, was one of a number of Japanese movies that won international plaudits in the period shortly after World War II. Like many other Japanese films of the era, it explored key aspects of human nature, often through the lens of snippets of life in medieval Japan. What made Rashomon unique was its portrayal of the elusive nature of truth, as the events surrounding the rape and murder of a young Japanese woman are presented through the eyes of a number of the participants.

Q *Japanese movie director Akira Kurosawa is notorious for having introduced a new cinematic technique in his 1950 film Rashomon. What was this technique, and can you think of any movies that you have seen that have successfully adopted it?*

MINDTAP See full-length Film & History feature in MindTap.
From Cengage

places, nor were they even (in the accepted wisdom) equal with men in the afterlife. One Buddhist commentary from the late thirteenth century said that a woman could not attain enlightenment because "her sin is grievous, and so she is not allowed to enter the lofty palace of the great Brahma, nor to look upon the clouds which hover over his ministers and people."⁴ Other Buddhist scholars were more egalitarian: "Learning the Law of Buddha and achieving release from illusion have nothing to do with whether one happens to be a man or a woman."⁵ Such views ultimately prevailed, and women were eventually allowed to participate fully in Buddhist activities in medieval Japan.

Although women did not possess the full legal and social rights of their male counterparts, they played an active role at various levels of Japanese society. Aristocratic women were prominent at court, and some like the author Murasaki Shikibu (MOO-rah-SAH-kee SHEE-kee-boo), known as Lady Murasaki (978–ca. 1016), became renowned for their artistic or literary talents (see Historical Voices, "Seduction of the Akashi Lady," p. 277). Though few commoners could aspire to such prominence, women often appear in the scroll paintings of the period along with men, doing the spring planting, threshing and hulling the rice, and acting as carriers, peddlers, salespersons, and entertainers.

Seduction of the Akashi Lady

Family & Society **OUT OF THE JAPANESE TRADITION** of female introspective prose appeared one of the world's truly great novels, *The Tale of Genji*, written around the year 1000 by diarist and court author Murasaki Shikibu (MOO-rah-SAH-kee SHEE-kee-boo), who was known as Lady Murasaki. The novel has influenced Japanese writing for more than a thousand years and even today is revered for its artistic refinement and sensitivity. A panoramic portrayal of court life in tenth-century Japan, it traces the life and loves of the courtier Genji as he strives to retain the favor of those in power while simultaneously pursuing his cult of love and beauty. The remarkable character of Genji is revealed to the reader through myriad psychological observations. In this excerpt, Genji has just seduced a lady at court and now feels misgivings at having betrayed his child bride. A koto is a Japanese stringed instrument similar to a zither.

Lady Murasaki, *The Tale of Genji*

A curtain string brushed against a koto, to tell him that she had been passing a quiet evening at her music.

"And will you not play for me on the koto of which I have heard so much?" . . .

This lady had not been prepared for an incursion and could not cope with it. She fled to an inner room. How she could have contrived to bar it he could not tell, but it was very firmly barred indeed. Though he did not exactly force his way through, it is not to be imagined that he left matters as they were. Delicate, slender—she was almost too beautiful. Pleasure was mingled with pity at the thought that he was imposing himself upon her. She was even more pleasing than reports from afar had had her. The autumn night, usually so long, was over in a trice. Not wishing to be seen, he hurried out, leaving affectionate assurances behind.

Genji called in secret from time to time. The two houses being some distance apart, he feared being seen by fishers, who were known to relish a good rumor, and sometimes several days would elapse between his visits. . . .

Genji dreaded having Murasaki [his bride] learn of the affair. He still loved her more than anyone, and he did not want her to make even joking reference to it. She was a quiet, docile lady, but she had more than once been unhappy with him. Why, for the sake of brief pleasure, had he caused her pain? He wished it were all his to do over again. The sight of the Akashi lady only brought new longing for the other lady.

He got off a more earnest and affectionate letter than usual, at the end of which he said: "I am in anguish at the thought that, because of foolish occurrences for which I have been responsible but have had little heart, I might appear in a guise distasteful to you. There has been a strange, fleeting encounter. That I should volunteer this story will make you see, I hope, how little I wish to have secrets from you. Let the gods be my judges.

> "It was but the fisherman's brush with the salty sea pine.
> Followed by a tide of tears of longing."

Her reply was gentle and unreproachful, and at the end of it she said: "That you should have deigned to tell me a dreamlike story which you could not keep to yourself calls to mind numbers of earlier instances.

> "Naive of me, perhaps; yet we did make our vows.
> And now see the waves that wash the Mountain of Waiting!"

It was the one note of reproach in a quiet, undemanding letter. He found it hard to put down, and for some nights he stayed away from the house in the hills.

 Why does this thousand-year-old passage still resonate with readers today?

Source: From *The Tale of the Genji* by Lady Murasaki, translated by Edward G. Seidensticker, copyright © 1976 by Edward G. Seidensticker (New York: Alfred A. Knopf).

11-1e In Search of the Pure Land: Religion in Early Japan

In Japan, as elsewhere, religious belief began with the worship of nature spirits. Early Japanese worshiped spirits called **kami** (KAH-mi) who resided in trees, rivers and streams, and mountains. They also believed in ancestral spirits present in the atmosphere. In Japan, these beliefs eventually evolved into a kind of state religion called **Shinto** (SHIN-toh) (the "Sacred Way" or the "Way of the Gods"), which is still practiced today. Shinto serves as an ideological and emotional force that knits the Japanese into a single people and nation.

Shinto does not have a complex metaphysical superstructure or an elaborate moral code. It does require certain ritual acts that are usually undertaken at a shrine and a process of purification, which may have originated in primitive concerns about death, childbirth, illness, and menstruation.

Another feature of Shinto is its stress on the beauty of nature and the importance of nature itself in Japanese life. Shinto shrines are usually located in places of exceptional beauty and are often dedicated to a nearby physical feature. As time passed, such primitive beliefs contributed to the characteristic Japanese love of nature. In this sense, early Shinto beliefs have been incorporated into the lives of all Japanese.

In time, Shinto evolved into a state doctrine that was linked with belief in the divinity of the emperor and the sacredness of the Japanese nation. A national shrine was established at Ise (EE-say) north of the early capital of Nara, where the emperor annually paid tribute to the sun goddess. Although Shinto had evolved well beyond its primitive origins, like its counterparts elsewhere it could not satisfy all the religious and emotional needs of the Japanese people. For those needs, the Japanese turned to Buddhism.

11.6 The Japanese Stone lantern. One of the most familiar artifacts found at Japanese Buddhist temples is the stone lantern. In Buddhist teachings, a burning lamp symbolizes Siddhartha Gautama himself as he brings light to humanity as a means of banishing ignorance. The first stone lanterns were brought to the Japanese islands from China in the sixth or seventh centuries C.E. and were originally used as votive lights to accompany symbolic offerings at Buddhist temples. Eventually they took on a secular purpose as a decorative element in private gardens and tea houses. The lanterns here are located at the Taiji Buddhist temple in Nara, Japan.

Buddhism As we have seen, Buddhism was introduced into Japan from China during the sixth century C.E. and had begun to spread beyond the court to the general population by the eighth century. As in China, most Japanese saw no contradiction between worshiping both the Buddha and their local nature gods (kami), many of whom were considered to be later manifestations of the Buddha. Most of the Buddhist sects that had achieved popularity in China were established in Japan, and many of them attracted powerful patrons at court. Great monasteries were established that competed in wealth and influence with the noble families that had traditionally ruled the country.

Perhaps the two most influential Buddhist sects were the Pure Land (Jodo) sect and **Zen** (in Chinese, Chan). The Pure Land sect, which taught that devotion alone could lead to enlightenment and release, was extremely popular among the common people, for whom monastic life was one of the few routes to upward mobility. Among the aristocracy, the most influential school was Zen, which exerted a significant impact on Japanese life and culture during the era of the warring states. In its emphasis on austerity, self-discipline, and communion with nature, Zen complemented many traditional beliefs in Japanese society and became an important component of the samurai warrior's code.

In Zen teachings, there were various ways to achieve enlightenment—*satori* (suh-TAWR-ee) in Japanese. Some stressed that it could be achieved suddenly. One monk, for example, reportedly achieved satori by listening to the sound of a bamboo striking against roof tiles; another, by carefully watching the opening of peach blossoms in the spring. But other practitioners, sometimes called *adepts*, said that enlightenment could come only through studying the scriptures and arduous self-discipline known as *zazen* (ZAH-ZEN), or "seated Zen." Seated Zen involved a lengthy process of meditation that cleansed the mind of all thoughts so that it could concentrate on the essential.

11-1f Sources of Traditional Japanese Culture

Nowhere is the Japanese genius for blending indigenous and imported elements into an effective whole better demonstrated than in culture. In such widely diverse fields as art, architecture, sculpture, and literature, the Japanese from early times showed an impressive capacity to borrow selectively from abroad without destroying essential native elements. Missions sent to China and Korea during the seventh and eighth centuries, for example, returned with examples of Tang literature, sculpture, and painting, all of which influenced the Japanese.

Literature Borrowing from Chinese literature was somewhat complicated, however, because the early Japanese had no writing system for recording their own spoken language and initially adopted the Chinese written language for writing. Eventually, however, they began to adapt the Chinese written characters for use in recording the Japanese language. But Chinese characters could not easily be used to record Japanese words, which normally contain more than one syllable. Sometimes the Japanese simply used Chinese characters as phonetic symbols that were combined to form Japanese words. Later they simplified the characters into phonetic symbols that were used alongside Chinese characters. This hybrid system continues to be used today. At first, most educated Japanese preferred to write in Chinese, and a court literature—essays, poetry, and official histories—appeared in the classical Chinese language. But spoken Japanese never totally disappeared among the educated classes and eventually became the instrument of a unique literature. With the lessening of Chinese cultural influence in the tenth century, poetry written in the Japanese language became popular. Initially, such poems they were written primarily by courtiers, but eventually the practice spread to all literate segments of society.

Japanese poetry is unique. It expresses its themes in a simple form, a characteristic stemming from traditional Japanese aesthetics, Zen religion, and the language itself. The aim of the Japanese poet in early times was to create a mood, perhaps the melancholic effect of gently falling cherry blossoms or leaves. With a few specific references, the poet suggested a whole world, just as Zen Buddhism sought enlightenment from a sudden perception. Poets often alluded to earlier poems by repeating their images with small changes, a technique that was viewed not as plagiarism but as an elaboration on the meaning of the earlier poem.

By the fourteenth century, the technique of the "linked verse" had become the most popular form of Japanese poetry. Known as *haiku* (HY-koo), it is composed of seventeen syllables divided into lines of five, seven, and five syllables, respectively. The poems in this period usually focused on images from nature and the mutability of life. Often the poetry was written by several individuals alternately composing verses and linking them together into long sequences of hundreds and even thousands of lines. The following example, by three poets named Sogi (SOH-gee), Shohaku (shoh-HAH-koo), and Socho (SOH-choh), is one of the most famous of the period:

Snow clinging to slope,	Sogi
On mist-enshrouded mountains	
At eveningtime.	
In the distance flows	Shohaku
Through plum-scented villages.	
Willows cluster	Socho
In the river breeze	
As spring appears[6]	

Poetry served a unique function at the Heian court, where it was the initial means of communication between lovers. By custom, aristocratic women were isolated from all contact with men outside their immediate family and spent their days hidden behind screens. In this situation, some amused themselves by writing poetry. When courtship began, poetic exchanges were the only means a woman had to attract her prospective lover, who would be enticed solely by her poetic art.

The famous classical Japanese drama known as *No* (NOH) also originated during this period. No developed out of a variety of entertainment forms such as dancing and juggling that were part of the native tradition or had been imported from China and other regions of Asia. The plots were normally based on stories from Japanese history or legend. Eventually, No evolved into a highly stylized drama in which the performers wore masks and danced to the accompaniment of instrumental music. Like much of Japanese culture, No was restrained, graceful, and refined.

Art and Architecture In art and architecture, as in literature, the Japanese pursued their interest in beauty, simplicity, and nature. To some degree, Japanese artists and architects were influenced by Chinese forms. As they became familiar with Chinese architecture, Japanese rulers and aristocrats tried to emulate the splendor of Tang civilization and began constructing their palaces and temples in Chinese style.

During the Heian period (794–1185), the search for beauty was reflected in various art forms, including narrative hand scrolls, screens, sliding door panels, fans, and lacquer decoration. As in literature, nature themes

Reflecting these chaotic times, the art of portraiture flourished, and a scroll would include a full gallery of warriors and holy men in starkly realistic detail, including such unflattering features as stubble, worry lines on a forehead, and crooked teeth. Japanese sculptors also produced naturalistic wooden statues of generals, nobles, and saints. By far the most distinctive, however, were the fierce heavenly "guardian kings" who still intimidate the viewer today.

11.7 The Golden Pavilion in Kyoto. Gardens, water, and architecture combine to create a magnificent setting for the Golden Pavilion. Constructed in the fourteenth century as a retreat where the shoguns could withdraw from their administrative chores, the pavilion derived its name from the gold foil that covered its exterior. Completely destroyed by an arsonist in 1950 as a protest against the commercialism of modern Buddhism, it was rebuilt and reopened in 1987. The use of water as a backdrop is especially noteworthy in Chinese and Japanese landscapes, as well as in the Middle East.

dominated: seashore scenes, a spring rain, moon and mist, or flowering wisteria and cherry blossoms. All were intended to evoke an emotional response on the part of the viewer. Japanese painting suggested the frail beauty of nature by presenting it on a smaller scale than that in Chinese art. The majestic mountain in a Chinese painting became a more intimate Japanese landscape with rolling hills and a rice field. Faces were rarely shown, and human drama was indicated by a woman lying prostrate or hiding her face in her sleeve. Tension was shown by two people talking at a great distance or with their backs to one another.

During the Kamakura period (1185–1333), the hand scroll with its physical realism and action-packed paintings of the new warrior class achieved great popularity.

11.8 Guardian Kings. Larger than life and intimidating in its presence, this thirteenth-century wooden statue departs from the refined atmosphere of the Heian court and pulsates with the masculine energy of the Kamakura period. Placed strategically at the entrance to Buddhist shrines, guardian kings such as this one protected the temple and the faithful. In contrast to the refined atmosphere of the Fujiwara court, the Kamakura era was a warrior's world.

In the Garden

IN TRADITIONAL CHINA AND JAPAN, gardens were meant to free the observer's mind from mundane concerns by offering spiritual refreshment in the quiet of nature. Chinese gardens were designed to reconstruct an orderly microcosm of nature where the harassed Confucian official could find spiritual renewal. Wandering through constantly changing perspectives of ponds, trees, rocks, and pavilions, he could imagine himself immersed in a monumental landscape. In the garden in Suzhou (Image 11.9a), the rocks represent towering mountains to suggest a Daoist sense of withdrawal and eternity, reducing the viewer to a tiny speck in the grand flow of life.

In Japan, the traditional garden reflected the Zen Buddhist philosophy of simplicity, restraint, allusion, and tranquility. Image 11.9b shows a garden at the Ryoanji (RYOH-ahn-jee) Temple in Kyoto. The rocks are meant to suggest mountains rising from a sea of pebbles. Such gardens served as an aid to meditation, inspiring the viewer to join with comrades in composing "linked verse" (see the poetry on p. 279).

 How do gardens in traditional China and Japan differ in form and purpose from gardens in Western societies? Why do you think this is the case?

11.9a

11.9b

Zen Buddhism, an import from China in the thirteenth century, also influenced Japanese aesthetics. With its emphasis on achieving enlightenment without recourse to intellectual analysis and elaborate ritual, Zen reinforced the Japanese predilection for simplicity and self-discipline. During this era, Zen philosophy found expression in the Japanese garden, the tea ceremony, the art of flower arranging, pottery and ceramics, and miniature plant display—the famous *bonsai* (bon-SY), literally "pot scenery."

Landscapes served as an important means of expression in both Japanese art and architecture. Japanese gardens were initially modeled on Chinese examples. Early court texts during the Heian period emphasized the importance of including a stream or pond when creating a garden. Because of the periodic shortage of water, later gardens concentrated on rock compositions using white pebbles to represent water (see the Comparative Illustration on above).

Like the Japanese garden, the tea ceremony represents the fusion of Zen and aesthetics. Developed in the fifteenth century, it was practiced in a simple room devoid of external ornament except for a tatami floor, sliding doors, and an alcove with a writing desk and asymmetrical shelves. The participants could therefore focus completely on the activity of pouring and drinking tea. "Tea and Zen have the same flavor," goes the Japanese saying. Considered the ultimate symbol of spiritual deliverance, the tea ceremony had great aesthetic value and moral significance in traditional times, just as it does today.

11-1g Japan and the Chinese Model

Few societies in Asia have historically been as isolated as Japan. Cut off from the mainland by 120 miles of frequently turbulent ocean, the Japanese had only minimal contact with the outside world during most of their early development.

Whether or not this isolation was ultimately beneficial to Japanese society cannot be determined. On the one hand, the lack of knowledge of developments taking place elsewhere probably delayed the process of change in Japan. On the other hand, the Japanese were spared the destructive invasions that afflicted other ancient civilizations. Certainly, once the Japanese became acquainted with Chinese culture at the height of the Tang era, they were quick to take advantage of the opportunity. In the space of a few decades, the young state adopted many aspects of Chinese society and culture and thereby introduced major changes into Japanese life.

Nevertheless, Japanese political institutions failed to follow all aspects of the Chinese pattern. Despite Prince Shotoku's effort to make effective use of the imperial traditions of Tang China, the decentralizing forces inside Japanese society remained dominant throughout the period under discussion in this chapter. Adoption of the Confucian civil service examination did not lead to a breakdown of Japanese social divisions; instead the examination was administered in a manner that preserved and strengthened them. Although Buddhist and Daoist doctrines made a significant contribution to Japanese religious practices, Shinto beliefs continued to play a major role in shaping the Japanese worldview.

Why Japan did not follow the Chinese road to centralized authority has been debated by some historians. Some argue that the answer lies in differing cultural traditions, whereas others suggest that Chinese institutions and values were introduced too rapidly to be assimilated effectively by Japanese society. A recent view suggests that diseases (such as smallpox and measles) imported inadvertently from China led to a marked decline in the population of the islands, reducing the food output and preventing the population from coalescing in more compact urban centers. A more likely factor was the absence of a foreign threat (except for the Mongols) in Japan. Fear of invasion can be a major factor in inducing a local population to coalesce around a single powerful figure in defense of the homeland.

In any event, Japan was not the only society in Asia to assimilate ideas from abroad while simultaneously preserving customs and institutions inherited from the past. Across the Sea of Japan to the west and several thousand miles to the south, other Asian peoples were embarked on a similar journey. We now turn to their experience.

11-2 KOREA: BRIDGE TO THE EAST

 Focus Question: What were the main characteristics of economic and social life in early Korea?

Few of the societies on China's periphery have been as directly influenced by the Chinese model as Korea. Nevertheless, the relationship between China and the peoples living on the Korean Peninsula has frequently been characterized by tension and conflict, and Koreans have often resented what they perceive to be Chinese chauvinism and arrogance.

A graphic example of this attitude has occurred in recent years as officials and historians in both countries have presented differing interpretations of the early history of the Korean people. Slightly larger than the state of Minnesota, the Korean Peninsula was probably first settled by Altaic-speaking fishing and hunting peoples from neighboring Manchuria during the Neolithic Age. Because the area is relatively mountainous (only around one-fifth of the peninsula is adaptable to cultivation), farming was apparently not practiced until around 2000 B.C.E. At that time, the peoples living in the area began to form organized communities.

It is this period that gives rise to scholarly disagreement. Official Chinese sources have recently claimed that the first organized kingdom in the area known as Koguryo (koh-GOOR-yoh) (37 B.C.E.–668 C.E.) occupied a wide swath of Manchuria as well as the northern section of the Korean Peninsula and was thus an integral part of Chinese history. Korean scholars, basing their contentions on both legend and limited historical evidence, have countered that a kingdom known as Gojoseon (goh-joh-SHAWN) had been created on the peninsula by a chieftain called Dangun (dan-GOON) in the mid-third millennium B.C.E. and that both he and his supporters were ethnically Korean. It was at that time, these scholars maintain, that the Bronze Age got under way in northeastern Asia.

Although this issue has not been resolved, most historians today agree that the northern part of the peninsula came under direct Chinese rule during the Han Dynasty, which divided the territory into provinces and introduced Chinese institutions. With the decline of the Han in the third century C.E., power gradually shifted to local tribal leaders, who evicted the Chinese administrators but continued to absorb Chinese cultural influence. Eventually, three separate kingdoms emerged on the peninsula: Koguryo in the north, Paekche (bayk-JEE) in the southwest, and Silla (SIL-uh) in the southeast.

11-2a The Three Kingdoms

From the fourth to the seventh centuries, the three kingdoms were bitter rivals for influence and territory on the peninsula. At the same time, all continued to absorb political and cultural institutions emanating from beyond their borders. Koguryo was the first to introduce Buddhism, and the first Confucian academy on the peninsula was established in the capital at Pyongyang (pyahng-YANG) in the late fourth century C.E. The kingdom of Silla, less exposed than its two rivals to Chinese influence, was at first the weakest of the three, but eventually it emerged as the dominant power on the peninsula. To pacify the haughty Chinese, Silla accepted tributary status under the Tang Dynasty, which still managed to exert a degree of influence over the entire area.

With the country unified for the first time, the rulers of Silla attempted to use political institutions and ideology introduced from China to forge a centralized state. Buddhism, now rising in popularity, became the state religion, and Korean monks followed the paths of their Japanese counterparts on journeys to Buddhist sites in the Middle Kingdom. Chinese architecture and art became dominant in the capital at Kyongju (KEE-yahng-joo) and other urban centers, and the written Chinese language became the official means of communication. Korean skilled workers made their own contributions in the fields of science and technology, especially in the area of metallurgy, ceramics, and astronomy (the earliest observatory in East Asia was established there in the seventh century). But the effort by Silla rulers to replicate the Chinese model faced strong headwinds, as powerful aristocratic families, long dominant in the southeastern part of the peninsula, were still influential at court. They were able to prevent the adoption of the Tang civil service examination system and resisted the distribution of manorial lands to the poor. The failure to adopt the Chinese model was fatal. Squabbling among noble families steadily increased, and after the assassination of the king of Silla in 780, civil war erupted.

Map 11.3 Korea's Three Kingdoms

The Rise of the Koryo Dynasty When the Silla Dynasty collapsed in the early tenth century, a new dynasty called Koryo (KAWR-yoh) (the root of the modern word for Korea) arose in the north. The new kingdom followed the Silla example by turning to Chinese political institutions in an effort to strengthen its power base and unify the peninsula. The civil service examination system was introduced in 958, but as in Japan the bureaucracy continued to be dominated by influential aristocratic families.

The Koryo Dynasty managed to retain power for 400 years, protected from invasion by the absence of a

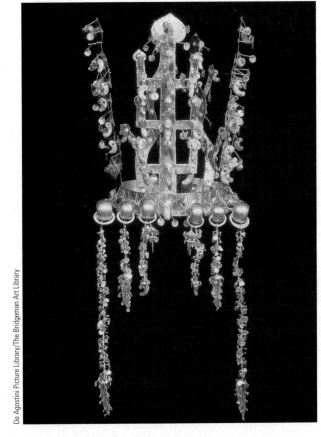

De Agostini Picture Library/The Bridgeman Art Library

11.10 Korean Royal Crown. The Silla Dynasty was renowned for the high quality of its gold, jewelry, crowns, and sword sheaths. Shown here is a jewel-inlaid royal crown of the fifth century C.E. that was excavated from a royal tomb in eastern Korea. Although much Silla artwork reflects Chinese influence, royal crowns located in Silla tombs often contain antler-like motifs, reflecting the animistic traditions of Korea's pre-Chinese past. The comma-shaped jewels symbolize the king's heaven-sanctioned authority on Earth.

Experience an interactive version of this period in ⋰᛫ MINDTAP strong dynasty in neighboring China. Under the Koryo, industry and commerce slowly began to develop, but as in China agriculture was the prime source of wealth. In theory, all land was the property of the king, but in actuality noble families controlled their holdings. The lands were worked by peasants who were subject to burdens similar to those of European serfs. At the bottom of society was a class of **chonmin** (CHAWN-min), or "base people," composed of slaves, artisans, and other specialized workers.

From a cultural perspective, the Koryo era was one of high achievement. Buddhist monasteries run by sects introduced from China, including Pure Land and Zen, controlled vast territories and their monks served as royal advisers at court. At first, Buddhist themes dominated in Korean art and sculpture, and the entire Tripitaka (tri-pih-TAH-kah) (the "three baskets" of the Buddhist canon) was printed using wooden blocks. Eventually, however, with the appearance of landscape painting and porcelain, Confucian themes began to predominate.

11-2b Resisting the Mongols

Like its predecessor in Silla, the kingdom of Koryo was unable to overcome the power of the nobility and the absence of a reliable tax base. In the thirteenth century, the Mongols seized the northern part of the country and assimilated it into the Yuan Empire. The weakened kingdom of Koryo became a tributary of the great khan in Khanbaliq (see Chapter 10).

The era of Mongol rule was one of profound suffering for the Korean people, but it also provided a conduit for the introduction of many new ideas and new technology from China and farther afield. When the Mongol Empire collapsed, Korean leaders were quick to take advantage of the opportunity. In 1392, military commander Yi Song-gye (YEE song-YEE) overthrew the weakened Koryo kingdom and established a new Choson (also known as Yi) Dynasty. Once again, the Korean people were in charge of their own destiny.

Always aware of potential threats emanating from more powerful neighbors, the Choson kingdom was actively interested in events taking place elsewhere in the region and was quick to follow up on technological advances taking place in China. Koreans were among the first to adopt the new invention of block printing, and Korean cartographers hastened to draw up regional and world maps based on Chinese originals. The famous Kangnido world map, based on Chinese models but produced in Korea in 1402, is considered to be the second oldest surviving map drawn up in Asia.

11-3 VIETNAM: THE SMALLER DRAGON

 Focus Questions: What were the main developments in Vietnamese history before 1500? Why were the Vietnamese able to restore their national independence after a millennium of Chinese rule?

Even as the Korean people were attempting to establish their own identity in the shadow of the powerful Chinese Empire, the peoples of Vietnam, on China's southern frontier, were seeking to do the same. The Vietnamese, the southernmost of a group of ethnically distinct peoples inhabiting a region stretching from the central China down to the Red River Valley, began to practice irrigated agriculture in the flooded regions of the Red River Delta at an early date and entered the Bronze Age sometime during the second millennium B.C.E. By around 200 B.C.E., a young state had begun to form in the area but immediately encountered the expanding power of China and, as we saw in the chapter opening (see also Chapter 3), they were eventually absorbed into the Han Empire.

At first, the Han were content to rule the delta as an autonomous region under the administration of the local landed aristocracy. But Chinese taxes were oppressive, and in 39 C.E. a revolt led by the Trungsisters (widows of local nobles who had been executed by the Chinese) briefly brought Han rule to an end (see Historical Voices, "The First Vietnam War," p. 285). The Chinese soon suppressed the rebellion, however, and began to rule the area directly through officials dispatched from China. The first Chinese officials to serve in the region became exasperated at the uncultured ways of the locals who wandered around "naked without shame."[7] In time, however, these foreign officials began to intermarry with the local nobility and form a Sino–Vietnamese ruling class who, though trained in Chinese culture, began to identify with the cause of Vietnamese autonomy.

For nearly a thousand years, the Vietnamese were exposed to the art, architecture, literature, philosophy, and written language of China as the Chinese attempted to integrate the area culturally, politically, and administratively into their empire. To all intents and purposes, the Red River Delta, then known to the Chinese as the "pacified South," or Annam (ahn-NAHM), became a part of China.

11-3a The Rise of Great Viet

Despite Chinese efforts to assimilate Vietnam, however, the latter's sense of ethnic and cultural identity proved

The First Vietnam War

Politics & Government

IN THE THIRD CENTURY B.C.E., the armies of the Chinese state of Qin (Ch'in) invaded the Red River Delta to launch an attack on the small Vietnamese state located there. As this passage from a Han dynasty philosophical text shows, the Vietnamese were not easy to conquer, and the new state soon declared its independence from the Qin. It was a lesson that was too often forgotten by would-be conquerors in later centuries.

Masters of Huai Nan

Ch'in Shih Huang Ti [the first emperor of Qin] was interested in the rhinoceros horn, the elephant tusks, the kingfisher plumes, and the pearls of the land of Yueh [Viet]; he therefore sent Commissioner T'u Sui at the head of five hundred thousand men divided into five armies.... For three years the sword and the cross-bow were in constant readiness. Superintendent Lu was sent; there was no means of assuring the transport of supplies so he employed soldiers to dig a canal for sending grain, thereby making it possible to wage war on the people of Yueh. The lord of Western Ou, I Hsu Sung, was killed; consequently, the Yueh people entered the wilderness and lived there with the animals; none consented to be a slave of Ch'in; choosing from among themselves men of valor, they made them their leaders and attacked the Ch'in by night, inflicting on them a great defeat and killing Commissioner T'u Sui; the dead and wounded were many. After this, the emperor deported convicts to hold the garrisons against the Yueh people.

The Yueh people fled into the depths of the mountains and forests, and it was not possible to fight them. The soldiers were kept in garrisons to watch over the abandoned territories. This went on for a long time, and the soldiers grew weary. Then the Yueh came out and attacked; the Ch'in soldiers suffered a great defeat. Subsequently, convicts were sent to hold the garrisons against the Yueh.

 How would the ancient Chinese military strategist Sun Tzu, mentioned in Chapter 3, have advised the Qin military commanders to carry out their operations? Would he have approved of the tactics adopted by the Vietnamese? Why or why not?

Source: From Keith W. Taylor, *The Birth of Vietnam* (Berkeley, 1983), p. 18.

---

difficult to extinguish, and in 939 the Vietnamese took advantage of the collapse of the Tang Dynasty in China to overthrow Chinese rule.

The new Vietnamese state, which called itself Dai Viet (dy VEE-et) (Great Viet), soon became a dynamic new force on the Southeast Asian mainland. Although the economic foundations of Vietnamese society had traditionally been founded on the cultivation of rice in the sediment-rich Red River Delta, Vietnamese merchants now became active participants in the commercial expansion that was taking place throughout the region. For centuries, the Vietnamese had been in active competition for territory and markets with the neighboring state of Champa (CHAHM-puh), a trading society based on Indian cultural traditions that had been been founded along the central coast of the peninsula in 192 C.E. Over the next several centuries, Champa played an active role in the regional trade network as an intermediary between China and Southeast Asia, as well as an exporter of forest products. But the emergence of Dai Viet brought the two competing states into frequent conflict, and in the fifteenth century Champa—a decentralized polity whose power base was centered on several small river estuaries along the coast—met its final destruction. The Vietnamese then launched their march southward, establishing agricultural settlements in the newly conquered territory. By the seventeenth century, the state of Dai Viet had reached the Gulf of Siam.

The Vietnamese, however, continued to confront a serious challenge from the north. Although the Song Dynasty in China, beset with its own problems on the northern frontier, had accepted the Dai Viet ruler's offer of tribute status, both the Yuan and Ming Dynasties attempted to reintegrate the Red River Delta into the Chinese Empire. The first effort was made in the late thirteenth century by the Mongols, who attempted on two occasions to conquer the Vietnamese. After a series of bloody battles, during which the Vietnamese displayed an impressive capacity for guerrilla warfare, the invaders were driven out. A little more than a century later, however, the Ming Dynasty tried again, and for twenty years

Vietnam was once more under Chinese rule. In 1428, the Vietnamese finally evicted the Chinese, an experience that has ever since contributed to the strong sense of Vietnamese identity.

CHRONOLOGY	Early Korea and Vietnam
Foundation of Gojoseon state in Korea	ca. 2333 B.C.E.
Chinese conquest of Korea and Vietnam	Second century B.C.E.
Trung sisters' revolt	39 C.E.
Founding of Champa	192
Era of Three Kingdoms in Korea	300s–600s
Restoration of Vietnamese independence	939
Mongol invasions of Korea and Vietnam	1257–1285
Founding of Choson (Yi) Dynasty in Korea	1392
Vietnamese conquest of Champa	1471

The Chinese Legacy Despite their stubborn resistance to Chinese rule, after the restoration of independence in the tenth century, Vietnamese rulers quickly discovered the convenience of the Confucian model in administering a river valley society and therefore sought to imitate Chinese practice in governing their own state. The ruler styled himself an emperor like his counterpart to the north (although he prudently termed himself a king in his direct dealings with the Chinese court), adopted Chinese court rituals, claimed the Mandate of Heaven, and arrogated to himself the same authority and privileges in his dealings with his subjects.

Like their Chinese counterparts, Vietnamese rulers fought to preserve their authority from the challenges of powerful aristocratic families and adopted the Chinese practice of using civil service examinations as a means of doing so. Under the pressure of strong monarchs, the concept of merit eventually took hold, and the power of the landed aristocracy was weakened if not entirely broken. The Vietnamese adopted much of the Chinese administrative structure, including the six ministries, the censorate, and the various levels of provincial and local administration.

Another aspect of the Chinese legacy was the spread of Buddhist, Daoist, and Confucian ideas that supplemented the traditional Vietnamese belief in nature spirits. Buddhist precepts became popular among the local population, who integrated the new faith into their existing belief system by founding Buddhist temples dedicated to the local village deity in the hope of guaranteeing an abundant harvest. Upper-class Vietnamese educated in the Confucian classics tended to follow the more agnostic Confucian doctrine, but some joined Buddhist monasteries. Daoism also flourished at all levels of society and, as in China, provided a structure for animistic beliefs and practices that still predominated at the village level.

During the early period of independence, Vietnamese culture also borrowed liberally from its larger neighbor. Educated Vietnamese tried their hand at Chinese poetry, wrote dynastic histories in the Chinese style, and followed Chinese models in sculpture, architecture, and porcelain. Many of the notable buildings of the medieval period such as the Temple of Literature and the famous One-Pillar Pagoda in Hanoi are classic examples of Chinese architecture.

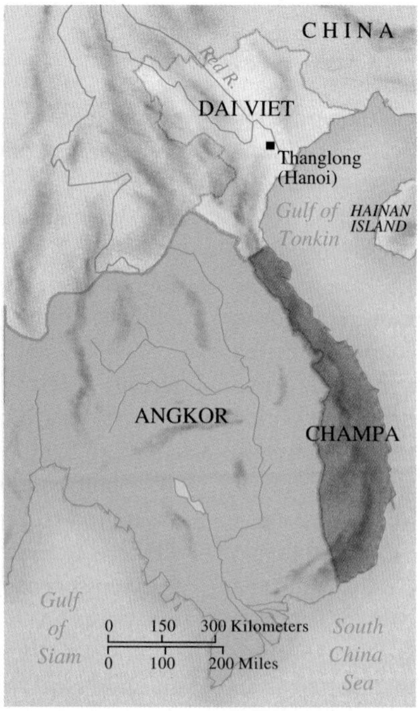

Map 11.4 The Kingdom of Dai Viet, 1100

But there were signs that Vietnamese creativity would eventually transcend the bounds of Chinese cultural norms. Although most classical writing was undertaken in literary Chinese, the only form of literary expression deemed suitable by Confucian conservatives, an adaptation of Chinese written characters called ***chu nom*** (CHOO nahm) ("southern characters"), was devised to provide a written system for spoken Vietnamese. In use by the early ninth century, it eventually began to be used for the composition of essays and poetry in the Vietnamese language. Such pioneering efforts would lead in later centuries to the emergence of a vigorous national literature totally independent of Chinese forms.

11-3b Society and Family Life

Vietnamese social institutions and customs were also strongly influenced by those of China. As in China, the introduction of a Confucian system and the adoption of civil service examinations undermined the role

Vietnam: On the Fault Line of Asia

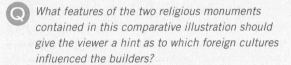

WAVES OF CULTURAL INFLUENCE from the great civilizations in China and India washed steadily over Southeast Asia beginning during the first millennium C.E. Nowhere was this process more in evidence than in the region of modern-day Vietnam, where Indian influence in the southern state of Champa contrasted with the influx of Chinese political institutions, philosophy, and culture to the north in the Red River Valley. The most visual example of this clash of culture appears in the field of architecture. Image 11.11a shows an eleventh-century shrine tower originally dedicated to the Indian deity Shiva in the city of Nha Trang clearly displays the influence of Indian models, whereas the distinctive one-pillar pagoda (Image 11.11b) reflects Chinese influence. The latter was built at the order of an eleventh-century Vietnamese monarch who had dreamed that the Buddhist goddess of mercy, known in China as Guan Yin, while seated on a lotus, had promised him a son. Shortly after the dream the emperor fathered a son. In gratitude he constructed this pagoda on one pillar, resembling a lotus blossom, the Buddhist symbol of purity, rising out of the mud.

Q *What features of the two religious monuments contained in this comparative illustration should give the viewer a hint as to which foreign cultures influenced the builders?*

William J. Duiker

11.11a

William J. Duiker

11.11b

of the old landed aristocrats and led eventually to their replacement by the scholar-gentry class. Also as in China, the examinations were open to most males, regardless of family background, which opened the door to a degree of social mobility unknown in most of the states elsewhere in the region. Candidates for the bureaucracy read many of the same Confucian classics and absorbed the same ethical principles as their counterparts in China. At the same time, they were also exposed to the classic works of Vietnamese history, which strengthened their sense that Vietnam was a distinct culture similar to, but separate from, that of China.

The vast majority of the Vietnamese people, however, were peasants. Most were small landholders or sharecroppers who rented their plots from wealthier farmers, but large estates were rare because of the systematic efforts of the central government to prevent the rise of a powerful local landed elite.

Family life in Vietnam was similar in many respects to that in China. The Confucian concept of family took hold during the period of Chinese rule, along with the related concepts of filial piety and gender inequality. Perhaps the most striking difference between family traditions in China and Vietnam was that Vietnamese women possessed more rights both in practice and by law. Since ancient times, wives had been permitted to own property and initiate divorce proceedings. One consequence of Chinese rule was a growing emphasis on male dominance, but the tradition of women's rights was never totally extinguished and was legally recognized in a law code promulgated in 1460.

Moreover, Vietnam had a strong historical tradition associating heroic women with the defense of the homeland. Perhaps it was not just symbolic that two of the greatest figures in Vietnamese history were the Trung sisters, who had given their lives in the struggle against Chinese conquest. As an eighteenth-century Vietnamese history noted,

> Were they not grand heroines? . . . Our two ladies brought forward an army of all the people, and, establishing a royal court that settled affairs in the territories of the sixty-five strongholds, shook their skirts over the Hundred Yueh [the Vietnamese people].[8]

CHAPTER SUMMARY

Like many other great civilizations, the Chinese were traditionally convinced of the superiority of their culture and, when the opportunity arose, sought to introduce it to neighboring peoples. Although the latter were viewed with a measure of condescension, the adoption of Confucian teachings suggested the possibility of redemption. As the Master had remarked in the *Analects,* "By nature, people are basically alike; in practice they are far apart."[9] As a result, Chinese policies in the region were often shaped by the desire to introduce Chinese values and institutions to non-Chinese peoples living on the periphery.

As this chapter has shown, when conditions were right, China's "civilizing mission" sometimes had marked success. All three countries that we have dealt with here borrowed liberally from the Chinese model. At the same time, all adapted Chinese institutions and values to the conditions prevailing in their own societies. They may have expressed admiration and respect for China's achievement, but they all sought to keep Chinese power at a distance.

As an island nation, Japan was the most successful of the three in protecting its political sovereignty and its cultural identity. Both Korea and Vietnam were compelled on various occasions to defend their independence by force of arms. That experience may have shaped their strong sense of national distinctiveness, which we shall discuss further in a later chapter.

The appeal of Chinese institutions can undoubtedly be explained by the fact that Japan, Korea, and Vietnam were all agrarian societies, much like their larger neighbor. But it is undoubtedly significant that the aspect of Chinese political culture that was least amenable to adoption abroad was the civil service examination system. The Confucian concept of meritocracy ran directly counter to the strong aristocratic tradition that flourished in all three societies during their early stage of development. Even when the system was adopted, it was put to quite different uses. Only in Vietnam did the concept of merit eventually triumph over that of birth as strong rulers of Dai Viet attempted to initiate the Chinese model as a means of creating a centralized system of government.

REFLECTION QUESTIONS

Q To what degree did the institutions and values of medieval Japan conform to the Chinese model? What factors explain the key differences?

Q How did the Korean Peninsula fit into the overall history of East Asia during the period under discussion in this chapter and the previous chapter?

Q In what ways was Vietnam's relationship with China during the early historical period similar to the relationship between China and the other two major civilizations in the region—Japan and Korea? In what ways was the Vietnamese relationship with China different?

CHAPTER TIMELINE

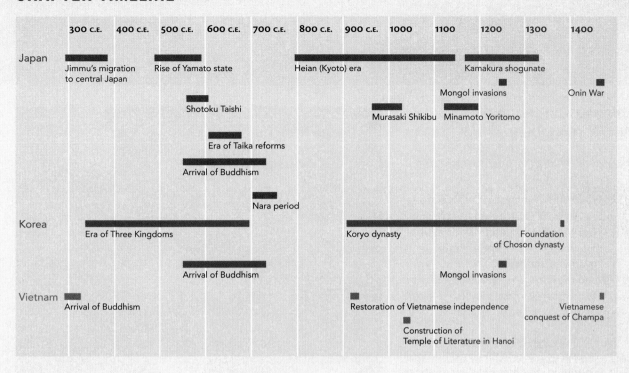

| | 300 C.E. | 400 C.E. | 500 C.E. | 600 C.E. | 700 C.E. | 800 C.E. | 900 C.E. | 1000 | 1100 | 1200 | 1300 | 1400 |

Japan

Jimmu's migration to central Japan

Rise of Yamato state

Heian (Kyoto) era

Kamakura shogunate

Mongol invasions

Onin War

Shotoku Taishi

Murasaki Shikibu   Minamoto Yoritomo

Era of Taika reforms

Arrival of Buddhism

Nara period

Korea

Era of Three Kingdoms

Koryo dynasty

Foundation of Choson dynasty

Arrival of Buddhism

Mongol invasions

Vietnam

Arrival of Buddhism

Restoration of Vietnamese independence

Vietnamese conquest of Champa

Construction of Temple of Literature in Hanoi

CHAPTER NOTES

1. Cited in C. Holcombe, *The Genesis of East Asia, 221 b.c.-a.d. 907* Honolulu, 2001), p. 41.
2. Quoted in D.J. Lu, *Sources of Japanese History,* vol. 1 (New York, 1974), p. 7.
3. From "The History of Wei," quoted in ibid., p. 10.
4. From "On the Salvation of Women," quoted in ibid., p. 127.
5. Quoted in B. Ruch, "The Other Side of Culture in Medieval Japan," in K. Yamamura, ed., *The Cambridge History of Japan,* vol. 3, *Medieval Japan* (Cambridge, 1990), p. 506.
6. H. P. Varley, "A Sample of Linked Verse," in K. Yamamura, ed., *The Cambridge History of Japan,* vol. 3, *Medieval Japan* (Cambridge, 1990), p. 480.
7. K. W. Taylor, *The Birth of Vietnam* (Berkeley, Calif., 1983), p. 76.
8. Quoted in ibid., pp. 336–337.
9. Confucius, *Analects,* 17:2.

MindTap® is a fully online, highly personalized learning experience built upon Cengage Learning content. MindTap combines student learning tools—readings, multimedia, activities, and assessments—into a singular Learning Path that guides students through the course and helps students develop the critical thinking, analysis, and communication skills that are essential to academic and professional success.

MINDTAP
From Cengage

Chapter Outline and Focus Questions

12-1 *The Emergence of Europe in the Early Middle Ages*

Q What contributions did the Romans, the Christian church, and the Germanic peoples make to the new civilization that emerged in Europe after the collapse of the Western Roman Empire? What was the significance of Charlemagne's coronation as emperor?

12-2 *Europe in the High Middle Ages*

Q What roles did aristocrats, peasants, and townspeople play in medieval European civilization, and how did their lifestyles differ? How did cities in Europe compare with those in China and the Middle East? What were the main aspects of the political, economic, spiritual, and cultural revivals that took place in Europe during the High Middle Ages?

12-3 *Medieval Europe and the World*

Q In what ways did Europeans begin to relate to peoples in other parts of the world after 1000 C.E.? What were the reasons for the crusades, and who or what benefited the most from the experience of the crusades?

12.1 **The coronation of Charlemagne by Pope Leo III.** Depiction of the event in a medieval French manuscript.

Scala/Art Resource, NY

Critical Thinking

Q *In what ways was the civilization that developed in Europe in the Middle Ages similar to those in China and the Middle East? How were they different?*

Connections to Today

Q *Do you think there is a the relationship between the crusades in the Middle Ages and contemporary events in the Middle East, including the Persian Gulf War and the activities of al-Qaeda and ISIS? If so, what do you think the relationship is?*

IN 800 C.E., CHARLEMAGNE, the king of the Franks, journeyed to Rome to help Pope Leo III, head of the Catholic Church, who was barely clinging to power in the face of rebellious Romans. On Christmas Day, Charlemagne and his family, attended by Romans and Franks, crowded into Saint Peter's Basilica to hear Mass. Quite unexpectedly, according to a Frankish writer, "as the king rose from praying before the tomb of the blessed apostle Peter, Pope Leo placed a golden crown on his head." The people in the church shouted, "Long life and victory to Charles Augustus, crowned by God the great and peace-loving Emperor of the Romans." Seemingly, the Roman Empire in the west had been reborn, and Charles had become the first Roman emperor since 476. But this "Roman emperor" was actually a German king, and he had been crowned by the head of the western Christian church. In truth, the coronation of Charlemagne was a sign not of the rebirth of the Roman Empire but of the emergence of a new European civilization that came into being in western Europe after the collapse of the Western Roman Empire.

This new civilization—European civilization—was formed by the coming together of three major elements:

the legacy of the Romans, the Christian church, and the Germanic peoples who moved in and settled the western empire. European civilization developed during a period that historians call the Middle Ages, or the medieval period, which lasted from roughly 500 to 1500. To the historians who first used the name, the Middle Ages was a middle period between the ancient world and the modern world. During the early Middle Ages, from around 500 to 1000 C.E., the Roman world of the western empire was slowly transformed into a new Christian European society.

12-1 THE EMERGENCE OF EUROPE IN THE EARLY MIDDLE AGES

 Focus Questions: What contributions did the Romans, the Christian church, and the Germanic peoples make to the new civilization that emerged in Europe after the collapse of the Western Roman Empire? What was the significance of Charlemagne's coronation as emperor?

As we saw in Chapter 10, China descended into political chaos and civil wars after the end of the Han Empire, and it was almost 400 years before a new imperial dynasty established political order. Similarly, after the collapse of the Western Roman Empire in the fifth century, it would also take hundreds of years to establish a new society.

12-1a The New Germanic Kingdoms

Already in the third century C.E., Germanic peoples in large numbers had begun to move into the lands of the Roman Empire; by 500, the Western Roman Empire had been replaced politically by a series of successor states ruled by German kings. The fusion of Romans and Germans took different forms in the various Germanic kingdoms. Both the kingdom of the Ostrogoths in Italy and the kingdom of the Visigoths in Spain (see Map 12.1) maintained the Roman structure for the larger native Roman populations, although a Germanic warrior caste came to dominate. Over a period of time, Germans and natives began to fuse. In Britain, however, after the Roman armies withdrew at the beginning of the fifth century, the Angles and Saxons, Germanic tribes from Denmark and northern Germany, moved in and settled there.

Only one of the German states on the European continent lasted very long: the kingdom of the Franks. The establishment of a Frankish kingdom was the work

of Clovis (KLOH-viss) (ca. 482–511 C.E.), who became a Catholic Christian around 500. By 510, Clovis had established a powerful new Frankish kingdom stretching from the Pyrenees in the west to German lands in the east (modern France and western Germany). After Clovis's death, however, as was the Frankish custom, his sons divided his newly created kingdom. During the sixth and seventh centuries, the once-united Frankish kingdom came to be divided into three major areas: Neustria (NOO-stree-uh) in northern Gaul; Austrasia (awss-TRAY-zhuh), which consisted of the ancient Frankish lands on both sides of the Rhine River; and the former kingdom of Burgundy.

12-1b The Role of the Christian Church

By the end of the fourth century, Christianity had become the dominant religion of the Roman Empire. As the official Roman state disintegrated, the Christian church played an increasingly important role in the growth of the new European civilization.

The Organization of the Church   By the fourth century, the Christian church had developed a system of government. A bishop, whose area of jurisdiction was known as a *bishopric*, or **diocese**, headed the Christian community, and the bishoprics of each Roman province were joined together under the direction of an archbishop. The bishops of four great cities—Rome, Jerusalem, Alexandria, and Antioch—held positions of special power in church affairs. Soon, however, one of them—the bishop of Rome—claimed that he was the sole leader of the western Christian church, which came to be known as the Roman Catholic Church. According to church tradition, Jesus had given the keys to the kingdom of heaven to Peter, who was considered the chief apostle and the first bishop of Rome. Subsequent bishops of Rome were considered Peter's successors and came to be known as popes (from the Latin word *papa*, meaning "father"). By the sixth century, popes had successfully extended papal authority over the Christian church in the west and converted the pagan peoples of Germanic Europe. Their primary instrument of conversion was the monastic movement.

The Monks and their Missions   A **monk** (in Latin, *monachus*, meaning "someone who lives alone") was a man who sought to live a life cut off from ordinary human society to pursue an idealized total dedication to God. As the monastic ideal spread, a new form of **monasticism** based on living together in a community soon became the dominant form. Saint Benedict (ca. 480 – ca. 543 C.E.), who founded a monastic house and wrote a set of rules for it (*The Rule of Saint Benedict*), established the basic form of monastic life in the western Christian church.

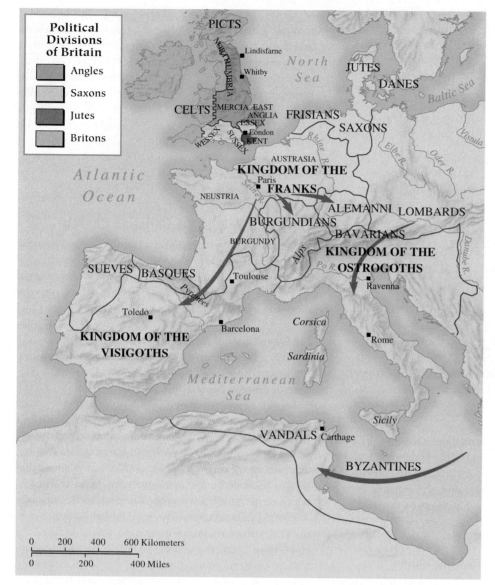

Political Divisions of Britain

- Angles
- Saxons
- Jutes
- Britons

PICTS

Lindisfarne

Whitby

NORTHUMBRIA

CELTS

MERCIA EAST ANGLIA

ESSEX

WESSEX SUSSEX

London KENT

North Sea

JUTES

DANES

FRISIANS

SAXONS

Baltic Sea

Elbe R. Oder R. Visula

AUSTRASIA

KINGDOM OF THE FRANKS

Paris

NEUSTRIA

Seine R.

Rhine R.

ALEMANNI LOMBARDS

BURGUNDIANS

BURGUNDY

Alps

BAVARIANS

KINGDOM OF THE OSTROGOTHS

Po R.

Danube R.

Ravenna

Atlantic Ocean

SUEVES BASQUES

Pyrenees

Toulouse

Toledo

Barcelona

Corsica

Rome

KINGDOM OF THE VISIGOTHS

Sardinia

Mediterranean Sea

Sicily

VANDALS Carthage

BYZANTINES

```
0    200    400    600 Kilometers
0        200        400 Miles
```

Map 12.1 The Germanic Kingdoms of the Old Western Empire. Germanic tribes filled the power vacuum caused by the demise of the Western Roman Empire by founding states that blended elements of Germanic customs and laws with those of Roman culture, including large-scale conversions to Christianity. The Franks established the most durable of these Germanic states.

Q *Which Germanic tribes settled in the present-day countries of Europe?*

An **abbot**, or "father" of the monastery, ruled each Benedictine monastery and had complete authority over his fellow monks. Unquestioning obedience to the will of the abbot was expected of every monk. Each Benedictine monastery held lands that enabled it to be a self-sustaining community, independent of the world surrounding it. Within the monastery, however, monks were to fulfill their vow of poverty: "Let all things be common to all, as it is written, lest anyone should say that anything is his own."[1] Only men could be monks, but women, called **nuns**, also began to withdraw from the world to dedicate themselves to God.

Monasticism played an indispensable role in early medieval civilization. Monks became the new heroes of Christian civilization, and their dedication to God became the highest ideal of Christian life. They were the social workers of their communities: monks provided schools for the young, hospitality for travelers, and hospitals for the sick. Monks also copied Latin works and passed on the legacy of the ancient world to the new European civilization. Monasteries became centers of learning wherever they were located, and monks worked to spread Christianity to all of Europe. Moreover, the monks were important in spreading Christianity to the entire European world. English and Irish monks were particularly enthusiastic missionaries who undertook the conversion of pagan peoples, especially in Germany.

One of the most famous of the Christian missionaries in the fifth century was Saint Patrick (ca. 390–461 C.E.).

Benedict's rule divided each day into a series of activities. All monks were required to do physical work of some kind for several hours a day as a means to reach God because idleness was "the enemy of the soul." At the very heart of community practice was prayer, the proper "work of God." Although this included private meditation and reading, all of the monks gathered together seven times during the day for common prayer and chanting of psalms. Living a communal life, monks ate, worked, slept, and worshiped together.

12-1c Charlemagne and the Carolingians

During the seventh and eighth centuries, as the kings of the Frankish kingdom gradually lost their power, the mayors of the palace—the chief officers of the king's household—assumed more control of the kingdom. One of these mayors, Pepin (PEP-in or pay-PANH), finally took the logical step of assuming the kingship of the Frankish state for himself and his family. Upon his death in 768, his son came to the throne of the Frankish kingdom.

This new king was the dynamic ruler known to history as Charles the Great (768–814 C.E.), or Charlemagne (SHAR-luh-mayn) (from the Latin for Charles the Great, *Carolus Magnus*). He was determined and decisive, intelligent and inquisitive, a strong statesman, and a pious Christian. Though he himself was unable to read or write, he was a wise patron of learning. In a series of military campaigns, he greatly expanded the territory he had inherited and created what came to be known as the Carolingian Empire. At its height, Charlemagne's empire covered much of western and central Europe; not until the time of Napoleon in the nineteenth century would an empire of its size be seen again in Europe (see Historical Voices, "The Achievements of Charlemagne," p. 294).

12.2 Saint Benedict. Benedict was the author of a set of rules that was instrumental in the development of monastic groups in the Catholic Church. In this sixth-century Latin manuscript miniature, an abbot is shown offering codes and possessions to Saint Benedict.

Son of a Romano-British Christian, Patrick was kidnapped as a young man by Irish raiders and kept as a slave in Ireland. After his escape to Gaul, he became a monk and chose to return to Ireland to convert the Irish to Christianity. Irish tradition ascribes to Patrick the title of "founder of Irish Christianity," a testament to his apparent success.

Women played an important role in the monastic missionary movement and the conversion of the Germanic kingdoms. Some served as **abbesses** (the heads of monasteries for nuns, which are known as *convents*). Many abbesses came from aristocratic families, especially in Anglo-Saxon England. In the kingdom of Northumbria, for example, Saint Hilda founded a monastery in 657 C.E. and, as abbess, made learning an important part of the life of the monastery.

Map 12.2 Charlemagne's Empire

Map legend:
- Frankish kingdom, 768
- Territories gained by Charlemagne

Labels: FRISIA, SAXONY, Aachen, Verdun, Mainz, BRITTANY, Paris, AUSTRASIA, TRIBUTARY SLAVIC, ALEMANNI, NEUSTRIA, BURGUNDY, BAVARIA, PEOPLES, Bordeaux, VENETIA, AQUITAINE, Milan, PAPAL STATES, SPANISH MARCH, Rome

HISTORIANS DEBATE

12-1d What Was the Significance of Charlemagne?

As Charlemagne's power grew, so did his prestige as the most powerful Christian ruler of what one monk called the "kingdom of Europe." In 800 C.E., Charlemagne acquired a new title: emperor of the Romans. The significance of this imperial coronation has been much debated by historians. We are not even sure if the pope or Charlemagne initiated the idea when they met in the summer of 799 in Paderborn in German lands or whether he was pleased or displeased. The crowning of an emperor by a pope is significant in

The Achievements of Charlemagne

Politics & Government

EINHARD (YN-HART), the biographer of Charlemagne, was born in the valley of the Main River in Germany about 775 C.E. Raised and educated in the monastery of Fulda, an important center of learning, he arrived at the court of Charlemagne in 791 or 792. Although he did not achieve high office under Charlemagne, he served as private secretary to Louis the Pious, Charlemagne's son and successor. In this selection, Einhard discusses some of Charlemagne's accomplishments.

Einhard, *Life of Charlemagne*

Such are the wars, most skillfully planned and successfully fought, which this most powerful king waged during the forty-seven years of his reign. He so largely increased the Frank kingdom, which was already great and strong when he received it at his father's hands, that more than double its former territory was added to it. . . . He subdued all the wild and barbarous tribes dwelling in Germany between the Rhine and the Vistula, the Ocean and the Danube, all of which speak very much the same language, but differ widely from one another in customs and dress. . . .

He added to the glory of his reign by gaining the good will of several kings and nations; so close, indeed, was the alliance that he contracted with Alfonso, King of Galicia and Asturias, that the latter, when sending letters or ambassadors to Charles, invariably styled himself his man. . . . The Emperors of Constantinople [the Byzantine emperors] sought friendship and alliance with Charles by several embassies; and even when the Greeks [the Byzantines] suspected him of designing to take the empire from them, because of his assumption of the title Emperor, they made a close alliance with him, that he might have no cause of offense. In fact, the power of the Franks was always viewed with a jealous eye, whence the Greek proverb, "Have the Frank for your friend, but not for your neighbor."

This King, who showed himself so great in extending his empire and subduing foreign nations, and was constantly occupied with plans to that end, undertook also very many works calculated to adorn and benefit his kingdom, and brought several of them to completion.

Among these, the most deserving of mention are the basilica of the Holy Mother of God at Aix-la-Chapelle [Aachen], built in the most admirable manner, and a bridge over the Rhine River at Mainz, half a mile long, the breadth of the river at this point. . . . Above all, sacred buildings were the object of his care throughout his whole kingdom; and whenever he found them falling to ruin from age, he commanded the priests and fathers who had charge of them to repair them, and made sure by commissioners that his instructions were obeyed. . . . Thus did Charles defend and increase as well as beautify his kingdom. . . .

He cherished with the greatest fervor and devotion the principles of the Christian religion, which had been instilled into him from infancy. Hence it was that he built the beautiful church at Aix-la-Chapelle, which he adorned with gold and silver and lamps, and with rails and doors of solid brass. He had the columns and marbles for this structure brought from Rome and Ravenna, for he could not find such as were suitable elsewhere. He was a constant worshiper at this church as long as his health permitted, going morning and evening, even after nightfall, besides attending mass. . . .

He was very forward in caring for the poor, so much so that he not only made a point of giving in his own country and his own kingdom, but when he discovered that there were Christians living in poverty in Syria, Egypt, and Africa, at Jerusalem, Alexandria, and Carthage, he had compassion on their wants, and used to send money over the seas to them. . . . He sent great and countless gifts to the popes, and throughout his whole reign the wish that he had nearest at heart was to reestablish the ancient authority of the city of Rome under his care and by his influence, and to defend and protect the Church of St. Peter, and to beautify and enrich it out of his own store above all other churches.

 How long did Einhard know Charlemagne? Does this excerpt reflect close, personal knowledge of the man, his court, and his works—or is it merely hearsay and legend?

Source: Einhard, *The Life of Charlemagne*, trans. S. E. Turner (New York, Harper and Brothers, 1880), pp. 50–54.

beginning a new era of the relationship between popes and emperors in the Middle Ages.

In any case, Charlemagne's coronation as Roman emperor demonstrated the strength, even after 300 years, of the concept of an enduring Roman Empire. More important, it symbolized the fusion of Roman, Christian, and Germanic elements. Did this fusion constitute the foundations of European civilization? A Germanic king had been crowned emperor of the Romans by the spiritual leader of western Christendom. Charlemagne had created an empire that stretched from the North Sea to Italy and from the Atlantic Ocean to the Danube River. This differed significantly from the Roman Empire, which encompassed much of the Mediterranean world. Had a new civilization emerged? And should Charlemagne be regarded as the "father of Europe," as one of his biographers has argued?[2]

Other historians disagree and argue that there was only a weak sense of community in Europe before 1000. As one has stated, "Europe was not born in the early Middle Ages. . . . There was no common European culture, and certainly not any Europe-wide economy."[3]

12-1e The World of Lords and Vassals

The Carolingian Empire began to disintegrate soon after Charlemagne's death in 814 C.E.; less than thirty years later, in 843, it was divided among his grandsons into three major sections. Invasions in different parts of the old Carolingian world added to the process of disintegration.

Invasions of the Ninth and Tenth Centuries   In the ninth and tenth centuries, western Europe was beset by a wave of invasions. Muslims attacked the southern coasts of Europe and sent raiding parties into southern France. The Magyars (MAG-yarz), a people from western Asia, moved into central Europe at the end of the ninth century and settled on the plains of Hungary; from there they made forays into western Europe. Finally crushed at the Battle of Lechfeld (LEK-feld) in Germany in 955 C.E., the Magyars converted to Christianity, settled down, and created the kingdom of Hungary.

The most far-reaching attacks of the time came from the Northmen or Norsemen of Scandinavia, also known to us as the Vikings. The Vikings were warriors whose love of adventure and search for booty and new avenues of trade may have led them to invade other areas of Europe. Viking ships were the best of the period. Their shallow draft enabled them to sail up European rivers and attack places at some distance inland. In the ninth century, Vikings sacked villages and towns, destroyed churches, and easily defeated small local armies.

The Pierpont Morgan Library/Art Resource, NY

12.3 The Vikings Attack England. This illustration from an eleventh-century English manuscript depicts a band of armed Vikings invading England. Two ships have already reached the shore, and a few Vikings are shown walking down a long gangplank onto English soil.

By the middle of the ninth century, groups of Norsemen from Norway had settled in Ireland, and Danes occupied northeastern England by 878 C.E. Beginning in 911, the ruler of the western Frankish lands gave one band of Vikings land at the mouth of the Seine River, forming a section of France that came to be known as Normandy. This policy of settling the Vikings and converting them to Christianity was a deliberate one; by their conversion to Christianity, the Vikings were soon made a part of European civilization.

HISTORIANS DEBATE   ### 12-1f What Was Feudalism?

The disintegration of central authority in the Carolingian world and the invasions by Muslims, Magyars, and Vikings led to the emergence of a new type of relationship between free individuals. When governments ceased to be able to defend their subjects, it became important to find some powerful lord who could offer protection in return for service. The contract sworn between a lord and his subordinate is the basis for what earlier generations of historians called *feudalism*, which they defined as a political and military system that applied to much of Europe in the Early Middle Ages.

In the 1970s, some historians denounced the use of the term *feudalism*, considering it an oversimplified model and not useful in describing medieval society. A later work maintained that historians had taken the feudal legal and social relations of the eleventh and twelfth centuries to falsely describe developments in the ninth and tenth centuries. Moreover, many historians argue that there were large differences from region to region in the relationship of service and duty based on land. To many historians today, feudalism was never a cohesive system, and they prefer to avoid using the term.

The Development of Fief-Holding   With the breakdown of royal governments, powerful nobles took control of large areas of land in many parts of Western Europe. Because they needed men to fight for them, the practice arose of giving grants of land to **vassals** who would fight for their lord in return. The Frankish army had originally consisted of foot soldiers armed with swords, but an eighth-century military change began to occur when larger horses and the stirrup were introduced. Earlier, horsemen had been throwers of spears. Now they came to be armored in coats of mail (the larger horse could carry the weight) and wielded long lances that enabled them to act as battering rams (stirrups kept them on their horses). For almost 500 years, warfare in Europe would be dominated by heavily armored cavalry, or *knights,* as they were called. The knights came to have the greatest social prestige and formed the backbone of the European aristocracy.

Of course, a horse, armor, and weapons were expensive, and it took time and much practice to learn to wield these instruments skillfully from horseback. Consequently, lords who wanted men to fight for them had to grant each vassal a piece of land that provided for the support of the vassal and his family. In return for the land, the vassal provided his lord with his fighting skills. Each needed the other. In the society of the Early Middle Ages, where there was little trade and wealth was based primarily on land, which became the most important gift a lord could give to a vassal in return for his loyalty and military service.

In some areas of Europe, the grant of land made to a vassal became known as a **fief** (FEEF) by the ninth century. A fief was a piece of land from the lord held by a vassal in return for military service, but vassals who held such grants of land also came to exercise rights of jurisdiction or political and legal authority within their fiefs. As the Carolingian world disintegrated politically under the impact of internal dissension and invasions, an increasing number of powerful lords arose who were now responsible for keeping order.

Fief holding came to be characterized by a set of practices that determined the relationship between a lord and his vassal. The major obligation of a vassal to his lord was to perform military service, usually around forty days a year. A vassal was also required to appear at his lord's court when summoned to give advice. He might also be asked to sit in judgment in a legal case because the important vassals of a lord were peers and only they could judge each other. Finally, vassals were also responsible for aids, or financial payments to the lord, on many occasions. In turn, a lord also had responsibilities toward his vassals. His major obligation was to protect his vassal, either by defending him militarily or by taking his side in a court of law. The lord was also responsible for the maintenance of the vassal, usually by granting him a fief (see the Comparative Essay "Feudal Orders Around the World" in Chapter 11, p. 272).

The Manorial System   The landholding class of nobles and knights contained a military elite whose ability to function as warriors depended on having the leisure time to pursue the arts of war. The manorial system provided the economic sustenance that made this way of life possible. A **manor** was an agricultural estate operated by a lord and worked by peasants. Although a large class of free peasants continued to exist, increasing numbers of free peasants became **serfs**—persons bound to the land and required to provide labor services, pay rents, and be subject to the lord's jurisdiction. By the ninth century, probably 60 percent of the population of western Europe had become serfs.

Labor services involved working the lord's **demesne** (duh-MAYN *or* duh-MEEN), the land retained by the lord, which might consist of one-third to one-half of the cultivated lands scattered throughout the manor. The peasants would use the rest for themselves. Building barns and digging ditches were also part of the labor services. Serfs usually worked about three days a week for their lord and paid rents by giving the lord a share of every product they raised.

Serfs were legally bound to the lord's lands and could not leave without his permission. Although free to marry, serfs could not marry anyone outside their manor without the lord's approval. Moreover, some lords exercised public rights or political authority on their lands, which gave them the right to try peasants in their own courts.

12-2 EUROPE IN THE HIGH MIDDLE AGES

 Focus Questions: What roles did aristocrats, peasants, and townspeople play in medieval European civilization, and how did their lifestyles differ? How did cities in Europe compare with those in China and the Middle East? What were the main aspects of the political, economic, spiritual, and cultural revivals that took place in Europe during the High Middle Ages?

The new European civilization that had emerged in the early Middle Ages began to flourish in the High Middle Ages (1000–1300). New agricultural practices that increased the food supply spurred commercial and urban expansion. Both lords and vassals recovered from the invasions and internal dissension of the early Middle Ages, and medieval kings began to exert a centralizing authority. The recovery of the Catholic church made it a forceful presence in every area of life. The High Middle Ages also gave birth to a cultural revival.

12-2a Land and People

In the early Middle Ages, Europe had a relatively small population of around 38 million; in the High Middle Ages, the number of people nearly doubled to 74 million. What accounted for this dramatic increase? For one thing, conditions in Europe were more settled and more peaceful after the invasions of the early Middle Ages had ended. For another, agricultural production surged after 1000.

The New Agriculture During the High Middle Ages, Europeans began to farm in new ways. An improvement in climate resulted in better growing conditions, and in the eleventh and twelfth centuries peasants also expanded cultivated or arable land by clearing forested areas and draining swamps.

Technological changes also furthered improvements in farming. The Middle Ages saw an explosion of laborsaving devices, many of which were made from iron mined in different areas of Europe. Iron was used to make scythes, axes, and hoes for use on farms, as well as saws, hammers, and nails for building purposes. Iron was crucial in making the *carruca* (kuh-ROO-kuh), a heavy, wheeled plow with an iron plowshare pulled by teams of horses that could turn over the heavy clay soil found north of the Alps.

Besides using horsepower, the High Middle Ages harnessed the power of water and wind to do jobs formerly done by humans or animals. Located along streams, mills powered by water were used to grind grains and produce flour. Where rivers were lacking or not easily dammed, Europeans developed windmills to harness the power of the wind.

The shift from a two-field to a three-field system also contributed to the increase in food production (see Comparative Illustration, "The New Agriculture in the Medieval World," p. 298). In the early Middle Ages, peasants planted one field while allowing another of equal size to lie fallow to regain its fertility. Now estates were divided into three parts. One field was planted in the fall with winter grains such as rye and wheat, and the second field was planted with spring grains such as oats or barley, and vegetables such as peas or beans. The third was allowed to lie fallow. When these fields were rotated, only one-third rather than one-half of the land lay fallow at any time. The rotation of crops also kept the soil from being exhausted so quickly, and more crops could now be grown.

Daily Life of the Peasantry The lifestyle of the peasants was quite simple. Their cottages of one or two rooms were made of wood frames surrounded by sticks, with the space between them filled with rubble and then plastered over with clay. Roofs were often thatched with reeds or straw.

Peasant women occupied both an important and a difficult position in manorial society. As mothers, they were expected to carry and bear their children as well as provide for their socialization and religious training. Peasant women also bore responsibility for doing the spinning and weaving that provided the household's clothes, tending the family's vegetable garden and chickens, and providing meals. A woman's ability to manage the household might determine whether a peasant family would starve or survive in difficult times. At the same time, peasant women often worked with men in the fields, especially at harvest time. Indeed, as one historian has noted, peasant marriage was an "economic partnership" in which both husbands and wives contributed their own distinctive labor. Peasant women also brewed ale for use in the household and for sale to help household finances.

Though simple, a peasant's daily diet was adequate when food was available. Bread was the staple of the peasant diet and the medieval diet in general. Women made the dough for the bread at home and then brought their loaves to be baked in community ovens, which were owned by the lord of the manor. Peasant bread was highly nutritious, containing not only wheat and rye but also barley, millet, and oats, giving it a dark appearance and a heavy, hard texture. Bread was supplemented by numerous vegetables from the household gardens, cheese from cow's or goat's milk, nuts and berries from woodlands, and fruits, such as apples, pears, and cherries. Chickens provided eggs and sometimes meat.

COMPARATIVE ILLUSTRATION

The New Agriculture in the Medieval World

Earth & Environment **NEW AGRICULTURAL METHODS AND TECHNIQUES** in the Middle Ages enabled peasants in both Europe and China to increase food production. This general improvement in diet was a factor in supporting noticeably larger populations in both areas. In Image 12.4a, a thirteenth-century painting shows Chinese peasants harvesting rice, which became the staple food in China. In Image 12.4b, a thirteenth-century illustration shows a group of English peasants harvesting grain under the direction of a bailiff, or manager.

Q *How important were staple foods (such as wheat and rice) to the diet and health of people in Europe and China during the Middle Ages?*

12.4a

12.4b

The Nobility of the Middle Ages In the High Middle Ages, European society, like that of Japan during the same period, was dominated by men whose chief concern was warfare. Like the Japanese samurai, many nobles loved war. The men of war were the lords and vassals of medieval society.

The lords were the kings, dukes, counts, barons, and viscounts (and even bishops and archbishops) who had extensive landholdings and wielded considerable political influence. They formed an **aristocracy** or nobility of people who held real political, economic, and social power. Both the great lords and ordinary knights were warriors united by the institution of knighthood. But there were also social divisions among them based on extremes of wealth and landholdings.

Although aristocratic women could legally hold property, most women remained under the control of men— their fathers until they married and their husbands after that. Nevertheless, these women had many opportunities for playing important roles. Because the lord was often away at war or at court, the lady of the castle had to manage the estate. Households could include large numbers of officials and servants, so this was no small responsibility.

Although women were legally expected to show deference to their husbands, many advised or even dominated their husbands. Perhaps the most famous was Eleanor of Aquitaine (ca. 1122–1204). Married to King Louis VII of France, Eleanor accompanied her husband on a crusade, but her alleged affair with her uncle during the crusade led Louis to have their marriage annulled. Eleanor then married Henry, duke of Normandy and count of Anjou (AHN-zhoo), who became King Henry II of England in 1154. She took an active role in politics, even assisting her sons in rebelling against Henry in 1173 and 1174 (see Film & History, *The Lion in Winter*).

12-2b The New World of Trade and Cities

Medieval Europe was overwhelmingly agrarian, with most people living in small villages. In the eleventh and twelfth centuries, however, new elements were introduced that began to transform the economic foundation of European civilization: a revival of trade, the emergence of specialized craftspeople and artisans, and the growth and development of towns. These changes were made possible by the new agricultural practices and subsequent increase in food production, which freed some European families from the need to produce their own food. Merchants and craftspeople could now buy their necessities. The increase in agricultural production also stimulated the development of trade. Crop surpluses made possible the export of food and the development of local markets and eventually regional markets to handle new trade possibilities.

The Revival of Trade The revival of trade was a gradual process. During the chaotic conditions of the early Middle Ages, large-scale trade had largely declined in western Europe. By the end of the tenth century, however, people were emerging in Europe with both the skills and the products for commercial activity. Cities in northern Italy took the lead in this revival of trade.

While the northern Italian cities were busy trading in the Mediterranean, the towns of Flanders were doing likewise in northern Europe. Flanders, the area along the coast of modern Belgium and northern France, was known for its high-quality woolen cloth. Its location made it an ideal center for the traders of northern Europe, and merchants from England, Scandinavia, France, and Germany converged there to trade their goods for woolen cloth. Flanders prospered in the eleventh and twelfth centuries. By the twelfth century, a regular exchange of goods had developed between Flanders and Italy, the two major centers of northern and southern European trade (see Opposing Viewpoints, "Two Views of Trade and Merchants," p. 300).

As trade increased, both gold and silver came to be in demand at fairs and trading markets of all kinds. Slowly, a money economy began to emerge. New trading companies and banking firms were set up to manage the exchange and sale of goods.

New techniques—including double-entry book-keeping, commercial contracts, and insurance—also appeared to facilitate the expansion of businesses. All of these new practices were part of a commercial revolution based on the growth of **capitalism**, an economic system in which commerce and industry are controlled by private owners who invest in trade and goods to make profits.

Trade Outside Europe In the High Middle Ages, Italian merchants became even more daring in their trade activities. They established trading posts in Cairo, Damascus, and several Black Sea ports, where they acquired spices, silks, jewelry, dyestuffs, and other goods brought by Muslim merchants from India, China, and Southeast Asia.

⊡ FILM & HISTORY

The Lion in Winter

Watch *The Lion in Winter* (1968), a film based on a play of the same name by James Goldman. The action takes place in a castle in Chinon, France, in 1183. The powerful but world-weary King Henry II, ruler of England and several French lands (the "Angevin Empire"), wants to establish his legacy and plans a Christmas gathering to decide which of his sons should succeed him. In contemporary terms, Henry and Eleanor are a dysfunctional married couple, and their family is acutely dysfunctional.

Everett Collection, Inc.

Q *In what ways is this film an accurate portrayal of a royal family's Christmas gathering? How realistic are the depictions of Henry II and his wife Eleanor?*

 MINDTAP See full-length Film & History feature in MindTap.
From Cengage

Two Views of Trade and Merchants

Interaction & Exchange **BY THE HIGH MIDDLE AGES,** the revival of trade in Europe had begun to expand dramatically. During the medieval period, trade already flourished in other parts of the world, especially in the Islamic world and in China. Nevertheless, many people in these societies, including rulers, nobles, and religious leaders, had some reservations about the success of merchants. The first selection is taken from the life of Godric, a twelfth-century European merchant who became a saint. The second selection is from the *Prolegomena,* the first part of a universal history written by Ibn Khaldun, a Muslim historian who traveled widely in the Muslim world in the fourteenth century.

Life of Saint Godric

At first, he lived as a peddler for four years in Lincolnshire, going on foot and carrying the smallest wares; then he traveled abroad, first to St. Andrews in Scotland and then for the first time to Rome. On his return, having formed a familiar friendship with certain other young men who were eager for merchandise, he began to launch upon bolder courses, and to coast frequently by sea to the foreign lands that lay around him. Thus, sailing often to and fro between Scotland and Britain, he traded in many divers wares and, amid these occupations, learned much worldly wisdom. . . .

Thus aspiring ever higher and higher, and yearning upward with his whole heart, at length his great labors and cares bore much fruit of worldly gain. For he labored not only as a merchant but also as a shipman . . . to Denmark and to Flanders and Scotland; in all which lands he found certain rare, and therefore more precious, wares, which he carried to other parts wherein he knew them to be least familiar, and coveted by the inhabitants beyond the price of gold itself; wherefore he exchanged these wares for others coveted by men of other lands; and thus he chaffered [traded] most freely and assiduously. Hence he made great profit in all his bargains, and gathered much wealth in the sweat of his brow; for he sold dear in one place the wares which he had bought elsewhere at a small price.

And now he had lived sixteen years as a merchant, and began to think of spending on charity, to God's honor and service, the goods which he had so laboriously acquired. He therefore took the cross as a pilgrim to Jerusalem. . . . [When he had returned to England] Godric, that he might follow Christ the more freely, sold all his possessions and distributed them among the poor [and began to live the life of a hermit].

Ibn Khaldun, *Prolegomena*

As for Trade, although it be a natural means of livelihood, yet most of the methods it employs are tricks aimed at making a profit by securing the difference between the buying and selling prices, and by appropriating the surplus. This is why [religious] Law allows the use of such methods, which, although they come under the heading of gambling, yet do not constitute the taking without return of other people's goods. . . .

Should their standard of living, however, rise, so that they begin to enjoy more than the bare necessities, the effect will be to breed in them a desire for repose and tranquility. They will therefore cooperate to secure superfluities; their food and clothing will increase in quantity and refinement; they will enlarge their houses and plan their towns for defense. A further improvement in their conditions will lead to habits of luxury, resulting in extreme refinement in cooking and the preparation of food; in choosing rich clothing of the finest silk; in raising lofty mansions and castles and furnishing them luxuriously, and so on. At this stage the crafts develop and reach their height. Lofty castles and mansions are built and decorated sumptuously, water is drawn to them and a great diversity takes place in the way of dress, furniture, vessels, and household equipment. Such are the townsmen, who earn their living in industry or trade.

 What did the biographers of Godric and Ibn Khaldun see as valuable in mercantile activity? What reservations did they have about trade? How are the two perspectives alike? How are they different, and how do you explain the differences? What generalizations can you make about Christian and Muslim attitudes toward trade?

Sources: Reginald of Durham, "Life of St. Godric," in G. G. Coulton, ed., *Social Life in Britain from the Conquest to the Reformation* (Cambridge: Cambridge University Press, 1918), pp. 415–420;. Ibn-Khaldun, *Prolegomena* in C. Issawi, ed. and trans. *An Arab Philosophy of History,* (New York: Darwin Press, 1987).

The spread of the Mongol Empire in the thirteenth century (see Chapter 10) also opened the door to Italian merchants in the markets of Central Asia, India, and China. As nomads who relied on trade with settled communities, the Mongols maintained safe trade routes for merchants moving through their lands. Two Venetian merchants, Niccolò and Maffeo Polo, began to travel in the Mongol Empire around 1260.

The creation of the crusader states in Syria and Palestine in the twelfth and thirteenth centuries (discussed later in this chapter) was especially favorable for Italian merchants. In return for taking the crusaders to the east, Italian merchant fleets received trading concessions in Syria and Palestine that enabled them to establish bases for carrying on lucrative trade.

The Growth of Cities   The revival of trade led to a revival of cities. Towns had experienced a great decline in the early Middle Ages, especially in Europe north of the Alps. Old Roman cities continued to exist but had dwindled in size and population. With the revival of trade, merchants began to settle in these old cities, followed by craftspeople or artisans, people who on manors or elsewhere had developed skills and now saw an opportunity to ply their trade and make goods that could be sold by the merchants. In the course of the eleventh and twelfth centuries, the old Roman cities came alive with new populations and growth.

Beginning in the late tenth century, many new cities or towns were also founded, particularly in northern Europe. Usually, a group of merchants established a settlement near some fortified stronghold such as a castle or monastery. (This explains why so many place names in Europe end in *borough*, *burgh*, *burg*, or *bourg*, all of which mean "fortress" or "walled enclosure.") Castles were particularly favored because they were generally located along trade routes; the lords of the castle also offered protection. If the settlement prospered and expanded, new walls were built to protect it.

Although lords wanted to treat towns and townspeople as they would their vassals and serfs, cities had totally different needs and a different perspective. Townspeople needed mobility to trade. Consequently, these merchants and artisans (who came to be called *burghers* or *bourgeois*, from the same root as *borough* and *burg*) needed their own unique laws to meet their requirements and were willing to pay for them. In many instances, lords and kings saw they could also make money and were willing to sell to the townspeople the liberties they were beginning to demand, including the right to bequeath goods and sell property, freedom from any military obligation to the lord, and written urban laws that guaranteed their freedom. Some towns also obtained the right to govern themselves by choosing their own officials and administering their own courts of law.

As time went on, medieval cities developed their own governments for running the affairs of the community. Only males who were born in the city or had lived there for a certain length of time could be citizens. In many cities, these citizens elected members of a city council who served as judges and city officials and passed laws.

Medieval cities remained relatively small in comparison to either ancient or modern cities (see Comparative Essay, "Cities in the Medieval World," p. 302). A large trading city might have 5,000 inhabitants. By 1200, London was the largest city in England with 30,000 people. On the continent of Europe north of the Alps, only a few urban centers of commerce, such as Bruges and Ghent, had populations close to 40,000. Italian cities tended to be larger, with Venice, Florence, Genoa, Milan, and Naples numbering almost 100,000.

Daily Life in the Medieval City   Medieval towns were surrounded by stone walls that were expensive to build, so the space within was precious. Consequently, most medieval cities featured narrow, winding streets with houses crowded against each other and second and third stories extending out over the streets. Because dwellings were built mostly of wood before the fourteenth century and candles and wood fires were used for light and heat, fire was a constant threat. Medieval cities burned rapidly once a fire started.

Most of the people who lived in cities were merchants involved in trade and artisans engaged in manufacturing a wide range of goods, such as cloth, metalwork, shoes, and leather goods. Generally, merchants and artisans had their own sections within a city. The merchant area included warehouses, inns, and taverns. Artisan sections were usually divided along craft lines. From the twelfth century on, craftspeople began to organize themselves into **guilds**; by the thirteenth century, virtually every craft had its own individual guild, as well as its own street where its activity was pursued.

The physical environment of medieval cities was not pleasant. They were dirty and smelled from animal and human wastes deposited in backyard privies or thrown into the streets. The rivers near most cities were polluted with wastes, especially from the tanning and butchering industries. Because of the pollution, cities did not use the rivers for drinking water but relied instead on wells.

In addition to supervising the household, purchasing food, preparing meals, raising the children, and managing the family finances, women in medieval cities were also often expected to help their husbands in their trades. Some women also developed their own trades to earn extra money such as brewing ale or making glass. When some master craftsmen died, their widows even carried on their

COMPARATIVE ESSAY

Cities in the Medieval World

Interaction & Exchange The exchange of goods between societies was a feature of both the ancient and medieval worlds. Trade routes crisscrossed the lands of the medieval world, and with increased trade came the growth of cities. In Europe, towns had dwindled after the collapse of the Western Roman Empire, but with the revival of trade in the eleventh and twelfth centuries, the cities came back to life. This revival occurred first in the old Roman cities, but soon new cities arose as merchants and artisans sought additional centers for their activities. As cities grew, so did the number of fortified houses, town halls, and churches whose towers punctuated the urban European skyline. Nevertheless, in the Middle Ages, cities in western Europe, especially north of the Alps, remained relatively small. Even the larger cities of Italy, with populations of 100,000, seemed insignificant in comparison with Constantinople and the great cities of the Middle East and China. With a population of possibly 300,000 people, Constantinople, the capital city of the Byzantine Empire (see Chapter 13), was the largest city in Europe in the early and High Middle Ages, and it was Europe's greatest commercial center, important for the exchange of goods between West and East, until the twelfth century. In addition to palaces, cathedrals, and monastic buildings, Constantinople had numerous gardens and orchards that occupied large areas inside its fortified walls. But despite the extensive open and cultivated spaces, the city was not self-sufficient and relied on imports of food under close government direction.

As trade flourished in the Islamic world, cities prospered. When the Abbasids were in power, Baghdad, with a population close to 700,000, was probably the largest city in the empire and one of the greatest cities in the world. After the rise of the Fatamids in Egypt, however, the focus of trade shifted to Cairo.

Islamic cities had a distinctive physical appearance. Usually, the most impressive urban buildings were the palaces for the caliphs or the local governors and the great mosques for worship. There were also public buildings with fountains and secluded courtyards, public baths, and bazaars. The bazaar, a covered market, was a crucial part of every Muslim settlement and an important trading center where goods from all the known world were available. Food prepared for sale at the market was carefully supervised. A rule in one Muslim city stated, "Grilled meats should only be made with fresh meat and not with meat coming from a sick animal and bought for its cheapness." The merchants were among the greatest beneficiaries of the growth of cities in the Islamic world.

During the medieval period, cities in China were the largest in the world. The southern port of Hangzhou had at least 1 million residents by 1000, and several other cities, including Chang'an and Kaifeng, may also have reached that size. Chinese cities were known for their broad canals and wide, tree-lined streets. They were no longer administrative centers dominated by officials and their families and now included a broader mix of officials, merchants, artisans, and entertainers. The prosperity of Chinese cities was well known. Marco Polo, in describing Hangzhou to unbelieving Europeans in the late thirteenth century, said, "so many pleasures can be found that one fancies himself to be in Paradise."

Robana/British Library Board/Art Resource, NY

12.5 Crime and Punishment in the Medieval City. Violence was a common feature of medieval life. Criminals, if apprehended, were punished quickly and severely, and public executions like the one shown here were considered deterrents to crime.

Q *Based on a comparison of these medieval cities, which of these civilizations do you think was the most advanced? Why?*

12.6 Shops in a Medieval Town. Most urban residents were merchants involved in trade and artisans who manufactured a wide variety of products. Master craftsmen had their workshops in the ground-level rooms of their homes. In this illustration, two well-dressed burghers are touring the shopping district of a French town. Tailors, furriers, a barber, and a grocer (from left to right) are visible at work in their shops.

Snark/Art Resource, NY

trades. Some women in medieval towns were thus able to lead lives of considerable independence and made important contributions to the market economy. Nevertheless, women often made less than men and faced obstacles that kept them from more rewarding opportunities. For example, women in textile production usually were given the most menial jobs. Many were forced to become domestic servants and given room and board in return for cooking, cleaning, and other domestic services.

12-2c Evolution of the European Kingdoms

The recovery and growth of European civilization in the High Middle Ages also affected the state. Although lords and vassals seemed forever mired in endless petty conflicts, some medieval kings inaugurated the process of developing new kinds of monarchical states that were based on the centralization of power rather than the decentralized political order that was characteristic of fief holding. By the thirteenth century, European monarchs were solidifying their governmental institutions in pursuit of greater power.

England in the High Middle Ages In late September 1066, an army of heavily armed knights under William of Normandy landed on the coast of England. A few weeks later, on October 14, they soundly defeated King Harold and his Anglo-Saxon foot soldiers in the Battle of Hastings. William (1066–1087) was crowned king of England at Christmastime in London and promptly began a process of combining Anglo-Saxon and Norman institutions that would change England forever. Many of the Norman knights were given parcels of land that they held as fiefs from the new English king. William made all nobles swear an oath of loyalty to him as sole ruler of England and insisted that all people owed loyalty to the king. All in all, William of Normandy established a strong, centralized monarchy.

In the twelfth century, the power of the English monarchy was greatly enlarged during the reign of Henry II (1154–1189). The new king was particularly successful in strengthening the royal courts. By increasing the number of criminal cases to be tried in the king's courts and taking other steps to expand the power of the royal courts, he expanded the power of the king. Moreover, because the royal courts were now found throughout England, a body of **common law** (law that was common to the whole kingdom) began to replace the different law codes that often varied from place to place.

Many English nobles came to resent the ongoing growth of the king's power and rose in rebellion during the reign of King John (1199–1216). At Runnymede in 1215, John was forced to accept the Magna Carta (Great Charter) guaranteeing feudal liberties. Feudal custom had always recognized that the relationship between king and vassals was based on mutual rights and obligations. The Magna Carta gave written recognition to that fact and was used in later years to support the idea that a monarch's power was limited.

During the reign of Edward I (1272–1307), an institution of great importance in the development of representative government—the English Parliament—emerged. Originally, the word *parliament* was applied to meetings of the king's Great Council, in which the greater barons and chief prelates of the church met with the king's judges and principal advisers to deal with judicial affairs. But needing money, in 1295 Edward I invited two knights from every county and two residents from each town to meet with the Great Council to consent to new taxes. This was the first Parliament.

Thus, the English Parliament came to be composed of two knights from every county and two burgesses from every borough as well as the barons and ecclesiastical lords. Eventually, the barons and church lords formed the House of Lords, and the knights and burgesses formed the House of Commons. The Parliaments of Edward I approved taxes, discussed politics, passed laws, and handled judicial business. The law of the realm was beginning to be determined not by the king alone but by the king in consultation with representatives of various groups that constituted the community.

Growth of the French Kingdom   In 843 C.E., the Carolingian Empire had been divided into three major sections. The western Frankish lands formed the core of the eventual kingdom of France. In 987, after the death of the last Carolingian king, the western Frankish nobles chose Hugh Capet (YOO ka-PAY) as the new king, thus establishing the Capetian (kuh-PEE-shun) Dynasty of French kings.

Although they carried the title of kings, the Capetians had little real power. They controlled as the royal domain only the lands around Paris known as the Île-de-France (EEL-duh-fronhss). As kings of France, the Capetians were formally the overlords of the great lords of France such as the dukes of Normandy, Brittany, Burgundy, and Aquitaine. In reality, however, many of the dukes were considerably more powerful than the Capetian kings. All in all, it would take the Capetian Dynasty hundreds of years to create a truly centralized monarchical authority in France.

The reign of King Philip II Augustus (1180–1223) was an important turning point in the growth of the French monarchy. Philip II waged war against the Plantagenet (plan-TAJ-uh-net) rulers of England, who also ruled the French territories of Normandy, Maine, Anjou, and Aquitaine, and he was successful in gaining control of most of these territories, thereby enlarging the power of the French monarchy (see Map 12.3). To administer justice and collect royal

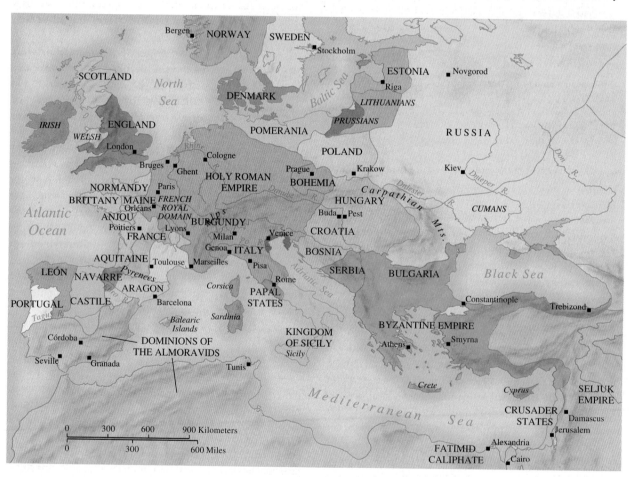

Map 12.3 Europe in the High Middle Ages. Although the nobility dominated much of European society in the High Middle Ages, kings began the process of extending their power in more effective ways, creating the monarchies that would form the European states.

 Which were the strongest monarchical states by 1300? Why?

revenues in his new territories, Philip appointed new royal officials, thus inaugurating a French royal bureaucracy in the thirteenth century.

Capetian rulers after Philip II continued to add lands to the royal domain. Philip IV the Fair (1285–1314) was especially effective in strengthening the French monarchy. He reinforced the royal bureaucracy and also brought a French parliament into being by asking representatives of the three estates, or classes—the clergy (First Estate), the nobles (Second Estate), and the townspeople (Third Estate)—to meet with him. They did so in 1302, inaugurating the Estates General, the first French parliament, although it had little real power. By the end of the thirteenth century, France was the largest, wealthiest, and best-governed monarchical state in Europe.

Christian Reconquest: The Iberian Kingdoms
Much of Spain had been part of the Islamic world since the eighth century. Starting in the tenth century, however, the most noticeable feature of Spanish history was the weakening of Muslim power and the beginning of a Christian reconquest that lasted until the final expulsion of the Muslims at the end of the fifteenth century.

Several small Christian kingdoms were established in northern Spain in the eleventh century, and within 100 years they had been consolidated into the Christian kingdoms of Castile (ka-STEEL), Navarre, Aragon, and Portugal, which first emerged as a separate kingdom in 1139. The southern half of Spain still remained under the control of the Muslims.

In the thirteenth century, Aragon, Castile, and Portugal made significant conquests of Muslim territory in the southern half of the Iberian Peninsula. The Muslims remained ensconced only in the kingdom of Granada in the southeast of the peninsula, which remained an independent Muslim state until its final conquest by the forces of Ferdinand of Aragon and Isabella of Castile in 1492.

The Spanish kingdoms did not follow a consistent policy in their treatment of the conquered Muslim population. In Aragon, Muslim farmers continued to work the land but were forced to pay extremely high rents. In Castile, King Alfonso X (1252–1284), who called himself the "King of Three Religions," encouraged the continued development of a cosmopolitan culture shared by Christians, Jews, and Muslims.

The Lands of the Holy Roman Empire
In the tenth century, the powerful dukes of the Saxons became kings of the eastern Frankish kingdom (or Germany, as it came to be called). The best known of the Saxon kings of Germany was Otto I (936–973 c.e.), who intervened in Italian politics and for his efforts was crowned emperor of the Romans by the pope in 962, reviving a title that had not been used since the time of Charlemagne.

As leaders of a new Roman Empire, the German kings attempted to rule both German and Italian lands. Frederick I Barbarossa (bar-buh-ROH-suh) (1152–1190) and Frederick II (1212–1250) tried to create a new kind of empire. Previous German kings had focused on building a strong German kingdom, but Frederick I planned to get his chief revenues from Italy as the center of a "holy empire," as he called it (hence the name *Holy Roman Empire*). But his attempt to conquer northern Italy ran into severe opposition from the pope and the cities of northern Italy. An alliance of these cities and the pope defeated Frederick's forces in 1176.

The main goal of Frederick II was the establishment of a strong centralized state in Italy, but he too became involved in a deadly conflict with the popes and the northern Italian cities. Frederick waged a bitter struggle in northern Italy, winning many battles but ultimately losing the war.

The struggle between popes and emperors had dire consequences for the Holy Roman Empire. By spending their time fighting in Italy, the German emperors left Germany in the hands of powerful German lords who ignored the emperor and created their own independent kingdoms. This ensured that the German monarchy would remain weak and incapable of building a centralized monarchical state; thus, the German Holy Roman emperor had no real power over either Germany or Italy. Unlike France and England, neither Germany nor Italy created a centralized national monarchy in the Middle Ages.

The Slavic Peoples of Central and Eastern Europe
The Slavs were originally a single people in central Europe, but they gradually divided into three major groups: the western, southern, and eastern Slavs (see Map 12.4). The western Slavs eventually formed the Polish and Bohemian kingdoms. German Christian missionaries converted both the Czechs in Bohemia and the Slavs in Poland by the tenth century. German Christians also converted the non-Slavic kingdom of Hungary, which emerged after the Magyars settled down after their defeat in 955 c.e. The Poles, Czechs, and Hungarians all accepted Catholic or western Christianity and became closely tied to the Roman Catholic Church and its Latin culture.

The southern and eastern Slavic populations took a different path: the Slavic peoples of Moravia were converted to the Orthodox Christianity of the Byzantine Empire (see Chapter 13) by two Byzantine missionary

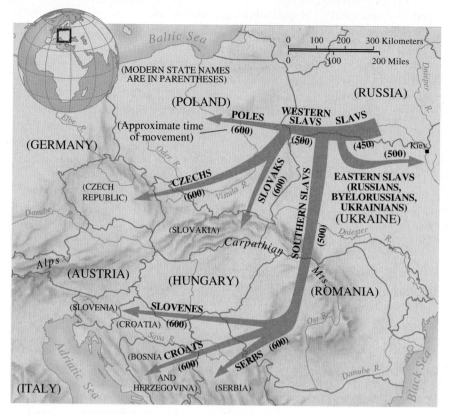

Map 12.4 The migrations of the Slavs. Originally from east-central Europe, the Slavic people broke into three groups. The western Slavs converted to Catholic Christianity, whereas most of the eastern and southern Slavs, under the influence of the Byzantine Empire, embraced the Eastern Orthodox faith.

Q *What connections do these Slavic migrations have with what we today characterize as eastern Europe?*

brothers, Cyril and Methodius (muh-THOH-dee-USS), who began their activities in 863 C.E.. The southern Slavic peoples included the Croats, Serbs, and Bulgarians. For the most part, they also embraced Eastern Orthodoxy, although the Croats came to accept the Roman Catholic Church. The acceptance of Eastern Orthodoxy by the Serbs and Bulgarians tied their cultural life to the Byzantine state.

The eastern Slavic peoples, from whom the modern Russians and Ukrainians are descended, had settled in the territory of present-day Ukraine and European Russia. There, beginning in the late eighth century, they began to encounter Swedish Vikings who were moving down the extensive network of rivers into the lands of the eastern Slavs in search of booty and new trade routes (see Historical Voices, "A Muslim's Description of the Rus," p. 307). These Vikings built trading settlements and eventually came to dominate the native peoples, who called them "the Rus" (ROOSS *or* ROOSH), from which the name *Russia* is derived.

The Development of Russia: Impact of the Mongols A Viking leader named Oleg (ca. 873–913 C.E.) settled in Kiev (KEE-yev) at the beginning of the tenth century and created the Rus state known as the Principality of Kiev. His successors extended their control over the eastern Slavs and expanded the territory of Kiev until it included the territory between the Baltic and Black Seas and the Danube and Volga Rivers. By marrying Slavic wives, the Viking ruling class was gradually assimilated into the Slavic population.

The growth of the Principality of Kiev attracted religious missionaries, especially from the Byzantine Empire. One Rus ruler, Vladimir (VLAD-ih-meer) (ca. 980–1015), married the Byzantine emperor's sister and officially accepted Christianity for himself and his people in 987. By the end of the tenth century, Byzantine Christianity had become the model for Russian religious life.

The Kievan Rus state prospered and reached its high point in the first half of the eleventh century. But civil wars and new invasions by Asiatic nomads caused the Principality of Kiev to collapse, and the sack of Kiev by north Russian princes in 1169 brought an end to the first Russian state, which had remained closely tied to the Byzantine Empire, not to Europe. In the thirteenth century, the Mongols conquered Russia and cut it off even more from Europe.

The Mongols had exploded onto the scene in the thirteenth century, moving east into China and west into the Middle East and central Europe. Although they conquered Russia, they were not numerous enough to settle the vast Russian lands. They occupied only part of Russia but required the Russian princes to pay tribute to them. One Russian prince soon emerged as more powerful than the others. Alexander Nevsky (NYEF-skee) (ca. 1220–1263), prince of Novgorod (NAHV-guh-rahd), defeated a German invading army in northwestern Russia in 1242. His cooperation with the Mongols won him their favor. The khan, leader of the western part of the Mongol Empire, rewarded Alexander Nevsky with the title of Grand Prince, enabling his descendants to

A Muslim's Description of the Rus

Family & Society | **DESPITE THE DIFFICULTIES** that travel presented in the early medieval period, some contact among the various cultures occurred through trade, diplomacy, or the conquest and migration of peoples. This document is a description of the Swedish Rus, who eventually merged with the native Slavic peoples to form the Principality of Kiev, commonly regarded as the first Russian state. It was written by Ibn Fadlan, a Muslim diplomat sent from Baghdad in 921 c.e. to a settlement on the Volga River. His comments on the filthiness of the Rus reflect the Muslim emphasis on cleanliness.

Ibn Fadlan, Description of the Rus

I saw the Rus folk when they arrived on their trading mission and settled at the river Atul [Volga]. Never had I seen people of more perfect physique. They are tall as date palms, and reddish in color. They wear neither coat nor kaftan, but each man carried a cape which covers one half of his body, leaving one hand free. No one is ever parted from his axe, sword, and knife. Their swords are Frankish in design, broad, flat, and fluted. Each man has a number of trees, figures, and the like from the fingernails to the neck. Each woman carried on her bosom a container made of iron, silver, copper, or gold—its size and substance depending on her man's wealth. They [the Rus] are the filthiest of God's creatures. They do not wash after discharging their natural functions, neither do they wash their hands after meals. They are as lousy as donkeys.

They arrive from their distant lands and lay their ships alongside the banks of the Atul, which is a great river, and there they build big houses on its shores. Ten or twenty of them may live together in one house, and each of them has a couch of his own where he sits and diverts himself with the pretty slave girls whom he had brought along for sale. He will make love with one of them while a comrade looks on; sometimes they indulge in a communal orgy, and, if a customer should turn up to buy a girl, the Rus man will not let her go till he has finished with her.

They wash their hands and faces every day in incredibly filthy water. Every morning the girl brings her master a large bowl of water in which he washes his hands and face and hair, then blows his nose into it and spits into it. When he has finished the girl takes the bowl to his neighbor—who repeats the performance. Thus, the bowl goes the rounds of the entire household. . . .

If one of the Rus folk falls sick they put him in a tent by himself and leave bread and water for him. They do not visit him, however, or speak to him, especially if he is a serf. Should he recover he rejoins the others; if he dies they burn him. But if he happens to be a serf they leave him for the dogs and vultures to devour. If they catch a robber they hang him to a tree until he is torn to shreds by wind and weather.

 What was Ibn Fadlan's impression of the Rus? Why do you think he was so critical of their behavior?

Source: J. Brøndsted *The Vikings*, trans. K. Skov (London: Penguin Books, 1965).

---

become the princes of Moscow and eventually leaders of all Russia.

12-2d Christianity and Medieval Civilization

Christianity was an integral part of the fabric of European society and the consciousness of Europe. Papal directives affected the actions of kings and princes alike, and Christian teachings and practices touched the lives of all Europeans.

Reform of the Papacy Since the fifth century, the popes of the Catholic Church had reigned supreme over church affairs. They also came to exercise control over the territories in central Italy that came to be known as the Papal States, which kept the popes involved in political matters, often at the expense of their spiritual obligations. At the same time, the church became increasingly entangled in the evolving feudal relationships. High officials of the church such as bishops and abbots came to hold their offices as fiefs from nobles. As vassals, they were obliged to carry out the usual duties, including military service. And because lords assumed the right to choose their vassals, they came to appoint bishops and abbots.

In the eleventh century, church leaders realized the need to free the church from the interference of lords in the appointment of church officials. **Lay investiture** was the practice by which secular rulers both chose nominees to church offices and invested them with (bestowed on them) the symbols of their office. Pope Gregory VII

England	
Norman conquest	1066
William the Conqueror	1066–1087
Henry II	1154–1189
John	1199–1216
Magna Carta	1215
Edward I	1272–1307
First Parliament	1295
France	
Philip II Augustus	1180–1223
Philip IV	1285–1314
First Estates-General	1302
Germany and the Empire	
Otto I	936–973
Frederick I Barbarossa	1152–1190
Frederick II	1212–1250
The Eastern World	
Mongol conquest of Russia	1230s
Alexander Nevsky, prince of Novgorod	ca. 1220–1263

(1073–1085), deciding to fight this practice, claimed that he as pope was God's "vicar on earth" and that the pope's authority extended over all of Christendom, including its rulers. In 1075, he issued a decree forbidding high-ranking clerics from receiving their investiture from lay leaders.

Gregory VII soon found himself in conflict with the king of Germany over his actions. King Henry IV (1056–1106) of Germany was also a determined man who had appointed high-ranking clerics, especially bishops, as his vassals in order to use them as administrators. Henry had no intention of obeying a decree that challenged the very heart of his administration.

The struggle between Henry IV and Gregory VII, which is known as the Investiture Controversy, was one of the great conflicts between church and state in the High Middle Ages. It dragged on until a new German king and a new pope reached a compromise in 1122 called the Concordat of Worms (kun-KOR-dat of WURMZ or VORMPS). Under this agreement, church officials first elected a bishop in Germany. After election, the nominee paid homage to the king as his lord, who then invested him with the symbols of temporal office. A representative of the pope, however, then invested the new bishop with the symbols of his spiritual office.

The Church Supreme: The Papal Monarchy   The popes of the twelfth century did not abandon the reform ideals of Pope Gregory VII, but they were more inclined to consolidate their power and build a strong administrative system. During the papacy of Pope Innocent III (1198–1216), the Catholic Church reached the height of its power. At the beginning of his pontificate, the pope made a clear statement of his views on papal supremacy in a letter to a priest:

> As God, the creator of the universe, set two great lights in the firmament of heaven, the greater light to rule the day, and the lesser light to rule the night, so He set two great dignities in the firmament of the universal church, . . . the greater to rule the day, that is, souls, and the lesser to rule the night, that is, bodies. These dignities are the papal authority and the royal power. And just as the moon gets her light from the sun, and is inferior to the sun . . . so the royal power gets the splendor of its dignity from the papal authority.[4]

Innocent III's actions were those of a man who believed that he, as pope, was the supreme judge of European affairs. To achieve his political ends, he did not hesitate to use the spiritual weapons at his command, especially the **interdict**, which forbade priests to dispense the **sacraments** of the church in the hope that the people, deprived of the comforts of religion, would exert pressure against their ruler.

New Religious Orders and new Spiritual Ideals   Between 1050 and 1150, a wave of religious enthusiasm seized Europe, leading to a spectacular growth in the number of monasteries and the emergence of new monastic orders. Most important was the Cistercian (sis-TUR-shun) order, which was founded in 1098 by a group of monks dissatisfied with the moral degeneration and lack of strict discipline at their own Benedictine monastery. The Cistercians were strict. They ate a simple diet and possessed only a single robe apiece. The Cistercians played a major role in developing a new, activist spiritual model for twelfth-century Europe.

Women were also actively involved in the spiritual movements of the age. The number of women joining religious houses grew dramatically in the High Middle Ages. Most nuns were from the ranks of the landed aristocracy. Convents were convenient for families unable or unwilling to find husbands for their daughters and for aristocratic women who did not wish to marry. Female intellectuals also found them a haven for their activities. Most of the learned women of the Middle Ages, especially in Germany, were nuns. One of the most distinguished was Hildegard of Bingen (HIL-duh-gard of BING-un) (1098–1179), who became abbess of a convent at Disibodenberg in western

Germany. Hildegard gained considerable renown as a mystic and prophet, and popes, emperors, kings, dukes, and bishops eagerly sought her advice.

In the thirteenth century, two new religious orders emerged that had a profound impact on the lives of ordinary people. Like their founder, Saint Francis of Assisi (uh-SEE-zee) (1182–1226), the Franciscans lived among the people, preaching repentance and aiding the poor. Their calls for a return to the simplicity and poverty of the early church, reinforced by their own example, were especially effective and made them popular.

The Dominicans arose out of the desire of a Spanish priest, Dominic de Guzmán (DAH-muh-nik duh gooz-MAHN) (1170–1221), to defend church teachings from **heresy**—beliefs contrary to official church doctrine. Dominic was an intellectual who came to believe that a new religious order of men who lived lives of poverty but were learned and capable of preaching effectively would best be able to attack heresy. The Dominicans became especially well known for their roles as the inquisitors of the papal Inquisition.

The Holy Office, as the papal Inquisition was formally called, was a court established by the church to find and try heretics. Anyone accused of heresy who refused to confess was still considered guilty and was turned over to the state for execution. To the Christians of the thirteenth century, who believed that there was only one path to salvation, heresy was a crime against God and against humanity. In their minds, force should be used to save souls from damnation.

12-2e The Culture of the High Middle Ages

The High Middle Ages was a time of extraordinary intellectual and artistic vitality. It witnessed the birth of universities and a building spree that left Europe bedecked with churches and cathedrals.

The Rise of Universities   The university as we know it—with faculty, students, and degrees—was a product of the High Middle Ages. The word *university* is derived from the Latin word *universitas* (yoo-nee-VAYR-see-tahss), meaning a corporation or guild, and referred to either a corporation of teachers or a corporation of students. Medieval universities were educational guilds or corporations that produced educated and trained individuals.

The first European university appeared in Bologna (boh-LOHN-yuh), Italy, where a great teacher named Irnerius (ur-NEER-ee-uss) (1088-1125), who taught Roman law, attracted students from all over Europe. To protect themselves, students at Bologna formed a guild or *universitas*, which was recognized by Emperor Frederick Barbarossa and given a charter in 1158. Kings, popes, and princes soon competed to found new universities, and by the end of the Middle Ages, there were eighty universities in Europe, most of them in England, France, Italy, and Germany (see Historical Voices, "University Students and Violence at Oxford," p. 310).

University students (all men—women did not attend universities in the Middle Ages) began their studies with the traditional **liberal arts** curriculum, which consisted of grammar, rhetoric, logic, arithmetic, geometry, music, and astronomy. Teaching was done by the lecture method. The word *lecture* is derived from the Latin verb for "read." Before the development of the printing press in the fifteenth century, books were expensive and few students could afford them, so teachers read from a basic text (such as a collection of laws if the subject was law) and then added their explanations. No exams were given after a series of lectures, but when a student applied for a degree, he was given a comprehensive oral examination by a committee of teachers. The exam was taken after a four- or six-year period of study. The first degree a student could earn was a bachelor of arts; later he might receive a master of arts.

The Development of Scholasticism   The importance of Christianity in medieval society ensured that theology would play a central role in the European intellectual world. Theology, the formal study of religion, was "queen of the sciences" in the new universities.

Beginning in the eleventh century, the effort to apply reason or logical analysis to the church's basic theological doctrines had a significant impact on the study of theology. The philosophical and theological system of the medieval schools is known as **Scholasticism** (skoh-LAS-tih-siz-uhm). Scholasticism tried to reconcile faith and reason to demonstrate that what was accepted on faith was in harmony with what could be learned by reason.

The overriding task of Scholasticism was to harmonize Christian teachings with the work of the Greek philosopher Aristotle. In the twelfth century, largely because of the work of Muslim and Jewish scholars in Spain, western Europe was introduced to a large number of Greek scientific and philosophical works, including the works of Aristotle. Aristotle's works threw many theologians into consternation, however. Aristotle had arrived at his conclusions by rational thought, not by faith, and some of his doctrines contradicted the teachings of the church. The most famous attempt to reconcile Aristotle and the doctrines of Christianity was that of Saint Thomas Aquinas (uh-KWY-nuss) (1225–1274).

Aquinas's reputation derives from his masterful attempt to reconcile faith and reason. He took it for granted that there were truths derived by reason and truths derived by faith. He was certain, however, that the two truths

University Students and Violence at Oxford

Art & Ideas **MEDIEVAL UNIVERSITIES** shared in the violent atmosphere of their age. Town and gown quarrels often resulted in bloody conflicts, especially during the universities' formative period. This selection is taken from an anonymous description of a student riot at Oxford at the end of the thirteenth century.

A Student Riot at Oxford

They [the townsmen] seized and imprisoned all scholars on whom they could lay hands, invaded their inns [halls of residence], made havoc of their goods and trampled their books under foot. In the face of such provocation the proctors [university officials] sent their assistants about the town, forbidding the students to leave their inns. But all commands and exhortations were in vain. By nine o'clock next morning, bands of scholars were parading the streets in martial array. If the proctors failed to restrain them, the mayor was equally powerless to restrain his townsmen. The great bell of St. Martin's rang out an alarm; oxhorns were sounded in the streets; messengers were sent into the country to collect rustic allies. The clerks [students and teachers], who numbered 3,000 in all, began their attack simultaneously in various quarters. They broke open warehouses in the Spicery, the Cutlery and elsewhere. Armed with bow and arrows, swords and bucklers, slings and stones, they fell upon their opponents. Three they slew, and wounded fifty or more. One band . . . took up a position in High Street between the Churches of St. Mary and All Saints' and attacked the house of a certain Edward Hales. This Hales was a longstanding enemy of the clerks. There were no half measures with him. He seized his crossbow, and from an upper chamber sent an unerring shaft into the eye of the pugnacious rector. The death of their valiant leader caused the clerks to lose heart. They fled, closely pursued by the townsmen and country-folk. Some were struck down in the streets, and others who had taken refuge in the churches were dragged out and driven mercilessly to prison, lashed with thongs and goaded with iron spikes.

Complaints of murder, violence and robbery were lodged straightway with the king by both parties. The townsmen claimed 3,000 pounds' damage. The commissioners, however, appointed to decide the matter, condemned them to pay 200 marks, removed the bailiffs, and banished twelve of the most turbulent citizens from Oxford.

 Who do you think was responsible for this conflict between town and gown? Why? Why do you think the king supported the university?

Source: C. Headlam, *The Story of Oxford*, 1907.

---

could not be in conflict. The natural mind, unaided by faith, could arrive at truths concerning the physical universe. Without the help of God's grace, however, reason alone could not grasp spiritual truths such as the Trinity (the manifestation of God in three separate yet identical persons—Father, Son, and Holy Spirit) or the Incarnation (Jesus's simultaneous identity as God and human).

The Gothic Cathedral Begun in the twelfth century and brought to perfection in the thirteenth, the **Gothic** cathedral remains one of the greatest artistic triumphs of the High Middle Ages. Soaring skyward, as if to reach heaven, it was a fitting symbol for medieval people's preoccupation with God.

Two fundamental innovations of the twelfth century made Gothic cathedrals possible. The combination of ribbed vaults and pointed arches replaced the barrel vault of earlier churches and enabled builders to make Gothic churches higher. The use of pointed arches and ribbed vaults created an impression of upward movement. Another technical innovation, the flying buttress, basically a heavy arched pier of stone built onto the outside of the walls, made it possible to distribute the weight of the church's vaulted ceilings outward and down and thus eliminate the heavy walls used in earlier churches to hold the weight of the massive barrel vaults. Thus, Gothic cathedrals could be built with thin walls containing magnificent stained-glass windows that created a play of light inside that varied with the sun at different times of the day. The use of light reflected the belief that natural light was a symbol of the divine light of God.

The first fully Gothic church was the abbey of Saint Denis (san-duh-NEE) near Paris, which was inspired by its famous Abbot Suger (soo-ZHAYR) (1122–1151) and built between 1140 and 1150. By the mid-thirteenth century, French Gothic architecture, most brilliantly executed in

12.7 The Gothic Cathedral. The Gothic cathedral was one of the great artistic triumphs of the High Middle Ages. Shown here is the cathedral of Notre Dame in Paris. Begun in 1163, it was not completed until the beginning of the fourteenth century.

cathedrals in Paris (Notre Dame), Reims, Amiens, and Chartres, had spread to virtually all of Europe.

A Gothic cathedral was the work of the entire community. All classes contributed to its construction. Master masons, who were both architects and engineers, designed the cathedrals, and stonemasons and other craftspeople were paid a daily wage and provided the skilled labor to build them. A Gothic cathedral symbolized the chief preoccupation of a medieval Christian community, its dedication to a spiritual ideal. As we have observed before, the largest buildings of an era reflect the values of its society. The Gothic cathedral, with its towers soaring toward heaven, gave witness to an age when a spiritual impulse underlay most aspects of its existence.

12-3 MEDIEVAL EUROPE AND THE WORLD

 Focus Questions: In what ways did Europeans begin to relate to peoples in other parts of the world after 1000 C.E.? What were the reasons for the crusades, and who or what benefited the most from the experience of the crusades?

As it developed, European civilization remained largely confined to its home continent, although Europe was never completely isolated. Some Europeans, especially merchants, had contacts with parts of Asia and Africa, and the goods of those lands made their way into medieval

castles. The Vikings were also daring explorers. After 860 C.E., they sailed westward in their long ships across the North Atlantic, reaching Iceland in 874. Some Vikings even landed in Newfoundland, the only known Viking site in North America, but it proved to be short lived as Viking expansion drew to a close by the end of the tenth century. Only at the end of the eleventh century did Europeans begin their first concerted attempt to expand beyond the frontiers of Europe by conquering the land of Palestine.

12-3a The Early Crusades

The Crusades were based on the idea of a holy war against the infidels (unbelievers). Christian wrath was directed against the Muslims, and Christian Europe found itself with a glorious opportunity to attack them at the end of the eleventh century. The immediate impetus for the Crusades came when the Byzantine emperor, Alexius I, asked Pope Urban II for help against the Muslim Seljuk Turks (see Chapter 13). The pope saw this as a chance to rally the warriors of Europe for the liberation of Jerusalem and the Holy Land of Palestine from the infidel. The Holy City of Jerusalem—where Jesus had lived and died—had long been the focus of Christian pilgrimages. At the Council of Clermont in southern France near the end of 1095, Urban II challenged Christians to take up their weapons and join in a holy war to recover the Holy Land.

In the First Crusade, begun in 1096, three organized crusading bands of noble warriors, most of them French, made their way eastward. After the capture of Antioch in 1098, much of the crusading host proceeded down the Palestinian coast, evading the well-defended coastal cities, and reached Jerusalem in June 1099. After a five-week siege, the Holy City was taken amid a horrible massacre of the inhabitants—men, women, and children.

After further conquest of Palestinian lands, the crusaders ignored the wishes of the Byzantine emperor and organized four Latin crusader states. Because the crusader kingdoms were surrounded by Muslims hostile to them, they grew increasingly dependent on the Italian commercial cities for supplies from Europe. Some Italian cities, such as Genoa, Pisa, and, above all, Venice, grew rich and powerful in the process.

But it was not easy for the crusader kingdoms to maintain themselves. Already by the 1120s, the Muslims had begun to strike back. The fall of one of the Latin kingdoms in

12.8 The First Crusade: The Capture of Jerusalem. Recruited from the noble class of western Europe, the first crusading army had taken Antioch by 1098. Working down the coast of Palestine, the crusaders captured Jerusalem in 1099. Shown here in a fifteenth-century manuscript illustration is a fanciful re-creation of the looting after its capture by the Christian crusaders.

1144 led to renewed calls for another Crusade, especially from the monastic firebrand Saint Bernard of Clairvaux (klayr-VOH). He exclaimed: "Now, on account of our sins, the enemies of the cross have begun to show their faces. . . . What are you doing, you servants of the cross? Will you throw to the dogs that which is most holy? Will you cast pearls before swine?"[5] Because of his reputation—he has been called the most widely respected holy man of the twelfth century—Bernard managed to enlist two powerful rulers. Nevertheless, the Second Crusade proved to be a total failure.

The Third Crusade was a reaction to the fall of the Holy City of Jerusalem to the Muslim forces under Saladin in 1187. Now all of Christendom was ablaze with calls for a new Crusade. Three major monarchs agreed to lead their forces in person: Emperor Frederick Barbarossa of Germany, Richard I the Lionhearted of England (1189–1199), and Philip II Augustus, king of France. Some of the crusaders finally arrived in the Holy Land by 1189 only to encounter problems. Frederick Barbarossa drowned while swimming in a local river, and his army quickly disintegrated.

The English and French arrived by sea and met with success against the coastal cities, where they had the support of their fleets; when they moved inland, they failed miserably. Eventually, after Philip went home, Richard the Lionhearted negotiated a settlement whereby Saladin agreed to allow Christian pilgrims free access to Jerusalem.

12-3b The Later Crusades

After the death of Saladin in 1193, Pope Innocent III initiated the Fourth Crusade. On its way to the east, the crusading army became involved in a dispute over the succession to the Byzantine throne. Although some historians believe the Venetian leaders of the Fourth Crusade saw an opportunity to neutralize their greatest commercial competitor, the Byzantine Empire, it is more likely that a series of unfortunate circumstances and misunderstandings led the western Crusaders to sack the great capital city of Constantinople in 1204 and set up the new Latin Empire of Constantinople (see Chapter 13). Not until 1261 did a Byzantine army recapture Constantinople. In the meantime, additional Crusades were undertaken to reconquer the Holy Land.

All of them were largely disasters, and the European military effort to capture Palestine was recognized as a complete failure by the end of the thirteenth century.

HISTORIANS DEBATE · **12-3c What Were the Effects of the Crusades?**

Whether the Crusades had much effect on European civilization is debatable. The crusaders made little long-term impact on the Middle East, where the only visible remnants of their conquests were their castles. There may have been some broadening of perspective that comes from the exchange between two cultures, but the interaction of Christian Europe with the Muslim world was actually both more intense and more meaningful in Spain and Sicily than in the Holy Land. Nevertheless, some historians believe there was some influence of the Crusades on Europe's intellectual development with the absorption of the advanced science and learning of the Islamic world.

Did the Crusades help stabilize European society by removing large numbers of young warriors who would have fought each other in Europe? Some historians think so and believe that Western monarchs established their control more easily as a result. However, historians today doubt this and argue that it was the wealthy and pious nobles who risked their lives and fortunes to help their fellow Christians. Taking the cross as a religious incentive was important to many nobles. As one prayed, "Lord, take me from wars between Christians in which I have spent much of my life; let me die in your service so I may share your kingdom in Paradise."[6]

The Crusades undoubtedly contributed to the economic growth of Italian port cities, especially Genoa, Pisa, and Venice. But it is important to remember that the growing wealth and population of twelfth-century Europe had made the Crusades possible in the first place. The Crusades may have enhanced Italian trade in the Mediterranean, but they certainly did not cause the revival of trade. Even without the Crusades, Italian merchants would have pursued new trade contacts with the eastern world. Moreover, there was little economic gain for many Crusaders, most of whom did not settle in the east but returned home after their initial success. Many faced economic ruin after selling their lands to finance their expeditions.

Did the Crusades have side effects that would haunt European society for generations? The Crusades did not lead, as some historians have suggested, to the decline of the Muslim world, which had little interest in the Crusades during the Middle Ages; after all, once united, the Muslim world had ended the crusader states in the Middle East. Not until the twentieth century, after believers in Western imperialism redefined the Crusades as the first effort of Western colonialism, did many in the Islamic world begin to view the Crusades as the first attempt of Western powers to colonize the Middle East, helping to lead to the troubled relationship between the Muslim world and the West today.

Another possible side effect is more apparent. The first widespread attacks on the Jews began with the Crusades. As some Christians argued, to undertake holy wars against infidel Muslims while the "murderers of Christ" ran free at home was unthinkable. With the crusades, the massacre of Jews became a regular feature of medieval European life.

CHAPTER SUMMARY

After the collapse of the Han Dynasty in the third century C.E., China experienced nearly four centuries of internal chaos until the seventh century C.E. when the Tang Dynasty attempted to follow the pattern of the Han Dynasty and restore the power of the Chinese Empire. The fall of the Western Roman Empire in the fifth century brought a quite different result as three new civilizations emerged out of the collapse of Roman power in the Mediterranean. In the east, a new world of Islam emerged that occupied large parts of the old Roman Empire and created its own flourishing civilization. As we shall see in Chapter 13, the eastern part of the old Roman Empire, increasingly Greek in culture, continued to survive as the Christian Byzantine Empire. At the same time, a new Christian European civilization was establishing its roots in the west. By the eleventh and twelfth centuries, these three heirs of Rome began their own conflict for control of the lands of the eastern Mediterranean.

When Charlemagne, the descendant of a Germanic tribe that converted to Christianity, was crowned emperor of the Romans in 800, the event symbolized the fusion of the three chief components of the new European civilization: the German tribes, the Roman legacy, and the Christian church. Charlemagne's

Carolingian Empire fostered the idea of a distinct European identity. With the disintegration of that empire, however, many different lords came to dominate Europe's political, economic, and social life, creating a world of castles and private power. During the High Middle Ages, kings gradually began to develop the machinery of government and accumulate political authority. Although they could not know it then, the actions of these medieval monarchs laid the foundation for the European states that in one form or another have dominated the European political scene ever since.

European civilization began to flourish in the High Middle Ages. The revival of trade, the expansion of towns and cities, and the development of a money economy did not mean the end of a predominantly rural European society, but they did open the door to new ways to make a living and new opportunities for people to expand and enrich their lives. At the same time, the High Middle Ages

also gave birth to a cultural revival that led to new centers of learning in the universities, to the use of reason to systematize the study of theology, and to a dramatic increase in the number and size of churches.

The Catholic Church shared in the challenge of new growth by reforming itself and striking out on a path toward greater papal power, both within the church and over European society. The High Middle Ages witnessed a spiritual renewal that enhanced papal leadership and the religious life of the clergy and laity. At the same time, this spiritual renewal also gave rise to the crusading "holy warrior," thereby creating an animosity between Christians and Muslims that still has repercussions today.

REFLECTION QUESTIONS

Q What impact did the Vikings have on the history and culture of medieval Europe?

Q What are the major political developments in Europe during the Middle Ages and how do they compare to developments in Asia, Africa, and the Middle East?

Q The medieval Catholic Church developed along new institutional lines in the High Middle Ages. What are the most important features of this development?

CHAPTER TIMELINE

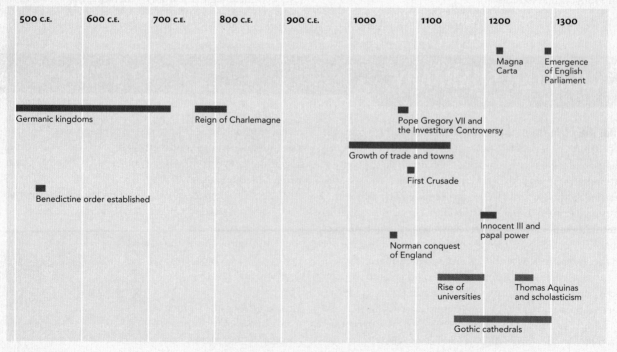

CHAPTER NOTES

1. N. F. Cantor, ed., *The Medieval World, 300–1300* (New York, 1963), p. 104.
2. A. Barbero, *Charlemagne: Father of a Continent*, trans. A. Cameron (Berkeley, Calif., 2004), p. 4.
3. Chris Wickham, *The Inheritance of Rome: A History of Europe from 400 to 1000* (New York, 2009), p. 4.
4. O. J. Thatcher and E. H. McNeal, eds., *A Source Book for Medieval History* (New York, 1905), p. 208.
5. Quoted in H. E. Mayer, *The Crusades*, trans. J. Gillingham (New York, 1972), pp. 99–100.
6. Quoted in Christopher Tyerman, *God's War: A New History of the Crusades* (Cambridge, Mass., 2006), p. 921.

MINDTAP
From Cengage

MindTap® is a fully online, highly personalized learning experience built upon Cengage Learning content. MindTap combines student learning tools—readings, multimedia, activities, and assessments—into a singular Learning Path that guides students through the course and helps students develop the critical thinking, analysis, and communication skills that are essential to academic and professional success.

CHAPTER 13

THE BYZANTINE EMPIRE AND CRISIS AND RECOVERY IN THE WEST

Chapter Outline and Focus Questions

Scala/Art Resource, NY

13.1 Justinian and Theodora

Critical Thinking

Q *In what ways did the Byzantine, European, and Islamic civilizations resemble and differ from each other? Were their relationships generally based on cooperation or conflict?*

Connections to Today

Q *How is the concept of the Renaissance relevant to the early twenty-first century?*

AT THE SAME TIME that medieval European civilization was emerging in the west, the eastern part of the late Roman Empire, increasingly Greek in culture, continued to survive. While serving as a buffer between Europe and the peoples to the east, especially the growing empire of Islam, the late Roman Empire in the east (Byzantine Empire) also preserved the intellectual and legal accomplishments of the Greeks and Romans.

In its early decades, the Eastern Roman Empire was beset by crises. Soon after the beginning of his reign, the emperor Justinian was faced with a serious revolt in the capital city of Constantinople. In 532 C.E., two factions—called the Blues and the Greens because they supported chariot teams bearing those colors when they competed in the Hippodrome (a huge amphitheater)—joined together and rioted to protest the emperor's taxation policies. The riots soon became a revolt as insurgents burned and looted the center of the city, shouting "Nika!" (victory), the word normally used to cheer on their favorite teams. Aristocratic factions joined the revolt and put forward a nobleman named Hypatius as a new emperor. Justinian seemed ready to flee, but his wife, the empress Theodora, strengthened his resolve by declaring, according to historian Procopius, "If now, it is your wish to save yourself, O Emperor, there is no difficulty. For we have much money, and there is the sea, here the boats. However, consider whether it will not come about after you have been saved that you would gladly exchange that safety for death. As for myself, I approve a certain ancient saying that royalty is a good burial shroud."[1] Shamed by his wife's words, Justinian resolved to fight. He ordered troops, newly returned from fighting the Persians, to attack a large crowd that had gathered in the Hippodrome to acclaim Hypatius as emperor. In the ensuing massacre, the imperial troops slaughtered 30,000 of the insurgents, some 5 percent of the city's population. After crushing the Nika Revolt, Justinian began a massive rebuilding program and continued the autocratic reign that established the foundations of the Byzantine Empire (as it came to known beginning in the eighth century).

Despite the early empire's reversals, the Macedonian emperors in the ninth, tenth, and eleventh centuries enlarged the empire, achieved economic prosperity, and expanded its cultural influence to eastern Europe and Russia. But after the Macedonian Dynasty ended in 1056 C.E., the empire began a slow but steady decline. Involvement in the crusades proved especially disastrous, leading to the occupation of Constantinople by western crusading forces in 1204. Byzantine rule was restored in 1261, and the empire survived in a weakened condition for another 190 years until the Ottoman Turks finally conquered it in 1453.

In the fourteenth century, Europe, too, sustained a series of crises and reversals after flourishing during the three centuries of the High Middle Ages. Unlike the Byzantine Empire, however, European civilization rebounded in the fifteenth century, experiencing an artistic and intellectual revival in the Renaissance as well as a renewal of monarchical authority among the western European states. Europe was poised to begin its dramatic entry into world affairs.

Focus Questions: How did the Byzantine Empire that had emerged by the eighth century differ from the empire of Justinian and from the Germanic kingdoms in the west? How were they alike?

As noted earlier, the western and eastern parts of the Roman Empire began to drift apart in the fourth century. As the Germanic peoples moved into the western part of the empire and established various kingdoms over the course of the fifth century, the late Roman Empire in the east solidified and prospered.

Constantinople, the imperial capital, viewed itself not only as the center of a world empire but also as a special Christian city. The inhabitants believed that the city was under the protection of God and the Virgin Mary. One thirteenth-century Byzantine said, "About our city you shall know: until the end she will fear no nation whatsoever, for no one will entrap or capture her, not by any means, for she has been given to the Mother of God and no one will snatch her out of Her hands. Many nations will break their horns against her walls and withdraw with shame."[2] The Byzantines saw their state as a Christian empire protected by God and the Virgin Mary.

13-1a The Reign of Justinian (527–565 c.e.)

In the sixth century, the empire in the east came under the control of one of its most remarkable rulers, the emperor Justinian (juh-STIN-ee-un). He married Theodora (thee-uh-DOR-uh), daughter of a lower-class circus trainer, who, as we have seen, proved to be a remarkably strong-willed woman during the revolt in 532. Justinian was determined to reestablish the Roman Empire in the entire Mediterranean world and began his attempt to reconquer the west within a year after the revolt had failed.

Justinian's army under Belisarius (bell-uh-SAH-ree-uss), probably the best general of the late Roman world, presented a formidable force. Belisarius sailed to North Africa and quickly defeated the Vandals in two major battles. From North Africa, he occupied Sicily in 535 c.e. and then led his forces onto the Italian Peninsula. But it was not until 552 that the Ostrogoths in Italy were finally defeated. Justinian appeared to have achieved his goals. He had restored the imperial Mediterranean world; his empire included Italy, part of Spain, North Africa, Asia Minor, Palestine, and Syria (see Map 13.1). But the conquest of the western empire proved fleeting. Only three years after Justinian's

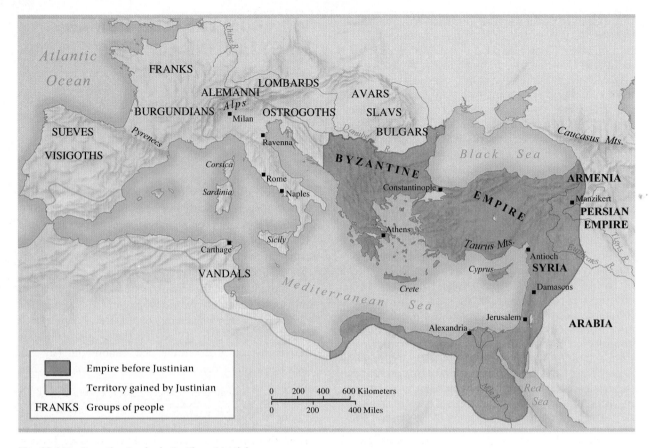

Map 13.1 The Byzantine Empire in the Time of Justinian

death, another Germanic people, the Lombards, entered Italy. Although the eastern empire maintained the fiction of Italy as a province, it controlled only a few small pockets.

The Codification of Roman Law Though his conquests proved short lived, Justinian made a lasting contribution to Western civilization through his codification of Roman law. The eastern empire was heir to a vast quantity of materials connected to the development of Roman law. Justinian had been well trained in imperial government and was thoroughly acquainted with Roman law. He wished to codify and simplify this mass of materials.

To accomplish his goal, Justinian authorized the jurist Trebonian (tre-BOHN-ee-un) to make a systematic compilation of imperial edicts. The result was the Code of Law, the first part of the *Corpus Iuris Civilis* (KOR-pus YOOR-iss SIV-i-liss) (Body of Civil Law), completed in 529 C.E. Four years later, two other parts of the *Corpus* appeared: the *Digest*, a compendium of writings of Roman jurists, and the *Institutes*, a brief summary of the chief principles of Roman law that could be used as a textbook. The fourth part of the *Corpus* was the *Novels*, a compilation of the most important new edicts issued during Justinian's reign.

Justinian's codification of Roman law became the basis of imperial law in the Byzantine Empire until its end in 1453. More important, however, because it was written in Latin, it was also eventually used in the west and became the basis of legal systems throughout continental Europe. In fact, the *Corpus* was last product of eastern Roman culture to be written in Latin, which was soon replaced by Greek.

The Emperor's Building Program After the riots destroyed much of Constantinople, Justinian rebuilt the city and gave it the appearance it would keep for almost a thousand years. The city was dominated by an immense palace complex, the huge arena known as the Hippodrome, and hundreds of churches. Justinian added many new buildings. His public works projects included roads, bridges, walls, public baths, law courts, and colossal underground reservoirs to hold the city's water supply. He also built hospitals, schools, monasteries, and churches. Churches were his special passion, and in Constantinople he built

13.2 The Emperor Justinian and his Court. As the seat of late Roman power in Italy, the town of Ravenna was adorned with late Roman art. The Church of San Vitale at Ravenna contains some of the finest examples of sixth-century mosaics. Small pieces of colored glass were set in mortar on the wall to form these figures and their surroundings. The emperor is depicted as both head of state (he wears a jeweled crown and a purple robe) and head of the church (he carries a gold bowl symbolizing the body of Jesus).

or rebuilt thirty-four of them. His greatest achievement was the famous Hagia Sophia (HAH-yuh soh-FEE-uh), the Church of the Holy Wisdom.

Completed in 537 C.E., Hagia Sophia was designed by two Greek scientists who departed radically from the simple, flat-roofed basilica of western architecture. The center of Hagia Sophia consisted of four huge piers crowned by an enormous dome, which seemed to be floating in space. In part, this impression was created by putting forty-two windows around the base of the dome, which allowed an incredible play of light within the cathedral. Light served to remind the worshipers of God; as Procopius (pruh-KOH-pee-USS), the court historian, commented: "Whoever enters there to worship perceives at once that it is not by any human strength or skill, but by the favor of God that this work has been perfected; his mind rises sublime to commune with God, feeling that He cannot be far off, but must especially love to dwell in the place which He has chosen."[3] As darkness is illuminated by invisible light, so, too, it was believed, the world is illuminated by invisible spirit.

The royal palace complex, Hagia Sophia, and the Hippodrome were the three greatest buildings in Constantinople. This last was a huge amphitheater constructed of brick covered by marble that could hold as many as 60,000 spectators. The main events were the chariot races; twenty-four would usually be presented in one day. The citizens of Constantinople were passionate fans of chariot racing. Crowds in the Hippodrome also took on political significance. Being a member of the two chief factions of charioteers—the Blues or the Greens—was the only real outlet for political expression. Even emperors had to be aware of their demands and attitudes: the loss of a race in the Hippodrome frequently resulted in bloody riots that could threaten the emperor's power.

13-1b A New Kind of Empire

Justinian's accomplishments had been spectacular, but he left the Eastern Roman Empire with serious problems when he died: too much distant territory to protect, an empty treasury, a smaller population after a devastating plague, and renewed threats to the frontiers. The seventh century proved to be an important turning point in the history of the empire.

Problems of the Seventh Century In the first half of the century, during the reign of Heraclius (he-ruh-KLY-uss or huh-RAK-lee-uss) (610–641 C.E.), the empire faced attacks from the Persians to the east and the Slavs to the north. A new system of defense was put in place, using a new and larger administrative unit—the *theme*—that combined civilian and military offices in the hands of the same person. Thus, the civil governor was also the military leader of the area. Although this innovation helped the empire survive, it also fostered an increased militarization of the empire.

13.3 Interior view of Hagia Sophia. Pictured here is the interior of the Church of the Holy Wisdom in Constantinople (modern Istanbul), which was constructed under Justinian by Anthemius of Tralles (an-THEE-mee-uss of TRAL-leez) and Isidore of Miletus (IH-zuh-dor of mih-LEE-tuss). This view gives an idea of how the windows around the base of the dome produced a special play of light within the cathedral. The pulpits and plaques bearing inscriptions from the Qur'an were introduced when the Turks converted this church to a mosque in the fifteenth century.

Bulgars defeated the eastern Roman forces and took possession of the lower Danube Valley, setting up a strong Bulgarian kingdom. By the beginning of the eighth century, the Eastern Roman Empire was greatly diminished in size, consisting only of a portion of the Balkans and Asia Minor.

It was now an eastern Mediterranean state. These external challenges had important internal repercussions as well. By the eighth century, the Eastern Roman Empire had been transformed into what historians call the Byzantine Empire, a civilization with its own unique character that would last until 1453 (Constantinople was built on the site of an older city named Byzantium, hence the name *Byzantine*).

The Byzantine Empire in the Eighth Century The Byzantine Empire was a Greek state. Latin fell into disuse as Greek became not only the common language of the empire but also its official language.

The Byzantine Empire was also a Christian state built on a faith in Jesus that was shared in a profound way by almost all its citizens. An enormous amount of artistic talent was poured into the construction of churches, church ceremonies, and church decoration. Spiritual principles deeply permeated Byzantine art. The importance of religion to the Byzantines explains why theological disputes took on an exaggerated form. The most famous of these disputes, the so-called iconoclastic controversy, threatened the stability of the empire in the first half of the eighth century.

By the mid-seventh century, it had become apparent that a restored Mediterranean empire was simply beyond the resources of the eastern empire, which now increasingly turned its back on the Latin west. A renewed series of external threats in the second half of the seventh century strengthened this development.

The most serious challenge to the empire was the rise of Islam, which unified the Arab tribes and created a powerful new force that swept through the region (see Chapter 7). The defeat of an eastern Roman army near the Yarmuk River in 636 C.E. meant the loss of the provinces of Syria and Palestine. The Arabs also moved into the old Persian Empire and conquered it. An Arab attempt to besiege Constantinople in 717 failed, leaving Arabs and eastern Roman forces facing each other along a frontier in southern Asia Minor.

Problems also arose along the northern frontier, especially in the Balkans, where an Asiatic people known as the *Bulgars* had arrived earlier in the sixth century. In 679, the

Map 13.2 The Byzantine Empire, ca. 750

Beginning in the sixth century, the use of religious images, especially in the form of icons or pictures of sacred figures, became so widespread that charges of idolatry, the worship of images, began to be heard. The use of images or icons had been justified by the argument that icons were not worshiped but were simply used to help illiterate people understand their religion. This argument failed to stop the **iconoclasts**, as the opponents of icons were called. **Iconoclasm** was not unique to the Byzantine Empire. In the neighboring Islamic empire, religious art did not include any physical representations of Muhammad (see Comparative Illustration, "Religious Imagery in the Medieval World," p. 322).

Beginning in 730 C.E., the Byzantine emperor Leo III (717–741) outlawed the use of icons. Strong resistance ensued, especially from monks. Leo also used the iconoclastic controversy to add to the prestige of the patriarch of Constantinople, the highest church official in the east and second in dignity only to the bishop of Rome. The Roman popes were opposed to the iconoclastic edicts, and their opposition created considerable dissension between the popes and the Byzantine emperors. Late in the eighth century, the Byzantine rulers reversed their stand on the use of images, but not before considerable damage had been done to the unity of the Christian church. Although the final separation between Roman Catholicism and Greek Orthodoxy (as the Christian church in the Byzantine Empire was called) did not occur until 1054, the iconoclastic controversy was important in moving both sides in that direction.

The emperor occupied a crucial position in the Byzantine state. Portrayed as chosen by God, the Byzantine emperor was crowned in an elaborate sacred ceremony, and his subjects were expected to prostrate themselves in his presence. The emperor's power was considered absolute and was limited in practice only by deposition or assassination. Because the emperor appointed the patriarch, he also exercised control over both church and state. The Byzantines believed that God had commanded their state to preserve the true faith, Orthodox Christianity. Emperor, clergy, and civic officials were all bound together in service to this ideal. It can be said that spiritual values truly held the Byzantine state together.

By 750 C.E., it was apparent that two of Rome's heirs, the Germanic kingdoms and the Byzantine Empire, were moving in different directions. Nevertheless, Byzantine influence on the Western world was significant. The images of a Roman imperial state that continued to haunt the west lived on in Byzantium. As noted earlier, the legal systems of the west came to owe much to Justinian's codification of Roman law. In addition, the Byzantine

Empire served in part as a buffer state, protecting the west for a long time from incursions from the east.

Intellectual Life   The intellectual life of the Byzantine Empire was greatly influenced by the traditions of classical civilization. Scholars actively strived to preserve the works of the ancient Greeks and based a great deal of their own literature on classical models. Although the Byzantines produced a substantial body of literature, much of it was of a highly practical nature. For example, manuals on war, providing instruction in the techniques of fighting, were a common type of Byzantine literature (see Historical Voices, "A Byzantine Emperor Gives Military Advice," p. 323). The most outstanding literary achievements of the early Byzantine Empire, however, were historical and religious works.

The empire's best-known historian was Procopius (ca. 500 – ca. 562 C.E.), court historian during the reign of Justinian. Procopius served as secretary to the great general Belisarius and accompanied him on his wars on behalf of Justinian. Procopius's best historical work, the *Wars*, is a firsthand account of Justinian's wars of reconquest in the western Mediterranean and his wars against the Persians in the east. Deliberately modeled after the work of his hero, the Greek historian Thucydides (see Chapter 4), Procopius's narrative features vivid descriptions of battle scenes, clear judgment, and noteworthy objectivity.

Life in Constantinople: The Importance of Trade   With a population in the hundreds of thousands, Constantinople was the largest city in Europe during the Middle Ages. Until the twelfth century, it was also Europe's greatest commercial center. The city was the chief entrepôt for the exchange of products between west and east, and trade formed the basis for its fabulous prosperity. Foreign merchants, however, largely carried on this trade. As one contemporary said:

> All sorts of merchants come here from the land of
> Babylon, from . . . Persia, Media, and all the sovereignty
> of the land of Egypt, from the lands of Canaan, and
> from the empire of Russia, from Hungaria, Khazaria [the
> Caspian region], and the land of Lombardy and Sepharad
> [Spain]. It is a busy city, and merchants come to it from
> every country by sea or land, and there is none like it in
> the world except Baghdad, the great city of Islam.[4]

Highly desired in Europe were the products of the east: silk from China, spices from Southeast Asia and India, jewelry and ivory from India (used by artisans for church items), wheat and furs from southern Russia, and flax and honey from the Balkans. Many of these eastern goods

13.4a

13.4b

COMPARATIVE ILLUSTRATION

Religious Imagery in the Medieval World

Art & Ideas

THE MIDDLE AGES WAS A GOLDEN AGE OF RELIGIOUS ART, reflecting the important role of religion itself in medieval society. These three illustrations show different aspects of medieval religious imagery. In Europe, much Christian art appeared in illuminated manuscripts. Image 13.4a shows a page depicting the figure of Jesus from *The Book of Kells,* a richly decorated manuscript of the Christian Gospels produced by the monks of Iona in the British Isles. Byzantine art was also deeply religious, as was especially evident in icons. Image 13.4b shows an icon of the Virgin and Child (Mary and Jesus) from the monastery of Saint Catherine at Mount Sinai in Egypt dating to around the year 600. Painted on wood, this icon shows the enthroned Virgin and Child between Saints Theodore and George

13.4c

with two angels behind them looking upward to a beam of light containing the hand of God. The figures are not realistic; the goal of the icon was to bridge the gap between the divine and the outer material world. Artists in the Muslim world faced a different challenge. Muslim clerics warned against imitating God by creating pictures of living beings, thus effectively prohibiting the representation of humans, especially Muhammad. Islamic religious artists therefore used decorative motifs based on geometric patterns and the Arabic script. The scriptural panel in Image 13.4c is an artistic presentation of a verse from the Qur'an, thus blending the spiritual and artistic spheres.

Q *How is the importance of religious imagery in the Middle Ages evident in these three illustrations?*

A Byzantine Emperor Gives Military Advice

Politics & Government

TO AN EMPIRE SURROUNDED BY ENEMIES on all sides, military prowess was an absolute necessity. Both Byzantine emperors and the ruling elite, however, also realized that military forces alone would not suffice and consequently fostered the art of diplomacy and military intelligence. This document is from an early-seventh-century work known as the *Strategikon* (stra-TEE-jih-kahn), a manual of strategy written by the emperor Maurice (582–602 C.E.), himself a strong military leader who led his troops into battle. The work is based on the assumption that a detailed knowledge of the habits and fighting skills of their enemies would give the Byzantines an advantage if they had to fight them.

Maurice, *Strategikon*

The light-haired races [Germanic peoples] place great value on freedom. They are bold and undaunted in battle. Daring and impetuous as they are, they consider any timidity and even a short retreat as a disgrace. They calmly despise death as they fight violently in hand-to-hand combat either on horseback or on foot. If they are hard pressed in cavalry actions, they dismount at a single prearranged sign and line up on foot. Although only a few against many horsemen, they do not shrink from the fight. They are armed with shields, lances, and short swords slung from their shoulders. They prefer fighting on foot and rapid charges.

Whether on foot or on horseback, they draw up for battle, not in any fixed measure and formation, or in regiments or divisions, but according to tribes, their kinship with one another, and common interest. Often, as a result, when things are not going well and their friends have been killed, they will risk their lives fighting to avenge them. In combat they make the front of their battle line even and dense. Either on horseback or on foot they are impetuous and undisciplined in charging, as if they were the only people in the world who are not cowards. They are disobedient to their leaders. They are not interested in anything that is at all complicated and pay little attention to external security and their own advantage. They despise good order, especially on horseback. They are easily corrupted by money, greedy as they are.

They are hurt by suffering and fatigue. Although they possess bold and daring spirits, their bodies are pampered and soft, and they are not able to bear pain calmly. In addition, they are hurt by heat, cold, rain, lack of provisions, especially of wine, and postponement of battle. When it comes to a cavalry battle, they are hindered by uneven and wooded terrain. They are easily ambushed along the flanks and to the rear of their battle line, for they do not concern themselves at all with scouts and the other security measures. Their ranks are easily broken by a simulated flight and a sudden turning back against them . . . .

Above all, therefore, in warring against them one must avoid engaging in pitched battles, especially in the early stages. Instead, make use of well-planned ambushes, sneak attacks, and stratagems. Delay things and ruin their opportunities. Pretend to come to agreements with them. Aim at reducing their boldness and zeal by shortage of provisions or the discomfort of heat or cold. This can be done when our army has pitched camp on rugged and difficult ground. On such terrain this enemy cannot attack successfully because they are using lances. But if a favorable opportunity for a regular battle occurs, line up the army as set forth in the book on formations.

 What did Maurice identify as the strengths and weaknesses of the Germanic peoples? Based on his analysis of their traits, what did he advise his military forces to do if they faced the Germans in battle?

Source: George T. Dennis, trans. *Maurice's Strategikon: Handbook of Byzantine Military Strategy, Book 11*, trans. G. T. Dennis (Philadelphia: University of Pennsylvania Press, 1984), pp. 118–119.

were then shipped to the Mediterranean area and northern Europe. Despite the Germanic incursions, trade with Europe never entirely ended.

Moreover, imported raw materials were used in Constantinople for local industries. During Justinian's reign, two Christian monks smuggled silkworms from China to begin a silk industry. The state had a monopoly on the production of silk cloth, and the workshops themselves were housed in Constantinople's royal palace complex. European demand for silk cloth made it the city's most lucrative product. Note that the upper classes, including emperors and empresses, were not discouraged from making money through trade and manufacturing. Indeed, one empress even manufactured perfumes in her bedroom.

13-2 THE ZENITH OF BYZANTINE CIVILIZATION (750–1025)

 Focus Question: What were the chief developments in the Byzantine Empire between 750 and 1025?

In the seventh and eighth centuries, the Byzantine Empire lost much of its territory to Slavs, Bulgars, and Muslims. By 750, the empire consisted only of Asia Minor, some lands in the Balkans, and a small amount of territory in Italy. Although Byzantium was beset with internal dissension and invasions in the ninth century, it was able to deal with them and not only endured but also expanded, reaching its high point in the tenth century, which some historians have called the golden age of Byzantine civilization.

13-2a The Beginning of a Revival

During the reign of Michael III (842–867 C.E.), the Byzantine Empire began to experience a revival. Iconoclasm was finally abolished in 843, and reforms were made in education, church life, the military, and the peasant economy. There was a noticeable intellectual renewal. But the empire was still plagued by persistent problems. The Bulgars mounted new attacks, and the Arabs continued to harass the periphery. Moreover, a new religious dispute with political repercussions erupted over differences between the pope as leader of the western Christian church and the patriarch of Constantinople as leader of the eastern Christian church.

13-2b The Macedonian Dynasty

The problems that arose during Michael's reign were effectively dealt with by a new dynasty of Byzantine emperors known as the Macedonians (867–1056). The Macedonian Dynasty managed to hold off Byzantium's external enemies and reestablish domestic order. Supported by the church, the emperors thought of the Byzantine Empire as a continuation of the Christian Roman Empire of late antiquity. Although for diplomatic reasons they occasionally recognized the imperial titles of earlier western emperors, such as Charlemagne and Otto I, they still regarded them as little more than barbarian parvenus.

Map 13.3 The Byzantine Empire, 1025

Economic and Religious Policies The Macedonian emperors could boast of a remarkable number of achievements in the late ninth and tenth centuries. They worked to strengthen the position of the free farmers, who felt threatened by the attempts of landed aristocrats to expand their estates at the farmers' expense. The emperors were well aware that the free farmers made up the rank and file of the Byzantine cavalry and provided the military strength of the empire.

The Macedonian emperors also fostered a burst of economic prosperity by expanding trade relations with western Europe, especially by selling silks and metalwork, and the city of Constantinople flourished. Foreign visitors continued to be astounded by its size, wealth, and physical surroundings. To western Europeans, it was the stuff of legends and fables (see Historical Voices, "A Western View of the Byzantine Empire," p. 325)

In this period of prosperity, Byzantine cultural influence expanded because of the active missionary efforts of eastern Byzantine Christians. Eastern Orthodox Christianity was spread to eastern European peoples such as the Bulgars and Serbs. Perhaps the greatest missionary success occurred when the prince of Kiev in Russia converted to Christianity in 987 C.E.

Political and Military Achievements Under the Macedonian rulers, Byzantium enjoyed a strong civil service, talented emperors, and military advances. Well-educated, competent aristocrats from Constantinople staffed the Byzantine civil service and oversaw the collection of taxes, domestic administration, and foreign policy. At the same time, the Macedonian Dynasty produced some truly outstanding emperors skilled in administration and law. Leo VI (886–912 C.E.), known as Leo the Wise, composed works on politics and theology, systematized rules for regulating both trade and court officials, and arranged for a new codification of all Byzantine law.

In the tenth century, competent emperors combined with several talented generals to mobilize the empire's

A Western View of the Byzantine Empire

Politics & Government

BISHOP LIUDPRAND OF CREMONA (LOO-id-prand of kray-MOH-nuh) undertook diplomatic missions to Constantinople on behalf of two western kings, Berengar of Italy and Otto I of Germany. This selection is taken from his description of his mission to the Byzantine emperor Constantine VII in 949 C.E. as an envoy for Berengar, king of Italy from 950 until his overthrow by Otto I of Germany in 964. Liudprand had mixed feelings about Byzantium: admiration, yet also envy and hostility because of its superior wealth.

Liudprand of Cremona, *Antapodosis*

Next to the imperial residence at Constantinople there is a palace of remarkable size and beauty which the Greeks call Magnavra . . . the name being equivalent to "Fresh breeze." In order to receive some Spanish envoys, who had recently arrived, as well as myself . . . , Constantine gave orders that this palace should be got ready. . . .

Before the emperor's seat stood a tree, made of bronze gilded over, whose branches were filled with birds, also made of gilded bronze, which uttered different cries, each according to its varying species. The throne itself was so marvelously fashioned that at one moment it seemed a low structure, and at another it rose high into the air. It was of immense size and was guarded by lions, made either of bronze or of wood covered over with gold, who beat the ground with their tails and gave a dreadful roar with open mouth and quivering tongue. Leaning upon the shoulders of two eunuchs I was brought into the emperor's presence. At my approach the lions began to roar and the birds to cry out, each according to its kind; but I was neither terrified nor surprised, for I had previously made enquiry about all these things from people who were well acquainted with them. So after I had three times made obeisance to the emperor with my face upon the ground, I lifted my head, and behold! The man whom just before I had seen sitting on a moderately elevated seat had now changed his raiment and was sitting on the level of the ceiling. How it was done I could not imagine, unless perhaps he was lifted up by some such sort of device as we use for raising the timbers of a wine press. On that occasion he did not address me personally, . . . but by the intermediary of a secretary he enquired about Berengar's doings and asked after his health. I made a fitting reply and then, at a nod from the interpreter, left his presence and retired to my lodging.

It would give me some pleasure also to record here what I did then for Berengar. . . . The Spanish envoys . . . had brought handsome gifts from their masters to the emperor Constantine. I for my part had brought nothing from Berengar except a letter and that was full of lies. I was very greatly disturbed and shamed at this and began to consider anxiously what I had better do. In my doubt and perplexity it finally occurred to me that I might offer the gifts, which on my account I had brought for the emperor, as coming from Berengar, and trick out my humble present with fine words. I therefore presented him with nine excellent cuirasses, seven excellent shields with gilded bosses, two silver gilt cauldrons, some swords, spears, and spits, and what was more precious to the emperor than anything, four carzimasia; that being the Greek name for young eunuchs who have had both their testicles and their penis removed. This operation is performed by traders at Verdun, who take the boys into Spain and make a huge profit.

 What impressions of the Byzantine court do you get from Liudprand's account? What is the modern meaning of the word byzantine? How does this account help explain the modern meaning of the word?

Source: *The Works of Liudprand of Cremona* by F. A. Wright (London: Routledge and Sons, 1930).

military resources and take the offensive. Especially important was Basil II (976–1025), who defeated the Bulgars and annexed Bulgaria to the empire. After his final victory over the Bulgars in 1014, Basil blinded 14,000 Bulgar captives before allowing them to return to their homes. The Byzantines went on to add the islands of Crete and Cyprus to the empire and defeat the Muslim forces in Syria, expanding the empire to the upper Euphrates River. By the end of Basil's reign in 1025, the Byzantine Empire was the largest it had been since the beginning of the seventh century.

13.5 Basil the Bulgar Slayer. Basil II became known as the Bulgar slayer after his devastating victory over the Bulgars in 1014. This frontispiece illustration from a religious prayer book shows the warrior Basil standing on top of bodies of the conquered Bulgarians. Both angels and warrior saints are shown protecting the emperor.

13-2c Women in the Byzantine Empire

In Byzantium, as in European society, women were regarded as inferior to men. In general, women were expected to remain at home. They could leave to shop, visit parents, and take part in civic celebrations, but they were supposed to wear veils on these occasions. Women were generally expected to fulfill three major functions: to marry and bear children, to maintain the household, and to weave clothes for their families. Contrary to these ideal female roles, some women in the Byzantine world worked outside the home as artisans and sellers, especially of foodstuffs, in the markets of Constantinople. Others served as midwives, bakers, cooks, and dancers, although some dancers also worked as prostitutes.

Upper-class women had greater opportunities to play important roles in the empire. Some aristocratic wives funded the establishment of monasteries, occupied important positions at court, and patronized the arts. Imperial wives could exercise considerable political power as regents for their sons; some even became empresses in their own right.

13-3 THE DECLINE AND FALL OF THE BYZANTINE EMPIRE (1025–1453)

Focus Questions: What impact did the crusades have on the Byzantine Empire? How and why did Constantinople and the Byzantine Empire fall?

The Macedonian Dynasty of the tenth and eleventh centuries had restored much of the power of the Byzantine Empire; its incompetent successors, however, reversed most of the gains.

13-3a New Challenges and New Responses

After the Macedonian Dynasty was extinguished in 1056, the empire was beset by internal struggles for power between ambitious military leaders and aristocratic families who bought the support of the great landowners of Anatolia by allowing them greater control over their peasants. This policy was self-destructive, however, because the peasant warrior was an important source of military strength in the Byzantine state. By the middle of the eleventh century, the Byzantine army began to decline.

A Christian Schism The growing division between the Roman Catholic Church of the west and the Eastern Orthodox Church of the Byzantine Empire also weakened the Byzantine state. The Eastern Orthodox Church was unwilling to accept the pope's claim that he was the sole head of the Christian church. This dispute reached a climax in 1054 when Pope Leo IX and Patriarch Michael Cerularius (sayr-yuh-LAR-ee-uss), head of the Byzantine church, formally excommunicated each other, initiating a schism between the two branches of Christianity that has not been healed to this day.

Islam and the Seljuk Turks The Byzantine Empire faced external threats to its security as well. In the west, the Normans were menacing the remaining Byzantine possessions in Italy. A much greater threat, however, came from the world of Islam.

A nomadic people from Central Asia, the Seljuk Turks had been converted to Islam. As their numbers increased, they moved into the eastern provinces of the Abbasid Empire (see Chapter 7), and in 1055 they captured Baghdad and occupied the rest of the empire. When they moved into Asia Minor—the heartland of the Byzantine Empire and its main source of food and manpower—the Byzantines were forced to react. Emperor Romanus IV led an army of recruits and mercenaries into Asia Minor in 1071 and met the Turkish forces at Manzikert (MANZ-ih-kurt), where the Byzantines were soundly defeated. The Seljuk Turks then went on to occupy much of Anatolia, where many peasants, already disgusted by their exploitation at the hands of Byzantine landowners, readily accepted Turkish control (see Map 7.4).

A New Dynasty After the loss at Manzikert, factional fighting erupted over the emperorship until the throne was seized by Alexius Comnenus (kahm-NEE-nuss) (1081–1118), who established a dynasty that breathed new life into the Byzantine Empire. Under Alexius, the Byzantines were victorious on the Greek Adriatic coast against the Normans, defeated their enemies in the Balkans, and stopped the Turks in Anatolia. In the twelfth century, the Byzantine Empire experienced a cultural revival and a period of prosperity that was fueled by an expansion of trade. But both the Comneni Dynasty and the revival of the twelfth century were ultimately threatened by Byzantium's encounters with crusaders from the west.

13-3b Impact of the Crusades

Lacking the resources to undertake additional campaigns against the Turks, Emperor Alexius turned to the west for military assistance and asked Pope Urban II for help against the Seljuk Turks. Instead of the military aid Alexius had expected, the pope set in motion the First Crusade (see Chapter 12), a decision that created enormous difficulties for the Byzantines.

Alexius requested that the military leaders of the First Crusade take an oath of loyalty to him and promise that any territory they conquered would be under Byzantine control. The crusaders ignored the emperor's wishes. After conquering Antioch, Jerusalem, and additional Palestinian lands, they organized the four crusading states of Edessa, Antioch, Tripoli, and Jerusalem. The Byzantines now had to worry not only about the Turks in Anatolia but also about westerners in the crusading states.

Even more disastrous was the Fourth Crusade. After the death of Saladin in 1193 (see Chapter 7), Pope Innocent III launched the Fourth Crusade. On its way to Palestine, however, the new crusading army became involved in a dispute over the succession to the Byzantine throne. Relations between the crusaders and the Byzantines deteriorated, leading to an attack on Constantinople by the crusaders in the spring of 1204. On April 12, they stormed and sacked the city. Christian crusaders took gold, silver, jewelry, and precious furs, and the Catholic clergy accompanying the crusaders stole as many relics as they could find.

The Byzantine Empire now disintegrated into a series of petty states ruled by crusading barons and Byzantine princes. The chief state was the new Latin Empire of Constantinople led by Count Baldwin of Flanders as emperor. The Venetians seized the island of Crete and assumed control of Constantinople's trade.

Revival of the Byzantine Empire The west was unable to maintain the Latin Empire, however, because the western rulers of the newly created principalities were soon engrossed in fighting each other. Some parts of the Byzantine Empire had managed to survive under Byzantine princes. In 1259, Michael Paleologus (pay-lee-AWL-uh-guss), a Greek military leader, took control of the kingdom of Nicaea in western Asia Minor, led a Byzantine army to recapture Constantinople two years later, and then established a new Byzantine dynasty, the Paleologi.

The Byzantine Empire had been saved, but it was no longer a Mediterranean power. The restored empire was a badly truncated entity, consisting of the city of Constantinople and its surrounding territory, some lands in Asia Minor, and part of Thessalonica. It was surrounded by enemies—Bulgarians, Mongols, Turks, and westerners, especially the resentful Venetians. Even in its reduced size, the empire limped along for another 190 years, but its enemies continued to multiply. The threat from the Turks finally doomed the aged empire.

13-3c The Ottoman Turks and the Fall of Constantinople

Beginning in northeastern Asia Minor in the thirteenth century, the Ottoman Turks spread rapidly, seizing the lands of the Seljuk Turks and the Byzantine Empire. In 1345, they bypassed Constantinople and moved into the Balkans. Under Sultan Murad (moo-RAHD), Ottoman forces moved through Bulgaria and into the lands of the Serbs; in 1389, at the Battle of Kosovo (KAWSS-suh-voh), Ottoman forces defeated the Serbs. By the beginning of the fifteenth century, the Byzantine Empire had been reduced to little more than Constantinople, now surrounded on all sides by the Ottomans. When Mehmet (meh-MET) II came to the throne in 1451 at the age of only nineteen, he was determined to capture Constantinople and complete the demise of the Byzantine Empire.

The siege began in April 1453 when Mehmet moved his forces—probably about 80,000 men—within striking distance of the 13-mile-long land walls along the western edge of the city. The Ottomans' main attack came against these walls. On April 6, the artillery onslaught began. The Ottoman invaders had a distinct advantage with their cannons. One constructed by a Hungarian engineer had a 26-foot barrel that fired stone balls weighing 1,200 pounds.

Revival under Michael III	842–867
Macedonian Dynasty	867–1056
Leo VI	886–912
Basil II	976–1025
Schism between Eastern Orthodox Church and Roman Catholic Church	1054
Turkish defeat of the Byzantines at Manzikert	1071
Revival under Alexius Comnenus	1081–1118
Latin Empire of Constantinople	1204–1261
Revival of Byzantine Empire	1261
Turkish defeat of Serbs at Kosovo	1389
Fall of the empire	1453

It took 60 oxen and 2,000 men to pull the great cannon into position. On May 29, Mehmet decided on a final assault and focused against the areas where the walls had been breached. When Ottoman forces broke into the city, the emperor became one of the first casualties. About 4,000 defenders were killed, and thousands of the inhabitants were sold into slavery. Early in the afternoon, Mehmet II rode into the city, exalted the power of Allah from the pulpit in the cathedral of Hagia Sophia, and ordered that it be converted into a mosque. He soon began rebuilding the city as the capital of the Ottoman Empire. The Byzantine Empire had come to an end.

HISTORIANS DEBATE 13-3d **Why Did the Eastern Roman Empire Last 1,000 Years Longer Than the Western Roman Empire?**

Historians have long debated why the Eastern Roman Empire lasted a thousand years longer than the Roman Empire in the West. Some have emphasized the political strengths of the Eastern Empire. A relatively stable monarchy was reinforced by a strong bureaucracy that helped avoid political instability even when there were deadly conflicts over who occupied the imperial throne. Then, too, a permanent war economy as well as the preoccupation of many emperors with military affairs and astute diplomacy kept the Byzantines well prepared when facing a considerable number of enemies.

Other historians have argued for the importance of the capital city of Constantinople. Its location surrounded by sea and land walls protected it (until 1453) from potential enemies at the heart of the empire. Some historians have also emphasized that Constantinople was in a good strategic position for trading activities. The volume of trade thus ensured the fabled prosperity of the empire over a long period of time.

Finally, some historians have also noted that the Eastern world in the Mediterranean was always more prosperous and literate than the Western Mediterranean world, giving the Byzantine Empire a distinct advantage.

13-4 THE CRISES OF THE FOURTEENTH CENTURY IN EUROPE

 Focus Questions: What impact did the Black Death have on Europe and Asia in the fourteenth century? What problems did Europeans face during the fourteenth century, and what impact did these crises have on European economic, social, and religious life?

At the beginning of the fourteenth century, changes in global weather patterns ushered in what has been called a "little ice age." Shortened growing seasons and disastrous weather conditions, including heavy storms and constant rain, led to widespread famine and hunger. Soon an even greater catastrophe struck.

13-4a The Black Death: From Asia to Europe

In the mid-fourteenth century, a disaster known as the Black Death struck in Asia, North Africa, and Europe. The most common and most important form of plague in the diffusion of the Black Death was bubonic plague, which was spread by black rats infested with fleas that were host to the deadly bacterium *Yersinia pestis* (yur-SIN-ee-uh PES-tiss).

Role of the Mongols This great plague originated in Asia. After disappearing from Europe and the Middle East in the early Middle Ages, bubonic plague continued to haunt areas of southwestern China. In the early 1300s, rats accompanying Mongol troops spread the plague into central China and by 1331 to northeastern China.

The establishment of the Mongol Empire in the thirteenth century facilitated long-distance trade throughout much of the Eurasian landmass, particularly along the Silk Road, now dominated by Muslim merchants from central Asia (see Chapter 10). But the flow of people and goods also facilitated the spread of the plague.

In the 1330s, the plague spread to Central Asia; by 1339 it had reached Samarkand, a caravan stop on the Silk Road.

From central Asia, trading caravans brought the plague to Caffa on the Black Sea in 1347 and to Constantinople by the following year (see Comparative Essay, "The Role of Disease in History," p. 330). Its arrival in the Byzantine Empire was noted in a work by Emperor John VI, who lost a son: "Upon arrival in Constantinople she [the empress] found Andronikos, the youngest born, dead from the invading plague, which . . . attacked almost all the sea coasts of the world and killed most of their people."[5] By 1348, the plague had spread to Egypt and also to Mecca and Damascus and other parts of the Middle East. Writing in the fourteenth century, Muslim historian Ibn Khaldun (IB-un kahl-DOON) commented, "Civilization in the East and West was visited by a destructive plague which devastated nations and caused populations to vanish. It swallowed up many of the good things of civilization and wiped them out."[6]

The Black Death in Europe The **Black Death** of the mid-fourteenth century was the most devastating natural disaster in European history. The plague reached Europe in October 1347 when Genoese merchants brought it from Caffa to the island of Sicily off the southwestern coast of Italy. It quickly spread to southern Italy and southern France by the end of 1347. Diffusion of the Black Death followed commercial trade routes. In 1348, it spread through Spain, France, and the Low Countries (modern-day Holland and Belgium) and into Germany. By the end of that year, it had moved to England, ravaging it in 1349. By the end of 1349, the plague had reached northern Europe and Scandinavia. Eastern Europe and Russia were affected by 1351.

Mortality figures for the Black Death were incredibly high. Especially hard hit were Italy's crowded cities, where 50 percent to 60 percent of the people died. One citizen of Florence wrote, "A great many breathed their last in the public streets, day and night; a large number perished in their homes, and it was only by the stench of their decaying bodies that they proclaimed their deaths to their neighbors. Everywhere the city was teeming with corpses."[7] In England and Germany, entire villages simply disappeared. Out of a total European population of 75 million, as many as an estimated 38 million people may have died of the plague between 1347 and 1351.

As contemporaries attempted to explain the Black Death and mitigate its harshness, some turned to extreme sorts of behavior. Many believed that the plague either had been sent by God as a punishment for humans' sins or had been caused by the Devil (see Opposing Viewpoints, "Causes of the Black Death," p. 331) Some, known as *flagellants* (FLAJ-uh-lunts), resorted to extreme measures to gain God's forgiveness. Groups of flagellants, both men and women, wandered from town to town, flogging each other with whips to beg the forgiveness of a God who they believed had sent the plague to punish humans for their sinful ways. One contemporary chronicler described their activities:

> The penitents went about, coming first out of Germany. They were men who did public penance and scourged themselves with whips of hard knotted leather with little iron spikes. Some made themselves bleed very badly between the shoulder blades and some foolish women had cloths ready to catch the blood and smear it on their eyes, saying it was miraculous blood. While they were doing penance, they sang very mournful songs about the nativity and the passion of Our Lord. The object of this penance was to put a stop to the mortality, for in that time . . . at least a third of all the people in the world died.[8]

The flagellants created mass hysteria wherever they went, and authorities worked overtime to crush the movement.

An outbreak of virulent anti-Semitism also accompanied the Black Death. Jews were accused of causing the plague by poisoning town wells. The worst **pogroms** against this minority were carried out in Germany, where more than sixty major Jewish communities had been exterminated by 1351. Many Jews fled eastward to Russia and especially to Poland, where the king offered them protection. Eastern Europe became home to large Jewish communities.

13-4b Economic Dislocation and Social Upheaval

The deaths of so many people in the fourteenth century had severe economic consequences. Trade declined, and some industries suffered greatly. A shortage of workers caused a dramatic rise in the price of labor, while the decline in the number of people lowered the demand for food, resulting in falling prices. Landlords were now paying more for labor at the same time that their rental income was declining. Concurrently, the decline in the number of peasants after the Black Death made it easier for some to convert their labor services to rent, thus freeing them from serfdom.

But there were limits to how much the peasants could advance. They faced the same economic hurdles as the lords, who also attempted to impose wage restrictions and reinstate old forms of labor service. Peasant complaints became widespread and soon gave rise to rural revolts. Although these revolts sometimes resulted in short-term gains for the participants, the uprisings were easily crushed and their gains quickly lost. Accustomed to ruling, the established classes easily combined with one another and stifled dissent.

The Role of Disease in History

Interaction & Exchange When Hernando Cortés and his fellow conquistadors arrived in Mesoamerica in 1519, the local inhabitants were frightened of the Spaniards' horses and firearms. What they did not know was that the most dangerous enemies brought by these strange new arrivals were invisible—the disease-bearing microbes that would soon kill them by the millions. Diseases have been the scourge of animal species since the dawn of prehistory, making the lives of human beings, in the words of English philosopher Thomas Hobbes, "nasty, brutish, and short." With the increasing sophistication of forensic evidence, archaeologists today have determined from recently discovered human remains that our immediate ancestors were plagued by such familiar ailments as anemia, arthritis, tuberculosis, and malaria.

With the explosive growth of the human population brought about by the agricultural revolution, the problems posed by the presence of disease intensified. As people began to congregate in villages and cities, bacteria settled in their piles of refuse and were carried by lice in their clothing. The domestication of animals made humans more vulnerable to diseases carried by their livestock. As population density increased, the danger of widespread epidemics increased with it.

As time went on, succeeding generations gradually developed partial or complete immunity to many of these diseases, which became chronic rather than fatal to their victims, as occurred, for example, with malaria in parts of Africa and chickenpox in the Americas. But when a disease was introduced to a particular society that had not previously been exposed to it, the consequences were often devastating. The most dramatic example was the famous Black Death, the plague that ravaged Europe and China during the fourteenth century, killing one-fourth to one-half of the inhabitants in the affected regions (and even greater numbers in certain areas). Smallpox had the same impact in the Americas after the arrival of Christopher Columbus, and malaria was fatal to many Europeans on their arrival in West Africa.

How were these diseases transmitted? In most instances, they followed the trade routes. Such was the case with the Black Death, which was initially carried by fleas living in the saddlebags of Mongol warriors as they advanced toward Europe in the thirteenth and fourteenth centuries and thereafter by rats in the holds of cargo ships. Smallpox and other diseases were brought to the Americas by the conquistadors. Epidemics, then, are a price that humans pay for having developed the network of rapid communication that has accompanied the evolution of human society.

What role has disease played in human history?

Snark/Art Resource, NY

13.6 Mass Burial of Plague Victims. The Black Death had spread to northern Europe by the end of 1348. Shown here is a mass burial of victims of the plague in Tournai in modern Belgium. As is evident in the illustration, at this stage of the plague, there was still time to make coffins for the victims' burial. Later, as the plague intensified, the dead were thrown into open pits.

Causes of the Black Death: Contemporary Views

Interaction & Exchange

THE BLACK DEATH WAS THE MOST TERRIFYING natural calamity of the Middle Ages and affected wide areas of Europe, North Africa, and Asia. People were often baffled by the plague, especially by its causes, and gave widely different explanations. The first selection is taken from the preface to the *Decameron* by fourteenth-century Italian writer Giovanni Boccaccio (joh-VAH-nee boh-KAH-choh). The other selections are from contemporary treatises that offered widely different explanations for the great plague.

Giovanni Boccaccio, *Decameron*

In the year of Our Lord 1348 the deadly plague broke out in the great city of Florence, most beautiful of Italian cities. Whether through the operation of the heavenly bodies or because of our own iniquities which the just wrath of God sought to correct, the plague had arisen in the East some years before, causing the death of countless human beings. It spread without stop from one place to another, until, unfortunately, it swept over the West. Neither knowledge nor human foresight availed against it, . . . Nor did humble supplications serve. Not once but many times they were ordained in the form of processions and other ways for the propitiation of God by the faithful, but, in spite of everything, toward the spring of the year the plague began to show its ravages.

On Earthquakes as the Cause of Plague

There is a fourth opinion, which I consider more likely than the others, which is that insofar as the mortality arose from natural causes its immediate cause was a corrupt and poisonous earthy exhalation, which infected the air in various parts of the world and, when breathed in by people, suffocated them and suddenly snuffed them out. . . .

It is a matter of scientific fact that earthquakes are caused by the exhalation of fumes enclosed in the bowels of the earth. When the fumes batter against the sides of the earth, and cannot get out, the earth is shaken and moves. I say that it is the vapor and corrupted air which has been vented—or so to speak purged—in the earthquake which occurred on St. Paul's day, 1347, along with the corrupted air vented in other earthquakes and eruptions, which has infected the air above the earth and killed people in various parts of the world; and I can bring various reasons in support of this conclusion.

Herman Gigas on Well Poisoning

In 1347 there was such a great pestilence and mortality throughout almost the whole world that in the opinion of well-informed men scarcely a tenth of mankind survived . . . . Some say that it was brought about by the corruption of the air; others that the Jews planned to wipe out all the Christians with poison and had poisoned wells and springs everywhere. And many Jews confessed as much under torture: that they had bred spiders and toads in pots and pans, and had obtained poison from overseas; and that not every Jew knew about this wickedness, only the more powerful ones, so that it would not be betrayed. As evidence of this heinous crime, men say that the bags full of poison were found in many wells and springs, and as a result, in cities, towns and villages throughout Germany, and in fields and woods too, almost all the wells and springs have been blocked up or built over, so that no one can drink from them or use the water for cooking, and men have to use rain or river water instead. God, the lord of vengeance, has not suffered the malice of the Jews to go unpunished. Throughout Germany, in all but a few places, they were burnt. For fear of that punishment many accepted baptism and their lives were spared. This action was taken against the Jews in 1349.

 What were the different explanations for the causes of the Black Death? How do you explain the differences, and what do these explanations tell you about the level of scientific knowledge in the later Middle Ages? Why do you think Jews became scapegoats?

Source: Giovanni Boccaccio, *The Decameron*, trans. F. Winwar (New York: Limited Editions, 1930, p. xxii-xxiv.; R. Horrox, ed., trans. *The Black Death* (Manchester, UK: University of Manchester Press, 1994), pp. 177–178, 207.

13-4c Political Instability

Famine, plague, economic turmoil, and social upheaval were not the only problems of the fourteenth century. War and political instability must also be added to the list. And of all the struggles that ensued in the fourteenth century, the Hundred Years' War was the most violent.

The Hundred Years' War In the thirteenth century, England still held one small possession in France known as the Duchy of Gascony. As duke of Gascony, the English king pledged loyalty as a vassal to the French king, but when King Philip VI of France (1328–1350) seized Gascony in 1337, the duke of Gascony—King Edward III of England (1327–1377)—declared war on Philip.

The Hundred Years' War began in a burst of knightly enthusiasm. The French army of 1337 still relied largely on heavily armed noble cavalrymen, who looked with contempt on foot soldiers and crossbowmen, whom they regarded as social inferiors. The English, too, used heavily armed cavalry, but they relied even more on large numbers of paid foot soldiers. Armed with pikes, many of these soldiers had also adopted the longbow. The longbow was first used by the Welsh, but the English, recognizing the longbow's power, soon adopted its use. A well-trained longbowman could shoot ten to twelve arrows per minutes, a more rapid speed of fire than the more powerful crossbow. And the arrows could pierce the armor of a knight at ranges of more than 250 yards. Although the English made use of heavily armed cavalry, they relied even more on large numbers of foot soldiers.

The first major battle of the war occurred in 1346 at Crécy (kray-SEE), just south of Flanders. The larger French army followed no battle plan but simply attacked the English lines in a disorderly fashion. The arrows of the English archers decimated the French cavalry. As the chronicler Froissart (frwah-SAR) described it, "[With their longbows] the English continued to shoot into the thickest part of the crowd, wasting none of their arrows. They impaled or wounded horses and riders, who fell to the ground in great distress, unable to get up again without the help of several men."[9] It was a stunning victory for the English and the foot soldier.

The Battle of Crécy was not decisive, however. The English simply did not possess the resources to subjugate all of France, but they continued to try. The English king, Henry V (1413–1422), was especially eager to achieve victory. At the Battle of Agincourt (AH-zhen-koor) in 1415, the heavy, armor-plated French knights attempted to attack across a field turned to mud by heavy rain; the result was a disastrous French defeat and the death of 1,500 French nobles. The English were masters of northern France.

The seemingly hopeless French cause then fell into the hands of the dauphin (DAH-fin or doh-FAN) Charles, the heir to the throne, who governed the southern two-thirds of French lands. Charles's cause seemed doomed until a French peasant woman quite unexpectedly saved the timid monarch. Born in 1412, the daughter of well-to-do peasants, Joan of Arc was a deeply religious person who came to believe that her favorite saints had commanded her to free France. In February 1429, Joan made her way to the dauphin's court and persuaded Charles to allow her to accompany a French army to Orléans (or-lay-AHN). Apparently inspired by the faith of the peasant girl called "the Maid of Orléans," the French armies found new confidence in themselves and liberated Orléans and the entire Loire Valley.

But Joan did not live to see the war concluded. Captured in 1430, she was turned over to the Inquisition on charges of witchcraft. In the fifteenth century, spiritual visions were thought to be inspired by either God or the Devil. Joan was condemned to death as a heretic and burned at the stake in 1431.

Joan of Arc's accomplishments proved decisive. Although the war dragged on for another two decades, defeats of English armies in Normandy and Aquitaine led to French victory by 1453. Important to the French success was the use of the cannon, a new weapon made possible by the invention of gunpowder. The Chinese had invented gunpowder in the tenth century and devised a simple cannon by the thirteenth century. The Mongols greatly improved this technology, developing more accurate cannons and cannonballs; both spread to the Middle East in the thirteenth century and to Europe by the fourteenth. The use of gunpowder eventually brought drastic changes to European warfare by making castles, city walls, and armored knights obsolete.

Political Disintegration By the fourteenth century, the feudal order had begun to break down. With money from taxes, kings could now hire professional soldiers, who tended to be more reliable than feudal knights anyway. Fourteenth-century kings had their own problems, however. Many dynasties in Europe failed to produce male heirs, and the founders of new dynasties had to fight for their positions as groups of nobles supported opposing candidates in efforts to gain advantages for themselves. Rulers encountered financial problems, too. Hiring professional soldiers left them always short of cash, adding yet another element of uncertainty and confusion to fourteenth-century politics.

13-4d The Decline of the Church

The papacy of the Roman Catholic Church reached the height of its power in the thirteenth century. But crises in the fourteenth century led to a serious decline for the church. By that time, the monarchies of Europe were no longer willing to accept papal claims of temporal supremacy, as is evident in the struggle between Pope Boniface VIII (1294–1303) and King Philip IV (1285–1314) of France. In his desire to acquire new revenues, Philip claimed the right to tax the clergy of France, but Boniface VIII insisted that the clergy of any state could not pay taxes to their secular ruler without the consent of the pope, who, he argued, was supreme over both the church and the state.

Philip IV refused to accept the pope's position and sent a small contingent of French forces to capture Boniface and bring him back to France for trial. The pope escaped but soon died from the shock of his experience. To ensure his position, Philip IV engineered the election of a Frenchman, Clement V (1305–1314), as pope. The new pope took up residence in Avignon (ah-veen- YOHN) on the east bank of the Rhône River.

From 1305 to 1377, the popes resided in Avignon, leading to an increase in antipapal sentiment. The city of Rome was the traditional capital of the universal church. The pope was the bishop of Rome, and it was unseemly that the head of the Catholic Church should reside in Avignon instead of Rome. Moreover, the splendor in which the pope and cardinals were living in Avignon led to highly vocal criticism of both clergy and papacy. At last, Pope Gregory XI (1370–1378), perceiving the disastrous decline in papal prestige, returned to Rome in 1377 but died there the spring after his return.

When the college of cardinals met to elect a new pope, the citizens of Rome threatened that the cardinals would not leave Rome alive unless they elected an Italian as pope. Indeed, the guards of the conclave warned the cardinals that they "ran the risk of being torn in pieces" if they did not choose an Italian. Wisely, the terrified cardinals duly elected the Italian archbishop of Bari as Pope Urban VI (1378–1389). Five months later, however, a group of dissenting cardinals—the French ones—declared Urban's election invalid and chose one of their number as pope, who promptly returned to Avignon. Because Urban remained in Rome, there were now two popes, beginning a crisis that has been called the Great Schism of the church.

The Great Schism divided Europe. France and its allies supported the pope in Avignon, whereas France's enemy England and its allies supported the pope in Rome. The Great Schism was also damaging to the faith of Christian believers. The pope was widely believed to be the true leader of Christendom; when both lines of popes denounced the other as the antichrist, people's faith in the papacy and the church was undermined. Finally, a church council met at Constance, Switzerland, in 1417. After the competing popes resigned or were deposed, a new pope was elected who was acceptable to all parties.

By the mid-fifteenth century, as a result of these crises, the church had lost much of its temporal power. Even worse, the papacy and the church had also lost much of their moral prestige.

13-5 RECOVERY: THE RENAISSANCE

 Focus Question: What were the main features of the Renaissance in Europe, and how did the period differ from the Middle Ages?

People who lived in Italy between 1350 and 1550 or so believed they were witnessing a rebirth of classical antiquity—the world of the Greeks and Romans. To them, this marked a new age, which historians later called the **Renaissance** (French for "rebirth") and viewed as a distinct period of European history, which began in Italy and then spread to the rest of Europe.

Renaissance Italy was largely an urban society. The city-states became the centers of Italian political, economic, and social life. Within this new urban society, a secular spirit emerged as increasing wealth created new possibilities for the enjoyment of worldly things.

The Renaissance was also an age of recovery from the disasters of the fourteenth century, including the Black Death, political disorder, and economic recession. In pursuing that recovery, Italian intellectuals became intensely interested in the glories of their own past, the Greco-Roman culture of antiquity.

A new view of human beings emerged as people in the Italian Renaissance began to emphasize individual ability. Fifteenth-century Florentine architect Leon Battista Alberti (LAY-un buh-TEESS-tuh al-BAYR-tee) expressed the new philosophy succinctly: "Men can do all things if they will."[10] This high regard for human worth and for individual potentiality gave rise to a new social ideal of the well-rounded personality or "universal person"— *l'uomo universale* (LWOH-moh OO-nee-ver-SAH-lay)—who was capable of achievements in many areas of life.

13-5a The Intellectual Renaissance

The emergence and growth of individualism and secularism as characteristics of the Italian Renaissance are most noticeable in the intellectual and artistic realms. The most important literary movement associated with the Renaissance was humanism.

Renaissance humanism was an intellectual movement based on the study of the classics, the literary works of

Greece and Rome. Humanists studied the liberal arts—grammar, rhetoric, poetry, moral philosophy or ethics, and history—all based on the writings of ancient Greek and Roman authors. We call these subjects the *humanities*.

Petrarch (PEE-trark or PET-trark) (1304–1374), who has often been called the father of Italian Renaissance humanism, did more than any other individual in the fourteenth century to foster its development. Petrarch sought to find forgotten Latin manuscripts and also began the humanist emphasis on the use of pure classical Latin. Humanists used the works of Cicero as a model for prose and those of Virgil for poetry. As Petrarch said, "Christ is my God; Cicero is the prince of the language."

In Florence, the humanist movement took a new direction at the beginning of the fifteenth century. Fourteenth-century humanists such as Petrarch had described the intellectual life as one of solitude. Now, however, the humanists who worked as secretaries for the city council of Florence took a new interest in civic life. They came to believe that intellectuals had a duty to live an active life for their state and that their study of the humanities should be put to the service of the state.

Also evident in the humanism of the first half of the fifteenth century was a growing interest in classical Greek civilization. One of the first Italian humanists to gain a thorough knowledge of Greek was Leonardo Bruni (leh-ah-NAHR-doh BROO-nee), who became an enthusiastic pupil of the Byzantine scholar Manuel Chrysoloras (man-WEL kriss-uh-LAHR-uss), who taught in Florence from 1396 to 1400.

HISTORIANS DEBATE 13-5b **Was There a Renaissance for Women?**

Historians have disagreed over whether women benefited from the Renaissance. Some maintain that during the Middle Ages upper-class women in particular had greater freedom to satisfy their emotional needs, whereas upper-class women in the Renaissance experienced a contraction of both social and personal options as they became even more subject to male authority. Other historians have argued that although conditions remained bleak for most women, some women—especially those in courtly, religious, and intellectual environments—found ways to develop a new sense of themselves as women. This may be especially true of women who were educated in the humanist fashion and went on to establish their own literary careers.

Isotta Nogarola (ee-ZAHT-uh noh-guh-ROH-luh) was born to a noble family in Verona, mastered Latin, and wrote numerous letters and treatises that brought her praise from male Italian intellectuals. Laura Cereta (say-REE-tuh) was educated in Latin by her father, a physician from Brescia. In a series of letters, Laura defended the ability of women to pursue scholarly pursuits.

13-5c The Artistic Renaissance

Renaissance artists sought to imitate nature in their works of art. Their search for naturalism became an end in itself: to persuade onlookers of the reality of the object or event they were portraying. At the same time, the new artistic standards reflected the new attitude of mind in which human beings became the focus of attention, the "center and measure of all things," as one artist proclaimed.

Florentine painters in the fifteenth century developed this new Renaissance style. Especially important were two major developments. One emphasized the technical side of painting—understanding the laws of perspective and the geometrical organization of outdoor space and light. The second development was the investigation of movement and anatomical structure. The realistic portrayal of the human nude became one of the foremost preoccupations of Italian Renaissance art.

By the end of the fifteenth century, Italian artists had mastered the new techniques for scientific observation of the world around them and were ready to move into new forms of creative expression. This marked the shift to the High Renaissance, which was dominated by the work of three artistic giants: Leonardo da Vinci (leh-ah-NAHR-doh dah VEEN-chee) (1452–1519), Raphael (RAFF-ee-ul) (1483–1520), and Michelangelo (my-kuh-LAN-juh-loh) (1475–1564). Leonardo carried on the fifteenth-century experimental tradition by studying everything and even dissecting human bodies to see how nature worked. But Leonardo also stressed the need to advance beyond such realism and initiated the High Renaissance's preoccupation with the idealization of nature, an attempt to generalize from realistic portrayal to an ideal form.

At twenty-five, Raphael was already regarded as one of Italy's best painters. He was acclaimed for his numerous madonnas, in which he attempted to achieve an ideal of beauty far surpassing human standards. He is well known for his frescoes in the Vatican palace, which reveal a world of balance, harmony, and order—the underlying principles of the classical art of Greece and Rome.

Michelangelo—an accomplished painter, sculptor, and architect—was fiercely driven by a desire to create, and he worked with great passion and energy on a remarkable number of projects. Michelangelo was influenced by Neoplatonism, which viewed the ideal beauty

13.7 Leonardo da Vinci, *The Last Supper*. Leonardo da Vinci was the impetus behind the High Renaissance concern for the idealization of nature, moving from a realistic portrayal of the human figure to an idealized form. Evident in Leonardo's *Last Supper* is his effort to depict a person's character and inner nature by the use of gesture and movement. Unfortunately, Leonardo used an experimental technique in this fresco, which soon led to its physical deterioration.

of the human form as a reflection of divine beauty; the more beautiful the body, the more godlike the figure. Another manifestation of Michelangelo's search for ideal beauty was his *David,* a colossal marble statue commissioned by the government of Florence in 1501 and completed in 1504.

The Artist and Social Status As in the Middle Ages, Early Renaissance artists were still largely viewed as artisans. Because guilds depended on commissions for their projects, patrons played an important role in the art of the Early Renaissance. The wealthy upper classes determined both the content and the purpose of the paintings and pieces of sculpture they commissioned.

By the end of the fifteenth century, a transformation in the position of the artist had occurred. Especially talented individuals such as Leonardo, Raphael, and Michelangelo were no longer regarded as artisans but as artistic geniuses with creative energies akin to the divine (see Historical Voices, "The Genius of Michelangelo," p. 336). Artists were heroes, individuals who were praised more for their creativity than for their competence as craftspeople. Michelangelo, for example, was frequently addressed as "Il Divino"—the Divine One. As society excused their eccentricities and valued their creative genius, the artists of the High Renaissance became the first to embody the modern concept of the artist.

13.8 Michelangelo, *David*. This statue of David was cut from an 18-foot-high piece of marble and exalts the beauty of the human body, a fitting symbol of the Italian Renaissance's affirmation of human power. Completed in 1504, *David* was moved by Florentine authorities to a special location in front of the Palazzo Vecchio, the seat of the Florentine government.

The Genius of Michelangelo

 DURING THE RENAISSANCE, artists came to be viewed as creative geniuses with almost divine qualities. One individual who helped create this image was himself a painter. Giorgio Vasari (JOR-joh vuh-ZAHR-ee) was an avid admirer of Italy's great artists and wrote a series of brief biographies of them. This excerpt is taken from his account of Michelangelo.

Giorgio Vasari, *Lives of the Artists*

Michelangelo was much inclined to the labors of art, seeing that everything, however difficult, succeeded with him, he having had from nature a genius very apt and ardent in the noble arts of design. Moreover, in order to be entirely perfect, innumerable times he made anatomical studies, dissecting men's bodies in order to see the principles of their construction and the arrangement of the bones, muscles, veins and nerves; the various movements and all the postures of the human body; and not of men only, but also of animals, and particularly of horses, . . . Of all these he desired to learn the principles and laws in so far as touched his art, and this knowledge he so demonstrated in the works that fell to him to handle that those who attend to no other study than this do now know more. He so executed his works, whether with the brush or with the chisel, that they are almost inimitable, and he gave to his labors such grace and loveliness that he surpassed and vanquished the ancients. He was able to wrest

things out of the greatest difficulties with such facility that they do not appear wrought with effort, although whoever draws his works after him finds it very hard to imitate them.

The genius of Michelangelo was recognized in his lifetime, and not, as happens to many, after death, for several of the popes always wished to have him near them, and also Suleiman, emperor of the Turks, Francis of Valois, king of France, the emperor Charles V, the signory of Venice, and finally Duke Cosimo de' Medici. All offered him honorable salaries, for no other reason but to avail themselves of his great genius. This does not happen except to men of great worth, such as he was. It is well known that all the three arts of painting, sculpture, and architecture were so perfect in him, that it is not found that among persons ancient or modern, in all the many years that the sun had been whirling round, God has granted this to any other but Michelangelo.

He had imagination of such a kind, and so perfect, and the things conceived by him in idea were such, that often, through not being able to express with the hands conceptions so terrible and grand, he abandoned his works—nay, destroyed many of them.

 How do you think Vasari's comments on Leonardo fostered the image of the Renaissance artist as a "creative genius with almost divine qualities"?

Source: Hutton Webster, *Readings in Medieval and Modern History* (Boston, 1917), pp. 191–192.

13-5d The State in the Renaissance

In the second half of the fifteenth century, attempts were made to reestablish the centralized power of monarchical governments after the political disasters of the fourteenth century. Some historians called these states the "new monarchies," especially those of France, England, and Spain.

The Italian States The Italian states provided the earliest examples of state building in the fifteenth century. During the Middle Ages, Italy had failed to develop a centralized territorial state, and by the fifteenth century five major powers dominated the Italian Peninsula: the duchy of Milan, the republics of Florence and Venice, the Papal States, and the kingdom of Naples.

Milan, Florence, and Venice proved especially adept at building strong, centralized states. Under a series of dukes, Milan became a highly centralized territorial state whose rulers devised systems of taxation that generated enormous revenues for the government. The maritime republic of Venice remained an extremely stable political entity governed by a small oligarchy of merchant aristocrats. Its commercial empire brought in vast revenues and gave it the status of an international power. In Florence, Cosimo de' Medici (KAH-zee-moh duh MED-ih-chee) took control of the merchant oligarchy in 1434. Through lavish patronage and careful courting of political allies, he and his family dominated the city at a time when Florence was the center of the cultural Renaissance.

As strong as these Italian states became, they still could not compete with the powerful monarchical states to the north and west. Beginning in 1494, Italy became a battlefield for the great power struggle between the French and Spanish monarchies, a conflict that led to Spanish domination of Italy in the sixteenth century.

Western Europe The Hundred Years' War left France prostrate. But it had also engendered a certain degree of French national feeling toward a common enemy that the kings could use to reestablish monarchical power. The development of a French territorial state was greatly advanced by King Louis XI (1461–1483), who strengthened the use of the *taille* (TY)—an annual direct tax usually on land or property—as a permanent tax imposed by royal authority, giving him a sound, regular source of income and creating the foundations of a strong French monarchy.

As the first Tudor king, Henry VII (1485–1509) worked to establish a strong monarchical government in England. Henry ended the petty wars of the nobility by abolishing their private armies. He was also incredibly thrifty. By not overburdening the nobility and the middle class with taxes, Henry won their favor, and they provided him much support.

Spain, too, experienced the growth of a strong national monarchy by the end of the fifteenth century. During the Middle Ages, several independent Christian kingdoms had emerged in the course of the long reconquest of the Iberian Peninsula from the Muslims. Two of the strongest were Aragon and Castile. The marriage of Isabella of Castile (1474–1504) and Ferdinand of Aragon (1479–1516) in 1469 was a major step toward unifying Spain. The two rulers worked to strengthen royal control of government. Ferdinand and Isabella also reorganized the military forces of Spain, making the new Spanish army the best in Europe by the sixteenth century.

Central and Eastern Europe Unlike France, England, and Spain, the Holy Roman Empire failed to develop a strong monarchical authority. The failure of the German emperors in the thirteenth century ended any chance of centralized monarchical authority, and Germany became a land of hundreds of virtually independent states. After 1438, members of the Habsburg (HAPS-burg) Dynasty held the position of Holy Roman emperor. Having gradually acquired many possessions along the Danube that were known collectively as *Austria*, the house of Habsburg had become one of the wealthiest landholders in the empire.

In eastern Europe, rulers struggled to achieve the centralization of the territorial states. Religious differences troubled the area as Roman Catholics, Eastern Orthodox Christians, and other groups, including the Mongols, confronted each other. In Poland, the nobles gained the upper hand and established the right to elect their kings, a policy that drastically weakened royal authority.

Since the thirteenth century, Russia had been under the domination of the Mongols. Gradually, the princes of Moscow rose to prominence by using their close relationship to the Mongol khans to increase their wealth and expand their possessions. During the reign of the great Prince Ivan III (1462–1505), a new Russian state was born. Ivan annexed other Russian principalities and took advantage of dissension among the Mongols to throw off their yoke by 1480.

Europe and the World For almost a millennium, Catholic Europe had largely been confined to one area. Of course, Europe had never completely lost contact with the outside world, but with the revival of trade in the High Middle Ages, European merchants began to travel more frequently to Asia and Africa. Nevertheless, Europe's contacts with non-European civilizations remained limited until the fifteenth century, when the growth of centralized monarchies in the Renaissance created new opportunities for expansion and opened the door to a remarkable series of overseas journeys. What caused European seafarers to undertake such dangerous voyages to the ends of Earth?

An economic motive looms large in Renaissance European expansion (see Chapter 14). In the fourteenth century, the conquests of the Ottoman Turks and then the breakup of the Mongol Empire reduced Western traffic to the East. With the closing of the overland routes, many people in Europe became interested in the possibility of reaching Asia by sea. Merchants, adventurers, and government officials had high hopes of finding precious metals and a direct source for the spices of the East. Another major reason for the overseas voyages was religious zeal. A crusading mentality was particularly strong in Portugal and Spain, where the Muslims had largely been driven out in the Middle Ages. Although most scholars believe that the religious motive was secondary to economic considerations, it would be foolish to overlook the genuine desire to convert so-called heathens to Christianity.

After the collapse of Roman power in the west, the late Roman Empire in the east—the Eastern Roman Empire centered in Constantinople—continued in the eastern Mediterranean and eventually emerged as the Byzantine Empire, which flourished for hundreds of years. Even as a new Christian civilization arose in Europe, the Byzantine Empire created its own unique Christian civilization.

And even as western Europe struggled in the early Middle Ages, the Byzantine world continued to prosper and flourish. Especially during the ninth, tenth, and eleventh centuries, under the Macedonian emperors, the Byzantine Empire expanded and achieved an economic prosperity that was evident to foreign visitors, who frequently praised the size, wealth, and physical surroundings of Constantinople.

During its heyday, Byzantium was a multicultural and multiethnic world empire that ruled a remarkable number of peoples who spoke different languages. Byzantine cultural and religious forms spread to the Balkans, parts of central Europe, and Russia. Byzantine scholars eventually spread the study of the Greek language to Italy, fostering the Renaissance humanists' interest in classical Greek civilization. The Byzantine Empire also interacted with the world of Islam to its east and the new European civilization of the west. Both interactions proved costly and ultimately fatal. Although European civilization and Byzantine civilization shared a common bond in Christianity, it proved incapable of keeping them in harmony politically. Indeed, the West's crusades to Palestine, ostensibly for religious motives, led to western control of the Byzantine Empire from 1204 to 1261. Although the empire was restored, it limped along until interactions with its other neighbor—the Muslim world—led to its demise in 1453 when the Ottoman Turks conquered the city of Constantinople and made it the center of their new empire.

Even as Byzantium was declining in the twelfth and thirteenth centuries, Europe was achieving new levels of growth and optimism. In the fourteenth century, however, Europe also experienced a time of troubles as it was devastated by the Black Death, economic dislocation, political chaos, and religious decline. But in the fifteenth century, while

Constantinople and the remnants of the Byzantine Empire finally fell to the world of Islam, Europe experienced a dramatic revival. Elements of recovery in the age of the Renaissance made the fifteenth century a period of significant artistic, intellectual, and political change in Europe. By the second half of the fifteenth century, as we shall see in the next chapter, the growth of strong, centralized monarchical states made possible the dramatic expansion of Europe into other parts of the world.

REFLECTION QUESTIONS

Q What were Justinian's major goals, and how did he try to achieve them? How successful was he in actually achieving these goals?

Q Why does the chapter use the phrase "zenith of Byzantine civilization" to describe the period from 750 to 1025?

Q Compare developments in the Byzantine world and Europe in the fourteenth and fifteenth centuries. What are their similarities and differences?

CHAPTER TIMELINE

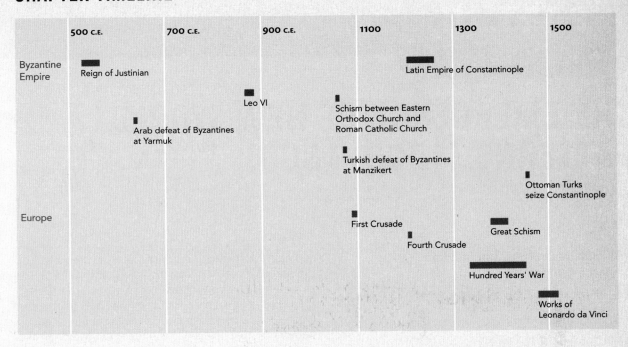

	500 C.E.	700 C.E.	900 C.E.	1100	1300	1500

Byzantine Empire
- Reign of Justinian
- Arab defeat of Byzantines at Yarmuk
- Leo VI
- Schism between Eastern Orthodox Church and Roman Catholic Church
- Turkish defeat of Byzantines at Manzikert
- Latin Empire of Constantinople
- Ottoman Turks seize Constantinople

Europe
- First Crusade
- Fourth Crusade
- Great Schism
- Hundred Years' War
- Works of Leonardo da Vinci

CHAPTER NOTES

1. Quoted in P. Cesaretti, *Theodora: Empress of Byzantium*, trans. R. M. Frongia (New York, 2004), p. 197.

2. Quoted in J. Harris, *Constantinople: Capital of Byzantium* (New York, 2007), p. 40.

3. Procopius, *Buildings of Justinian* (London, 1897), pp. 9, 6–7.

4. Quoted in Harris, *Constantinople*, p. 118.

5. Quoted in C. S. Bartsocas, "Two Fourteenth-Century Descriptions of the 'Black Death,'" *Journal of the History of Medicine* (October 1966): 395.

6. Quoted in M. Dols, *The Black Death in the Middle East* (Princeton, N.J., 1977), p. 270.

7. G. Boccaccio, *The Decameron*, trans. F. Winwar (New York, 1955), p. xiii.

8. J. Froissart, *Chronicles*, ed. and trans. G. Brereton (Harmondsworth, England, 1968), p. 111.

9. Ibid., p. 89.

10. Quoted in J. Burckhardt, *The Civilization of the Renaissance in Italy*, trans. S. G. C. Middlemore (London, 1960), p. 81.

MINDTAP
From Cengage

MindTap® is a fully online, highly personalized learning experience built upon Cengage Learning content. MindTap combines student learning tools—readings, multimedia, activities, and assessments—into a singular Learning Path that guides students through the course and helps students develop the critical thinking, analysis, and communication skills that are essential to academic and professional success.

THE EMERGENCE OF NEW WORLD PATTERNS (1500–1800)

HISTORIANS OFTEN REFER to the period from the sixteenth through eighteenth centuries as the *early modern era*. During these years, several factors were at work that created the conditions of our own time.

From a global perspective, perhaps the most noteworthy event of the period was the extension of the maritime trade network throughout the entire populated world. Traders from the Middle East had spearheaded the process with their voyages to East Asia and southern Africa in the first millennium c.e., and the Chinese had followed suit with Zheng He's groundbreaking voyages to India and East Africa, as mentioned in Chapter 10. By the end of the fifteenth century, a thriving trade network stretched from the Middle East through the Indian Ocean and all the way to China and the islands of Japan. It was at this time that a resurgent Europe suddenly exploded onto the world scene when the Portuguese discovered a maritime route to the East and Spanish adventurers opened the first European contacts with peoples of the Western Hemisphere. Although the Europeans were late to the game, they were quick learners; over the next three centuries, they gradually managed to dominate much of the shipping on international trade routes.

Some contemporary historians argue that it was this sudden burst of energy from Europe that created the first truly global economic network. Although it is true that European explorers were responsible for opening communications with the vast new world of the Americas, other historians note that it was the rise of the Arab Empire in the Middle East and the Mongol expansion a few centuries later that had played the greatest role in creating a widespread communications network by enabling goods and ideas to travel from one end of the Eurasian supercontinent to the other.

Whatever the truth of this debate, many reasons remain to consider the end of the fifteenth century a crucial date in world history. By marking the end of the long isolation of the Western Hemisphere from the rest of the inhabited world, this period led to the creation of the first truly global network of ideas and commodities that would introduce plants, ideas, and (unfortunately) many new diseases to all humanity (see Comparative Essay, "The Columbian Exchange," later in this chapter). In fact, the era gave birth to a stunning increase in trade and manufacturing that stimulated major political, economic, and social changes not only in Europe but also in other parts of the world.

But the period from 1500 to 1800 was not only an incubation period for the modern world but also the launching pad for an era of European domination that would reach fruition in the nineteenth century. To understand why the West emerged as the leading force in the world at that time, it is necessary to grasp what factors were at work in Europe that differentiated its actions from those of other major civilizations around the globe. For example, historians have identified improvements in navigation, shipbuilding, and weaponry as essential elements in promoting the European Age of Exploration. As we have seen, many of these technological advances were based on earlier discoveries that had taken place elsewhere—in China, India, and the Middle East—and had then been brought to Europe on Muslim ships or along the trade routes through Central Asia. But it was the determination of the Europeans to make practical use of the discoveries of others that was

III.1

the decisive factor in the equation, thus enabling them to dominate international sea-lanes and ultimately to create vast colonial empires in the Western Hemisphere.

What explains the sudden explosion of Europe across the international scene? As with Arab expansion several hundred years previously, European expansion was not fueled solely by economic considerations but by religious motives as well. In the fifteenth century, the world of Christendom was in the midst of a major period of conflict with the forces of Islam, a rivalry that had been exacerbated by the conquest of the Byzantine Empire by the Ottoman Turks in 1453 (see Chapter 13). Although the claims of Portuguese and Spanish adventurers that their activities were motivated primarily by a desire to bring the word of God to non-Christian peoples certainly contained a considerable measure of hypocrisy, there seems no reason to doubt that religious motives played a meaningful role in the process, as King Manuel of Portugal's letter to his Spanish counterpart makes clear (see Historical Voices, "For God, Gold, and Glory in the Age of Exploration," in Chapter 14).

While Europe was on the cusp of a dynamic era of political, economic, and cultural expansion, conditions in other parts of the world were less conducive to such developments. In China, for example, the Ming Dynasty, after launching a major effort to extend its power and influence throughout the Indian Ocean in the early fifteenth century, suddenly abandoned the quest and turned inward. Smugly confident of its superiority to all potential rivals, it continued to rely on a prosperous agricultural sector as the economic foundation of the empire. In India and the Middle East, manufacturing and commerce had played a vital role in the life of societies since the emergence of the Indian Ocean trade network in the first centuries C.E. But beginning in the eleventh century, the area had suffered through an extended period of political instability marked by invasions by nomadic peoples from Central Asia. Although the emergence of the Ottoman Empire and the rise to power of the Mughals in India signaled the revival of Islam as a major force within the region, the relative lack of interest shown by Ottoman and Mughal elites in manufacturing, technology, and commerce placed them as a significant disadvantage in their competition with Christian rivals.

In the early modern era, then, Europe was best placed to take advantage of the technological innovations that had become increasingly available as other regions were still beset by internal obstacles or had deliberately turned inward to seek their destiny. Europe now turned outward to seek a new and dominant position in the world. This does not imply, however, that significant changes were not taking place in other parts of the world as well, and many of these changes had relatively little to do with the situation in the West. As we shall see, the impact of European expansion on the rest of the world was still limited at the end of the eighteenth century. Though European political authority was firmly established in a few key areas such as the Spice Islands and Latin America, traditional societies remained relatively intact in most regions of Africa and Asia. And processes at work in these societies often operated independently of events in Europe and would later give birth to forces that acted to restrict or shape the Western impact. One of these forces was the progressive emergence of centralized states, some of them built on the concept of ethnic unity.

NEW ENCOUNTERS: THE CREATION OF A WORLD MARKET

Chapter Outline and Focus Questions

14-1 *An Age of Exploration and Expansion*

Q How did Muslim merchants expand the world trade network at the end of the fifteenth century? How did their achievements extend the era of commercial expansion that took place under the Mongols in the thirteenth and fourteenth centuries?

14-2 *The Portuguese Maritime Empire*

Q Why were the Portuguese so successful in taking over the spice trade? Why was their period of hegemony in Asia so brief?

14-3 *The Conquest of the "New World"*

Q How did Portugal and Spain acquire their empires in the Americas, and why were they so much more successful in setting down deep roots there than was the case in Asia?

14-4 *Africa in Transition*

Q What were the main features of the African slave trade, and what effects did European participation have on traditional African practices?

14-5 *Southeast Asia in the Era of the Spice Trade*

Q What were the main characteristics of Southeast Asian societies, and how were they affected by the coming of Islam and the Europeans?

14.1 The Vasco da Gama Pillar at Malindi

William J. Duiker

Critical Thinking

Q *Christopher Columbus has recently become a controversial figure in world history? Why do you think this is so, and how would you evaluate his contribution to the modern world?*

Connections to Today

Q *In hindsight, do you think that European explorers can be held accountable for transmitting Old World diseases to the peoples of the Western Hemisphere?*

IN THE SPRING OF 1498, when the Portuguese fleet arrived at the town of Calicut (KAL-ih-kuht) (now known as Kozhikode) on the western coast of India, the fleet commander Vasco da Gama (VAHSH-koh dah GAHM-uh) ordered a landing party to go ashore to contact local authorities. The first to greet them, a Muslim merchant from Tunisia, said, "May the Devil take thee! What brought thee hither?" "Christians and spices," replied the visitors. "A lucky venture, a lucky venture," replied the Muslim. "Plenty of

rubies, plenty of emeralds! You owe great thanks to God, for having brought you to a country holding such riches!"[1]

Such words undoubtedly delighted the Portuguese, who explored the immediate vicinity of the town and soon convinced themselves that the local population appeared to be Christians originally converted by the apostle Thomas in the first century C.E. Although it later turned out that they were mistaken—the local faith was a form of Hinduism—their spirits were probably not seriously dampened because the conversion of the indigenous population was probably less important than gold and glory to sailors who had undergone considerable hardships to become the first Europeans since the ancient Greeks to sail across the Indian Ocean. They left two months later with a cargo of spices and the determination to return soon with a second and larger fleet.

Vasco da Gama's voyage to India inaugurated a period of European expansion into Asia that lasted several hundred years and had effects that are still felt today. His tiny fleet had rounded the Cape of Good Hope and sailed up the eastern coast of Africa, where his sailors encountered an Arab navigator in the port of Malindi who promised to take them across the Indian Ocean to seek the riches of Asia. To memorialize the occasion and mark the spot for their return voyage, the Portuguese erected a pillar of coral stone mounted by a cross that still stands on the site today (see the chapter-opening illustration).

Da Gama's voyage was a fateful one because it eventually led to a Western takeover of existing trade routes in the Indian Ocean and the establishment of colonies throughout the region, as well as in Africa and Latin America. In later years, Western historians would begin to describe the era as an "Age of Discovery" that significantly broadened the maritime trade network and set the stage for the emergence of the modern world.

As we now know, of course, the voyages of Vasco da Gama and his European successors were a discovery only in the sense that Europeans for the first time began to take part in a regional trade network that had existed for centuries and was already flourishing at a time when European maritime commerce was still essentially restricted to the Mediterranean Sea and the stormy waters of the North Atlantic Ocean. By that time, Chinese fleets had roamed the Indian Ocean and linked the Ming Empire with societies as distant as the Middle East and the coast of East Africa. Arab and Indian ships regularly passed between India, Southeast Asia, eastern Africa, and the Middle East, bringing goods from one part of the region to another. Elsewhere, Muslim caravans snaked across the Sahara Desert from the Mediterranean to the civilizations that flourished along the banks of the Niger River.

The Europeans, then, were not the trailblazers their chroniclers announced they were, but late-comers to the process. It was, after all, a Muslim from North Africa who greeted the Portuguese on their first appearance off the coast of India. In this chapter, we turn our attention to the stunning expansion in the scope and volume of commercial and cultural contacts that took place in the generations preceding and following da Gama's historic voyage to India as well as the factors that brought about this expansion.

14-1 AN AGE OF EXPLORATION AND EXPANSION

 Focus Questions: How did Muslim merchants expand the world trade network at the end of the fifteenth century? How did their achievements extend the era of commercial expansion that took place under the Mongols in the thirteenth and fourteenth centuries?

Western historians have customarily regarded the voyage of Vasco da Gama as a crucial step in the opening of trade routes to the East. This view has merit in the sense that the voyage was a harbinger of future European participation in the spice trade and that a new maritime route between the Atlantic and the Indian Oceans had been discovered. In fact, however, the Indian Ocean had been a busy thoroughfare for centuries. The spice trade had been carried on by sea in the region since the days of the legendary Queen of Sheba, and Chinese junks had sailed to the area in search of cloves and nutmeg since the Tang Dynasty (see Chapter 10).

14-1a Islam and the Spice Trade

For centuries, Arabs or Indian converts to Islam had also taken part in the Indian Ocean trade, and by the thirteenth century Islam had established a presence in seaports on the islands of Sumatra and Java. In 1292, Venetian traveler Marco Polo observed that Muslims were engaging in missionary activity in Sumatra: "This kingdom is so much frequented by the Saracen merchants that they have converted the natives to the Law of Mahomet—I mean the townspeople only, for the hill people live for all the world like beasts, and eat human flesh, as well as other kinds of flesh, clean or unclean."[2]

But the major impetus for the spread of Islam in Southeast Asia came in the early fifteenth century with the foundation of a new sultanate at Malacca (muh-LAK-uh) on the strait that now bears that name. The founder was Paramesvara (pahr-uh-muss-VAHR-uh), a vassal of the Hindu state of Majapahit (mah-jah-PAH-hit) on Java. Paramesvara's previous base of operations had been at Tumasik (tuh-MAH-sik) (modern Singapore) at the tip of the Malay Peninsula, but in 1390 he moved his base to Malacca to take advantage of its strategic location (see Map 14.1). As a sixteenth-century visitor from Portugal would observe, Malacca "is a city that was made for commerce; . . . the trade and commerce between the different nations for a thousand leagues on every hand must come to Malacca."[3]

Shortly after its founding, Malacca was visited by a Chinese fleet under the command of Admiral Zheng He (see Chapter 10). To protect his patrimony from local rivals, Paramesvara accepted Chinese vassalage and cemented the new relationship by making an official visit to the Ming emperor in Beijing. Later, he converted to Islam, a move that enhanced Malacca's ability to participate in the trade that passed through the strait, much of which was dominated by Muslim merchants. Within a few years, Malacca had become the leading economic power in the region and helped promote the spread of Islam to trading ports throughout the islands of Southeast Asia.

Map 14.1 The Strait of Malacca

14-1b The Spread of Islam in West Africa

In the meantime, Muslim commercial and religious influence continued to expand south of the Sahara into the Niger River Valley in West Africa. Muslim traders—first Arabs and later African converts—crossed the desert carrying Islamic values, political culture, and legal traditions along with their goods.

The Empire of Songhai The early stage of state formation in Africa had culminated with the kingdom of Mali under the renowned Mansa Musa (see Chapter 8). With the decline of Mali in the late fifteenth century, a new power

eventually appeared: the empire of Songhai (song-GY). Its founder was Sonni Ali, a local chieftain who seized Timbuktu from its Berber overlords in 1468 and then sought to restore the formidable empire of his predecessors. Under his rule, Songhai emerged as a major trading state (see Map 14.2).

Shortly after Sonni Ali's death in 1492, one of his military commanders seized power as king under the name Askia Mohammed (r. 1493–1528). While Sonni Ali had been criticized by Muslim scholars for supporting traditional religious practices, the new ruler, a fervent Muslim, increasingly relied on Islamic institutions and ideology to strengthen national unity and centralize authority. After his return from a pilgrimage to Mecca, Askia Mohammed tried to revive Timbuktu as a major center of Islamic learning, although many of his subjects—especially in rural areas—continued to resist conversion to Islam. During his rule, trans-Saharan trade (the exchange of gold for salt) greatly increased, providing a steady source of income to Songhai (see Historical Voices, "The Great City of Timbuktu," p. 345). After Mohammed's death, however, centrifugal forces within Songhai eventually led to its breakup. In 1591,

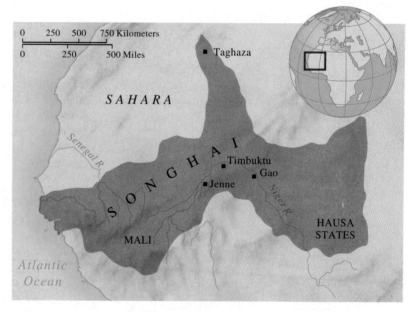

Map 14.2 The Songhai Empire. Songhai was the last of the great states to dominate the region of the Niger River Valley before the European takeover in the nineteenth century.

Q *What were the predecessors of the Songhai Empire in the region? What explains the importance of the area in African history?*

The Great City of Timbuktu

Interaction & Exchange **AFTER ITS FOUNDING IN THE TWELFTH CENTURY,** Timbuktu became a great center of Islamic learning and a fabled city of mystery and riches to Europeans. In the sixteenth century, Timbuktu was still a major commercial center on the trade route through the Sahara. This description of the city was written in 1526 by Leo Africanus, a Muslim from the Islamic state of Granada and one of the great travelers of his time.

Leo Africanus, *History and Description of Africa*

Here are many shops of artificers and merchants, and especially of such as weave linen and cotton cloth. And hither do the Barbary merchants bring cloth of Europe. All the women of this region, except the maid-servants, go with their faces covered, and sell all necessary victuals. The inhabitants, and especially strangers there residing, are exceeding rich, insomuch that the king that now is, married both his daughters to rich merchants. Here are many wells containing sweet water; and so often as the river Niger overfloweth, they convey the water thereof by certain sluices into the town. Corn, cattle, milk, and butter this region yieldeth in great abundance: but salt is very scarce here; for it is brought hither by land from Taghaza which is 500 miles distant. When I myself was here, I saw one camel's load of salt sold for 80 ducats. The rich king of Timbuktu hath many plates and scepters of gold, some whereof weigh 1,300 pounds: and he keeps a magnificent

and well-furnished court. When he travelleth any whither he rideth upon a camel which is led by some of his noblemen; and so he doth likewise when he goeth forth to warfare, and all his soldiers ride upon horses. Whoever will speak unto this king must first fall down before his feet, and then taking up earth must first sprinkle it upon his own head and shoulders: which custom is ordinarily observed by . . . ambassadors from other princes. He hath always 3,000 horsemen, and a number of footmen that shoot poisoned arrows, attending upon him. They have often skirmishes with those that refuse to pay tribute, and so many as they take, they sell unto the merchants of Timbuktu. . . . Here are great store of doctors, judges, priests, and other learned men, that are bountifully maintained at the king's cost and charges, and hither are brought divers manuscripts or written books out of Barbary, which are sold for more money than any other merchandise. The coin of Timbuktu is of gold without any stamp or superscription but in matters of small value they use certain shells brought hither out of the kingdom of Persia. . . . The inhabitants are people of gentle and cheerful disposition, and spend a great part of the night singing and dancing through all the streets of the city.

 What role did the city of Timbuktu play in regional commerce, according to this author? What were the chief means of payment?

Source: From *The History and Description of Africa,* by Leo Africanus (New York: Burt Franklin).

Moroccan forces armed with firearms conquered the city to gain control over the gold trade in the region. At this point, Timbuktu and the trade route that enabled its rise began a long period of decline.

14-1c A New Player: Europe

The rise of Songhai in the mid-fifteenth century coincided with the appearance of a new competitor in the region. Europeans had long been attracted to the East. Myths and legends of an exotic land of great riches were widespread in the Middle Ages, largely sparked by the dramatic account of adventurer Marco Polo. But the conquests of the Ottoman Turks in Anatolia and the Mediterranean Sea temporarily reduced Western traffic to the East. With the closing of the overland routes,

many Europeans became interested in the possibility of reaching Asia by sea.

As we saw in Chapter 13, by the mid-fifteenth century Europe was in the process of recovering from the turmoil of the recent past. A new spirit of adventure and confidence combined with political consolidation and a vigorous economic recovery stimulated Europeans' desires to look for wealth and trading opportunities beyond their frontiers. As one Spanish conquistador (kahn-KEES-tuh-dor) explained, he and his kind went to the Americas to "serve God and His Majesty, to give light to those who were in darkness, and to grow rich, as all men desire to do."[4]

The desire for economic gain was supplemented by a renewed spirit of rivalry between the worlds of Christendom and Islam. The Ottoman seizure of the great city of Constantinople in 1453 sent shock waves

14.2 The City of Timbuktu. Timbuktu sat astride one of the major trade routes that passed through the Sahara between the kingdoms of West Africa and the Mediterranean Sea. Caravans transported food and various manufactured articles southward in exchange for salt, gold, copper, skins, agricultural goods, and slaves. Salt was at such a premium in Timbuktu that a young Moroccan wrote in 1513 that one camel's load brought 500 miles by caravan sold for 80 gold ducats, while a horse sold for only 40 ducats. Timbuktu became a prosperous city and a great center of Islamic scholarship. By 1550, it had three universities connected to its principal mosques and 180 Qur'anic schools. This pen-and-ink sketch was done by French traveler Rene Caillie in 1828 when the city was long past its peak of prosperity and renown.

readings, the portolani proved of great value for voyages in European waters. Unfortunately, because they were drawn on a flat surface and did not account for Earth's curvature, they were of little use for longer overseas voyages. Only when seafarers began to venture beyond the coasts of Europe did they begin to accumulate information about the actual shape of the earth and how to measure it.

By the end of the fifteenth century, cartography had developed to the point that Europeans possessed fairly accurate knowledge of the known world. Portuguese sailors venturing into the North Atlantic opened the process by discovering that circular wind patterns enabled them to tack against the wind and eventually return to their home ports. In addition, Europeans had developed remarkably seaworthy ships as well as new navigational techniques. Shipbuilders had mastered the use of the sternpost rudder, an import from China, and learned how to combine the use of lateen sails with a square rig. With these innovations, they could construct **caravels** (KER-uh-velz), ships mobile enough to sail against the wind and engage in naval warfare and also large enough to be armed with heavy cannons and carry substantial amounts of goods (see Image 14.3). In addition, new navigational aids such as the compass (a Chinese invention) and the astrolabe (an instrument adapted by Arab sailors from Greek examples that measured the altitude of the sun and the stars above the horizon) enabled sailors to explore the high seas with confidence.

throughout Europe and provoked a growing desire for military action to prevent the Mediterranean from becoming "a Muslim lake." A European takeover of the spice routes from Asia would not only result in massive profits to merchants and adventurers but also undercut the growing power of Islam and open the door for missionary efforts to convert the heathen masses of Asia to Christianity. Christian zealots had long dreamed of spreading the word of the Gospel beyond the bounds of Europe to Africa, the Middle East, and elsewhere. With the opening of the Age of Exploration, the opportunity beckoned (see Historical Voices, "For God, Gold, and Glory in the Age of Exploration," p. 347).

The Means If "Christians and spices" were the primary motives, as Vasco da Gama allegedly contended, what made the voyages possible? By the end of the fifteenth century European states had a level of knowledge and technology that enabled them to regularly engage in voyages beyond Europe. Although the highly schematic and symbolic maps popular in the medieval era (see Chapter 7) were of little help to sailors, detailed charts drawn by navigators and mathematicians and known as *portolani* (pohr-tuh-LAH-nee) were more useful. With detailed information on coastal contours, distances between ports, and compass

14-2 THE PORTUGUESE MARITIME EMPIRE

 Focus Questions: Why were the Portuguese so successful in taking over the spice trade? Why was their period of hegemony in Asia so brief?

Portugal took the lead in exploration when it began exploring the coast of Africa under the sponsorship of Prince Henry the Navigator (1394–1460), who hoped to find an ally against the Muslims and acquire new trade opportunities for Portugal. In 1419, he founded a school for navigators; shortly thereafter, Portuguese fleets began probing

For God, Gold, and Glory in the Age of Exploration

Interaction & Exchange

MUCH HAS BEEN WRITTEN BY MODERN HISTORIANS about the motives behind the European Age of Exploration. Some researchers stress the desire for fame and riches, while others point to the importance of the missionary effort to spread the message of Christianity. As this letter from King Manuel of Portugal to the king and queen of Castile suggests, the motives for European expansion were not always subject to simple interpretation. As the slogan often voiced by participants in the Spanish conquest of the Americas suggests, the motives behind the process were a complex mixture of "God, Gold, and Glory," and not necessarily in that order.

Letter from King Manuel of Portugal

Your Highnesses already know that we had ordered Vasco da Gama, a nobleman of our household, and his brother Paulo da Gama, with four vessels to make discoveries by sea, and that two years have now elapsed since their departure. And as the principal motive of this enterprise has been . . . the service of God our Lord . . . it pleased Him in His mercy to speed them on their route. From a message which has now been brought to this city by one of the captains, we learn that they did reach and discover India and other kingdoms and lordships bordering upon it; that they entered and navigated its sea, finding large cities, large edifices and rivers, and great populations, among whom is carried on all the trade in spices and precious stones, which are forwarded in ships . . . to Mecca, and thence to Cairo, whence they are dispersed throughout the world. Of these they have brought a quantity, including cinnamon, cloves, ginger, nutmeg, and pepper . . . also many fine stones of all sorts, such as rubies and others.

And they also came to a country in which there are mines of gold, of which, as of the spices and precious stones, they did not bring as much as they could have done, for they took no merchandise with them.

As we are aware that your Highnesses will hear of these things with much pleasure and satisfaction, we thought well to give this information. And your Highnesses may believe, in accordance with what we have learnt concerning the Christian people whom these explorers reached, that it will be possible, notwithstanding that they are not as yet strong in the faith or possessed of a thorough knowledge of it, to do much in the service of God and the exaltation of the Holy Faith, once they shall have been converted and fully fortified in it. And when they shall have thus been fortified in the faith there will be an opportunity for destroying the Moors of those parts. Moreover, we hope, with the help of God, that the great trade which now enriches the Moors of those parts, through whose hands it passes without the intervention of other persons or peoples, shall, in consequence of our regulations be diverted to the natives and ships of our own kingdom, so that henceforth all Christendom, in this part of Europe, shall be able , in a large measure, to provide itself with these spices and precious stones. . . . This . . . will cause our designs and intentions to be pushed with more ardour . . . the war upon the Moors of the territories conquered by us in these parts. . . .

 Based on what you have learned in this chapter, how would you rate the various motives for European expansion as identified in this document?

Source: Letter from King Manuel of Portugal to their Highnesses Ferdinand and Isabella of Castile, from *A Journal of the First Voyage of Vasco da Gama, 1497–1499* (London: Hakluyt Society, 1898), tr. E.G. Ravenstein, pp. 113–114, and cited in Nigel Cliff, *The Last Crusade: The Epic Voyages of Vasco da Gama* (New York: Harper, 2011), pp. 277–278.

southward along the western coast of Africa in search of gold. In 1441, Portuguese ships reached the Senegal River just north of Cape Verde. They found no gold but brought home a cargo of black Africans, most of whom were sold as slaves to wealthy buyers elsewhere in Europe. Within a few years, an estimated thousand slaves were shipped annually from the area back to Lisbon.

Continuing southward, in 1471 the Portuguese discovered a new source of gold along the southern coast of the hump of West Africa, where they leased land from local rulers and built forts along what would henceforth be labeled the Gold Coast.

14-2a En Route to India

Hearing reports of a route to India around the southern tip of Africa, Portuguese sea captains continued their probing. In 1487, Bartolomeu Dias (bar-toh-loh-MAY-oo

14.3 The Caravel, Workhorse of the Age of Exploration. Before the fifteenth century, most European ships were either small craft with triangular, lateen sails used in the Mediterranean or slow, unwieldy square-rigged vessels operating in the North Atlantic. By the sixteenth century, European naval architects began to build caravels that combined the maneuverability and speed offered by lateen sails (widely used by sailors in the Indian Ocean) with the carrying capacity and seaworthiness of the square-riggers. For a century, caravels were the feared "raiders of the oceans." Eventually, as naval technology progressed, the carrack, a larger European warship with greater firepower and both lateen and square-rigged sails, became used (see the Part Opener, p. 338).

DEE-uhs) rounded the Cape of Good Hope but returned home without continuing onward because he feared his crew was about to mutiny. Ten years later, a fleet under the command of Vasco da Gama rounded the cape and stopped at several ports controlled by Muslim merchants along the coast of East Africa, including Sofala, Kilwa, and Mombasa. Then da Gama's fleet crossed the Arabian Sea and arrived at Calicut on the Indian coast on May 18, 1498. The Portuguese crown had sponsored the voyage with the clear objective of destroying the Muslim monopoly over the spice trade, which had intensified since the Ottoman conquest of Constantinople in 1453 (see Chapter 13). Calicut was a major entrepôt on the route from the Spice Islands to the Mediterranean, but the ill-informed Europeans believed it was the source of the spices themselves (see Map 14.3). Da Gama returned to Europe with a cargo of ginger and cinnamon that earned the investors a profit of several thousand percent.

14-2b The Search for the Source of Spices

Encouraged by the results of Vasco da Gama's maiden voyage, the Portuguese set out to gain control of the spice trade. In 1510, Admiral

Map 14.3 The Spice Islands

Afonso de Albuquerque (ah-FAHN-soh day AL-buh-kur-kee) established his headquarters at Goa (GOH-uh), on India's western coast. From there, the Portuguese raided Arab shippers, provoking the following comment from an Arab source: "[The Portuguese] took about seven vessels, killing those on board and making some prisoner. This was their first action, may God curse them."[5] In 1511, Albuquerque seized Malacca and put the local Muslim population to the sword. Control of Malacca not only provided the Portuguese with a way station en route to the Spice Islands, which are known today as the Moluccas (muh-LUHK-uhz), but also gave them a means to disrupt the Arab spice trade network by blocking passage through the Strait of Malacca.

From Malacca, the Portuguese sent expeditions farther east to China in 1514 and the Spice Islands. There they signed a treaty with a local sultan for the purchase of cloves for the European market. Within a few years, they had managed to seize control of the spice trade from Muslim traders and had garnered substantial profits for the Portuguese monarchy.

Why were the Portuguese so successful? Basically, their success was a matter of guns and seamanship. The Portuguese by no means possessed a monopoly on the use of firearms and explosives, but they used the maneuverability of their light ships to maintain their distance while bombarding the enemy with their powerful cannons. Such tactics gave them a military superiority over lightly armed rivals that they were able to exploit until the arrival of other European forces several decades later.

14-2c New Rivals Enter the Scene

Portugal's efforts to dominate the trade of the Indian Ocean were never entirely successful, however. The Portuguese lacked both the numbers and the wealth to overcome local resistance and colonize Asian regions. Moreover, their massive investments in ships and laborers for their empire (hundreds of ships and hundreds of thousands of workers in shipyards and overseas bases) proved extremely costly. The empire was simply too large and Portugal too small to maintain it, and by the end of the sixteenth century, the Portuguese were being severely challenged by both local rivals and new entrants on the scene.

The Spanish First on the scene was Spain. Queen Isabella had already signaled her intent to enter the competition in 1492 when she sponsored the voyage of Christopher Columbus into the Atlantic Ocean in search of a westward route to the Indies. That led to a dispute between the two Iberian nations over the rights to newly conquered territories. In 1494, the Treaty of Tordesillas (tor-day-SEE-yass) divided the newly discovered world into separate Portuguese and Spanish spheres of influence. Thereafter, the route east around the Cape of Good Hope was reserved for the Portuguese, while the route across the Atlantic (except for the eastern hump of South America) was assigned to Spain (see Map 14.4).

Eventually convinced that the lands Columbus had reached were not the Indies but an unknown land that possessed its own attractions, the Spanish continued to seek a route to the Spice Islands. In 1519, a Spanish fleet

under the command of Portuguese sea captain Ferdinand Magellan sailed around the southern tip of South America, proceeded across the Pacific Ocean, and landed in the Philippine Islands. Although Magellan and some forty of his crew were killed in a skirmish with the local population, one of the two remaining ships sailed on to the Moluccas and thence around the world via the Cape of Good Hope. In the words of a contemporary historian, they arrived in Cádiz "with precious cargo and fifteen men surviving out of a fleet of five sail."[6]

As it turned out, the Spanish could not follow up on Magellan's accomplishment, and in 1529 they sold their rights in the Moluccas to the Portuguese. But Magellan's voyage was not a total loss because Spain soon managed

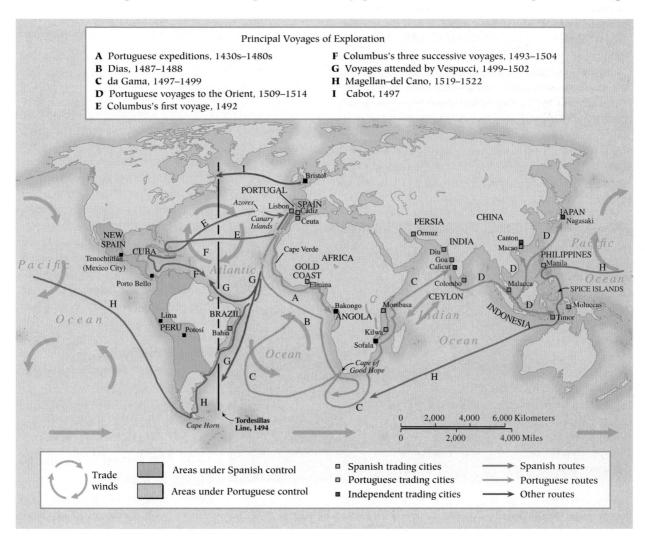

Principal Voyages of Exploration

A Portuguese expeditions, 1430s–1480s
B Dias, 1487–1488
C da Gama, 1497–1499
D Portuguese voyages to the Orient, 1509–1514
E Columbus's first voyage, 1492

F Columbus's three successive voyages, 1493–1504
G Voyages attended by Vespucci, 1499–1502
H Magellan–del Cano, 1519–1522
I Cabot, 1497

Trade winds
Areas under Spanish control
Areas under Portuguese control
Spanish trading cities
Portuguese trading cities
Independent trading cities
Spanish routes
Portuguese routes
Other routes

Map 14.4 European Voyages and Possessions in the Sixteenth and Seventeenth Centuries. This map indicates the most important voyages launched by Europeans during their momentous Age of Exploration in the sixteenth and seventeenth centuries.

Why did Vasco da Gama sail so far into the South Atlantic on his voyage to Asia?

to consolidate its control over the Philippines, which eventually became a major base in the carrying trade across the Pacific. Spanish galleons made use of the Pacific trade winds to carry silk and other luxury goods to Acapulco in exchange for silver from the mines of Mexico.

The English and the Dutch   The primary threat to the Portuguese toehold in Southeast Asia, however, came from the English and the Dutch. In 1591, the first English expedition to the Indies through the Indian Ocean returned to London with a cargo of pepper. Nine years later, a private joint stock enterprise, the East India Company, was founded to provide a stable source of capital for future voyages. In 1608, an English fleet landed at Surat (SOOR-et) on the northwestern coast of India. Trade with Southeast Asia soon followed.

The Dutch were quick to follow suit, and the first Dutch fleet arrived in India in 1595. In 1602, the Dutch East India Company was established under government sponsorship and was soon actively competing with the English and the Portuguese. In 1611, a Dutch fleet made history by sailing directly east on the "roaring forties" (the powerful westerly winds circling the globe at that southern latitude) from South Africa to the Indonesian Archipelago. In 1641, they seized Malacca, one of the linchpins of Portugal's trading empire in Asia, thus earning for themselves a dominant position in the spice trade (see Image 14.4).

14.4 The Port of Malacca in 1726. In 1641, the Dutch took over the seaport of Malacca from the Portuguese. Over the next several decades, the new owners gradually replaced their Catholic rivals in controlling the spice trade between Europe and the Indies. One of the most prominent chroniclers of this process was Dutch naturalist and author Francis Valentijn. Born in 1666, he spent many years in the Dutch East Indies and wrote a highly respected study of the Indonesian archipelago. His engraving of Malacca, shown here with European ships floating in the harbor, appeared shortly before his death in 1727. In the early nineteenth century, Malacca was ceded by treaty to Great Britain.

Photograph by William J. Duiker/Engraving of the city of Malacca by Francis Valentijn

14-3 **THE CONQUEST OF THE "NEW WORLD"**

Focus Question: How did Portugal and Spain acquire their empires in the Americas, and why were they so much more successful in setting down deep roots there than was the case in Asia?

While the Portuguese were seeking access to the spice trade by sailing eastward through the Indian Ocean, the Spanish attempted to reach the same destination by sailing westward across the Atlantic. Although the Spanish came to overseas discovery and exploration later than the Portuguese, their greater resources enabled them to establish a far grander overseas empire.

14-3a **The Voyages**

In the late fifteenth century, knowledgeable Europeans were aware that Earth was round but were still uncertain about its size and the extent of the continent of Asia (see Map 14.5). Convinced that Earth's circumference was smaller than contemporaries believed, Christopher Columbus (1451–1506), an Italian from Genoa, maintained that Asia could be reached by sailing due west instead of eastward around Africa. He persuaded Queen Isabella of Spain to finance an expedition, which reached the Americas in October 1492 and explored the coastline of Cuba and the neighboring island of Hispaniola (his-puhn-YOH-luh or ees-pahn-YAH-luh). Columbus believed that he had reached Asia and in three subsequent voyages (1493, 1498, and 1502) sought in vain to find a route through the outer islands to the Asian mainland.

14-3b **The Arrival of Hernando Cortés in Mexico**

Other navigators, however, soon realized that Columbus had discovered a new frontier altogether and joined the race to benefit from the opportunity. A Venetian, John Cabot, explored the New England coastline under a license from King Henry VII of England. While en route to Asia, Portuguese captain Pedro Cabral (PAY-droh kuh-BRAHL) accidentally discovered the continent of South America in 1500. Amerigo Vespucci (ahm-ay-REE-goh vess-POO-chee), a Florentine, accompanied Cabral's voyage and wrote a series of letters describing the lands he observed. The publication of these letters led to the name *America* (after Vespucci's first name) for the new lands.

Map 14.5 Cape Horn and the Strait of Magellan

14-3c The Conquests

The territories that Europeans referred to as the "New World" actually contained flourishing civilizations populated by millions of people. But the Americas were new to the Europeans, who quickly saw opportunities for conquest and exploitation. With Portugal clearly in the lead in the race to exploit the riches of the Indies, the importance of these lands was magnified in the minds of the Spanish.

The Spanish **conquistadors** (kahn-KEES-tu-dors), as they were called, were a hardy lot of adventurous individuals motivated by a typical sixteenth-century blend of glory, greed, and religious zeal. Their superior weapons, organizational skills, and determination brought the conquistadors incredible success in their new environment. In 1519, a Spanish expedition led by Hernando Cortés landed at Veracruz on the Gulf of Mexico. Marching to Tenochtitlán (teh-nahch-teet-LAHN) with a small contingent of troops, Cortés received a friendly welcome from the Aztec monarch Moctezuma Xocoyotzin (mahk-tuh-ZOO-muh shoh-koh-YAHT-seen) (often called *Montezuma*).

But tensions soon erupted between the Spaniards and the Aztecs. When the Spanish took Moctezuma hostage and began to destroy Aztec religious shrines, the local population revolted and drove the invaders from the city. Meanwhile, the Aztecs were beginning to suffer the

first effects of the diseases brought by the Europeans, which would eventually wipe out the majority of the local residents. With assistance from the state of Tlaxcallan (tuh-lah-SKAH-lahn), Cortés finally succeeded in vanquishing the Aztecs (see Comparative Illustration, "The Spaniards Conquer a New World," p. 352). Within months, their magnificent city and its temples, believed by the conquerors to be the work of Satan, had been destroyed.

A similar fate awaited the powerful Inka Empire in South America. Between 1531 and 1536, an expedition led by Francisco Pizarro (frahn-SEES-koh puh-ZAHR-oh) (1470–1541) destroyed Inka power high in the Peruvian Andes. Here, too, the Spanish conquests were undoubtedly facilitated by the previous arrival of European diseases, which had decimated the local population.

The Portuguese in Brazil Meanwhile, the Portuguese crown had established the colony of Brazil, basing its claim on the Treaty of Tordesillas, which had allocated the eastern coast of South America to the Portuguese

14.5 The Catholic Cathedral at Cuzco. After the total destruction of the Inka Empire, the Spanish conquistadors rebuilt the Inkan capital of Cuzco in their own image. Among the many changes that they implemented, the sacred Inkan pyramid in the heart of the city was dismantled and an impressive Spanish Baroque cathedral was erected on its base. As a final humiliation, many of the materials originally used for the pyramid were later put to use in building its replacement.

14.6a

COMPARATIVE ILLUSTRATION

The Spaniards Conquer a New World

Politics & Government **THE PERSPECTIVE THAT THE SPANISH BROUGHT** to their arrival in the Americas was quite different from that of the indigenous peoples. In the European painting shown in Image 14.6a, the encounter was a peaceful one, and the upturned eyes of Columbus and his fellow voyagers imply that their motives were spiritual rather than material. Image 14.6b, drawn by an Aztec artist, expresses a dramatically different point of view, as the Spanish invaders, assisted by their Indian allies, use superior weapons against the bows and arrows of their adversaries to bring about the conquest of Mexico.

14.6b

 What does the Aztec painting presented here show the viewer about the nature of the conflict between the two contending armies?

sphere of influence. Like their Spanish rivals, the Portuguese initially saw their new colony as a source of gold and silver, but they soon discovered that profits could be made in other ways as well. A formal administrative system was instituted in Brazil in 1549, and Portuguese migrants arrived to establish plantations to produce sugar, coffee, and other tropical products for export to Europe.

14-3d Governing the Empires

As Portugal came to dominate Brazil, Spain established a colonial empire that included Central America, most of South America, and parts of North America. Within the lands of Central and South America, a new civilization arose that we have come to call *Latin America* (see Map 14.6).

The State and the Church in Colonial Latin America In administering their colonial empires in the Americas, both Portugal and Spain tried to keep the most important posts of colonial government in the hands of Europeans (known as *peninsulares*). At the head of the Portuguese and the Spanish administrative pyramid was a **viceroy**. The Spanish created viceroyalties for New Spain (Mexico) in 1535 and for Peru in 1543. Viceroyalties were in turn subdivided into smaller units. All of the major government positions were held by Spaniards. For **creoles**—American-born descendants of Europeans—the chief opportunity to hold a government post was in city councils.

From the beginning, the Spanish and Portuguese rulers were determined to convert the indigenous peoples of the Americas to Christianity (see Film & History, *The Mission*, p. 354). Consequently, the Catholic Church played an important role in the colonies, building hospitals, orphanages, and schools to instruct the Indians in the rudiments of reading, writing, and arithmetic. To facilitate their efforts, missionaries often brought Indians to live in mission villages where they could be converted, taught trades, and encouraged to grow crops, all under the control of the church.

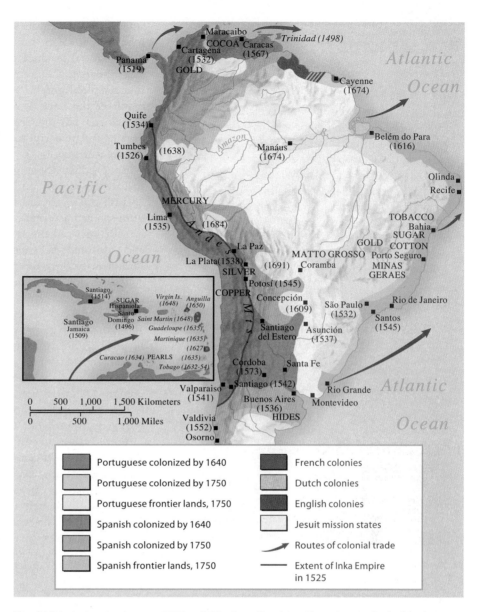

Map 14.6 Latin America from ca. 1500 to 1750. From the sixteenth century on, Latin America was largely the colonial preserve of the Spanish, although Portugal dominated Brazil. The Latin American colonies supplied the Spanish and Portuguese with gold, silver, sugar, tobacco, cotton, and animal hides.

How do you explain the ability of Europeans to dominate such large areas of Latin America?

For women in the colonies, Catholic nunneries provided outlets other than marriage. Women in religious orders, many of them of aristocratic background, often operated outside their establishments by running schools and hospitals. The nun Sor Juana Inés de la Cruz (SAWR HWAH-nuh ee-NAYSS day lah KROOZ) (1651–1695), who became one of seventeenth-century Latin America's best-known literary figures, wrote poetry and prose and urged that women be educated.

The Mission

The film *The Mission* (1986), directed by Roland Joffe, is a moving portrayal of a tragic era in the European conquest of the Western Hemisphere. As the local Amerindian population in parts of Latin America is victimized by European settlers seeking to seize their lands and force them into slavery, members of the Jesuit order establish religious missions to protect the most threatened peoples from a heinous fate. The Catholic Church, caught in the twisted web of competing national interests, fails to protect the Jesuits and their charges, and the missions are destroyed. This is a sobering film, and not for the fainthearted.

Q *Why do you think that the Jesuit missionaries stationed in Latin America were not given greater support by their superiors, or by the civilian administrators in the area?*

Warner Brothers/Courtesy Everett Collection, Inc.

MINDTAP See full-length Film & History feature in MindTap.
From Cengage

Exploiting the Riches of the Americas Economic exploitation was the prime purpose of Spanish and Portuguese rule in the Americas. One source of wealth came from the gold and silver the Europeans sought so avidly. One Aztec observer commented that the Spanish conquerors "longed and lusted for gold. Their bodies swelled with greed, and their hunger was ravenous; they hungered like pigs for that gold."[7] Rich silver deposits were exploited in Mexico and southern Peru (modern Bolivia). Between 1503 and 1650, an estimated 16 million kilograms (17,500 tons) of silver and 185,000 kilograms (200 tons) of gold entered the port of Seville in Spain.

In the long run, however, agriculture proved to be more rewarding. The American colonies became sources of raw materials for Spain and Portugal as sugar, tobacco, chocolate, precious woods, animal hides, and other natural products made their way to Europe. In turn, the mother countries supplied their colonists with manufactured goods. Both Spain and Portugal closely regulated the trade of their American colonies to keep others out, but the English and the French eventually became too powerful to be excluded from this lucrative market (see Map 14.7).

To produce these goods, colonial authorities initially tried to rely on local sources of human labor. Spanish policy toward the Indians was a combination of misguided paternalism and cruel exploitation. Queen Isabella declared the Indians to be subjects of Castile and instituted the **encomienda system**, under which European settlers received grants of land and could collect tribute from the indigenous peoples and use them as laborers. In return, the holders of an *encomienda* (en-koh-MYEN-duh) were supposed to protect the Indians and supervise their spiritual and material needs. In practice, this meant that the settlers were free to implement the system as they pleased. Spanish settlers largely ignored their distant government and brutally used the Indians to pursue their own economic interests. Indians were put to work on sugar plantations and in gold and silver mines.

Forced labor, starvation, and especially disease took a fearful toll on Indian lives. With little or no natural resistance to European diseases, the Indians were ravaged by smallpox, measles, and typhus brought by the Europeans. Although estimates vary, in some areas at least half of the local population probably died of European diseases. In 1542, largely in response to the publications of Bartolomé de Las Casas (bahr-toh-loh-MAY day lahs KAH-sahs), the government abolished the encomienda system and provided more protection for the Indians (see Opposing Viewpoints, "The March of Civilization," p. 355). By then, however, the indigenous population had been decimated by disease, causing the Spanish and eventually the Portuguese to import African slaves to replace Indians in the sugar fields.

14-3e The Competition Intensifies

The success of the Spanish and the Portuguese in exploiting the riches of the Americas soon attracted competition from other European states. In 1607, the English established their first permanent colony at Jamestown near the mouth of the Chesapeake Bay, and other settlements appeared shortly afterward. Within a few years other European states had followed suit and soon occupied much of the eastern seaboard of North America.

The March of Civilization

Interaction & Exchange — **AS EUROPEANS BEGAN TO EXPLORE** new parts of the world in the fifteenth century, they were convinced that it was their duty to introduce civilized ways to the heathen peoples they encountered. This attitude is reflected in the first selection, which describes the Spanish captain Vasco Núñez de Balboa (BAHS-koh NOON-yez day bal-BOH-uh) in 1513, when from a hill on the Isthmus of Panama he first laid eyes on the Pacific Ocean.

Bartolomé de Las Casas (1474–1566) was a Dominican monk who participated in the conquest of Cuba and received land and Indians in return for his efforts. But in 1514, he underwent a radical transformation that led him to believe that the Indians had been cruelly mistreated by his fellow Spaniards. He spent the remaining years of his life fighting for the Indians. The second selection is taken from his most influential work, *Brevísima Relación de la Destrucción de las Indias,* known to English readers as *The Tears of the Indians.* This work was largely responsible for the reputation of the Spanish conquistadors as cruel and murderous fanatics.

Gonzalo Fernández de Ovieda, *Historia General y Natural de las Indias*

On Tuesday, the twenty-fifth of September of the year 1513, at ten o'clock in the morning, Captain Vasco Núñez, having gone ahead of his company, climbed a hill with a bare summit, and from the top of this hill saw the South Sea. Of all the Christians in his company, he was the first to see it. He turned back toward his people, full of joy, lifting his hands and his eyes to Heaven, praising Jesus Christ and his glorious Mother the Virgin, Our Lady. Then he fell upon his knees on the ground and gave great thanks to God for the mercy He had shown him, in allowing him to discover that sea, and thereby to render so great a service to God and to the most serene Catholic Kings of Castile, our sovereigns . . . .

And he told all the people with him to kneel also, to give the same thanks to God, and to beg Him fervently to allow them to see and discover the secrets and great riches of that sea and coast, for the greater glory and increase of the Christian faith, for the conversion of the Indians, natives of those southern regions, and for the fame and prosperity of the royal throne of Castile and of its sovereigns present and to come. All the people cheerfully and willingly did as they were bidden; and the Captain made them fell a big tree and make from it a tall cross, which they erected in that same place, at the top of the hill from which the South Sea had first been seen.

Bartolomé de Las Casas, *The Tears of the Indians*

There is nothing more detestable or more cruel than the tyranny which the Spaniards use toward the Indians for the getting of pearl. Surely the infernal torments cannot much exceed the anguish that they endure, by reason of that way of cruelty; for they put them under water some four or five ells deep, where they are forced without any liberty of respiration, to gather up the shells wherein the Pearls are; sometimes they come up again with nets full of shells to take breath, but if they stay any while to rest themselves, immediately comes a hangman row'd in a little boat, who as soon as he hath well beaten them, drags them again to their labor. Their food is nothing but filth, and the very same that contains the Pearl, with small portion of that bread which that Country affords; in the first whereof there is little nourishment; and as for the latter, it is made with great difficulty, besides that they have not enough of that neither for sustenance; they lie upon the ground in fetters, lest they should run away; and many times they are drown'd in this labor, and are never seen again till they swim upon the top of the waves; oftentimes they also are devoured by certain sea monsters, that are frequent in those seas. Consider whether this hard usage of the poor creatures be consistent with the precepts which God commands concerning charity to our neighbor. . . .

 Can the sentiments expressed by Vasco Núñez be reconciled with the treatment accorded to the Indians as described by Las Casas? Which selection do you think better describes the behavior of the Spaniards in the Americas?

Source: From *The Age of Reconnaissance* by J. H. Parry (International Thomson Publishing, 1969), pp. 233–234. From *The Tears of the Indians,* Bartolomé de Las Casas. Copyright © 1970 by The John Lilburne Company Publishers.

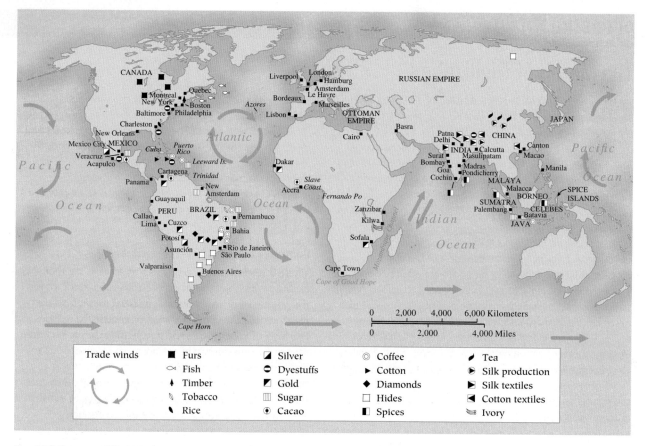

Map 14.7 Patterns of World Trade Between 1500 and 1800. This map shows the major products that were traded by European merchants throughout the world during the era of European exploration.

Q *What were the primary sources of gold and silver so sought after by Columbus and his successors?*

But the main arena of competition was farther to the south, where the lure of profits from the sugar trade was difficult to resist. By the end of the seventeenth century, several European nations competed actively for control of the islands of the Caribbean Sea, where sugar plantations were producing fabulous profits for their owners. Several islands shifted control several times during the course of the seventeenth and eighteenth centuries (see Chronology, "Spanish and Portuguese Activities in the Americas").

CHRONOLOGY	Spanish and Portuguese Activities in the Americas
Christopher Columbus's first voyage to the Americas	1492
Portuguese fleet arrives in Brazil	1500
Columbus's last voyages	1502–1504
Spanish conquest of Mexico	1519–1522
Francisco Pizarro's conquest of the Inkas	1531–1536
Viceroyalty of New Spain established	1535
Formal colonial administrative system established in Brazil	1549

HISTORIANS DEBATE 14-3f **Christopher Columbus: Hero or Villain?**

For centuries, explorer Christopher Columbus has generally been viewed in a positive light. By discovering the Western Hemisphere, he opened up the world and laid the foundations for the modern global economy. Recently, however, some historians have challenged the prevailing image of Columbus as a heroic figure and view him as a symbol of European colonial repression and a prime mover in the virtual extinction of the peoples and cultures of the Americas (see Comparative Essay, "The Columbian Exchange," p. 357).

The Columbian Exchange

Interaction & Exchange In the Western world, the discovery of the Americas has traditionally been viewed as a positive development, the first step in a process that expanded the global trade network and eventually led to increased economic well-being and the spread of civilization throughout the world. In recent years, however, that view has been sharply attacked by observers who point out that the primary legacy of the European conquest for the peoples of the Americas was not improved living standards but harsh colonial exploitation and the spread of pestilential diseases that devastated local populations.

Certainly, the record of European conquistadors leaves much to be desired, and the voyages of Columbus did not universally benefit his contemporaries or later generations. They not only destroyed vibrant civilizations in the Americas but also led to the enslavement of millions of Africans, who were separated from their families and shipped to a far-off world in deplorable, inhumane conditions.

But to focus solely on the evils committed in the name of exploration and civilization misses a larger point and obscures the long-term ramifications of the events taking place. The age of European expansion that began in the fifteenth century was only the latest in a series of population movements that included the spread of nomadic peoples across Central Asia and the expansion of Islam out of the Middle East after the death of the prophet Muhammad. In fact, the migration of peoples in search of a better livelihood has been a central theme in the evolution of the human race since the dawn of prehistory. Virtually all of the migrations involved acts of unimaginable cruelty and the forcible displacement of peoples and societies.

In retrospect, the consequences of such broad population movements are too complex to be summed up in moral or ideological simplifications. The Mongol invasions and the expansion of Islam are two examples of movements that brought benefits as well as costs for the peoples who were affected. By the same token, the European conquest of the Americas not only brought the destruction of cultures and dangerous new diseases but also initiated the exchange of plant and animal species that have ultimately fed millions and been of widespread benefit to peoples throughout the globe. The introduction of the horse, the cow, and various grain crops vastly increased food production in the Americas. The cultivation of corn, manioc, and potato, all products of the Western Hemisphere, has had the same effect in Asia, Africa, and Europe. The **Columbian Exchange**, as it is sometimes labeled, has had far-reaching consequences that transcend facile moral judgments.

The opening of the Americas had other long-term ramifications as well. The importation of vast amounts of gold and silver into Europe was a crucial factor in the growth of commercial capitalism that helped finance the Industrial Revolution and set the stage for the modern global economy (see Chapter 19).

Viewed in that context, the Columbian Exchange, whatever its moral failings, ultimately brought tangible benefits to peoples throughout the world. For some, the costs were high, and it can be argued that the indigenous peoples of the Americas might have better managed the transformation on their own. But the "iron law" of history operates at its own speed and does not wait for laggards. For good or ill, the Columbian Exchange marked a major stage in the transition between the traditional and the modern world.

The Granger Collection, NYC

14.7 A Sugar Plantation. For African slaves brought to the Americas, few occupations were as murderous and dehumanizing as the work on the sugar plantations. Shown here, slaves on the island of Hispaniola are cutting the cane to prepare it for transformation into cane sugar.

 How can the costs and benefits of the Columbian Exchange be measured? What standards would you apply in attempting to measure them?

As we have seen, the immediate consequences of Columbus's voyages were tragic for many of the indigenous peoples. Columbus himself viewed those whom he encountered with condescension, describing them as naïve innocents who could be exploited to increase the wealth and power of Spain. As a consequence, his men frequently treated the local population brutally.

But is it fair to blame Columbus for possessing many of the character traits and prejudices common to his era? To do so is to demand that an individual transcend the limitations of his time and adopt the values of a future generation. Perhaps it is better to note simply that Columbus and his contemporaries showed relatively little understanding and sympathy for the cultural values of peoples who lived beyond the borders of their own civilization, a limitation that would probably apply to one degree or another to all generations, including our own. Whether Columbus was a hero or a villain will remain a matter of debate. That he and his contemporaries played a key role in the emergence of the modern world is a matter on which there can be no doubt.

14-4 AFRICA IN TRANSITION

 Focus Question: What were the main features of the African slave trade, and what effects did European participation have on traditional African practices?

Although the primary objective of the Portuguese in rounding the Cape of Good Hope was to find a sea route to the Spice Islands, they soon discovered that profits were to be made en route along the eastern coast of Africa.

14-4a Europeans in Africa

In the early sixteenth century, a Portuguese fleet seized several East African port cities, including Kilwa, Sofala, and Mombasa, and built forts along the coast in an effort to control the trade in the area (see Map 14.5). Above all, the Portuguese wanted to monopolize the trade in gold, which was mined by Bantu workers in the hills and then shipped to Sofala on the coast (see Chapter 8). For centuries, the gold trade had been monopolized by local Bantu-speaking Shona peoples at Zimbabwe. In the fifteenth century, it had come under the control of a Shona Dynasty known as the Mwene Mutapa (MWAY-nay moo-TAH-puh). At first, the Mwene Mutapa found the Europeans useful as an ally against local rivals, but by the end of the sixteenth century the Portuguese had forced the local ruler to grant them large tracts of land. The Portuguese lacked the personnel, the capital, and the expertise to dominate the local trade, however, and a vassal of the Mwene Mutapa succeeded in driving them from the plateau in the late seventeenth century.

The first Europeans to settle in southern Africa were the Dutch. In 1652, they set up a way station at the Cape of Good Hope to serve as a base for their fleets en route to the East Indies. Eventually, the settlement developed into a permanent colony as Dutch farmers known as **Boers** (BOORS or BORS), who spoke a Dutch dialect that evolved into Afrikaans, began to settle outside the city of Cape Town. With its temperate climate and absence of tropical diseases, the territory was practically the only land south of the Sahara that the Europeans had found suitable for habitation.

14-4b The Slave Trade

The European exploration of the African coastline had little apparent significance for most peoples living in the interior of the continent, except for a few who engaged in direct or indirect trade with the foreigners. But for peoples living on or near the coast, the impact was often great indeed. As the trade in slaves increased during the sixteenth through the eighteenth centuries, thousands and then millions of Africans were removed from their homes and forcibly exported to plantations in the Western Hemisphere.

The Arrival of the Europeans As we saw in Chapter 8, slavery existed in various forms in Africa before the arrival of the Europeans. Some slaves were used as agricultural laborers, others as household servants. After the expansion of Islam south of the Sahara in the eighth century, a vigorous traffic in slaves developed as Arab merchants traded for slaves to be transported to the Middle East. A few were sent to Europe, where, along with Slavic-speaking peoples captured in war in the regions near the Black Sea (the English word *slave* derives from "Slav"), they were used for domestic purposes or as agricultural workers.

With the arrival of the Europeans in the fifteenth century, the African slave trade changed dramatically. At first, the Portuguese simply replaced European slaves with African slaves. But the discovery of the Americas changed the situation. The cause was sugar. Cane sugar had been introduced to Europeans from the Middle East during the crusades, but when the Ottoman Empire seized much of the eastern Mediterranean (see Chapter 13), the Europeans needed to seek out new areas suitable for cultivation. In 1490, the Portuguese established sugar plantations on São Tomé, an island off the central coast of Africa.

It soon became clear that the climate and soil of West Africa were not especially conducive to the cultivation of sugar, so during the sixteenth century plantations were established along the eastern coast of Brazil and on several Caribbean islands. Because the cultivation of cane sugar is an arduous process demanding large quantities of labor, the new plantations required more workers than could be provided by the local Indian population, many of whom (as described earlier) had died of diseases, so African slaves began to be shipped to Brazil and the Caribbean to work on the plantations. The first were sent from Portugal, but in 1518 a Spanish ship carried the first boatload of African slaves directly from Africa to the Americas.

The Middle Passage   Over the next two centuries, the trade in slaves saw massive increases. An estimated 275,000 enslaved Africans were exported to other countries during the sixteenth century, more than two-thirds of them to the Americas. The total climbed to more than 1 million during the next century and jumped to 6 million in the eighteenth century when the trade spread from West and Central Africa to East Africa. As many as 10 million African slaves are estimated to have been transported to the Americas between the early sixteenth and the late nineteenth centuries (see Map 14.8). As many as 2 million were exported to other areas during the same period.

One reason for these astonishing numbers was the tragically high death rate. In what is often called the **Middle Passage**, the arduous voyage from Africa to the Americas, losses were frequently appalling. Although figures on the number of slaves who died on the journey are almost entirely speculative, during the first shipments as many as one-third may have died of disease or malnourishment. Even among crew members, mortality rates were sometimes as high as one in four. Later merchants became more efficient and reduced losses to around 10 percent. Still, the future slaves were treated inhumanely, chained together in the holds of ships

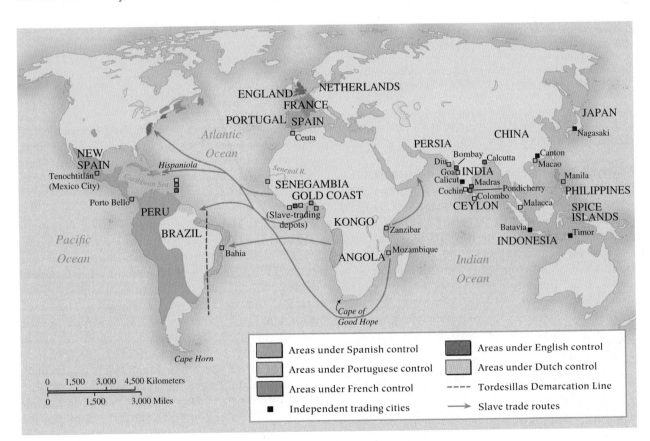

Map 14.8 The Slave Trade. Beginning in the sixteenth century, the trade in African slaves to the Americas became a major source of profit for European merchants. This map traces the routes taken by slave-trading ships, as well as the territories and ports of call of European powers in the seventeenth century.

Q *What were the major destinations for the slave trade?*

Experience an interactive version of this period in **MINDTAP**

14.8 Gateway to Slavery. Of the 12 million slaves shipped from Africa to other parts of the world, some passed through Gorée (GOR-ay) prison on a small island just off the coast of Senegal near Cape Verde. Beginning in the sixteenth century, European traders began to ship African captives from the region of West Africa to the Americas to be used as slave labor on sugar plantations. Although the number of individuals shipped from Gorée was relatively small, the prison has been promoted as a poignant symbol of the cruelty afflicted by the slave trade on millions of innocent Africans. As a sign on a doorway in the prison reads, "From this door, they would embark on a voyage with no return, eyes fixed on an infinity of suffering." The modern African city of Dakar looms in the distance.

reeking with the stench of human waste and diseases carried by vermin (see Image 14.8).

Slavery in the Americas Ironically, African slaves who survived the brutal voyage fared somewhat better than whites after their arrival. Mortality rates for Europeans in the West Indies were ten to twenty times higher than in Europe, and death rates for new arrivals in the islands averaged more than 125 per 1,000 annually. But the figure for Africans, many of whom had developed at least a partial immunity to yellow fever, was only around 30 per 1,000.

The reason for these staggering death rates was clearly more than maltreatment, although that was certainly a factor. As we have seen, the transmission of diseases from one continent to another brought high death rates among those lacking immunity. African slaves were somewhat less susceptible to European diseases than the American Indian populations. Indeed, they seem to have possessed a degree of immunity, perhaps because their ancestors had developed antibodies to diseases common to the Old World from centuries of contact via the trans-Saharan trade. Still, working conditions for slaves were onerous, especially on sugar plantations, where laborers were forced to cut the sugarcane in the heat of the tropical sun

and then bring it to the mill for crushing and transformation into raw sugar. Desperate to escape such conditions, thousands of slaves escaped into the wilderness, where they set up communities safe from control of European colonial authorities.

Sources of Slaves For the most part, Europeans obtained their slaves by traditional means, purchasing them from local African merchants at the infamous slave markets in exchange for gold, guns, or other European manufactured goods such as textiles or copper or iron utensils. The "third leg" of this **Triangular Trade** took place when slave owners in the Americas paid for their slaves with sugar or its by-products (such as rum or molasses) exported to buyers in Europe. At first, local slave traders obtained their supply from the immediate surrounding regions, but as demand increased they had to move farther inland to locate their victims. A few local rulers became concerned about the impact of the slave trade on the political and economic well-being of their societies (see Historical Voices, "A Plea Between Friends," p. 361). More frequently, however, local monarchs viewed the slave trade as a source of income, and many launched forays against defenseless villages in search of victims.

A Plea Between Friends

Interaction & Exchange

KING AFONSO I OF THE STATE OF KONGO was one of Portugal's chief African allies during the early sixteenth century. A convert to Christianity, he used his relationship with the Portuguese to extend the territory of his kingdom at the expense of neighboring states in the region. Captives obtained during his military campaigns were sold to merchants and then exported abroad as slaves. As the demand for slaves increased, however, traders began to trap and enslave Afonso's own subjects while flooding the country with goods from abroad that undermined his royal authority.

In this letter, written in 1526, Afonso appealed to his "brother" sovereign, Dom João III, king of Portugal, to prevent such unscrupulous merchants from seizing his subjects and selling them as slaves to European sea captains. The letter is vivid testimony to how the slave trade destabilized African societies on or near the coast during the sixteenth and seventeenth centuries.

A Letter to King João

[1526] Sir, your Highness [of Portugal] should know how our Kingdom is being lost in so many ways that it is convenient to provide for the necessary remedy, since this is caused by the excessive freedom given by your factors and officials to the men and merchants who are allowed to come to this Kingdom to set up shops with goods and many things which have been prohibited by us, and which they spread throughout our Kingdoms and Domains in such an abundance that many of our vassals, whom we had in obedience, do not comply because they have the things in greater abundance than we ourselves; and it was with these things that we had them content and subjected under our vassalage and jurisdiction, so it is doing a great harm not only to the service of God, but the security and peace of our Kingdoms and State as well.

And we cannot reckon how great the damage is, since the mentioned merchants are taking every day our natives, sons of the land and the sons of our noblemen and vassals and our relatives, because the thieves and men of bad conscience grab them wishing to have the things and wares of this Kingdom which they are ambitious of; they grab them and get them to be sold; and so great, Sir, is the corruption and licentiousness that our country is being completely depopulated, and Your Highness should not agree with this nor accept it as in your service. And to avoid it we need from those [your] Kingdoms no more than some priests and a few people to teach in schools, and no other goods except wine and flour for the holy sacrament. That is why we beg of Your Highness to help and assist us in this matter, commanding your factors that they should not send here either merchants or wares, because it is our will that in these Kingdoms there should not be any trade of slaves nor outlet for them. Concerning what is referred above, again we beg of Your Highness to agree with it, since otherwise we cannot remedy such an obvious damage. Pray Our Lord in His mercy to have Your Highness under His guard and let you do for ever the things of His service. I kiss your hand many times.

At our town of Congo, written on the sixth day of July.

João Teixeira did it in 1526.

The King, Dom Afonso.

[On the back of this letter the following can be read: To the most powerful and excellent prince Dom João, King our Brother.]

 In what ways were the European merchants destabilizing the kingdom of Kongo? What remedy did Afonso propose?

Source: From *The African Past: Chronicles from Antiquity to Modern Times* by Basil Davidson (Boston: Little, Brown and Company, 1964), pp. 191–192.

The Effects of the Slave Trade The effects of the slave trade varied from area to area. One assumes the practice would have led to the depopulation of vast areas of the continent, and this did occur in some areas, notably in modern Angola, south of the mouth of the Congo River, and in thinly populated areas in East Africa. It was less true, however, in West Africa. High birthrates there were often able to counterbalance the loss of able-bodied adults, and the introduction of new crops from the Western Hemisphere such as maize, peanuts, and manioc led to an increase in food production that made it possible to support a larger population. One of the many cruel ironies of history is that while the institution of slavery was a tragedy for many, it benefited others.

Still, there is no denying that from a moral point of view, the slave trade represented a tragic loss for millions of Africans, for families as well as individuals. As many as 20 percent of those sold to European slavers were children, a statistic that may be partly explained by the fact that many European countries had enacted regulations that permitted more children than adults to be transported aboard the ships.

How did Europeans justify cruelty of such epidemic proportions? Some rationalized that slave traders were only carrying on a tradition that had existed for centuries throughout the Mediterranean and African world. In fact, African intermediaries were active in the process and were often able to dictate the price, volume, and availability of slaves to European purchasers. Other Europeans eased their consciences by noting that slaves would now be exposed to the Christian faith.

14-4c Political and Social Structures in a Changing Continent

Of course, the Western economic penetration of Africa had other dislocating effects. The importation of manufactured goods from Europe undermined the foundations of the local cottage industry and impoverished countless families. The introduction of firearms intensified political instability and civil strife. As the European demand for slaves increased, African slave traders began to use their newly purchased guns to raid neighboring villages in search of captives, initiating a chain of violence that created a climate of fear and insecurity. Old polities were undermined, and new regimes ruled by rapacious "merchant princes" began to proliferate on the coast.

At the same time, the impact of the Europeans on the African continent as a whole should not be exaggerated. Only in a few isolated areas, such as South Africa and Mozambique, were permanent European settlements established. Elsewhere, at the insistence of African rulers and merchants, European influence generally did not penetrate beyond the coastal regions. Nevertheless, inland areas were often affected by events taking place elsewhere. In the western Sahara, for example, the diversion of trade routes toward the coast led to the weakening of the old Songhai trading empire and its eventual conquest by a vigorous new Moroccan dynasty in the late sixteenth century.

European influence had a more direct impact along the coast of West Africa, but no European colonies were established there before 1800. Most of the numerous African states in the area from Cape Verde to the delta of the Niger River were sufficiently strong to resist Western encroachments. Some, like the powerful Ashanti kingdom, established in 1680 on the Gold Coast, profited substantially from the rise in seaborne commerce. Some states, particularly along the so-called Slave Coast in what are now Benin and Togo or in the densely populated Niger River Delta

CHRONOLOGY	The Penetration of Africa	
Life of Prince Henry the Navigator	1394–1460
Portuguese ships reach the Senegal River	1441
Bartolomeu Dias sails around the tip of Africa	1487
First boatload of slaves to the Americas	1518
Dutch way station established at Cape of Good Hope	1652
Ashanti kingdom established in West Africa	1680
Portuguese expelled from Mombasa	1728

took an active part in the slave trade. The demands of slavery and the temptations to profit, however, also contributed to the increase in conflict among the states in the area.

This was especially true in the region of the Congo River, where Portuguese activities eventually led to the splintering of the Kongo Empire and two centuries of strife among its successor states. Similarly, in East Africa, Portuguese activities led to the decline and eventual collapse of the Mwene Mutapa. Northward along the coast in present-day Kenya and Tanzania, African rulers were assisted by Arab forces from the Arabian Peninsula and expelled the Portuguese from Mombasa in 1728. Swahili culture now regained some of its earlier dynamism, but with much shipping now diverted to the route around the Cape of Good Hope the area never completely recovered and was increasingly dependent on the export of slaves and ivory obtained through contacts with African states in the interior. (See Chronology, "The Penetration of Africa," above.)

14-5 SOUTHEAST ASIA IN THE ERA OF THE SPICE TRADE

Focus Question: What were the main characteristics of Southeast Asian societies, and how were they affected by the coming of Islam and the Europeans?

As noted earlier, Southeast Asia was affected in various ways by the expansion of the global trade network that began to accelerate in the fifteenth century. Not only did the Muslim faith begin to make inroads in the region, but the seizure of Malacca by the Portuguese in 1511 inaugurated a period of conflict among various European competitors for control of the spice trade. At first, the rulers of most of the local states were able to fend off these challenges and maintain their independence. As we shall see in a later chapter, however, the reprieve was only temporary.

14-5a The Arrival of the West

Where the Portuguese had trod, others soon followed. By the seventeenth century, the Dutch, the English, and the French had begun to join the scramble for rights to the lucrative spice trade. Within a short time, the Dutch appeared to seize the advantage. Formed in 1602, the aggressive and well-financed East India Company (Vereenigde Oost-Indische Compagnie or VOC) soon succeeded in elbowing rivals out of the spice trade and the Dutch began to consolidate their control over the area. On the island of Java, where they established a fort at Batavia (buh-TAY-vee-uh) (today's Jakarta) in 1619, the Dutch found it necessary to bring the inland regions under their control to protect their position. Rather than establishing a formal colony, however, they tried to rule through the local aristocracy. On Java and Sumatra, the VOC established pepper plantations, which became the source of massive profits for Dutch merchants in Amsterdam. Elsewhere they attempted to monopolize the clove trade by limiting cultivation of the crop to one island. By the end of the eighteenth century, the Dutch had succeeded in bringing much of the Indonesian Archipelago under their control. (See Chronology, "The Spice Trade.")

The arrival of the Europeans initially had somewhat less impact on the states of mainland Southeast Asia, where cohesive monarchies in Burma, Thailand (then known as Ayuthaya) (see Image 14.9), and Vietnam (then Dai Viet) vigorously resisted foreign encroachment. Local ruling elites were interested in exploiting trade opportunities, however, and by the seventeenth century several European nations began to compete actively commercial and missionary privileges within the region. As was the case elsewhere, the European powers characteristically began to intervene in local politics, supporting different sides in civil wars in Burma (now Myanmar) and Vietnam as a means of obtaining political and commercial advantage. By the end of the seventeenth century, however, when it became clear that economic opportunities were limited, most European states abandoned

CHRONOLOGY	The Spice Trade	
Vasco da Gama lands at Calicut in southwestern India	1498
Albuquerque establishes base at Goa	1510
Portuguese seize Malacca	1511
Portuguese ships land in southern China	1514
Magellan's voyage around the world	1519–1522
English East India Company established	1600
Dutch East India Company established	1602
English arrive at Surat in northwestern India	1608
Dutch fort established at Batavia	1619

their factories (trading stations) in the area, although some missionaries sought to persevere in their efforts to convert locals to the Christian faith.

14-5b State and Society in Precolonial Southeast Asia

Between 1500 and 1800, Southeast Asia experienced the last flowering of traditional culture before the advent of European rule in the nineteenth century. Although the arrival of the Europeans had an immediate and direct impact in some areas, notably in the Philippines and parts of the Malay world, in most areas Western influence was

William J. Duiker

14.9 The Thai Capital at Ayuthaya. The longest-lasting Thai capital was at Ayuthaya, which was one of the finest cities in Asia from the fourteenth to eighteenth centuries. After the Burmese invasion in 1767, most of Ayuthaya's inhabitants were killed, and all official Thai records were destroyed. Here the remains of some Buddhist stupas, erected in a ceremonial precinct in the center of the city, remind us of the greatness of Thai civilization.

Experience an interactive version of this period in ⁂ MINDTAP still relatively limited. Europeans occasionally dabbled in local politics and commerce, but they generally were not a decisive factor in the evolution of local political or social systems.

Nevertheless, Southeast Asian societies were changing in subtle ways—in their trade patterns, their means of livelihood, and their religious beliefs. In some ways, these changes accentuated the differences between individual states in the region. Yet beneath these differences was an underlying commonality of life for most people. Despite the diversity of cultures and religious beliefs, Southeast Asians were in most respects closer to each other than to peoples outside the region. For the most part, the states and peoples of Southeast Asia were still in control of their own destiny.

Religion and Kingship   During the early modern era, Buddhism and Islam continued to earn the allegiance of most of the population of the states in Southeast Asia, although Christianity began to make some inroads, especially in port cities directly occupied by Europeans and the Philippines. Buddhism was dominant in lowland areas on the mainland from Burma to Vietnam. Muslim influence was prevalent mainly on the Malay Peninsula and along the northern coast of Java and Sumatra, where local traders regularly encountered Muslim merchants from foreign lands. Elsewhere, traditional religious beliefs continued to survive, especially in inland areas, where the local populations either ignored the new doctrines and or integrated them into their habitual forms of spirit worship.

Buddhism and Islam also helped shape Southeast Asian political institutions. The Buddhist style of kingship took shape between the eleventh and the fifteenth centuries as Theravada teachings spread throughout the area. It became the predominant political system in the Buddhist states of mainland Southeast Asia—Burma, Ayuthaya, Laos, and Cambodia. Perhaps the most dominant feature of the Buddhist model was the godlike character of the monarch, who was considered by virtue of his karma to be innately superior to other human beings and served as a link between humans and the cosmos.

On the island of Java, kingship often took the form of a blend of Buddhist and Islamic political traditions. Like their Buddhist counterparts, Javanese monarchs originally possessed a sacred quality and maintained the balance between the sacred and the material world, but as Islam penetrated the Indonesian islands in the fifteenth and sixteenth centuries the monarchs began to lose their semidivine status. On the Malay Peninsula and along the coast of the Indonesian Archipelago, a more purely Islamic model prevailed. In this pattern, the head of state was a sultan, who was viewed as a mortal although he still possessed some magical qualities. The sultan served as a defender of the faith and staffed his bureaucracy mainly with aristocrats, but he also frequently relied on the Muslim community of scholars—the *ulama*—and was expected to rule according to the Shari'a (see Chapter 7). A display in the restored Sultan's Palace in Malacca shows the local sultan sitting on a raised dais before his advisers and assembled guests.

The Economy   During the early period of European penetration, the economy of most Southeast Asian societies was based primarily on agriculture—as it had been for thousands of years. Still, manufacturing and commercial activities were on the rise as the region increasingly served as a focal point in a widespread trading network between East Asia and the Indian Ocean. Agriculture itself was becoming more commercialized as cash crops like sugar and spices replaced subsistence farming in rice or other cereals in some areas. Spices, of course, were the mainstay of the interregional trade, but other products were exchanged as well. Tin (which had been mined in Malaya since the tenth century), copper, gold, tropical fruits and other agricultural products, cloth, gems, and luxury goods were exported in exchange for manufactured goods, ceramics, and high-quality textiles such as silk from China.

Society   In general, Southeast Asians probably enjoyed a higher living standard than most of their contemporaries elsewhere in Asia. Although most of the population was poor by modern Western standards, hunger was not widespread. Several factors help explain this relative prosperity. First, most of Southeast Asia has been blessed by a salubrious climate. Uniformly high temperatures and abundant rainfall led to the proliferation of tropical fruits and enabled farmers to grow as many as two and even three crops of rice each year. Second, although the soil in some areas is poor, the alluvial deltas on the mainland are fertile, and the volcanoes of Indonesia periodically spew forth rich volcanic ash that renews the soil of Sumatra and Java. Finally, with some exceptions, most of Southeast Asia was relatively thinly populated. Only in a few areas such as the Red River Delta in northern Vietnam was overpopulation a serious problem.

Social institutions tended to be fairly homogeneous throughout Southeast Asia. Compared with China and India, there was little social stratification, and the nuclear family predominated. In general, women fared better in the region than elsewhere in Asia. Daughters often had the same inheritance rights as sons, and family property

14.10 The Sultan of Malacca and his Court. Before the conquest of Malacca by the Portuguese in 1511, the city and its surroundings were ruled by a Muslim sultan, who ruled from a spacious palace that has now been restored as a museum. In the display in this illustration, the sultan is seated on a raised dais and attending to official business in the Royal Audience Hall; his advisers and other officials are seated at his feet. It was also in this hall that he greeted visiting merchants as well as emissaries from other countries in the region.

was held jointly between husband and wife. Wives were often permitted to divorce their husbands, and monogamy was the rule rather than the exception. Although women were usually restricted to specialized work such as making ceramics, weaving, and transplanting rice seedlings into the main paddy fields, and they rarely possessed legal rights equal to those of men, they still enjoyed a comparatively high degree of freedom and status in most societies in the region and were sometimes involved in commerce.

CHAPTER SUMMARY

Beginning in the fifteenth century, the pace of international commerce throughout the world increased dramatically. Chinese fleets embarked on several visits to the Indian Ocean while Muslim traders extended their activities into the Spice Islands and sub-Saharan West Africa. Then the Europeans burst onto the world scene. Beginning with the seemingly modest ventures of the Portuguese ships that sailed southward along the West African coast, the process accelerated with the epoch-making voyages of Christopher Columbus to the Americas and Vasco da Gama to the Indian Ocean in the 1490s. Soon several other European states had entered the fray helping to create a global trade network that distributed foodstuffs, textile goods, spices, and precious minerals from one end of the globe to the other.

In less than 300 years, the expansion of the global trade network changed the face of the world. In some areas such as the Americas and the Spice Islands, it led to the destruction of indigenous civilizations and the establishment of European colonies. In others—Africa, South Asia, and mainland Southeast Asia—it left local regimes intact but had a strong impact on local societies and regional trade patterns. In some areas, it led to an irreversible decline in traditional institutions and values, setting in motion a corrosive process that has not been reversed to this day.

At the time, most European observers probably viewed the process in a favorable light. It not only led to an expansion of world trade and foster the exchange of new crops and discoveries between the Old and New Worlds but also introduced Christianity to peoples around the globe. Some modern historians have been much more critical of the process, concluding that European activities during the sixteenth and seventeenth centuries created a "tributary mode of production" based on European profits from unequal terms of trade that foreshadowed the exploitative relationship characteristic of the later colonial period. Other scholars have questioned that contention, however, and argue that although Western commercial operations had a significant impact on global trade patterns, they did not—at least not before the nineteenth century—usher in an era of

dominance over the rest of the world. Muslim merchants were long able to evade European efforts to eliminate them from the spice trade, while local traders, some of them migrants from China and South Asia, dominated commercial activities in many of the port cities within the region. In Africa, the trans-Saharan caravan trade was relatively unaffected by European merchant shipping along the western coast of the continent.

In the meantime, traditional empires continued to hold sway over many of the lands washed by the Muslim faith. Beyond the Himalayas, Chinese emperors in their northern capital of Beijing retained proud dominion over all the vast territory of continental East Asia. In Chapters 16 and 17, we shall deal with these regions and how they confronted the challenges of a changing world.

REFLECTION QUESTIONS

Q What were some of the key features of the Columbian Exchange, and what effects did they have on the world trade network?

Q How did the expansion of European power during the Age of Exploration compare with the expansion of the Islamic empires in the Middle East a few centuries earlier?

Q Why were the Spanish conquistadors able to complete their conquest of Latin America so quickly when their contemporaries failed to do so in Africa and Southeast Asia?

CHAPTER TIMELINE

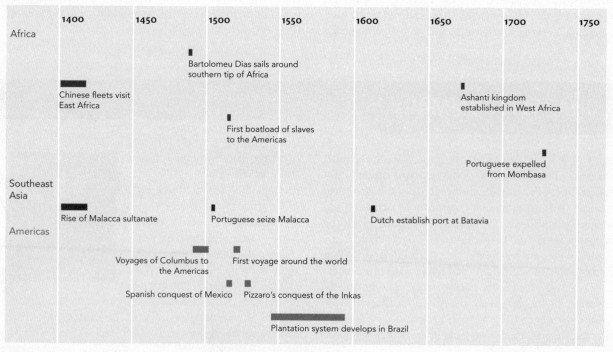

	1400	1450	1500	1550	1600	1650	1700	1750

Africa

Bartolomeu Dias sails around southern tip of Africa

Chinese fleets visit East Africa

Ashanti kingdom established in West Africa

First boatload of slaves to the Americas

Portuguese expelled from Mombasa

Southeast Asia

Rise of Malacca sultanate

Portuguese seize Malacca

Dutch establish port at Batavia

Americas

Voyages of Columbus to the Americas

First voyage around the world

Spanish conquest of Mexico   Pizzaro's conquest of the Inkas

Plantation system develops in Brazil

CHAPTER NOTES

1. From *A Journal of the First Voyage of Vasco da Gama* (London, 1898), cited in J. H. Parry, *The European Reconnaissance: Selected Documents* (New York, 1968), p. 82.
2. H. J. Benda and J. A. Larkin, eds., *The World of Southeast Asia: Selected Historical Readings* (New York, 1967), p. 13.
3. Parry, *European Reconnaissance*, quoting from A. Cortesão, *The Summa Oriental of Tomé Pires*, vol. 2 (London, 1944), pp. 283, 287.
4. Quoted in J. H. Parry, *The Age of Reconnaissance: Discovery, Exploration, and Settlement, 1450 to 1650* (New York, 1963), p. 33.
5. K. N. Chaudhuri, *Trade and Civilization in the Indian Ocean: An Economic History from the Rise of Islam to 1750* (Cambridge, 1985), p. 65.
6. Quoted in Parry, *Age of Reconnaissance*, pp. 176–177.
7. Quoted in M. Leon-Portilla, ed., *The Broken Spears: The Aztec Account of the Conquest of Mexico* (Boston, 1969), p. 51.

MINDTAP
From Cengage

MindTap® is a fully online, highly personalized learning experience built upon Cengage Learning content. MindTap combines student learning tools—readings, multimedia, activities, and assessments—into a singular Learning Path that guides students through the course and helps students develop the critical thinking, analysis, and communication skills that are essential to academic and professional success.

CHAPTER 15

EUROPE TRANSFORMED: REFORM AND STATE BUILDING

Chapter Outline and Focus Questions

Critical Thinking

Q *What was the relationship between European overseas expansion (as traced in Chapter 14) and political, economic, and social developments in Europe?*

Connections to Today

Q *How does the exercise of state power in the seventeenth century compare with the exercise of state power in the twenty-first century? What, if anything, has changed?*

Art Resource, NY

15.1 A Nineteenth-Century Engraving Showing Luther before the Diet of Worms

ON APRIL 18, 1521, A LOWLY MONK stood before the emperor and princes of Germany in the city of Worms (VAWRMZ). He had been called before this august gathering to answer charges of heresy, charges that could threaten his very life. The monk was confronted with a pile of his books and asked if he wished to defend them all or reject a part. Courageously, Martin Luther defended them all and asked to be shown where any part was in error on the basis of "Scripture and plain reason." The emperor was outraged by Luther's response and made his own position clear the next day: "Not only I, but you of this noble German nation, would be forever disgraced if by our negligence not only heresy but the very suspicion of heresy were to survive. After having heard yesterday the obstinate defense of Luther, I regret that I have so long delayed in proceeding against him and his false teaching. I will have no more to do with him." Luther's appearance at Worms set the stage for a serious challenge to the authority of the Catholic Church. This was by no means the first crisis in the church's 1,500-year history, but its consequences were more far-reaching than any one at Worms in 1521 could have imagined.

After the disintegrative patterns of the fourteenth century, Europe began a remarkable recovery that encompassed a revival of arts and letters in the fifteenth century, a period known as the Renaissance, and a religious renaissance in the sixteenth century known as the Reformation. The resulting religious division of Europe (Catholics versus Protestants) was instrumental in beginning a series of wars that dominated much of European history from 1560 to 1650 and exacerbated the economic and social crises besetting the region.

One response to the crises of the seventeenth century was a search for order. The most general trend was an extension of monarchical power as a stabilizing force. This development, which historians have called **absolutism** or *absolute monarchy,* was most evident in France during the flamboyant reign of Louis XIV, regarded by some as the perfect embodiment of an absolute monarch.

But absolutism was not the only response to the search for order in the seventeenth century. Other states such as England reacted quite differently to domestic crises, and another system emerged in which monarchs were limited by the power of their representative assemblies. Absolute and limited monarchy were the two poles of seventeenth-century state building.

15-1 THE REFORMATION OF THE SIXTEENTH CENTURY

 Focus Question: What were the main tenets of Lutheranism, Zwinglianism, and Calvinism, and how did they differ from each other and from Catholicism?

The **Protestant Reformation** is the name given to the religious reform movement that divided the western Christian church into Catholic and Protestant groups. Although the Reformation began with Martin Luther in the early sixteenth century, several earlier developments had set the stage for religious change.

15-1a Background to the Reformation

Changes in the fifteenth century—the age of the Renaissance—helped prepare the way for the dramatic upheavals in sixteenth-century Europe.

The Growth of State Power In the second half of the fifteenth century, attempts had been made to reestablish the centralized power of monarchical governments. To characterize the results, some historians have used the label "Renaissance states"; others have spoken of the "**new monarchies**"—especially those of France, England, and Spain—at the end of the fifteenth century (see Chapter 13).

What was new about these Renaissance monarchs was their concentration of royal authority, their attempts to suppress the nobility, their efforts to control the church in their lands, and their desire to obtain new sources of revenue to increase royal power and enhance the military forces at their disposal. Like the rulers of fifteenth-century Italian states, the Renaissance monarchs were often crafty men obsessed with the acquisition and expansion of political power.

No one gave better expression to the Renaissance preoccupation with political power than Niccolò Machiavelli (nee-koh-LOH mahk-ee-uh-VEL-ee) (1469–1527), an Italian who wrote *The Prince* (1513), one of the most influential works on political power in the Western world. Machiavelli's major concerns in *The Prince* were the acquisition, maintenance, and expansion of political power as the means to restore and maintain order. In the Middle Ages, many political theorists stressed the ethical side of a prince's activity—how a ruler ought to behave based on Christian moral principles. Machiavelli bluntly contradicted this approach: "For the gap between how people actually behave and how they ought to behave is so great that anyone who ignores everyday reality in order to live up to an ideal will soon discover he had been taught how to destroy himself, not how to preserve himself."[1] Machiavelli was among the first Western thinkers to abandon morality as the basis for the analysis of political activity, thus emphasizing the ends justifying the means, or on achieving results regardless of the methods employed.

Social Changes in the Renaissance Social changes in the fifteenth century also helped create an environment in which the Reformation of the sixteenth century could occur. After the severe economic reversals and social upheavals of the fourteenth century, the European economy gradually recovered as manufacturing and trade increased in volume.

As noted in Chapter 12, society in the Middle Ages was divided into three estates: the clergy, or First Estate, whose preeminence was grounded in the belief that people should be guided to spiritual ends; the nobility, or Second Estate, whose privileges rested on the principle that nobles provided security and justice for society; and the peasants and inhabitants of the towns and cities, the Third Estate. Although this social order continued into the Renaissance, some changes also became evident.

Throughout much of Europe, the landholding nobles faced declining real incomes during most of the fourteenth and fifteenth centuries. Many members of the old nobility survived, however, and new blood also infused their ranks. By 1500, the nobles, old and new, who constituted between 2 percent and 3 percent of the population in most countries, still dominated society, as they had done in the Middle Ages, holding important political posts and serving as advisers to the king.

Except in the heavily urban areas of northern Italy and Flanders, peasants made up the overwhelming mass of the Third Estate, constituting 85 percent to 90 percent of the total European population. Serfdom had decreased as the labor dues owed by peasants to their lord were increasingly converted into rents paid in money. By 1500, especially in western Europe, more and more peasants were becoming legally free. At the same time, peasants in many areas resented their social superiors and sought a greater share of the benefits coming from their labor. In the sixteenth century, the grievances of the peasants, especially in Germany, led many of them to support religious reform movements.

Inhabitants of towns and cities, originally merchants and artisans, constituted the remainder of the Third Estate. But by the fifteenth century, the Renaissance town or city had become more complex. At the top of urban society were the patricians, whose wealth from capitalistic enterprises in trade, industry, and banking enabled them to dominate their urban communities economically, socially, and politically. Below them were the petty burghers—the shopkeepers, artisans, guild masters, and guildsmen—who were largely concerned with providing goods and services for local consumption. Below these two groups were the propertyless workers earning pitiful wages and the unemployed, living squalid and miserable lives. These poor city dwellers made up 30 to 40 percent of the urban population. The pitiful conditions of the lower groups in urban society often led them to support calls for radical religious reform in the sixteenth century.

The Impact of Printing

The Renaissance witnessed the development of printing, which made an immediate impact on European intellectual life and thought. Printing from hand-carved wooden blocks had been done in the West since the twelfth century and in China even before that. What was new in the fifteenth century in Europe was multiple printing with movable metal type. The development of printing from movable type was a gradual process that culminated sometime between 1445 and 1450; Johannes Gutenberg (yoh-HAH-nuss GOO-ten-bayrk) of Mainz (MYNTS) played an important role in bringing the process to completion. Gutenberg's Bible, completed in 1455 or 1456, was the first true book produced from movable type.

By 1500, there were more than 1,000 printers in Europe, who collectively had published almost 40,000 titles (between 8 million and 10 million copies).

The printing of books encouraged scholarly research but also stimulated the development of an ever-expanding lay reading public, a development that had an enormous impact on European society. Indeed, the printing press enabled the new religious ideas of the Reformation to spread as rapidly as they did in the sixteenth century. Moreover, printing allowed European civilization to compete for the first time with the civilization of China.

Prelude to Reformation

During the second half of the fifteenth century, the new classical learning of the Italian Renaissance spread to the European countries north of the Alps and spawned a movement called **Christian humanism** or **northern Renaissance humanism**, whose major goal was the reform of Christendom. The Christian humanists believed in the ability of human beings to reason and improve themselves and thought that through education in the sources of classical, and especially Christian, antiquity, they could instill an inner piety or an inward religious feeling that would bring about a reform of the church and society. To change society, then, they believed they must first change the human beings who composed it.

The most influential of all the Christian humanists was Desiderius Erasmus (dez-i-DEER-ee-us i-RAZZ-mus) (1466–1536), who formulated and popularized the reform program of Christian humanism. He called his conception of religion "the philosophy of Christ," by which he meant that Christianity should be a guiding philosophy for the direction of daily life rather than the system of dogmatic beliefs and practices that the medieval church seemed to stress. No doubt his work helped prepare the way for the Reformation; as contemporaries proclaimed, "Erasmus laid the egg that Luther hatched."

Church and Religion on the Eve of the Reformation

Considerable corruption in the Catholic Church was another factor that encouraged people to want reform. Between 1450 and 1520, a series of popes known as the *Renaissance popes* largely failed to meet the church's spiritual needs. The popes were supposed to be the spiritual leaders of the Catholic Church, but as rulers of the Papal States, they were all too often involved in worldly concerns. Julius II (1503–1513), the fiery "warrior pope," personally led armies against his enemies, much to the disgust of pious Christians, who viewed the pope as a spiritual leader. As one intellectual wrote, "How, O bishop standing in the room of the Apostles, dare you teach the people the things that pertain to war?" Many high church officials regarded their church offices mainly as opportunities to advance their careers and wealth, and many ordinary parish priests seemed ignorant of their spiritual duties.

While many leaders of the church were failing to meet their responsibilities, many ordinary people were clamoring for meaningful religious expression and certainty of salvation. As a result, for some the process of salvation became almost mechanical. As more and more people sought certainty of salvation through veneration of **relics** (bones or other objects intimately association with the saints), collections of relics grew. Frederick the Wise, elector of Saxony and Martin Luther's prince, had amassed nearly 19,000 relics to which were attached **indulgences** that could reduce one's time in purgatory by 1,443 years. (An indulgence is a remission, after death, of all or part of the punishment resulting from sin.)

15-1b Martin Luther and the Reformation in Germany

Martin Luther (1483–1546) was a monk and a professor at the University of Wittenberg (VIT-ten-bayrk), where he lectured on the Bible. Probably sometime between 1513 and 1516, through his study of the Bible, he arrived at an answer to a problem—the assurance of salvation—that had disturbed him since his entry into the monastery.

Catholic doctrine had emphasized that both faith and good works were required for a Christian to achieve personal salvation. In Luther's eyes, human beings, weak and powerless in the sight of an almighty God, could never do enough good works to merit salvation. Through his study of the Bible, Luther came to believe that humans are saved not through their good works but through faith in the promises of God, which was made possible by the sacrifice of Jesus on the cross. This doctrine of salvation, or justification by grace through faith alone, became the primary doctrine of the Protestant Reformation (**justification by faith** is the act by which a person is made deserving of salvation). Because Luther had arrived at this doctrine from his study of the Bible, the Bible became for Luther, as for all other Protestants, the chief guide to religious truth.

Luther did not see himself as a revolutionary innovator or a heretic, but he was greatly upset by the widespread selling of indulgences. Especially offensive in his eyes was the monk Johann Tetzel, who hawked indulgences with the slogan: "As soon as the coin in the coffer [money box] rings, the soul from purgatory springs." Greatly angered, in 1517 Luther issued a stunning indictment of the abuses in the sale of indulgences known as the Ninety-Five Theses. Thousands of copies were printed and quickly spread to all parts of Germany.

Unable to accept Luther's ideas, the church excommunicated him in January 1521. He was also summoned to appear before the imperial diet or Reichstag (RYKHSS-tahk) of the Holy Roman Empire convened by the newly elected Emperor Charles V (1519–1556). Ordered to recant the heresies he had espoused, Luther refused and made the famous reply that became the battle cry of the Reformation:

> Unless I am convicted by Scripture and plain reason—I do not accept the authority of popes and councils, for they have contradicted each other—my conscience is captive to the Word of God. I cannot and I will not recant anything, for to go against conscience is neither right nor safe. Here I stand, I cannot do otherwise. God help me. Amen.[2]

Members of the Reichstag were outraged and demanded that Luther be arrested and delivered to the emperor. But Luther's ruler, Elector Frederick of Saxony, stepped in and protected him.

During the next few years, Luther's movement began to grow and spread. As it made an impact on the common people, it also created new challenges. This was especially true when the Peasants' War erupted in 1524. Social discontent created by their pitiful conditions became entangled with religious revolt as the German peasants looked to Martin Luther for support. But when the peasants took up arms and revolted against their landlords, Luther proved to be a conservative on economic and social issues. He turned against the peasants and called on the German princes, who in Luther's eyes were ordained by God to maintain peace and order, to crush the rebels. By May 1525, the German princes had ruthlessly suppressed the peasant hordes. By this time, Luther found himself dependent on the state authorities for the growth of his reformed church.

Luther now succeeded in gaining the support of many of the rulers of the 300 or so German states that made up the Holy Roman Empire. These rulers quickly took control of the churches in their territories. The Lutheran churches in Germany (and later in Scandinavia) became territorial or state churches in which the state supervised the affairs of the church. As part of the development of these state-dominated churches, Luther also instituted new religious services to replace the Catholic Mass. These focused on Bible reading, preaching the word of God, and singing hymns. Following his own denunciation of clerical celibacy, Luther married a former nun, Katherina von Bora, in 1525. Their union provided a model of married and family life for the new Protestant minister.

Politics and Religion in the German Reformation From its very beginning, the fate of Luther's movement was closely tied to political affairs. In 1519, Charles I, king

15.2 A Reformation Woodcut. In the 1520s, after Luther's return to Wittenberg, his teachings began to spread rapidly, ending ultimately in a reform movement supported by state authorities. Pamphlets containing picturesque woodcuts were important in the spread of Luther's ideas. In the woodcut shown here, the crucified Jesus attends Luther's service on the left, while on the right the pope is at a table selling indulgences.

of Spain and the grandson of Emperor Maximilian, was elected Holy Roman emperor as Charles V. As Charles V, he ruled over an immense empire consisting of Spain and its overseas possessions, the traditional Austrian Habsburg lands, Bohemia, Hungary, the Low Countries, and the kingdom of Naples in southern Italy. Politically, Charles wanted to maintain his enormous empire; religiously, he hoped to preserve the unity of his empire in the Catholic faith.

The internal political situation in the Holy Roman Empire was not in Charles's favor, however. Although all the German states owed loyalty to the emperor, in the Middle Ages these states had become quite independent of imperial authority. By the time Charles V was able to bring military forces to Germany in 1546, Lutheranism had become well established, and the Lutheran princes were well organized. Unable to defeat them, Charles was forced to negotiate a truce. In 1555, the Peace of Augsburg (OUKS-boork) formally acknowledged the division of Christianity; Lutheran states were to have the same legal rights as Catholic states. Although the German states were now free to choose between Catholicism and Lutheranism, the peace settlement did not recognize the principle of

religious toleration for individuals. The right of each German ruler to determine the religion of his subjects was accepted, but not the right of the subjects to choose their own religion. With the Peace of Augsburg, what had at first been merely feared was now certain: the ideal of Christian unity was forever lost. The rapid spread of new Protestant groups made this a certainty for all of Europe.

15-1c The Spread of the Protestant Reformation

Switzerland was home to two major Reformation movements: Zwinglianism and Calvinism. Ulrich Zwingli (OOL-rikh TSFING-lee) (1484–1531) was ordained a priest in 1506 and accepted an appointment as a cathedral priest in the Great Minster of Zürich (ZOOR-ik or TSIH-rikh) in 1518. Zwingli's preaching of the Gospel caused such unrest that in 1523 the city council decided to institute evangelical reforms. Relics and images were abolished. All paintings and decorations were removed from the churches and replaced by whitewashed walls. A new liturgy consisting of scripture reading, prayer, and sermons replaced the Mass. Monasticism, pilgrimages, the veneration of saints,

A Reformation Debate: Conflict at Marburg

Religion & Philosophy

DEBATES PLAYED A CRUCIAL ROLE IN THE REFORMATION PERIOD. They were a primary instrument for introducing the Reformation in innumerable cities as well as a means of resolving differences among like-minded Protestant groups. This selection contains an excerpt from the vivacious and often brutal debate between Luther and Zwingli over the sacrament of the Lord's Supper at Marburg in 1529. The two protagonists failed to reach agreement.

The Marburg Colloquy, 1529

The Hessian Chancellor Feige: My gracious prince and lord [Landgrave Philip of Hesse] has summoned you for the express and urgent purpose of settling the dispute over the sacrament of the Lord's Supper.... Let everyone on both sides present his arguments in a spirit of moderation.... Now then, Doctor Luther, you may proceed.

Luther: Noble prince, gracious lord! Undoubtedly the colloquy is well intentioned.... Although I have no intention of changing my mind, which is firmly made up, I will nevertheless present the grounds of my belief and show where the others are in error.... Your basic contentions are these: In the last analysis you wish to prove that a body cannot be in two places at once, and you produce arguments about the unlimited body which are based on natural reason. I do not question how Christ can be God and man and how the two natures can be joined. For God is more powerful than all our ideas, and we must submit to his word. Prove that Christ's body is not there where the Scripture says, "This is my body!" Rational proofs I will not listen to.... It is God who commands, "Take, eat, this is my body." I request, therefore, valid scriptural proof to the contrary.

Zwingli: I insist that the words of the Lord's Supper must be figurative. This is ever apparent, and even required by the article of faith: "taken up into heaven, seated at the right hand of the Father."

Otherwise, it would be absurd to look for him in the Lord's Supper at the same time that Christ is telling us that he is in heaven. One and the same body cannot possibly be in different places. . . .

Luther: I call upon you as before: your basic contentions are shaky. Give way, and give glory to God!

Zwingli: And we call upon you to give glory to God and to quit begging the question! The issue at stake is this: Where is the proof of your position? I am willing to consider your words carefully—no harm meant! You're trying to outwit me. . . . You'll have to sing another tune.

Luther: You're being obnoxious.

Zwingli: (excitedly) Don't you believe that Christ was attempting in John 6 to help those who did not understand?

Luther: You're trying to dominate things! You insist on passing judgment! Leave that to someone else! . . . It is your point that must be proved, not mine. But let us stop this sort of thing. It serves no purpose.

Zwingli: It certainly does! It is for you to prove that the passage in John 6 speaks of a physical repast.

Luther: You express yourself poorly and make about as much progress as a cane standing in a corner. You're going nowhere.

Zwingli: No, no, no! This is the passage that will break your neck!

Luther: Don't be so sure of yourself. Necks don't break this way. You're in Hesse, not Switzerland.

 How did the positions of Zwingli and Luther on the sacrament of the Lord's Supper differ? What was the purpose of this debate? How does this example show why many Reformation debates led to further hostility rather than compromise and unity between religious and sectarian opponents? What implication did this have for the future of the Protestant Reformation?

Source: "The Marburg Colloquy," edited by Donald Ziegler, from *Great Debates of the Reformation*, edited by Donald Ziegler, copyright © 1969 by Donald Ziegler.

clerical celibacy, and the pope's authority were all abolished as remnants of papal Christianity.

As his movement began to spread to other cities in Switzerland, Zwingli sought an alliance with Martin Luther and the German reformers. Although both the German and the Swiss reformers realized the need for unity to defend against the opposition of the Catholic authorities, they were unable to agree on the interpretation of the Lord's Supper, the sacrament of Communion (see Opposing Viewpoints, "A Reformation Debate," above). Zwingli believed that the

Experience an interactive version of this period in **MINDTAP**

scriptural words "This is my body, this is my blood" should be taken figuratively, not literally, and refused to accept Luther's insistence on the real presence of the body and blood of Christ "in, with, and under the bread and wine." In October 1531, war erupted between the Swiss Protestant and Catholic states. Zürich's army was routed, and Zwingli was found wounded on the battlefield. His enemies killed him, cut up his body, burned the pieces, and scattered the ashes. The leadership of Swiss Protestantism now passed to John Calvin, the systematic theologian and organizer of the Protestant movement.

Calvin and Calvinism John Calvin (1509–1564) was educated in his native France, but after converting to Protestantism he was forced to flee to the safety of Switzerland. In 1536, he published the first edition of the *Institutes of the Christian Religion*, a masterful synthesis of Protestant thought that immediately secured his reputation as one of the new leaders of Protestantism.

On most important doctrines, Calvin stood close to Luther. He adhered to the doctrine of justification by faith alone to explain how humans achieved salvation. But Calvin also placed much emphasis on the absolute sovereignty of God or the all-powerful nature of God— what Calvin called the "power, grace, and glory of God." One idea derived from his emphasis on the absolute sovereignty of God—**predestination**—gave a unique cast to Calvin's teachings. This "eternal decree," as Calvin called it, meant that God had predestined some people to be saved (the elect) and others to be damned (the reprobate). According to Calvin, "He has once for all determined, both whom He would admit to salvation, and whom He would condemn to destruction."[3] Although Calvin stressed that there could be no absolute certainty of salvation, his followers did not always make this distinction, and later Calvinists had an unshakable conviction that they were doing God's work on earth, making Calvinism a dynamic and activist faith.

In 1536, Calvin began working to reform the city of Geneva. He was able to fashion a tightly organized church order that employed both clergy and laymen in the service of the church. The Consistory, a special body for enforcing moral discipline, functioned as a court to oversee the moral life, daily behavior, and doctrinal orthodoxy of Genevans and to admonish and correct deviants. Citizens of Geneva were punished for such varied "crimes" as dancing, singing obscene songs, being drunk, swearing, and playing cards.

Calvin's success in Geneva enabled the city to become a vibrant center of Protestantism. Following Calvin's lead, missionaries trained in Geneva were sent to all parts of Europe. Calvinism became established in France, the Netherlands, Scotland, and central and eastern Europe.

15.3 John Calvin. After a conversion experience, John Calvin abandoned his life as a humanist and became a reformer. In 1536, Calvin began working to reform the city of Geneva, where he remained until his death in 1564. This is a seventeenth-century portrait of Calvin done by a member of the Swiss school.

By the mid-sixteenth century, Calvin's Geneva stood as the fortress of the Reformation.

The English Reformation The English Reformation was rooted in politics, not religion. King Henry VIII (1509–1547) had a strong desire to divorce his first wife, Catherine of Aragon, with whom he had a daughter, Mary, but no male heir. The king wanted to marry Anne Boleyn (BUH-lin or buh-LIN), with whom he had fallen in love. Impatient with the pope's unwillingness to grant him an annulment of his marriage, Henry turned to England's own church courts. As archbishop of Canterbury and head of the highest church court in England, Thomas Cranmer ruled in May 1533 that the king's marriage to Catherine was "absolutely void." At the beginning of June, Anne was crowned queen, and three months later, a child was born; much to the king's disappointment, the baby was a girl (the future Queen Elizabeth I).

In 1534, at Henry's request, Parliament moved to finalize the break of the Church of England with Rome. The Act of Supremacy of 1534 declared that the king was "the only supreme head on earth of the Church of England," a position that gave him control of doctrine, clerical appointments, and discipline. Although Henry VIII had broken with the papacy, little change occurred in matters of doctrine, theology, and ceremony. Some of his supporters, including Archbishop Cranmer, sought a religious reformation as well as an administrative one, but Henry was unyielding. When he died in 1547, he was succeeded by his son, the underage and sickly Edward VI (1547–1553). During Edward's reign, Cranmer and others inclined toward Protestant doctrines were able to move the Church of England (or Anglican Church) in a more Protestant direction. New acts of Parliament gave the clergy the right to marry and created a new Protestant church service.

Edward VI was succeeded by Mary (1553–1558), a Catholic who attempted to return England to Catholicism. Her actions aroused much anger, however, especially when "bloody Mary" burned more than 300 Protestant heretics. By the end of Mary's reign, England was more Protestant than it had been at the beginning.

15-1d The Social Impact of the Protestant Reformation

The Protestants were especially important in developing a new view of the family. Because Protestantism had eliminated any idea of special holiness for celibacy and had abolished both monasticism and a celibate clergy, the family could be placed at the center of human life, and a new stress on "mutual love between man and wife" could be extolled (see the Comparative Essay, "Marriage in the Early Modern World," p. 376).

But were doctrine and reality the same? Most often, reality reflected the traditional roles of husband as the ruler and wife as the obedient servant whose chief duty was to please her husband. Luther stated it clearly: "The rule remains with the husband, and the wife is compelled to obey him by God's command. He rules the home and the state, wages war, defends his possessions, tills the soil, builds, plants, etc. The woman on the other hand . . . [looks] after the affairs of the household."[4]

Obedience to her husband was not a wife's only role; her other important duty was to bear children. To Calvin and Luther, this function of women was part of the divine plan; for most Protestant women, family life was their only destiny. Overall, the Protestant Reformation did not noticeably alter women's subordinate place in society.

15-1e The Catholic Reformation

By the mid-sixteenth century, Lutheranism had become established in Germany and Scandinavia and Calvinism in Scotland, Switzerland, France, the Netherlands, and eastern Europe. In England, the split from Rome had resulted in the creation of a national church. The situation in Europe did not look particularly favorable for the Roman Catholic Church. Nevertheless, the Catholic Church underwent a revitalization in the sixteenth century that gave it new strength.

HISTORIANS DEBATE ## 15-1f Catholic Reformation or Counter-Reformation?

But was this revitalization a **Catholic Reformation** or a counter-reformation? Some historians prefer the term *counter-reformation* to focus on the aspects that were a direct reaction against the Protestant movement. Historians who prefer the term *Catholic Reformation* point out that elements of reform were already present in the Catholic Church at the end of the fifteenth century and the beginning of the sixteenth century. Especially noticeable were the calls for reform from the religious orders of the Franciscans, Dominicans, and Augustinians. Members of these groups put particular emphasis on preaching to laypeople. Another example was the Oratory of Divine Love. First organized in Italy in 1497, the Oratory was an informal group of clergy and laymen who worked to foster reform by emphasizing personal spiritual development and outward acts of charity.

No doubt, both positions on the nature of the reformation of the Catholic Church contain elements of truth. The Catholic Reformation revived the best features of medieval Catholicism and then adjusted them to meet new conditions, as is most apparent in the emergence of a new mysticism, closely tied to the traditions of Catholic piety, and the revival of monasticism by the regeneration of older religious orders and the founding of new orders.

The Society of Jesus Of all the new religious orders, the most important was the Society of Jesus, known as the Jesuits, founded by a Spanish nobleman, Ignatius of Loyola (ig-NAY-shuss of loi-OH-luh) (1491–1556). Loyola brought together a small group of individuals who were recognized as a religious order by the pope in 1540. The new order was grounded on the principles of absolute obedience to the papacy, a strict hierarchical order for the society, the use of education to achieve its goals, and a dedication to engage in "conflict for God." A special vow of absolute obedience to the pope made the Jesuits an important instrument for papal policy. Jesuit missionaries proved

Marriage in the Early Modern World

Family & Society

Marriage is an ancient institution. In China, myths about the beginnings of Chinese civilization maintained that the rites of marriage began with the primordial couple Fuxi and Nugun and that these rites actually preceded such discoveries as fire, farming, and medicine. In the early modern world, family and marriage were inseparable and at the center of all civilizations.

During this period, the family was still at the heart of Europe's social organization. For the most part, people viewed the family in traditional terms as a patriarchal institution in which the husband dominated his wife and children. The upper classes in particular thought of the family as a "house," an association whose collective interests were more important than those of its individual members. Parents (especially fathers) generally selected marriage partners for their children based on the interests of the family. When the son of a French noble asked about his upcoming marriage, the father responded, "Mind your own business." Details were worked out well in advance, sometimes when children were only two or three years old, and were set out in a legally binding contract. An important negotiating point was the size of the dowry, money presented by the wife's family to the groom upon marriage. The dowry could be a large sum, and all families were expected to provide dowries for their daughters.

Arranged marriages were not unique to Europe but were common throughout the world. In China, marriages were normally arranged for the benefit of the family, and the groom and bride were usually not consulted. Frequently, they did not meet until the marriage ceremony. Love was obviously not a reason for marriage and in fact was often viewed as a detriment because it could distract the married couple from their responsibility to the larger family unit. In Japan, too, marriages were arranged, often by the heads of dominant families in rural areas, and the new wife moved in with the family of her husband. In India, marriages were not only arranged but also not uncommon for women before age ten. In colonial Latin America, parents selected marriage partners for their children. In many areas, before members of the lower classes could marry, they had to offer gifts to the powerful noble landlords in the region and obtain their permission. These nobles often refused to allow women to marry in order to keep them as servants.

15.4a   15.4b

Iberfoto/Iberfoto/Superstock

The Granger Collection, NYC

15.4 Marriage Ceremonies. Image 15.4a is a detail of a marriage ceremony in Italy from a fresco painted by Dominico di Bartolo in 1443. Image 15.4b is a seventeenth-century Mughal painting showing Shah Jahan, the Mughal emperor (with halo). He is riding to the wedding celebration of his son, who rides before him.

Arranged marriages were the logical result of a social system in which men dominated and women's primary role was to bear children, manage the household, and work in the fields. Not until the nineteenth century did a feminist movement emerge in Europe to improve the rights of women. By the beginning of the twentieth century, that movement had spread to other parts of the world. The New Culture Movement in China, for example, advocated the free choice of spouses. Although the trend throughout the world is toward allowing people to choose their mates, in some places, especially in rural communities, families continue to play an active role in selecting marriage partners.

 In what ways were marriage practices similar in the West and East during the early modern period? Were there any significant differences?

singularly successful in restoring Catholicism to parts of Germany and eastern Europe.

Another prominent Jesuit activity was the propagation of the Catholic faith among non-Christians. Francis Xavier (ZAY-vee-ur) (1506–1552), one of the original members of the Society of Jesus, carried the message of Catholic Christianity to the East. After attracting tens of thousands of converts in India, he traveled to Japan in 1549. He spoke highly of the Japanese: "They are a people of excellent morals—good in general and not malicious."[5] Thousands of Japanese, especially in the southernmost islands, became Christians. Although conversion efforts in Japan proved short lived, Jesuit activity in China was longer lasting. The Jesuits attempted to draw parallels between Christian and Confucian concepts and to show the similarities between Christian morality and Confucian ethics. For their part, the missionaries were much impressed with many aspects of Chinese civilization, and reports of their experiences heightened European curiosity about this great society on the other side of the world.

The Jesuits were also determined to carry the Catholic banner and fight Protestantism. Jesuit missionaries succeeded in restoring Catholicism to parts of Germany and eastern Europe. Poland was largely won back for the Catholic Church through Jesuit efforts.

A Reformed Papacy A reformed papacy was another important factor in the development of the Catholic Reformation. The involvement of Renaissance popes in dubious finances and Italian political and military affairs had created numerous sources of corruption. It took the jolt of the Protestant Reformation to bring about serious reform. Pope Paul III (1534–1549) perceived the need for change and took the audacious step of appointing a reform commission to ascertain the church's ills. The commission's report in 1537 blamed the church's problems on the corrupt policies of popes and cardinals. Paul III also formally recognized the Jesuits and summoned the Council of Trent.

The Council of Trent In March 1545, a group of high church officials met in the city of Trent on the border between Germany and Italy and initiated the Council of Trent, which met intermittently from 1545 to 1563 in three major sessions. The final decrees of the council reaffirmed traditional Catholic teachings in opposition to Protestant beliefs. Scripture and tradition were affirmed as equal authorities in religious matters; only the church could interpret scripture. Both faith and good works were declared necessary for salvation. Belief in purgatory and in the use of indulgences was strengthened, although the selling of indulgences was prohibited.

After the Council of Trent, the Roman Catholic Church possessed a clear body of doctrine and a unified structure under the acknowledged supremacy of the popes. Although it had become one Christian denomination among many, the church entered a new phase of its history with a spirit of confidence.

15-2 EUROPE IN CRISIS, 1560–1650

 Focus Question: Why is the period between 1560 and 1650 in Europe considered an age of crisis?

Between 1560 and 1650, Europe experienced religious wars, revolutions and constitutional crises, economic and social disintegration, and a witchcraft craze. It was truly an age of crisis.

15-2a Politics and the Wars of Religion in the Sixteenth Century

By 1560, Calvinism and Catholicism had become activist religions dedicated to spreading the word of God as they interpreted it. Although their struggle for the minds and hearts of Europeans was at the center of the religious wars of the sixteenth century, economic, social, and political forces also played important roles in these conflicts.

The French Wars of Religion (1562–1598) Religion was central to the French civil wars of the sixteenth century. The growth of Calvinism had led to persecution by the French kings, but the latter did little to stop the spread of Calvinism. Huguenots (HYOO-guh-nots) (as the French Calvinists were called) constituted only some 7 percent of the population, but 40 percent to 50 percent of the French nobility became Huguenots, including the house of Bourbon (boor-BOHN), which stood next to the Valois (val-WAH) in the royal line of succession. The conversion of so many nobles made the Huguenots a potentially dangerous political threat to monarchical power. Still, the Calvinist minority was greatly outnumbered by the Catholic majority, and the Valois monarchy was staunchly Catholic.

For thirty years, battles raged in France between Catholic and Calvinist parties. Finally, in 1589, Henry of Navarre, the political leader of the Huguenots and a member of the Bourbon Dynasty, succeeded to the throne as Henry IV (1589–1610). Realizing, however, that he would never be accepted by Catholic France, Henry converted to Catholicism. With his coronation in 1594, the wars of religion had finally come to an end. The Edict of Nantes (NAHNT) in 1598 solved the religious problem by acknowledging Catholicism as the official religion of France while guaranteeing the Huguenots the right to worship and to enjoy all political privileges, including the holding of public offices.

Philip II and Militant Catholicism The greatest advocate of militant Catholicism in the second half of the sixteenth century was King Philip II of Spain (1556–1598), the son and heir of Charles V. Philip's reign ushered in an age of Spanish greatness, both politically and culturally. Philip II had inherited from his father Spain, the Netherlands, and possessions in Italy and the Americas. To strengthen his control, Philip insisted on strict conformity to Catholicism and strong monarchical authority. Achieving the latter was not an easy task, because each of the lands of his empire had its own structure of government.

Philip's attempt to strengthen his control over the Spanish Netherlands, which consisted of seventeen provinces (modern-day Netherlands and Belgium), soon led to a revolt. The nobles, who stood to lose the most politically, strongly opposed Philip's efforts. Religion also became a major catalyst for rebellion when Philip attempted to crush Calvinism. Violence erupted in 1566, and the revolt became organized, especially in the northern provinces, where the Dutch, under the leadership of William of Nassau, the prince of Orange, offered growing resistance. The struggle dragged on for decades until 1609, when the war ended with a twelve-year truce that virtually recognized the independence of the northern provinces. These seven northern provinces, which called

themselves the United Provinces of the Netherlands, became the core of the modern Dutch state. Spain continued to play the role of a great power, but much power had shifted to England.

The England of Elizabeth When Elizabeth Tudor, the daughter of Henry VIII and Anne Boleyn, ascended the throne in 1558, England was home to fewer than 4 million people. Yet during her reign (1558–1603), the small island kingdom became the leader of the Protestant nations of Europe and laid the foundations for a world empire.

Intelligent, cautious, and self-confident, Elizabeth moved quickly to solve the difficult religious problem she inherited from her half-sister, Queen Mary. She repealed the Catholic laws of Mary's reign, and a new Act of Supremacy designated Elizabeth as "the only supreme governor" of both church and state. The Church of England under Elizabeth was basically Protestant, but it was of a moderate bent that kept most people satisfied.

Elizabeth proved as adept in government and foreign policy as in religious affairs. Assisted by competent officials, she handled Parliament with considerable skill. Caution and moderation also dictated Elizabeth's foreign policy. Nevertheless, Elizabeth was gradually drawn into conflict with Spain. Having resisted for years the idea of invading England as too impractical, Philip II of Spain was finally persuaded to do so by advisers who assured him that the people of England would rise against their queen when the Spaniards arrived. A successful invasion of England would mean the overthrow of heresy and the return of England to Catholicism. Philip ordered preparations for a fleet of warships, the *armada*, to spearhead the invasion of England.

The armada was a disaster. The Spanish fleet that finally set sail had neither the ships nor the manpower that Philip had planned to send. Battered by several encounters with British ships in the English Channel, the Spanish fleet sailed back to Spain by a northward route around Scotland and Ireland, where it was further pounded by storms.

15-2b Economic and Social Crises

The period of European history from 1560 to 1650 witnessed severe economic and social crises as well as political upheaval. Economic contraction began to be evident in some parts of Europe by the 1620s. In the 1630s and 1640s, as imports of silver from the Americas declined, economic recession intensified, especially in the Mediterranean area. Once the industrial and financial center of Europe in the age of the Renaissance, Italy was now facing economic difficulties.

Population Decline Population trends of the sixteenth and seventeenth centuries also reveal Europe's worsening

15.5 **Procession of Queen Elizabeth I.** Intelligent and learned, Elizabeth Tudor was familiar with Latin and Greek and spoke several European languages. Served by able administrators, Elizabeth ruled for nearly forty-five years and generally avoided open military action against any major power. This painting done near the end of her reign shows the queen in a ceremonial procession.

conditions. The population of Europe increased from 60 million in 1500 to 85 million by 1600, the first major recovery of the European population since the devastation of the Black Death in the mid-fourteenth century. By 1650, however, records indicate a decline in the population, especially in central and southern Europe. Europe's long-time adversaries—war, famine, and plague—continued to affect population levels. These problems created social tensions, some of which were manifested in an obsession with witches.

Witchcraft Mania Hysteria over witchcraft affected the lives of many Europeans in the sixteenth and seventeenth centuries. Perhaps more than 100,000 people were prosecuted throughout Europe on charges of witchcraft. As more and more people were brought to trial, the fear of witches, as well as the fear of being accused of witchcraft, escalated to frightening levels (see Historical Voices, "A Witchcraft Trial in France," p. 380).

Common people—usually those who were poor and without property—were more likely to be accused of

witchcraft. Indeed, where lists are given, those mentioned most often are milkmaids, peasant women, and servant girls. In the witchcraft trials of the sixteenth and seventeenth centuries, more than 75 percent of the accused were women, most of them single or widowed and many fifty years of age and older.

That women were most often the victims of the witch hunt has led some scholars to argue that the witch hunt was really a woman hunt or "genderized mass murder," arguing that men hunted witches because they caused disorder and were sexual beings in a patriarchal society. Other scholars have rejected this approach and argue first that men were also accused of witchcraft and second that women accused other women of witchcraft. These scholars believe that people in the sixteenth and seventeenth century believed in witchcraft as a constant threat in their society.

Despite scholarly differences about the nature of the witch hunts, there is no doubt that women were the primary victims. Current estimates are that there were 100,000 to 110,000 witch trials between 1450 and 1750

A Witchcraft Trial in France

Art & Ideas

PERSECUTIONS FOR WITCHCRAFT reached their high point in the sixteenth and seventeenth centuries, when tens of thousands of people were brought to trial. In this excerpt from the minutes of a trial in France in 1652, we can see why the accused witch stood little chance of exonerating herself.

The Trial of Suzanne Gaudry

28 May, 1652. . . . Interrogation of Suzanne Gaudry, prisoner at the court of Rieux. . . . [During interrogations on May 28 and May 29, the prisoner confessed to a number of activities involving the devil.]

Deliberation of the Court—June 3, 1652

The undersigned advocates of the Court have seen these interrogations and answers. They say that the aforementioned Suzanne Gaudry confesses that she is a witch, that she had given herself to the devil, that she had renounced God, Lent, and baptism, that she has been marked on the shoulder, that she has cohabited with the devil and that she has been to the dances, . . .

Third Interrogation, June 27

This prisoner being led into the chamber, she was examined to know if things were not as she had said and confessed at the beginning of her imprisonment.

—Answers no, and that what she has said was done so by force.

Pressed to say the truth, that otherwise she would be subjected to torture . . .

—Answers that she is not a witch. . . .

She was placed in the hands of the officer in charge of torture . . .

The Torture

On this same day, being at the place of torture.

This prisoner, before being strapped down, was admonished to maintain herself in her first confessions . . . .

—Says that she denies everything she has said, ...

Feeling herself being strapped down, says that she is not a witch, . . . and being a little stretched [on the rack] screams ceaselessly that she is not a witch.

Asked if she did not confess that she had been a witch for twenty-six years.

—Says that she said it, that she retracts it, crying that she is not a witch . . . .

The mark having been probed by the officer, . . . it was adjudged by the aforesaid doctor and officer truly to be the mark of the devil.

Being more tightly stretched upon the torture rack, urged to maintain her confessions.

—Said that it was true that she is a witch. . . . Asked how long she has been in subjugation to the devil.

—Answers that it was twenty years ago that the devil appeared to her, being in her lodgings in the form of a man dressed in a little cowhide and black breeches. . . .

Verdict

July 9, 1652. In the light of the interrogations, answers, and investigations made into the charge against Suzanne Gaudry, . . . seeing by her own confessions that she is said to have made a pact with the devil, received the mark from him, . . . and that following this, she . . . had let herself be known carnally by him, in which she received satisfaction. Also, seeing that she is said to have been a part of nocturnal carols and dances.

For expiation of which the advice of the undersigned is that the office of Rieux can legitimately condemn the aforesaid Suzanne Gaudry to death, tying her to a gallows, and strangling her to death, then burning her body and burying it here in the environs of the woods.

 Why were women, particularly older women, especially vulnerable to accusations of witchcraft? What "proofs" are offered here that Suzanne Gaudry had consorted with the devil? What does this account tell us about the spread of witchcraft persecutions in the seventeenth century?

Source: A. Kors and E. Peters, eds., *Witchcraft in Europe, 1100–1700: A Documentary History* (Philadelphia: The University of Pennsylvania Press, 1972).

with about 50 percent of the trials leading to executions. Of those executed, 75 percent to 80 percent were women, many of them older women.

That women should be the chief victims of witchcraft trials was hardly accidental. To one witchcraft judge in France it came as no surprise that witches would confess to sexual experiences with Satan: "The Devil uses them so, because he knows that women love carnal pleasures, and he means to bind them to his allegiance by such agreeable provocations."[6]

By the mid-seventeenth century the witchcraft hysteria had begun to subside. As governments grew stronger, fewer magistrates were willing to accept the unsettling and divisive conditions generated by the trials of witches. Moreover, by the beginning of the eighteenth century, more and more people were questioning altogether their old attitudes toward religion and found it especially contrary to reason to believe in the old view of a world haunted by evil spirits.

Economic Trends in the Seventeenth Century In the course of the seventeenth century, new economic trends also emerged. Historians refer to the economic practices of the seventeenth century as **mercantilism**. According to the mercantilists, the prosperity of a nation depended on a plentiful supply of bullion (gold and silver). For this reason, it was desirable to achieve a favorable balance of trade in which goods exported were of greater value than those imported, promoting an influx of gold and silver payments that would increase the quantity of bullion. Furthermore, to encourage exports, governments should stimulate and protect export industries and trade by granting trade monopolies, encouraging investment in new industries through subsidies, and improving transportation systems by building roads, bridges, and canals. By placing high tariffs on foreign goods, a government could reduce imports and prevent them from competing with domestic industries. Colonies were also deemed valuable as sources of raw materials and markets for finished goods.

Mercantilist theory on the role of colonies was matched in practice by Europe's overseas expansion. With the development of colonies and trading posts in the Americas and the East, Europeans embarked on an adventure in international commerce in the seventeenth century. Although some historians speak of a nascent world economy, we should remember that local, regional, and intra-European trade still predominated. What made the transoceanic trade rewarding, however, was not the volume of goods but their value. Dutch, English, and French merchants were bringing back products that were still consumed largely by the wealthy but were beginning to make their

way into the lives of artisans and merchants. Pepper and spices from the Indies, West Indian and Brazilian sugar, and Asian coffee and tea were becoming more readily available to European consumers.

Despite the growth of capitalism, most of the European economy still depended on an agricultural system that had experienced few changes since the thirteenth century. At least 80 percent of Europeans still worked on the land. Almost all of the peasants of western Europe were free of serfdom, although many saw little or no improvement in their lot as they faced increased rents and fees and higher taxes imposed by the state.

15-2c Seventeenth-Century Crises: Revolution and War

During the first half of the seventeenth century, a series of rebellions and civil wars rocked the domestic stability of many European governments. A devastating war that affected much of Europe also added to the sense of crisis.

The Thirty Years' War (1618–1648) The Thirty Years' War began in 1618 in the Germanic lands of the Holy Roman Empire as a struggle between Catholic forces, led by the Habsburg Holy Roman emperors, and Protestant—primarily Calvinist—nobles in Bohemia who rebelled against Habsburg authority (see Map 15.1). What began as a struggle over religious issues soon became a wider conflict perpetuated by political motivations as both minor and major European powers—Denmark, Sweden, France, and Spain—entered the war. The competition for European leadership between the Bourbon Dynasty of France and the Habsburg Dynasties of Spain and the Holy Roman Empire was an especially important factor. Nevertheless, most of the battles were fought on German soil, with considerable damage. The Thirty Years' War was undoubtedly the most destructive conflict Europe had yet experienced (see Historical Voices, "The Destruction of Magdeburg in the Thirty Years' War," p. 383).

The war in Germany was officially ended in 1648 by the Peace of Westphalia, which proclaimed that all German states, including the Calvinist ones, were free to determine their own religion. The major contenders gained new territories, and France emerged as the dominant nation in Europe. The more than 300 entities that made up the Holy Roman Empire were recognized as independent states, and each was given the power to conduct its own foreign policy; this brought an end to the Holy Roman Empire and ensured German disunity for another 200 years. The Peace of Westphalia made it clear that political motives, not religious convictions, had become the guiding force in public affairs.

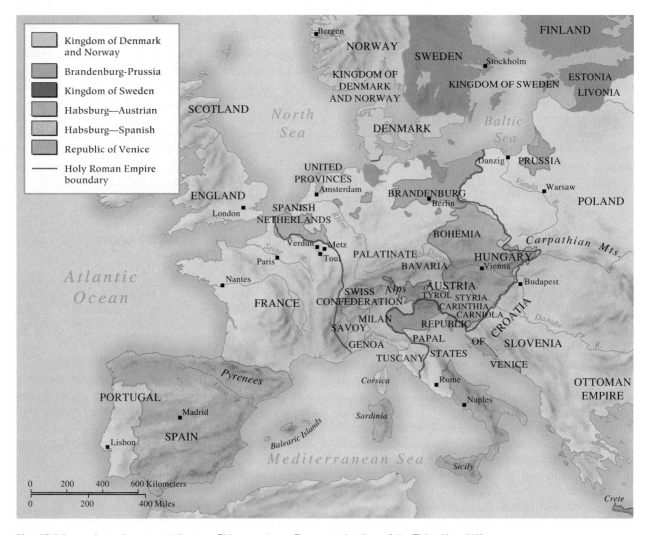

Map 15.1 Europe in the Seventeenth Century. This map shows Europe at the time of the Thirty Years' War (1618–1648). Although the struggle began in Bohemia and much of the fighting took place in the Germanic lands of the Holy Roman Empire, the conflict became a continent-wide struggle.

 Which countries engaged in the war were predominantly Protestant, which were Catholic, and which were mixed?

HISTORIANS DEBATE

15-2d Was There a Military Revolution?

By the seventeenth century, war was playing an increasingly important role in European affairs. Military power was considered essential to a ruler's reputation and power, so the pressure to build an effective military machine was intense. Some historians believe that the changes that occurred in the science of warfare between 1560 and 1650 constituted a military revolution. Other historians have questioned the use of the phrase "military revolution" to describe the military changes from 1560 to 1660, arguing instead that military developments were gradual. In any

case, for the rest of the seventeenth century, warfare continued to change.

These changes included increased use of firearms and cannons, greater flexibility and mobility in tactics, and better-disciplined and better-trained armies. These innovations necessitated standing armies, based partly on conscription, which grew ever larger and more expensive as the seventeenth century progressed. Such armies could be maintained only by levying heavier taxes, making war an economic burden and an ever more important part of the early modern European state. The creation of large bureaucracies to supervise the military resources of the state contributed to the growth in the power of governments.

The Destruction of Magdeburg in the Thirty Years' War

Politics & Government **AFTER KING GUSTAVUS ADOLPHUS OF SWEDEN** entered the war, he was finally joined by German Protestant forces after the fall of the Protestant city of Magdeburg to the imperial forces. In the excerpt below, a writer of this period gives a vivid description of what happened to Magdeburg and its inhabitant.

An Account of the Destruction of Magdeburg

Thus it came about that the city and all its inhabitants fell into the hands of the enemy, whose violence and cruelty were due in part to their common hatred of the adherents of the Augsburg Confession [Lutherans], and in part to their being embittered by the chain shot which had been fired at them and by the derision and insults that the Magdeburgers had heaped upon them from the ramparts.

Then was there naught but beating and burning, plundering, torture, and murder. Most especially was every one of the enemy bent on securing much booty. When a marauding party entered a house, if its master had anything to give he might thereby purchase respite and protection for himself and his family till the next man, who also wanted something should come along. It was only when everything had been brought forth and there was nothing left to give that the real trouble commenced. Then, what with blows and threats of shooting, stabbing, and hanging, the poor people were so terrified that if they had had anything left they would have brought it forth if it had been buried in the earth or hidden away in a thousand castles. In this frenzied rage, the great and splendid city that had stood like a fair princess in the land was now, in its hour of direct need and unutterable distress

and woe, given over to the flames, and thousands of innocent men, women, and children, in the midst of a horrible din of heartrending shrieks and cries, were tortured and put to death in so cruel and shameful a manner that no words would suffice to describe, nor no tears to bewail it. . . .

Thus, in a single day this noble and famous city, the pride of the whole country, went up in fire and smoke; and the remnant of its citizens, with their wives and children, were taken prisoner and driven away by the enemy with a noise of weeping and wailing that could be heard from afar, while the cinders and ashes from the town were carried by the wind to . . . distant places. . . .

In addition to all this, quantities of sumptuous and irreplaceable house furnishings and movable property of all kinds, such as books, manuscripts, paintings, memorials of all sorts . . . which money could not buy, were either burned or carried away by the soldiers as booty. The most magnificent garments, hangings, silk stuffs, gold and silver lace, linen of all sorts, and other household goods were bought by the army sutlers for a mere song and peddled about the by cart load all throughout the archbishopric of Magdeburg. . . . Gold chains and rings, jewels, and every kind of gold and silver utensils were to be bought from the common soldiers for a tenth of their real value. . . .

 What does this document reveal about the effect of war on ordinary Europeans? Compare this description with the descriptions of the treatment of civilians in other wars. Does this author exaggerate, or is this description similar to the others?

Source: James Harvey Robinson, *Readings in European History*, Vol. 2 (Boston: Ginn and Company, 1906), pp. 211–212.

15-3 RESPONSE TO CRISIS: THE PRACTICE OF ABSOLUTISM

 Focus Question: What was absolutism, and what were the main characteristics of the absolute monarchies that emerged in France, Prussia, Austria, and Russia?

Many people responded to the crises of the seventeenth century by searching for order. An increase in monarchical power became an obvious means for achieving stability. The result was what historians have called *absolutism*

or *absolute monarchy* in which the sovereign power or ultimate authority in the state rested in the hands of a king who claimed to rule by divine right—the idea that kings received their power from God and were responsible to no one but God. Late-sixteenth-century political theorists believed that sovereign power consisted of the authority to make laws, levy taxes, administer justice, control the state's administrative system, and determine foreign policy.

15-3a France Under Louis XIV

France during the reign of Louis XIV (1643–1715) has traditionally been regarded as the best example of the

Sun Kings, West and East

Politics & Government   **AT THE END OF THE SEVENTEENTH CENTURY,** two powerful rulers held sway in kingdoms that dominated the affairs of the regions around them. Both rulers saw themselves as favored by divine authority—Louis XIV of France as a divine-right monarch and Kangxi (GANG-zhee) of China as possessing the Mandate of Heaven. Thus, both rulers saw themselves not as divine beings but as divinely ordained beings whose job was to govern organized societies. In Image 15.6a, Louis, who ruled France from 1643 to 1715, is seen in a portrait by Hyacinthe Rigaud (ee-ah-SANT ree-GOH) that captures the king's sense of royal dignity

and grandeur. One person at court said of the king: "Louis XIV's vanity was without limit or restraint." In Image 15.6b, Kangxi, who ruled China from 1661 to 1722, is seen in a portrait that shows him seated in majesty on his imperial throne. A dedicated ruler, Kangxi once wrote, "One act of negligence may cause sorrow all through the country, and one moment of negligence may result in trouble for hundreds and thousands of generations."

Q *Although these rulers practiced profoundly different religions, are there any differences or similarities in the way they justify their power?*

15.6a

15.6b

RMN-Grand Palais/Art Resource, NY

Hu Weibiao/Panorama/The Image Works

practice of absolute or **divine-right monarchy** in the seventeenth century (see the Comparative Illustration, "Sun Kings, West and East," above). French culture, language, and manners reached into all levels of European society. French diplomacy and wars overwhelmed the political affairs of western and central Europe. The court of Louis XIV seemed to be imitated everywhere in Europe.

Political Institutions   One key to Louis's power was his ability to control the central policy-making machinery of government because it was part of his own court and household. The royal court, located in the magnificent palace at Versailles (vayr-SY), served three purposes simultaneously: it was the personal household of the king, the location of central governmental machinery, and the place where powerful subjects came to find favors and offices for themselves and their clients. The greatest danger to Louis's personal rule came from the highest nobles and princes of the blood (the royal princes), who considered it natural to assert the policy-making role of royal ministers. Louis eliminated this threat by removing them from the royal council, the chief administrative body of the king, and enticing them to his court at Versailles, where he could keep them preoccupied with court life and out of politics. Instead of the high nobility and royal princes, Louis relied for his ministers on nobles who came from relatively new aristocratic families. His ministers were expected to be subservient: "I had no intention of sharing my authority with them," Louis said.

Louis's domination of his ministers and secretaries gave him control of the central policy-making machinery of government and thus authority over the traditional areas of monarchical power: the formulation of foreign policy, the making of war and peace, the assertion of the secular power of the crown against any religious authority, and the ability to levy taxes to fulfill these functions. Louis had considerably less success with the internal administration of the kingdom, however.

The Economy and the Military   The cost of building palaces, maintaining his court, and pursuing his wars made finances a crucial issue for Louis XIV. He was most fortunate in having the services of Jean-Baptiste Colbert (ZHAHN-bap-TEEST kohl-BAYR) (1619–1683) as controller general of finances. Colbert sought to increase the wealth and power of France by generally adhering to mercantilism. To decrease imports and increase exports, Colbert granted subsidies to individuals who established new industries. To improve communications and the transportation of goods internally, he built roads and canals. To decrease imports directly, Colbert raised tariffs on foreign goods.

The increase in royal power that Louis pursued led the king to develop a professional army numbering 100,000 men in peacetime and 400,000 in time of war. To achieve the prestige and military glory befitting an absolute monarch as well as to ensure the domination of his Bourbon Dynasty over European affairs, Louis waged four wars between 1667 and 1713. His ambitions roused much of Europe to form coalitions that were determined to prevent the certain destruction of the European balance of power by Bourbon hegemony. Although Louis added some

territory to France's northeastern frontier and established a member of his own Bourbon Dynasty on the throne of Spain, he also left France impoverished and surrounded by enemies.

15-3b Absolutism in Central and Eastern Europe

During the seventeenth century, a development of great importance for the modern Western world took place with the appearance in central and eastern Europe of three new powers: Prussia, Austria, and Russia.

Prussia   Frederick William the Great Elector (1640–1688) laid the foundation for the Prussian state. Realizing that the land he had inherited— Brandenburg-Prussia— was a small, open territory with no natural frontiers for defense, Frederick William built an army of 40,000 men, the fourth largest in Europe. To sustain this force, he established the General War Commissariat to levy taxes for the army and oversee its growth. The commissariat soon evolved into an agency for civil government as well. The new bureaucratic machine became the elector's chief instrument for governing the state. Many of its officials were members of the Prussian landed aristocracy, the Junkers (YOONG-kers), who also served as officers in the all-important army.

In 1701, Frederick William's son Frederick (1688–1713) officially gained the title of king. Elector Frederick III became King Frederick I, and Brandenburg-Prussia simply Prussia. In the eighteenth century, Prussia emerged as a great power in Europe.

Austria   The Austrian Habsburgs had long played a significant role in European politics as Holy Roman emperors, but their hopes of creating an empire in Germany had been dashed by the end of the Thirty Years' War. In the seventeenth century, the house of Austria created a new empire in eastern and southeastern Europe.

The nucleus of the new Austrian Empire remained the traditional Austrian hereditary possessions: Lower and Upper Austria, Carinthia, Carniola, Styria, and Tyrol. To these had been added the kingdom of Bohemia and parts of northwestern Hungary. After the defeat of the Turks in 1687 (see Chapter 16), Austria took control of all of Hungary, Transylvania, Croatia, and Slovenia, thus establishing the Austrian Empire in southeastern Europe. By the beginning of the eighteenth century, the house of Austria had assembled an empire of considerable size.

The Austrian monarchy, however, never became a highly centralized, absolutist state, primarily because it contained so many different national groups. The Austrian Empire remained a collection of territories held together by the Habsburg emperor, who was archduke of Austria, king of Bohemia, and king of Hungary. Each of these regions had its own laws and political life.

From Muscovy to Russia A new Russian state had emerged in the fifteenth century under the leadership of the Principality of Muscovy and its grand dukes. In the sixteenth century, Ivan IV (1533–1584) became the first ruler to take the title of *tsar* (the Russian word for *Caesar*). When Ivan's dynasty came to an end in 1598, it was followed by a period of anarchy that did not end until the Zemsky Sobor (ZEM-skee suh-BOR), or national assembly, chose Michael Romanov (ROH-muh-nahf) as the new tsar, establishing a dynasty that lasted more than 300 years. One of its most prominent members was Peter the Great.

Peter the Great (1689–1725) was an unusual character. A towering, strong man at six feet nine inches tall, he enjoyed a low kind of humor—belching contests and crude jokes—and vicious punishments, including floggings, impalings, and roastings. Peter got a firsthand view of the West when he made a trip there in 1697–1698, and he returned to Russia with a firm determination to westernize or Europeanize Russia. He was especially eager to borrow European technology to create the army and navy he needed to make Russia a great power.

As could be expected, one of Peter's first priorities was the reorganization of the army and the creation of a navy. Employing both Russians and Europeans as officers, he conscripted peasants for 25-year stints of service to build a standing army of 210,000 men and at the same time formed the first-ever Russian navy.

To impose the rule of the central government more effectively throughout the land, Peter divided Russia into provinces. Although he hoped to create a well-ordered community governed in accordance with law, few of his bureaucrats shared his concept of loyalty to the state. Peter hoped to evoke a sense of civic duty among his people, but his own forceful personality created an atmosphere of fear that prevented any such sentiment.

The object of Peter's domestic reforms was to make Russia into a great state and military power. His primary goal was to "open a window to the west," meaning an ice-free port easily accessible to Europe. This could only be achieved on the Baltic, but at that time, the Baltic coast was controlled by Sweden, the most important power in northern Europe. A long and hard-fought war with Sweden won Peter the lands he sought. In 1703, Peter began the construction of a new city, St. Petersburg, his window to the west and a symbol that Russia was looking

westward to Europe. Under Peter, Russia became a great military power and an important European state by his death in 1725.

15-4 ENGLAND AND LIMITED MONARCHY

 Focus Question: How and why did England avoid the path of absolutism?

Not all states were absolutist in the seventeenth century. One prominent example of resistance to absolute monarchy came in England, where king and Parliament struggled to determine the roles each should play in governing England.

15-4a Conflict Between King and Parliament

With the death of Queen Elizabeth I in 1603, the Tudor Dynasty became extinct, and the Stuart line of rulers was inaugurated with the accession to the throne of Elizabeth's cousin, King James VI of Scotland, who became James I (1603–1625) of England. James espoused the divine right of kings, a viewpoint that alienated Parliament, which had grown accustomed under the Tudors to act on the premise that monarch and Parliament together ruled England as a "balanced polity." Then, too, the Puritans—Protestants within the Anglican Church who, inspired by Calvinist theology, wished to eliminate every trace of Roman Catholicism from the Church of England—were alienated by the king's strong defense of the Anglican Church. Many of England's gentry, mostly well-to-do landowners, had become Puritans, and they formed an important and substantial part of the House of Commons, the lower house of Parliament. It was not wise to alienate these men.

The conflict that had begun during the reign of James came to a head during the reign of his son Charles I (1625–1649). Like his father, Charles believed in divine-right monarchy, and religious differences also added to the hostility between Charles I and Parliament. The king's attempt to impose more ritual on the Anglican Church struck the Puritans as a return to Catholic practices. When Charles tried to force the Puritans to accept his religious policies, thousands of them went off to the "howling wildernesses" of America.

15-4b Civil War and Commonwealth

Grievances mounted until England finally slipped into a civil war (1642–1648), which was won by the parliamentary forces largely because of Oliver Cromwell's New

Model Army. This army was composed primarily of more extreme Puritans known as the Independents, who, in typical Calvinist fashion, believed they were doing battle for God. As Cromwell wrote in one of his military reports, "Sir, this is none other but the hand of God; and to Him alone belongs the glory." We might give some credit to Cromwell; his soldiers were well trained in the new military tactics of the seventeenth century.

After the execution of Charles I on January 30, 1649, Parliament abolished the monarchy and the House of Lords and proclaimed England a republic or commonwealth. But Cromwell and his army, unable to work effectively with Parliament, dispersed it by force and established a military dictatorship. After Cromwell's death in 1658, the army decided that military rule was no longer feasible and restored the monarchy in the person of Charles II (1660–1685), the son of Charles I.

15-4c Restoration and a Glorious Revolution

Charles II was sympathetic to Catholicism, and Parliament's suspicions were aroused in 1672 when he took the audacious step of issuing the Declaration of Indulgence, which suspended the laws that Parliament had passed against Catholics and Puritans after the restoration of the monarchy. Parliament forced the king to suspend the declaration.

The accession of James II (1685–1688) to the crown virtually guaranteed a new constitutional crisis for England. An open and devout Catholic, his attempt to further Catholic interests made religion once more a primary cause of conflict between king and Parliament. James named Catholics to high positions in the government, army, navy, and universities. Parliamentary outcries against James's policies stopped short of rebellion because the members knew that he was an old man and that his successors were his Protestant daughters Mary and Anne, born to his first wife. But on June 10, 1688, a son was born to James II's second wife, also a Catholic. Suddenly, the specter of a Catholic hereditary monarchy loomed large. A group of prominent English noblemen invited the Dutch chief executive, William of Orange, husband of James's daughter Mary, to invade England. William and Mary raised an army and invaded England while James, his wife, and their infant son fled to France. With little bloodshed, England had undergone its "Glorious Revolution."

In January 1689, Parliament offered the throne to William and Mary, who accepted it along with the provisions of the Bill of Rights (see Historical Voices, "The Bill of Rights," p. 388). The Bill of Rights affirmed Parliament's right to make laws and levy taxes. The rights of citizens to keep arms and have a jury trial were also confirmed. By deposing one king and establishing another, Parliament had destroyed the divine-right theory of kingship

CHRONOLOGY	Absolute and Limited Monarchy
France	
Louis XIV	1643–1715
Brandenburg-Prussia	
Frederick William the Great Elector	1640–1688
Elector Frederick III (King Frederick I)	1688–1713
Russia	
Ivan IV the Terrible	1533–1584
Peter the Great	1689–1725
First trip to the West	1697–1698
Construction of St. Petersburg begins	1703
England	
Civil wars	1642–1648
Commonwealth	1649–1653
Charles II	1660–1685
Declaration of Indulgence	1672
James II	1685–1688
Glorious Revolution	1688
Bill of Rights	1689

(William was, after all, king by grace of Parliament, not God) and asserted its right to participate in the government. Parliament did not have complete control of the government, but it now had the right to participate in affairs of state. Over the next century, it would gradually prove to be the real authority in the English system of **limited (constitutional) monarchy**.

15-5 THE FLOURISHING OF EUROPEAN CULTURE

Focus Question: How did the artistic and literary achievements of this era reflect the political and economic developments of the period?

Despite religious wars and the growth of absolutism, European culture continued to flourish. The era was blessed with many prominent artists and writers.

15-5a Art: The Baroque

The artistic movement known as the **Baroque** (buh-ROHK) dominated the Western artistic world for a century and a half. The Baroque began in Italy in the last quarter of the

The Bill of Rights

Politics & Government **IN 1688, THE ENGLISH EXPERIENCED** a bloodless revolution in which the Stuart king James II was replaced by Mary, James's daughter, and her husband, William of Orange. After William and Mary had assumed power, Parliament passed a Bill of Rights that specified the rights of Parliament and laid the foundation for a constitutional monarchy.

The Bill of Rights

Whereas the said late King James II having abdicated the government, and the throne being thereby vacant, his Highness the prince of Orange (whom it hath pleased Almighty God to make the glorious instrument of delivering this kingdom from popery and arbitrary power) did (by the device of the lords spiritual and temporal, and diverse principal persons of the Commons) cause letters to be written to the lords spiritual and temporal, being Protestants, and other letters to the several counties, cities, universities, boroughs, and Cinque Ports, for the choosing of such persons to represent them, as were of right to be sent to parliament, to meet and sit at Westminster upon the two and twentieth day of January, in this year 1689, in order to such an establishment as that their religion, laws, and liberties might not again be in danger of being subverted; upon which letters elections have been accordingly made.

And thereupon the said lords spiritual and temporal and Commons, pursuant to their respective letters and elections, being now assembled in a full and free representation of this nation, taking into their most serious consideration the best means for attaining the ends aforesaid, do in the first place (as their ancestors in like case have usually done), for the vindication and assertion of their ancient rights and liberties, declare:

1. That the pretended power of suspending laws, or the execution of laws, by regal authority, without consent of parliament is illegal.

2. That the pretended power of dispensing with the laws, or the execution of law by regal authority, as it hath been assumed and exercised of late, is illegal.

3. That the commission for erecting the late court of commissioners for ecclesiastical causes, and all other commissions and courts of like nature, are illegal and pernicious.

4. That levying money for or to the use of the crown by pretense of prerogative, without grant of parliament, for longer time or in other manner than the same is or shall be granted, is illegal.

5. That it is the right of the subjects to petition the king, and all commitments and prosecutions for such petitioning are illegal.

6. That the raising or keeping a standing army within the kingdom in time of peace, unless it be with consent of parliament, is against law.

7. That the subjects which are Protestants may have arms for their defense suitable to their conditions, and as allowed by law.

8. That election of members of parliament ought to be free.

9. That the freedom of speech, and debates or proceedings in parliament, ought not to be impeached or questioned in any court or place out of parliament.

10. That excessive bail ought not to be required, nor excessive fines imposed, nor cruel and unusual punishments inflicted.

11. That jurors ought to be duly impaneled and returned, and jurors which pass upon men in trials for high treason ought to be freeholders.

12. That all grants and promises of fines and forfeitures of particular persons before conviction are illegal and void.

13. And that for redress of all grievances, and for the amending, strengthening, and preserving of the laws, parliament ought to be held frequently.

 How did the Bill of Rights lay the foundation for a constitutional monarchy in England?

Source: *The Statutes: Revised Edition* (London: Eyre & Spottiswoode, 1871), Vol. 2, pp. 10–12.

sixteenth century and spread to the rest of Europe and Latin America. Baroque artists sought to harmonize the classical ideals of Renaissance art with the spiritual feelings of the sixteenth-century religious revival. In large part, Baroque art and architecture reflected the search for power that was characteristic of much of the seventeenth century. Baroque churches and palaces featured richly ornamented facades, sweeping staircases, and an overall splendor meant to impress people. Kings and princes wanted not only their subjects but also other kings and princes to be in awe of their power.

Baroque painting was known for its use of dramatic effects to arouse the emotions. Perhaps the greatest figure of the Baroque was Italian architect and sculptor Gian Lorenzo Bernini (ZHAHN loh-RENT-zoh bur-NEE-nee) (1598–1680), who completed Saint Peter's Basilica at the Vatican and designed the vast colonnade enclosing the piazza in front of it. In his most striking sculptural work, the *Ecstasy of Saint Theresa*, Bernini depicts a moment of mystical experience in the life of the sixteenth-century Spanish saint. The elegant draperies

and the expression on her face create a sensuously real portrayal of physical ecstasy

15-5b Art: Dutch Realism

A brilliant flowering of Dutch painting paralleled the supremacy of Dutch commerce in the seventeenth century. Wealthy patricians and burghers of Dutch urban society commissioned works of art for their guildhalls, town halls, and private dwellings. The interests of this burgher society were reflected in the subject matter of many Dutch paintings: portraits of themselves, landscapes, seascapes, genre scenes, still lifes, and the interiors of their residences. Neither classical nor Baroque, Dutch painters were primarily interested in the realistic portrayal of secular everyday life.

This interest in painting scenes of everyday life is evident in the work of Judith Leyster (LESS-tur) (ca. 1609–1660), who established her own independent painting career, a remarkable achievement for a woman in seventeenth-century Europe. Musicians playing their instruments, women sewing, children laughing while playing games, and actors performing all form the subject matter of Leyster's portrayals of everyday Dutch life.

Scala/Art Resource, NY

15.7 Gian Lorenzo Bernini, *Ecstasy of Saint Theresa*. The *Ecstasy of Saint Theresa*, created for the Cornaro Chapel in the Church of Santa Maria della Vittoria in Rome, was one of Bernini's most famous sculptures. Bernini sought to convey visually Theresa's mystical experience when, according to her description, an angel pierced her heart repeatedly with a golden arrow.

National Gallery of Art, Washington, DC

15.8 Judith Leyster, *Self-Portrait*. Although Judith Leyster was a well-known artist to her Dutch contemporaries, her fame diminished soon after her death. In the late nineteenth century, a Dutch art historian rediscovered her work. In her *Self-Portrait*, painted in 1635, she is seen pausing in her work in front of one the scenes of daily life that made her such a popular artist in her own day.

Experience an interactive version of this period in ⚫ MINDTAP

15-5c A Golden Age of Literature in England

In England, writing for the stage reached new heights between 1580 and 1640. The golden age of English literature is often called the *Elizabethan Era* because much of the English cultural flowering occurred during Elizabeth's reign. Elizabethan literature exhibits the exuberance and pride associated with English exploits at the time. Of all the forms of Elizabethan literature, none expressed the energy and intellectual versatility of the era better than drama. And no dramatist is more famous or more accomplished than William Shakespeare (1564–1614).

Shakespeare was a "complete man of the theater." Although best known for writing plays, he was also an actor and a shareholder in the chief acting company of the time, the Lord Chamberlain's Company, which played in various London theaters. Shakespeare is to this day hailed as a genius. A master of the English language, he imbued its words with power and majesty. And his technical proficiency was matched by incredible insight into human psychology. Whether writing tragedies or comedies, Shakespeare exhibited a remarkable understanding of the human condition.

CHAPTER SUMMARY

In Chapter 14, we observed how the movement of Europeans beyond Europe began to change the shape of world history. But what had made this development possible? After all, the Reformation of the sixteenth century, initially begun by Martin Luther, had brought about the religious division of Europe into Protestant and Catholic camps. By

the middle of the sixteenth century, it was apparent that the religious passions of the Reformation era had brought an end to the religious unity of medieval Europe. The religious division (Catholics versus Protestants) was instrumental in beginning a series of religious wars that were complicated by economic, social, and political forces.

The crises of the sixteenth and seventeenth centuries soon led to a search for a stable, secular order of politics and made possible the emergence of a system of nation-states in which power politics took on increasing significance. Within those states, there slowly emerged some of the machinery that made possible a growing centralization of power. In states called *absolutist*, strong monarchs with the assistance of their aristocracies took the lead in providing the leadership for greater centralization. In this so-called age of absolutism, Louis XIV, the Sun King of France, was the model for other rulers. Strong monarchy also prevailed in central and eastern

Europe, where three new powers made their appearance: Prussia, Austria, and Russia.

But not all European states followed the pattern of absolute monarchy. Especially important were developments in England, where a series of struggles between king and Parliament took place in the seventeenth century. In the long run, the landed aristocracy gained power at the expense of the monarchs, thus laying the foundations for a constitutional government in which Parliament provided the focus for the institutions of centralized power.

In every major European state, a growing concern for power and dynamic expansion led to larger armies and greater conflict, stronger economies, and more powerful governments. From a global point of view, Europeans—with their strong governments, prosperous economies, and strengthened military forces—were beginning to dominate other parts of the world, leading to a growing belief in the superiority of their civilization.

Yet despite Europeans' increasing domination of global trade markets, they had not achieved their goal of diminishing the power of Islam, a goal first pursued during the crusades. In fact, as we shall see in the next chapter, in the midst of European expansion and exploration, three new and powerful Muslim empires were taking shape in the Middle East and South Asia.

REFLECTION QUESTIONS

Q What role did politics play in the success of the Protestant Reformation?

Q What did Louis XIV hope to accomplish in his domestic and foreign policies? To what extent did he succeed?

Q Compare and contrast the development of states in Europe and the world of Islam (see Chapter 16). What are the similarities and differences in these developments? How do you explain the similarities and differences?

CHAPTER TIMELINE

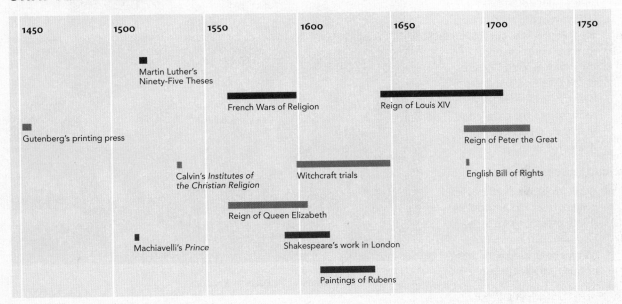

CHAPTER NOTES

1. N. Machiavelli, *The Prince,* trans. D. Wootton (Indianapolis, Ind., 1995), p. 48.
2. Quoted in R. Bainton, *Here I Stand: A Life of Martin Luther* (New York, 1950), p. 144.
3. J. Calvin, *Institutes of the Christian Religion,* trans. J. Allen (Philadelphia, 1936), vol. 1, p. 228; vol. 2, p. 181.
4. Quoted in B. S. Anderson and J. P. Zinsser, *A History of Their Own: Women in Europe from Prehistory to the Present,* vol. 1 (New York, 1988), p. 259.
5. Quoted in J. O'Malley, *The First Jesuits* (Cambridge, Mass., 1993), p. 76.
6. Quoted in J. Klaits, *Servants of Satan: The Age of Witch Hunts* (Bloomington, Ind., 1985), p. 68.

MINDTAP
From Cengage

MindTap® is a fully online, highly personalized learning experience built upon Cengage Learning content. MindTap combines student learning tools—readings, multimedia, activities, and assessments—into a singular Learning Path that guides students through the course and helps students develop the critical thinking, analysis, and communication skills that are essential to academic and professional success.

Chapter Outline and Focus Questions

16-1 The Ottoman Empire

Q What were the chief reasons for the success of the Ottoman Turks in consolidating their influence throughout the Middle East and the Balkans. Why were they more successful at the effort than their predecessors, the Byzantine Empire?

16-2 The Safavids

Q What problems did the Safavid Empire face, and how did its rulers attempt to solve them? How did their success and failures compared with those of other Muslim empires?

16-3 The Grandeur of the Mughals

Q What role did Islam play in the Mughal Empire, and how did the Mughals' approach to religion compare with that of the Ottomans and the Safavids? What might explain the differences?

Critical Thinking

Q *What were the main characteristics of each Muslim empire, and in what ways did they resemble each other? How were they distinct from their European counterparts?*

Connections to Today

Q *How would you compare the position of Islam in the world today with its position in the era described in this chapter?*

Universal Images Group / Art Resource, NY

16.1 Turks Fight Christians at the Battle of Mohács

THE OTTOMAN ARMY, led by Sultan Suleyman the Magnificent, arrived at Mohács, on the plains of Hungary, on an August morning in 1526. The Turkish force numbered about 100,000 men, and its weapons included 300 new long-range cannons. Facing them was a somewhat larger European force clothed in heavy armor but armed with only 100 older cannons.

The battle began at noon and was over in two hours. The flower of the Hungarian cavalry had been destroyed, and 20,000 foot soldiers had drowned in a nearby swamp. The Ottomans had lost fewer than 200 men. Two weeks later, they seized the Hungarian capital at Buda and prepared to lay siege to the nearby Austrian city of Vienna. Europe was in a panic, but Mohács would end up being the high point of Turkish expansion in Europe.

In launching their Age of Exploration, European rulers had hoped that they could cripple the power of Islam and reduce its threat to the security of Europe by controlling global markets. But their strategy had not been entirely successful because the Muslim world, which appeared to have entered a period of decline with the collapse of the

Abbasid caliphate, managed to revive itself with the rise of three great Muslim empires. These powerful Muslim states—the Ottomans, the Safavids, and the Mughals—dominated the Middle East and the South Asian subcontinent and brought a measure of stability to a region that had been in turmoil for centuries.

16-1 THE OTTOMAN EMPIRE

 Focus Questions: What were the chief reasons for the success of the Ottoman Turks in consolidating their influence throughout the Middle East and the Balkans? Why were they more successful at the effort than their predecessors, the Byzantine Empire?

The Ottoman Turks were among the many Turkic-speaking nomadic peoples who had spread westward from Central Asia in the ninth through the eleventh centuries. The first to appear in the Middle East were the Seljuk Turks, who initially attempted to revive the declining Abbasid caliphate in Baghdad. Later they established themselves in the Anatolian Peninsula at the expense of the Byzantine Empire. Turks served as warriors or administrators, whereas the peasants who tilled the farmland were mainly Greek.

16-1a The Rise of the Ottoman Turks

In the late thirteenth century, a new group of Turks under the tribal leader Osman (os-MAHN) (r. 1280–1326) began to consolidate their power in the northwestern corner of the Anatolian Peninsula. At first, the Osman Turks were relatively peaceful and engaged in pastoral pursuits, but as the Seljuk Empire began to disintegrate in the early fourteenth century, they began to expand and founded the Osmanli (os-MAHN-lee) Dynasty, with its capital at Bursa (BURR-suh). The Osmanlis later came to be known as the Ottomans.

The Byzantine Empire, of course, had controlled the area for centuries, but it had been severely weakened by the 1204 sacking of Constantinople in the Fourth Crusade and the Western occupation of much of the empire for the next half-century. In 1345, Ottoman forces under their leader Orkhan (or-KHAHN) I (r. 1326–1360) crossed the Bosporus for the first time to support a usurper against the Byzantine emperor in Constantinople. Setting up their first European base at Gallipoli (gah-LIP-poh-lee) at the Mediterranean entrance to the Dardanelles, Turkish troops expanded gradually into the Balkans and allied with fractious Serbian and Bulgar forces against the Byzantines. In these unstable conditions, the Ottomans established permanent settlements throughout the area, where Turkish provincial governors, called **beys** (BAYS) (from the Turkish *beg*, "knight"), drove out the previous landlords and collected taxes from the local Slavic peasants. The Ottoman leader now began to claim the title of **sultan** (SUL-tun) or sovereign of his domain.

In 1360, Orkhan was succeeded by his son Murad (moo-RAHD) I (r. 1360–1389), who consolidated Ottoman power in the Balkans and steadily reduced the Byzantine emperor to a vassal. Murad now began to build up a strong military administration based on the creation of a new elite guard. Called **janissaries** (JAN-nih-say-reez) (from the Turkish *yeni cheri*, "new troops"), they were recruited from the local Christian population in the Balkans and then converted to Islam and trained as foot soldiers or administrators. One major advantage of the janissaries was that they were directly subordinated to the sultanate and therefore owed their loyalty to the person of the sultan. Other military forces were organized by the beys and were thus loyal to their local tribal leaders.

The janissary corps also represented a response to changes in warfare. As the knowledge of firearms spread in the late fourteenth century, the Turks began to master the new technology, including siege cannons and muskets (see Comparative Essay, "The Changing Face of War," p. 394). The traditional nomadic cavalry charge was now outmoded and was superseded by infantry forces armed with muskets. Thus, the janissaries provided a well-armed infantry who served both as an elite guard to protect the palace and as a means of extending Turkish control in the Balkans. With his new forces, Murad defeated the Serbs at the famous Battle of Kosovo (KAWSS-suh-voh) in 1389 and ended Serbian hegemony in the area.

16-1b Expansion of the Empire

Under Murad's successor, Bayazid (by-uh-ZEED) I (r. 1389–1402), the Ottomans annexed Bulgaria. When Mehmet (meh-MET) II (r. 1451–1481) succeeded to the throne, he was determined to capture Constantinople. Already in control of the Dardanelles, he ordered the construction of a major fortress on the Bosporus just north of the city, which put the Turks in a position to strangle the Byzantines.

The Fall of Constantinople In desperation, the last Byzantine emperor called for help from the Europeans, but only the Genoese came to his defense.

With massive cannons (see Chapter 13) and 80,000 troops ranged against only 7,000 defenders, Mehmet laid siege to Constantinople in 1453. The defenders stretched heavy chains across the Golden Horn, the inlet that forms the city's harbor, to prevent a naval attack from the north

The Changing Face of War

Science & Technology

"War," as renowned French historian Fernand Braudel once observed, "has always been a matter of arms and techniques. Improved techniques can radically alter the course of events." Braudel's remark was directed to the situation in the Mediterranean region during the sixteenth century when the adoption of artillery changed the face of warfare and gave enormous advantages to those countries that stood at the head of the new technological revolution. But it could as easily have been applied to the present day when potential adversaries possess weapons capable of reaching across oceans and continents.

One crucial aspect of military superiority, of course, lies in the nature of weaponry. From the invention of the bow and arrow to the advent of the atomic era, the possession of superior instruments of war has provided a distinct advantage against a poorly armed enemy. It was at least partly the possession of bronze weapons, for example, that enabled the invading Hyksos to conquer Egypt during the second millennium B.C.E.

Mobility is another factor of vital importance. During the second millennium B.C.E., horse-drawn chariots revolutionized the art of war from the Mediterranean Sea to the Yellow River Valley in northern China. Later, the invention of the stirrup enabled mounted warriors to shoot bows and arrows from horseback, a technique applied with great effect by the Mongols as they devastated civilizations across the Eurasian supercontinent.

To protect themselves from marauding warriors, settled societies began to erect massive walls around their cities and fortresses. That, in turn, led to the invention of siege weapons such as the catapult and the battering ram. The Mongols allegedly even came up with an early form of chemical warfare, hurling human bodies infected with the plague into the bastions of their enemies.

The invention of explosives launched the next great revolution in warfare. First used as a weapon of war by the Tang Dynasty in China, explosives were brought to the West by the Turks, who used them with great effectiveness in the fifteenth century against the

William J. Duiker

16.2 Angkor Troops Advance Against their Enemies in Champa

Byzantine Empire. But the Europeans quickly mastered the new technology and took it to new heights, inventing handheld firearms and mounting iron cannons on their warships. The latter represented a significant advantage to European fleets as they began to compete with rivals for control of the Indian and Pacific Oceans.

The twentieth century saw revolutionary new developments in the art of warfare from armored vehicles to airplanes to nuclear arms. But as weapons grow ever more fearsome, they are more risky to use, resulting in the paradox of the Vietnam War—lightly armed Viet Cong guerrilla units were able to fight the world's mightiest army to a virtual standstill. The lessons of Vietnam have been effectively absorbed in our own day as lightly armed insurgents rely on terror and assassination to promote their goals against more powerful enemies. As Chinese military strategist Sun Tzu had long ago observed, victory in war often goes to the smartest, not the strongest.

 Why were the Europeans rather than other peoples able to make effective use of firearms to expand their influence throughout the rest of the world?

and prepared to make their final stand behind the thirteen-mile-long wall along the western edge of the city. But Mehmet's forces seized the tip of the peninsula north of the Golden Horn and then dragged their ships overland across the peninsula from the Bosporus and put them into the water behind the chains. Finally, the walls were breached; the Byzantine emperor died in the final battle.

The Advance into Western Asia and Africa

With their new capital at Constantinople, eventually renamed Istanbul, the Ottoman Turks became a dominant force in the Balkans and the Anatolian Peninsula. They now began to advance to the east against the Shi'ite kingdom of the Safavids (sah-FAH-weeds) in Persia (see Section 16-2, "The Safavids," p. 401), which had been promoting rebellion among the Anatolian tribal population and disrupting Turkish trade through the Middle East. After defeating the Safavids at a major battle in 1514, Emperor Selim (seh-LEEM) I (1512–1520) consolidated Turkish control over the territory that had been ancient Mesopotamia and then turned his attention to the Mamluks (MAM-looks) in Egypt, who had failed to support the Ottomans in their struggle against the Safavids. Cairo fell in 1517, and Selim declared himself to be the new caliph or successor to Muhammad. During the next few years, Turkish armies and fleets advanced westward along the African coast, occupying Tripoli, Tunis, and Algeria, and eventually penetrating almost to the Strait of Gibraltar (see Map 16.1).

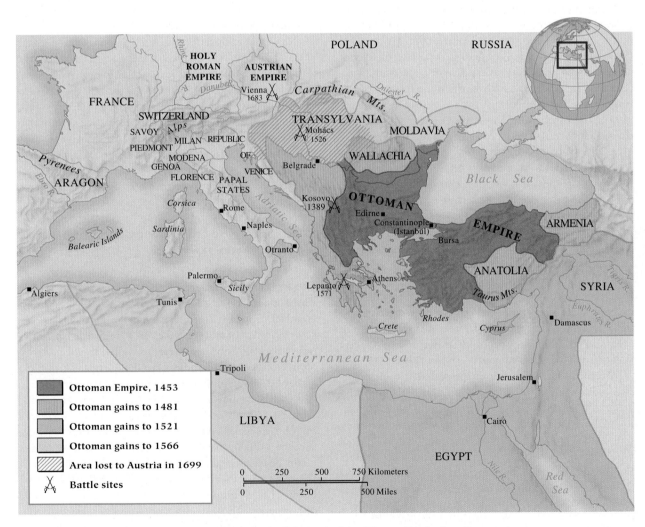

Map 16.1 The Ottoman Empire. This map shows the territorial growth of the Ottoman Empire from the eve of the conquest of Constantinople in 1453 to the end of the seventeenth century when a defeat at the hands of Austria led to the loss of a substantial portion of central Europe.

 Where did the Ottomans come from?

The impact of Turkish rule on the peoples of North Africa was relatively light. Like their predecessors, the Turks were Muslims, and they preferred where possible to administer their conquered regions through local rulers known as **pashas** (PAH-shuz), who collected taxes (with a fixed percentage sent to the central government), maintained law and order, and were directly responsible to Istanbul. The Turks ruled from coastal cities such as Algiers, Tunis, and Tripoli and made no attempt to control the interior beyond maintaining the trade routes through the Sahara to the trading centers along the Niger River. Meanwhile, local pirates along the Barbary Coast—the northern coast of Africa from Egypt to the Atlantic Ocean—competed with their Christian rivals in raiding shipping in the Mediterranean.

By the seventeenth century, the links between the imperial court in Istanbul and its appointed representatives in North Africa had begun to deteriorate. Some pashas were dethroned by local elites, while others such as the bey of Tunis became hereditary rulers. Even Egypt, whose agricultural wealth and control over the route to the Red Sea made it the most important country in the area to the Turks, gradually became autonomous under a new official class of janissaries.

Turkish Expansion in Europe   After their conquest of Constantinople in 1453, the Turks turned their attention back to Europe. Under the leadership of Suleyman (SOO-lay-mahn) I the Magnificent (r. 1520–1566), Turkish forces advanced up the Danube, seizing Belgrade in 1521 and winning a major victory over the Hungarians at the Battle of Mohács (MOH-hach) on the Danube in 1526. Subsequently, the Turks overran most of Hungary, moved into Austria, and advanced as far as Vienna, where they were finally repelled in 1529. At the same time, they extended their power into the western Mediterranean and threatened to turn it into a Turkish lake until the Spanish destroyed a large Turkish fleet at Lepanto (LEH-pahn-toh or LIH-pan-toh) in 1571.

A century later, the Ottomans resumed their offensive, advancing through the Hungarian plain to the gates of Vienna. Repulsed by a coalition of European forces, the Turks retreated once again. Although they retained the core of their empire, the Ottoman Turks would never again be a threat to Europe. The Turkish Empire held together for the rest of the seventeenth and the eighteenth centuries, but it faced new challenges from the ever-growing Austrian Empire in southeastern Europe and the new Russian giant to the north.

16-1c The Nature of Turkish Rule

Like other Muslim empires in Persia and India, the Ottoman political system was the result of the evolution of tribal institutions into a sedentary empire. At the apex of the Ottoman system was the sultan, who was the supreme authority both politically and militarily. The origins of this system can be traced back to the bey, who, as tribal leader, was a first among equals, and could claim loyalty from his chiefs only as long as he could provide them with booty and grazing lands. Disputes were settled by tribal law, and Muslim laws were secondary. Tribal leaders collected taxes—or booty—from areas under their control and sent one-fifth on to the bey. Both administrative and military powers were centralized under the bey, and the capital was wherever the bey and his administration happened to be.

In a manner reminiscent of the Abbasids, however, the rise of empire brought the adoption of Byzantine traditions of rule. The status and prestige of the sultan now increased relative to the subordinate tribal leaders and, with Suleyman the Magnificent—perhaps the empire's greatest ruler—the position took on the trappings of imperial rule (see Historical Voices, "A Portrait of Suleyman the Magnificent," p. 397). Court rituals inherited from the Byzantines and Persians were adopted, as was a centralized administrative system that increasingly isolated the sultan in his palace. The position of the sultan was hereditary, with a son always succeeding the father, although not necessarily the eldest. This practice led to chronic succession struggles on the death of individual sultans, and the losers were often executed (strangled with a silk bowstring) or imprisoned. Heirs to the throne were assigned as provincial governors to provide them with experience.

The Harem   The heart of the sultan's power was in the Topkapi (tahp-KAH-pee) Palace in the center of Istanbul. Topkapi (meaning "cannon gate") was constructed in 1459 and served as an administrative center (known as the **Sublime Porte**) as well as the private residence of the sultan and his family. Eventually, it had a staff of 20,000 employees. The sultan's private domain was called the **harem** ("sacred place"). Here he resided with his concubines. Normally, a sultan did not marry but chose several concubines as his favorites; they were accorded this status after they gave birth to sons. When a son became a sultan, his mother became known as the queen mother and administered the royal household. This tradition, initiated by the influential wife of Suleyman the Magnificent, often resulted in considerable authority for the queen mother in affairs of state. Queen mothers also controlled the marital alliances of their daughters with senior officials or with members of other royal families to cement alliances with other states.

A Portrait of Suleyman the Magnificent

Politics & Government SULEYMAN I WAS PERHAPS THE GREATEST of all Ottoman sultans. Like King Louis XIV of France and Emperor Kangxi of China, he presided over his domain at the peak of its military and cultural achievement. This description of him was written by Ghislain de Busbecq (GEE-lan duh booz-BEK), the Habsburg ambassador to Constantinople. Busbecq observed Suleyman firsthand and was highly impressed by the Turkish ruler, as this selection indicates.

Ghislain de Busbecq, *The Turkish Letters*

The Sultan was seated on a rather low sofa, no more than a foot from the ground and spread with many costly coverlets and cushions embroidered with exquisite work. Near him were his bow and arrows. His expression, as I have said, is anything but smiling, and has a sternness which, though sad, is full of majesty. On our arrival we were introduced into his presence by his chamberlains, who held our arms—a practice which has always been observed since a Croatian sought an interview and murdered the Sultan Amurath in a revenge for the slaughter of his master, Marcus the Despot of Serbia. After going through the pretense of kissing his hand, we were led to the wall facing him backwards, so as not to turn our backs or any part of them toward him. He then listened to the recital of my message, but, as it did not correspond [to] his expectations (for the demands of my imperial master [the Habsburg emperor Ferdinand I] were full of dignity and independence, and, therefore, far from acceptable to one who thought that his slightest wishes ought to be obeyed), he assumed an expression of disdain, and merely answered *"Giusel, giusel,"* that is, Well, well." We were then dismissed to our lodging. . . .

You will probably wish me to describe the impression which Suleyman made upon me. He is beginning to feel the weight of years, but his dignity of demeanor and his general physical appearance are worthy of the ruler of so vast an empire. He has always been frugal and temperate, and was so even in his youth, when he might have erred without incurring blame in the eyes of the Turks. Even in his earlier years he did not indulge in wine or in those unnatural vices to which the Turks are often addicted. Even his bitterest critics can find nothing more serious to allege against him than his undue submission to his wife and its result in his somewhat precipitate action in putting Mustapha [his firstborn son, by another wife] to death, which is generally imputed to her employment of love potions and incantations. It is generally agreed that ever since he promoted her to the rank of his lawful wife, he has possessed no concubines, although there is no law to prevent his doing so. He is a strict guardian of his religion and its ceremonies, being not less desirous of upholding his faith than of extending his dominions. For his age—he has almost reached his sixtieth year—he enjoys quite good health, though his bad complexion may be due to some hidden malady; and indeed it is generally believed that he has an incurable ulcer or gangrene on his leg. This defect of complexion he remedies by painting his face with a coating of red powder, when he wishes departing ambassadors to take with them a strong impression of his good health; for he fancies that it contributes to inspire greater fear in foreign potentates if they think that he is well and strong.

 What were the main achievements of Suleyman that caused him to be called "the Magnificent"? Is this description the work of an admirer or a critic? Why do you think so?

Members of the harem, like the janissaries, were often of slave origin and formed an elite element in Ottoman society. Because the enslavement of Muslims was forbidden, slaves were taken among non-Islamic peoples. Some concubines were prisoners selected for the position, while others were purchased or offered to the sultan as a gift. They were then trained and educated like the janissaries in a system called *devshirme* (dev-SHEER-may) ("collection"). Devshirme had originated in the practice of requiring local clan leaders to provide prisoners to the sultan as part of their tax obligation. Talented males were given special training for eventual placement in military or administrative positions, while their female counterparts were trained for service in the harem, with instruction in reading and the Qur'an, sewing and embroidery, and musical performance. They were ranked according to their status, and some were permitted to leave the harem to marry officials.

Unique to the Ottoman Empire from the fifteenth century onward was the exclusive use of slaves to produce its royal heirs. Contrary to myth, few of the women of the imperial harem were used for sexual purposes, as the majority were members of the sultan's extended family—sisters,

Claire L. Duiker

Yvonne V. Duiker

16.3a   16.3b

16.3 The Sultan's Chambers in Topkapi Palace. After his conquest of Constantinople in 1453, Mehmet II constructed the extensive palace compound known as *Topkapi* as his royal residence and the seat of the new government. Set on a high promontory overlooking the Bosporus and the Sea of Marmara, this self-contained city housed more than 4,000 people and included a royal harem, dormitories, libraries, schools, mosques, a hospital, and gardens with fountains. Shown here (Image 16.3a) is the sultan's imperial throne room. The walls of the harem are covered with magnificent tile work designs, including this design of colorful flowers in vases (Image 16.3b). Ottoman artists were renowned for the high quality of their glazed tile art, which was produced in many colors including their own secret "tomato red," which adorned palaces as well as mosques.

daughters, widowed mothers, and in-laws, with their own personal slaves and entourage. Contemporary European observers compared the atmosphere in the Topkapi harem to a Christian nunnery, with its hierarchical organization, enforced chastity, and rule of silence.

Administration of the Government The sultan ruled through an imperial council that met four days a week and was chaired by the chief minister known as the **grand vizier** (veh-ZEER) (Turkish *vezir*). The sultan often attended behind a screen, whence he could privately indicate his desires to the grand vizier. The latter presided over the imperial bureaucracy. Like the palace guard, the bureaucrats were not an exclusive group but were chosen at least partly by merit from a palace school for training officials. Most officials were Muslims by birth, but some talented janissaries became senior members of the bureaucracy, and almost all the later grand viziers came from the devshirme system.

Local administration during the imperial period was a product of Turkish tribal tradition and was similar in some respects to fief holding in Europe. The empire was divided into provinces and districts governed by officials who, like their tribal predecessors, combined civil and military functions. Senior officials were assigned land in fief by the sultan and were then responsible for collecting taxes and supplying armies to the empire. These lands were then farmed out to the local cavalry elite called the **sipahis** (suh-pah-heez), who obtained their salaries by exacting taxes from all peasants in their fiefdoms.

16-1d Religion and Society in the Ottoman World

The Ottoman ruling elites were Sunni Muslims. Having assumed the title of *caliph* ("defender of the faith"), Ottoman sultans were theoretically responsible for guiding the flock and maintaining Islamic law, the shari'a. In practice, the sultan assigned these duties to a supreme religious authority who administered the law and maintained schools for educating Muslims. Islamic law and customs were applied to all Muslims in the empire. Like their rulers, most Turkic-speaking people were Sunni Muslims, but some communities were attracted to Sufism (see Chapter 7) or other heterodox doctrines. The government tolerated such activities as long as their practitioners remained loyal to the state, but unrest among these groups—some of whom converted to the Shi'ite version of Islam—outraged the conservative ulama and eventually led to war against the Safavids (see Section 16-2 "The Safavids" later in this chapter).

The Treatment of Minorities Non-Muslims—mostly Orthodox Christians (Greeks and Slavs), Jews, and Armenian Christians—formed a significant minority

16.4 Recruitment of the Children. The Ottoman Empire, like its Chinese counterpart, sought to recruit its officials on the basis of merit. Through the system called *devshirme* ("collection"), youthful candidates were selected from the non-Muslim population in villages throughout the empire. In this painting, an imperial officer is counting coins to pay for the children's travel expenses to Istanbul, where they will undergo extensive academic and military training. Note the concern of two of the mothers and a priest as they question the official, who undoubtedly underwent the process himself as a child. As they leave their family and friends, the children carry their worldly possessions in bags slung over their shoulders.

within the empire, which treated them with relative tolerance. Each religious group was organized as a separate administrative unit called a **millet** (mi-LETT) that governed the community according to its own laws. Non-Muslims were compelled to pay a head tax, but they were permitted to practice their religion or convert to Islam. Most of the population in European areas of the empire remained Christian, but some converted to Islam, most notably in parts of the Balkans.

Social Classes The subjects of the Ottoman Empire were also divided by occupation and place of residence. In addition to the ruling class, there were four main occupational groups: peasants, artisans, merchants, and pastoral peoples. The first three were classified as "urban" residents. Peasants tilled land that was leased to them by the state (ultimate ownership of all land resided with the sultan), but the land was deeded to them, so they were able to pass it to their heirs. They were not allowed to sell the land and thus in practice were forced to remain on the soil. Taxes were based on the amount of land the peasants possessed and were paid to the local sipahis, who held the district in fief.

Artisans were organized according to craft guilds. Each guild was headed by a council of elders and was responsible not only for dealing with the governmental authorities but also for providing financial services, social security, and training for its members. Outside the ruling elite, merchants were the most privileged class in Ottoman society. They were largely exempt from government regulations and taxes and were therefore able in many cases to amass large fortunes. Charging interest was technically illegal under Islamic law, but the rules were often ignored in practice. In the absence of regulations, merchants often established monopolies and charged high prices, which caused bitter resentment by other subjects of the empire.

Nomadic peoples were placed in a separate millet and were subject to their own regulations and laws. They were divided into the traditional nomadic classifications of tribes, clans, and "tents" (individual families) and were governed by their hereditary chiefs, the beys. As we have seen, the beys were responsible for administration and for collecting taxes for the state.

CHRONOLOGY	The Ottoman Empire
Reign of Osman I	1280–1326
Ottoman Turks cross the Bosporus	1345
Murad I consolidates Turkish power in the Balkans	1360
Ottomans defeat the Serbian army at Kosovo	1389
Reign of Mehmet II the Conqueror	1451–1481
Turkish conquest of Constantinople	1453
Turks defeat the Mamluks in Syria and seize Cairo	1516–1517
Reign of Suleyman I the Magnificent	1520–1566
Turks defeat the Hungarians at Battle of Mohács	1526
Defeat of the Turks at Vienna	1529
Battle of Lepanto	1571
Second siege of Vienna	1683

The Position of Women Women in the Ottoman Empire were subject to the same restrictions that afflicted their counterparts in other Muslim societies, but their position was ameliorated to some degree by various factors. First, non-Muslims were subject to the laws and customs of their own religions; thus, Orthodox Christian, Jewish, and Armenian Christian women were spared some of the restrictions applied to their Muslim sisters (although they were then subject to restrictions imposed by their own faith). Second, Islamic laws as applied in the Ottoman Empire defined the legal position of women comparatively tolerantly, perhaps because Turkish tribal tradition had adopted a more egalitarian view of gender roles than was the case in the sedentary societies around them. Women were permitted to own and inherit property, including their dowries. They could not be forced into marriage and in certain cases were permitted to seek a divorce. As we have seen, women often exercised considerable influence in the palace and in a few instances even served in such senior official positions as governors of provinces.

HISTORIANS DEBATE 16-1e **The Ottoman Empire: A Civilization in Decline?**

By the late seventeenth century, the expansionist tendencies of earlier eras had largely disappeared, and the empire began to lose many of its territorial gains in the region. Many observers have interpreted these conditions as symptoms of a civilization in decline. Recently, however, some historians have taken issue with this paradigm, maintaining that in many respects the empire remained relatively healthy up to the early twentieth century when the final collapse occurred.

The issue is partly a matter of the interpretation of facts. In many respects, the dynamic forces that had predominated during the early stages of growth were no longer present. First, the quality of leadership had begun to decline. Talented early leaders such as Mehmet II and Suleyman the Magnificent gave way to incompetent sultans who lacked interest in the affairs of state and turned responsibility for governing over to administrators or members of the harem. Palace intrigue was the result.

Second, the administrative system began to break down as talented officials selected through the meritocratic devshirme system were gradually transformed into a privileged and often degenerate hereditary caste. Local administrators were corrupted, and taxes rose as the central bureaucracy lost its links with rural areas. Constant wars depleted the treasury, and transport and communications were neglected. In addition, the empire was beset by economic difficulties caused by the diversion of trade routes away from the eastern Mediterranean and the price inflation brought about by the influx of cheap American silver.

Most important, perhaps, was the failure of the Ottomans to take an interest in the technological advances that were being introduced from the scientific revolution in Europe. The adoption of printed books produced from movable type, for example, was resisted vigorously by conservative Muslim clerics, who argued that they were objectionable on religious and aesthetic grounds. Similarly, the use of mechanical clocks to keep accurate time was opposed in favor of the traditional use of the water clock and the sundial. Imports of military technology lagged as well, and the vaunted Ottoman superiority in cannonry gradually disappeared. At root, the Ottomans lacked an interest in events taking place elsewhere in the world and adopted instead an attitude of smug complacency based on the alleged superiority of traditional Islamic civilization.

Ottoman society was by no means totally isolated from the outside world. As familiarity with European civilization gradually increased, cosmopolitan officials and merchants began to mimic the habits and lifestyles of their European counterparts, dressing in the European fashion, purchasing Western furniture and art objects, and ignoring Muslim strictures against the consumption of alcohol and sexual activities outside marriage. Coffee and tobacco had been introduced into polite Ottoman society by the sixteenth century, and cafés for their consumption began to appear in the major cities (see Historical Voices, "A Turkish Discourse on Coffee," p. 401). One sultan in the early seventeenth century issued a decree prohibiting the consumption of both coffee and tobacco, arguing (correctly, no doubt) that many cafés were nests of antigovernment intrigue. He even began to wander incognito through the streets of Istanbul at night. Any of his subjects detected in immoral or illegal acts were summarily executed and their bodies left on the streets as examples to others.

16-1f Ottoman Art

The Ottoman sultans were enthusiastic patrons of the arts. In the period from Mehmet II in the fifteenth century to the early eighteenth century, pottery, rugs, silk and other textiles, jewelry, arms and armor, and calligraphy all flourished. They adorned the palaces of the rulers, testifying to their opulence and exquisite taste. The artists came from all parts of the realm and beyond.

Architecture The greatest contribution of the Ottoman Empire to world art was probably its architecture,

A Turkish Discourse on Coffee

Interaction & Exchange | **COFFEE WAS FIRST INTRODUCED** to Turkey from the Arabian Peninsula in the mid-sixteenth century and supposedly came to Europe during the Turkish siege of Vienna in 1529. The following account was written by Katib Chelebi (kah-TEEB CHEL-uh-bee), a seventeenth-century Turkish author who compiled an extensive encyclopedia and bibliography. In *The Balance of Truth,* he describes how coffee entered the empire and the problems it caused for public morality. In the Muslim world, as in Europe and later in colonial America, rebellious elements often met in coffeehouses to promote antigovernment activities. Chelebi died in Istanbul in 1657, reportedly while drinking a cup of coffee.

Katib Chelebi, The *Balance of Truth*

[Coffee] originated in Yemen and has spread, like tobacco, over the world. Certain sheikhs, who lived with their dervishes in the mountains of Yemen, used to crush and eat the berries . . . of a certain tree. Some would roast them and drink their water. Coffee is a cold dry food, suited to the ascetic life and sedative of lust. . . .

It came to Asia Minor by sea, about 1543, and met with a hostile reception, *fetwas* [decrees] being delivered against it. For they said, Apart from its being roasted, the fact that it is drunk in gatherings, passed from hand to hand, is suggestive of loose living. It is related of

Abul-Suud Efendi that he had holes bored in the ships that brought it, plunging their cargoes of coffee into the sea. But these strictures and prohibitions availed nothing. One coffeehouse was opened after another, and men would gather together, with great eagerness and enthusiasm, to drink. Drug addicts in particular, finding it a life-giving thing, which increased their pleasure, were willing to die for a cup.

Storytellers and musicians diverted the people from their employments, and working for one's living fell into disfavor. Moreover the people, from prince to beggar, amused themselves with knifing one another. Toward the end of 1633, the late Ghazi Gultan Murad, becoming aware of the situation, promulgated an edict, out of regard and compassion for the people, to this effect: Coffeehouses throughout the Guarded Domains shall be dismantled and not opened hereafter. Since then, the coffeehouses of the capital have been as desolate as the heart of the ignorant. . . . But in cities and towns outside Istanbul, they are opened just as before. As has been said above, such things do not admit of a perpetual ban.

 Why did coffee come to be regarded as a dangerous substance in the Ottoman Empire? Were the authorities successful in suppressing its consumption?

Source: From The *Balance of Truth* by Katib Chelebi, translated by G. L. Lewis, copyright 1927.

---

especially the magnificent mosques erected throughout the empire. Traditionally, prayer halls in mosques were divided by numerous pillars that supported small individual domes to create a private, forestlike atmosphere. The Turks, however, modeled their new mosques on the open floor plan of the Byzantine church of Hagia Sophia, which had been turned into a mosque by Mehmet II, and they began to push the pillars toward the outer wall to create a prayer hall with an uninterrupted central area under one large dome. With this plan, large numbers of believers could worship in unison in accordance with Muslim preference. By the mid-sixteenth century, the great Ottoman architect Mimar Sinan (si-NAHN) began erecting the first of his eighty-one mosques with an uncluttered prayer area topped by an imposing dome and framed with towering narrow minarets. The interiors were characterized by delicate plasterwork and tile decoration that transformed the mosque into a monumental oasis of spirituality, opulence, and power (see Comparative Illustration, "Hagia Sophia and the Suleymaniye Mosque," p. 402).

16-2 THE SAFAVIDS

 Focus Questions: What problems did the Safavid Empire face, and how did its rulers attempted to solve them? How did their successes and failures compare with those in the other Muslim empires?

After the collapse of the empire of Tamerlane in the early fifteenth century, the area extending from Persia into Central Asia lapsed into anarchy. The Uzbeks (ooz-BEKS),

Hagia Sophia and the Suleymaniye Mosque

Art & Ideas

THE MAGNIFICENT MOSQUES built under the patronage of Suleyman the Magnificent are a great legacy of the Ottoman Empire and a fitting supplement to Hagia Sophia, the cathedral built by Byzantine emperor Justinian in the sixth century C.E. Towering under a central dome, these mosques seem to defy gravity and, like Gothic cathedrals throughout Europe, convey a sense of weightlessness. The Suleymaniye Mosque (Image 16.5a), constructed in the mid-sixteenth century on a design by great architect Sinan, borrowed many elements from its great predecessor (Image 16.5b) and today is one of the most impressive and most graceful in Istanbul. A far cry from the seventh-century desert mosques constructed of palm trunks, the Ottoman mosques stand among the architectural wonders of the world.

Q *How would you compare the mosques built by the architect Sinan and his successors with the Gothic cathedrals that were being built at the same time in Europe? What do you think accounts for the differences?*

16.5a

Fergus O'Brien/The Image Bank/Getty Images

16.5b

William J. Duiker

Turkic-speaking peoples from Central Asia, were the chief political and military force in the area. From their capital at Bukhara (boh-KAHR-uh or boo-KAH-ruh), east of the Caspian Sea, they sought to control the highly fluid tribal alignments until the emergence of the Safavid Dynasty in Persia at the beginning of the sixteenth century.

The Safavid Dynasty was founded by Shah Ismail (IS-mah-eel) (r. 1487–1524), the descendant of Sheikh Safi al-Din (SAH-fee ul-DIN) (hence the name *Safavid*) (1252-1334), who traced his origins to Ali, the fourth imam of the Muslim faith. In the early fourteenth century, Safi had been the leader of one of the many mystical Sufi communities of Turkic-speaking nomadic people in Azerbaijan west of the Caspian Sea. Safi's community was only one of many Sufi mystical religious groups throughout the area. In time, the doctrine spread throughout the region and was gradually transformed into the more activist Shi'ite version of Islam. Its adherents were known as "red heads" because they wore a distinctive red cap with twelve folds that symbolized allegiance to the twelve imams of the Shi'ite faith.

In 1501, Ismail seized much of the old Abbasid Empire and proclaimed himself the shah of a new Persian state that was to be called *Iran* in deference to the ancient term derived from the ethnic word *Aryan*. Baghdad was subdued in 1508, as were the Uzbeks in Bukhara. Ismail now promoted the Shi'ite faith among the primarily Sunni local population and sent Shi'ite preachers into Anatolia to proselytize among Turkish peoples in the Ottoman Empire. In retaliation, the Ottoman sultan Selim I invaded Safavid territory and won a major battle near Tabriz (tah-BREEZ) in 1514. But Selim could not maintain control of the area, and Ismail regained the city a few years later.

The Ottomans returned to the attack in the 1580s and forced the new Safavid shah, Abbas (uh-BAHS) I the Great (r. 1587–1629), to sign a punitive peace acceding to the loss of much territory. The Safavid capital was subsequently moved for defensive reasons from Tabriz in the northwest to Isfahan (is-fah-HAHN) in the south, where the Safavids attained the zenith of their glory. Shah Abbas established a system similar to the janissaries in Turkey to train administrators to replace the traditional warrior elite. He also used the interval to build up his army, now armed with modern weapons, and attempted to regain the lost territories. War resumed in the 1620s, and a lasting peace was not achieved until 1638 (see Map 16.2).

By centralizing power in his hands and broadening the nation's economy, Abbas the Great managed to consolidate his power base, and Iran was stable and vigorous at his death in 1629. But succession conflicts plagued the dynasty, contributing to an increase in the influence of militant Shi'ites within the court and in Safavid society at large. The intellectual freedom that had characterized the empire at its height was increasingly curtailed under the pressure of religious orthodoxy; Iranian women, who had enjoyed considerable freedom and influence during the early period, were forced to withdraw into seclusion behind the veil. Meanwhile, attempts to suppress the religious beliefs of minorities led to increased popular unrest. In the early eighteenth century, rebellious Afghan warriors seized the capital of Isfahan, forcing the Safavid ruling family to retreat to Azerbaijan, their original homeland. Order was briefly restored by military adventurer Nadir

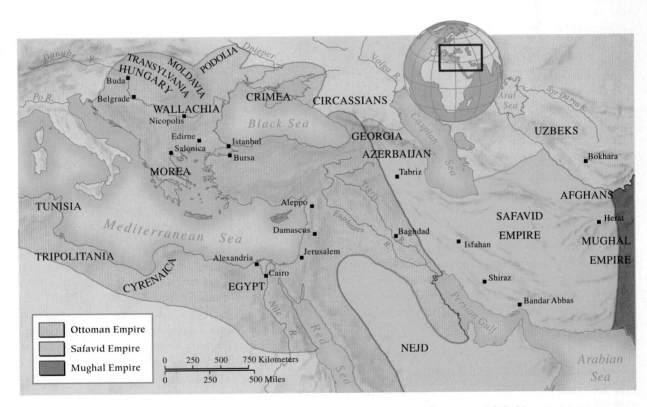

Map 16.2 The Ottoman and Safavid Empires ca. 1683. During the seventeenth century, the Ottoman and Safavid Empires contested vigorously for hegemony in the eastern Mediterranean and the Middle East. This map shows the territories controlled by each state in the late seventeenth century.

Q *Which states shared control over the ancient lands in the Tigris and Euphrates Valleys? In which modern-day countries are those lands?*

Experience an interactive version of this period in MINDTAP

The Religious Zeal of Shah Abbas the Great

Religion & Philosophy **SHAH ABBAS I,** probably the greatest of the Safavid rulers, expanded the borders of his empire into areas of the southern Caucasus inhabited by Christians and other non-Muslim peoples. After Persian control was ensured, he instructed that local populations be urged to convert to Islam for their own protection and the glory of God. In this passage, his biographer, Persian historian Eskander Beg Monshi (es-KAHN-der bayg MAHN-shee), recounts the story of that effort.

Eskander Beg Monshi, "The Conversion of a Number of Christians to Islam"

This year the Shah decreed that those Armenians and other Christians who had been settled in [the southern Caucasus] and had been given agricultural land there should be invited to become Muslims. Life in this world is fraught with vicissitudes, and the Shah was concerned lest, in a period when the authority of the central government was weak, these Christians . . . might be subjected to attack by the neighboring Lor tribes (who are naturally given to causing injury and mischief), and their women and children carried off into captivity. In the areas in which these Christian groups resided, it was the Shah's purpose that the places of worship which they had built should become mosques, and the muezzin's call should be heard in them, so that these Christians might assume the guise of Muslims, and their future status accordingly be assured. . . .

Some of the Christians, guided by God's grace, embraced Islam voluntarily; others found it difficult to abandon their Christian faith and felt revulsion at the idea. They were encouraged by their monks and priests to remain steadfast in their faith. After a little pressure had been applied to the monks and priests, however, they desisted, and these Christians saw no alternative but to embrace Islam, though they did so with reluctance. The women and children embraced Islam with great enthusiasm, vying with one another in their eagerness to abandon their Christian faith and declare their belief in the unity of God. Some five thousand people embraced Islam. As each group made the Muslim declaration of faith, it received instruction in the Koran and the principles of the religious law of Islam, and all bibles and other Christian devotional material were collected and taken away from the priests.

In the same way, all the Armenian Christians who had been moved to [the area] were also forcibly converted to Islam . . . . Most people embraced Islam with sincerity, but some felt an aversion to making the Muslim profession of faith. True knowledge lies with God! May God reward the Shah for his action with long life and prosperity!

 How do Shah Abbas's efforts to convert nonbelievers to Islam compare with similar programs by Muslim rulers in India, as described in Chapter 9? What did the author of this selection think about the conversions?

Source: From Eskander Beg Monshi in *History of Shah Abbas the Great*, Vol. II by Roger M. Savory by Westview Press, 1978.

Shah Afshar (NAH-der shah ahf-SHAR), who launched an extended series of campaigns that recovered lost territory and even occupied the Mughal capital of Delhi (see "The Shadows Lengthen" later in this chapter). After his death, the Zand Dynasty took over and ruled until the end of the eighteenth century.

16-2a Safavid Politics and Society

Like the Ottoman Empire, Iran under the Safavids was a mixed society The dynasty had come to power with the support of Turkic-speaking pastoral peoples, and leading elements from those groups retained considerable influence. The majority of the population, however, was Persian—most were farmers or townspeople—and their attitudes often reflected the relatively sophisticated and urbanized culture of pre-Safavid Iran. Faced with the problem of integrating unruly nomadic peoples with the sedentary Persian-speaking population, the Safavids used the Shi'ite faith as a unifying force (see Historical Voices, "The Religious Zeal of Shah Abbas the Great," above). The shah himself acquired an almost divine quality and claimed to be the spiritual leader of all Islam. Shi'ism was declared the state religion.

Although there was a landed aristocracy, power and influence gravitated toward strong-minded shahs who confiscated aristocratic estates and brought them under the control of the crown. Appointment to senior positions in the bureaucracy was now by merit rather than by birth.

The Safavid shahs took a direct interest in the local economy and actively engaged in commercial and manufacturing activities, although there was also a large and affluent urban bourgeoisie, many of them of Armenian or Indian extraction. The currency was reformed, and exports such as silk products, horses, and almonds were promoted. Like the Ottoman sultan, one shah regularly traveled the city streets incognito to check on the honesty of his subjects. When he discovered that a baker and butcher were overcharging for their products, he had the baker cooked in his own oven and the butcher roasted on a spit.

At its height, Safavid Iran was a worthy successor to the great Persian empires of the past, although it was undoubtedly not as wealthy as its Mughal and Ottoman neighbors. Hemmed in by the sea power of the Europeans to the south and the land power of the Ottomans to the west, the early Safavids had no navy and were forced to divert overland trade with Europe through southern Russia to avoid an Ottoman blockade. The situation improved when Persian forces working with the English seized the island of Hormuz (hawr-MOOZ) from Portugal and established a new seaport on the southern coast at Bandar Abbas (BUHN-der uh-BAHS). As a consequence, commercial ties with Europe began to increase.

George Holton/Science Source

16.6 The Royal Academy of Isfahan. Along with institutions such as libraries and hospitals, theological schools were often included in the mosque compound. One of the most sumptuous was the Royal Academy of Isfahan, which was built by the shah of Persia in the early eighteenth century. This view shows the large courtyard surrounded by arcades of student rooms, which are reminiscent of the arrangement of monks' cells in European cloisters.

16-2b Safavid Art and Literature

Persia witnessed an extraordinary flowering of the arts under the Safavids. Abbas the Great's new capital of Isfahan was a grandiose planned city with wide visual perspectives and a sense of order almost unique in the region. Shah Abbas ordered his architects to position his palaces, mosques, and bazaars around a massive rectangular polo ground. The immense mosques are richly decorated with imaginative metalwork and elaborate blue tiles.

The palaces are delicate structures with unusual slender wooden columns. These architectural wonders of Isfahan epitomize the grandeur, delicacy, and color that defined the Safavid golden age.

Textiles and painting were also areas of great achievement. Silk weaving based on new techniques became a national industry. Carpet weaving flourished, stimulated by the great demand for Persian carpets in Europe. The long tradition of Persian painting also continued, although with some changes. Taking advantage of the official toleration of portraiture, painters began to highlight the inner character of their subjects. Artists also sought to attract an audience beyond the royal court by producing individual paintings that promoted their own distinctive styles and proudly bore their own signatures.

16-3 THE GRANDEUR OF THE MUGHALS

Focus Questions: What role did Islam play in the Mughal Empire, and how did the Mughals' approach to religion compare with that of the Ottomans and the Safavids? What might explain the differences?

The Mughal (MOO-gul) Dynasty, which seized power in northern India in the early sixteenth century, has often been viewed as a high point of traditional culture in India. Unifying the bulk of the subcontinent for the first time in

CHRONOLOGY	The Safavids
Ismail seizes Persia and Iraq and becomes shah of Persia	1501
Ismail conquers Baghdad and defeats Uzbeks	1508
Reign of Shah Abbas I	1587–1629
Truce achieved between Ottomans and Safavids	1638
Collapse of the Safavid Empire	1723

more than a millennium, the Mughals created a common culture that inspired admiration and envy throughout the entire region.

16-3a The Founding of the Empire

When the Portuguese fleet led by Vasco da Gama arrived at the port of Calicut in 1498, the Indian subcontinent was still divided into many Hindu and Muslim kingdoms. But it was on the verge of a new era of unity that would be brought about by a foreign dynasty—the Mughals. Like so many of their predecessors, the founders of the Mughal Empire were not natives of India but came from the mountainous region north of the Ganges River. The founder of the dynasty, known to history as Babur (BAH-burr) (1483–1530), had an illustrious pedigree. His father was descended from the great Asian conqueror Tamerlane, his mother from the Mongol conqueror Genghis Khan.

Babur had inherited a fragment of Tamerlane's empire in a valley of the Syr Darya (SEER DAHR-yuh) River. Driven south by the rising power of the Uzbeks and then the Safavid Dynasty in Persia, Babur and his warriors seized Kabul in 1504 and crossed the Khyber Pass to India thirteen years later.

Following a pattern we have seen before, Babur began his rise to power by offering to help an ailing dynasty against its opponents. Although his own forces were far smaller than those of his adversaries, he possessed advanced weapons, including artillery, and used them to great effect. His use of mobile cavalry, supplemented by mounted elephants, was particularly successful against the massed forces of his enemy. In 1526, with only 12,000 troops against an enemy force nearly ten times that size, Babur captured Delhi (DEL-ee). Over the next years, he continued his conquests in northern India until his early death in 1530 at age forty-seven.

Babur's success was partly the result of his vigor and his charismatic personality, which earned him the undying loyalty of his followers. His son and successor Humayun (hoo-MY-yoon) (r. 1530–1556) was, in the words of one British historian, "intelligent but lazy." In 1540, he was forced to flee to Persia, where he lived in exile for sixteen years. Finally, with the aid of the Safavid shah of Persia, he returned to India and reconquered Delhi in 1555 but died the following year, reportedly from injuries suffered in a fall after smoking opium.

Humayun was succeeded by his son Akbar (r. 1556–1605). Born while his father was in exile, Akbar was only fourteen when he mounted the throne. Highly intelligent and industrious, Akbar set out to extend his domain, then limited to the Punjab (puhn-JAHB) and the upper Ganges River Valley. "A monarch," he remarked, should be ever intent on conquest; otherwise his neighbors rise in arms against him. The army "should be exercised in warfare, lest from want of training they become self-indulgent."[1] By the end of his life, he had brought Mughal rule to most of the subcontinent—from the Himalaya Mountains to central India and from Kashmir to the mouths of the Brahmaputra (brah-muh-POO-truh) and Ganges Rivers. In so doing, Akbar had created the greatest Indian empire since the Mauryan Dynasty nearly 2,000 years earlier (see Map 16.3). Though it appeared highly centralized from the outside, the empire was actually a collection of semiautonomous principalities ruled by provincial elites and linked together by the overarching majesty of the Mughal emperor.

16-3b Akbar and Indo-Muslim Civilization

Although Akbar was probably the greatest of the conquering Mughal monarchs, he was like his famous predecessor Ashoka and best known for the humane character of his rule. Above all, he accepted the diversity of Indian society and took steps to reconcile his Muslim and Hindu subjects.

Religion and the State Though raised an orthodox Muslim, Akbar had been exposed to other beliefs during his childhood and had little patience with the pedantic views of Muslim scholars at court. As emperor, he displayed a keen interest in other religions, not only tolerating Hindu practices and taking a Hindu princess as one of his wives but also welcoming the expression of Christian views by his Jesuit advisers (the Jesuits first sent a mission to Agra in 1580). He patronized classical Indian arts and architecture and abolished many of the restrictions faced by Hindus in a Muslim-dominated society.

During his later years, Akbar became steadily more hostile to Islam. To the dismay of many Muslims at court, he sponsored a new form of worship called the Divine Faith (*Din-i-ilahi*), which combined characteristics of several religions with a central belief in the infallibility of all decisions reached by the emperor. The new faith aroused deep hostility in Muslim circles and rapidly vanished after his death.

Administrative Reforms Akbar also extended his innovations to the imperial administration. Although the upper ranks of the government continued to be dominated by nonnative Muslims, a substantial proportion of lower-ranking officials were Hindus, and a few were appointed to positions of importance. The same element of religious tolerance extended to the legal system. Although Muslims were subject to the Islamic codes (the shari'a), Hindu law was applied in areas settled by Hindus, who after 1579 were no longer required to pay the unpopular jizya (JIZ-yuh), or

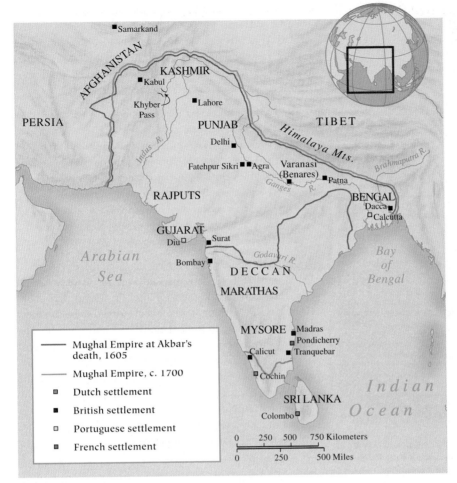

Map 16.3 The Mughal Empire. This map shows the expansion of the Mughal Empire from the death of Akbar in 1605 to the rule of Aurangzeb at the end of the seventeenth century.

Q *In which cities on the map were European settlements located? When did each group of Europeans arrive, and how did the settlements spread?*

and manufacturing flourished. Foreign trade in particular thrived as Indian goods—notably textiles, tropical food products, spices, and precious stones—were exported in exchange for gold and silver. Tariffs on imports were low. Much of the foreign commerce was handled by Arab traders because the Indians, like their Mughal rulers, did not care for travel by sea. Internal trade, however, was dominated by large merchant castes, who also were active in banking and handicrafts.

16-3c Akbar's Successors

Akbar died in 1605 and was succeeded by his son Jahangir (juh-HAHN-geer) (r. 1605–1628). During the early years of his reign, Jahangir continued to strengthen central control over the vast empire. Eventually, however, his grip began to weaken (according to his memoirs, he "only wanted a bottle of wine and a piece of meat to make merry"), and the court fell under the influence of one of his wives, Persian-born Nur Jahan (NOOR juh-HAHN). The empress took advantage of her position to enrich her own family and arranged for her niece Mumtaz Mahal (MOOM-tahz muh-HAHL) to marry her husband's third son and ultimate successor, Shah Jahan (r. 1628–1657). When Shah Jahan succeeded to the throne, he quickly demonstrated the single-minded quality of his grandfather (albeit in a much more brutal manner), ordering the assassination of all of his rivals to secure his position.

The Reign of Shah Jahan During a reign of three decades, Shah Jahan maintained the system established by his predecessors while expanding the boundaries of the empire by successful campaigns in the Deccan Plateau and against Samarkand, north of the Hindu Kush. But Shah Jahan's rule was marred by his failure to deal with the growing domestic problems. He had inherited a nearly empty treasury because of Empress Nur Jahan's penchant for luxury and ambitious charity projects. Though the majority of his subjects lived in

poll tax on non-Muslims. Punishments for crime were mild by the standards of the day, and justice was administered in a relatively impartial and efficient manner.

To cover the costs of administration, Akbar assigned plots of farmland to local civilian and military officials for their temporary use. These officials, known as *zamindars* (zuh-meen-DAHRZ), were expected to collect taxes from peasants tilling the lands under their control and forward them to the central government at its capital in Agra. They often accumulated considerable power in their localities. Although all Indian peasants were required to pay around one-third of their annual harvest to the state through the zamindars, in general the system was applied fairly; when drought struck in the 1590s, the taxes were reduced or even suspended altogether. Thanks to a long period of relative peace and political stability, commerce

16.7 Jahangir the Magnificent. In 1615, the English ambassador to the Mughal court presented an official portrait of King James I to Shah Jahangir, who returned the favor with a portrait of himself. Thus was established a long tradition of exchanging paintings between the two empires. As it turned out, the practice altered the style of Mughal portraiture, which had previously shown the emperor in action—hunting, participating at official functions, or engaging in battle. Henceforth, portraits of the ruler followed European practice by focusing on the opulence and spiritual power of the empire. In this painting, Jahangir has chosen spiritual over earthly power by offering a book to a sheikh while ignoring the Ottoman sultan, King James I, and the Hindu artist who painted the picture. Even the cherubs, a European artifice, are dazzled by the shah's divine character, which is further demonstrated by an enormous halo.

grinding poverty, Shah Jahan's frequent military campaigns and expensive building projects put a heavy strain on the imperial finances and compelled him to raise taxes. At the same time, the government did little to improve rural conditions. In a country where transport was primitive (it often took three months to travel the 600 miles between Patna, in the middle of the Ganges River Valley, and Delhi) and drought conditions frequent, the dynasty made few efforts to increase agricultural

efficiency or to improve the roads, although a grand trunk road was eventually constructed between the capital Agra (AH-gruh) and Lahore (luh-HOHR), a growing city several hundred miles to the northwest. A Dutch merchant in Gujarat (goo-juh-RAHT) described conditions during a famine in the mid-seventeenth century:

> As the famine increased, men abandoned towns and villages and wandered helplessly. It was easy to recognize their condition: eyes sunk deep in head, lips pale and covered with slime, the skin hard, with the bones showing through, the belly nothing but a pouch hanging down empty, knuckles and kneecaps showing prominently. One would cry and howl for hunger, while another lay stretched on the ground dying in misery; wherever you went, you saw nothing but corpses.[2]

In 1648, Shah Jahan moved his capital from Agra to Delhi and built the famous Red Fort in his new capital city. But he is best known for the Taj Mahal (tahj muh-HAHL) in Agra, which is widely considered to be the most beautiful building in India if not in the entire world. The story is a romantic one—the Taj was built by the emperor in memory of his wife Mumtaz Mahal, who had died giving birth to her thirteenth child at age thirty-nine. But the reality has a less attractive side: the expense of the building, which employed 20,000 masons over twenty years, forced the government to raise agricultural taxes, further impoverishing many Indian peasants.

Rule of Aurangzeb Succession struggles returned to haunt the dynasty in the mid-1650s when Shah Jahan's illness led to a struggle for power between his sons Dara Shikoh (DA-ruh SHIH-koh) and Aurangzeb (ow-rang-ZEB). Dara Shikoh was described by his contemporaries as progressive and humane, but he apparently lacked political acumen and was outmaneuvered by Aurangzeb (r. 1658–1707), who had Dara Shikoh put to death and then imprisoned his father in the fort at Agra.

Aurangzeb is one of the most controversial individuals in the history of India. A man of high principle, he attempted to eliminate many of what he considered to be India's social evils, prohibiting the immolation of widows on their husband's funeral pyre (a practice known as *sati*), the castration of eunuchs, and the exaction of illegal taxes. With less success, he tried to forbid gambling, drinking, and prostitution. But Aurangzeb, a devout and somewhat doctrinaire Muslim, also adopted several measures that reversed the policies of religious tolerance established by his predecessors. The building of new Hindu temples was prohibited, and the Hindu poll tax was restored. Forced conversions to Islam were

16.8 The Taj Mahal: symbol of the exotic East. Completed in 1653, the Taj Mahal was built by Mughal Emperor Shah Jahan as a tomb to commemorate his beloved wife, Mumtaz Mahal. Raised on a marble platform above the Yamuna River, the Taj is dramatically framed by contrasting twin red sandstone mosques, magnificent gardens, and a long reflecting pool that mirrors and magnifies its beauty. The effect is one of monumental size, near blinding brilliance, and delicate lightness, a startling contrast to the heavier and more masculine Baroque style then popular in Europe. The entire exterior and interior surface of the Taj is decorated with cut-stone geometric patterns, delicate black stone tracery, or intricate inlay of colored precious stones in floral and Qur'anic arabesques.

resumed, and non-Muslims were driven from the court. Aurangzeb's heavy-handed religious policies led to a revival of Hindu fervor. The last years of his reign saw considerable domestic unrest and several revolts against imperial authority.

The Shadows Lengthen During the eighteenth century, Mughal power was threatened from both within and without. Fueled by the growing power and autonomy of the local gentry and merchants, rebellious groups throughout the empire—from the Deccan to the Punjab—began to reassert local authority and reduce the power of the Mughal emperor to that of a "tinsel sovereign." Increasingly divided, India was vulnerable to attack from abroad. In 1739, Delhi was sacked by the Persians, who left it in ashes.

We can identify several obvious reasons for the virtual collapse of the Mughal Empire, including a drain on the imperial treasury and the decline in competence of the Mughal rulers. But also note that even at its height under Akbar, the empire was a loosely knit collection of heterogeneous principalities held together by the authority of the throne, which tried to combine Persian concepts of kingship with the Indian tradition of decentralized power. Decline set in when centrifugal forces gradually began to predominate over centripetal ones.

16-3d The Impact of European Power in India

As we have seen, the first Europeans to arrive were the Portuguese. Although they established a virtual monopoly over regional trade in the Indian Ocean, they did not seek to penetrate the interior of the subcontinent but focused on establishing way stations en route to China and the Spice Islands. The situation changed at the end of the sixteenth century when the English and the Dutch appeared on the scene. Soon both powers were in active competition with Portugal and with each other for trading privileges in the region (see Opposing Viewpoints, "The Capture of Port Hoogly," p. 410).

Penetration of the new market was not easy. When the first English fleet arrived at Surat (SOOR-et), a thriving port on India's northwestern coast, in 1608, their request for trading privileges was rejected by Emperor Jahangir. Needing lightweight Indian cloth to trade for spices in the East Indies, the English persisted, and they were finally permitted to install their own ambassador at the imperial court in Agra in 1616. Three years later, the first English factory (trading station) was established at Surat.

During the next several decades, the English presence in India steadily increased while Mughal power gradually waned. By midcentury, additional English factories had been established at Fort William (now the city of Kolkata,

The Capture of Port Hoogly

Interaction & Exchange

IN 1632, THE MUGHAL RULER, SHAH JAHAN, ORDERED AN ATTACK on the city of Hoogly (HOOG-lee), a fortified Portuguese trading post on the northeastern coast of India. For the Portuguese, who had profited from half a century of triangular trade between India, China, and various countries in the Middle East and Southeast Asia, the loss of Hoogly at the hands of the Mughals hastened the decline of their influence in the region. Presented here are two contemporary versions of the battle. The first is from the *Padshahnama* (pad-shah-NAHM-uh) (*Book of Kings*) and relates the course of events from the Mughal point of view. The second account is by John Cabral, a Jesuit missionary who was resident in Hoogly at the time.

The *Padshahnama*

During the reign of the Bengalis, a group of Frankish [European] merchants . . . settled in a place one *kos* from Satgaon . . . and, on the pretext that they needed a place for trading, they received permission from the Bengalis to construct a few edifices. Over time, due to the indifference of the governors of Bengal, many Franks gathered there and built dwellings of the utmost splendor and strength, fortified with cannons, guns, and other instruments of war. It was not long before it became a large settlement and was named Hoogly. . . . The Franks' ships trafficked at this port, and commerce was established, causing the market at the port of Satgaon to slump. . . . Of the peasants of those places, they converted some to Christianity by force and others through greed and sent them off to Europe in their ships. . . .

Since the improper actions of the Christians of Hoogly Port toward the Muslims were accurately reflected in the mirror of the mind of the Emperor before his accession to the throne, when the imperial banners cast their shadows over Bengal, and inasmuch as he was always inclined to propagate the true religion and eliminate infidelity, it was decided that when he gained control over this region he would eradicate the corruption of these abominators from the realm.

John Cabral, *Travels of Sebastian Manrique, 1629–1649*

Hugli continued at peace all the time of the great King Jahangir. For, as this Prince, by what he showed, was more attached to Christ than to Mohammad and was a Moor in name and dress only. . . . Sultan Khurram [Shah Jahan] was in everything unlike his father, especially as regards the latter's leaning towards Christianity. . . . He declared himself the mortal enemy of the Christian name and the restorer of the law of Mohammad. . . . He sent a *firman* [order] to the Viceroy of Bengal, commanding him without reply or delay, to march upon the Bandel of Hugli and put it to fire and the sword. He added that, in doing so, he would render a signal service to God, to Mohammad, and to him. . . .

Consequently, on a Friday, September 24, 1632, . . . all the people [the Portuguese] embarked with the utmost secrecy. . . . Learning what was going on, and wishing to be able to boast that they had taken Hugli by storm, they [the imperialists] made a general attack on the Bandel by Saturday noon. They began by setting fire to a mine, but lost in it more men than we. Finally, however, they were masters of the Bandel.

 How do these two accounts of the Battle of Hoogly differ? Is there any way to reconcile the two accounts into a single narrative?

Source: From *King of the World: A Mughal Manuscript from the Royal Library, Windsor Castle,* trans. by Wheeler Thackston, text by Milo Cleveland Beach and Ebba Koch (London: Thames and Hudson, 1997), p. 59.

formerly Calcutta) on the Hoogly River near the Bay of Bengal and in 1639 at Madras (muh-DRAS or muh-DRAHS) (Chennai) on the southeastern coast. From there, English ships carried Indian-made cotton goods to the East Indies, where they were bartered for spices that were shipped back to England.

English success in India attracted rivals, including the Dutch and the French. The Dutch eventually abandoned their interests in India to concentrate on the spice trade, but the French were more persistent and established factories of their own. For a brief period, under the ambitious empire builder Joseph François Dupleix (zho-ZEF frahn-SWAH doo-PLAY), the French competed successfully with the British, even capturing Madras from a British garrison in 1746. But the French government was reluctant to support Dupleix's ambitious plans, and eventually the British, under the leadership of Sir Robert Clive (CLYV), an aggressive administrator and empire builder with the East India Company, drove the French out of South India, leaving them only their fort at Pondicherry (pon-duh-CHEH-ree) and a handful of small territories on the southeastern coast.

Clive's victory over the French marked the opening stage in an intensive effort to consolidate British influence in other parts of the Mughal Empire. When a local potentate attacked the British settlement at Fort William and imprisoned the local British population in the infamous Black Hole of Calcutta (an underground prison for holding prisoners, many of whom died in captivity), the British retaliated by defeating a Mughal-led army more than ten times its size in the Battle of Plassey (PLASS-ee). As part of the spoils of victory, the British East India Company exacted from the now-decrepit Mughal court the authority to collect taxes from extensive lands in the area surrounding Calcutta (Kolkata). Less than a decade later, British forces seized the reigning Mughal emperor in a skirmish at Buxar (buk-SAHR), and the British began to consolidate their economic and administrative control over Indian territory through the surrogate power of the now powerless Mughal court (see Map 16.4).

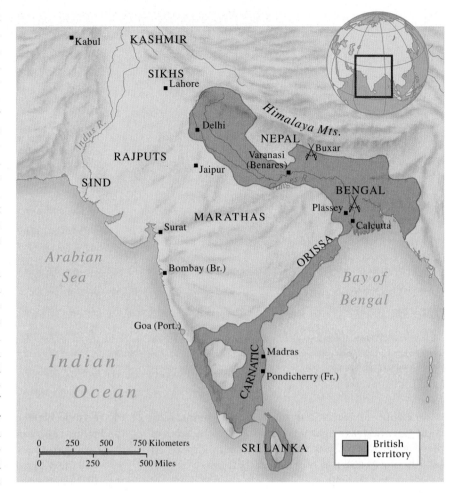

Map 16.4 India in 1805. By the early nineteenth century, much of the Indian subcontinent had fallen under British domination.

Q *Where was the capital of the Mughal Empire located?*

Economic Difficulties The Company's takeover of vast landholdings, notably in the eastern Indian states of Orissa (uh-RIH-suh) and Bengal (ben-GAHL), may have been a windfall for enterprising British officials, but it was a disaster for the Indian economy. First, it transferred capital from the local Indian aristocracy to company officials, most of whom sent their profits back to Britain. Second, it hastened the destruction of once healthy local industries because British goods such as machine-made textiles were imported duty-free into India to compete against local products. Finally, British expansion hurt the peasants. As the British took over the administration of the land tax, they also applied British law, which allowed the lands of those unable to pay the tax to be confiscated. In the 1770s, a series of massive famines led to the death of an estimated one-third of the population in the areas under company administration. The British government attempted to resolve the problem by assigning tax lands to the local revenue collectors (zamindars) in the hope of transforming them into English-style rural gentry, but many collectors themselves fell into bankruptcy and sold their lands to absentee bankers while the now landless peasants remained in abject poverty. It was hardly an auspicious beginning to "civilized" British rule.

16.9 A Pepper Plantation. During the Age of Exploration, pepper was one of the spices most sought by European adventurers. Unlike cloves and nutmeg, it was found in other areas of Asia besides the Indonesian archipelago. Shown here is a medieval European portrayal of a pepper plantation in southern India. The illustration appeared in a fifteenth-century edition of *The Travels of Marco Polo*.

Unfortunately for India, most Indian commanders could not effectively fight the British. In the last years of the eighteenth century, the stage was set for the final consolidation of British rule over the subcontinent.

HISTORIANS DEBATE 16-3e The Mughal Dynasty: A "Gunpowder Empire"?

To some recent historians, the success of the Mughals, like that of the Ottomans and the Safavids, was the result of their mastery of modern warfare techniques, especially the use of firearms. In this view, firearms played a central role in the rise of all three empires to regional hegemony. Accordingly, some scholars have labeled them "gunpowder empires." Although technical prowess in the art of warfare was undoubtedly a key element in their success, we should not forget that other factors such as dynamic leadership, political acumen, and ardent followers motivated by religious zeal were at least equally important. Even today, many Indians regard Akbar as the country's greatest ruler, a tribute not only to his military success but also to the humane policies adopted during his reign.

Unlike the Ottoman Turks, however, the Mughals were inconsistent in applying a policy of tolerance for the non-Muslim peoples within their borders. Aurangzeb's policy of actively converting peoples of other faiths to the reigning ideology of Islam was undoubtedly a factor in the rise of Hindu insurgent groups seeking to break away from Mughal rule during his reign. In other respects, the Mughals suffered from the same limitations that afflicted their counterparts in Isfahan and Istanbul. Smugly confident in the superiority of their culture to that of potential rivals, they expressed little interest in the dramatic changes taking place in the fields of science and technology. Eventually, even their vaunted superiority in the art of war abandoned them as they failed to realize the importance of adopting modern naval technology and tactics, a tragic mistake that placed them as a disadvantage in an era when naval warfare was becoming the key to national survival.

16-3f Society Under the Mughals: A Synthesis of Cultures

The Mughals were the last of the great traditional Indian dynasties. Like so many of their predecessors since the fall of the Guptas nearly a thousand years before, the Mughals were Muslims. But like the Ottoman Turks, the best Mughal rulers did not simply impose Islamic institutions and beliefs on the predominantly Hindu population; they combined Muslim with Hindu and even Persian concepts and cultural values in a unique social and cultural synthesis. The new faith of Sikhism, founded in the early sixteenth

16.10 The Astronomical Observatory of Jai Singh. Although Mughal elites generally expressed little interest in science and technology, one Indian ruler who broke the mold was the Hindu ruler of Jaipur, Jai Singh. In the 1720s, he ordered the construction of an astronomical observatory in his palace to study the movement of the heavenly bodies. Unfortunately, much of the equipment—some of which is shown here—consisted of outdated instruments and lacked the capacity to compete with the accurate telescopic observations then being carried out in Europe. The observatory was closed a few years later and is now merely a curiosity.

that the mystical and devotional qualities promoted by Sufi missionaries corresponded to local traditions. This was especially true in Bengal, on the eastern edge of the Indian subcontinent, where Hindu practices were not as well established and where forms of religious devotionalism had long been popular.

The Economy Although much of the local population in the subcontinent lived in poverty punctuated by occasional periods of widespread famine, the first centuries of Mughal rule were in some respects a period of relative prosperity for the region. India was a leading participant in the growing foreign trade that crisscrossed the Indian Ocean from the Red Sea and the Persian Gulf to the Strait of Malacca and the Indonesian Archipelago. High-quality cloth from India was especially prized, and the country's textile industry made it, in the words of one historian, "the industrial workshop of the world."

Long-term stability led to increasing commercialization and the spread of wealth to new groups within Indian society. The Mughal era saw the emergence of an affluent landed

century in an effort to blend both faiths (see Chapter 9), undoubtedly benefited from the mood of syncretism promoted by the Mughal court.

To be sure, Hindus sometimes attempted to defend themselves and their religious practices against the efforts of some Mughal monarchs to impose the Islamic religion and Islamic mores on the indigenous population. In some cases, despite official prohibitions, Hindu men forcibly married Muslim women and then converted them to the native faith, while converts to Islam normally lost all of their inheritance rights within the Indian family. Government orders to destroy Hindu temples were often ignored by local officials, sometimes as the result of bribery or intimidation. Although the founding emperor Babur expressed little admiration for the country he had subjected to his rule, ultimately Indian practices had an influence on the Mughal elites as many Mughal chieftains married Indian women and adopted Indian forms of dress.

In some areas, Emperor Akbar's tireless effort to bring about a blend of Middle Eastern and South Asian religious and cultural values paid rich dividends as substantial numbers of Indians converted to Islam during the centuries of Mughal rule. Some were undoubtedly attracted to the religion's egalitarian characteristics, but others found

CHRONOLOGY	The Mughal Era
Arrival of Vasco da Gama at Calicut	1498
Babur seizes Delhi	1526
Death of Babur	1530
Humayun recovers throne in Delhi	1555
Death of Humayun and accession of Akbar	1556
First Jesuit mission to Agra	1580
Death of Akbar and accession of Jahangir	1605
Arrival of English at Surat	1608
English embassy to Agra	1616
Reign of Emperor Shah Jahan	1628–1657
Foundation of English factory at Madras	1639
Aurangzeb succeeds to the throne	1658
Death of Aurangzeb	1707
Sack of Delhi by the Persians	1739
French capture Madras	1746
Battle of Plassey	1757

gentry and a prosperous merchant class. Members of prestigious castes from the pre-Mughal period reaped many of the benefits of the increasing wealth, but some of these changes transcended caste boundaries and led to the emergence of new groups who achieved status and wealth on the basis of economic achievement rather than traditional kinship ties. During the late eighteenth century, this economic prosperity was shaken by the decline of the Mughal Empire and the increasing European presence. But many prominent Indians reacted by establishing commercial relationships with the foreigners. For a time, such relationships often worked to the Indians' benefit. As we shall see, they would later have cause to regret the arrangement.

The Position of Women Whether Mughal rule had much effect on the lives of ordinary Indians seems somewhat problematic. The treatment of women is a good example. Women had traditionally played an active role in Mongol tribal society—many actually fought on the battlefield alongside men—and Babur and his successors often relied on the women in their families for political advice. Women from aristocratic families were often awarded honorific titles, received salaries, and were permitted to own land and engage in business. Women at court sometimes received an education, and aristocratic women often expressed their creative talents by writing poetry, painting, or playing music. Women of all classes were adept at spinning thread, either for their own use or to sell to weavers to augment the family income. They sold simple cloth to local villages and fine cottons, silks, and wool to the Mughal court.

To a certain degree, these Mughal attitudes toward women may have affected Indian society. Women were allowed to inherit land, and some even possessed zamindar rights. Women from mercantile castes sometimes took an active role in business activities. At the same time, however, as Muslims, the Mughals subjected women to certain restrictions under Islamic law. On the whole, these Mughal practices coincided with and even accentuated existing tendencies in Indian society. The Muslim practice of isolating women and preventing them from associating with men outside the home (*purdah*) was adopted by many upper-class Hindus as a means of enhancing their status or protecting their women from unwelcome advances by Muslims in positions of authority. In other ways, Hindu practices were unaffected. The custom of sati continued to be practiced despite efforts by the Mughals to abolish it, and child marriage (most women were betrothed before age ten) remained common. Women were still instructed to obey their husbands without question and to remain chaste.

16-3g Mughal Culture

The era of the Mughals was one of synthesis in culture, politics, and religion. The Mughals combined Islamic themes with Persian and indigenous motifs to produce a unique style that enriched and embellished Indian art and culture. The Mughal emperors were zealous patrons of the arts and enticed painters, poets, and artisans from as far away as the Mediterranean. Apparently, the generosity of the Mughals made it difficult to refuse a trip to India. It was said that they would reward a poet with his weight in gold.

Architecture Undoubtedly, the Mughals' most visible achievement was in architecture. Here they integrated Persian and Indian styles in a new and sometimes breathtakingly beautiful form best symbolized by the Taj Mahal, which was built by the emperor Shah Jahan in the mid-seventeenth century. Although the human and economic cost of the Taj tarnishes the romantic legend of its construction, there is no denying the beauty of the building. Ironically, after Shah Jahan was deposed by his son Aurangzeb, he spent his last years imprisoned in a room in the adjacent Red Fort at Agra; from his windows, he could see the beautiful memorial to his beloved wife.

The Taj was not the only magnificent building erected during the Mughal era. Akbar, who, in the words of a contemporary, "[dressed] the work of his mind and heart in the garment of stone and clay," was the first of the great Mughal builders. His first palace at Agra, the Red Fort, was begun in 1565. A few years later, he ordered the construction of a new palace at Fatehpur Sikri (fah-tay-POOR SIK-ree), twenty-six miles west of Agra. The new palace was built in honor of a Sufi mystic who had correctly forecast the birth of a son to the emperor. In gratitude, Akbar decided to build a new capital city and palace on the site of the mystic's home in the village of Sikri. Over fifteen years, from 1571 to 1586, a magnificent new city in red sandstone was constructed. Although the city was abandoned before completion and now stands almost untouched, it is a popular destination for tourists and pilgrims.

Painting The other major artistic achievement of the Mughal period was painting. Like so many other aspects of Mughal India, painting blended two cultures. While living in exile, Emperor Humayun had learned to admire Persian miniatures. On his return to India in 1555, he invited two Persian masters to live in his palace and introduce the technique to his adopted land. His successor Akbar appreciated the new style and popularized it with his patronage. He established a state workshop at Fatehpur Sikri for 200 artists, mostly Hindus, who worked under the guidance of the Persian masters to create the Mughal school of painting.

Literature The development of Indian literature was held back by the absence of printing, which was not introduced until the end of the Mughal era. Literary works were inscribed by calligraphers, and one historian has estimated that the library of Agra contained more than 24,000 volumes. Poetry, in particular, flourished under the Mughals, who established poet laureates at court. Poems were written in the Persian style and in the Persian language. In fact, Persian became the official language of the court until the sack of Delhi in 1739.

Another aspect of the long Mughal reign was a revival of Hindu devotional literature, much of it dedicated to Krishna and Rama. The retelling of the *Ramayana* in the vernacular culminated in the sixteenth-century Hindi version by the great poet Tulsidas (tool-see-DAHSS) (1532–1623). His *Ramcaritmanas* (RAM-kah-rit-MAH-nuz) presents the devotional story with a deified Rama and Sita. Tulsidas's genius was in combining the conflicting cults of Vishnu and Shiva into a unified and overwhelming love for the divine, which he expressed in some of the most moving of all Indian poetry. The *Ramcaritmanas* has eclipsed its 2,000-year-old Sanskrit ancestor in popularity and even became the basis of an Indian television series in the late 1980s.

CHAPTER SUMMARY

The three empires discussed in this chapter exhibited several striking similarities. First, they were Muslim in their religious affiliation, although the Safavids were Shi'ite rather than Sunni, a distinction that often led to mutual tensions and conflict. More important, perhaps, they were all nomadic in origin, and the political and social institutions they adopted carried the imprint of their preimperial past. Once they achieved imperial power, however, all three ruling dynasties displayed an impressive capacity to administer large empires and brought a degree of stability to peoples who had all too often lived in conditions of internal division and war.

The rise of these powerful Muslim states coincided with the opening period of European expansion at the end of the fifteenth century and the beginning of the sixteenth. The military and political talents of these empires helped protect much of the Muslim world from the resurgent forces of Christianity. In fact, the Ottoman Turks carried their empire into the heart of Christian Europe and briefly reached the gates of the great city of Vienna. By the end of the eighteenth century, however, the Safavid Dynasty had imploded, and the powerful Mughal Empire was in a state of virtual collapse. Only the Ottoman Empire was still functioning. Yet it too had lost much of its early expansionistic vigor and was showing signs of internal decay.

Why these empires declined has inspired considerable debate among historians. One factor was undoubtedly the expansion of European power into the Indian Ocean and the Middle East. But internal causes were probably more important in the long run. All three empires experienced growing factionalism within the ruling elite, incompetent leadership, and the emergence of divisive forces in the empire at large—factors that have marked the passing of traditional empires since early times. Climate change (the region was reportedly hotter and drier after the beginning of the seventeenth century) may have been a contributing factor. Paradoxically, one of the greatest strengths of these empires—their mastery of gunpowder—may have simultaneously been a serious weakness because it allowed them to develop a complacent sense of security. With little incentive to turn their attention to new developments in science and technology, they were increasingly vulnerable to attack by the advanced nations of the West.

The Muslim empires, however, were not the only states in the Old World that were able to resist the first outward thrust of European expansion. Farther to the east, the mature civilizations in China and Japan faced down a similar challenge from Western merchants and missionaries. Unlike their counterparts in South Asia and the Middle East, as the nineteenth century dawned, they continued to thrive.

REFLECTION QUESTIONS

Q How did the social policies adopted by the Ottomans compare with those of the Mughals and the Safavids? What similarities and differences do you detect, and what might account for them?

Q What is meant by the phrase "gunpowder empires," and to what degree did the Muslim states discussed here conform to this description? Can the concept be applied to other parts of the world as well?

Q What role did women play in the Ottoman, Safavid, and Mughal Empires? What might explain the similarities and differences? How did the treatment of women in these states compare with their treatment in other parts of the world?

CHAPTER TIMELINE

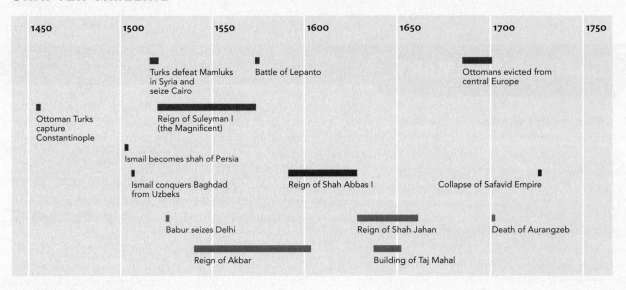

| 1450 | 1500 | 1550 | 1600 | 1650 | 1700 | 1750 |

Turks defeat Mamluks in Syria and seize Cairo

Battle of Lepanto

Ottomans evicted from central Europe

Ottoman Turks capture Constantinople

Reign of Suleyman I (the Magnificent)

Ismail becomes shah of Persia

Ismail conquers Baghdad from Uzbeks

Reign of Shah Abbas I

Collapse of Safavid Empire

Babur seizes Delhi

Reign of Shah Jahan

Death of Aurangzeb

Reign of Akbar

Building of Taj Mahal

CHAPTER NOTES

1. V. A. Smith, *The Oxford History of India* (Oxford, 1967), p. 341.

2. Quoted in M. Edwardes, *A History of India: From the Earliest Times to the Present Day* (London, 1961), p. 188.

MINDTAP
From Cengage

MindTap® is a fully online, highly personalized learning experience built upon Cengage Learning content. MindTap combines student learning tools—readings, multimedia, activities, and assessments—into a singular Learning Path that guides students through the course and helps students develop the critical thinking, analysis, and communication skills that are essential to academic and professional success.

Chapter Outline and Focus Questions

17-1 *China at Its Apex*

Q Why were the Manchus so successful establishing a foreign dynasty in China, and what were the main characteristics of Manchu rule?

17-2 *Changing China*

Q How did the economy and society of China change during the Ming and Qing eras, and to what degree did these changes seem to be leading toward an industrial revolution on the European model?

17-3 *Tokugawa Japan*

Q How did the society and economy of Japan change during the Tokugawa era, and how did Japanese culture reflect those changes?

17-4 *Korea and Vietnam*

Q To what degree did developments in Korea during this period reflect conditions in China and Japan? What were the unique aspects of Vietnamese civilization?

Critical Thinking

Q *How did China and Japan respond to the coming of the Europeans, and what explains the differences in their approach? What impact did European contacts have on these two East Asian civilizations through the end of the eighteenth century?*

Connections to Today

Q *The world population was increasing dramatically in parts of the world during the eighteenth century, just as it is today. What were the main reasons for this expansion, and what lessons does it suggest for dealing with the issue in our own day?*

Hu Weibiao/Panorama/The Image Works

17.1 Emperor Kangxi

IN DECEMBER 1717, Emperor Kangxi (KANG-shee) returned from a hunting trip north of the Great Wall and began to suffer from dizzy spells. Conscious of his approaching date with mortality—he was now nearly seventy years old—the emperor called together his sons and leading government officials in the imperial palace and issued an edict summing up his ideas on the art of statecraft. Rulers, he declared, should sincerely revere heaven's laws as their fundamental strategy for governing the country. Among other things, those laws required that the ruler show concern for the welfare of the people, practice diligence, protect the state from its enemies, choose able advisers, and strike a careful balance between leniency and strictness, principle and expedience. That, he concluded, was all there was to it.[1]

Any potential successor to the throne would have been well advised to attend to the emperor's advice. Kangxi was not only one of the longest reigning of all Chinese rulers but also one of the wisest. His era was one of peace and prosperity, and the empire was now at the zenith of its power and influence after a half-century of his rule. As his life approached its end, heaven must indeed have been pleased at the quality of his stewardship.

Kangxi reigned during one of the most glorious eras in the long history of China. Under the Ming (MING) and the early Qing (CHING) Dynasties, the empire expanded its borders to a degree not seen since the Han and the Tang. Chinese culture was the envy of its neighbors and earned the admiration of many European visitors, including Jesuit priests and Enlightenment philosophes.

On the surface, China appeared to be an unchanging society patterned after the Confucian vision of a "golden age" in the remote past. This indeed was the image presented by China's rulers, who referred constantly to tradition as a model for imperial institutions and cultural values. Although few observers could have been aware of it at the time, however, China was changing—and rather rapidly.

A similar process was under way in neighboring Japan. A vigorous new shogunate (SHOH-gun-ut or SHOH-gun-ayt) called the Tokugawa (toh-goo-GAH-wah) rose to power in the early seventeenth century and managed to revitalize the traditional system in a somewhat more centralized form that enabled it to survive for another 250 years. But major structural changes were taking place in Japanese society, and tensions were growing as the gap between theory and reality widened by the nineteenth century. As always, Korea and Vietnam sought to reconcile their own indigenous traditions with the powerful influence of Chinese culture.

17-1 CHINA AT ITS APEX

Focus Question: Why were the Manchus so successful establishing a foreign dynasty in China, and what were the main characteristics of Manchu rule?

In 1514, a Portuguese fleet dropped anchor off the coast of China, just south of the Pearl River estuary and present-day Hong Kong. It was the first direct contact between the Chinese Empire and the West since the arrival of Venetian adventurer Marco Polo two centuries earlier, and it opened an era that would eventually change the face of China and, indeed, all the world.

17-1a The Later Ming

Marco Polo had reported on the magnificence of China after visiting Beijing (bay-ZHING) during the reign of Khubilai Khan, the great Mongol ruler. By the time the Portuguese fleet arrived off the coast of China, of course, the Yuan Dynasty had long since disintegrated. It had gradually weakened after the death of Khubilai Khan and was finally overthrown in 1368 by a massive peasant rebellion

under the leadership of Zhu Yuanzhang (JOO yoo-wen-JAHNG), who had declared himself the founding emperor of a new Ming (Bright) Dynasty (1369–1644).

As we have seen, the Ming inaugurated a period of territorial expansion westward into Central Asia and southward into Vietnam while consolidating control over China's vast heartland. At the same time, between 1405 and 1433 the dynasty sponsored a series of voyages that spread Chinese influence far into the Indian Ocean. Then suddenly the voyages were discontinued, and the dynasty turned its attention to domestic concerns (see Chapter 10). To underline the new policy, Emperor Yongle (YOONG-luh) transplanted his capital to Beijing, where he ordered the construction of a new home—known as the Imperial City—on the grounds of Khubilai's old palace under the Yuan dynasty (see Image 17.2).

First Contacts with the West Despite the Ming's retreat from active participation in maritime trade, China was in command of a vast empire that stretched from the steppes of Central Asia to the China Sea, from the Gobi Desert to the tropical rain forests of Southeast Asia when the Portuguese arrived in 1514. From the lofty perspective of the imperial throne in Beijing, the Europeans could only have seemed like an unusually exotic form of barbarian to be inserted within the familiar framework of the tributary system, the hierarchical arrangement in which rulers of all other countries were regarded as "younger brothers" of the Son of Heaven. Indeed, the bellicose and uncultured behavior of the Portuguese so outraged Chinese officials that they initially expelled the Europeans. After further negotiations, however, the Portuguese were permitted to occupy the tiny territory of Macao (muh-KOW) on the coast of southern China, a foothold they would retain until the end of the twentieth century.

At first, the arrival of the Europeans had little effect on Chinese society. Chinese interest in European goods was limited, so Portuguese ships became involved in the regional trade network, carrying silk from China to Japan in return for Japanese silver. Eventually, the Spanish also began to participate, using the Philippines as an anchor in the galleon trade between China and the great silver mines in the Americas.

More influential than trade, perhaps, were the ideas introduced by Christian missionaries, who received permission to reside in China beginning in the last quarter of the sixteenth century. Among the most active and the most effective were highly educated Jesuits, who were familiar with European philosophical and scientific developments. Court officials were particularly impressed by the visitors' ability to predict the exact time of a solar eclipse, an event the Chinese viewed with extreme reverence.

17.2 The Imperial City in Beijing. During the fifteenth century, the Ming Dynasty erected an immense imperial city on the remnants of the palace of Khubilai Khan in Beijing. Surrounded by 6.5 miles of walls, the enclosed compound is divided into a maze of private apartments and offices; it also includes an imposing ceremonial quadrangle with stately halls for imperial audiences and banquets. Because it was off-limits to commoners, the compound was known as the Forbidden City.

The Ming Brought to Earth During the late sixteenth century, the Ming Dynasty began to decline as a series of weak rulers led to an era of corruption, concentration of land-ownership, and ultimately peasant rebellions and tribal unrest along the northern frontier. The inflow of vast amounts of foreign silver to pay for Chinese goods resulted in an alarming increase in inflation. Then the arrival of the English and the Dutch, whose ships preyed on the Spanish galleon trade between Asia and the Americas, disrupted the silver trade; silver imports plummeted, severely straining the Chinese economy by raising the value of the metal relative to that of copper. Crop yields declined because of harsh weather, and the resulting scarcity made it difficult for the government to provide food in times of imminent starvation. High taxes, necessitated in part because corrupt officials siphoned off revenues, led to rural unrest and violent protests among urban workers.

Recognizing the Chinese pride in their own culture, the Jesuits sought to draw parallels between Christian and Confucian concepts (for example, they identified the Western concept of God with the Chinese character for heaven) and to show the similarities between Christian morality and Confucian ethics. European inventions such as the clock, the prism, and various astronomical and musical instruments impressed Chinese officials, who had hitherto been deeply imbued with a sense of the superiority of Chinese civilization, and that helped Western ideas win acceptance at court. An elderly Chinese scholar expressed his wonder at the miracle of eyeglasses:

> *White glass from across the Western Seas*
> *Is imported through Macao:*
> *Fashioned into lenses big as coins,*
> *They encompass the eyes in a double frame.*
> *I put them on—it suddenly becomes clear;*
> *I can see the very tips of things!*
> *And read fine print by the dim-lit window*
> *Just like in my youth.*[2]

For their part, the missionaries were much impressed with many aspects of Chinese civilization, and their reports home heightened European curiosity about this great society on the other side of the world. By the late seventeenth century, European philosophers and political thinkers had begun to praise Chinese civilization and to hold up Confucian institutions and values as a mirror to criticize their counterparts in the West.

As always, internal problems were accompanied by unrest along the northern frontier. Following long precedent, the Ming had attempted to pacify the frontier tribes by forging alliances with them and granting trade privileges. One alliance was with the Manchus (man-CHOOZ)—also known as the Jurchen (roor-ZHEN)—the descendants of peoples who had briefly established a kingdom in northern China during the early thirteenth century. The Manchus, a mixed agricultural and hunting people, lived northeast of the Great Wall in the area known today as Manchuria (man-CHUR-ee-uh).

At first, the Manchus were satisfied with consolidating their territory and made little effort to extend their rule south of the Great Wall. But during the first decades of the seventeenth century, a major epidemic devastated the population in many areas of the country. The suffering brought on by the epidemic, combined with widespread drought conditions, helped spark a vast peasant uprising led by the former postal worker Li Zicheng (lee zuh-CHENG) (1604–1651). By the 1630s, the revolt had spread throughout the country, and Li's forces finally occupied the capital of Beijing in 1644. The last Ming emperor committed suicide by hanging himself from a tree in the palace gardens.

Emboldened by the overthrow of the Ming Dynasty, the Manchus attacked Beijing on their own (see Map 17.1). Li Zicheng's army disintegrated, and the Manchus declared

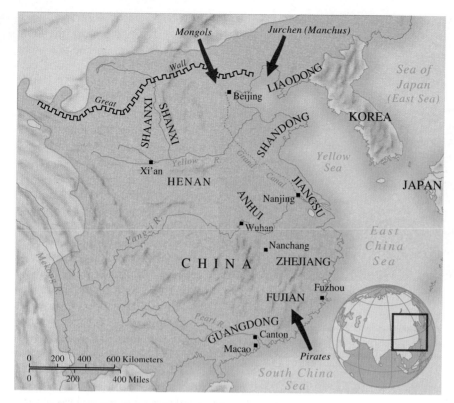

Mongols
Jurchen (Manchus)
Wall
Great
Beijing
LIAODONG
Sea of Japan (East Sea)
SHAANXI
SHANXI
SHANDONG
KOREA
Xi'an
Yellow R.
HENAN
Grand Canal
Yellow Sea
JIANGSU
JAPAN
Nanjing
ANHUI
Yang-zi R.
Wuhan
East China Sea
Nanchang
C H I N A
ZHEJIANG
Fuzhou
FUJIAN
Pearl R.
GUANGDONG
Canton
Macao
Pirates
South China Sea
Mekong R.

0   200   400   600 Kilometers
0   200   400 Miles

Map 17.1 China and its Enemies During the Late Ming Era. During the seventeenth century, the Ming Dynasty faced challenges on two fronts: from China's traditional adversaries, nomadic groups north of the Great Wall, and from new arrivals, European merchants who had begun to press for trading privileges along the southern coast.

 How did these threats differ from those faced by previous dynasties in China?

the creation of a new dynasty: the Qing (or Pure), which lasted from 1644 until 1911. Once again, China was under foreign rule.

17-1b The Greatness of the Qing

The accession of the Manchus to power in Beijing was not universally applauded. Some Ming loyalists fled to Southeast Asia, but others continued their resistance to the new rulers from inside the country. To make it easier to identify the rebels, the government ordered all Chinese to adopt Manchu dress and hairstyles. All Chinese males were to shave their foreheads and braid their hair into a queue (KYOO); those who refused were to be executed. As a popular saying put it, "Lose your hair or lose your head."[3]

Like all of China's great dynasties, however, the Qing was blessed with a series of strong early rulers who pacified the country, rectified many of the most obvious social and economic inequities, and restored peace and prosperity. For the Ming Dynasty, these strong emperors had been Zhu Yuanzhang and Yongle; under the Qing, they would be Kangxi and Qianlong (CHAN-loong).

The two Qing monarchs ruled China for well over a century and were responsible for much of the success achieved by the Qing Empire.

The Reign of Kangxi Kangxi (r. 1661–1722) was arguably the greatest ruler in Chinese history. Ascending to the throne at age seven, he was blessed with diligence, political astuteness, and a strong character and began to take charge of Qing administration while he was still an adolescent. During the six decades of his reign, Kangxi not only stabilized imperial rule by pacifying the restive peoples along the northern and western frontiers but also managed to make the dynasty acceptable to the general population. As an active patron of arts and letters, he cultivated the support of scholars through many major projects.

During Kangxi's reign, the activities of the Western missionaries—Dominicans and Franciscans as well as Jesuits—reached their height. The emperor was quite tolerant of the Christian presence, and several Jesuit missionaries became influential at court. Several hundred officials converted to Christianity, as did an estimated 300,000 ordinary Chinese. But the Christian effort was ultimately undermined by resentment from Confucian officials at court as well as by squabbling among the Western religious orders over the Jesuit policy of accommodating local beliefs and practices to facilitate conversion (see Opposing Viewpoints, "The Debate over Christianity," p. 421). Jealous Dominicans and Franciscans complained to the pope, who issued an edict ordering all missionaries and converts to conform to the official orthodoxy set forth in Europe. At first, Kangxi attempted to resolve the problem by appealing directly to the Vatican, but the pope was uncompromising. After Kangxi's death, his successor began to suppress Christian activities throughout China.

The Reign of Qianlong Kangxi's achievements were carried on by his successors, Yongzheng (YOONG-jehng) (r. 1722–1736) and Qianlong (r. 1736–1795). Like Kangxi, Qianlong was known for his diligence, tolerance, and intellectual curiosity, and he too combined vigorous military action against

The Debate over Christianity

Religion & Philosophy

THE ARRIVAL OF CHRISTIAN MISSIONARIES at the Ming imperial court in Beijing caused a major tumult among Chinese officials there. Although some were attracted to the new faith, others expressed alarm that these strange new ideas could corrupt traditional neo-Confucian doctrine. As the following passages indicate, both supporters and opponents had only a rudimentary understanding of Christian teachings and the Western culture from which they had sprung.

Xu Guangqi: A Memorial in Defense of the [Western] Teaching (1616)

Because the teaching of the men from afar [i.e., Christian missionaries from Europe] is most correct, and because your humble servant knows from experience that it is right, he earnestly begs to memorialize the throne, to the end that blessings may last forever and peace may be handed on to all generations. . . .

[Y]our servant . . . has studied with and learned from these [Western] tributary officials, and I know that they are most honest and solid. There is nothing whatsoever about them that is dubious. Truly, they are all disciples of the sages. Their way is very correct, their discipline strict, their learning very broad, their knowledge superior, their affections true, and their views very stable. . . .

Now in their countries, men of the church all cultivate personal virtue in order to serve the Lord of Heaven. . . . This teaching has as its basic tenet serving the Lord on High; to save the body and soul is the most essential principle, while one's practice should consist in loyalty, filial piety, love, and compassion. The way to begin is to choose good and repent, and the way to advance and improve is to confess and reform. True blessing in Heaven is the glorious reward of doing good, while eternal retribution in hell is the bitter recompense of doing evil. . . .

Now there are more than thirty countries in the West, and they have accepted and practiced this teaching for a thousand and several hundred years, right up to the present time, great and small living together in harmony, superior and inferior at peace with each other. The borders are not guarded, and the rulers of the states are all of the same family. . . . As for revolt and rebellion, not even once has there been such a thing or such people. . . .

Yang Guangxian: I Cannot Do Otherwise (1665)

According to a book by [the Christian scholar] Li Zubo, the Qing dynasty is nothing but an offshoot of Judea; our ancient Chinese rulers, sages, and teachers were but the off-shoots of a heterodox sect; and our classics and the teachings of the sages propounded generation after generation are no more than the remnants of a heterodox teaching. How can we abide these calumnies! They really aim to inveigle the people of the Qing into rebelling against the Qing and following this heterodox sect, which would lead all-under-Heaven to abandon respect for rulers and fathers. . . .

Our Confucian teaching is based on the Five Relationships (between parent and child, ruler and minister, husband and wife, older and younger brothers, and friends), whilst the Lord of Heaven Jesus was crucified because he plotted against his own country, showing that he did not recognize the relationship between ruler and subject. Mary, the mother of Jesus had a husband named Joseph, but she said Jesus was not conceived by him.

Those who follow this teaching [Christianity] are not allowed to worship their ancestors and ancestral tablets. They do not recognize the relationship of parent and child. Their teachers oppose the Buddhists and Daoists, who do recognize the relationship between ruler and subject and father and son. Jesus did not recognize the relationship between ruler and subject and parent and child. . . . What arrant nonsense! . . .

 To what degree do you feel that the authors of these two passages misrepresent Christian teachings and the influence that such ideas have had in European society?

Source: W. T. de Bary and R. Lufrano, *Sources of Chinese Tradition: From 1600 Through the Twentieth Century*, Vol. II (New York: Columbia University Press, 2000), pp. 148–151.

the unruly tribes along the frontier with active efforts to promote economic prosperity, administrative efficiency, and scholarship and artistic excellence. The result was continued growth for the Qing Empire throughout much of the eighteenth century.

But it was also under Qianlong that the first signs of the internal decay of the Qing Dynasty began to appear. The clues were familiar. Qing military campaigns along the frontier were expensive and placed heavy demands on the imperial treasury. As the emperor aged, he became less astute in selecting his subordinates and fell under the influence of corrupt elements at court. Corruption at the center led inevitably to unrest in rural areas, where higher taxes, bureaucratic venality, and rising pressure on the land because of the growing population had produced economic hardship. The heart of the unrest was in central China, where discontented peasants who had recently been settled on infertile land launched a revolt known as the White Lotus Rebellion (1796–1804). The revolt was eventually suppressed but at great expense.

Qing Political Institutions   One reason for the success of the Manchus was their ability to adapt to their new environment. They retained the Ming political system with relatively few changes. They also tried to establish their legitimacy as China's rightful rulers by stressing their devotion to the principles of Confucianism. Emperor Kangxi ostentatiously studied the sacred Confucian classics and issued a "sacred edict" that proclaimed to the entire empire the importance of the moral values established by the master (see Opposing Viewpoints, "Some Confucian Commandments," later in this chapter, and Image 17.3).

Still, like the Mongols, the Manchus were ethnically, linguistically, and culturally different from their subject population. The Qing attempted to cope with this reality by adopting a two-pronged strategy. As one part of this strategy, the Manchus—representing less than 2 percent of the entire population—were legally defined as distinct from everyone else in China. The Manchu nobles retained their aristocratic privileges, and their economic base was protected by extensive landholdings and revenues provided from the state treasury. Other Manchus were assigned farmland and organized into military units called **banners**, which were stationed as separate units in various strategic positions throughout China. These "bannermen" were the primary fighting force of the empire. Ethnic Chinese were prohibited from settling in Manchuria and were still compelled to wear their hair in a queue as a sign of submission to the ruling dynasty.

Although the Manchus attempted to protect their distinct identity within an alien society, they also recognized the need to bring ethnic Chinese into the top ranks of imperial administration. Their solution was to create a **dyarchy**, a system in which all important administrative positions were shared equally by Chinese and Manchu. Meanwhile, the Manchus themselves, despite official efforts to preserve their separate language and culture, were increasingly assimilated into Chinese civilization.

China on the Eve of the Western Onslaught   Unfortunately for China, the first signs of the Qing Dynasty's decline

17.3 The Temple of Heaven. Located in the capital city of Beijing, this temple is one of the most significant historical structures in China. Built in 1420 at the order of the Ming emperor Yongle, it was the site of the emperor's annual appeal to heaven for a good harvest. In this important ceremony, the emperor demonstrated to his subjects that he was their protector and would ward off the evil forces in nature. Yongle's temple burned to the ground in 1889 but was immediately rebuilt following the original design.

CHRONOLOGY	China During the Early Modern Era
Rise of Ming Dynasty	1369
Voyages of Zheng He	1405–1433
Portuguese arrive in southern China	1514
Matteo Ricci arrives in China	1601
Li Zicheng occupies Beijing	1644
Manchus seize China	1644
Reign of Kangxi	1661–1722
Treaty of Nerchinsk	1689
First English trading post at Canton	1699
Reign of Qianlong	1736–1795
Lord Macartney's mission to China	1793
White Lotus Rebellion	1796–1804

occurred just as China's modest relationship with the West was about to give way to a new era of military confrontation and increased pressure for trade. The initial challenges came in the north, where Russian traders seeking skins and furs began to penetrate the region between Siberian Russia and Manchuria. Earlier the Ming Dynasty had attempted to deal with the Russians by the traditional method of placing them in a tributary relationship. But the tsar refused to play by Chinese rules. His envoys to Beijing ignored the tribute system and refused to perform the **kowtow** (the ritual of prostration and touching the forehead to the ground before the emperor), the classic symbol of fealty demanded of all foreign ambassadors to the Chinese court. Formal diplomatic relations were finally established in 1689 when the Treaty of Nerchinsk (ner-CHINSK) settled the boundary dispute and provided for regular trade between the two countries. Through such arrangements,

the Qing were able to not only pacify the northern frontier but also extend their rule over Xinjiang (SHIN-jyahng) and Tibet to the west and southwest (see Map 17.2).

Dealing with foreigners who arrived by sea was more difficult. By the end of the seventeenth century, the English had replaced the Portuguese as the dominant force in European trade. Operating through the East India Company, which served as both a trading unit and administrator of English territories in Asia, the English established their first trading post at Canton (KAN-tun) in 1699. Over the next decades, trade with China increased rapidly, notably the export of tea and silk to Great Britain. Chinese imports of European goods was much smaller. To limit contact between Chinese and Europeans, the Qing licensed Chinese trading firms at Canton to be the exclusive conduit for trade with the West, and the Qing confined the Europeans to a small island just outside the city

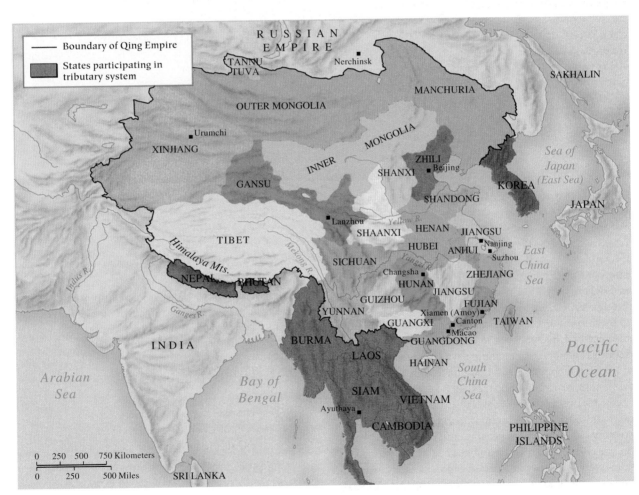

Map 17.2 The Qing Empire in the Eighteenth Century. This map shows the boundaries of the Chinese empire at the height of the Qing Dynasty in the eighteenth century.

Q *What areas were linked in tributary status to the Chinese empire, and how did they benefit the empire?*

The Art Archive/Marine Museum Stockholm/Collection Dagli Orti

17.4 European Warehouses at Canton. Aggravated by the growing presence of foreigners in the eighteenth century, the Chinese court severely restricted the movement of European traders in China. They were permitted to live only in a compound near Canton during the six months of the trading season and could go into the city only three times a month. In this painting, foreign flags (including, from the left, those of the United States, Sweden, Great Britain, and Holland) fly over the warehouses and residences of the foreign community while Chinese sampans and junks sit anchored in the river.

wall, where they were permitted to reside from October through March (see Image 17.4).

By the end of the eighteenth century, the British government had become restive at the uneven balance of trade between the two countries, which forced the British to ship vast amounts of silver bullion to China in exchange for its silks, porcelains, and teas. In 1793, a mission under Lord Macartney visited Beijing to press for liberalization of trade restrictions. A compromise was reached on the kowtow (Macartney was permitted to bend on one knee, the prevailing British custom), but Qianlong expressed no interest in British manufactured products (see Historical Voices, "The Tribute System in Action," p. 425). An exasperated Macartney compared the Chinese empire to "an old, crazy, first-rate man-of-war" that had once awed its neighbors "merely by her bulk and appearance" but was now destined under incompetent leadership to be "dashed

to pieces on the shore."[4] With his contemptuous dismissal of the British request, the emperor had inadvertently sowed the seeds for a century of humiliation.

17-2 CHANGING CHINA

 Focus Question: How did the economy and society of China change during the Ming and Qing eras, and to what degree did these changes seem to be leading toward an industrial revolution on the European model?

During the Ming and Qing Dynasties, China remained a predominantly agricultural society; nearly 85 percent of its people were farmers. Even though most Chinese

The Tribute System in Action

Interaction & Exchange **IN 1793, THE BRITISH EMISSARY** Lord Macartney visited the Qing Empire to request the opening of formal diplomatic and trading relations between his country and China. Emperor Qianlong's reply to King George III of Britain illustrates how the imperial court in Beijing viewed the world. King George could not have been pleased. The document provides a good example of the complacent view the Celestial Empire had of the world beyond its borders.

A Decree of Emperor Qianlong

An Imperial Edict to the King of England: You, O King, are so inclined toward our civilization that you have sent a special envoy across the seas to bring to our Court your memorial of congratulations on the occasion of my birthday and to present your native products as an expression of your thoughtfulness. On perusing your memorial, so simply worded and sincerely conceived, I am impressed by your genuine respectfulness and friendliness and greatly pleased.

As to the request made in your memorial, O King, to send one of your nationals to stay at the Celestial Court to take care of your country's trade with China, this is not in harmony with the state system of our dynasty and will definitely not be permitted. Traditionally people of the European nations who wished to render some service under the Celestial Court have been permitted to come to the capital. But after their arrival they are obliged to wear Chinese court costumes, are placed in a certain residence, and are never allowed to return to their own countries. This is the established rule of the Celestial Dynasty with which presumably you, O King, are familiar. Now you, O King, wish to send one of your nationals to live in the capital, but he is not like the Europeans who come to Peking [Beijing] as Chinese employees, live there, and never return home again, nor can he be allowed to go and come and maintain any correspondence. This is indeed a useless undertaking.

Moreover the territory under the control of the Celestial Court is very large and wide. There are well-established regulations governing tributary envoys from the outer states to Peking, giving them provisions (of food and traveling expenses) by our post-houses and limiting their going and coming. There has never been a precedent for letting them do whatever they like. Now if you, O King, wish to have a representative in Peking, his language will be unintelligible and his dress different from the regulations; there is no place to accommodate him. . . .

The Celestial Court has pacified and possessed the territory within the four seas. Its sole aim is to do its utmost to achieve good government and to manage political affairs, attaching no value to strange jewels and precious objects. The various articles presented by you, O King, this time are accepted by my special order to the office in charge of such functions in consideration of the offerings having come from a long distance with sincere good wishes. As a matter of fact, the virtue and prestige of the Celestial Dynasty having spread far and wide, the kings of the myriad nations come by land and sea with all sorts of precious things. Consequently there is nothing we lack, as your principal envoy and others have themselves observed. We have never set much store on strange or ingenious objects, nor do we need any more of your country's manufactures.

 What reasons did the emperor give for refusing Macartney's request to have a permanent British ambassador in Beijing? How did the tribute system differ from the principles of international relations as practiced in the West?

Source: Reprinted by permission of the publisher from *China's Response to the West: A Documentary Survey, 1839–1923,* by Ssu-yu Teng and John King Fairbank, pp. 24–27, Cambridge, Mass.: Harvard University Press, Copyright © 1954, 1979 by the President and Fellows of Harvard College, copyright renewed 1982 by Ssu-yu Teng and John King Fairbank.

still lived in rural villages, the economy was undergoing many changes.

17-2a The Population Explosion

In the first place, the center of gravity was continuing to shift steadily from the north to the south. In the early centuries of Chinese civilization, the administrative and economic center of gravity was clearly in the north. By the early Qing Dynasty, the economic breadbasket of China was located along the Yangzi River and regions to the south. One concrete indication of this shift occurred during the Ming Dynasty when Emperor Yongle ordered the

The Population Explosion

Earth & Environment Between 1700 and 1800, Europe, China, and, to a lesser degree, India and the Ottoman Empire experienced a dramatic growth in population. In Europe, the population grew from 120 million people to almost 200 million by 1800; the Chinese population grew from less than 200 million to 300 million during the same period.

Four developments in particular contributed to this population explosion. First, better growing conditions—made possible by an improvement in climate—affected wide areas of the world and enabled people to produce more food. Both China and Europe experienced warmer summers beginning in the early eighteenth century. Second, by the eighteenth century, people had begun to develop immunities to the epidemic diseases that had caused such widespread loss of life between 1500 and 1700. The increase in travel by ship after 1500 had led to devastating epidemics. For example, the arrival of Europeans in Mexico introduced smallpox, measles, and chicken pox to a native population that had no immunities to European diseases. In 1500, between 11 million and 20 million people lived in the area of Mexico; by 1650, only 1.5 million remained. Gradually, however, people developed resistance to these diseases.

A third factor in the population increase was the introduction of new foods. As a result of the Columbian Exchange (see Comparative Essay, "The Columbian Exchange," p. 355 in Chapter 14), American food crops such as corn, potatoes, and sweet potatoes were transported to other parts of the world, where they became important food sources. China imported a new species of rice from Southeast Asia that had a shorter harvest cycle than existing varieties. These new foods provided additional sources of nutrition that enabled more people to live longer. At the same time, land development and canal building in the eighteenth century enabled government authorities to move food supplies to areas threatened with crop failure and famine.

Finally, the use of new weapons based on gunpowder allowed states to control larger territories and ensure a new degree of order. The early rulers of the Qing

Dynasty, for example, pacified the Chinese empire and ensured a long period of peace and stability. Absolute monarchs achieved similar goals in several European states. Less violence resulted in fewer deaths at the same time that an increase in food supplies and a decrease in deaths from diseases were occurring, thus making possible in the eighteenth century the beginning of the world population explosion that persists to this day.

Q *What were the main reasons for the dramatic expansion in the world's population during the early modern era?*

© British Museum, London/The Bridgeman Art Library

17.5 **Festival of the Yam.** With the spread of a few major food crops, new sources of nutrition became available to feed more people. The importance of the yam to the Ashanti people of West Africa is evident in this celebration of a yam festival at harvest time in 1817.

renovation of the Grand Canal to facilitate the shipment of rice from the Yangzi Delta to the food-starved north.

Moreover, the population was beginning to increase rapidly (see Comparative Essay, "The Population Explosion," above). For centuries, China's population had remained within a range of 50 million to 100 million, rising in times of peace and prosperity and falling in periods of foreign invasion and internal anarchy. By 1800, however, the population had increased from an estimated 70 million to 80 million in 1390 to more than 300 million. There were probably several reasons for this population increase: the relatively long period of peace and stability under the early Qing; the introduction of new crops from the Americas, including peanuts, sweet potatoes, and maize;

and the planting of a new species of faster-growing rice from Southeast Asia.

Of course, this population increase meant much greater population pressure on the land, smaller farms, and a razor-thin margin of safety in case of climatic disaster. The imperial court attempted to deal with the problem through various means, most notably by preventing the concentration of land in the hands of wealthy landowners. Nevertheless, by the eighteenth century, almost all the land that could be irrigated was already under cultivation, and the problems of rural hunger and landlessness became increasingly serious.

© Peabody Essex Museum, Salem, Massachusetts, USA/The Bridgeman Art Library

17.6 Haggling Over the Price of Tea. An important item in the China trade of the eighteenth and early nineteenth centuries was tea, which had become extremely popular in Great Britain. The painting depicts the various stages of growing, processing, and marketing tea leaves. In the background, workers are removing tender young leaves from the bushes. In the foreground, British and Chinese merchants bargain over the price. After being dried, the leaves are packed into chests and loaded on vessels for shipment abroad.

17-2b Seeds of Industrialization

The steady growth of manufacturing and commerce was another change that took place during the early Qing era. Taking advantage of the long era of peace and prosperity, merchants and manufacturers began to expand their operations beyond their immediate provinces. Commercial networks began to operate on a regional and sometimes even a national basis as trade in silk, metal and wood products, porcelain, cotton goods, and cash crops like cotton and tobacco developed rapidly. Foreign trade also expanded after the Ming court in 1567 suspended its prohibition of such activities. Chinese merchants began to establish extensive contacts with countries in Southeast Asia. As Chinese tea, silk, and porcelain became ever more popular in other parts of the world, the trade surplus grew as the country's exports greatly outnumbered its imports (see Image 17.6).

HISTORIANS DEBATE **The Qing Economy: Ready for Takeoff?** For many years, Western historians commonly believed that conditions in early modern China were not conducive to the onset of an industrial revolution along the Western model. In recent years, however, some have suggested that because of the impressive advances achieved during the early Qing Dynasty, China was poised to make the transition from an agricultural to a predominantly manufacturing and commercial economy by the end of the eighteenth century. The same transition began to take place in western Europe with the onset of the Industrial Revolution in the late eighteenth century (see Chapter 19).

Certainly, in most respects the Chinese economy in 1800 was as advanced as any of its counterparts around the world. China's achievements in technology over the past centuries were unsurpassed. A perceptive observer at the time might well have concluded that the Qing Empire would be highly competitive with the most advanced nations around the world for the indefinite future.

Nevertheless, several factors raise doubts that China was ready to advance rapidly into the industrial age. The mercantile class was not as independent in China as in some European societies. Trade and manufacturing remained under the firm control of the state, and political and social prejudices against commercial activity remained strong. Reflecting an ancient preference for agriculture over manufacturing and trade, the state levied heavy taxes on manufacturing and commerce while attempting to keep agricultural taxes low.

At the root of such attitudes was the lingering influence of Neo-Confucianism, which remained the official state doctrine in China down to the end of the Qing Dynasty. Although the founding fathers of Neo-Confucianism had originally focused on the "investigation of things," as time passed its practitioners tended to emphasize the elucidation of moral principles rather than the expansion of scientific knowledge. As historian Toby Huff has noted, the civil service examination during the early Qing contained no questions on science or technology, and Chinese interest in European scientific advances in areas like astronomy was limited to a few officials at court. Though the Chinese economy was gradually being transformed from an agricultural to a commercial and industrial giant, scholars tended to look back to antiquity rather than to empirical science as the prime source for knowledge of the natural world and human events. The result was an intellectual environment that valued continuity over change and tradition over innovation. In effect, although the conditions for a transition to a modern industrial economy were present in early Qing China, the motivation to do so was lacking.

The Chinese reaction to European clock-making techniques provides an example. In the early seventeenth century, Matteo Ricci, a Jesuit priest, introduced advanced European clocks driven by weights or springs. The emperor was fascinated and found the clocks more reliable than Chinese timekeepers. Over the next decades, European timepieces became a popular novelty at court, but the Chinese expressed little curiosity about the technology involved, provoking one European observer to remark that playthings like cuckoo clocks "will be received here with much greater interest than scientific instruments or *objets d'art*."[5]

17-2c Daily Life in Qing China

Daily life under the Ming and early Qing Dynasties continued to follow traditional patterns with families and the roles of women.

The Family Traditionally, Chinese society was organized around the family. The ideal social unit was the joint family in which as many as three or four generations lived under the same roof. When sons married, they brought their wives to live with them in the family homestead. Aging parents and grandparents, as well as unmarried daughters, remained under the same roof and were cared for by younger members of the household until they died. This ideal did not always correspond to reality, however, because many families did not possess sufficient land to support a large household.

The family retained its importance under the Qing for many of the same reasons as in earlier times. As a labor-intensive society based primarily on the cultivation of rice, China needed large families to help with the harvest and to provide security for parents too old to work in the fields. Sons were particularly prized, not only because they had strong backs but also because they would raise their own families under the parental roof. With few opportunities for employment outside the family, sons had little choice but to remain with their parents and help on the land. Within the family, the oldest male was king, and his wishes theoretically had to be obeyed by all family members. Arranged marriages were the norm, and the primary consideration in selecting a spouse was whether the union would benefit the family as a whole. The couple themselves usually had no say in the matter and might not even meet until the marriage ceremony. Romantic feelings were not considered unimportant

in marriage but were often viewed as undesirable because they would draw the attention of the husband and wife away from their primary responsibility to the larger family unit.

In theory, the obligations were not all on the side of the children. The father was expected to provide support for his wife and children and, like the ruler, was supposed to treat those in his care with respect and compassion. All too often, however, the male head of the family was able to exact his privileges without performing his responsibilities in return.

Beyond the joint family was the clan, which was an extended kinship unit consisting of dozens or even hundreds of joint and nuclear families linked together by a clan council of elders and a variety of other common social and religious functions. The clan served many useful purposes. Some clans possessed lands that could be rented out to poorer families, or richer families within the clan might provide land for the poor. Because there was no general state-supported educational system, sons of poor families might be invited to study in a school established in the home of a more prosperous relative. If the young man succeeded in becoming an official, he would be expected to provide favors and prestige for the clan as a whole.

The Role of Women In traditional China, the role of women had always been inferior to that of men. A sixteenth-century Spanish visitor to South China observed that Chinese women were "very secluded and virtuous, and it was a very rare thing for us to see a woman in the cities and large towns, unless it was an old crone."[6] Women were more visible, he said, in rural areas, where they frequently could be seen working in the fields.

The concept of female inferiority had deep roots in Chinese history. This view was embodied in the belief that only a male would carry on sacred family rituals and that men alone had the talent to govern others. Only males could aspire to a career in government or scholarship. Within the family system, the wife was clearly subordinated to the husband. Legally, she could not divorce her husband or inherit property. The husband, however, could divorce his wife if she did not produce male heirs, and he could take a second wife as well as a concubine for his pleasure. A widow suffered especially because she had to either raise her children on a single income or fight off her former husband's greedy relatives, who would coerce her to remarry because they could legally inherit all of her previous property and her original dowry.

Female children were less desirable because of their limited physical strength and because a girl's parents would have to pay a dowry to the parents of her future husband. Female children normally did not receive an education, and daughters might even be put to death in times of scarcity when food was in short supply.

The Art of Printing

Art & Ideas

EUROPEANS OBTAINED MUCH OF THEIR EARLY INFORMATION ABOUT CHINA from the Jesuits who served at the Ming court in the sixteenth and seventeenth centuries. Clerics such as the Italian Matteo Ricci (ma-TAY-oh REE-chee) (1552–1610), who arrived in China in 1601, found much to admire in Chinese civilization. Here Ricci expresses a keen interest in Chinese printing methods, which at that time were well in advance of the techniques used in the West. Later Christian missionaries expressed strong interest in Confucian philosophy and Chinese ideas of statecraft.

Matteo Ricci, *The Diary of Matthew Ricci*

The art of printing was practiced in China at a date somewhat earlier than that assigned to the beginning of printing in Europe, which was about 1405. It is quite certain that the Chinese knew the art of printing at least five centuries ago, and some of them assert that printing was known to their people before the beginning of the Christian era, about 50 B.C.E. Their method of printing differs widely from that employed in Europe, and our method would be quite impracticable for them because of the exceedingly large number of Chinese characters and symbols. . . .

Their method of making printed books is quite ingenious. The text is written in ink, with a brush made of very fine hair, on a sheet of paper which is inverted and pasted on a wooden tablet. When the paper has become thoroughly dry, its surface is scraped off quickly and with great skill, until nothing but a fine tissue bearing the characters remains on the wooden tablet. Then, with a steel graver, the workman cuts away the surface following the outlines of the characters until these alone stand out in low relief. From such a block a skilled printer can make copies with incredible speed, turning out as many as fifteen hundred copies in a single day. . . . This scheme of engraving wooden blocks is well adapted for the large and complex nature of the Chinese characters, but I do not think it would lend itself very aptly to our European type, which could hardly be engraved upon wood because of its small dimensions.

Their method of printing has one decided advantage, namely, that once these tablets are made, they can be preserved and used for making changes in the text as often as one wishes. Additions and subtractions can also be made as the tablets can be readily patched. . . . We have derived great benefit from this method of Chinese printing, as we employ the domestic help in our homes to strike off copies of the books on religious and scientific subjects which we translate into Chinese from the languages in which they were written originally. In truth, the whole method is so simple that one is tempted to try it for himself after once having watched the process. The simplicity of Chinese printing is what accounts for the exceedingly large numbers of books in circulation here and the ridiculously low prices at which they are sold.

 How did the Chinese method of printing differ from that used in Europe at that time? What were its advantages?

Source: From *China in the Sixteenth Century*, by Matthew Ricci, translated by Louis J. Gallagher. Copyright © 1942 and renewed 1970 by Louis J. Gallagher, S.J.

Though women were clearly inferior to men in theory, this was not always the case in practice. Capable women often compensated for their legal inferiority by playing a strong role within the family. Women were often in charge of educating the children and handling the family budget. Some privileged women also received training in the Confucian classics, although their schooling was generally for a shorter time and was less rigorous than that of their male counterparts. A few produced significant works of art and poetry.

17-2d Cultural Developments

During the late Ming and the early Qing Dynasties, traditional culture in China reached new heights of achievement.

With the rise of a wealthy urban class, the demand for art, porcelain, textiles, and literature grew significantly.

The Rise of the Chinese Novel   During the Ming Dynasty, a new form of literature first appeared that would eventually evolve into the modern Chinese novel. Although considered less respectable than poetry and nonfiction prose, these groundbreaking works (often written anonymously or under pseudonyms) were enormously popular, especially among well-to-do urban dwellers. Rapid advances in printing were a major factor in spreading the availability of books to the general population (see Historical Voices, "The Art of Printing," above).

Written in a colloquial style, the new fiction was characterized by a realism that resulted in vivid portraits of

Chinese society. Many of the stories sympathized with society's downtrodden—often helpless maidens—and dealt with such crucial issues as love, money, marriage, and power. Adding to the realism were sexually explicit passages that depicted the private side of Chinese life. Readers delighted in sensuous tales that, no matter how pornographic, always professed a moral lesson; the villains were punished and the virtuous were rewarded.

Dream of the Red Chamber is generally considered China's most distinguished popular novel. Published in 1791, it tells of the tragic love between two young people caught in the financial and moral disintegration of a powerful Chinese clan. The hero and the heroine, both sensitive and spoiled, represent the inevitable decline of the Chia family and come to an equally inevitable tragic end, she in death and he in an unhappy marriage to another.

The Art of the Ming and the Qing   During the Ming and the early Qing Dynasties, traditional China produced its last outpouring of artistic brilliance. Although most of the creative work was modeled on past examples, the art of this period is impressive for its technical perfection and breathtaking quantity.

In architecture, the most outstanding example is the Imperial City in Beijing. Building on the remnants of the palace of the Yuan Dynasty, the Ming emperor Yongle ordered renovations when he returned the capital to Beijing in 1421. Succeeding emperors continued to add to the palace, but the basic design has not changed since the Ming era. Surrounded by high walls, the immense compound is divided into a maze of private apartments and offices and an imposing ceremonial quadrangle with a series of stately halls for imperial audiences and banquets. The grandiose scale, richly carved marble, spacious gardens, and graceful upturned roofs all contribute to the splendor of the "Forbidden City" (see Image 17.2, p. 419).

Decorative arts flourished in this period, especially the intricately carved lacquerware and boldly shaped and colored cloisonné (kloi-zuh-NAY or KLWAH-zuh-nay), a type of enamel work in which thin metal bands separate the areas of colored enamel. Silk production reached its zenith, and the best-quality silks were highly prized in Europe, where chinoiserie (sheen-wah-zuh-REE or sheen-nwahz-REE), as Chinese art of all kinds was called, was in vogue. Perhaps the most famous of all the achievements of the Ming era was its blue-and-white porcelain, which is still prized by collectors throughout the world. During the Qing Dynasty, artists produced great quantities of paintings, mostly for home consumption. Inside the Forbidden City in Beijing, court painters worked alongside Jesuit artists and experimented with Western techniques. Most scholarly painters and the literati, however, totally rejected

17.7 A Japanese Castle. Imitating European castle architecture, the Japanese perfected a new type of fortress palace in the early seventeenth century. Strategically placed high on a hilltop, these strongholds were constructed of heavy stone with tiny windows and were fortified by numerous watchtowers and massive walls, making them impregnable to arrows and catapults. They served as a residence for the local daimyo, and castle compounds also housed his army and contained the seat of local government. Osaka Castle was built by Toyotomi Hideyoshi essentially as a massive stage set to proclaim his power and grandeur. In 1615, the powerful warlord Tokugawa Ieyasu seized the castle, and it remained in his family's control for nearly 250 years.

foreign techniques and became obsessed with traditional Chinese styles. As a result, Qing painting became progressively more repetitive and stale.

17-3 TOKUGAWA JAPAN

 Focus Question: How did the society and economy of Japan change during the Tokugawa era, and how did Japanese culture reflect those changes?

At the end of the fifteenth century, the traditional Japanese system was at a point of near anarchy. With the decline in the authority of the Ashikaga (ah-shee-KAH-guh) Shogunate at

Kyoto (KYOH-toh), clan rivalries had exploded into an era of warring states. Even at the local level, power was frequently diffuse. The typical daimyo (DYM-yoh) (great lord) domain had often become little more than a coalition of fief holders held together by a loose allegiance to the manor lord. Nevertheless, Japan was on the verge of an extended era of national unification and peace under the rule of its greatest shogunate—the Tokugawa.

17-3a The Three Great Unifiers

The process began in the mid-sixteenth century with the emergence of three extremely powerful political figures: Oda Nobunaga (1568–1582), Toyotomi Hideyoshi (1582–1598), and Tokugawa Ieyasu (1598–1616). In 1568, Oda Nobunaga (OH-dah noh-buh-NAH-guh), the son of a samurai (SAM-uh-ry) and a military commander under the Ashikaga Shogunate, seized the imperial capital of Kyoto and placed the reigning shogun (SHOH-gun) under his domination. During the next few years, the brutal and ambitious Nobunaga consolidated his rule throughout the central plains by defeating his rivals and suppressing the power of the Buddhist estates, but he was killed by one of his generals in 1582 before the process was complete. He was succeeded by Toyotomi Hideyoshi (toh-yoh-TOH-mee hee-day-YOH-shee), a farmer's son who had worked his way up through the ranks to become a military commander. Hideyoshi built a castle at Osaka (oh-SAH-kuh) (see Image 17.7) to accommodate his headquarters and gradually extended his power outward to the southern islands of Shikoku (shee-KOH-koo) and Kyushu (KYOO-shoo) (see Map 17.3). By 1590, he had persuaded most of the daimyo on the Japanese islands to accept his authority and created a national currency. Then he invaded Korea in an abortive effort to export his rule to the Asian mainland (see section 17-4a, "Korea: In a Dangerous Neighborhood" later in this chapter).

Despite their efforts, however, neither Nobunaga nor Hideyoshi was able to eliminate the power of the local daimyo. Both were compelled to form alliances with some daimyo so they could destroy other more powerful rivals. By 1590, Toyotomi Hideyoshi could claim to be the supreme proprietor of all registered lands in areas under his authority. He then reassigned those lands as fiefs to the local daimyo, who declared their allegiance to him. The daimyo in turn began to pacify the countryside, carrying out extensive "sword hunts" to disarm the population and attracting samurai to their service. The

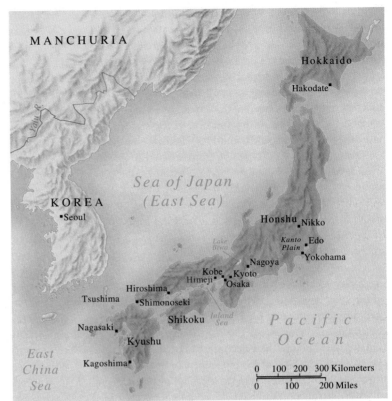

Map 17.3 Tokugawa Japan. This map shows the Japanese islands and its key cities, including the shogun's capital of Edo (Tokyo), during the long era of the Tokugawa Shogunate.

 Where was the imperial court located?

Japanese tradition of decentralized rule had not yet been overcome.

After Hideyoshi's death in 1598, Tokugawa Ieyasu (toh-koo-GAH-wah ee-yeh-YAH-soo), the powerful daimyo of Edo (EH-doh) (modern Tokyo), moved to fill the vacuum. In 1603, Ieyasu named himself shogun, initiating the most powerful and long lasting of all Japanese shogunates; it remained in power until 1868, when a war dismantled the entire system. As a contemporary phrased it, "Oda pounds the national rice cake, Hideyoshi kneads it, and in the end Ieyasu sits down and eats it."[7]

17-3b Opening to the West

The unification of Japan took place almost simultaneously with the coming of the Europeans. Portuguese traders sailing in a Chinese junk that may have been blown off course by a typhoon had landed on the islands in 1543. Within a few years, Portuguese ships were stopping at Japanese ports on a regular basis to take part in the regional trade between Japan, China, and Southeast Asia. The first Jesuit missionary, Francis Xavier (ZAY-vee-ur), arrived in 1549.

Initially, the visitors were welcomed. Although Japanese leaders were somewhat ambivalent about establishing relations with the outside world, Japanese merchants were active in the regional trade network, and some ventured as far as Southeast Asia, where they quickly earned the reputation as ferocious competitors. The arrival of the Europeans added a new dimension to the equation. The curious Japanese were fascinated by tobacco, clocks, spectacles, and other European goods, and local daimyo were interested in purchasing all types of European weapons and armaments. Oda Nobunaga and Toyotomi Hideyoshi found the new firearms helpful in defeating their enemies and unifying the islands. The effect on Japanese military architecture was particularly striking, as local lords began to erect castles on the European model, many of which still exist today.

The missionaries also had some success in converting many local daimyo to the Christian faith, some of whom may have been partly motivated by the desire for commercial profits. By the end of the sixteenth century, thousands of Japanese in the southernmost islands of Kyushu and Shikoku had become Christians. But papal claims to the loyalty of all Japanese Christians and the European habit of intervening in local politics soon began to arouse suspicion in official circles. Missionaries added to the problem by deliberately destroying local idols and shrines and turning some temples into Christian schools or churches.

The Expulsion of the Christians   Inevitably, local authorities reacted. In 1587, Toyotomi Hideyoshi issued an edict prohibiting further Christian activities within his domains. Japan, he declared, was "the land of the Gods," and the destruction of shrines by the foreigners was "something unheard of in previous ages."[8] The Jesuits were ordered to leave the country within twenty days. Hideyoshi was careful to distinguish missionary from trading activities, however, and merchants were permitted to continue their operations.

The Jesuits protested the expulsion, and eventually Hideyoshi relented, permitting them to continue proselytizing as long as they were discreet. But he refused to repeal the edicts, and when the aggressive activities of newly arrived Spanish Franciscans aroused his ire, he ordered the execution of nine missionaries and several of their Japanese converts. When the missionaries continued to interfere in local politics, Tokugawa Ieyasu ordered the eviction of all missionaries in 1612.

At first, Japanese authorities hoped to maintain commercial relations with European countries even while suppressing the Western religion, but eventually they decided to regulate foreign trade more closely, restricting European access to the small island of Deshima (deh-SHEE-muh *or* deh-JEE-muh) in Nagasaki harbor, where a small Dutch community was given permission to engage in limited trade with Japan (the Dutch, unlike the Portuguese and the Spanish, had not allowed missionary activities to interfere with their commercial interests) (see Image 17.7, p. 430).

17.8 **Arrival of the Portuguese at Nagasaki.** Portuguese traders, dressed in billowing pantaloons and broad-brimmed hats, landed in Japan by accident in 1543. In a few years, they were arriving regularly, taking part in a regional trade network involving Japan, China, and Southeast Asia. In these panels done in black lacquer and gold leaf, we see a late-sixteenth-century Japanese interpretation of Portuguese merchants at Nagasaki. Normally, Japanese screens are read from right to left, but this one is read left to right. Having arrived by ship, the Portuguese proceed in splendor to the Jesuit priests waiting in a church on the right.

Dutch ships were permitted to dock at Nagasaki harbor only once a year and were allowed to remain for two or three months after close inspection. Nor were the Japanese free to engage in foreign trade, as the *bakufu* (buh-KOO foo or bah KOO fuh)—the central government—now sought to restrict the ability of local authorities to carry out commercial transactions with foreign merchants. Skittish about maintaining official contacts with European nations because of their tendency to interfere in Japanese domestic affairs, shogunate officials resisted efforts to lure them into the establishment of formal diplomatic relations with European governments. A small amount of commerce took place with China and other parts of Asia, but Japanese were forbidden to leave the country on penalty of death.

17-3c The Tokugawa "Great Peace"

Once in power, the Tokugawa attempted to strengthen the system that had governed Japan for more than 300 years. They followed precedent in ruling through the bakufu, which was now composed of a coalition of daimyo and a council of elders. But the system was more centralized than it had been previously. Now the shogunate government played a dual role. It set national policy on behalf of the emperor in Kyoto while simultaneously governing the shogun's own domain, which included about one-quarter of the national territory as well as the three great cities of Edo, Kyoto, and Osaka. As before, the state was divided into separate territories called *domains* that were ruled by some 250 individual daimyo.

Daimyo and Samurai   In theory, the daimyo were essentially autonomous in that they were able to support themselves from taxes on their lands. In actuality, the shogunate was able to guarantee their loyalty by compelling the daimyo to maintain two residences, one in their own domains and the other at Edo, and to leave their families in Edo as hostages for the daimyo's good behavior. Keeping up two residences also put the Japanese nobility in a difficult economic position. Some were able to defray the high costs by concentrating on cash crops such as sugar, fish, and forestry products; but most were rice producers, and their revenues remained roughly the same throughout the period. The daimyo were also able to protect their economic interests by depriving their samurai retainers of their proprietary rights over the land and transforming them into salaried officials. The fief became a stipend, and the personal relationship between the daimyo and his retainers gradually gave way to a bureaucratic authority.

Thus the samurai gradually ceased to be a warrior class and were required to live in the castle towns. As a gesture to their glorious past, samurai were still permitted to wear their two swords, and a rigid separation was maintained between persons of samurai status and the nonaristocratic segment of the population.

Seeds of Capitalism   The long period of peace under the Tokugawa Shogunate made possible a dramatic rise in commerce and manufacturing, especially in the growing cities of Edo, Kyoto, and Osaka. The growth of trade and industry was stimulated by a rising standard of living—driven in part by technological advances in agriculture and an expansion of arable land—and the voracious appetites of the aristocrats for new products.

Most of this commercial expansion took place in the major cities and castle towns where the merchants and artisans lived along with the samurai, who were clustered in neighborhoods surrounding the daimyo's castle. Banking flourished, and paper money became the normal medium of exchange in commercial transactions. Merchants formed guilds not only to control market conditions but also to facilitate government control and the collection of taxes. Under the benign if somewhat contemptuous supervision of Japan's noble rulers, a Japanese merchant class gradually began to emerge from the shadows to play a significant role in the life of the Japanese nation.

Eventually, the increased pace of industrial activity spread from the cities into rural areas. As in Great Britain, cotton was a major factor. Cotton had been introduced to China during the Song Dynasty and was introduced to Korea and Japan shortly thereafter. Traditionally, cotton

CHRONOLOGY	Japan and Korea During the Early Modern Era
First phonetic alphabet in Korea	Fifteenth century
Portuguese merchants arrive in Japan	1543
Francis Xavier arrives in Japan	1549
Rule of Oda Nobunaga	1568–1582
Seizure of Kyoto	1568
Rule of Toyotomi Hideyoshi	1582–1598
Edict prohibiting Christianity in Japan	1587
Japan invades Korea	1592
Death of Hideyoshi and withdrawal of the Japanese army from Korea	1598
Rule of Tokugawa Ieyasu	1598–1616
Creation of Tokugawa Shogunate	1603
Dutch granted permission to trade at Nagasaki	1609
Order evicting Christian missionaries	1612
Choson Dynasty of Korea declares fealty to China	1630s

cloth had been too expensive for the common people, who instead wore clothing made of hemp, but technological advances reduced the cost and specialized communities for producing cotton cloth began to appear in the countryside and in small towns. By the eighteenth century, cotton had firmly replaced hemp as the cloth of choice for most Japanese.

The expansion of trade was facilitated by the construction of a new and expanded system of roads and bridges ordered by Tokugawa Ieyasu himself. The main trunk road—known as the Tokaido, or "Eastern Coastal Highway"—connected the imperial city in Kyoto with the administrative capital of Edo, and fifty-three post stations were established along the route to provide travelers with food stalls and rest facilities to ease their journey to their destinations.

Not everyone benefited from the economic changes of the seventeenth and eighteenth centuries, however; most notable were the samurai, who were barred by tradition and prejudice from commercial activities. Most samurai still relied on their revenues from rice lands, which were often insufficient to cover their rising expenses; consequently, they fell heavily into debt. Others were released from servitude to their lord and became "masterless samurai." Occasionally, these unemployed warriors—known as **ronin** (ROH-nihn), or "wave men"—revolted or plotted against local authorities.

Land Problems The effects of economic developments on the rural population during the Tokugawa era are harder to estimate. Some farm families benefited by exploiting the growing demand for cash crops. But not all prospered. Most peasants continued to rely on rice cultivation and were whipsawed between declining profits and rising costs and taxes (as daimyo expenses increased, land taxes often took as much as 50 percent of the annual harvest). Many were forced to become tenants or to work as wage laborers on the farms of wealthy neighbors or in village industries. When rural conditions in some areas became desperate, peasant revolts erupted. According to one estimate, nearly 7,000 disturbances took place during the Tokugawa era.

Some Japanese historians, influenced by a Marxist view of history, have interpreted such evidence as an indication that the Tokugawa economic system was highly exploitative, with feudal aristocrats oppressing powerless peasants. Recent scholars, however, have tended to adopt a more balanced view, maintaining that in addition to agriculture, manufacturing and commerce experienced extensive growth, with benefits that extended to the rural population. Some point out that although the population of the country doubled in the seventeenth century, a relatively low rate for the time period, so did the amount of cultivable land, with agricultural technology making significant advances.

17-3d Life in the Village

The changes that took place during the Tokugawa era had a major impact on the lives of ordinary Japanese. In some respects, the result was an increase in the power of the central government at the village level. The shogunate increasingly relied on Confucian maxims advocating obedience and hierarchy to enhance its authority with the general population. Decrees from the bakufu instructed the peasants on all aspects of their lives, including their eating habits and their behavior (see Opposing Viewpoints, "Some Confucian Commandments," p. 435). At the same time, the increased power of the government gave peasants more autonomy from the local daimyo. Villages now had more control over their local affairs.

At the same time, the Tokugawa era saw the emergence of the nuclear family—the *ie*—as the basic unit in Japanese society. In previous times, Japanese peasants had few legal rights. Most were too poor to keep their conjugal family unit intact or to pass property to their children. Many lived at the manorial residence or worked as servants in the households of more affluent villagers. Now, with farm income on the rise, the nuclear family took on the same form as in China, although without the joint family concept. The Japanese system of inheritance was based on primogeniture (pry-moh-JEN-ih-chur). Family property was passed to the eldest son, although younger sons often received land from their parents to set up their own families after marriage.

The Role of Women Another result of the changes under the Tokugawa was that women were somewhat more restricted than they had been previously. The rights of females were especially restricted in the samurai class, where Confucian values were highly influential. Male heads of households had broad authority over property, marriage, and divorce; wives were expected to obey their husbands on pain of death. Males often took concubines or homosexual partners, but females were expected to remain chaste. The male offspring of samurai parents studied the Confucian classics in schools established by the daimyo; females were reared at home, where only the fortunate might receive a rudimentary training in reading and writing Chinese characters. Nevertheless, some women were able to become accomplished poets and painters because, in aristocratic circles, female literacy was prized for its ability to enhance the refinement, social graces, and moral virtue of the home.

Women were similarly at a disadvantage among the common people. Marriages were arranged, and as in

Some Confucian Commandments

Family & Society — **ALTHOUGH THE QING DYNASTY WAS OF FOREIGN ORIGIN**, its rulers found Confucian maxims convenient for maintaining the social order. In 1670, the great emperor Kangxi issued the Sacred Edict to popularize Confucian values among the common people. The edict was read publicly at periodic intervals in every village in China and set the standard for behavior throughout the empire. Like the Qing Dynasty in China, the Tokugawa shoguns attempted to keep their subjects in line with decrees that carefully prescribed all kinds of behavior. Yet a subtle difference in tone can be detected between these two documents. While Kangxi's edict tended to encourage positive behavior, the decree of the Tokugawa Shogunate focused more on actions that were prohibited or discouraged.

Kangxi's Sacred Edict

1. Esteem most highly filial piety and brotherly submission, in order to give due importance to the social relations.
2. Behave with generosity toward your kindred, in order to illustrate harmony and benignity.
3. Show that you prize moderation and economy, in order to prevent the lavish waste of your means.
4. Extirpate strange principles, in order to exalt the correct doctrine.
5. Lecture on the laws, in order to warn the ignorant and obstinate.
6. Labor diligently at your proper callings, in order to stabilize the will of the people.
7. Instruct sons and younger brothers, in order to prevent them from doing what is wrong.
8. Put a stop to false accusations, in order to preserve the honest and good.
9. Fully remit your taxes, in order to avoid being pressed for payment.
10. Remove enmity and anger, in order to show the importance due to the person and life.

Maxims for Peasant Behavior in Tokugawa Japan

1. Young people are forbidden to congregate in great numbers.
2. Entertainments unsuited to peasants, such as playing the samisen or reciting ballad dramas, are forbidden.
3. Staging sumo matches is forbidden for the next five years.
4. Frugality . . . must be observed.
5. If a person has to leave the village for business or pleasure, that person must return by ten at night.
6. Father and son are forbidden to stay overnight at another person's house. An exception is to be made if it is to nurse a sick person.
7. Corvée [obligatory labor] assigned by the [local officials] must be performed faithfully.
8. Children who practice filial piety must be rewarded.
9. One must never get drunk and cause trouble for others.
10. Peasants who neglect farm work and cultivate their paddies and upland fields in a slovenly and careless fashion must be punished.
11. Fights and quarrels are forbidden in the village.
12. The deteriorating customs and morals of the village must be rectified.
13. Peasants who are suffering from poverty must be identified and helped.
14. This village has a proud history compared to other villages, but in recent years bad times have come upon us. Everyone must rise at six in the morning, cut grass, and work hard to revitalize the village.
15. The punishments to be meted out to violators of the village code and gifts to be awarded the deserving are to be decided during the last assembly meeting of the year.

 In what ways did Kangxi's set of commandments conform to the principles of State Confucianism? How do Kangxi's standards compare with those applied in Japan?

Source: From *Popular Culture In Late Imperial China* by David Johnson et al. Copyright © 1985 The Regents of the University of California. From Chi Nakane and Oishi Shinsabura, *Tokugawa Japan: The Social and Economic Antecedents of Modern Japan* (Japan, University of Tokyo, 1990), pp. 51–52. Translated by Conrad Totman. Copyright 1992 by Columbia University Press.

Experience an interactive version of this period in **MINDTAP**

China, the new wife moved in with the family of her husband. A wife who did not meet the expectations of her spouse or his family was likely to be divorced. Still, gender relations were more egalitarian than among the nobility. Women were generally valued as childbearers and homemakers, and both men and women worked in the fields. Poor families, however, often put infant daughters to death or sold them into prostitution.

Such attitudes toward women operated within the context of the increasingly rigid stratification of Japanese society. Deeply conservative in their social policies, the Tokugawa rulers established strict legal distinctions between the four main classes in Japan (warriors, artisans, peasants, and merchants). Intermarriage between classes was forbidden in theory, although sometimes the prohibitions were ignored in practice. Below these classes were Japan's outcasts, the **eta** (AY-tuh). Formerly, they were permitted to escape their status, at least in theory. The Tokugawa made their status hereditary and enacted severe discriminatory laws against them, regulating their place of residence, dress, and even hairstyles.

17-3e Tokugawa Culture

Under the Tokugawa, a vital new set of cultural values began to appear, especially in the cities. This innovative era witnessed the rise of popular literature written by and for the townspeople. With the development of woodblock printing in the early seventeenth century, literature became available to the common people, literacy levels rose, and lending libraries increased the accessibility of the printed word.

The Literature of the New Middle Class The best examples of this new urban fiction are the works of Saikaku (SY-kah-koo) (1642–1693), considered one of Japan's finest novelists. Saikaku's greatest novel, *Five Women Who Loved Love*, relates the amorous exploits of five women of the merchant class. Based partly on real-life experiences, it broke from the Confucian ethic of wifely fidelity to her husband and portrayed women who were willing to die for love—and all but one eventually did. Despite the tragic circumstances, the tone of the novel is upbeat and sometimes comic, and the author's wry comments prevent the reader from becoming emotionally involved with the heroines' misfortunes.

In the theater, the rise of Kabuki (kuh-BOO-kee) threatened the long dominance of the No (NOH) play, replacing the somewhat restrained and elegant thematic and stylistic approach of the classical drama with a new emphasis on violence, music, and dramatic gestures. Significantly, the new drama emerged not from the rarefied world of the court but from the new world of entertainment and amusement (see Comparative Illustration, "Popular Culture: East and West," p. 437). Its commercial success, however, led to difficulties with the government, which periodically attempted to restrict or even suppress it. Early Kabuki was often performed by prostitutes, and shogunate officials—fearing that such activities could have a corrupting effect on the nation's morals—prohibited women from appearing on the stage. As a result, a new professional class of male actors emerged to impersonate female characters on stage.

In contrast to the popular literature of the Tokugawa period, poetry persevered in its more serious tradition. The most exquisite poetry was produced in the seventeenth century by the greatest of all Japanese poets, Basho (BAH-shoh) (1644–1694). He was concerned with the search for the meaning of existence and the poetic expression of his experience. With his love of Daoism and Zen Buddhism, Basho found answers to his quest for the meaning of life in nature, and his poems are grounded in seasonal imagery. The following is among his most famous poems:

> *The ancient pond*
> *A frog leaps in*
> *The sound of the water.*
> *On the withered branch*
> *A crow has alighted—*
> *The end of autumn.*

Tokugawa Art Art also reflected the dynamism and changes in Japanese culture under the Tokugawa regime. The shogun's order that all daimyo and their families live every other year in Edo set off a burst of building as provincial rulers competed to erect the most magnificent mansion. And the prosperity of the newly rising merchant class added fuel to the fire. Japanese paintings, architecture, textiles, and ceramics all flourished during this affluent era.

Although Japan was isolated from the Western world during much of the Tokugawa era, Japanese art was enriched by ideas from other cultures. Japanese pottery makers borrowed both techniques and designs from Korea to produce handsome ceramics. The passion for "Dutch learning" inspired Japanese to study Western medicine, astronomy, and languages and led to experimentation with oil painting and Western ideas of perspective and the interplay of light and dark. Europeans desired Japanese lacquerware and metalwork inlaid with ivory and mother-of-pearl and especially the ceramics, which were now as highly prized as those of the Chinese.

Perhaps the most famous of all Japanese art of the Tokugawa era is the woodblock print. With a new literate mercantile class eager for illustrated texts that presented a visual documentation of the times, artists began to mass-produce woodblock prints to satisfy their needs. Some portrayed the "floating world" of the entertainment quarter with scenes of carefree revelers enjoying the pleasures of

Popular Culture, East and West

Family & Society

BY THE SEVENTEENTH CENTURY, a popular culture distinct from the elite culture of the nobility was beginning to emerge in the urban worlds of both the East and the West. Image 17.9a shows a festival scene from the pleasure district of Kyoto known as the Gion. Spectators on a balcony are enjoying a colorful parade of floats and costumed performers. The festival originated as a celebration of the passing of a deadly epidemic in medieval Japan. Image 17.9b shows a scene from the celebration of Carnival on the Piazza Sante Croce in Florence, Italy. Carnival was a period of festivities before Lent, celebrated primarily in Roman Catholic countries. It became an occasion for indulgence in food, drink, games, and practical jokes as a prelude to the austerity of the forty-day Lenten season from Ash Wednesday to Easter.

 Do festivals such as these still exist in our own day? What purpose might they serve?

17.9a

Newark Museum/Art Resource, NY

Scala/Art Resource, NY

17.9b

Getty Images

17.10 Hokusai: from *Thirty-Six Views of Mount Fuji*. Along with Ando Hiroshige, Matsushika Hokusai became enormously popular in nineteenth-century Japan because of his colorful block prints portraying the people and the geography of the country. His series titled *Thirty-Six Views of Mount Fuji* were among his admired works, not least because of the symbolic importance of that symmetrical mount in Japanese culture. Long considered to be the home of the gods, Fuji became the focus of a sect of Shintoism, and even today thousands of Japanese make a pilgrimage to the peak of the mountain to view the sunrise over the eastern sea. The print shown here is entitled *Tama River in Musashi Province*.

life. Others such as Utamaro (OO-tah-mah-roh) (1754–1806) painted erotic and sardonic women in everyday poses— walking down the street, cooking, or drying their bodies after a bath. Two of the most popular, Hokusai (HOH-kuh-sy) (1760–1849) and Ando Hiroshige (AHN-doh hee-roh-SHEE-gay) (1797–1858), became famous for their bold interpretation of the Japanese landscape (see Image 17.10).

17-4 KOREA AND VIETNAM

Q **Focus Questions:** To what degree did developments in Korea during this period reflect conditions in China and Japan? What were the unique aspects of Vietnamese civilization?

On the fringes of the East Asian mainland, two of China's close neighbors sought to preserve their fragile independence from the expansionistic tendencies of the powerful Ming and Qing Dynasties.

17-4a Korea: In a Dangerous Neighborhood

As Japan under the Tokugawa Shogunate moved steadily out from the shadows of the Chinese empire by creating a unique society with its own special characteristics, the Choson Dynasty in Korea continued to pattern itself after the Chinese model— at least on the surface. The dynasty had been founded by military commander Yi Song Gye (YEE song yee) in the late fourteenth century and immediately set out to establish close political and cultural relations with the Ming Dynasty. From their new capital at Seoul (SOHL) on the Han (HAHN) River in the center of the peninsula, the Choson rulers accepted a tributary relationship with their powerful neighbor and engaged in the wholesale adoption of Chinese institutions and values. As in China, the civil service examinations tested candidates on their knowledge of the Confucian classics, and success was viewed as an essential step toward upward mobility.

There were differences, however. As in Japan, the dynasty continued to restrict entry into the bureaucracy to members of the aristocratic class, which were known in

Korea as the *yangban* (YAHNG-ban) (or "two groups," civil servants and military). At the same time, the peasantry remained locked in serflike conditions, working on government estates or on the manor holdings of the landed elite. A class of slaves called **chonmin** (CHAWN-min) labored on government plantations or served in certain occupations such as butchers and entertainers, which were considered beneath the dignity of other groups in the population.

Eventually, Korean society began to show signs of independence from Chinese orthodoxy. In the fifteenth century, a phonetic alphabet for writing the Korean spoken language (*hangul*) was devised. Although it was initially held in contempt by the elites and used primarily as a teaching device, eventually it became the medium for private correspondence and the published fiction intended for a popular audience. At the same time, changes were taking place in the economy, where rising agricultural production contributed to a population increase and the appearance of a small urban industrial and commercial sector, and in society, where the long domination of the Yangban class began to weaken. As their numbers increased and their power and influence declined, some Yangban became merchants or even moved into the ranks of the peasantry, further blurring the distinction between the aristocratic class and the common people.

Meanwhile, the Choson Dynasty faced continual challenges to its independence from its neighbors. Throughout much of the sixteenth century, the main threat came from the north, where Manchu forces harassed Korean lands just south of the Yalu (YAH-loo) River (refer back to Map 17.3). By the 1580s, however, the larger threat came from the east in the form of a newly united Japan. During much of the sixteenth century, leading Japanese daimyo had been involved in a protracted civil war as Oda Nobunaga, Toyotomi Hideyoshi, and Tokugawa Ieyasu strove to solidify their control over the islands. Of the three, only Hideyoshi lusted for an empire beyond the seas. Although born to a commoner family, he harbored visions of grandeur and in the late 1580s announced plans to attack the Ming Empire. When the Korean king Sonjo (SOHN-joe) (1567–1608) refused Hideyoshi's offer of an alliance, in 1592 the latter launched an invasion of the Korean Peninsula.

At first the campaign went well, and Japanese forces, wreaking death and devastation throughout the countryside, advanced as far as the Korean capital at Seoul. But eventually the Koreans under the inspired leadership of military commander Yi Sunshin (YEE soon-SHIN) (1545–1598), who designed fast but heavily armed ships that could destroy the more cumbersome landing craft of the invading forces, managed to repel the attack and safeguard their independence. The respite was brief, however. By

the 1630s, a new threat from the Manchus had emerged from across the northern border. A Manchu force invaded northern Korea and eventually compelled the Choson Dynasty to promise allegiance to the new imperial government in Beijing.

Korea was relatively untouched by the arrival of European merchants and missionaries, although information about Christianity was brought to the peninsula by Koreans returning from tribute missions to China, and a small Catholic community was established there in the late eighteenth century.

17-4b Vietnam: The Perils of Empire

Vietnam—or Dai Viet (dy VEE-et), as it was known at the time—had managed to avoid the fate of many of its neighbors during the seventeenth and eighteenth centuries. Less directly located on the major maritime routes that passed through the region, the country was only peripherally involved in the spice trade with the West and had not suffered the humiliation of losing territory to European colonial powers. In fact, Dai Viet followed an imperialist path of its own, defeating the trading state of Champa to the south and imposing its suzerainty over the rump of the old Angkor Empire—today known as Cambodia. The state of Dai Viet now extended from the Chinese border to the shores of the Gulf of Siam.

But expansion undermined the cultural integrity of traditional Vietnamese society as migrants from the north who settled in the marshy Mekong River Delta developed a "frontier spirit" far removed from the communal values long practiced in the old national heartland of the Red River Valley. At the same time, thousands of non-Vietnamese subjects were now placed under the suzerainty of the dynasty in the north. By the seventeenth century, a civil war had split Dai Viet into two squabbling territories in the north and south, providing European powers with the opportunity to meddle in the country's internal affairs to their own benefit. In 1802, with the assistance of a French adventurer long active in the region, a member of the southern royal family managed to reunite the country under the new Nguyen (NGWEN) Dynasty, which lasted until 1945.

To placate China, the country was renamed Vietnam (South Viet), and the new imperial capital was established in the city of Hué (HWAY), a small river port roughly equidistant from the two rich river valleys that provided the country with its chief sustenance, wet rice. The founder of the new dynasty, who took the reign title of Gia Long, fended off French efforts to promote Christianity among his subjects and sought to promote traditional Confucian values among an increasingly diverse population.

CHAPTER SUMMARY

When the first European ships began to appear off the coast of China and Japan, the new arrivals were welcomed—even if only as curiosities. Eventually, several European nations established trade relations with China and Japan, and Christian missionaries of various religious orders were active in both countries and in Korea and Vietnam as well. But their welcome was short lived. Europeans eventually began to be perceived as detrimental to law and order, and the majority of the foreign merchants and missionaries were evicted from all four countries during the seventeenth century. From then until the middle of the nineteenth century, the East Asian states were minimally affected by events taking place beyond their borders.

That fact led many observers to assume that the traditional societies in the region were essentially stagnant, characterized by agrarian institutions and values reminiscent of those of the feudal era in Europe. As we have seen, however, that picture is misleading because all four countries were evolving and by the early nineteenth century were quite different from what they had been three centuries earlier.

Ironically, these changes were especially marked in Tokugawa Japan, a seemingly "closed" country, but one

where traditional classes and institutions were under increasing strain, not only from the emergence of a new merchant class but also from the centralizing tendencies of the powerful Tokugawa Shogunate. On the mainland as well, the popular image in the West of a "changeless China" was increasingly divorced from reality as social and economic conditions were marked by a growing complexity that gave birth to tensions that would strain the Qing Dynasty to its very core by the middle of the nineteenth century.

By the beginning of the nineteenth century, then, powerful tensions, reflecting a growing gap between ideal and reality, were at work in all the societies on the eastern fringe of the Eurasian supercontinent. Under these conditions, all four countries were soon forced to face a new challenge from the aggressive power of an industrializing Europe.

REFLECTION QUESTIONS

Q What factors at the end of the eighteenth century might have served to promote or impede China's transition to an advanced industrial and market economy? Which factors do you think were the most important? Why?

Q Some historians have declared that during the Tokugawa era the Japanese government essentially sought to close the country to all forms of outside influence. Is that claim justified? Why or why not?

Q What was the nature of Sino–Korean relations during the early modern era? How did they compare with Chinese policies toward Vietnam?

CHAPTER TIMELINE

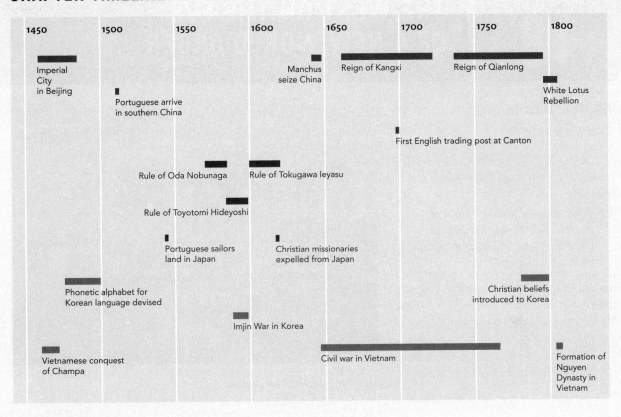

1450	1500	1550	1600	1650	1700	1750	1800

Imperial City in Beijing

Portuguese arrive in southern China

Manchus seize China

Reign of Kangxi

Reign of Qianlong

White Lotus Rebellion

First English trading post at Canton

Rule of Oda Nobunaga

Rule of Tokugawa Ieyasu

Rule of Toyotomi Hideyoshi

Portuguese sailors land in Japan

Christian missionaries expelled from Japan

Phonetic alphabet for Korean language devised

Christian beliefs introduced to Korea

Imjin War in Korea

Vietnamese conquest of Champa

Civil war in Vietnam

Formation of Nguyen Dynasty in Vietnam

CHAPTER NOTES

1. From J. D. Spence, *Emperor of China: Self-Portrait of K'ang Hsi* (New York, 1974), pp. 143–144.
2. R. Strassberg, *The World of K'ang Shang-jen: A Man of Letters in Early Ch'ing China* (New York, 1983), p. 275.
3. L. Struve, *The Southern Ming, 1644–1662* (New Haven, Conn., 1984), p. 61.
4. J. L. Cranmer-Byng, *An Embassy to China: Lord Macartney's Journal, 1793–1794* (London, 1912), p. 340.
5. Quoted in D. J. Boorstin, *The Discoverers: A History of Man's Search to Know His World and Himself* (New York, 1983), p. 63.
6. C. R. Boxer, ed., *South China in the Sixteenth Century* (London, 1953), p. 265.
7. C. Nakane and S. Oishi, eds., *Tokugawa Japan* (Tokyo, 1990), p. 14.
8. Quoted in J. Elisonas, "Christianity and the Daimyo," in J. W. Hall, ed., *The Cambridge History of Japan*, vol. 4 (Cambridge, 1991), p. 360.

MINDTAP
From Cengage

MindTap® is a fully online, highly personalized learning experience built upon Cengage Learning content. MindTap combines student learning tools—readings, multimedia, activities, and assessments—into a singular Learning Path that guides students through the course and helps students develop the critical thinking, analysis, and communication skills that are essential to academic and professional success.

CHAPTER 18

THE WEST ON THE EVE OF A NEW WORLD ORDER

Chapter Outline and Focus Questions

18.1 The Storming of the Bastille

CCI/The Art Archive at Art Resource, NY

Critical Thinking

Q *In what ways were the American Revolution, the French Revolution, and the seventeenth-century English revolutions alike? In what ways were they different?*

Connections to Today

Q *What are the similarities and differences between the French Revolution and contemporary revolutions?*

IN PARIS ON THE MORNING OF JULY 14, 1789, a mob of 8,000 men and women in search of weapons streamed toward the Bastille (bass-STEEL), a royal armory filled with arms and ammunition. The Bastille was also a state prison, and although it held only seven prisoners at the time, it was a glaring symbol of the government's despotic policies in the eyes of these angry Parisians. The building was defended by the Marquis de Launay (mar-KEE duh loh-NAY) and a small garrison of 114 men. The attack on the Bastille began in earnest in the early afternoon, and de Launay and the garrison surrendered after three hours of fighting. Angered by the loss of ninety-eight protesters, the victors beat de Launay to death, cut off his head, and carried it aloft in triumph through the streets of Paris. When King Louis XVI was told the news of the fall of the Bastille by the duc de La Rochefoucauld-Liancourt (dook duh lah-RUSH-foo-koh-lee-ahn-KOOR), he exclaimed, "Why, this is a revolt." "No, Sire," replied the duc. "It is a revolution."

The French Revolution was a key factor in the emergence of a new world order. Historians have often portrayed the eighteenth century as the final phase of an old Europe that would be forever changed by the violent upheaval and reordering of society associated with the French Revolution. Before the Revolution, the old order—still largely agrarian, dominated by kings and landed aristocrats, and grounded in privileges for nobles, clergy, towns, and provinces—seemed to continue a basic pattern that had prevailed in Europe since medieval times. As the century drew to a close, however, a new intellectual order based on rationalism and secularism emerged, and demographic, economic, social, and political patterns were beginning to change in ways that proclaimed the arrival of a new and more modern order.

The French Revolution demolished the institutions of the old regime and established a new order based on individual rights, representative institutions, and a concept of loyalty to the nation rather than to the monarch. The revolutionary upheavals of the era, especially in France, created new liberal and national political ideals that were summarized in the French revolutionary slogan "Liberté, Egalité, Fraternité" ("Liberty, Equality, Fraternity") that transformed France and then spread to other European countries and the rest of the world.

18-1 TOWARD A NEW HEAVEN AND A NEW EARTH: AN INTELLECTUAL REVOLUTION IN THE WEST

 Focus Question: Who were the leading figures of the Scientific Revolution and the Enlightenment, and what were their main contributions?

In the seventeenth century, a group of scientists set the Western world on a new path known as the **Scientific Revolution**, which gave Europeans a new way of viewing the universe and their place in it. The Scientific Revolution affected only a small number of Europe's educated elite.

But in the eighteenth century, this changed dramatically as a group of intellectuals popularized the ideas of the Scientific Revolution and used them to undertake a dramatic re-examination of all aspects of life. The widespread impact of these ideas on their society has caused historians ever since to call the eighteenth century in Europe the Age of Enlightenment.

18-1a The Scientific Revolution

The Scientific Revolution ultimately challenged conceptions and beliefs about the nature of the external world that had become dominant by the late Middle Ages.

Toward a New Heaven: A Revolution in Astronomy Medieval philosophers had used the ideas of Aristotle, Ptolemy (the greatest astronomer of antiquity, who lived in the second century C.E.), and Christianity to form the Ptolemaic (tahl-uh-MAY-ik) or **geocentric theory** of the universe. In this conception, the universe was seen as a series of concentric spheres with a fixed or motionless Earth at its center. Composed of material substance, Earth was imperfect and constantly changing. The spheres surrounding Earth were made of a crystalline, transparent substance and moved in circular orbits around Earth. The heavenly bodies, believed to number ten in 1500, were pure orbs of light that were embedded in the moving, concentric spheres. Working outward from Earth, the first eight spheres contained the moon, Mercury, Venus, the sun, Mars, Jupiter, Saturn, and the fixed stars. The ninth sphere imparted to the eighth sphere of the fixed stars its daily motion, while the tenth sphere was frequently described as the prime mover that moved itself and imparted motion to the other spheres. Beyond the tenth sphere was the Empyrean Heaven—the location of God and all the saved souls. Thus, God and the saved souls were at one end of the universe and humans were at the center.

Polish mathematician Nicolaus Copernicus (NEE-koh-lowss kuh-PURR-nuh-kuss) (1473–1543) felt that Ptolemy's geocentric system of the heavenly bodies was wrong and offered his iwn **heliocentric** (sun-centered) **theory** as a more accurate explanation. Copernicus argued that the sun was motionless at the center of the universe. The planets revolved around the sun in the order of Mercury, Venus, Earth, Mars, Jupiter, and Saturn. The moon, however, revolved around Earth. Moreover, what appeared to be the movement of the sun around Earth was really explained by Earth's daily rotation on its axis and its journey around the sun each year. But Copernicus did not reject the idea that the heavenly spheres moved in circular orbits.

Johannes Kepler (yoh-HAHN-us KEP-lur) (1571–1630) took the next step in destroying the Ptolemaic system. A brilliant German mathematician and astronomer, Kepler

18.2 Medieval Conception of the Universe. As this sixteenth-century illustration shows, the medieval cosmological view placed Earth at the center of the universe surrounded by a series of concentric spheres. Earth was imperfect and constantly changing, whereas the heavenly bodies that surrounded it were perfect and incorruptible. Beyond the tenth and final sphere was heaven, where God and all the saved souls were located. [From the center outward, the circles read: (1) moon, (2) Mercury, (3) Venus, (4) sun, (5) Mars, (6) Jupiter, (7) Saturn, (8) firmament of the stars, (9) crystalline sphere, (10) prime mover, and at the end Empyrean Heaven—Home of God and All the Elect—that is, saved souls.]

18.3 The Copernican System. The Copernican system was presented in *On the Revolutions of the Heavenly Spheres*, which was published shortly before Copernicus's death. As shown in this illustration from the first edition, Copernicus maintained that the sun was the center of the universe while the planets, including Earth, revolved around it. Moreover, Earth rotated daily on its axis. [From the center outward, the circles read: sun: (VII) Mercury, orbit of eighty days; (VI) Venus; (V) Earth, with the moon, orbit of one year; (IIII) Mars, orbit of two years; (III) Jupiter, orbit of twelve years; (II) Saturn, orbit of thirty years; and (I) Immobile Sphere of the Fixed Stars.]

arrived at laws of planetary motion that confirmed Copernicus's heliocentric theory. In his first law, however, he revised Copernicus by showing that the orbits of the planets around the sun were not circular but elliptical, with the sun at one focus of the ellipse rather than at the center.

Kepler's work destroyed the basic structure of the Ptolemaic system. People could now think in new terms of the actual paths of planets revolving around the sun in elliptical orbits. But important questions remained; for example, what were the planets made of? An Italian scientist achieved the next important breakthrough to a new cosmology by answering that question.

Galileo Galilei (gal-li-LAY-oh GAL-li-lay) (1564–1642) taught mathematics and was the first European to make systematic observations of the heavens by means of a telescope, inaugurating a new age in astronomy. Galileo turned his telescope to the skies and made a remarkable series of discoveries: mountains on the moon, four moons revolving around Jupiter, and sunspots. Galileo's observations seemed to destroy yet another aspect of the traditional cosmology in that the universe seemed to be composed of material similar to that of Earth rather than a perfect, unchanging substance.

Galileo's revelations, published in *The Starry Messenger* in 1610, made Europeans aware of a new picture of the universe. But the Catholic church condemned Copernicanism and ordered Galileo to abandon the Copernican thesis. The church attacked the Copernican system because it threatened not only Scripture but also an entire conception of the universe. The heavens were no longer a spiritual world but a world of matter.

By the 1630s and 1640s, most astronomers had come to accept the new conception of the universe. Nevertheless, the problem of explaining motion in the universe and tying together the ideas of Copernicus, Galileo, and Kepler had not yet been done. This would be the work of an Englishman who has long been considered the greatest genius of the Scientific Revolution.

Isaac Newton (1642–1727) taught at Cambridge University, where he wrote his major work, *Mathematical Principles of Natural Philosophy*, known simply as the *Principia* (prin-SIP-ee-uh) by the first word of its Latin title. In the *Principia*, Newton defined the three laws of motion that govern the planetary bodies as well as objects on Earth. Crucial to his argument was the universal law of gravitation, which explained why planetary bodies did not travel in straight lines but continued in elliptical orbits around the sun. In mathematical terms, Newton explained that every object in the universe is attracted to every other object by a force called *gravity*.

Newton had demonstrated that one mathematically proven universal law could explain all motion in the universe. At the same time, the Newtonian synthesis created a new cosmology in which the universe was seen as one huge, regulated machine that operated according to natural laws in absolute time, space, and motion. Newton's **world-machine** concept dominated the modern worldview until the twentieth century when Albert Einstein's concept of relativity created a new picture of the universe.

Europe, China, and Scientific Revolutions A question that arises is why the Scientific Revolution occurred in Europe and not in China. In the Middle Ages, China had been the most technologically advanced civilization in the world. After 1500, that distinction passed to the West (see Comparative Essay, "The Scientific Revolution," p. 446). Historians are not sure why. Some have contrasted the sense of order in Chinese society with the competitive spirit existing in Europe. Others have emphasized China's ideological viewpoint that favored living in harmony with nature rather than trying to dominate it. One historian has even suggested that China's civil service system drew the "best and the brightest" into government service to the detriment of other occupations.

18-1b Background to the Enlightenment

The impetus for political and social change in the eighteenth century stemmed in part from the **Enlightenment**, a movement of intellectuals who were greatly impressed with the accomplishments of the Scientific Revolution. When they used the word *reason*—one of their favorite words—they were advocating the application of the **scientific method** to the understanding of all life. All institutions and all systems of thought were subject to the rational, scientific way of thinking if people would only free themselves from the shackles of outmoded traditions, especially religious ones. If Isaac Newton could discover the natural laws regulating the world of nature, by using reason they also could find the laws that governed human society. This belief in turn led them to hope that they could create a better society than the one they had inherited. *Reason, natural law, hope, progress*—these were the buzzwords in the heady atmosphere of eighteenth-century Europe.

Major sources of inspiration for the Enlightenment were Isaac Newton and his fellow Englishman John Locke (1632–1704). Newton had contended that the world and everything in it worked like a giant machine. Enchanted by the grand design of this world-machine, the intellectuals of the Enlightenment were convinced that by following Newton's rules of reasoning, they could discover the natural laws that governed politics, economics, justice, and religion.

John Locke's theory of knowledge also made a great impact. In his *Essay Concerning Human Understanding* (1690), Locke denied the existence of innate ideas and argued that every person was born with a *tabula rasa* (TAB-yuh-luh RAH-suh), a blank mind. By denying innate ideas, Locke implied that people were molded by their environment, by whatever they perceived through their senses from their surrounding world. If the environment were changed and people were subjected to proper influences, they could be changed and a new society created. And how should the environment be changed? Newton had paved the way: reason enabled enlightened people to discover the natural laws to which all institutions should conform.

18-1c The Philosophes and Their Ideas

The intellectuals of the Enlightenment were known by the French term *philosophes* (fee-loh-ZAHFS), although they were not all French and few were philosophers in the strict sense of the term. The **philosophes** were literary people, professors, journalists, economists, political scientists, and, above all, social reformers. Although it was a truly international and cosmopolitan movement, the Enlightenment also enhanced the dominant role being played by French culture; Paris was its recognized capital, and most of the leaders of the Enlightenment were French. The French philosophes, in turn, affected intellectuals elsewhere and created a movement that touched the entire Western world, including the British and Spanish colonies in the Americas. (The terms *British* and *Great Britain* began to be used after 1707 when the Act of Union united England and Scotland.)

To the philosophes, the role of philosophy was not just to discuss the world but also to change it. A spirit of rational criticism was to be applied to everything, including religion and politics. Spanning almost a century, the Enlightenment evolved with each succeeding generation, becoming more radical as new thinkers built on the contributions of their predecessors. A few individuals, however, dominated the landscape so completely that we can gain insight into the core ideas of the philosophes by focusing on the three French giants—Montesquieu, Voltaire, and Diderot.

Montesquieu Charles de Secondat (SHARL duh suh-KAHN-da), the baron de Montesquieu (MOHN-tess-kyoo) (1689–1755), came from the French nobility. In his most

COMPARATIVE ESSAY

The Scientific Revolution

Science & Technology When Catholic missionaries began to arrive in China during the sixteenth century, they marveled at the many accomplishments of Chinese civilization, including woodblock printing and the civil service examination system. In turn, their hosts were impressed with European inventions such as the spring-driven clock and eyeglasses.

It is not surprising that the Western visitors were impressed with what they saw in China, for that country had long been at the forefront of human achievement. After the sixteenth century, however, Europe would take the lead in science and technology, a phenomenon that would ultimately bring about the Industrial Revolution and begin a transformation of human society that would lay the foundations of the modern world.

18.4 The Telescope, a European Invention

Why did Europe suddenly become the engine for rapid change in the seventeenth and eighteenth centuries? One factor was the shift in the European worldview from a metaphysical to a materialist perspective and the growing inclination among European intellectuals to question first principles. In contrast to China, empirical scientists in early modern Europe rejected received religious ideas, developed a new conception of the universe, and sought ways to improve material conditions around them.

Why were European thinkers more interested in practical applications of their discoveries than their counterparts elsewhere? No doubt the literate mercantile and propertied elites of Europe were attracted to the new science because it offered new ways to exploit resources for profit. Some early scientists made it easier for these groups to accept the new ideas by showing how they could be applied to specific industrial and technological needs. Galileo, for example, consciously appealed to the material interests of the educated elite when he explained that the science of mechanics would be quite useful "when it becomes necessary to build bridges or other structures over water, something occurring mainly in affairs of great importance."

Finally, the political changes taking place in Europe may also have contributed. Many European states enlarged their bureaucratic machinery and consolidated their governments to collect revenues and amass the armies needed to compete militarily with rivals. Political leaders desperately sought ways to enhance their wealth and power and grasped eagerly at new tools that might guarantee their survival and prosperity.

 Why did the Scientific Revolution emerge in Europe and not in China?

famous work, *The Spirit of the Laws* (1748), Montesquieu attempted to apply the scientific method to the comparative study of governments to ascertain the "natural laws" governing the social and political relationships of human beings. Montesquieu distinguished three basic kinds of governments: republic, monarchy, and despotism.

Montesquieu used England as an example of monarchy, and his analysis of England's constitution led to his most lasting contribution to political thought—the importance of checks and balances achieved by means of a **separation**

of powers. He believed that England's system, with its separate executive, legislative, and judicial powers that served to limit and control each other, provided the greatest freedom and security for a state. American political leaders incorporated his separation of powers into the U.S. Constitution.

Voltaire The greatest figure of the Enlightenment was François-Marie Arouet (frahn-SWAH-ma-REE ahr-WEH), known simply as Voltaire (vohl-TAYR) (1694–1778). Son of a prosperous middle-class family from Paris, he studied law but achieved his first success as a playwright. Voltaire wrote an almost endless stream of pamphlets, novels, plays, letters, philosophical essays, and histories.

Voltaire was especially well known for his criticism of traditional religion and his strong attachment to the ideal of religious toleration. "Crush the infamous thing," he thundered—the infamous thing being religious fanaticism, intolerance, and superstition.

Throughout his life, Voltaire championed not only religious tolerance but also **deism**, a religious outlook shared by most other philosophes. Deism was built on the Newtonian world-machine, which implied the existence of a mechanic (God) who had created the universe. To Voltaire, the universe was like a clock, and God was the clockmaker who had created it, set it in motion, and allowed it to run according to its own natural laws.

Diderot Denis Diderot (duh-NEE dee-DROH) (1713–1784), the son of a skilled craftsman, became a writer so that he could be free to study many subjects and languages. One of Diderot's favorite topics was Christianity, which he condemned as fanatical and unreasonable.

Diderot's most famous contribution was the *Encyclopedia*, or *Classified Dictionary of the Sciences, Arts, and Trades*, a twenty-eight-volume compendium of knowledge that he edited and referred to as the "great work of his life." Its purpose, according to Diderot, was to "change the general way of thinking." It did precisely that, becoming a major weapon of the philosophes' crusade against the old French society. The contributors included many philosophes who attacked religious intolerance and advocated social, legal, and political improvements that would lead to a society that was more cosmopolitan, more tolerant, more humane, and more reasonable. The *Encyclopedia* was sold to doctors, clergymen, teachers, lawyers, and even military officers, thus spreading the ideas of the Enlightenment.

Toward a New "Science of Man" The Enlightenment belief that Newton's scientific methods could be used to discover the natural laws underlying all areas of human life led to the emergence of what the philosophes called a "science of man," or what we would call the social sciences. In many areas—especially economics, politics, and education—the philosophes arrived at natural laws that they believed governed human actions.

Adam Smith (1723–1790), often viewed as one of the founders of the discipline of economics, believed that individuals should be free to pursue their own economic self-interest. Through their actions, all society would ultimately benefit. Consequently, the state should in no way interrupt the free play of natural economic forces by imposing government regulations on the economy but should leave it alone, a doctrine that subsequently became known as **laissez-faire** (less-ay-FAYR) (French for "leave it alone"). In Smith's view, government had only three basic functions: to protect society from invasion (army), to defend its citizens from injustice (police), and to keep up certain public works such as roads and canals that private individuals could not afford.

The Later Enlightenment By the late 1760s, a new generation of philosophes began to move beyond their predecessors' beliefs. Most famous was Jean-Jacques Rousseau (ZHAHNH-ZHAHK roo-SOH) (1712–1778), whose political beliefs were presented in two major works. In his *Discourse on the Origins of the Inequality of Mankind*, Rousseau argued that people had adopted laws and governors to preserve their private property. In the process, government enslaved them. What, then, should people do to regain their freedom? In his celebrated treatise *The Social Contract* (1762), Rousseau found an answer in the concept of the social contract whereby an entire society agreed to be governed by its general will. Each individual might have a particular will contrary to the general will, but if the individual put his particular will (self-interest) above the general will, he should be forced to abide by the general will. "This means nothing less than that he will be forced to be free," said Rousseau, because the general will, being ethical and not just political, represented what the entire community ought to do.

Another influential treatise by Rousseau was his novel *Émile*, one of the Enlightenment's most important works on education. Rousseau's fundamental concern was that education should foster rather than restrict children's natural instincts. But Rousseau did not necessarily practice what he preached. His own children were sent to orphanages, where many children died at a young age. Rousseau also viewed women as "naturally" different from men. In *Émile*, Sophie, Émile's intended wife, was educated for her role as wife and mother by learning obedience and nurturing skills that would enable her to provide loving care for her husband and children. Not everyone in the eighteenth century, however, agreed with Rousseau.

The "Woman Question" in the Enlightenment For centuries, many male intellectuals had argued that the nature of women made them inferior to men and made male domination of women necessary and right. These biases restricted women's access to education. Despite these educational limitations, many women made notable contributions to the Scientific Revolution. Maria Winkelmann (VINK-ul-mahn) in Germany, for example, was an outstanding

HISTORICAL VOICES

The Rights of Women

Art & Ideas | **MARY WOLLSTONECRAFT RESPONDED TO AN UNHAPPY CHILDHOOD** in a large family by seeking to lead an independent life. Few occupations were available for middle-class women in her day, but she survived by working as a governess to aristocratic children. All the while, she wrote and developed her ideas on the rights of women. This excerpt is taken from her *Vindication of the Rights of Woman*, written in 1792, which established her reputation as the foremost British feminist thinker of the eighteenth century.

Mary Wollstonecraft, *Vindication of the Rights of Woman*

It is a melancholy truth [that] the most respectable women are the most oppressed; and, unless they have understandings far superior to the common run of understandings, taking in both sexes, they must, from being treated like contemptible beings, become contemptible. How many women thus waste life away the prey of discontent, who might have practiced as physicians, regulated a farm, managed a shop, and stood erect, supported by their own industry, instead of hanging their heads surcharged with the dew of sensibility, that consumes the beauty to which it at first gave luster. . . .

Proud of their weakness, however, [women] must always be protected, guarded from care, and all the rough toils that dignify the mind. If this be the fiat of fate, if

they will make themselves insignificant and contemptible, sweetly to waste "life away," let them not expect to be valued when their beauty fades, for it is the fate of the fairest flowers to be admired and pulled to pieces by the careless hand that plucked them. In how many ways do I wish, from the purest benevolence, to impress this truth on my sex; yet I fear that they will not listen to a truth that dear-bought experience has brought home to many an agitated bosom, nor willingly resign the privileges of rank and sex for the privileges of humanity, to which those have no claim who do not discharge its duties. . . .

Would men but generously snap our chains, and be content with rational fellowship instead of slavish obedience, they would find us more observant daughters, more affectionate sisters, more faithful wives, and more reasonable mothers—in a word, better citizens. We should then love them with true affection, because we should learn to respect ourselves; and the peace of mind of a worthy man would not be interrupted by the idle vanity of his wife.

 What picture did Wollstonecraft paint of the women of her day? Why were they in such a deplorable state? Why did Wollstonecraft suggest that both women and men were at fault for the "slavish" situation of females?

Source: From *First Feminists: British Women, 1578–1799* by Moira Ferguson. Copyright © 1985 Indiana University Press.

---

practicing astronomer. Nevertheless, when she applied for a position as assistant astronomer at the Berlin Academy, for which she was highly qualified, she was denied the post by the academy's members, who feared that hiring her would establish a precedent ("mouths would gape").

Female thinkers in the eighteenth century disagreed with this attitude and offered suggestions for improving conditions for women. The strongest statement of the rights of women was advanced by English writer Mary Wollstonecraft (WULL-stun-kraft) (1759–1797), who is viewed by many historians as the founder of modern European **feminism**.

In her *Vindication of the Rights of Woman* (1792), Wollstonecraft pointed out two contradictions in the views of women held by such Enlightenment thinkers as

Rousseau. To argue that women must obey men, she said, was contrary to the beliefs of those same individuals that a system based on the arbitrary power of monarchs over their subjects or slave owners over their slaves was wrong. The subjection of women to men was equally wrong. Furthermore, the Enlightenment was based on an ideal of reason innate in all human beings. If women have reason, then they should have the same rights as men to obtain an education and engage in economic and political life (see Historical Voices, "The Rights of Women,").

18-1d Culture in an Enlightened Age

Although the Baroque style that had dominated the seventeenth century continued to be popular, by the 1730s a

18.5 Antoine Watteau, *Return from Cythera.* Antoine Watteau was one of the most gifted painters in eighteenth-century France. His portrayal of aristocratic life reveals a world of elegance, wealth, and pleasure. In this painting, Watteau depicts a group of aristocratic lovers about to depart from the island of Cythera, where they have paid homage to Venus, the goddess of love.

new style of decoration and architecture known as **Rococo** (ruh-KOH-koh) had spread throughout Europe. Unlike the Baroque, which stressed power, grandeur, and movement, Rococo emphasized grace, charm, and gentle action. Rococo rejected strict geometrical patterns and had a fondness for curves; it liked to follow the wandering lines of natural objects such as seashells and flowers. Highly secular, its lightness and charm spoke of the pursuit of pleasure, happiness, and love.

Some of Rococo's appeal is evident in the work of Antoine Watteau (AHN-twahn wah-TOH) (1684–1721), who created a specific type of Rococo art (see Image 18.5). His paintings portrayed a lyrical view of aristocratic life, refined, sensual, and civilized, with gentlemen and ladies in elegant dress—reflecting a world of upper-class pleasure and joy. Underneath that exterior, however, was an element of sadness as the artist revealed the fragility and transitory nature of pleasure, love, and life. Watteau relied on the use of color rather than representational form to highlight his subjects. Later artists such as Jean-Honoré Fragonard (FRA-go-NARD) (1732–1806) continued Watteau's use of color and subject matter (see Image 18.6).

High Culture Historians have grown accustomed to distinguishing between a civilization's high culture and its popular culture. **High culture** is the literary and artistic culture of the educated and wealthy ruling classes; **popular culture** is the written and unwritten culture of the masses, most of which has traditionally been passed down orally. By the eighteenth century, the two forms were beginning to blend, owing to the expansion of both the reading public and publishing. While French publishers issued 300 titles in 1750, about 1,600 were being published yearly in the 1780s. Although many of these books were still aimed at small groups of the educated elite, many were also directed to the new reading public of the middle classes, which included women and even urban artisans.

Popular Culture The distinguishing characteristic of popular culture is its collective nature. Group activity was especially common in the *festival*, a broad name used to cover a variety of celebrations: community festivals, annual festivals such as Christmas and Easter, and the ultimate festival, Carnival, which was celebrated in the Mediterranean world of Spain, Italy, and France as well as in Germany and Austria.

18.6 Jean-Honoré Fragonard, *The Swing*. In this painting, Fragonard portrays a young lady being pushed on a swing as her suitor sits below her, capturing the frivolity and decadence of French aristocracy. The lush environs and curvilinear landscape epitomize Rococo's love of nature; the delicate light and color of the lady's dress highlight the playful moment of her kicking off her shoe.

Carnival began after Christmas and lasted until the start of Lent, the forty-day period of fasting and purification leading up to Easter. Because people were expected to abstain from meat, sex, and most recreations during Lent, Carnival was a time of great indulgence when heavy consumption of food and drink was the norm. It was a time of intense sexual activity as well.

18-2 ECONOMIC CHANGES AND THE SOCIAL ORDER

 Focus Question: What changes occurred in the European economy in the eighteenth century, and to what degree were these changes reflected in social patterns?

The eighteenth century in Europe witnessed the beginning of economic changes that ultimately had a strong impact on the rest of the world.

18-2a New Economic Patterns

Europe's population began to grow around 1750 and continued to increase steadily. The total European population was probably around 120 million in 1700, 140 million in 1750, and 190 million in 1790. A falling death rate was perhaps the most important reason for this population growth. Of great significance in lowering death rates was the disappearance of bubonic plague, diet was also significant. More plentiful food and better transportation of food supplies led to improved nutrition and relief from devastating famines (see section 18-2b, "Was There an Agricultural Revolution?" p. 451).

In European industry in the eighteenth century, textiles were the most important product and were still mostly produced by master artisans in guild workshops. But in many areas textile production was shifting to the countryside through the "putting-out" or "domestic" system. A merchant–capitalist entrepreneur bought the raw materials, mostly wool and flax, and "put them out" to rural workers who spun them into yarn and then wove the yarn into cloth on simple looms. The entrepreneurs sold the finished product, made a profit, and used it to purchase more raw materials. This system also became known as the **cottage industry** because the spinners and weavers did their work in their own cottages.

Overseas trade boomed in the eighteenth century. Some historians speak of the emergence of a true global economy with patterns of trade that interlocked Europe, Africa, the East, and the Americas (see Map 18.1). One important pattern involved the influx of gold and silver into Spain from its colonial American empire. Much of this gold and silver made its way to Britain, France, and the Netherlands in return for manufactured goods. British, Dutch, and French merchants in turn used their profits to buy tea, spices, silk, and cotton goods from China and India to sell in Europe.

As a result of the growth in trade, historians have argued that during the eighteenth century, England and parts of northern Europe experienced a "consumer revolution" in which ordinary people greatly increased their consumption of consumer goods. Expensive porcelain had been imported from China for centuries; however, by the eighteenth century, factories on the Continent and in England had surpassed Chinese production. Large showrooms opened in London; the most notable was that of Josiah Wedgewood. By the late eighteenth century, Wedgewood exported nearly 80 percent of its wares. In addition to porcelain, imports of inexpensive Indian fabric increased the sale of clothing. By the end of the eighteenth century, most ordinary families could consume tea, sugar, tobacco, furniture, cutlery, and clothing, goods that were once considered luxuries.

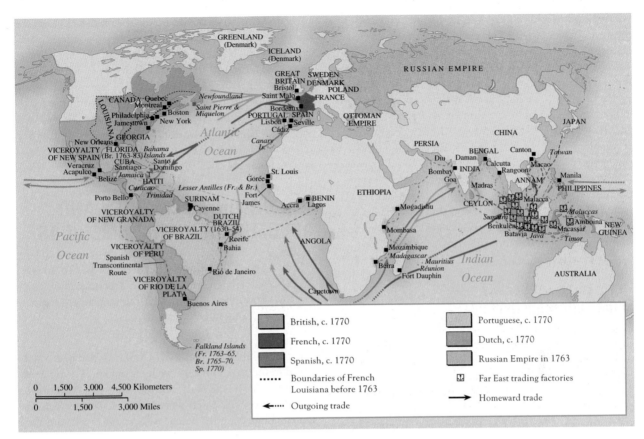

Map 18.1 Global Trade Patterns of the European States in the Eighteenth Century. New patterns of trade interlocked Europe, Africa, the East, and the Americas. Dutch, English, French, Spanish, and Portuguese colonies had been established in North and South America, and the ships of these nations followed the trade routes across the Atlantic, Pacific, and Indian Oceans.

Q *With what regions did Britain conduct most of its trade?*

Capitalism created enormous prosperity for some European countries. By 1700, Spain, Portugal, and the Dutch Republic, which had earlier monopolized overseas trade, found themselves increasingly overshadowed by France and England, which built enormously profitable colonial empires during the eighteenth century. After the French lost the Seven Years' War in 1763, Britain emerged as the world's strongest overseas trading nation, and London became the world's greatest port.

HISTORIANS DEBATE 18-2b **Was There an Agricultural Revolution?**

Did improvements in agricultural practices and methods in the eighteenth-century lead to an **agricultural revolution**? The topic is much debated. Some historians have noted the beginning of agrarian changes already in the seventeenth century, especially in the Low Countries. Others, however, have questioned the use of the term, arguing that significant changes occurred only in England and that even there

the upward trend in agricultural production was not maintained after 1750. Traditional interpretations of the agricultural revolution are characterized by four interrelated factors: more farmland, increased crop yields per acre, healthier and more abundant livestock, and an improved climate.

Historians dispute the increase of the amount of land under cultivation and the rate at which more land entered cultivation. One argument for greater land availability was the abandoning of the old open-field system in which part of the land was allowed to lie fallow (unplanted) to renew the soil. The formerly empty fields were now planted with new crops such as alfalfa, turnips, and clover that stored nitrogen in their roots and thereby restored the soil's fertility, allowing for a greater yield of crops. This shift in choice of plant crops certainly contributed to the higher yield of food. The increase of the new crops served another purpose: they provided winter fodder for livestock, enabling landlords to maintain ever-larger numbers of animals.

Experience an interactive version of this period in MINDTAP

The eighteenth century witnessed greater yields of meat and vegetables. The more numerous livestock increased the amount of meat in the European diet and enhanced food production by producing animal manure. Animal manure is a prime fertilizer, and its use increased agricultural production. Landed aristocrats with an interest in the scientific experimentation of the age also adopted innovations that increased yields. Importation of vegetables from America, especially the potato and maize (Indian corn), increased food yields.

Historians also debate the role of climate in food production during the eighteenth century. Climatologists believe that the "little ice age" of the seventeenth century declined in the eighteenth, which is especially evident in moderate summers that provided more ideal growing conditions.

18-2c European Society in the Eighteenth Century

First established in the Middle Ages, the pattern of Europe's social organization continued well into the eighteenth century. Society was still divided into the traditional "orders" or "estates" determined by heredity.

Because society was still mostly rural in the eighteenth century, the peasantry constituted the largest social group, approximately 85 percent of Europe's population. There were rather wide differences within this group, however, especially between free peasants and serfs. In eastern Germany, eastern Europe, and Russia, serfs remained tied to the lands of their noble landlords. In contrast, peasants in Britain, northern Italy, the Low Countries, Spain, most of France, and some areas of western Germany were largely free.

The nobles, who constituted only 2 percent to 3 percent of the European population, played a dominating role in society. Being born a noble automatically guaranteed a place at the top of the social order with all of its attendant privileges and rights. Nobles, for example, were exempt from many forms of taxation. Since medieval times, landed aristocrats had functioned as military officers, and eighteenth-century nobles held most of the important offices in the administrative machinery of state and controlled much of the life of their local districts.

Townspeople were still a distinct minority of the total population except in the Dutch Republic, Britain, and parts of Italy. At the end of the eighteenth century, approximately one-sixth of the French population lived in towns of 2,000 people or more. The biggest city in Europe was London with 1 million inhabitants; Paris was a little more than half that size.

Many cities in western and even central Europe had a long tradition of **patrician** oligarchies that dominated town and city councils. Just below the patricians stood the upper crust of the middle classes: non-noble officeholders, financiers and bankers, merchants, wealthy *rentiers* (rahn-TYAYS) who lived off their investments, and important professionals, including lawyers. Another large urban group consisted of the lower middle class, which comprised master artisans, shopkeepers, and small traders. Below them were the laborers or working classes and a large group of unskilled workers who served as servants, maids, and cooks at pitifully low wages.

18-3 COLONIAL EMPIRES AND REVOLUTION IN THE AMERICAS

 Focus Question: What colonies did the British and French establish in the Americas, and how did their methods of administering their colonies differ?

The first colonial empires in the Americas had been established in the sixteenth century by Spain and Portugal (see Chapter 14). By the early seventeenth century, however, both Portugal and Spain were facing challenges from the Dutch, English, and French, who sought to create their own colonial empires on the North American continent.

18-3a British North America

Although Spain had claimed all of North America as part of its empire, other nations largely ignored its claims. In 1606 the Virginia Company of London sponsored the first permanent English settlement in America. A ship carrying 105 passengers departed England in December 1606, landing in Jamestown in what is now Virginia in 1607. The settlers barely survived, making it clear that colonizing American lands would not necessarily mean quick profits. The Massachusetts colony fared much better; its initial 4,000 settlers had increased to 40,000 by 1660. By the eighteenth century, British North America consisted of thirteen colonies. They were thickly populated, containing some 1.5 million people by 1750, and were also prosperous.

18-3b French North America

The French also established a colonial empire in North America. In 1534, French explorer Jacques Cartier (ZHAHK kar-TYAY) had discovered the Saint Lawrence River and laid claim to Canada as a French possession. Not until Samuel de Champlain (sa-my-ELL duh shahm-PLAN or SHAM-playn) established a settlement at Quebec in 1608, however, did the French begin to take a serious interest in Canada as a colony. In 1663, Canada was made property of the French crown and administered by a French governor like any other French province.

French North America was run autocratically as a vast trading area, where valuable furs, leather, fish, and timber were acquired. The inability of the French state to persuade its people to emigrate to its Canadian possessions, however, left the territory thinly populated. Already in 1713, the French began to cede some of their American possessions to their British rival. As a result of the Seven Years' War, they surrendered the rest of their Canadian lands to Britain in 1763 (see section 18-4e, "Changing Patterns of War: Global Confrontation," p. 456).

18-3c The American Revolution

By the mid-eighteenth century, increasing trade and industry had led to a growing middle class in Britain that favored expansion of trade and world empire. These people found a spokesman in William Pitt the Elder (1708–1778), who became prime minister in 1757 and began to expand the British Empire. In North America, after the end of the Seven Years' War, Great Britain controlled Canada and the lands east of the Mississippi.

The Americans and the British had different conceptions of how the empire should be governed, however. In eighteenth-century Britain, the king or queen and Parliament shared power, with Parliament gradually gaining the upper hand. The monarch chose ministers who were responsible to the crown and who set policy and guided Parliament. Parliament had the power to make laws, levy taxes, pass budgets, and indirectly influence the ministers. The British envisioned Parliament as the supreme authority throughout the empire, but the Americans had their own representative assemblies. They believed that neither king nor Parliament should interfere in their internal affairs and that no tax could be levied without the consent of their own assemblies. After the Seven Years' War, the British tried to obtain new revenues from the colonies to pay for the cost of defending them, but the colonists resisted.

Crisis followed crisis until 1776, when the colonists declared their independence from Great Britain. On July 4, 1776, the Second Continental Congress approved a declaration of independence drafted by Thomas Jefferson. A stirring political document, the Declaration of Independence affirmed the Enlightenment's natural rights of "life, liberty, and the pursuit of happiness" and declared the colonies to be "free and independent states absolved from all allegiance to the British crown." The war for American independence had formally begun.

Of great importance to the colonies' cause was support from foreign countries eager to gain revenge for earlier defeats at the hands of the British. French officers and soldiers served in the American Continental Army under George Washington as commander in chief. When the army of British General Cornwallis was forced to surrender to a combined American and French army and French fleet under Washington at Yorktown in 1781, the British decided to call it quits. The Treaty of Paris, signed in 1783, recognized the independence of the American colonies and granted the Americans control of the territory from the Appalachians to the Mississippi River.

Birth of a New Nation The thirteen American colonies had gained their independence, but fear of concentrated power meant they had little enthusiasm for a strong central government, and so the Articles of Confederation, ratified in 1781, did not create one. A movement for a different form of national government soon arose. In the summer of 1787, fifty-five delegates—wealthy, politically experienced, and well educated—convened in Philadelphia to revise the Articles of Confederation but decided instead to devise a new constitution.

The proposed U.S. Constitution established a central government distinct from and superior to governments of the individual states. The central or federal government was divided into three branches, each with some power to check the others. A president would serve as the chief executive with the power to execute laws, veto the legislature's acts, supervise foreign affairs, and direct military forces. Legislative power was vested in the second branch of government, a bicameral legislature composed of the Senate, with its members elected by the state legislatures, and the House of Representatives, whose members would be elected directly by the people. A supreme court and other courts "as deemed necessary" by Congress provided the third branch of government. They would enforce the Constitution as the "supreme law of the land."

The Constitution was approved by the states—by a slim margin. Important to its success was a promise to add a bill of rights as the new government's first piece of business. Accordingly, in March 1789, the new Congress enacted the first ten amendments to the Constitution. Known as the Bill of Rights, they guaranteed freedom of religion, speech, press, petition, and assembly, as well as the right to bear arms, protection against unreasonable searches and arrests, trial by jury, due process of law, and protection of property rights. Many of these rights were derived from the **natural rights** philosophy of the eighteenth-century philosophes. Is it any wonder that many European intellectuals saw the American Revolution as the embodiment of the Enlightenment's political dreams?

18-4 TOWARD A NEW POLITICAL ORDER AND GLOBAL CONFLICT

 Focus Question: What do historians mean by the term *enlightened absolutism*, and to what degree did eighteenth-century Prussia, Austria, and Russia exhibit its characteristics?

Enlightenment thought undoubtedly had some impact on the political development of European states in the eighteenth century. The philosophes believed there were certain natural rights that should not be withheld from any person. These rights included equality before the law, freedom of religious worship, freedom of speech and press, and the rights to assemble, hold property, and pursue happiness. But how were these natural rights to be established and preserved? Most philosophes believed that people needed to be ruled by an enlightened ruler, by which they meant a ruler who would allow religious toleration, freedom of speech and press, and the rights of private property; foster the arts, sciences, and education; and, above all, obey the laws and enforce them fairly. Only strong monarchs seemed capable of overcoming vested interests and effecting the needed reforms. Therefore, reforms should come from above (from absolute rulers) rather than from below (from the people).

Many historians once assumed that a new type of monarchy emerged in the later eighteenth century, which they called *enlightened despotism* or **enlightened absolutism**. Monarchs such as Frederick II of Prussia, Catherine the Great of Russia, and Joseph II of Austria supposedly followed the philosophes' advice and ruled by enlightened principles. Recently, however, scholars have questioned the usefulness of the concept of enlightened absolutism. We can determine the extent to which it can be applied by examining the major "enlightened absolutists" of the late eighteenth century.

18-4a Prussia

Frederick II, known as Frederick the Great (1740–1786), was well versed in Enlightenment thought and even invited Voltaire to live at his court for several years (see Historical Voices, "Frederick the Great and His Father," p. 455). A believer in the king as the "first servant of the state," Frederick was a conscientious ruler who enlarged the Prussian army (to 200,000 men) and kept a strict watch over the bureaucracy.

For a time, Frederick seemed quite willing to make enlightened reforms. He abolished the use of torture except in treason and murder cases and also granted limited freedom of speech and press, as well as complete religious toleration. He did exclude Jews, levying special taxes on Jewish subjects and barring them from civil service. Frederick attempted to improve the lives of peasants by increasing agricultural productivity; he imported clover and potatoes from Western Europe and the iron plow to help drain swamps in the lower Oder Valley. His efforts were limited, however, because he kept Prussia's rigid social structure and serfdom intact and avoided any additional reforms.

18-4b The Austrian Empire of the Habsburgs

The Austrian Empire had become one of the great European states by the beginning of the eighteenth century. Because it was a sprawling conglomerate of nationalities, languages, religions, and cultures, however, it was difficult to rule (see Map 18.2).

Joseph II (1780–1790) believed in the need to sweep away anything standing in the path of reason. As he said, "I have made Philosophy the lawmaker of my empire; her logical applications are going to transform Austria." Joseph's reform program was far-reaching. He abolished serfdom, abrogated the death penalty, and established the principle of equality of all before the law. Joseph instituted drastic religious reforms as well, including complete religious toleration.

Joseph's program proved overwhelming for Austria, however. He alienated the nobility by freeing the serfs and alienated the church by his attacks on the monastic establishment. Joseph realized his failure when he wrote the epitaph for his own gravestone: "Here lies Joseph II, who was unfortunate in everything that he undertook." His successors undid many of his reforms.

18-4c Russia Under Catherine the Great

Catherine II the Great (1762–1796) was an intelligent woman who was familiar with the works of the philosophes and seemed to favor enlightened reforms. But she was skeptical about impractical theories. She considered the idea of a new law code that would recognize the principle of the equality of all people in the eyes of the law, but in the end she did nothing because she knew her success depended on the support of the Russian nobility. In 1785, she gave the nobles a charter that exempted them from taxes. Catherine's policy of favoring the landed nobility led to even worse conditions for the Russian peasants and sparked a rebellion that soon faltered and collapsed.

Above all, Catherine proved a worthy successor to Peter the Great in her policies of territorial expansion westward into Poland and southward to the Black Sea. Russia spread southward by defeating the Turks. Russian expansion

HISTORICAL VOICES

Frederick the Great and His Father

AS A YOUNG MAN, the future Frederick the Great was quite different from his strict and austere father, Frederick William I. Possessing a high regard for French culture, poetry, and flute playing, Frederick resisted his father's wishes that he study governmental and military affairs. Eventually, Frederick capitulated to his father's will and accepted the need to master affairs of state. These letters, written when Frederick was sixteen, illustrate the difficulties in their relationship.

Frederick to His Father, Frederick William I (September 11, 1728)

I have not ventured for a long time to present myself before my dear papa, partly because I was advised against it, but chiefly because I anticipated an even worse reception than usual and feared to vex my dear papa still further by the favor I have now to ask; so I have preferred to put it in writing.

I beg my dear papa that he will be kindly disposed toward me. I do assure him that after long examination of my conscience I do not find the slightest thing with which to reproach myself; but if, against my wish and will, I have vexed my dear papa, I hereby beg most humbly for forgiveness, and hope that my dear papa will give over the fearful hate which has appeared so plainly in his whole behavior and to which I cannot accustom myself. I have always thought hitherto that I had a kind father, but now I see the contrary. However, I will take courage and hope that my dear papa will think this all over and take me again into his favor. Meantime I assure him that I will never, my life long, willingly fail him, and in spite

of his disfavor I am still, with most dutiful and childlike respect, my dear papa's

Most obedient and faithful servant and son,
Frederick

Frederick William I to His Son Frederick

A bad, obstinate boy, who does not love his father; for when one does one's best, and especially when one loves one's father, one does what he wishes not only when he is standing by but when he is not there to see. Moreover you know very well that I cannot stand an effeminate fellow who has no manly tastes, who cannot ride or shoot (to his shame be it said!), is untidy about his person, and wears his hair curled like a fool instead of cutting it; and that I have condemned all these things a thousand times, and yet there is no sign of improvement. For the rest, haughty, offish as a country lout, conversing with none but a favored few instead of being affable and popular, grimacing like a fool, and never following my wishes out of love for me but only when forced into it, caring for nothing but to have his own way, and thinking nothing else is of any importance. This is my answer.

Frederick William

 Based on these documents, why was the relationship between Frederick II and his father so difficult? What does this troubled relationship tell you about the effects of ruling on the great monarchs of Europe and their families? What new duties and concerns of rulers (such as Frederick William) may have reshaped relations between kings and sons?

Source: From *Readings in European History*, vol. 2, by James Harvey Robinson (Lexington, Mass.: Ginn and Co., 1906).

---

westward occurred at the expense of neighboring Poland. In three partitions of Poland, Russia gained some 50 percent of Polish territory.

18-4d Enlightened Absolutism Reconsidered

Of the rulers discussed thus far, only Joseph II sought truly radical changes based on Enlightenment ideas. Both Frederick II and Catherine II liked to talk about enlightened reforms and even attempted some, but neither ruler's policies seemed seriously affected by Enlightenment thought. Necessities of state and maintenance of the existing system took precedence over

reform. Indeed, many historians maintain that Joseph, Frederick, and Catherine were all primarily concerned for the power and well-being of their states. In the final analysis, heightened state power was used to create armies and wage wars to gain more power.

At the same time, the ability of enlightened rulers to make reforms was limited by political and social realities. Everywhere in Europe, the hereditary aristocracy was still the most powerful class. As the chief beneficiaries of a system based on traditional rights and privileges, the nobles were not willing to support a political ideology that trumpeted the principle of equal rights for all. The first serious

Map 18.2 Europe in 1763. By the mid-eighteenth century, five major powers dominated Europe: Prussia, Austria, Russia, Britain, and France. Each sought to enhance its domestic powers through a bureaucracy that collected taxes and ran the military as well as internationally by capturing territory or preventing other powers from doing so.

Q *Given the distribution of Prussian and Habsburg holdings, in what areas of Europe were they most likely to compete for land and power?*

challenge to their supremacy would come with the French Revolution, an event that blew open the door to the world of modern politics.

18-4e Changing Patterns of War: Global Confrontation

The philosophes condemned war as a foolish waste of life and resources. Despite their words, the rivalries and costly struggles among the European states continued unabated in the eighteenth century. Europe consisted of many self-governing states that were chiefly guided by the self-interests of their rulers. As Frederick the Great of Prussia said, "The fundamental rule of governments is the principle of extending their territories."

By far the most dramatic confrontation was the Seven Years' War. Although it began in Europe, it soon turned into a global conflict fought in Europe, India, and North America. In Europe, the British and Prussians fought the

Austrians, Russians, and French. With his superb army and military skill, Frederick the Great of Prussia was able for some time to defeat the Austrian, French, and Russian armies. Gradually, however, his forces were worn down and faced utter defeat until a new Russian tsar withdrew Russia's troops from the conflict. A stalemate ensued, ending the European conflict in 1763.

The struggle between Britain and France in the rest of the world had more decisive results. In India, local rulers allied with British and French troops fought several battles. Ultimately, the British under Robert Clive won out, not because they had better forces but because they were more persistent (see Image 18.7). By the Treaty of Paris in 1763, the French withdrew and left India to the British.

The greatest conflicts of the Seven Years' War took place in North America, where it was known as the French and Indian War. Despite initial French successes, the British went on to seize Montreal, the Great Lakes area, and the Ohio River Valley. The French were forced to make peace. By the

18.7 Robert Clive in India. Robert Clive was the leader of the army of the British East India Company. He had been commanded to fight the rule of Bengal in order to gain trading privileges. After the Battle of Plassey in 1757, Clive and the East India Company took control of Bengal. In this painting by Edward Penny, Clive is shown receiving a grant of money for his injured soldiers from the local nabob or governor of Bengal.

Treaty of Paris, they ceded Canada and the lands east of the Mississippi to Britain. Their ally Spain transferred Spanish Florida to British control; in return, the French gave their Louisiana territory to the Spanish. By 1763, Great Britain had become the world's greatest colonial power. British victories cost Great Britain substantially; the national debt of Great Britain rose from 75 million pounds in 1756 to 133 million pounds by 1763. Great Britain's attempts to raise revenue by taxing the American colonies led to the American Revolution. For France, the loss of its empire was soon followed by an even greater internal upheaval.

18-5 THE FRENCH REVOLUTION

Focus Question: What were the causes, the main events, and the results of the French Revolution?

The year 1789 witnessed two far-reaching events: the beginning of a new United States of America under its revamped constitution and the eruption of the French Revolution. Compared with the American Revolution a decade earlier, the French Revolution was more complex, more violent, and far more radical in its attempt to construct new political and social orders.

18-5a Background to the French Revolution

The root causes of the French Revolution must be sought in the condition of French society. Before the revolution, France was a society grounded in privilege and inequality. During the eighteenth century, the population had increased by 44 percent from 18 million to 26 million. It was a young country, with 36 percent of citizens under age twenty and 40 percent between twenty and forty. It was divided, as it had been since the Middle Ages, into three orders or estates.

Social Structure of the Old Regime The First Estate consisted of the clergy and numbered some 130,000 people who owned approximately 10 percent of the land. Clergy were exempt from the *taille* (TY), France's chief tax. The church was extremely wealthy; income from church property and other investments produced almost 300 million *livres* (Leev-RUH) annually—half the income of the royal crown. Clergy were also radically divided: the higher-ranking clergy came from aristocratic families and shared the interests of the nobility and lived in palaces and townhouses, while the parish priests were often poor commoners.

The Second Estate consisted of the nobility, composed of some 350,000 people who owned between 25 percent and 30 percent of the land. The nobility continued to play an important role in French society, holding many of the leading positions in the government, the military, the law courts, and the higher church offices. The nobles sought to expand their power at the expense of the monarchy and to maintain their positions in the military, church, and government. Common to all nobles were tax exemptions, especially from the taille.

The Third Estate—the commoners—constituted the overwhelming majority of the French population. They were divided by vast differences in occupation, level of education, and wealth. The peasants constituted 75 percent to 80 percent of the total population and were by far the largest segment of the Third Estate. They owned some 35 percent to 40 percent of the land, although more than half had little or no land on which to survive. The landless peasants were day laborers who increasingly migrated to Paris in search of work; they were the first to suffer in difficult times. Serfdom no longer existed on any large scale in France, but French peasants still had obligations to their local landlords whom they deeply resented. These "relics of feudalism," or aristocratic privileges, had survived from an earlier age and included the payment of fees for the use of village facilities such as the flour mill, community oven, and winepress.

© British Library Board/Robana/Art Resource, NY

Another part of the Third Estate consisted of skilled craftspeople, shopkeepers, and other urban wage earners. In the eighteenth century, these groups suffered a decline in purchasing power as consumer prices rose faster than wages. Their daily struggle for survival led many of these people to play an important role in the revolution, especially in Paris.

Some 8 percent of the population, or 2.3 million people, constituted the bourgeoisie or middle class, who owned 20 percent to 25 percent of the land. This group included merchants, industrialists, and bankers who had benefited from the economic prosperity after 1730. The bourgeoisie also included professional people—lawyers, holders of public offices, doctors, and writers. Many members of the bourgeoisie had their own grievances because they were often excluded from the social and political privileges monopolized by nobles.

Moreover, the new political ideas of the Enlightenment proved attractive to both the aristocracy and the bourgeoisie. Both elites, long accustomed to a new socioeconomic reality based on wealth and economic achievement, were increasingly frustrated by a monarchical system resting on privileges and on an old and rigid social order based on the concept of estates. The opposition of these elites to the **old order** led them ultimately to drastic action against the monarchical **old regime**. In a real sense, the revolution had its origins in political grievances.

Other Problems Facing the French Monarchy Although France had enjoyed fifty years of economic expansion, bad harvests in 1787 and 1788 and the beginnings of a manufacturing depression had resulted in food shortages, rising prices for food and other goods, and unemployment in the cities. The number of poor, estimated at almost one-third of the population, reached crisis proportions on the eve of the revolution.

The French monarchy seemed incapable of dealing with the new social realities. Louis XVI (1774–1792) had become king in 1774 at age twenty; he knew little about the operations of the French government and lacked the energy to deal decisively with state affairs. His wife, Marie Antoinette (ma-REE ahn-twahn-NET), was a spoiled Austrian princess who devoted much of her time to court intrigues (see Film & History, "*Marie Antoinette*,"). As France's crises worsened, neither Louis nor his queen seemed able to fathom the depths of despair and discontent that soon led to violent revolution.

The immediate cause of the French Revolution was the near collapse of government finances. France experienced a depression from 1778 to 1787 as a result of a loss of overseas markets and overproduction. Peasants faced increasing uncertainty as rent prices remained high because of a

 FILM & HISTORY

Marie Antoinette

Watch *Marie Antoinette* (2006), a film based on Antonia Fraser's book *Marie Antoinette: A Journey* (2001). The film begins with the marriage of Marie Antoinette, the daughter of Empress Maria Theresa of Austria, to the dauphin Louis, heir to the French throne. Filmed at Versailles, the movie chronicles the young life of Marie Antoinette at court and the challenges she faced in France. The film incorporates contemporary music and material goods to engage modern viewers, yet the elaborate sets and costumes capture the grandeur and splendor of court life in eighteenth-century France.

Q *What can you discern about courtly life by watching this film? What challenges did Marie Antoinette face at court?*

Columbia/American Zoetrope/Sony/The Kobal Collection

MINDTAP See full-length Film & History feature in MindTap.
From Cengage

rapidly growing population, while poor harvests in 1788 and 1789 sent prices of wheat and rye soaring—leaving many people desperate. Costly wars and royal extravagance drove French governmental expenditures ever higher. The government responded by borrowing. Poor taxation policy contributed to the high debt, with most of the monarchy's funds coming from the peasantry. Unlike Britain, where the Bank of England financed the borrowing of money at low interest rates, France had no central bank and instead relied on private loans. By 1788, the interest on the debt alone constituted half of all government spending.

On the verge of a complete financial collapse, the government of Louis XVI was finally forced to call a meeting of the Estates-General, the French parliamentary body that had not met since 1614. The Estates-General consisted of representatives from the three orders of French society. In the elections for the Estates-General, the government had ruled that the Third Estate should get double representation (it did—after all, it constituted 97 percent of the population). Consequently, while both the First Estate (the clergy) and the Second Estate (the nobility) had some 300 delegates each, the Third Estate had almost 600 representatives, most of whom were lawyers from French towns.

18-5b From Estates-General to National Assembly

The Estates-General opened at Versailles on May 5, 1789. The first issue was whether voting should be by order or by head (each delegate having one vote). Traditionally, each order would vote as a group and have one vote. That meant that the First and Second Estates could outvote the Third Estate two to one. The Third Estate demanded that each deputy have one vote. With the assistance of liberal nobles and clerics, that would give the Third Estate a majority. When the First Estate declared in favor of voting by order, the Third Estate responded dramatically. On June 17, 1789, the Third Estate declared itself the "National Assembly" and prepared to draw up a constitution. This was the first step in the French Revolution because the Third Estate had no legal right to act as the National Assembly. Louis XVI sided with the First Estate and prepared to use force to dissolve the Estates-General.

The common people, however, saved the Third Estate from the king's forces. On July 14, a mob of Parisians stormed the Bastille, a royal armory, and proceeded to dismantle it brick by brick. Soon informed that the royal troops were unreliable, Louis XIV accepted this reality, signaling the collapse of royal authority. The king could no longer enforce his will.

At the same time, popular revolts broke out throughout France in both cities and countryside (see Comparative Illustration, "Revolution and Revolt in France and China," p. 460). Behind the popular uprising was a growing resentment of the entire landholding system with its fees and obligations. The fall of the Bastille and the king's apparent capitulation to the demands of the Third Estate now led peasants to take matters into their own hands. The peasant rebellions that occurred throughout France had a great impact on the National Assembly meeting at Versailles.

18-5c Destruction of the Old Regime

One of the National Assembly's first acts abolished the rights of landlords and the fiscal exemptions of nobles, clergy, towns, and provinces. Three weeks later, the National Assembly adopted the Declaration of the Rights of Man and the Citizen. This charter of basic liberties proclaimed freedom and equal rights for all men and access to public office based on talent. All citizens were to have the right to take part in the legislative process. Freedom of speech and the press was coupled with the outlawing of arbitrary arrests.

But did the declaration's ideal of equal rights for "all men" also include women? Many deputies insisted that it did, provided that, as one said, "women do not hope to exercise political rights and functions." Olympe de Gouges (oh-LAMP duh GOOZH), a playwright, rejected this exclusion of women from political rights. Echoing the words of the official declaration, she penned the Declaration of the Rights of Woman and the Female Citizen, in which she insisted that women should have all the same rights as men (see Opposing Viewpoints, "The Natural Rights of the French People: Two Views," p. 461). The National Assembly ignored her demands.

Because the Catholic church was seen as an important pillar of the old order, it too was reformed. Most of the church's lands were seized. Under the Civil Constitution of the Clergy, which was adopted on July 12, 1790, bishops and priests were to be elected by the people and paid by the state. The Catholic church, still an important institution in the life of the French people, now became an enemy of the revolution.

By 1791, the National Assembly had completed a new constitution that established a limited constitutional monarchy. There was still a monarch—now called "king of the French"—but sovereign power was vested in the new Legislative Assembly, which would make the laws. The Legislative Assembly was to sit for two years and consisted of 745 representatives elected by an indirect system that preserved power in the hands of the more affluent members of society. A small group of 50,000 electors chose the deputies.

Thus, the old order had been destroyed, but the new order had many opponents—Catholic priests, nobles, lower classes hurt by the rising cost of living, peasants opposed to dues that had still not been eliminated, and political clubs like the Jacobins (JAK-uh-binz) that offered more radical solutions. The king also made things difficult for the new government when he sought to flee France in June 1791 and almost succeeded before being recognized, captured, and brought back to Paris. The flight to Varennes shattered the illusion of a loyal king. In this unsettled situation, under a discredited and seemingly disloyal monarch, the new Legislative Assembly held its first session in October 1791. France's relations with the rest of Europe soon led to Louis' downfall.

On August 27, 1791, the monarchs of Austria and Prussia, fearing that revolution would spread to their countries, invited other European monarchs to use force to reestablish monarchical authority in France. The French fared badly in the fighting in the spring of 1792, and a frantic search for scapegoats began. As one observer noted,

Revolution and Revolt in France and China

Politics & Government

BOTH FRANCE AND CHINA EXPERIENCED REVOLUTIONARY UPHEAVAL in the late eighteenth and nineteenth centuries. In both countries, common people often played an important role. Image 18.8b shows a scene from the storming of the Bastille in 1789. This early action by the people of Paris ultimately led to the overthrow of the French monarchy. Image 18.8a is an episode during the Taiping Rebellion, a major peasant revolt in the mid-nineteenth century in China. An imperial Chinese army is shown recapturing the city of Nanjing from Taiping rebels in 1864.

 What role did common people play in revolutionary upheavals in France and China in the eighteenth and nineteenth centuries?

18.8a

The Art Archive/School of Oriental & African Studies/Eileen Tweedy

18.8b

Chateau de Versailles, France/Giraudon/The Bridgeman Art Library

"Everywhere you hear the cry that the king is betraying us, the generals are betraying us, that nobody is to be trusted; . . . that Paris will be taken in six weeks by the Austrians. . . . We are on a volcano ready to spout flames."[1] Defeats in war coupled with economic shortages led to renewed political demonstrations, especially against the king. In August 1792, radical political groups in Paris took the king captive and forced the Legislative Assembly to suspend the monarchy and call for a national convention, chosen on the basis of universal male suffrage, to decide on the future form of government. The French Revolution was about to enter a more radical stage.

The Natural Rights of the French People: Two Views

Politics & Government ONE OF THE IMPORTANT DOCUMENTS OF THE FRENCH REVOLUTION, the Declaration of the Rights of Man and the Citizen was adopted on August 26, 1789, by the National Assembly. Olympe de Gouges was a butcher's daughter who wrote plays and pamphlets. She argued that the Declaration of the Rights of Man and the Citizen did not apply to women and composed her own Declaration of the Rights of Woman and the Female Citizen in 1791.

Declaration of the Rights of Man and the Citizen

1. Men are born and remain free and equal in rights. Social distinctions can only be founded upon the general good.

2. The aim of all political association is the preservation of the natural and imprescriptible rights of man. These rights are liberty, property, security, and resistance to oppression.

3. The principle of all sovereignty resides essentially in the nation. No body or individual may exercise any authority which does not proceed directly from the nation.

4. Liberty consists in being able to do everything which injures no one else. . . .

6. Law is the expression of the general will. Every citizen has a right to participate personally or through his representative in its formation. It must be the same for all, whether it protects or punishes. All citizens being equal in the eyes of the law are equally eligible to all dignities and to all public positions and occupations according to their abilities and without distinction except that of their virtues and talents.

7. No person shall be accused, arrested, or imprisoned except in the cases and according to the forms prescribed by law. . . .

10. No one shall be disturbed on account of his opinions, including his religious views, provided their manifestation does not disturb the public order established by law.

11. The free communication of ideas and opinions is one of the most precious of the rights of man. Every citizen may, accordingly, speak, write and print with freedom, being responsible, however, for such abuses of this freedom as shall be defined by law. . . .

16. A society in which the observance of the law is not assured nor the separation of powers defined has no constitution at all.

17. Property being an inviolable and sacred right, no one shall be deprived thereof except where public necessity, legally determined, shall clearly demand it, and then only on condition that the owner shall have been previously and equitably indemnified.

Declaration of the Rights of Woman and the Female Citizen

Mothers, daughters, sisters and representatives of the nation demand to be constituted into a national assembly. Believing that ignorance, omission, or scorn for the rights of woman are the only causes of public misfortunes and of the corruption of governments, the women have resolved to set forth in a solemn declaration the natural, inalienable, and sacred rights of woman in order that this declaration, constantly exposed before all the members of the society, will ceaselessly remind them of their rights and duties. . . .

Consequently, the sex that is as superior in beauty as it is in courage during the sufferings of maternity recognizes and declares in the presence and under the auspices of the Supreme Being, the following.

Rights of Woman and of Female Citizens

1. Woman is born free and lives equal to man in her rights. Social distinctions can be based only on the common utility.

2. The purpose of any political association is the conservation of the natural and imprescriptible rights of woman and man; these rights are liberty, property, security, and especially resistance to oppression.

3. The principle of all sovereignty rests essentially with the nation, which is nothing but the union of woman and man; no body and no individual can exercise any authority which does not come expressly from [the nation].

4. Liberty and justice consist of restoring all that belongs to others; thus, the only limits on the exercise of the natural rights of woman are perpetual male tyranny; these limits are to be reformed by the laws of nature and reason. . . .

6. The law must be the expression of the general will; all female and male citizens must contribute either personally or through representatives to its formation; it must be the same for all: male and female citizens, being equal in the eyes of the law, must be equally

(continued)

admitted to all honors, positions, and public employment according to their capacity and without other distinctions besides those of their virtues and talents.

7. No woman is an exception; she is accused, arrested, and detained in cases determined by law. Women, like men, obey this rigorous law. . . .

10. No one is to be disquieted for his very basic opinions; woman has the right to mount the scaffold; she must equally have the right to mount the rostrum, provided that her demonstrations do not disturb the legally established public order.

11. The free communication of thought and opinions is one of the most precious rights of woman, since that liberty assured the recognition of children by their fathers. . . .

16. No society has a constitution without the guarantee of rights and the separation of powers; the constitution is null if the majority of individuals comprising the nation have not cooperated in drafting it.

17. Property belongs to both sexes whether united or separate; for each it is an inviolable and sacred right; no one can be deprived of it, since it is the true patrimony of nature, unless the legally determined public need obviously dictates it, and then only with a just and prior indemnity.

Q *What "natural rights" does the first document proclaim? To what extent was this document influenced by the writings of the philosophes? What rights for women does the second document enunciate? Given the nature and scope of the arguments in favor of natural rights and women's rights in these two documents, what key effects on European society would you attribute to the French Revolution?*

Sources: Excerpt from Thomas Carlyle, *The French Revolution: A History, Vol. I* (George Bell and Sons, London, 1902), pp. 346–348. From *Women in Revolutionary Paris, 1789–1795: Selected Documents Translated with Notes and Commentary*. Translated with notes and commentary by Darline Gay Levy, Harriet Branson Applewhite, and Mary Durham Johnson. Copyright © 1979 by the Board of Trustees of the University of Illinois. Used with permission of the editors and the University of Illinois Press.

18-5d The Radical Revolution

In September 1792, the newly elected National Convention began its sessions. Dominated by lawyers and other professionals, two-thirds of its deputies were under age forty-five, and almost all had gained political experience as a result of the revolution. Almost all distrusted the king. As a result, the convention's first step on September 21 was to abolish the monarchy and establish a republic. On January 21, 1793, the king was executed, and the destruction of the old regime was complete. But the execution of the king created new enemies for the revolution both at home and abroad.

In Paris, the local government, known as the Commune, whose leaders came from the working classes, favored radical change and put constant pressure on the convention, pushing it to ever more radical positions. Meanwhile, peasants in the west and inhabitants of the major provincial cities refused to accept the authority of the convention.

A foreign crisis also loomed. By the beginning of 1793, after the king had been executed, most of Europe—an informal coalition of Austria, Prussia, Spain, Portugal, Britain, the Dutch Republic, and even Russia—aligned militarily against France. Grossly overextended, the French armies began to experience reverses; by late spring, France was threatened with invasion.

A Nation in Arms To meet these crises, the convention gave broad powers to an executive committee of twelve known as the Committee of Public Safety, which came to be dominated by Maximilien Robespierre (mak-see-meel-YENH ROHBZ-pyayr). For a twelve-month period—from 1793 to 1794—the Committee of Public Safety took control of France. To save the republic from its foreign foes, on August 23, 1793, the committee decreed a levy-in-mass, or universal mobilization of the nation:

Young men will fight, young men are called to conquer. Married men will forge arms, transport military baggage and guns and will prepare food supplies. Women, who at long last are to take their rightful place in the revolution and follow their true destiny, will forget their futile tasks: their delicate hands will work at making clothes for soldiers; they will make tents and they will [help the wounded]. Children will make lint of old cloth. It is for them that we are fighting: children, those beings destined to gather all the fruits of the revolution, will raise their pure hands toward the skies. And old men, performing their missions again, as of yore, will be guided to the public squares of the cities where they will kindle the courage of young warriors and preach the doctrines of hate for kings and the unity of the Republic.[2]

In less than a year, the French revolutionary government had raised an army of 650,000 and had pushed the allies back across the Rhine and even conquered the Austrian Netherlands by 1795.

The French revolutionary army was an important step in the creation of modern **nationalism**. Previously, wars had been fought between governments or ruling dynasties by relatively small armies of professional soldiers. The new French army was the creation of a "people's" government; its wars were now "people's" wars that involved the entire nation. But when dynastic wars became people's wars, warfare increased in ferocity while being less restrained. The wars of the French revolutionary era opened the door to the total war of the modern world.

Reign of Terror   To meet the domestic crisis, the National Convention and the Committee of Public Safety launched a period of bloodshed that came to be called the Reign of Terror. Revolutionary courts were instituted to protect the republic from its internal enemies. Robespierre passed a law that denied suspects sent before the Revolutionary Tribunal all rights to defend themselves. This law increased the pace of executions. In the course of nine months, 16,000 people were officially killed under the blade of the guillotine—a revolutionary device designed for the quick and efficient separation of heads from bodies.

Revolutionary armies were set up to bring recalcitrant cities and districts back under the control of the National Convention. The Committee of Public Safety decided to make an example of Lyons (LYOHNH), which had defied the authority of the National Convention. By April 1794, some 1,880 citizens of Lyons had been executed. When the guillotine proved too slow, cannon fire was used to blow condemned men into open graves. As one German observed,

> Whole ranges of houses, always the most handsome, burnt. The churches, convents, and all the dwellings of the former patricians were in ruins. When I came to the guillotine, the blood of those who had been executed a few hours beforehand was still running in the street. . . . I said to a group of [radicals] that it would be decent to clear away all this human blood. Why should it be cleared? one of them said to me. It's the blood of aristocrats and rebels. The dogs should lick it up.[3]

Equality and Slavery: Revolution in Haiti   Early in the French Revolution, the desire for equality led to a discussion of what to do about slavery. A club called Friends of the Blacks advocated the abolition of slavery, which was achieved in France in September 1791. But French planters in the West Indies, who profited greatly from the use of slaves on their sugar plantations, opposed the abolition of slavery in colonial French territories. On February 4, 1794, however, the National Convention, guided by ideas of equality, abolished slavery in the colonies.

18-5e Reaction and the Directory

By the summer of 1794, the French had been successful on the battlefield against their foreign foes, making the Terror less necessary. But the Terror continued because Robespierre, who had come to dominate the Committee of Public Safety, became obsessed with purifying the body politic of all the corrupt. Many deputies in the National Convention began to fear they were not safe while Robespierre was free to act and gathered enough votes to condemn him. Robespierre was guillotined on July 28, 1794.

After Robespierre's death, a reaction set in as more moderate middle-class leaders took control. The Reign of Terror came to a halt, and the National Convention reduced the power of the Committee of Public Safety. In August, a new constitution was drafted that reflected the desire for a stability that did not sacrifice the ideals of 1789. Five directors—the Directory—acted as the executive authority.

The period of the Revolution under the Directory (1795–1799) was an era of stagnation and corruption. At the same time, the Directory faced political enemies from both the left and the right of the political spectrum. On the right, royalists continued their efforts to restore the monarchy. On the left, radical hopes of power were revived by continuing economic problems. Battered from both sides, unable to solve the country's economic problems, and still carrying on the wars inherited from the Committee of Public Safety, the Directory increasingly relied on the military to maintain its power. This led to a coup d'état in 1799 in which the popular military general Napoleon Bonaparte seized power.

CHRONOLOGY	The French Revolution
Meeting of Estates-General	May 5, 1789
Formation of National Assembly	June 17, 1789
Fall of the Bastille	July 14, 1789
Declaration of the Rights of Man and the Citizen	August 26, 1789
Civil Constitution of the Clergy	July 12, 1790
Flight of the king	June 20–21, 1791
Attack on the royal palace	August 10, 1792
Abolition of the monarchy	September 21, 1792
Execution of the king	January 21, 1793
Levy-in-mass	August 23, 1793
Execution of Robespierre	July 28, 1794
Adoption of Constitution of 1795 and the Directory	August 22, 1795

Experience an interactive version of this period in ⋮ MINDTAP

Napoleon and Psychological Warfare

 IN 1796, AT AGE TWENTY-SEVEN, Napoleon Bonaparte was given command of the French army in Italy, where he won a series of stunning victories. His use of speed, deception, and surprise to overwhelm his opponents is well known. In this selection from a proclamation to his troops in Italy, Napoleon also appears as a master of psychological warfare.

Napoleon Bonaparte, Proclamation to French Troops in Italy (April 26, 1796)

Soldiers:

In a fortnight you have won six victories, taken twenty-one standards [flags of military units], fifty-five pieces of artillery, several strong positions, and conquered the richest part of Piedmont [in northern Italy]; you have captured 15,000 prisoners and killed or wounded more than 10,000 men You have won battles without cannon, crossed rivers without bridges, made forced marches without shoes, camped without brandy and often without bread. Soldiers of liberty, only republican troops could have endured what you have endured. Soldiers, you have our thanks! The grateful *Patrie* [nation] will owe its prosperity to you.

The two armies which but recently attacked you with audacity are fleeing before you in terror; the wicked men who laughed at your misery and rejoiced at the thought of the triumphs of your enemies are confounded and trembling.

But, soldiers, as yet you have done nothing compared with what remains to be done. . . . Undoubtedly the greatest obstacles have been overcome; but you still have battles to fight, cities to capture, rivers to cross. Is there one among you whose courage is abating? No. . . . All of you are consumed with a desire to extend the glory of the French people; all of you long to humiliate those arrogant kings who dare to contemplate placing us in fetters; all of you desire to dictate a glorious peace, one which will indemnify the *Patrie* for the immense sacrifices it has made; all of you wish to be able to say with pride as you return to your villages, "I was with the victorious army of Italy!"

 What themes did Napoleon use to play on the emotions of his troops and inspire them to greater efforts? Do you think Napoleon believed these words? Why or why not?

Source: From James Harvey Robinson, *Readings in European History* (Lexington, Mass.: Ginn and Co., 1906), p. 471.

18-6 THE AGE OF NAPOLEON

 Focus Question: Which aspects of the French Revolution did Napoleon preserve, and which did he destroy?

Napoleon dominated both French and European history from 1799 to 1815. He had been born in Corsica in 1769 shortly after France had annexed the island. The young Napoleone Buonaparte (his birth name) was sent to France to study in one of the new military schools and was a lieutenant when the revolution broke out in 1789. The revolution and the European war that followed gave him new opportunities, and Napoleon rose quickly through the ranks. In 1794, at age twenty-five, he was made a brigadier general. Two years later, he commanded the French armies in Italy, where he won a series of victories and returned to France as a conquering hero (see Historical Voices, "Napoleon and Psychological Warfare,"). After a disastrous expedition to Egypt, Napoleon returned to Paris, where he participated in the coup that gave him control of France. He was only thirty years old.

After the coup of 1799, a new form of the republic called the Consulate was proclaimed in which Napoleon, as first consul, controlled the entire executive authority of government. He had overwhelming influence over the legislature, appointed members of the administrative bureaucracy, commanded the army, and conducted foreign affairs. In 1802, Napoleon was made consul for life, and in 1804, he returned France to monarchy when he became Emperor Napoleon I.

18-6a Domestic Policies

One of Napoleon's first domestic policies was to establish peace with the oldest and most implacable enemy of the revolution: the Catholic Church. In 1801, Napoleon arranged a concordat with the pope that recognized Catholicism as the religion of a majority of the French people. In return, the pope agreed not to challenge the confiscation of church lands during the revolution.

Napoleon's most enduring domestic achievement was his codification of the laws. Before the Revolution, France had some 300 local legal systems. During the revolution, efforts were made to prepare a single code of laws for the nation, but it remained for Napoleon to bring the work to completion in the famous Civil Code. It preserved most of the revolutionary gains by recognizing the equality of all citizens before the law, abolishing serfdom and feudalism, and promoting religious toleration. Property rights were also protected.

Napoleon also developed a powerful, centralized administration and worked hard to develop a bureaucracy of capable officials. Early on, the regime showed that it cared little whether officials had acquired their expertise in royal or revolutionary bureaucracies. Promotion, whether in civil or military offices, was based not on rank or birth but on ability only. This principle of a government career open to talent was, of course, what many bourgeois had wanted before the revolution.

In his domestic policies, then, Napoleon both destroyed and preserved aspects of the Revolution. Although equality was preserved in the law code and the opening of careers to talent, the creation of a new aristocracy, the strong protection accorded to property rights, and the use of conscription for the military made it clear that much equality had been lost. Liberty was replaced by an initially benevolent despotism that grew increasingly arbitrary. Napoleon shut down sixty of France's seventy-three newspapers.

18-6b Napoleon's Empire

When Napoleon became consul in 1799, France was at war with a second European coalition of Russia, Great Britain, and Austria. Napoleon realized the need for a pause and made a peace treaty in 1802. But in 1803 war was renewed with Britain, which was soon joined by Austria, Russia, and Prussia in the Third Coalition. In a series of battles from 1805 to 1807, Napoleon's Grand Army defeated the Austrian, Prussian, and Russian armies, giving Napoleon the opportunity to create a new European order.

The Grand Empire From 1807 to 1812, Napoleon was the master of Europe. His Grand Empire was composed of three major parts: the French Empire, dependent states, and allied states (see Map 18.3). Dependent states were ruled by Napoleon's relatives; these came to include Spain, the Netherlands, the kingdom of Italy, the Swiss Republic, the Grand Duchy of Warsaw, and the Confederation of the

Reunion des Musees Nationaux/Art Resource, NY

18.9 The Coronation of Napoleon. In 1804, Napoleon restored monarchy to France when he became Emperor Napoleon I. In the coronation scene painted by Jacques-Louis David, Napoleon is shown crowning his wife, Empress Josephine, while the pope looks on. The painting shows Napoleon's mother seated in the box in the background, even though she was not at the ceremony.

Experience an interactive version of this period in MINDTAP

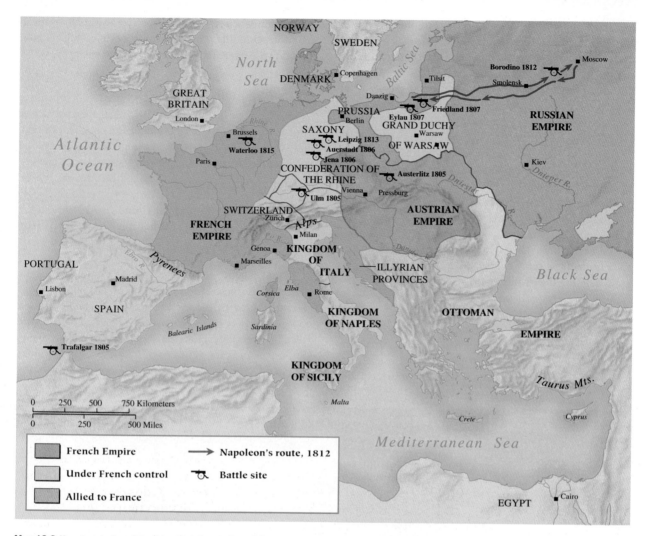

Map 18.3 Napoleon's Grand Empire. Napoleon's Grand Army won a series of victories against Austria, Prussia, and Russia that gave the French emperor full or partial control over much of Europe by 1807.

Q *On the European continent, what was the overall relationship between distance from France and degree of French control, and how can you account for this?*

Rhine (a union of every German state except Austria and Prussia). Allied states were those defeated by Napoleon and included Prussia, Austria, Russia, and Sweden. They were forced to join his struggle against Britain.

Within his empire, Napoleon sought acceptance of certain revolutionary principles, including legal equality, religious toleration, and economic freedom. In the inner core and dependent states of his Grand Empire, Napoleon tried to destroy the old order. Nobility and clergy everywhere in these states lost their special privileges. He decreed equality of opportunity with offices open to talent, equality before the law, and religious toleration.

Napoleon hoped that his Grand Empire would last for centuries, but it collapsed almost as rapidly as it had been formed. As long as Britain ruled the waves, it was not subject to military attack. Napoleon hoped to invade Britain, but he could not overcome the British navy's decisive defeat of a combined French–Spanish fleet at Trafalgar in 1805. To defeat Britain, Napoleon turned to his **Continental System**. An alliance put into effect between 1806 and 1808, it attempted to prevent British goods from reaching the European continent in order to weaken Britain economically and destroy its capacity to wage war. But the Continental System failed. Allied states resented it, and some began to cheat and others to resist.

Napoleon also encountered new sources of opposition. His conquests made the French hated oppressors and aroused the patriotism of the conquered people. A Spanish uprising, aided by the British, kept a French force of 200,000 pinned down for years.

The Fall of Napoleon The beginning of Napoleon's downfall came in 1812 with his invasion of Russia. The refusal of the Russians to remain in the Continental System left Napoleon with little choice. Although aware of the risks in invading such a huge country, he knew that if the Russians were allowed to challenge the Continental System unopposed, other nations would follow suit. In June 1812, he led his Grand Army of more than 600,000 men into Russia. His hopes for victory depended on quickly defeating the Russian armies, but the Russian forces retreated and refused to give battle, torching their own villages to keep Napoleon's army from finding food. When the Russians did stop to fight at Borodino, Napoleon won an indecisive and costly victory. When the remaining troops of the Grand Army arrived in Moscow, they found the city ablaze. Lacking food and supplies, Napoleon abandoned Moscow late in October and made a retreat across Russia in terrible winter conditions. Only 40,000 of the original 600,000 men arrived back in Poland in January 1813.

This military disaster led other European states to rise up and attack the crippled French army. Paris was captured in March 1814, and Napoleon was sent into exile on the island of Elba off the coast of Italy. Meanwhile, the Bourbon monarchy was restored in the person of Louis XVIII, brother of the executed king. (Louis XVII, son of Louis XVI, had died in prison at age ten.) Bored on Elba, Napoleon slipped back into France. When troops were sent to capture him, Napoleon opened his coat and addressed them: "Soldiers of the 5th regiment, I am your Emperor. . . . If there is a man among you would kill his Emperor, here I am!" No one fired a shot. Shouting "Vive l'Empereur! Vive l'Empereur," the troops went over to his side, and Napoleon entered Paris in triumph on March 20, 1815. The powers that had defeated him pledged once more to fight him. Napoleon raised another army and moved to attack the allied forces stationed in what is now Belgium. At Waterloo on June 18, Napoleon met a combined British and Prussian army under the duke of Wellington and suffered a bloody defeat. This time, the victorious allies exiled him to Saint Helena, a small, forsaken island in the South Atlantic off the coast of Africa. Only the memory of Napoleon's reign continued to haunt French political life.

CHAPTER SUMMARY

In the Scientific Revolution, the Western world overthrew the medieval Ptolemaic worldview and arrived at a new conception of the universe: the sun at the center, the planets as material bodies revolving around the sun in elliptical

orbits, and an infinite rather than finite world. With the changes in the conception of "heaven" came changes in the conception of "Earth." Highly influenced by the new worldview created by the Scientific Revolution, the philosophes of the eighteenth century hoped to create a new society by using reason to discover the natural laws that governed it. They attacked traditional religion as the enemy and developed the new "sciences of man" in economics, politics, and education. Together, the Scientific Revolution of the seventeenth century and the Enlightenment of the eighteenth century constituted an intellectual revolution that laid the foundations for a modern worldview based on rationalism and secularism.

Everywhere in Europe at the beginning of the eighteenth century, the old order remained strong. Nobles, clerics, towns, and provinces all had privileges. Everywhere in the eighteenth century, monarchs sought to enlarge their bureaucracies to raise taxes to support large standing armies. The existence of these armies led to wars on a worldwide scale. Although the wars resulted in few changes in Europe, British victories enabled Great Britain to emerge as the world's greatest naval and colonial power. Meanwhile in Europe, increased demands for taxes to support these wars led to attacks on the old order and a desire for change not met by the ruling monarchs. At the same time, a growing population as well as changes in finance, trade, and industry created tensions that undermined the foundations of the old order.

Its inability to deal with these changes led to a revolutionary outburst at the end of the eighteenth century that marked the beginning of the end for the old order.

The revolutionary era of the late eighteenth century was a time of dramatic political transformations. Revolutionary upheavals, beginning in North America and continuing in France, spurred movements for political liberty and equality. The documents promulgated by these revolutions (the Declaration of Independence and the

Declaration of the Rights of Man and the Citizen) embodied the fundamental ideas of the Enlightenment and created a liberal political agenda based on a belief in popular sovereignty—the people as the source of political power—and the principles of liberty and equality. In theory, liberty meant freedom from arbitrary power as well as the freedom to think, write, and worship as one chose. Equality meant equality in rights, although it did not include equality between men and women.

REFLECTION QUESTIONS

Q What was the impact of the intellectual revolution of the seventeenth and eighteenth centuries on European society?

Q How was France changed by the revolutionary events between 1789 and 1799, and who benefited the most from these changes?

Q In what ways did Napoleon's policies reject the accomplishments of the French Revolution? In what ways did his policies strengthen those accomplishments?

CHAPTER TIMELINE

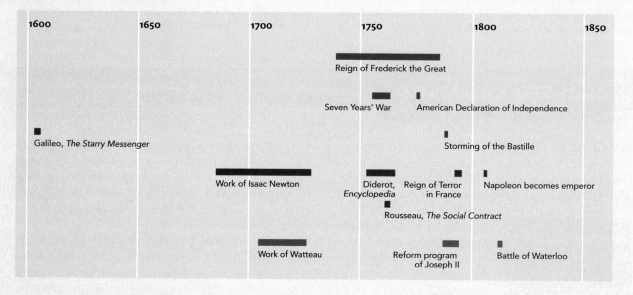

CHAPTER NOTES

1. Quoted in W. Doyle, *The Oxford History of the French Revolution* (Oxford, 1989), p. 184.

2. Quoted in L. Gershoy, *The Era of the French Revolution* (Princeton, N.J., 1957), p. 157.

3. Quoted in Doyle, *The Oxford History of the French Revolution*, p. 254.

MINDTAP
From Cengage

MindTap® is a fully online, highly personalized learning experience built upon Cengage Learning content. MindTap combines student learning tools—readings, multimedia, activities, and assessments—into a singular Learning Path that guides students through the course and helps students develop the critical thinking, analysis, and communication skills that are essential to academic and professional success.

GLOSSARY

abbess   the head of a convent or monastery for women.

abbot   the head of a monastery.

absolutism   a form of government where the sovereign power or ultimate authority rested in the hands of a monarch who claimed to rule by divine right and was therefore responsible only to God.

Abstract Expressionism   a post–World War II artistic movement that broke with all conventions of form and structure in favor of total abstraction.

abstract painting   an artistic movement that developed early in the twentieth century in which artists focused on color to avoid any references to visual reality.

African Union   the organization that replaced the Organization of African Unity in 2001; designed to bring about increased political and economic integration of African states.

Amerindians   earliest inhabitants of North and South America. Original theories suggested migration from Siberia across the Bering Land Bridge; more recent evidence suggests migration also occurred by sea from regions of the South Pacific to South America.

apartheid   the system of racial segregation practiced in the Republic of South Africa until the 1990s, which involved political, legal, and economic discrimination against nonwhites.

aristocracy   a class of hereditary nobility in medieval Europe; a warrior class who shared a distinctive lifestyle based on the institution of knighthood, although there were social divisions within the group based on extremes of wealth.

ASEAN   the Association of Southeast Asian Nations, formed in 1967 to promote the prosperity and political stability of its member nations. Currently, Brunei, Cambodia, Indonesia, Laos, Malaysia, Myanmar, the Philippines, Singapore, Thailand, and Vietnam are members. Other countries in the region participate as "observer" members.

assimilation   the concept, originating in France, that the colonial peoples should be assimilated into the parent French culture.

association   the concept developed by French colonial officials that colonial peoples should be permitted to retain their precolonial cultural traditions.

Atman   in Brahmanism, the individual soul.

Ausgleich   the "Compromise" of 1867 that created the dual monarchy of Austria-Hungary. Austria and Hungary each had its own capital, constitution, and legislative assembly, but were united under one monarch.

bakufu   the centralized government set up in Japan in the twelfth century. *See also* shogunate system.

banners   originally established in 1639 by the Qing Dynasty, the eight banners were administrative divisions into which all Manchu families were placed. Banners quickly evolved into the basis of Manchu military organization, with each required to raise and support a prescribed number of troops.

bard   in Africa, a professional storyteller.

Baroque   a style that dominated Western painting, sculpture, architecture, and music from about 1580 to 1730, generally characterized by elaborate ornamentation and dramatic effects. Important practitioners included Bernini, Rubens, Handel, and Bach.

Bedouins   nomadic tribes originally from northern Arabia, who became important traders after the domestication of the camel during the first millennium B.C.E. Early converts to Islam, their values and practices deeply affected the religion of Islam.

Berbers   an ethnic group indigenous to western North Africa.

bey   a provincial governor in the Ottoman Empire.

bhakti   in Hinduism, devotion as a means of religious observance open to all persons regardless of class.

Black Death   the outbreak of plague (mostly bubonic) in the mid-fourteenth century that killed from 25 to 50 percent of Europe's population.

blitzkrieg   "lightning war." A war conducted with great speed and force, as in Germany's advance at the beginning of World War II.

bodhi   wisdom in India. Sometimes described as complete awareness of the true nature of the universe.

bodhisattvas   in some schools of Buddhism, individuals who have achieved enlightenment but, because of their great compassion, have chosen to renounce Nirvana and to remain on earth in spirit form to help all human beings achieve release from reincarnation.

Boers   the Afrikaans-speaking descendants of Dutch settlers in southern Africa who left the Cape Colony in the nineteenth century to settle in the Orange Free State and Transvaal; defeated by the British in the Boer War (1899–1902) and ultimately incorporated into the Union of South Africa.

bonsai   the cultivation of stunted trees and shrubs to create exquisite nature scenes in miniature; originated in China in the first millenium B.C.E. and imported to Japan between 700 and 900 C.E.

Brahman   the Hindu word roughly equivalent to God; the Divine basis of all being; regarded as the source and sum of the cosmos.

Brahmanism   the early religious beliefs of the Aryan people in India, which eventually gave rise to Hinduism.

brahmin   a member of the Hindu priestly caste or class; literally "one who has realized or attempts to realize Brahman." Traditionally, duties of a *brahmin* include studying Hindu religious scriptures and transmitting them to others orally. The priests of Hindu temples are *brahmin*.

Brezhnev Doctrine   the doctrine, enunciated by Leonid Brezhnev, that the Soviet Union had a right to intervene if socialism was threatened in another socialist state; used to justify the use of Soviet troops in Czechoslovakia in 1968.

Buddhism   a religion and philosophy based on the teachings of Siddhartha Gautama in about 500 B.C.E. Principally practiced in China, India, and other parts of Asia, Buddhism has 360 million followers and is considered a major world religion.

Burakumin   a Japanese minority similar to *dalits* (untouchables) in Indian culture. Past and current discrimination has resulted in lower educational attainment and socioeconomic status for members of this group. Movements with objectives ranging from "liberation" to integration have tried over the years to change this situation.

Bushido   the code of conduct observed by samurai warriors; comparable to the European concept of chivalry.

470

caliph   the secular leader of the Islamic community.

calpulli   in Aztec society, a kinship group, often of a thousand or more, which served as an intermediary with the central government, providing taxes and conscript labor to the state.

capitalism   beginning in the Middle Ages, an economic system in which people invested in trade and goods in order to make profits.

caravels   mobile sailing ships with both lateen and square sails that began to be constructed in Europe in the sixteenth century.

caste system   a system of rigid social hierarchy in which all members of that society are assigned by birth to specific "ranks" and inherit specific roles and privileges.

Catholic Reformation   a movement for the reform of the Catholic Church in the sixteenth century.

caudillos   strong leaders in nineteenth-century Latin America who were usually supported by the landed elites and ruled chiefly by military force, though some were popular; they included both modernizers and destructive dictators.

centuriate assembly   the chief popular assembly of the Roman republic. It passed laws and elected the chief magistrates.

chaebol   a South Korean business structure similar to the Japanese *keiretsu*.

Chan   a Chinese sect (Zen in Japanese) influenced by Daoist ideas that called for mind training and a strict regimen as a means of seeking enlightenment.

chinampas   in Mesoamerica, artificial islands crisscrossed by canals that provided water for crops and easy transportation to local markets.

chonmin   in Korea, the lowest class in society consisting of slaves and workers in certain undesirable occupations such as butchers; literally, "base people."

Christian (northern Renaissance) humanism   an intellectual movement in northern Europe in the late fifteenth and early sixteenth centuries that combined the interest in the classics of the Italian Renaissance with an interest in the sources of early Christianity, including the New Testament and the writings of the church fathers.

chu nom   an adaptation of Chinese written characters to provide a writing system for spoken Vietnamese; in use by the ninth century C.E.

civil disobedience   the tactic of using illegal but nonviolent means of protest; designed by the Indian nationalist leader Mohandas Gandhi to resist British colonial rule.

civilization   a complex culture in which large numbers of humans share a variety of common elements, including cities; religion; political, military, and social structures; material complexity; writing; and significant artistic and intellectual activity.

civil service examination   an elaborate Chinese system of selecting bureaucrats on merit, first introduced in 165 C.E., developed by the Tang Dynasty in the seventh century C.E. and refined under the Song Dynasty; later adopted in Vietnam and with less success in Japan and Korea. It contributed to efficient government, upward mobility, and cultural uniformity.

class struggle   the basis of the Marxist analysis of history, which says that the owners of the means of production have always oppressed the workers and predicts an inevitable revolution. See *also* Marxism.

Cold War   the ideological conflict between the Soviet Union and the United States after World War II.

Columbian Exchange   the exchange of animals, plants, and culture, but also communicable diseases and human populations including slaves, between the Western and Eastern Hemispheres that occurred after Columbus's voyages to the Americas.

common law   law common to the entire kingdom of England; imposed by the king's courts beginning in the twelfth century to replace the customary law used in county and feudal courts, which varied from place to place.

communalism   in South Asia, the tendency of people to band together in mutually antagonistic social subgroups; elsewhere used to describe unifying trends in the larger community.

Communist International (Comintern)   a worldwide organization of Communist parties, founded by Lenin in 1919, dedicated to the advancement of world revolution; also known as the Third International.

Confucianism   a system of thought based on the teachings of Confucius (551–479 B.C.E.) that developed into the ruling ideology of the Chinese state. See *also* Neo-Confucianism.

conquistadors   "conquerors." Leaders in the Spanish conquests in the Americas, especially Mexico and Peru, in the sixteenth century.

conscription   a military draft.

conservatism   an ideology based on tradition and social stability that favored the maintenance of established institutions, organized religion, and obedience to authority and resisted change, especially abrupt change.

consuls   the chief executive officers of the Roman republic. Two were chosen annually to administer the government and lead the army in battle.

consumer society   a term applied to Western society after World War II as the working classes adopted the consumption patterns of the middle class and installment plans, credit cards, and easy credit made consumer goods such as appliances and automobiles widely available.

containment   a policy adopted by the United States in the Cold War. It called for the use of any means, but hopefully short of all-out war, to limit Soviet expansion.

Continental system   Napoleon's effort to bar British goods from the continent of Europe in the hope of weakening Britain's economy and destroying its capacity to wage war.

Contras   in Nicaragua in the 1980s, an anti-Sandinista guerrilla movement supported by the U.S. Reagan administration.

Coptic   a form of Christianity, originally Egyptian, that has thrived in Ethiopia since the fourth century C.E.

cottage industry   a system of textile manufacturing in which spinners and weavers worked at home in their cottages using raw materials supplied to them by capitalist entrepreneurs.

council of the plebs   in the Roman republic, a council only for the plebeians. After 287 B.C.E., its resolutions were binding on all Romans.

creoles   in Latin America, American-born descendants of Europeans.

crusade   in the Middle Ages, a military campaign in defense of Christendom.

Cubism   an artistic style developed at the beginning of the twentieth century, especially by Pablo Picasso, that used geometric designs to re-create reality in the viewer's mind.

cuneiform   "wedge-shaped." A system of writing developed by the Sumerians that consisted of wedge-shaped impressions made by a reed stylus on clay tablets.

Dadaism an artistic movement in the 1920s and 1930s by artists who were revolted by the senseless slaughter of World War I and used their "anti-art" to express contempt for the Western tradition.

daimyo prominent Japanese families who provided allegiance to the local shogun in exchange for protection; similar to vassals in Europe.

dalits commonly referred to as untouchables; the lowest level of Indian society, technically outside the caste system and considered less than human; named *harijans* ("children of God") by Gandhi, they remain the object of discrimination despite affirmative action programs.

Dao a Chinese philosophical concept, literally "the Way," central to both Confucianism and Daoism, that describes the behavior proper to each member of society; somewhat similar to the Indian concept of *dharma*.

Daoism a Chinese philosophy traditionally ascribed to the perhaps legendary Lao Tzu, which holds that acceptance and spontaneity are the keys to harmonious interaction with the universal order; an alternative to Confucianism.

decolonization the process of becoming free of colonial status and achieving statehood; occurred in most of the world's colonies between 1947 and 1962.

deficit spending the concept, developed by John Maynard Keynes in the 1930s, that in times of economic depression governments should stimulate demand by hiring people to do public works, such as building highways, even if this increases the public debt.

deism belief in God as the creator of the universe who, after setting it in motion, ceased to have any direct involvement in it and allowed it to run according to its own natural laws.

demesne the part of a manor retained under the direct control of the lord and worked by the serfs as part of their labor services.

denazification after World War II, the Allied policy of rooting out any traces of Nazism in German society by bringing prominent Nazis to trial for war crimes and purging any known Nazis from political office.

de-Stalinization the policy of denouncing and undoing the most repressive aspects of Stalin's regime; begun by Nikita Khrushchev in 1956.

détente the relaxation of tension between the Soviet Union and the United States that occurred in the 1970s.

developed nations a term used to refer to rich nations, primarily in the Northern Hemisphere, that have well-organized industrial and agricultural systems, advanced technologies, and effective educational systems.

developing nations a term used to refer to poor nations, mainly in the Southern Hemisphere, that have primarily agricultural economies with little technology and serious over-population problems.

devshirme in the Ottoman Empire, a system (literally, "collection") of training talented children to be administrators or members of the sultan's harem; originally meritocratic, by the seventeenth century, it degenerated into a hereditary caste.

dharma in Hinduism and Buddhism, the law that governs the universe, and specifically human behavior.

dictator in the Roman republic, an official granted unlimited power to run the state for a short period of time, usually six months, during an emergency.

diffusion hypothesis the hypothesis that the Yellow River Valley was the ancient heartland of Chinese civilization and that technological and cultural achievements radiated from there to other parts of East Asia. Recent discoveries of other early agricultural communities in China have led to some modification of the hypothesis to allow for other centers of civilization.

diocese the area under the jurisdiction of a Christian bishop; based originally on Roman administrative districts.

direct rule a concept devised by European colonial governments to rule their colonial subjects without the participation of local authorities. It was most often applied in colonial societies in Africa.

divine-right monarchy a monarchy based on the belief that monarchs receive their power directly from God and are responsible to no one except God.

dyarchy during the Qing Dynasty in China, a system in which all important national and provincial administrative positions were shared equally by Chinese and Manchus, which helped to consolidate both Manchu rule and their assimilation.

Einsatzgruppen in Nazi Germany, special strike forces in the SS that played an important role in rounding up and killing Jews.

El Niño periodic changes in water temperature at the surface of the Pacific Ocean, which can lead to major environmental changes and may have led to the collapse of the Moche civilization in what is now Peru.

emir "commander" in Arabic; a title used by Muslim rulers in southern Spain and elsewhere.

encomienda a grant from the Spanish monarch to colonial conquistadors.

encomienda system the system by which Spain first governed its American colonies. Holders of an *encomienda* were supposed to protect the Indians while using them as laborers and collecting tribute, but in practice they exploited them.

enlightened absolutism an absolute monarchy where the ruler follows the principles of the Enlightenment by introducing reforms for the improvement of society, allowing freedom of speech and the press, permitting religious toleration, expanding education, and ruling in accordance with the laws.

Enlightenment an eighteenth-century intellectual movement, led by the philosophes, that stressed the application of reason and the scientific method to all aspects of life.

Epicureanism a philosophy founded by Epicurus in the fourth century B.C.E. that taught that happiness (freedom from emotional turmoil) could be achieved through the pursuit of pleasure (intellectual rather than sensual pleasure).

eta in feudal Japan, a class of hereditary slaves who were responsible for what were considered degrading occupations, such as curing leather and burying the dead.

ethnic cleansing the policy of killing or forcibly removing people of another ethnic group; used by the Serbs against Bosnian Muslims in the 1990s.

eunuch a man whose testicles have been removed; a standard feature of the Chinese imperial system, the Ottoman Empire, and the Mughal Dynasty, among others.

existentialism a philosophical movement that arose after World War II that emphasized the meaninglessness of life, born of the desperation caused by two world wars.

fascism an ideology or movement that exalts the nation above the individual and calls for a centralized government with a dictatorial leader, economic and social regimentation, and forcible suppression of opposition; in particular, the ideology of Mussolini's Fascist regime in Italy.

feminism   the belief in the social, political, and economic equality of the sexes; also, organized activity to advance women's rights.

fief   a landed estate granted to a vassal in exchange for military services.

filial piety   in traditional China, in particular, a hierarchical system in which every family member has his or her place, subordinate to a patriarch who has in turn reciprocal responsibilities.

Final Solution   the physical extermination of the Jewish people by the Nazis during World War II.

Five Pillars of Islam   the core requirements of the Muslim faith: belief in Allah and his Prophet Muhammad; prescribed prayers; observation of Ramadan; pilgrimage to Mecca; and giving alms to the poor.

five relationships   in traditional China, the hierarchical interpersonal associations considered crucial to social order, within the family, between friends, and with the king.

foot binding   an extremely painful process, common in China throughout the second millenium C.E., that compressed girls' feet to half their natural size, representing submissiveness and self-discipline, which were considered necessary attributes for an ideal wife.

Four Modernizations   the slogan for radical reforms of Chinese industry, agriculture, technology, and national defense, instituted by Deng Xiaoping after his accession to power in the late 1970s.

genin   landless laborers in feudal Japan, who were effectively slaves.

genro   the ruling clique of aristocrats in Meiji Japan.

geocentric theory   the idea that the earth is at the center of the universe and that the sun and other celestial objects revolve around the earth.

glasnost   "openness." Mikhail Gorbachev's policy of encouraging Soviet citizens to openly discuss the strengths and weaknesses of the Soviet Union.

global climate change   the changes in climate, including an increase in the temperature of the earth's atmosphere, caused by the greenhouse effect.

global economy   an interdependent economy in which the production, distribution, and sale of goods are accomplished on a worldwide scale.

globalization   a term referring to the trend by which peoples and nations have become more interdependent; often used to refer to the development of a global economy and culture.

good emperors   the five emperors who ruled from 96 to 180 (Nerva, Trajan, Hadrian, Antoninus Pius, and Marcus Aurelius), a period of peace and prosperity for the Roman Empire.

Good Neighbor policy   a policy adopted by the administration of President Franklin D. Roosevelt to practice restraint in U.S. relations with Latin American nations.

Gothic   a term used to describe the art and especially the architecture of Europe in the twelfth, thirteenth, and fourteenth centuries.

Gothic literature   a form of literature used by Romantics to emphasize the bizarre and unusual, especially evident in horror stories.

Grand Council   the top of the government hierarchy in the Song Dynasty in China.

grand vizier   the chief executive in the Ottoman Empire, under the sultan.

Great Leap Forward   a short-lived, radical experiment in China, started in 1958, that created vast rural communes and attempted to replace the family as the fundamental social unit.

Great Proletarian Cultural Revolution   an attempt to destroy all vestiges of tradition in China in order to create a totally egalitarian society. Launched by Mao Zedong in 1966, it devolved into virtual anarchy and lasted only until Mao's death in 1976.

greenhouse effect   the warming of the earth caused by the buildup of carbon dioxide in the atmosphere as a result of human activity.

guest workers   foreign workers working temporarily in European countries.

guided democracy   the name given by President Sukarno of Indonesia in the late 1950s to his style of government, which theoretically operated by consensus.

guild   an association of people with common interests and concerns, especially people working in the same craft. In medieval Europe, guilds came to control much of the production process and to restrict entry into various trades.

guru   teacher, especially in the Hindu, Buddhist and Sikh religious traditions, where it is an important honorific.

Hadith   a collection of the sayings of the Prophet Muhammad, used to supplement the revelations contained in the Qur'an.

harem   the private domain of a ruler such as the sultan in the Ottoman Empire or the caliph of Baghdad, generally large and mostly inhabited by the extended family.

Hegira   the flight of Muhammad from Mecca to Medina in 622, which marks the first date on the official calendar of Islam.

heliocentric theory   the idea that the sun (not the earth) is at the center of the universe.

helots   serfs in ancient Sparta, who were permanently bound to the land that they worked for their Spartan masters.

heresy   the holding of religious doctrines different from the official teachings of the church.

hieroglyphics   a highly pictorial system of writing most often associated with ancient Egypt. Also used (with different "pictographs") by other ancient peoples such as the Maya.

high colonialism   the more formal phase of European colonial policy in Africa after World War I when the colonial administrative network was extended to outlying areas and more emphasis was placed on improving social services and fostering economic development, especially the exploitation of natural resources, to enable the colonies to achieve self-sufficiency.

high culture   the literary and artistic culture of the educated and wealthy ruling classes.

Hinayana   the scornful name for Theravada Buddhism ("lesser vehicle") used by devotees of Mahayana Buddhism.

Hinduism   the main religion in India. It emphasizes reincarnation, based on the results of the previous life, and the desirability of escaping this cycle. Its various forms feature both asceticism and the pleasures of ordinary life, and encompass a multitude of gods as different manifestations of one ultimate reality.

hominids   the earliest humanlike creatures. They flourished in East and South Africa as long as 3 to 4 million years ago.

Hopewell culture   a Native American society that flourished from about 200 B.C.E. to 400 C.E., noted for large burial mounds and extensive manufacturing. Largely based in Ohio, its traders ranged as far as the Gulf of Mexico.

hoplites   heavily armed infantry soldiers used in ancient Greece in a phalanx formation.

hydraulic society   a society organized around a large irrigation system to control the allocation of water.

iconoclasm   an eighth-century Byzantine movement against the use of icons (pictures of sacred figures), which was condemned as idolatry.

iconoclast a member of an eighth-century Byzantine movement against the use of icons (pictures of sacred figures), which it condemned as idolatry.

imam an Islamic religious leader. Some traditions say there is only one per generation; others use the term more broadly.

Impressionism an artistic movement that originated in France in the 1870s. Impressionists sought to capture their impressions of the changing effects of light on objects in nature.

indirect rule a colonial policy of foreign rule in cooperation with local political elites. Though implemented in much of India and Malaya and in parts of Africa, it was not feasible where resistance was strong.

indulgence the remission of part or all of the temporal punishment in purgatory due to sin; granted for charitable contributions and other good deeds. Indulgences became a regular practice of the Christian church in the High Middle Ages, and their abuse was instrumental in sparking Luther's reform movement in the sixteenth century.

informal empire the growing presence of Europeans in Africa during the first decades of the nineteenth century. During this period, most African states were nonetheless still able to maintain their independence.

interdict in the Catholic Church, a censure by which a region or country is deprived of receiving the sacraments.

intervention, principle of the idea, after the Congress of Vienna, that the Great Powers of Europe had the right to send armies into countries experiencing revolution to restore legitimate monarchs to their thrones.

intifada the "uprising" of Palestinians living under Israeli control, especially in the 1980s and 1990s.

Jainism an Indian religion, founded in the fifth century B.C.E., that stresses extreme simplicity.

Janissaries an elite core of eight thousand troops personally loyal to the sultan of the Ottoman Empire.

jati a kinship group, the basic social organization of traditional Indian society, to some extent specialized by occupation.

jihad in Islam, "striving in the way of the Lord." The term is ambiguous and has been subject to varying interpretations, from the practice of conducting raids against local neighbors to the conduct of "holy war" against unbelievers.

justification by faith the primary doctrine of the Protestant Reformation; taught that humans are saved not through good works, but by the grace of God, bestowed freely through the sacrifice of Jesus.

kami spirits worshiped in early Japan that resided in trees, rivers, and streams. *See also* Shinto.

karma a fundamental concept in Hindu (and later Buddhist, Jain, and Sikh) philosophy, that rebirth in a future life is determined by actions in this or other lives. The word refers to the entire process, to the individual's actions, and also to the cumulative result of those actions, for instance, a store of good or bad *karma.*

keiretsu a type of powerful industrial or financial conglomerate that emerged in post–World War II Japan following the abolition of the *zaibatsu.*

khanates Mongol kingdoms, in particular the subdivisions of Genghis Khan's empire ruled by his heirs.

kokutai the core ideology of the Japanese state, particularly during the Meiji Restoration, stressing the uniqueness of the Japanese system and the supreme authority of the emperor.

kowtow the ritual of prostration and touching the forehead to the ground, demanded of all foreign ambassadors to the Chinese court as a symbol of submission.

kshatriya originally, the warrior class of Aryan society in India; ranked below (sometimes equal to) *brahmins;* in modern times, often government workers or soldiers.

laissez-faire "to let alone." An economic doctrine that holds that an economy is best served when the government does not interfere but allows the economy to self-regulate according to the forces of supply and demand.

latifundia large landed estates in the Roman Empire (singular: *latifundium*).

lay investiture the practice in which a layperson chose a bishop and invested him with the symbols of both his temporal office and his spiritual office; led to the Investiture Controversy, which was ended by compromise in the Concordat of Worms in 1122.

Legalism a Chinese philosophy that argued that human beings were by nature evil and would follow the correct path only if coerced by harsh laws and stiff punishments. Adopted as official ideology by the Qin Dynasty, it was later rejected but remained influential.

legitimacy, principle of the idea that after the Napoleonic wars peace could best be reestablished in Europe by restoring legitimate monarchs who would preserve traditional institutions; guided Metternich at the Congress of Vienna.

liberal arts the seven areas of study that formed the basis of education in medieval and early modern Europe. Following Boethius and other late Roman authors, they consisted of grammar, rhetoric, and dialectic or logic (the *trivium*) and arithmetic, geometry, astronomy, and music (the *quadrivium*).

liberalism an ideology based on the belief that people should be as free from restraint as possible. Economic liberalism is the idea that the government should not interfere in the workings of the economy. Political liberalism is the idea that there should be restraints on the exercise of power so that people can enjoy basic civil rights in a constitutional state with a representative assembly.

limited (constitutional) monarchy a system of government in which the monarch is limited by a representative assembly and by the duty to rule in accordance with the laws of the land.

lineage group the descendants of a common ancestor; relatives, often as opposed to immediate family.

Longshan a Neolithic society from near the Yellow River in China, sometimes identified by its black pottery.

maharaja originally, a king in the Aryan society of early India (a great raja); later used more generally to denote an important ruler.

Mahayana a school of Buddhism that promotes the idea of universal salvation through the intercession of bodhisattvas; predominant in north Asia.

majlis a council of elders among the Bedouins of the Roman era.

Malayo-Polynesian a family of languages whose speakers originated on Taiwan or in southeastern China and spread from there to the Malay Peninsula, the Indonesian Archipelago, and many islands of the South Pacific.

Mandate of Heaven the justification for the rule of the Zhou Dynasty in China. The king was charged to maintain order as a representative of Heaven, which was viewed as an impersonal law of nature.

mandates a system established after World War I whereby a nation officially administered a territory (mandate) on behalf of the League of Nations. Thus, France administered Lebanon and Syria as mandates, and Britain administered Iraq and Palestine.

manor an agricultural estate operated by a lord and worked by peasants who performed labor services and paid various rents and fees to the lord in exchange for protection and sustenance.

mansa in the West African state of Mali, a chieftain who served as both religious and administrative leader and was responsible for forwarding tax revenues from the village to higher levels of government.

Marshall Plan the European Recovery Program, under which the United States provided financial aid to European countries to help them rebuild after World War II.

Marxism the political, economic, and social theories of Karl Marx, which included the idea that history is the story of class struggle and that ultimately the proletariat will overthrow the bourgeoisie and establish a dictatorship en route to a classless society.

mass education a state-run educational system, usually free and compulsory, that aims to ensure that all children in society have at least a basic education.

mass leisure forms of leisure that appeal to large numbers of people in a society, including the working classes; emerged at the end of the nineteenth century to provide workers with amusements after work and on weekends; used during the twentieth century by totalitarian states to control their populations.

mass politics a political order characterized by mass political parties and universal male and (eventually) female suffrage.

mass society a society in which the concerns of the majority— the lower classes—play a prominent role; characterized by extension of voting rights, an improved standard of living for the lower classes, and mass education.

matrilinear passing through the female line, for example, from a father to his sister's son rather than his own, as practiced in some African societies; not necessarily, or even usually, combined with matriarchy, in which women rule.

megaliths large stones, widely used in Europe from around 4000 to 1500 B.C.E. to create monuments, including sophisticated astronomical observatories.

Meiji Restoration the period during the late nineteenth and early twentieth centuries in which fundamental economic and cultural changes occurred in Japan, tranforming it from a feudal and agrarian society to an industrial and technological society.

mercantilism an economic theory that held that a nation's prosperity depended on its supply of gold and silver and that the total volume of trade is unchangeable; therefore, advocated that the government play an active role in the economy by encouraging exports and discouraging imports, especially through the use of tariffs.

Mesoamerica the region stretching roughly from modern central Mexico to Honduras, in which the Olmec, Maya, Aztec, and other civilizations developed.

Middle Passage the journey of slaves from Africa to the Americas as the middle leg of the triangular trade.

Middle Path a central concept of Buddhism, which advocates avoiding extremes of both materialism and asceticism; also known as the Eightfold Way.

mihrab the niche in a mosque's wall that indicates the direction of Mecca, usually containing an ornately decorated panel representing Allah.

militarism a policy of aggressive military preparedness; in particular, the large armies based on mass conscription and complex, inflexible plans for mobilization that most European nations had before World War I.

millet an administrative unit in the Ottoman Empire used to organize religious groups.

Modernism the new artistic and literary styles that emerged in the decades before 1914 as artists rebelled against traditional efforts to portray reality as accurately as possible (leading to Impressionism and Cubism) and writers explored new forms.

monasticism a movement that began in early Christianity whose purpose was to create communities of men or women who practiced a communal life dedicated to God as a moral example to the world around them.

monk a man who chooses to live a communal life divorced from the world in order to dedicate himself totally to the will of God.

monotheistic/monotheism having only one god; the doctrine or belief that there is only one god.

Multiculturalism a term referring to the connection of several cultural or ethnic groups within a society.

multinational corporation a company with divisions in more than two countries.

nationalism a sense of national consciousness based on awareness of being part of a community—a "nation"—that has common institutions, traditions, language, and customs and that becomes the focus of the individual's primary political loyalty.

nation-state a form of political organization in which a relatively homogeneous people inhabits a sovereign state, as opposed to a state containing people of several nationalities.

natural law a body of laws or specific principles held to be derived from nature and binding upon all human society even in the absence of positive laws.

natural rights certain inalienable rights to which all people are entitled; include the right to life, liberty, and property, freedom of speech and religion, and equality before the law.

natural selection Darwin's idea that organisms that are most adaptable to their environment survive and pass on the variations that enabled them to survive, while other, less adaptable organisms become extinct; "survival of the fittest."

neocolonialism the use of economic rather than political or military means to maintain Western domination of developing nations.

Neo-Confucianism the dominant ideology of China during the second millennium C.E. It combined the metaphysical speculations of Buddhism and Daoism with the pragmatic Confucian approach to society, maintaining that the world is real, not illusory, and that fulfillment comes from participation, not withdrawal. It encouraged an intellectual environment that valued continuity over change and tradition over innovation.

Neolithic Revolution the shift from gathering plants and hunting animals for sustenance to producing food by systematic agriculture that occurred gradually between 10,000 and 4000 B.C.E. (the Neolithic or "New Stone" Age).

New Culture Movement a protest launched at Peking University after the failure of the 1911 revolution, aimed at abolishing the remnants of the old system and introducing Western values and institutions into China.

New Democracy the initial program of the Chinese Communist government, from 1949 to 1955, focusing on honest government, land reform, social justice, and peace rather than on the utopian goal of a classless society.

New Economic Policy a modified version of the old capitalist system introduced in the Soviet Union by Lenin in 1921 to revive the economy after the ravages of the civil war and war communism.

new imperialism the revival of imperialism after 1880 in which European nations established colonies throughout much of Asia and Africa.

new monarchies the governments of France, England, and Spain at the end of the fifteenth century, where the rulers were successful in reestablishing or extending centralized royal authority, suppressing the nobility, controlling the church, and insisting upon the loyalty of all peoples living in their territories.

Nirvana in Buddhist thought, enlightenment, the ultimate transcendence from the illusion of the material world; release from the wheel of life.

Nok culture in northern Nigeria, one of the most active early ironworking societies in Africa, artifacts from which date back as far as 500 B.C.E.

Nonaligned Movement an organization of neutralist nations established in the 1950s to provide a counterpoise between the socialist bloc, headed by the Soviet Union, and the capitalist nations led by the United States. Chief sponsors of the movement were Jawaharlal Nehru of India, Gamal Abdul Nasser of Egypt, and Sukarno of Indonesia.

noncentralized societies societies characterized by autonomous villages organized by clans and ruled by a local chieftain or clan head; typical of the southern half of the African continent before the eleventh century C.E.

nongovernmental organizations (NGOs) organizations that have no government ties and work to address world problems.

nun a woman who withdraws from the world and joins a religious community; the female equivalent of a monk.

old regime/old order the political and social system of France in the eighteenth century before the Revolution.

oligarchy rule by a few.

Open Door Notes a series of letters sent in 1899 by U.S. Secretary of State John Hay to Great Britain, France, Germany, Italy, Japan, and Russia, calling for equal economic access to the China market for all states and for the maintenance of the territorial and administrative integrity of the Chinese Empire.

organic evolution Darwin's principle that all plants and animals have evolved over a long period of time from earlier and simpler forms of life.

Paleolithic Age the period of human history when humans used simple stone tools (ca. 2,500,000–10,000 B.C.E.).

Pan-Africanism the concept of African continental unity and solidarity in which the common interests of African countries transcend national boundaries.

Pan-Arabism a movement promoted by Egyptian president Gamal Abdul Nasser and other Middle Eastern leaders to unify all Arab peoples in a single supra-national organization. After Nasser's death in 1971, the movement languished.

pantheism a doctrine that equates God with the universe and all that is in it.

pariahs members of the lowest level of traditional Indian society, technically outside the class system itself; also known as untouchables.

pasha an administrative official of the Ottoman Empire, responsible for collecting taxes and maintaining order in the provinces; later, some became hereditary rulers.

paterfamilias the dominant male in a Roman family whose powers over his wife and children were theoretically unlimited, though they were sometimes circumvented in practice.

patriarchal/patriarchy a society in which the father is supreme in the clan or family; more generally, a society dominated by men.

patricians great landowners who became the ruling class in the Roman republic.

patrilinear passing through the male line, from father to son; often combined with patriarchy.

pax Romana "Roman peace." A term used to refer to the stability and prosperity that Roman rule brought to the Mediterranean world and much of western Europe during the first and second centuries C.E.

peaceful coexistence the policy adopted by the Soviet Union under Khrushchev in 1955, and continued by his successors, that called for economic and ideological rivalry with the West rather than nuclear war.

perestroika "restructuring." A term applied to Mikhail Gorbachev's economic, political, and social reforms in the Soviet Union.

permissive society a term applied to Western society after World War II to reflect the new sexual freedom and the emergence of a drug culture.

phalanx a rectangular formation of tightly massed infantry soldiers.

pharaoh the most common title used for ancient Egyptian kings. Pharaohs possessed absolute power and were seen as divine.

philosophes intellectuals of the eighteenth-century Enlightenment who believed in applying a spirit of rational criticism to all things, including religion and politics, and who focused on improving and enjoying this world, rather than on the afterlife.

plebeians the class of Roman citizens who included nonpatrician landowners, craftspeople, merchants, and small farmers in the Roman republic. Their struggle for equal rights with the patricians dominated much of the republic's history.

pogroms organized massacres of Jews.

polis an ancient Greek city-state encompassing both an urban area and its surrounding countryside; a small but autonomous political unit where all major political and social activities were carried out in a central location.

polygyny the practice of having more than one wife at a time.

polytheistic/polytheism having many gods; belief in or the worship of more than one god.

popular culture as opposed to high culture, the unofficial, written and unwritten culture of the masses, much of which was passed down orally; centers on public and group activities such as festivals. In the twentieth and twenty-first centuries, the entertainment, recreation, and pleasures that people purchase as part of mass consumer society.

portolani charts of landmasses and coastlines made by navigators and mathematicians in the thirteenth and fourteenth centuries.

Post-Impressionism an artistic movement that began in France in the 1880s. Post-Impressionists sought to use color and line in their art to express inner feelings and produce a personal statement of reality.

Postmodernism a term used to cover a variety of artistic and intellectual styles and ways of thinking prominent since the 1970s.

poststructuralism (deconstruction) a theory formulated by Jacques Derrida in the 1960s, holding that there is no fixed, universal truth because culture is created and can therefore be analyzed in various ways.

praetorian guard the military unit that served as the personal bodyguard of the Roman emperors.

praetors the two senior Roman judges, who had executive authority when the consuls were away from the city and could also lead armies.

Prakrit an ancient Indian language, a simplified form of Sanskrit.

predestination the belief, associated with Calvinism, that God, as a consequence of his foreknowledge of all events, has predetermined those who will be saved (the elect) and those who will be damned.

proletariat the industrial working class; in Marxism, the class that will ultimately overthrow the bourgeoisie.

Protestant Reformation the western European religious reform movement in the sixteenth century that divided Christianity into Catholic and Protestant groups.

psychoanalysis a method developed by Sigmund Freud to resolve a patient's psychic conflict.

pueblo a three-story adobe communal house with a timbered roof. Pueblos were constructed by the Ancient Pueblo people in what is now the southwestern United States starting around the ninth century C.E.

Pueblo Bonito a large settlement built by the Ancient Pueblo people in what is now New Mexico in the ninth century C.E. It contained several hundred compounds housing several thousand residents.

puja in India, a popular tradition focused on personal worship that began to replace the Brahmanical emphasis on court sacrifice and asceticism during the early centuries of the first millennium C.E.; an aspect of the transition from Brahmanism to Hinduism.

purdah the Indian term for the practice among Muslims and some Hindus of isolating women and preventing them from associating with men outside the home.

Pure Land a Buddhist sect, originally Chinese but later popular in Japan, which taught that devotion alone could lead to enlightenment and release.

quipu an Inka record-keeping system that used knotted strings rather than writing.

raj the British colonial regime in India.

raja originally, a chieftain in the Aryan society of early India, a representative of the gods; later used more generally to denote a ruler.

Ramadan the holy month of Islam, during which believers fast from dawn to sunset. Since the Islamic calendar is lunar, Ramadan migrates through the seasons.

Realism in the nineteenth century, a school of painting that emphasized the everyday life of ordinary people, depicted with photographic realism.

Realpolitik "politics of reality." Politics based on practical concerns rather than theory or ethics.

reincarnation the idea that the individual soul is reborn in a different form after death. In Hindu and Buddhist thought, release from this cycle is the objective of all living souls.

relativity theory Einstein's theory that holds, among other things, that (1) space and time are not absolute but are relative to the observer and interwoven into a four-dimensional space-time continuum and (2) matter is a form of energy ($E = mc^2$).

relics the bones of Christian saints or objects intimately associated with saints that were considered worthy of veneration.

Renaissance the "rebirth" of classical culture that occurred in Italy between ca. 1350 and ca. 1550; also, the earlier revivals of Classical culture that occurred under Charlemagne and in the twelfth century.

Renaissance humanism an intellectual movement in Renaissance Italy based on the study of the Greek and Roman classics.

rentier a person who lives on income from property and is not personally involved in its operation.

revisionism a socialist doctrine that rejected Marx's emphasis on class struggle and revolution and argued instead that workers should work through political parties to bring about gradual change.

revolutionary socialism the socialist doctrine that violent action was the only way to achieve the goals of socialism.

rococo a style, especially of decoration and architecture, that developed from the Baroque and spread throughout Europe by the 1730s. While still elaborate, it emphasized curves, lightness, and charm in the pursuit of pleasure, happiness, and love.

Romanticism a nineteenth-century intellectual and artistic movement that rejected the Enlightenment's emphasis on reason. Instead, Romantics stressed the importance of intuition, feeling, emotion, and imagination as sources of knowing.

ronin Japanese warriors made unemployed by developments in the early modern era, since samurai were forbidden by tradition to engage in commerce.

rural responsibility system post-Maoist land reform in China, under which collectives leased land to peasant families, who could consume or sell their surplus production and keep the profits.

sacraments rites considered imperative for a Christian's salvation. By the thirteenth century consisted of the Eucharist or Lord's Supper, baptism, marriage, penance, extreme unction, holy orders, and confirmation of children; Protestant reformers of the sixteenth century generally recognized only two—baptism and communion (the Lord's Supper).

sakoku during the Tokugawa Shogunate in Japan, the policy of closing the country to trade with Europe and encouraging domestic production of goods that had previously been imported.

samurai literally "retainers"; similar to European knights. Usually in service to a particular shogun, these Japanese warriors lived by a strict code of ethics and duty.

Sanskrit an early Indo-European language, in which the Vedas were composed, beginning in the second millenium B.C.E. It survived as the language of literature and the bureaucracy in India for centuries after its decline as a spoken tongue.

sati the Hindu ritual requiring a wife to throw herself upon her deceased husband's funeral pyre.

satori enlightenment, in the Japanese, especially Zen, Buddhist tradition.

satrap/satrapy a governor with both civil and military duties in the ancient Persian Empire, which was divided into satrapies, or provinces, each administered by a satrap.

satyagraha the Hindi term for the practice of nonviolent resistance, as advocated by Mohandas Gandhi; literally, "hold fast to the truth."

scholar-gentry in Song Dynasty China, candidates who passed the civil service examinations and whose families were nonaristocratic landowners; eventually, a majority of the bureaucracy.

Scholasticism the philosophical and theological system of the medieval schools, which emphasized rigorous analysis of contradictory authorities; often used to try to reconcile faith and reason.

School of Mind a philosophy espoused by Wang Yangming during the mid-Ming era of China, which argued that mind and the universe were a single unit and knowledge was therefore obtained through internal self-searching rather than through investigation of the outside world; for a while, a significant but unofficial rival to Neo-Confucianism.

scientific method a method of seeking knowledge through inductive principles; uses experiments and observations to develop generalizations.

Scientific Revolution the transition from the medieval worldview to a largely secular, rational, and materialistic perspective; began in the seventeenth century and was popularized in the eighteenth.

secularization the process of becoming more concerned with material, worldly, temporal things and less with spiritual and religious things.

self-strengthening a late-nineteenth-century Chinese policy by which Western technology would be adopted while Confucian principles and institutions were maintained intact.

senate/senators the leading council of the Roman republic; composed of about three hundred men (senators) who served for life and dominated much of the political life of the republic.

separation of powers a doctrine enunciated by Montesquieu in the eighteenth century that separate executive, legislative, and judicial powers serve to limit and control each other.

sepoys native troops hired by the East India Company to protect British interests in South Asia; formed the basis of the British Indian Army.

serf a peasant who is bound to the land and obliged to provide labor services and pay various rents and fees to the lord; considered unfree but not a slave because serfs could not be bought and sold.

shari'a a law code, originally drawn up by Muslim scholars shortly after the death of Muhammad, that provides believers with a set of prescriptions to regulate their daily lives.

sheikh originally, the ruler of a Bedouin tribe; later, also used as a more general honorific.

Shi'ite the second largest tradition of Islam, which split from the majority Sunni soon after the death of Muhammad, in a disagreement over the succession; especially significant in Iran and Iraq.

Shinto a kind of state religion in Japan, derived from beliefs in nature spirits and until recently linked with belief in the divinity of the emperor and the sacredness of the Japanese nation.

shogun a powerful Japanese leader, originally military, who ruled under the titular authority of the emperor.

shogunate system the system of government in Japan in which the emperor exercised only titular authority while the shogun (regional military dictators) exercised actual political power.

Sikhism a religion, founded in the early sixteenth century in the Punjab that began as an attempt to reconcile the Hindu and Muslim traditions and developed into a significant alternative to both.

sipahis in the Ottoman Empire, local cavalry elites, who held fiefdoms and collected taxes.

Social Darwinism the application of Darwin's principle of organic evolution to the social order; led to the belief that progress comes from the struggle for survival as the fittest advance and the weak decline.

Socratic method a form of teaching that uses a question-and-answer format to enable students to reach conclusions by using their own reasoning.

soviets councils of workers' and soldiers' deputies formed throughout Russia in 1917; played an important role in the Bolshevik Revolution.

sphere of influence a territory or region over which an outside nation exercises political or economic influence.

Star Wars nickname of the Strategic Defense Initiative, proposed by President Reagan, which was intended to provide a shield that would destroy any incoming missiles; named after a popular science-fiction movie.

State Confucianism the integration of Confucian doctrine with Legalist practice under the Han Dynasty in China, which became the basis of Chinese political thought until the modern era.

Stoicism a philosophy founded by Zeno in the fourth century B.C.E. that taught that one could obtain happiness by accepting one's lot and living in harmony with the will of God, thereby achieving inner peace.

stupa originally a stone tower holding relics of the Buddha; more generally a place for devotion, often architecturally impressive and surmounted with a spire.

Sublime Porte the office of the grand vizier in the Ottoman Empire.

sudras the classes that represented the great bulk of the Indian population from ancient times, mostly peasants, artisans or manual laborers; ranked below *brahmins, kshatriyas,* and *vaisyas,* but above the pariahs.

suffragists those who advocate the extension of the right to vote (suffrage), especially to women.

Sufism a mystical school of Islam, noted for its music, dance, and poetry, which became prominent in about the thirteenth century.

sultan "holder of power," a title commonly used by Muslim rulers in the Ottoman Empire, Egypt, and elsewhere; still in use in parts of Asia, sometimes for regional authorities.

Sunni the largest tradition of Islam, from which the Shi'ites split soon after the death of Muhammad, in a disagreement over the succession.

Supreme Ultimate according to Neo-Confucianists, a transcendent world, distinct from the material world in which humans live, but to which humans may aspire; a set of abstract principles, roughly equivalent to the Dao.

Surrealism an artistic movement that arose between World War I and World War II. Surrealists portrayed recognizable objects in unrecognizable relationships in order to reveal the world of the unconscious.

Swahili a mixed African-Arabian culture that developed by the twelfth century along the east coast of Africa; also, the national language of Kenya and Tanzania.

Taika reforms the seventh-century "great change" reforms that established the centralized Japanese state.

taille a French tax on land or property, developed by King Louis XI in the fifteenth century as the financial basis of the monarchy. It was largely paid by the peasantry; the nobility and the clergy were exempt.

Taisho democracy   the era of the 1920s in Japan when universal (male) suffrage was instituted, political parties expanded, and other democratic institutions appeared to flourish. The process of democratization proved fragile, however, and failed to continue into the 1930s.

Tantrism   a mystical Buddhist sect that emphasized the importance of magical symbols and ritual in seeking a path to enlightenment.

Theravada   a school of Buddhism that stresses personal behavior and the quest for understanding as a means of release from the wheel of life, rather than the intercession of bodhisattvas; predominant in Sri Lanka and Southeast Asia.

three obediences   the traditional duties of Japanese women, in permanent subservience: child to father, wife to husband, and widow to son.

three people's principles   the three principles on which the program of Sun Yat-sen's Revolutionary Alliance (Tongmenghui) was based: nationalism (meaning primarily the elimination of Manchu rule over China), democracy, and people's livelihood.

totalitarian state   a state characterized by government control over all aspects of economic, social, political, cultural, and intellectual life; the subordination of the individual to the state; and insistence that the masses be actively involved in the regime's goals.

total war   warfare in which all of a nation's resources, including civilians at home as well as soldiers in the field, are mobilized for the war effort.

transnational corporation   another term for a "multinational corporation," or a company with divisions in more than two countries.

trench warfare   warfare in which the opposing forces attack and counterattack from a relatively permanent system of trenches protected by barbed wire; characteristic of World War I.

Triangular Trade   a term used to describe a form of international trade taking place between three countries or regions of the world.

tribunes of the plebs   beginning in 494 B.C.E., Roman officials who were given the power to protect plebeians against arrest by patrician magistrates.

Truman Doctrine   the doctrine enunciated by Harry Truman in 1947 that the United States would provide economic aid to countries that were threatened by Communist expansion.

twice-born   the males of the higher castes in traditional Indian society, who underwent an initiation ceremony at puberty.

tyrant/tyranny   in an ancient Greek *polis* (or an Italian city-state during the Renaissance), a ruler who came to power in an unconstitutional way and ruled without being subject to the law.

uhuru   "freedom" in Swahili; a key slogan in the African independence movements, especially in Kenya.

uji   a clan in early Japanese tribal society.

ulama   a convocation of leading Muslim scholars, the earliest of which shortly after the death of Muhammad drew up a law code, called the *shari'a*, based largely on the Qur'an and the sayings of the Prophet, to provide believers with a set of prescriptions to regulate their daily lives.

umma   the Muslim community, as a whole.

uninterrupted revolution   the goal of the Great Proletarian Cultural Revolution launched by Mao Zedong in 1966.

vaisya   the third-ranked class in traditional Indian society, usually merchants.

varna   Indian classes, or castes.

vassal   a person granted a fief, or landed estate, in exchange for providing military services to the lord and fulfilling certain other obligations, such as appearing at the lord's court when summoned and making a payment on the knighting of the lord's eldest son.

veneration of ancestors   the extension of filial piety to include care for the deceased, for instance, by burning replicas of useful objects to accompany them on their journey to the next world.

viceroy   the administrative head of the provinces of New Spain and Peru in the Americas.

Viet Cong   the popular name applied to the resistance forces led by the National Front for the Liberation of South Vietnam (NLF) in South Vietnam. Literally, "Viet Communists."

Vietnam syndrome   the presumption, from the 1970s on, that the U.S. public would object to a protracted military entanglement abroad, such as another Vietnam-type conflict.

vizier   the prime minister in the Abbasid caliphate and elsewhere, a chief executive.

war communism   Lenin's policy of nationalizing industrial and other facilities and requisitioning the peasants' produce during the civil war in Russia.

welfare state   a social/political system in which the government assumes the primary responsibility for the social welfare of its citizens by providing such things as social security, unemployment benefits, and health care.

well-field system   the theoretical pattern of land ownership in early China, named for the appearance of the Chinese character for "well," in which farmland was divided into nine segments and a peasant family would cultivate one for their own use and cooperate with seven others to cultivate the ninth for the landlord.

White Lotus   a Chinese Buddhist sect, founded in 1133 C.E., that sought political reform; in 1796–1804, a Chinese peasant revolt.

women's liberation movement   the struggle for equal rights for women, which has deep roots in history but achieved new prominence under this name in the 1960s, building on the work of, among others, Simone de Beauvoir and Betty Friedan.

world-machine   Newton's conception of the universe as one huge, regulated, and uniform machine that operated according to natural laws in absolute time, space, and motion.

yangban   the aristocratic class in Korea. During the Choson Dynasty, entry into the bureaucracy was limited to members of this class.

Yangshao   a Neolithic society from near the Yellow River in China, sometimes identified by its painted pottery.

yoga   "union"; the practice of body training that evolved from the early asceticism and remains an important element of Hindu religious practice.

Young Turks   a successful Turkish reformist group in the late nineteenth and early twentieth centuries.

zaibatsu   powerful business cartels formed in Japan during the Meiji era and outlawed following World War II.

zamindars   Indian tax collectors, who were assigned land, from which they kept part of the revenue. The British revived the system in a misguided attempt to create a landed gentry.

Zen Buddhism   (in Chinese, Chan or Ch'an) a school of Buddhism particularly important in Japan, some of whose adherents stress that enlightenment *(satori)* can be achieved suddenly, though others emphasize lengthy meditation.

ziggurat   a massive stepped tower upon which a temple dedicated to the chief god or goddess of a Sumerian city was built.

Zionism   an international movement that called for the establishment of a Jewish state or a refuge for Jews in Palestine.

Zoroastrianism   a religion founded by the Persian Zoroaster in the seventh century B.C.E.; characterized by worship of a supreme god Ahuramazda who represents the good against the evil spirit, identified as Ahriman.

INDEX

A

al-Andaluz, 172, 174. *See also* Spain
al-Bakri, 199
al-dis (reeds), 197
al-Ma'mun, 170–71, 176
al-Mas'udi, 171, 180, 182, 196–97 201–2
al-Bakri, 199
al-Biruni, 219
al-Din, Ismail, 402–3
al-dis (reeds), 197
al-Idrisi, 181
Abacuses, 248
al-Abbas, Abu, 170
Abbas I the Great, 170–73, 403–5
Abbasid Empire
    in Baghdad, 393
    bureaucracy in, 170–71
    corruption in, 170–71
    frontier with Byzantine Empire, 171
    Genghis Khan and, 251
    Great Mosque of Samarra, 172
    homosexuality in, 171
    instability and division, 171–72
    Mongol defeat of, 173
    rule of, 170–71
    Seljuk Turks and, 172
    sexuality and, 171
    trade in, 170
    view of Islam, 170
Abbesses, 292–93
Abbots, 292
al-Abbas, Abu, 170
Aborigines, 228
Absolutism
    in Austria, 385
    in Central and Eastern Europe, 384–85
    enlightened, 454–55
    in France, 369, 390
Abu Bakr, 167
Academies
    in Athens, 98
    in China, 72, 246
    Islamic, 179, 246
Accla, 157
Achaemenid Dynasty, 26
Achilles, 86–87, 103
Acre, 173
Acropolis, 88
Act of Supremacy, 375, 378
Act of Union (1707), 445
Adal, Muslim state of, 197, 200
Administration. *See* Government
Admonitions for Women (Ban Zhao), 124
Adrianople, 127
Adriatic Sea, 111
Adshead, Samuel, 254
Adulis, port of, 190
Adultery
    Hammurabi's Code on, 13
    Hebrew Law Code on, 23, 25

in Islamic society, 178
in Japan, 276
Adventures of Marco Polo, The (film), 254
Aegean Sea. *See names of specific countries*
Aegospotami, battle at, 94
Aeneas, 122
Aeneid, The (Virgil), 122
Aeolian Greeks, 86
Aequi, 113
Aeschylus, 95
Afghanistan
    as Bactria, 50
    seizure of Isfahan, 402–3
Afonso I (Kongo), 361
Africa. *See* also Central Africa; also East Africa;
    also *names of specific countries and regions*;
    also North Africa; also Slavery; also
    South Africa
    agriculture and farming in, 197, 201–2, 204,
      346, 358, 396
    aristocracy in, 190, 199, 203
    birthrate in, 360, 740
    camels in, 177–78, 191–92, 194, 198, 201,
      205, 345–46
    civilizations of, 188–193
    clans in, 198, 201–3, 207
    climate of, 189–193
    cotton and cotton industry in, 189, 194,
      199, 353
    culture in, 190–91, 193, 195, 197–98,
      205–7
    economy in, 201
    education in, 201,
    elites in, 207
    Europeans and, 204, 294, 311
    foods in, 192, 200
    gold in, 177, 355–57
    history of, 188–208
    housing in, 203–4
    Islam in, 167, 194–201, 205, 207, 344–45
    languages in, 190, 198–99, 202, 207
    leaders in, 200
    marriage in, 20, 198, 205
    merchants in, 203
    Muslims in, 193–200, 205, 207
    noncentralized societies in, 201–2
    Ottomans and, 395–96
    political and social structures in, 189–190,
      193, 198
    Portugal and, 358
    pottery in, 189, 191, 203
    rural areas in, 193, 203
    sexuality and, 171
    slave trade and, 198, 204
    states in, 189–191, 193, 197–202, 204, 207
    timeline, 209, 366
    trade in, 190–204
    wealth in, 190, 200–202
Africa, ancient
    agriculture and farming in, 7, 188–89,
      191–93, 195

camels in, 177–78, 191–92
clans in, 194
family in, 202–4
first humans, 4–6
foods in, 189
housing in, 194
marriage in, 20
Phoenicians and, 22
political and social structures in, 193
states in, 193
Africa, culture in
    architecture in, 207–8
    literature in, 208
    music in, 206–7
    painting and sculpture, 205–6
Africa, early society
    slavery in, 204
    urban life, 202–3
    village life in, 203–4
    women in, 204–5
Africa, emergence of civilization
    agriculture in, 17, 19, 188–89
    ancient, 188–193
    Arabs in, 195
    Axum and Meroë, 188–190
    Chinese view of, 194
    early chronology, 195
    first farmers, 188–89
    history of, 202
    Kingdom of Ethiopia, 195–97
    land in, 187
    noncentralized societies in, 200–201
    religion in, before Islam, 193–95
    Sahara Desert region, 190–93
Africa, in transition
    political and social structures in, 362
    slave trade and, 358–361
Africanus, Leo, 177, 205, 345
Afshar, Nadir Shah, 404
Afterlife. *See also* Pyramids
    in Africa, 193
    in Americas, 154
    in Buddhism, 276
    in China, 56, 58–59, 79
    in Egypt, 18–20
    in India, 43–46
    in Islam, 165
Agamemnon, 86
Agatharchides, 196
Agave, 140–41
Age of Augustus, 117–18
"Age of Discovery," 343
Age of Exploration, 347, 392–93, 412
Age of Pericles, 93
Agincourt, Battle of, 332
Agora, 88
Agra, India, 408
Agrarian societies. *See names of specific*
    countries
Agricultural Revolution, 451–52

arts in, 400
Balkans and, 495
bureaucracy in, 398, 400
Byzantine Empire and, 317, 327–28, 393–96, 401, 403
children in, 399
chronology of, 399
culture in, 400–401
decline of, 400
defeat by Tammerlane, 221
Europe and, 392–93, 396
expansion of, 392–93, 396
fall of Cairo, 396
fall of Constantinople to Ottoman Turks, 393–95
government of, 396, 398
laws in, 396, 399–400
Mediterranean region and, 393–94
minorities in, 398–99
Muslims in, 398–400
nature of Turkish rule, 396–98
religion in, 398–400
rise of Ottoman Turks, 393
rule in, 396, 398
Safavids and, 395
Seljuk Turks in, 393
sexuality and, 397, 400
silk and silk industry in, 400
social classes in, 399
society in, 398–400
textiles in, 400
treatment of minorities, 398–99
women in, 400
Outcastes. *See* Untouchables
Outer Mongolia, 251, 423
Out-of-Africa theory, 5–6
Oxford University, 310

P

Pacal, 143, 145
Pachakuti, 156
Pachamama, 158
Pacific, expansion into, 236
Padshahnama (Book of Kings), 410
Paekche kingdom, 283
Pagan, Kingdom of, 230, 235. *See also* Southeast Asia
Pagodas, 271, 286–87
Painted Portico, 106
Painting. *See also names of specific artists and works*
    in Aztec society, 149
    China, 73, 241, 243, 261, 263
    in India, 42, 47
    Mughal Empire, 414–15
Pakistan. *See also* India
    Alexander the Great and, 107
Palace of the Large Masks, 15
Palembang, Sumatra, 231
Palenque, 143, 145–46
Paleolithic Age, 6–7
Paleologi Dynasty, 327
Paleologus, Michael, 327
Palestine, 317, 327, 611. *See also* Arabs and Arab world; Middle East
    Alexander the Great in, 102
Pallava people, 214–15, 218
Pamir Mountains, 221–22, 248
Pandya kingdom, 220

Panhellenic celebrations, 98
Pantheism, 194
Pantheon, 123
Papacy. *See names of specific popes;* Popes
Papal Inquisition. *See* Inquisition
Papal supremacy, 308
Paper, 20, 73, 137, 150, 170, 174, 180, 182, 248–49, 261, 263, 275, 429, 433
Papermaking, 73
Papyrus, 20, 50, 180
Paramesvara, 344
Pariahs (outcastes), 39
Parliaments, 303–4
Parma, 485, 488–89
Parnassus, Mount, 85, 99
Parsis, 225
Parthenon, 95
Pashas, 396
Pataliputra, India, 37
Paterfamilias, 122
Patriarchs of Constantinople. *See also names of specific patriarchs,* 321, 324, 326
Patriarchy, 9
Patrician oligarchies, 452
Patricians, 114, 452
Patrilineal society, 204
Patriotism, 127, 466. *See also* Nationalism
Paul III, 377
Pax Mongolica, 255
Pax Romana, 118–120
Peace of Augsburg, 371–72
Peace of Westphalia, 381
Pearl River, 418
Peas, 33, 177, 296
Peasant economy, 324
Peasants. *See also* Revolts and rebellions; Serfs and serfdom
    in Asia, 62, 72, 75, 247, 254, 261–62
    Black Death and, 328–330
    in China, 62, 72, 75, 247, 254, 261–62
    in Europe, 296–98, 369–371, 379, 381, 386
Peasants' War, 371
Peking. *See* Beijing, China
Peloponnesian War, 85, 92–96
Peloponnesus region, 84
    Dorian Greeks in, 86
Pemba, 197
Peninsulares, 353
Penny, Edward, 457
Pensions, 171, 176
Pepin, 293
Pepper plantation, 412
Pergamum, 104
Pericles, 83–84, 93
Periplus (travel account), 193, 213
Persecution of Christians, 130–31, 195
Persepolis, 26, 28, 102–3, 105
Persia. *See also* Iran; Persian Empire
    aristocracy in, 170
    Mongols in, 251
    timeline, 30
Persian Empire. *See also names of specific ruler;* Persia
    Alexander the Great and, 102
    Arabs in, 167
Persian Empire, ancient
    civil administration of, 27
    military of, 27–28
    religion in, 28–29

Persian Gulf, 11, 13, 33, 37, 102, 105, 163–64, 169–171, 179, 194, 196, 212, 403, 413
Persian language, 415
Persian miniatures, 414
Personal worship (*puja*), 218
Peru
    Caral civilization in, 152–53
    Chimor kingdom in, 153–55
    Inka in, 155–57
    Moche in, 153
    Wari people in, 153–55
Peter the Great, 386, 454
Petrarch, 334
Phalanx, 88
Pharaohs. *See names of specific rulers; See* Egypt, ancient
Philadelphia Convention, 453
Philip II Augustus (France), 304, 312
Philip II (Macedonian king), 92, 101
Philip II (Spain), 378
Philip IV (France), 305, 333
Philip VI (France), 332
Philippines, 363–64
    Buddism in, 264
    Chinese traders in, 234
Philosophes (French intellectuals)
    baron de Montesquieu (Charles de Secondat), 445–46
    definition of, 445
    Denis Diderot, 447
    later Enlightenment, 447
    new "Science of Man," 447
    Voltaire (Francois-Marie Arouet), 446–47
    and women, 447–48
Philosophy. *See also* Intellectual thought
    in Axial Age, 97
    early China, 63–68
    in Greece, 105–6
    in Hellenistic world, 105–6
    Islam (Muslim) civilization, early, 179–182
    philosophy in, 64–68
Phoenicians, 22
Phonetic script, 35
Pictographs, 22, 35
Pilate, Pontius, 128
Pillars, 37, 49, 51–53, 119, 183, 207–8, 227, 286–87, 342–43, 401
Ping (peace), 218
Pisa, 171, 304, 311, 313
Pisistratus, 92
Pitt, William, the Elder, 453
Pizarro, Francisco, 351
Plague. *See* Black Death; Bubonic plague
Planetary motion, 444–45. *See also* Astronomy; Universe
Plantagenets, 304
Plantations
    in Africa, 358–360
    in Americas, 354–58
    in Brazil, 351–53
    in Haiti, 463–64
    in India, 223
    in Korea, 439
    slaves on, 204
    in Southeast Asia, 363
    workers for, 358–59
Plants, 6–8, 77, 140, 149–150, 185, 189, 225, 231, 281, 340, 357, 375, 451. *See also* Agriculture and farming; Crops

tomb of First Emperor, 79
Qin Shi Huang-di, 55–56, 69–71
    Great Wall and, 71
    mausoleum of, 81
    tomb of, 79
Qing (Pure) Dynasty
    Emperor Kangzi, 417–418
    arts of, 431
    boundaries of, 423
    economy under, 428–29
    lifestyle under, 429–430
    political institutions in, 422
    rejects trade with Great Britain,
        550–51
    western onslaught of, 422–23
Quechua language, 158
Quetzalcoatl, 146
Queue (braid), 420
Quipu (Inka record-keeping system), 157–58
Qur'an, 162–65, 167–68, 172, 179, 182–84,
    200, 320
Quraysh, 164, 169

R

Race and racism. *See also* Slave trade; Slavery
    color of skin in Indian society, 38–39
Raga (musical scale), 228
Raid (*razzia*), 167
Raja (prince), 36, 222–23
Rajputs (Hindu clans), 219
Rama, 50–51
Ramadan, 165
Ramayana (Tusidas), 50–51, 231, 415
Ramcaritmanas, 415
Ramesses I, 15
Ramesses II, 19
Raphael, 334–35
al-Rahshid, Harun, 170, 172
Rashomon (Kurosawa), 275–76
Rasputin, 587
al-Rathman, Abd, 174–75
Rationalism, 443, 445
Ravenna, 292, 294, 318–19
Raw materials
    from Americas, 354
    Berenike, 178
    in Byzantine Empire, 323
    colonialism and, 381
    in England, 381
    in Japan, 275
Razzia (raid), 167
Re (Egyptian sun god), 17–18
Rebellions. *See* Revolts and rebellions
Recession, 333, 378. *See also* Great Depression
Reconquista (reconquest), 174
Records of Foreign Nations (Chau Ju-kau), 229
Records of Western Countries (Xuan), 217
Red Fort, 408, 414
Red River Delta, 364
Red River region, 228
Red Sea, 174, 190
Reformation, 16th century
    Catholic Reformation, 375
    Church and religion, prior to, 370–71
    growth of state power, 369
    impact of printing, 370
    Martin Luther and, 371–72

politics and religion in German
    Reformation, 371–72
prelude to, 370
reformation of the papacy, 377
social changes in the Renaissance, 369–370
social impact of, 375
spread of Protestant Reformation, 372–75
Reforms. *See names of specific reforms and reform
    movements*
Regional trade, 3, 42, 50, 137, 150, 177–78,
    195, 212, 215, 230, 233–34, 285, 343, 409,
    418, 431–32
Reichstag, 371
Relics, 370
Reign of Terror, 463
Reims, 311
Reincarnation, 43–46, 49, 97, 215
Religion. *See also* Secularization; *also names of
    specific religions*, 8–9, 386–87
    in Asia, 32–33, 38–39, 43–49, 51, 61–68, 75,
        215–19, 221–23, 225, 227, 231–36, 242,
        245, 257–59, 277–78, 364, 421, 432
    Aztec, 148
    in Byzantine Empire, 320–22, 324, 327–28
    as characteristic of civilization, 7, 9
    in China, 242, 245, 257–59
    emergence of, 2
    in Europe, 291–94, 305, 307–9, 370–74,
        377–78, 381, 384, 387–88
    in Greece, 84, 97–99
    in India, 32–33, 38–39, 43–49, 51
    in Mesopotamia, 13–14
    Mughal Empire, 406
    Protestant Reformation, 372–75
    rulers and gods, 129
    and society, 753
    in Southeast Asia, 215–19, 221–23, 225, 227,
        231–36
Religious imagery, 322
Religious orders. *See names of specific orders*
Religious toleration, 372, 447, 454, 465–66
Renaissance, 317
    architecture in, 333–34, 336
    artistic, 334–35
    central and eastern Europe, 337
    economy in, 369–370
    Europe and the world, 337
    intellectual Renaissance, 333–34
    Italian states, 336–37
    social status of artists, 335–36
    western Europe, 337
    women in, 334
Renaissance humanism, 333–34
Rentiers, 452
Republic, The (Plato), 98
Res Gestae (Augustus), 119
Resistance. *See names of specific movements;
    Revolts and rebellions*
Resources. *See names of specific resources*
Return from Cythera (Watteau), 448
Returned Sword Lake, Vietnam, 266–67
Revolts and rebellions. *See also* Protests;
    Revolutions
    in China, 59, 75, 244, 461
    in India, 409
    Jewish, 120
    by Roman slaves, 125
    White Lotus sect, 242, 257

Revolution and Revolt in France and China,
    461
Revolutionary Tribunal (Reign of Terror), 463
Revolutionary War in America. *See* American
    Revolution
Revolutions. *See also* Revolts and rebellions;
    Scientific Revolution
    in France, 443
    in Russia. *See* Russian Revolutions
On the Revolutions of the Heavenly Spheres
    (Copernicus), 444
Reza Khan, 608–9. *See also* Pahlavi Dynasty
Rhapta (Dar es Salaam), 193
Rhee, Syngman, 786
Rhine, Confederation of, 465–66
Rhine River region, 120
Ricci, Matteo, 427, 429
Rice
    in early China, 75–77
    in India, 42
    in Southeast Asia, 225, 229–231, 233–34
    wet rice culture, ancient China, 56, 58, 62
Richard I the Lionhearted, 312
Rig Veda, 44
Rigaud, Hyacinth, 384
Rights. *See also names of specific rights*; Women,
    of women, 288, 462
Rights of women, 448
Rites of Zhou, 61, 64, 80
Rituals in Byzantine court, 396
River valley civilizations. *See names of specific
    civilizations*
Roads and highways, in China, 254, 260
Robespierre, Maximilien, 462–63
Rock architecture, 226
Rock art, 46, 189, 192, 205. *See also* Cave art
    camels in, 205
    in Sahara, 192
Rock chambers, 51–52
Roger II (Sicily), 181
Roman Catholic Church. *See also names of
    specific orders*, 291, 375, 386, 464
    decline of, 332–33
    in France, 332
    iconoclasm and, 321
    in slavic countries, 305–6
Roman Confederation, 112–13, 116
Roman Empire. *See also* Roman Republic;
    Rome (ancient); Western Roman Empire
    in Carthage, 195
    China and, 131
    Christianity in, 126, 128–131
    compared to Han Empire, 132–33
    economy in, 328
    spice trade and, 121
Roman Empire, crisis in
    culture in, 122–26
    end of Western, 127–28
    Germany and, 127
    plague and, 126
    reforms in, 126–27
Roman Empire, early and the Republic
    aristocracy in, 114, 116
    army in, 116–17
    Battle of Zama, 115
    bureaucracy in, 118–19
    Carthage and, 114–15
    chronology of conquests, 115